AMERICAN SLAVERY AS IT WAS IN 1839
TESTIMONY OF A THOUSAND WITNESSES

"Behold the wicked abominations that they do I"—Ezekiel,viii. 9.
"The righteous considereth the cause of the poor; but the wicked regardeth not to know it."—Prov. 29,7.
"True humanity consists not in a Squeamish Ear, but in listening to the story of human suffering and endeavoring to relieve it."—Charles Jambs Fox.

Originally Written By

Theodore D. Weld

And Published By
THE AMERICAN ANTI-SLAVERY SOCIETY
In the Year 1839
as
American Slavery as it is in 1839
Testimony of a Thousand Witnesses

Re-created, Re-edited and Re-published
With additional photos, illustrations and annotations by

C. Stephen Badgley

In the year 2013

ISBN 978-0615764405

AMERICAN SLAVERY AS IT WAS IN 1839 ----------------------1

ADVERTISEMENT TO THE READER --i

NOTE-- iii

INTRODUCTION---v

PERSONAL NARRATIVES --1
   NARRATIVE OF MR. CAULKINS --3
   NARRATIVE AND TESTIMONY OF REV. HORACE MOULTON --------------------- 19
   NARRATIVE AND TESTIMONY OF SARAH M. GRIMKE------------------------------ 33
   TESTIMONY OF THE LATE REV. JOHN GRAHAM ---------------------------------- 39
   TESTIMONY OF MR. WILLIAM POE-- 43

PRIVATIONS OF THE SLAVES-- 47
   I. FOOD -- 47
   II. LABOR -- 67
   THE SLAVES ARE OVERWORKED -- 67
   III. CLOTHING -- 81
   IV. DWELLINGS --- 88
   V. TREATMENT OF THE SICK. -- 92

PERSONAL NARRATIVES-PART II -- 97
   TESTIMONY OF THE REV. WILLIAM T. ALLAN, LATE OF ALABAMA ------------- 97
   NARRATIVE OF MR. WILLIAM LEFTWICH, A NATIVE OF VIRGINIA. ----------- 103
   TESTIMONY OF MR. LEMUEL SAPINGTON --- 106
   A NATIVE OF MARYLAND --- 106
   TESTIMONY OF MRS. NANCY LOWRY, A NATIVE OF KENTUCKY ------------- 108
   TESTIMONY OF MR. WM. C. GILDERSLEEVE--- 109
   A NATIVE OF GEORGIA -- 109
   TESTIMONY OF MR. HIRAM WHITE--- 110
   A NATIVE OF NORTH CAROLINA --- 110
   TESTIMONY OF MR. JOHN M. NELSON -- 111
   A NATIVE OF VIRGINIA --- 111
   TESTIMONY OF ANGELINA GRIMKE WELD--- 113

GENERAL TESTIMONY TO THE -- 127

CRUELTIES INFLICTED UPON SLAVES --- **127**

TESTIMONY OF REV. GEORGE WHITEFIELD --- 127

TESTIMONY OF THE -- 128

'MARYLAND JOURNAL AND BALTIMORE ADVERTISER' --------------------------- 128

OF MAY 30, 1788 --- 128

TESTIMONY OF THE HON. WILLIAM PINCKNEY OF MARYLAND -------------- 128

EXTRACT FROM A SPEECH BY MR. RICE --- 129

in the Convention for forming the Constitution of Kentucky in 1790 ------- 129

PRESIDENT EDWARDS, THE YOUNGER --- 129

GEORGE BUCHANAN, M. D. --- 129

TESTIMONY OF HON. JOHN RANDOLPH, OF ROANOKE ---------------------- 129

A SLAVEHOLDER --- 129

Major Stoddard, of the United States Army ------------------------------------ 130

MONSIEUR C. C. ROBIN --- 131

WHITMAN MEAD. Esq. --- 133

TESTIMONY OF REV. JOHN RANKIN --- 133

TESTIMONY OF THE AMERICAN COLONIZATION SOCIETY -------------------- 134

TESTIMONY OF THE -- 134

GRADUAL EMANCIPATION SOCIETY OF NORTH CAROLINA ------------------- 134

FROM NILES' BALTIMORE REGISTER FOR 1829, VOL. 35, p. 4. -------------- 135

JUDGE RUFFIN, OF THE SUPREME COURT OF NORTH CAROLINA ----------- 135

MR. MOORE OF VIRGINIA --- 135

TESTIMONY.OF B. SWAIN, ESQ., OF NORTH CAROLINA ---------------------- 135

TESTIMONY OF DR. JAMES C. FINLEY --- 136

TESTIMONY OF REV. WILLIAM ALLAN, OF ILLINOIS ---------------------------- 136

MR. NATHAN COLE OF ST. LOUIS, MISSOURI ------------------------------------ 137

TESTIMONY OF REV. JAMES A. THOME -- 137

TESTIMONY OF THE MARYVILLE (TENNESSEE) INTELLIGENCER, OF OCT. 4, 1835 --- 137

TESTIMONY OF THE PRESBYTERIAN SYNOD OF KENTUCKY ------------------ 137

TESTIMONY OF THE REV. N. H. HARDING -- 138

MR. ASA A. STONE --- 139

TESTIMONY OF REV. PHINEAS SMITH -- 139

REV. JOSEPH M. SADD -- 139

SARAH M. GRIMKE --- 140

PUNISHMENTS -- **143**

I. FLOGGINGS --- 143

II. TORTURES, IRON COLLARS, CHAINS, FETTERS, HANDCUFFS, &c. --------- 172

III. BRANDINGS, MAIMINGS, GUN-SHOT WOUNDS, &c. ----------------------- 187

PERSONAL NARRATIVES-PART III -- **241**

NARRATIVE AND TESTIMONY OF REV. FRANCIS HAWLEY ---------------------- 241

TESTIMONY OF REUBEN G. MACY AND RICHARD MACY----------------------- 250

TESTIMONY ON THE AUTHORITY OF REV. WM. SCALES ----------------------- 256

LYNDON, VT. -- 256

TESTIMONY OF JOSEPH IDE, ESQ. -- 257

TESTIMONY OF REV. PHINEAS SMITH--- 259

TESTIMONY OF PHILEMON BLISS, ESQ. -- 261

TESTIMONY OF REV. WILLIAM A. CHAPIN ------------------------------------- 267

TESTIMONY OF MESSRS. T. D. M. AND F. C. MACY ---------------------------- 269

TESTIMONY OF A CLERGYMAN -- 273

OBJECTIONS CONSIDERED --- **281**

Objection I—"SUCH CRUELTIES ARE INCREDIBLE."-------------------------- 281

Objection II—"SLAVEHOLDERS PROTEST THAT------------------------------ 306

THEY TREAT THEIR SLAVES WELL."--- 306

Objection III—"SLAVEHOLDERS ARE PROVERBIAL FOR THEIR KINDNESS,

HOSPITALITY, BENEVOLENCE, AND GENEROSITY." --------------------------- 315

Objection IV—"NORTHERN VISITORS AT THE SOUTH ------------------------ 322

TESTIFY THAT THE SLAVES ARE NOT CRUELLY TREATED." ------------------- 322

Objection V—"IT IS FOR THE INTEREST-- 329

OF THE MASTERS TO TREAT THEIR SLAVES WELL."-------------------------- 329

Objection VI—"THE FACT THAT THE SLAVES MULTIPLY SO RAPIDLY PROVES

THAT THEY ARE NOT INHUMANLY TREATED, BUT ARE IN A COMFORTABLE

CONDITION."--- 345

Objection VIII.—"PUBLIC OPINION-- 355

IS A PROTECTION TO THE SLAVE." --- 355

THE PROTECTION EXTENDED BY 'PUBLIC OPINION,'--------------------------- 397

TO THE HEALTH* OF THE SLAVES --- 397

THE 'PROTECTION' VOUCHSAFED BY 'PUBLIC OPINION,'----------------------- 399

TO LIBERTY.-- 399

THE PROTECTION OF "PUBLIC OPINION" TO DOMESTIC TIES. --------------- 405

THE "PROTECTION" AFFORDED BY 'PUBLIC OPINION'------------------------- 413

TO CHILDHOOD AND OLD AGE. --- 413

SLAVE BREEDING--- 447

THAT SLAVES MUST HABITUALLY SUFFER GREAT CRUELTIES------------------ 462
ARKANSAS --- 464
MISSOURI --- 469
ALABAMA --- 472
MISSISSIPPI -- 479
LOUISIANA -- 487
KENTUCKY -- 498

INDEX --- **517**

ADVERTISEMENT TO THE READER

A Majority of the facts and testimony contained in this work rests upon the authority of Slaveholders, whose names and residences are given to the public, as vouchers for the truth of their statements. That they should utter falsehoods, for the sake of proclaiming their own infamy, is not probable.

Their testimony is taken, mainly, from recent newspapers, published in the slave states. Most of those papers will be deposited at the office of the American Anti-Slavery Society, 143 Nassau Street, New-York City. Those who think the atrocities, which they describe, incredible, are invited to call and read for themselves. We regret that all of the original papers are not in our possession. The idea of preserving them on file for the inspection of the incredulous, and the curious, did not occur to us until after the preparation of the work was in a state of forwardness; in consequence of this, some of the papers cannot be recovered. Nearly all of them however have been preserved. In all cases the name of the paper is given, and, with very few exceptions, the place and time, (year, month, and day) of publication. Some of the extracts, however not being made with reference to this work, and before its publication was contemplated, are without date; but this class of extracts is exceedingly small, probably not a thirtieth of the whole The statements, not derived from the papers and other periodicals, letters, books, &c., published by slaveholders, have been furnished by individuals who have resided in slave states, many of whom are natives of those states, and have been slaveholders. The names, residences, &c, of the witnesses generally are given. A number of them, however, still reside in slave states. To publish their names would be, in most cases, to make them the victims of popular fury. *New-York, May* 4, 1839.

NOTE

The Executive Committee of the American Anti-Slavery Society, while tendering their grateful acknowledgments, in the name of American Abolitionists, and in behalf of the slave, to those who have furnished for this publication the result of their residence and travel in the slave states of this Union, announce their determination to publish, from time to time, as they may have the materials and the funds, Tracts, containing well authenticated facts, testimony, personal narratives, &c. fully setting forth the *condition* of American slaves. In order that they may be furnished with the requisite materials, they invite all who have had personal knowledge of the condition of slaves in any of the states of this Union, to forward their testimony with their names and residences. To prevent imposition, it is indispensable that persons forwarding testimony, who are not personally known to any of the Executive Committee, or to the Secretaries or Editors of the American Antislavery Society, should furnish references to some person or persons of respectability, with whom, if necessary, the Committee may communicate respecting the writer.

Facts and testimony respecting the condition of slaves, in *all respects,* are desired; their food, (kinds, quality, and quantity,) clothing, lodging, dwellings, hours of labor and rest, kinds of labor, with the mode of exaction, supervision, &c.—the number and time of meals each day, treatment when sick, regulations respecting their social intercourse, marriage and domestic ties, the system of torture to which they are subjected, with its various modes; and *in* detail, their intellectual and moral condition. Great care should be observed in the statement of facts. Well-weighed testimony and well-authenticated facts, with a responsible name, the Committee earnestly desire and call for. Thousands of persons in the Free States have ample knowledge on this subject, derived from their own observation in the midst of slavery. Will such hold their peace? That which maketh manifest is light; he who keepeth his candle under a bushel at such a time and in such a cause as this, forges fetters for himself, as well as for the slave. Let no one withhold his testimony because others have already testified to similar facts. The value of testimony is by no means to be measured by the novelty of the horrors which it describes. Corroborative testimony,—facts, similar to those established by the testimony of others,—is highly valuable. Who that can give it and has a heart of flesh, will refuse to the slave so small a boon?

Communications maybe addressed to

Theodore D. Weld,
143 Nassau-street, \
New York.

New York, May, 1839.

INTRODUCTION

Reader, you are empanelled as a juror to try a plain case and bring in an honest verdict. The question at issue is not one of law, but of fact—"What is the actual condition of the slaves in the United States?" A plainer case never went to a jury. Look at It. Twenty-Seven-Hundred Thousand-persons in this country, men, women, and children, are in slavery. Is slavery, as a condition for human beings, good, bad, or indifferent? We submit the question without argument. You have common sense, and conscience, and a human heart;—pronounce upon it. You have a wife, or a husband, a child, a father, a mother, a brother or a sister— make the case your own, make it theirs, and bring in your verdict. The case of Human Rights against Slavery has been adjudicated in the court of conscience times innumerable. The same verdict has always been rendered—" Guilty;" the same sentence has always been pronounced, "Let it be accursed;" and human nature, with her million echoes, has rung it round the world in every language under heaven, "Let it be accursed. Let it be accursed." His heart is false to human nature, who will not say "Amen." There is not a man on earth who does not believe that slavery is a curse. Human beings may be inconsistent, but. human nature is true to herself. She has uttered her testimony against slavery with a shriek ever since the monster was begotten; and till it perishes amidst the execrations of the universe, she will traverse the world on its track, dealing her bolts upon its head, and dashing against it her condemning brand. We repeat it; every man knows that slavery is a curse. Whoever denies this, his lips libel his heart. Try him; clank the chains in his ears, and tell him they are for him. Give him an hour to prepare his wife and children for a life of slavery. Bid him make haste and get ready their necks for the yoke, and their wrists for the coffle chains, then look at his pale lips and trembling knees, and you have nature's testimony against slavery.

Two million seven hundred thousand persons in these States are in this condition. They were made slaves and are held such by force, and by being put in fear, and this for no crime! Reader, what have you to say of such treatment? Is it right, just, benevolent? Suppose I should seize you, rob you of your liberty, drive you into the field, and make you work without pay as long as you live, would that be justice and kindness, or monstrous injustice and cruelty? Now, everybody knows that the slaveholders do these things to the slaves every day, and yet it is stoutly affirmed that they treat them well and kindly, and that their tender regard for their slaves restrains the masters from inflicting cruelties upon them. We shall go into no metaphysics to show the absurdity of this pretence. The man who robs you every day, is, forsooth, quite too tenderhearted ever to cuff or kick you! True, he can snatch your money, but he does it gently lest he should hurt you. He can empty your pockets without qualms, but if your stomach is empty, it cuts him to the quick. He can make you work a life time without pay, but loves you too well to let you go hungry. He fleeces you of your rights with a relish, but is shocked if you work bareheaded in summer, or in winter without warm stockings. He can make you go without your liberty, but never without a shirt. He can crush, in you, all hope of bettering your condition, by vowing that you shall die his slave, but though he can coolly torture your feelings, he is too compassionate to lacerate your back—he can break your heart, but he is very tender of your skin. He can strip you of all protection and thus expose you to all outrages, but if you are exposed to the weather, half clad and half sheltered, how his tender bowels yearn! What! slaveholders talk of treating men well, and yet not only rob them of all they get, and as fast as they get it, but rob them of themselves, also; their very hands and feet, all their muscles, and limbs, and senses, their bodies and minds, their time and liberty and earnings, their free speech and rights of conscience, their right to acquire knowledge, and property, and reputation;—and yet they, who plunder them of all these, would fain make us believe that their soft hearts ooze out so lovingly toward their slaves that they always keep them well housed and well clad, never push them too hard in the field, never make their dear backs smart, nor let their dear stomachs get empty.

But there is no end to these absurdities. Are slaveholders dunces, or do they take all the rest of the world to be, that they think to bandage our eyes with such thin gauzes? Protesting their kind regard for those whom they hourly plunder of all they have and all they get! What! When they have seized their victims, and annihilated all their rights, still claim to be the special guardians of their happiness. Plunderers of their liberty, yet the careful suppliers of their wants? Robbers of their earnings, yet watchful sentinels round their interests, and kind providers of their comforts? Filching all their time, yet granting generous donations for rest and sleep? Stealing the use of their muscles, yet thoughtful of their ease? Putting them under drivers, yet careful that they are not hard-pushed. Too humane forsooth to stint the stomachs of their slaves, yet force their minds to starve, and brandish over them pains and penalties, if they dare to reach forth for the smallest crumb of knowledge, even a letter of the alphabet!

It is no marvel that slaveholders are always talking of their kind treatment of their slaves. The only marvel is that men of sense can be gulled by such professions. Despots always insist that they are merciful. The greatest tyrants that ever dripped with blood have assumed the titles of "most gracious," "most clement," "most merciful," &c., and have ordered their crouching vassals to accost them thus. When did not vice lay claim to those virtues which are the opposites of its habitual crimes? The guilty, according to their own showing, are always innocent, and cowards brave, and drunkards sober, and harlots chaste, and pickpockets honest to a fault. Everybody understands this. When a man's tongue grows thick, and he begins to hiccough and walk cross-legged, we expect him, as a matter of course, to protest that he is not drunk; so when a man is always singing the praises of his own honesty, we instinctively watch his movements and look out for our pocket-books. Whoever is simple enough to be hoaxed by such professions should never be trusted in the streets without somebody to take care of him. Human nature works out in slaveholders just as it does in other men, and in American slaveholders just as in English, French, Turkish, Algerian, Roman and Grecian. The Spartans boasted of their kindness to their slaves, while they whipped them to death by thousands at the altars of their gods. The Romans lauded their own mild treatment of their bondmen, while they branded their names on their flesh with hot irons, and when old, threw them into their fish ponds, or like Cato "The Just," starved them to death. It is the boast of the Turks that they treat their slaves as though they were their children, yet their common name for them is "dogs," and for the merest trifles, their feet are bastinadoed to a jelly, or their heads clipped off with the scimitar. The Portuguese pride themselves on their gentle bearing toward their slaves, yet the streets of Rio Janeiro are filled with naked men and women yoked in pairs to carts and wagons, and whipped by drivers like beasts of burden.

Slaveholders, the world over, have sung the praises of their tender mercies towards their slaves. Even the wretches that plied the African slave trade, tried to rebut Clarkson's proofs of their cruelties, by speeches, affidavits, and published pamphlets, setting forth the accommodations of the "middle passage," and their kind attentions to the comfort of those whom they had stolen from their homes, and kept stowed away under hatches, during a voyage of four thousand miles. So, according to the testimony of the autocrat of the Russians, he exercises great clemency towards the Poles, though he exiles them by thousands to the snows of Siberia, and tramples them down by millions, at home. Who discredits the atrocities perpetrated by Ovando in Hispaniola, Pizarro in Peru, and Cortez in Mexico,—because they filled the ears of the Spanish Court with protestations of their benignant rule? While they were yoking the enslaved natives like beasts to the draught, working them to death by thousands in their mines, hunting them with bloodhounds, torturing them on racks, and broiling them on beds of coals, their representations to the mother country teemed with eulogies of their parental sway! The bloody atrocities of Philip II in the expulsion of his Moorish subjects are matters of imperishable history. Who disbelieves or doubts them? And yet his courtiers magnified his virtues and chanted his clemency and his mercy, while the wail of a million victims, smitten down by a tempest of fire and slaughter let loose at his bidding, rose above the *Te Deums* that thundered from all Spain's cathedrals. When Louis XIV revoked the edict of Nantz, and proclaimed two millions of his subjects free plunder for persecution,—when from the English channel to the Pyrenees the mangled bodies of the Protestants were dragged on reeking hurdles by a shouting populace, he claimed to be "the father of his people," and wrote himself "His most *Christian M*ajesty."

But we will not anticipate topics, the full discussion of which more naturally follows than cedes the inquiry into the actual condition and treatment of slaves in the United States. As slaveholders and their apologists are volunteer witnesses in their own cause, and are flooding the world with testimony that their slaves are kindly treated; that they are well fed, well clothed, well housed, well lodged, moderately worked, and bountifully provided with all things needful for their comfort, we propose—first, to disprove their assertions by the testimony of a multitude of impartial witnesses, and then to put slaveholders themselves through a course of cross-questioning which shall draw their condemnation out their of own mouths. We will prove that the slaves of the United States are treated with barbarous inhumanity; that they are overworked, underfed, wretchedly clad and lodged, and have insufficient sleep; that they are often made to wear around their necks iron collars armed with prongs, to drag heavy chains and weights at their feet while working in the field, and to wear yokes, and bells, and iron horns; that they are often kept confined in the stocks day and night for weeks together, made to wear gags in their mouths for hours or days, have some of their front teeth torn out or broken off, that they may be easily detected when they run away; that they are frequently flogged with terrible severity, have red pepper rubbed into their lacerated flesh, and hot brine, spirits of turpentine, &c., poured over the gashes to increase the torture; that they are often stripped naked, their backs and limbs cut with knives, bruised and mangled by scores and hundreds of blows with the paddle, and terribly torn by the claws of cats, drawn over them by their tormentors; that they are often hunted with bloodhounds and shot down like beasts, or torn in pieces by dogs; that they are often suspended by the arms and whipped and beaten till they faint, and when revived by restoratives, beaten again till they faint, and sometimes till they die; that their ears are often cut off, their eyes knocked out, their bones broken, their flesh branded with red hot irons; that they are maimed, mutilated and burned to death over slow fires. All these things, and more, and worse, we shall *prove*. Reader, we know whereof we affirm, we have weighed it well; *more and worse* WE WILL PROVE. Mark these words, and read on; we will establish all these facts by the testimony of scores and hundreds of eye witnesses, by the testimony of *slaveholders* in all parts of the slave states, by slaveholding members of Congress and of state legislatures, by ambassadors to foreign courts, by judges, by doctors of divinity, and clergymen of all denominations, by merchants, mechanics, lawyers and physicians, by presidents and professors in colleges and *professional* seminaries, by planters, overseers and drivers. We shall show, not merely that such deeds are committed, but that they are frequent; not done in corners, but before the sun; not in one of the slave states, but in all of them; not perpetrated by brutal overseers and drivers merely, but by magistrates, by legislators, by professors of religion, by preachers of the gospel, by governors of states, by "gentlemen of property and standing," and by delicate females moving in the "highest circles of society." We know, full well, the outcry that will be made by multitudes, at these declarations; the multiform cavils, the flat denials, the charges of "exaggeration" and "falsehood" so often bandied the sneers of affected contempt at the credulity that can believe such things, and the rage and imprecations against those who give them currency. We know, too, the threadbare sophistries by which slaveholders and their apologists seek to evade such testimony. If they admit that such deeds are committed, they tell us that they are exceedingly rare, and therefore furnish no grounds for judging of the general treatment of slaves; that occasionally a brutal wretch in the *free* states barbarously butchers his wife, but that no one thinks of inferring from that, the general treatment of wives at the North and West.

They tell us, also, that the slaveholders of the South are proverbially hospitable, kind, and generous, and it is incredible that they can perpetrate such enormities upon human beings; further, that it is absurd to suppose that they would thus injure their own property, that self interest would prompt them to treat their slaves with kindness, as none but fools and madmen wantonly destroy their own property; further, that Northern visitors at the South come back testifying to the kind treatment of the slaves, and that the slaves themselves corroborate such representations. All these pleas, and scores of others, are bruited in every corner of the free States; and who that hath eyes to see, has not sickened at the blindness that saw not, at the palsy of heart that felt not, or at the cowardice and sycophancy that dared not expose such shallow fallacies. We are not to be turned from our purpose by such vapid babblings. In their appropriate places, we propose to consider these objections and various others, and to show their emptiness and folly.

The foregoing declarations touching the inflictions upon slaves, are not haphazard assertions, nor the exaggerations of fiction conjured up to carry a point; nor are they the rhapsodies of enthusiasm, nor crude conclusions, jumped at by hasty and imperfect investigation, nor the aimless outpourings either of sympathy or poetry; but they are proclamations of deliberate, well-weighed convictions, produced by accumulations of proof, by affirmations and affidavits, by written testimonies and statements of a cloud of witnesses who speak what they know and testify what they have seen, and all these impregnably fortified by proofs innumerable, in the relation of the slaveholder to his slave, the nature of arbitrary power, and the nature and history of man.

Of the witnesses whose testimony is embodied in the following pages, the majority are slaveholders, many of the remainder have been slaveholders, but now reside in free States.

Another class, whose testimony will be given, consists of those who have furnished the results of their own observation during periods of residence and travel in the slave States.

We will first present the reader with a few Personal Narratives furnished by individuals, natives of slave states and others, embodying, in the main, the results of their own observation in the midst of slavery—facts and scenes of which they were eye-witnesses.

In the next place, to give the reader as clear and definite a view of the actual condition of slaves as possible, we propose to make specific points, to pass in review the various particulars in the slave's condition, simply presenting sufficient testimony under each head to settle the question in every candid mind. The examination will be conducted by stating distinct propositions, and in the following order of topics:

1. The Food of The Slaves, The Kinds, Quality and Quantity, Also, the Number And Time of Meals Each Day, &c.

2. Their Hours of Labor and Rest.

3. Their Clothing.

4. Their Dwellings.

5. Their Privations and Inflictions.

6. In conclusion, a variety of Objections and Arguments will be considered which are used by the advocates of slavery to set aside the force of testimony, and to show that the slaves are kindly treated.

Between the larger divisions of the work, brief personal narratives will be inserted, containing a mass of facts and testimony, both general and specific.

PERSONAL NARRATIVES

Mr. Nehemiah Caulkins, of Waterford, New London Co., Connecticut, has furnished the Executive Committee of the American Anti-Slavery Society, with the following statements relative to the condition and treatment of slaves, in the south eastern part of North Carolina. Most of the facts related by Mr. Caulkins fell under his personal observation. The air of candor and honesty that pervades the narrative, the manner in which Mr. C. has drawn it up, the good sense, just views, conscience and heart which it exhibits, are sufficient of themselves to commend it to all who have ears to hear.

The Committee has no personal acquaintance with Mr. Caulkins, but they have ample testimonials from the most respectable sources; all of which represent him to be a man whose long established character for sterling integrity, sound moral principle and piety, have secured for him the uniform respect and confidence of those who know him.

Without further preface the following testimonials are submitted to the reader:

"This may certify, that we the subscribers have lived for a number of years past in the neighborhood with Mr. Nehemiah Caulkins, and have no hesitation in stating that we consider him a man of high respectability and that his character for truth and veracity is unimpeachable."\
Peter Comstock, D. G. Otis, A. P. Perkins, M.D., Philip Morgan, Isaac Beebe, Lodowick Beebe, James Rogers, M. D."
Waterford, Connecticut, January 16, 1839

Mr. Comstock is a Justice of the Peace. Mr. L. Beebe is the Town Clerk of Waterford. Mr. I. Beebe is a member of the Baptist Church. Mr. Otis is a member of the Congregational Church. Mr. Morgan is a Justice of the Peace, and Messrs. Perkins and Rogers are designated by their titles. All those gentlemen are citizens of Waterford, Connecticut.

"To whom it may concern:
This may certify that Mr. Nehemiah Caulkins, of Waterford, in New London County, is a near neighbor to the subscriber, and has been for many years. I do consider him a man of *unquestionable* veracity and certify that he is so considered by people to whom he is personally known.
Edward R. Warren." *Jan. 15th,* 1839

~ 1 ~

Mr. Warren is a Commissioner (Associate Judge) of the County Court, for New London County.

"This may certify that Mr. Nehemiah Caulkins, of the town of Waterford, County of New London, and State of Connecticut, is a member of the first Baptist Church in said Waterford, is in good standing, and is esteemed by us a man of truth and veracity.

Francis Darrow, Pastor of said Church."
Waterford, Jan. 16th, 1839.

"This may certify that Nehemiah Caulkins, of Waterford, lives near me, and I always esteemed him, and believe him to be a man of truth and veracity.

Elisha Beckwith."
Jan. 16th 1839

Mr. Beckwith is a Justice of the Peace, a Post Master, and a Deacon of the Baptist Church.

Mr. Dwight P. Janes, a member of the Second Congregational Church in the city of New London, in a recent letter, says:

"Mr. Caulkins is a member of the Baptist Church in Waterford, and in every respect a very worthy citizen. I have labored with him in the Sabbath School, and know him to be a man of active piety. The most *entire confidence* may be placed in the truth of his statements. Where he is known, no one will call them in question."

We close these testimonials with an extract, of a letter from William Bolles, Esq., a well known and respected citizen of New London, Ct:

"Mr. Nehemiah Caulkins resides in the town of Waterford, about six miles from this City. His opportunities to acquire exact knowledge in relation to Slavery, in that section of our country, to which his narrative is confined, have been very great. He is a carpenter, and was employed principally on the plantations, working at his trade, being thus almost constantly in the company of the slaves as well as of their masters. His full heart readily responded to the call, [for information relative to slavery,] for, as he expressed it, he had long desired that others might know what he had seen, being confident that a general knowledge of facts as they exist, would greatly promote the overthrow of the system. He is a man of undoubted character; and where known, his statements need no corroboration.

Yours, &c .William Bolles.

NARRATIVE OF MR. CAULKINS

I feel it my duty to tell some things that I know about slavery, in order, if possible, to awaken more feeling at the North in behalf of the slave. The treatment of the slaves on the plantation where I had the greatest opportunity of getting knowledge, *as not so bad* as that on some neighboring estates, where the owners were noted for their cruelty. There were, however, other estates in the vicinity, where the treatment was better; the slaves were better clothed and fed, were not worked so hard, and more attention was paid to their quarters.

The scenes that I have witnessed are enough to harrow up the soul; but could the slave be permitted to tell the story of his sufferings, which no white man, not linked with slavery, *is allowed to know* the land would vomit out the horrible system, slaveholders and all, if they would not un-clinch their grasp upon their defenseless victims.

I spent eleven winters, between the years 1824 and 1835, in the state of North Carolina, mostly in the vicinity of Wilmington; and four out of the eleven on the estate of Mr. John Swan, five or six miles from that place. There were on his plantation about seventy slaves, male and female: some were married, and others lived together as man and wife, without even a mock ceremony. With their owners generally, it is a matter of indifference; the marriage of slaves not being recognized by the slave code. The slaves, however, think much of being married by a clergyman.

The cabins or huts of the slaves were small, and were built principally by the slaves themselves, as they could find time on Sundays and moonlight nights; they went into the swamps, cut the logs, backed or *hauled* them to the quarters, and put up their cabins.

When I first knew Mr. Swan's plantation, his overseer was a man who had been a Methodist minister. He treated the slaves with great cruelty. His reason for leaving the ministry and becoming an overseer, as I was informed, was this: his wife died, at which providence he was so enraged, that he swore he would not preach for the Lord another day. This man continued on the plantation about three years; at the close of which, on settlement of accounts, Mr. Swan owed him about $400, for which he turned him out a negro woman, and about twenty acres of land. He built a log hut, and took the woman to live with him; since which, I have been at his hut, and seen four or five mulatto children. He has been appointed a *justice of the peace,* and his place as overseer was afterwards occupied by a Mr. Galloway.

It is customary in that part of the country, to let the hogs run in the woods. On one occasion a slave caught a pig about two months old, which he carried to his quarters. The overseer, getting information of the fact, went to the field where he was at work, and ordered him to come to him. The slave at once suspected it was something about the pig, and fearing punishment, dropped his hoe and ran for the woods. He had got but a few rods, when the overseer raised his gun, loaded with duck shot, and brought him down. It is a common practice for overseers to go into the field armed with a gun or pistols, and sometimes both. He was taken up by the slaves and carried to the plantation hospital, and the physician sent for. A physician was employed by the year to take care of the sick or wounded slaves. In about six weeks this slave got better, and was able to come out of the hospital. He came to the mill where I was at work, and asked me to examine his body, which I did, and counted twenty-six duck shot still remaining in his flesh, though the doctor had removed a number while he was laid up.

There was a slave on Mr. Swan's plantation, by the name of Harry, who, during the absence of his master, ran away and secreted himself in the woods. This the slaves sometimes do, when the master is absent for several weeks, to escape the cruel treatment of the overseer. It is common for them to make preparations, by secreting a mortar, a hatchet, some cooking utensils, and whatever things they can get that will enable them to live while they are in the woods or swamps. Harry staid about three months, and lived by robbing the rice grounds, and by such other means as came in his way. The slaves generally know where the runaway is secreted, and visit him at night and on Sundays. On the return of his master, some of the slaves were sent for Harry. When he came home he was seized and confined in the stocks. The stocks were built in the barn, and consisted of two heavy pieces of timber, ten or more feet in length, and about seven inches wide; the lower one, on the floor, has a number of holes or places cut in it, for the ankles; the upper piece, being of the same dimensions, is fastened at one end by a hinge, and is brought down after the ankles are placed in the holes, and secured by a clasp and padlock at the other end. In this manner the person is left to sit on the floor. Harry was kept in the stocks *day and night for a week,* and flogged *every morning.* After this, he was taken out one morning, a log chain fastened around his neck, the two ends dragging on the ground, and he was sent to the field, to do his task with the other slaves. At night he was again put in the stocks, in the morning he was sent to the field in the same manner, and thus dragged out another week.

The overseer was a very miserly fellow, and restricted his wife in what are considered the comforts of life—such as tea, sugar, &c. To make up for this, she set her wits to work, and, by the help of a slave, named Joe, used to take from the plantation whatever she could conveniently, and watch her opportunity during her husband's absence, and send Joe to sell them and buy for her such things as she directed. Once when her husband was away, she told Joe to kill and dress one of the pigs, sell it, and get her some tea, sugar, &c. Joe did as he was bid, and she gave him the offal for his services. When Galloway returned, not suspecting his wife, he asked her if she knew what had become of his pig. She told him she suspected one of the slaves, naming him, had stolen it, for she had heard a pig squeal the evening before. The overseer called the slave up, and charged him with the theft. He denied it, and said he knew nothing about it. The overseer still charged him with it, and told him he would give him one week to think of it, and if he did not confess the theft, or find out who did steal the pig, he would flog every negro on the plantation; before the week was up it was ascertained that Joe had killed the pig. He was called up and questioned, and admitted that he had done so, and told the overseer that he did it by the order of Mrs. Galloway, and that she directed him to buy some sugar, &c. with the money. Mrs. Galloway gave Joe the lie; and he was terribly flogged. Joe told me he had been several times to the smoke-house with Mrs. G, and taken hams and sold them, which her husband told me he supposed were stolen by the negroes on a neighboring plantation. Mr. Swan, hearing of the circumstance, told me he believed Joe's story, but that his statement would not be taken as proof; and if every slave on the plantation told the same story it could not be received as evidence against a white person.

To show the manner in which old and worn out slaves are sometimes treated, I will state a fact Galloway owned a man about seventy years of age. The old man was sick and went to his hut; laid himself down on some straw with his feet to the fire, covered by a piece of an old blanket, and there lay four or five days, groaning in great distress, without any attention being paid him by his master, until death ended his miseries; he was then taken out and buried with as little ceremony and respect as would be paid to a brute.

There is a practice prevalent among the planters, of letting a negro off from severe and long continued punishment on account of the intercession of some white person, who pleads in his behalf, that he believes the negro will behave better; that he promises well, and he believes he will keep his promise, &c. The planters sometimes get tired of punishing a negro, and, wanting Ins services in the field, they get some white person to come, and, in the presence of the slave, intercede for him. At one time a negro, named Charles, was confined in the stocks in the building where I was at work, and had been severely whipped several times. He begged me to intercede for him and try to get him released. I told him I would; and when his master came in to whip him again, I went up to him and told him I had been talking with Charles, and he had promised to behave better, &c., and requested him not to punish him anymore, but to let him go. He then said to Charles, "As Mr. Caulkins has been pleading for you, I will let you go on his account;" and accordingly released him. Women are generally shown some little indulgence for three or four weeks previous to childbirth; they are at such times not often punished if they do not finish the task assigned them; it is, in some cases, passed over with a severe reprimand, and sometimes without any notice being taken of it. They are generally allowed four weeks after the birth of a child, before they are compelled to go into the field, they then take the child with them, attended sometimes by a little girl or boy, from the age of four to six, to take care of it while the mother is at work. When there is no child that can be spared, or not young enough for this service, the mother, after nursing, lays it under a tree, or by the side of a fence, and goes to her task, returning at stated intervals to nurse it. While I was on this plantation, a little negro girl, six years of age, destroyed the life of a child about two months old, which was left in her care. It seems this little nurse, so called, got tired of her charge and the labor of carrying it to the quarters at night, the mother being obliged to work as long as she could see. One evening she nursed the infant at sunset as usual, and sent it to the quarters. The little girl, on her way home, had to cross a run, or brook, which led down into the swamp; when she came to the brook she followed it into the swamp, then took the infant and plunged it head foremost into the water and mud, where it stuck fast; she there left it and went to the negro quarters. When the mother came in from the field, she asked the girl where the child was; she told her she had brought it home, but did not know where it was; the overseer was immediately informed, search was made, and it was found as above stated, and dead. The little girl was shut up in the barn, and confined there two or three weeks, when a speculator came along and bought her for two hundred dollars.

The slaves are obliged to work from daylight till dark, as long as they can see. When they have tasks assigned, which is often the case, a few of the strongest and most expert, sometimes finish them before sunset; others will be obliged to work till eight or nine o'clock in the evening. All must finish their tasks or take a flogging. The whip and gun, or pistol, are companions of the overseer; the former he uses very frequently upon the negroes, during their hours of labor without regard to age or sex. Scarcely a day passed while I was on the plantation, in which some of the slaves were not whipped; I do not mean that they were *struck a few blows* merely, but lad a *set flogging*. The same labor is commonly assigned to men and women,—such as digging ditches in the rice marshes, clearing up land, chopping cord-wood, threshing, &c. I have known the women go into the barn as soon as they could see in the morning, and work as late as they could see at night, threshing rice with the flail, (they now have a threshing machine,) and when they could see to thresh no longer, they had to gather up the rice, carry it up stairs, and deposit it in the granary.

The allowance of clothing on this plantation to each slave, was given out at Christmas for the year, and consisted of one pair of coarse shoes, and enough coarse cloth to make a jacket and trowsers. If the man has a wife she makes it up; if not, it is made up in the house. The slaves on this plantation, being near Wilmington, procured themselves extra clothing by working Sundays and moonlight nights, cutting cordwood in the swamps, which they had to back about a quarter of a mile to the river; they would then get a permit from their master, and taking the wood in their canoes, carry it to Wilmington, and sell it to the vessels, or dispose of it as they best could, and with the money buy an old jacket of the sailors, some coarse cloth for a shirt, &c. They sometimes gather the moss from the trees, which they cleanse and take to market. The women receive their allowance of the same kind of cloth which the men have. This they make into a frock; if they have any under garments *they* must *procure them for* *themselves* .When the slaves get a permit to leave the plantation, they sometimes make all ring again by singing the following significant ditty, which shows that after all there is a flow of spirits in the human breast which for a while, at least, enables them to forget their wretchedness.*

> Hurra, for good ole Massa,
> He giv me de pass to go to de city
> Hurra, for good ole Missis,
> She bile de pot, and giv me de licker.
> Hurra, I'm goin to de city.

*Slaves sometimes sing, and so do convicts in jails under sentence, and both for the same reason. Their singing proves that they *want to* be happy not that they *are* so. It is the *means* that they use to make themselves happy, not the evidence that they are so already. Sometimes, doubtless, the excitement of song whelms their misery in momentary oblivion. He who argues from this that they have no conscious misery to forget, knows as little of human nature as of slavery.—Editor.

Every Saturday night the slaves receive their allowance of provisions, which must last them till the next Saturday night. "Potato time," as it is called, begins about the middle of July. The slave may measure for himself, the overseer being present, half a bushel of sweet potatoes, and heap the measure as long as they will lie on; I have, however, seen the overseer, if he think the negro is getting too many, kick the measure; and if any fall off, tell him he has got his measure. No salt is furnished them to eat with their potatoes. When rice or corn is given, they give them a little salt; sometimes half a pint of molasses is given, but not often. The quantity of rice, which is of the small, broken, unsalable kind, is one peck. When corn is given them, their allowance is the same, and if they get it ground, (Mr. Swan had a mill on his plantation,) they must give one quart for grinding, thus reducing their weekly allowance to seven quarts. When fish (mullet) were plenty, they were allowed, in addition, one fish. As to meat, they seldom had any. I do not think they had an allowance of meat oftener than once in two or three months, and then the quantity was very small. When they went into the field to work, they took some of the meal or rice and a pot with them; the pots were given to an old woman, who placed two poles parallel, set the pots on them, and kindled a fire underneath for cooking; she took salt with her and seasoned the messes as she thought proper. When their breakfast was ready, which was generally about ten or eleven o'clock, they were called from labor, ate, and returned to work; in the afternoon, dinner was prepared in the same way. They had but two meals a day while in the field; if they wanted more, they cooked for themselves after they returned to their quarters at night. At the time of killing hogs on the plantation, the pluck, entrails, and blood were given to the slaves.

When I first went upon Mr. Swan's plantation, I saw a slave in shackles or fetters, which were fastened around each ankle and firmly riveted, connected together by a chain. To the middle of this chain he had fastened a string, so as in a manner to suspend them and keep them from galling his ankles. This slave, whose name was Frank, was an intelligent, good looking man, and a very good mechanic. There was nothing vicious in his character, but he was one of those high-spirited and daring men, that whips, chains, fetters, and all the means of cruelty in the power of slavery, could not subdue. Mr. S. had employed a Mr. Beckwith to repair a boat, and told him Frank was a good mechanic, and he might have his services. Frank was sent for, his *shackles still on.* Mr. Beckwith set him to work making *trunnels,* &c. I was employed in putting up a building, and after Mr. Beckwith had done with Frank, he was sent for to assist me. Mr. Swan sent him to a blacksmith's shop and had his shackles cut off with a cold chisel. Frank was afterwards sold to a cotton planter.

I will relate one circumstance, which shows the little regard that is paid to the feelings of the slave. During the time that Mr. Isaiah Rogers was superintending the building of a rice machine, one of the slaves complained of a severe toothache. Swan asked Mr. Rogers to take his hammer and *knock out the tooth.*

There was a slave on the plantation named Ben, a waiting man. I occupied a room in the same hut, and had frequent conversations with him. Ben was a kind-hearted man, and, I believe, a Christian; he would always ask a blessing before he sat down to eat, and was in the constant practice of praying morning and night.— One day when I was at the hut, Ben was sent for to go to the house. Ben sighed deeply and went. He soon returned with a girl about seventeen years of age, whom one of Mr. Swan's daughters had ordered him to flog. He brought her into the room where I was, and told her to stand there while he went into the next room: I heard him groan again as he went. While there I heard his voice, and he was engaged in prayer. After a few minutes he returned with a large cowhide, and stood before the girl, without saying a word. I concluded he wished me to leave the hut, which I did; and immediately after I heard the girl scream. At every blow she would shriek, "Do, Ben! Oh do, Ben!" This is a common expression of the slaves to the person whipping them: "Do, Massa!" or, "Do, Missus!"

After she had gone, I asked Ben what she was whipped for: he told me she had done something to displease her young missus; and in boxing her ears, and otherwise beating her, she had scratched her finger by a pin in the girl's dress, for which she sent her to be flogged. I asked him if he stripped her before flogging; he said, yes; he did not like to do this, but was *obliged* to: he said he was once ordered to whip a woman, which he did without stripping her: on her return to the house, her mistress examined her back; and not seeing any marks, he was sent for, and asked why he had not whipped her: he replied that he had; she said she saw no marks, and asked him if he had made her pull her clothes off; he said, No. She then told him, that when he whipped any more of the women, he must make them strip off their clothes, as well as the men, and flog them on their bare backs, or he should be flogged himself.

Ben often appeared very gloomy and sad: I have frequently heard him, when in his room, mourning over his condition, and exclaim, "Poor African slave! Poor African slave!" Whipping was so common an occurrence on this plantation, that it would be too great a repetition to state the *many* and *severe* floggings I have seen inflicted on the slaves. They were flogged for not performing their tasks, for being careless, slow, or not in time, for going to the fire to warm, &c. &c.; and it often seemed as if occasions were sought as an excuse for punishing them.

On one occasion, I heard the overseer charge the hands to be at a certain place the next morning at sun-rise. I was present in the morning, in company with my brother, when the hands arrived. Joe, the slave already spoken of, came running, all out of breath, about five minutes behind the time, when, without asking any questions, the overseer told him to take off his jacket. Joe took off his jacket. He had on a piece of a shirt; he told him to take it off: Joe took it off: he then whipped him with a heavy cow-hide full six feet long. At every stroke Joe would spring from the ground, and scream, "O my God! Do, Massa Galloway!" My brother was so exasperated, that he turned to me and said, "If I were Joe, I would kill the overseer (even) if I knew I should be shot the next minute."

In the winter the horn blew at about four in the morning, and all the threshers were required to be at the threshing floor in fifteen minutes after. They had to go about a quarter of a mile from their quarters. Galloway would stand near the entrance, and all who did not come in time would get a blow over the back or head as heavy as he could strike. I have seen him, at such times, follow after them, striking furiously a number of blows, and every one followed by their screams. I have seen the women go to their work after such a flogging, crying and taking on most piteously.

It is almost impossible to believe that human nature can endure such hardships and sufferings as the slaves have to go through: I have seen them driven into a ditch in a rice swamp to bail out the water, in order to put down a flood-gate, when they had to break the ice, and there stand in the water among the ice until it was bailed out. I have *often* known the hands to be taken from the field, sent down the river in flats or boats to Wilmington, absent from twenty-four to thirty hours, *without anything to eat,* no provision being made for these occasions.

Galloway kept medicine on hand, that in case any of the slaves were sick, he could give it to them without sending for the physician; but he always kept a good look out that they did not sham sickness. When any of them excited his suspicions, he would make them take the medicine in his presence, and would give them a rap on the top of the head, to make them swallow it. A man once came to him, of whom he said he was suspicious. He gave him two potions of salts, and fastened him in the stocks for the night. His medicine soon began to operate; and *there he lay in all his filth till he was taken out the next* day.

One day, Mr. Swan beat a slave severely, for alleged carelessness in letting a boat get adrift. The slave was told to secure the boat: whether he took sufficient means for this purpose I do not know; he was not allowed to make any defense. Mr. Swan called him up, and asked why he did not secure the boat; he pulled off his hat and began to tell his story. Swan told him he was a damned liar, and commenced beating him over the head with a hickory cane, and the slave retreated backwards; Swan followed him about two rods, threshing him over the head with the hickory as he went.

As I was one day standing near some slaves who were threshing, the driver, thinking one of the women did not use her flail quick enough, struck her over the head: the end of the whip hit her in the eye. I thought at the time he had put it out; but, after poulticing and doctoring for some days, she recovered. Speaking to him about it, he said that he once struck a slave so as to put one of her eyes entirely out.

A patrol is kept upon each estate, and every slave found off the plantation without a pass is whipped on the spot. I knew a slave who started without a pass, one night, for a neighboring; plantation, to see his wife: he was caught, tied to a tree, and flogged. He stated his business to the patrol, who was well acquainted with him, but all to no purpose. I spoke to the patrol about it afterwards: he said he knew the negro, that he was a very clever fellow, but he had to whip him, for, if he let him pass, he must another, &c. He stated that he had sometimes caught and flogged four in a night.

In conversation with Mr. Swan about runaway slaves, he stated to me the following fact:

A slave, by the name of Luke, was owned in Wilmington; he was sold to a speculator and carried to Georgia. After an absence of about two months the slave returned; he watched an opportunity to enter his old master's house when the family was absent, no one being at home but a young waiting man. Luke went to the room where his master kept his arms; took his gun, with some ammunition, and went into the woods. On the return of his master, the waiting man told him what had been done: this threw him into a violent passion; he swore he would kill Luke, or lose his own life. He loaded another gun, took two men, and made search, but could not find him: he then advertised him, offering a large reward if delivered to him or lodged in jail. His neighbors, however, advised him to offer a reward of two hundred dollars for him *dead or alive,* which he did. Nothing however was heard of him for some months. Mr. Swan said one of his slaves ran away, and was gone eight or ten weeks; on his return he said he had found Luke, and that he had a rifle, two pistols, and a sword.

I left the plantation in the spring, and returned to the north; when I went out again, the next fall, I asked Mr. Swan if anything had been heard of Luke; he said he was *shot,* and related to me the manner of his death, as follows:—Luke went to one of the plantations, and entered a hut for something to eat. Being fatigued, he sat down and fell asleep. There was only a woman in the hut at the time. As soon as she found he was asleep, she ran and told her master, who took his rifle, and called two white men on another plantation: the three, with their rifles, then went to the hut, and posted themselves in different positions, so that they could watch the door.

When Luke waked up he went to the door to look out, and saw them with their rifles, he stepped back and raised his gun to his face. They called to him to surrender; and stated that they had him in their power, and said he had better give up. He said he would not; and if they tried to take him, he would kill one of them; for, if he gave up, he knew they would kill him, and he was determined to sell his life as dear as he could. They told him, if he should shoot one of them, the other two would certainly kill him: he replied, he was determined not to give up, and kept his gun moving from one to the other; and while his rifle was turned toward one, another, standing in a different direction, shot him through the head, and he fell lifeless to the ground.

There was another slave shot while I was there; this man had run away, and had been living in the woods a long time, and it was not known where he was, till one day he was discovered by two men, who went on the large island near Belvidere to hunt turkeys; they shot him and carried his head home.

It is common to keep dogs on the plantations, to pursue and catch runaway slaves. I was once bitten by one of them. I went to the overseer's house, the dog lay in the piazza, as soon as I put my foot upon the floor, he sprang and bit me just above the knee, but not severely; he tore my pantaloons badly. The overseer apologized for his dog, saying he never knew him to bite a *white* man before. He said he once had a dog, when he lived on another plantation, that was very useful to him in hunting runaway negroes. He said that a slave on the plantation once ran away; as soon as he found the course he took, he put the dog on the track, and he soon came so close upon him that the man had to climb a tree; he followed with his gun, and brought the slave home.

The slaves have a great dread of being sold and carried south. It is generally said, and I have no doubt of its truth, that they are much worse treated farther south.

The following are a few among the many facts related to me while I lived among the slaveholder. The names of the planters and plantations, I shall not give, *as they did not come under my own observation.* I however place the fullest confidence in their truth.

A planter not far from Mr. Swan's employed an overseer to whom he paid $400 a year; he became dissatisfied with him, because he did not drive the slaves hard enough and get more work out of them. He therefore sent to

South Carolina, or Georgia, and got a man to whom he paid I believe $800 a year. He proved to be a cruel fellow and drove the slaves almost to death. There was a slave on this plantation who had repeatedly run away, and had been severely flogged every time. The last time he was caught, a hole was dug in the ground, and he buried up to the chin, his arms being secured down by his sides. He was kept in this situation four or five days. The following was told me by an intimate friend; it took place on a plantation containing about one hundred slaves. One day the owner ordered the women into the barn, he then went in among them, whip in hand, and told them he meant to flog them all to death; they began immediately to cry out "What have I done Massa?" What have I done Massa?" He replied; "D—n you, I will let you know what you have done, you don't breed, I haven't had a young one from one of you for several months." They told him they could not breed while they had to work in the rice ditches. (The rice grounds are low and marshy, and have to be drained, and while digging or clearing the ditches, the women had to work in mud and water from one to two feet in depth; they were obliged to draw up and secure their frocks about their waist, to keep them out of the water, in this manner they frequently had to work from daylight in the morning till it was so dark they could see no longer.) After swearing and threatening for some time, he told them to tell the overseer's wife, when they got in that way, and he would put them upon the land to work. This same planter had a female slave who was a member of the Methodist Church; for a slave she was intelligent and conscientious. He proposed a criminal intercourse with her. She would not comply. He left her and sent for the overseer, and told him to have her flogged. It was done. Not long after, he renewed his proposal. She again refused. She was again whipped. He then told her why she had been twice flogged, and told her he intended to whip her till she should yield. The girl, seeing that her case was hopeless, her back smarting with the scourging she had received, and dreading a repetition, gave herself up to be the victim of his brutal lusts.

One of the slaves on another plantation gave birth to a child which lived but two or three weeks. After its death the planter called the woman to him, and asked her how she came to let the child die; said it was all owing to her carelessness, and that he meant to flog her for it. She told, him with all the feeling of a mother, the circumstances of its death. But her story availed her nothing against the savage brutality of her master. She was severely whipped. A healthy child four months old was then considered worth $100 in North Carolina.

The foregoing facts were related to me by white persons of character and respectability. The following fact was related to me on a plantation where I have spent considerable time and where the punishment was inflicted. I have no doubt of its truth. A slave ran away from his master, and got as far as Newbern. He took provisions that lasted him a week; but having eaten all, he went to a house to get something to satisfy his hunger. A white man suspecting him to be a runaway demanded his pass: as he had none he was seized and put in Newbern jail. He was there advertised, his description given, &c. His master saw the advertisement and sent for him; when he was brought back; his wrists were tied together and drawn over his knees. A stick was then passed over his arms and under his knees, and he was secured in this manner, his trousers were then stripped down, and he turned over on his side, and severely beaten with the paddle, then turned over and severely beaten on the other side, and then turned back again, and tortured by another bruising and beating. He was afterwards kept in the stocks a week, and whipped every morning.

To show the disgusting pollutions of slavery, and how it covers with moral filth everything it touches, I will state two or three facts, which I have on such evidence I cannot doubt their truth. A planter offered a white man of my acquaintance twenty dollars for every one of his female slaves, whom he would get in the family way. This offer was no doubt made for the purpose of improving the stock, on the same principle that farmers endeavor to improve their cattle by crossing the breed.

Slaves belonging to merchants and others in the city, often hire their own time, for which they pay various prices per week or month, according to the capacity of the slave. The females who thus hire their time, pursue various modes to procure the money; their masters making no inquiry how they get it, provided the money comes. If it is not regularly paid they are flogged. Some take in washing, some cook on board vessels, pick oakum, sell peanuts, &c., while others, younger and more comely, often resort to the vilest pursuits. I knew a man from the north who, though married to a respectable southern woman, kept two of these mulatto girls in an upper room at his store; his wife told some of her friends that he had not lodged at home for two weeks together, I have seen these two *kept misses,* as they are there called, at his store; he was afterwards stabbed in an attempt to arrest a runaway slave, and died in about ten days.

The clergy at the north cringe beneath the corrupting influence of slavery, and their moral courage is borne down by it. Not the hypocritical and unprincipled alone, but even such as can hardly be supposed to be destitute of sincerity.

Going one morning to the Baptist Sunday school, in Wilmington, in which I was engaged, I fell in with the Rev. Thomas P. Hunt, who was going to the Presbyterian school. I asked him how he could bear to see the little negro children beating their hoops, hallooing, and running about the streets, as we then saw them, their moral condition entirely neglected, while the whites were so carefully gathered into the schools. His reply was substantially this: "I can't bear it, Mr. Caulkins. I feel as deeply as anyone can on this subject, but what can I do? My hands are tied."

Now, if Mr. Hunt was guilty of neglecting his duty, as a servant of Him who never failed to rebuke sin in high places, what shall be said of those clergymen at the north, where the power that closed his mouth is comparatively unfelt, who refuse to tell their people how God abhors oppression, and who seldom open their mouths on this subject, but to denounce the friends of emancipation, thus giving the strongest support to the accursed system of slavery. I believe Mr. Hunt has since become an agent of the Temperance Society.

In stating the foregoing facts, my object has been to show the practical workings of the system of slavery, and if possible to correct the misapprehension on this subject, so common at the north. In doing this I am not at war with slaveholders. No, my soul is moved for them as well as for the poor slaves. May God send them repentance to the acknowledgment of the truth! Principle, on a subject of this nature, is dearer to me than the applause of men, and should not be sacrificed on any subject, even though the ties of friendship may be broken. We have too long been silent on this subject, the slave has been too much considered, by our northern states, as being kept by necessity in his present condition.—Were we to ask, in the language of Pilate, "What evil have they done?"—We may search their history, we cannot find that they have taken up arms against our government, nor insulted us as a nation—that they are thus compelled to drag out a life in chains! Subjected to the most terrible inflictions if in any way they manifest a wish to be released.—Let us reverse the question.

What evil has been done to them by those who call themselves masters? First let us look at their persons, "neither clothed nor naked"—I have seen instances where this phrase would not apply to boys and girls, and that too, in winter. I knew one young man seventeen years of age, by the name of Dave, on Mr. J. Swan's plantation, worked day after day in the rice machine as naked as when he was born. The reason of his being so, his master said in my hearing, was that he could not keep clothes on him—he would get into the fire and burn them off.

Follow them next to their huts; some with and some without floors:— Go at night, view their means of lodging, see them lying on benches, some on the floor or ground, some sitting on stools, dozing away the night. Others, of younger age with a bare blanket wrapped about them; and one or two lying in the ashes. These things *I have often seen with my own eyes.*

Examine their means of subsistence, which consists generally of seven quarts of meal or eight quarts of small rice for one week; then follow them to their work, with driver and overseer pushing them to the utmost of their strength, by threatening and whipping.

If they are sick from fatigue and exposure, go to their huts, as I have often been, and see them groaning under a burning fever or pleurisy, lying on some straw, their feet to the fire with barely a blanket to cover them; or on some boards nailed together in form of a bedstead.

And after seeing all this and hearing them tell of their sufferings, need I ask, is there any evil connected with their condition? And if so; upon whom is it to be charged? I answer for myself, and the reader can do the same. Our government stands first chargeable for allowing slavery to exist, under its own jurisdiction. Second, the states for enacting laws to secure their victim. Third, the slaveholder for carrying out such enactments in horrid form enough to chill the blood. Fourth, every person who knows what slavery is, and does not raise his voice against this crying sin, but by silence gives consent to its continuance, is chargeable with guilt in the sight of God. "The blood of Zacharias who was slain between the temple and altar," says Christ, "WILL I REQUIRE OF THIS GENERATION."

Look at the slave, his condition but little, if at all, better than that of the brute; chained down by the law, and the will of his master; and every avenue closed against relief; and the names of those who plead for him, cast out as evil;—must not humanity let its voice be heard, and tell Israel their transgressions and Judah their sins?

May God look upon their afflictions, and deliver them from their cruel task-masters! I verily believe he will, if there be any efficacy in prayer. I have been to their prayer meetings and with them offered prayer in their behalf. I have heard some of them in their huts before day-light praying in their simple broken language, telling their heavenly Father of their trials in the following and similar language.

"Fader in heaven, look upon de poor slave dat have to work all de day long, dat cant have de time to pray only in de night, and den massa mus not know it.* Fader, have mercy on massa and missus. Fader, when shall poor slave get through the world? When will death come, and de poor slave go to heaven?" And in their meetings they frequently add, "Fader, bless de white man dat come to hear de slave pray, bless his family," and so on. They uniformly begin their meetings by singing the following:

"And are we yet alive
To see each other's face," &c.

* At this time there was some fear of insurrection and the slaves were forbidden to hold meetings.

Is the ear of the Most High deaf to the prayer of the slave? I do firmly believe that their deliverance will come, and that the prayer of this poor afflicted people will be answered.

Emancipation would be safe. I have had eleven winters to learn the disposition of the slaves, and am satisfied that they would peaceably and cheerfully work for pay. Give them education, equal and just laws, and they will become a most interesting people. Oh, let a cry be raised which shall awaken the conscience of this guilty nation, to demand for the slaves immediate and unconditional emancipation.

Nehemiah Caulkins

NARRATIVE AND TESTIMONY OF REV. HORACE MOULTON

Mr. Moulton is an esteemed minister of the Methodist Episcopal Church, in Marlborough, Mass. He spent five years in Georgia, between 1817 and 1824. The following communication has been recently received from him.

Marlborough, Mass., Feb. 18, 1839.

Dear Brother,

Yours of Feb. 2d, requesting me to write out a few facts on the subject of slavery, as it exists at the south, has come to hand. I hasten to comply with your request. Were it not, however, for the claims of those "who are drawn unto death," and the responsibility resting upon me, in consequence of this request, I should forever hold my peace. For I well know that I shall bring upon myself a flood of persecution, for attempting to speak out for the dumb. But I am willing to be set at nought by men, if I can be the means of promoting the welfare of the oppressed of our land. I shall not relate many particular cases of cruelty, though I might a great number; but shall give some general information as to their mode of treatment, their food, clothing, dwellings, deprivations, &c.

Let me say, in the first place, that I spent nearly five years in Savannah, Georgia, and in its vicinity, between the years 1817 and 1824. My object in going to the south was to engage in making and burning brick; but not immediately succeeding, I engaged in no business of much profit until late in the winter, when I took charge of a set of hands and went to work. During my leisure, however, I was an observer, at the auctions, upon the plantations, and in almost every department of business. The next year, during the cold months, I had several two-horse teams under my care, with which we used to haul brick, boards, and other articles from the wharf into the city, and cotton, rice, corn, and wood from the country. This gave me an extensive acquaintance with merchants, mechanics and planters. I had slaves under my control some portions of every year when at the south. All the brick-yards, except one, on which I was engaged, were connected either with a cornfield, potato patch, rice field, cotton field, tan-works, or with a wood lot. My business, usually, was to take charge of the brick-making department. At those jobs I have sometimes taken in charge both the field and brick-yard hands. I have been on the plantations in South

Carolina, but have never been an overseer of slaves in that state, as has been said in the public papers. I think the above facts and explanations are necessary to be connected with the account I may give of slavery, that the reader may have some knowledge of my acquaintance with *practical* slavery: for many mechanics and merchants who go to the South, and stay there for years, know but little of the dark side of slavery. My account of slavery will apply to *field hands,* who compose much the largest portion of the black population, (probably nine-tenths,) and not to those who are kept for kitchen maids, nurses, waiters, &c., about the houses of the planters and public hotels, where persons from the north obtain most of their knowledge of the evils of slavery. I will now proceed to take up specific points.

I. THE LABOR OF THE SLAVES

Males and females work together promiscuously on all the plantations. On many plantations *tasks* are given them. The best working hands can have some leisure time; but the feeble and unskillful ones, together with slender females, have indeed a hard time of it, and very often answer for non-performance of tasks at the *whipping-posts.* None who worked with me had tasks at any time. The rule was to work them from sun to sun. But when I was burning brick, they were obliged to take turns, and *sit up all night* about every other night, and work all day. On one plantation, where I spent a few weeks, the slaves were called up to work long before daylight, when business pressed, and worked until late at night; and sometimes some of them *all night.* A large portion of the slaves are owned by masters who keep them on purpose to hire out—and they usually let them to those who will give the highest wages for them, irrespective of their mode of treatment; and those who hire them, will of course try to get the greatest possible amount of work performed, with the least possible expense. Women are seen bringing their infants into the field to their work, and leading others who are not old enough to stay at the cabins with safety. When they get there, they must set them down in the dirt, and go to work. Sometimes they are left to cry until they fall asleep. Others are left at home, shut up in their huts. Now, is it not barbarous, that the mother, with her child or children around her, half starved, must be whipped at night if she does not perform her task? But so it is. Some who have very young ones, fix a little sack, and place the infants on their backs, and work. One reason, I presume is, that they will not cry so much when they can hear their mother's voice. Another is, the mothers fear that the poisonous vipers and snakes will bite them. Truly, I never knew any place where the land is so infested with all kinds of the most venomous snakes, as in the low lands round about Savannah. The moccasin snakes, so called, and water rattle-snakes—the bites of both of which are as poisonous as our upland rattle-snakes at the north,—are found in myriads about the stagnant waters and swamps of the South. The females, in order to secure their infants from these poisonous snakes, do, as I have said, often work with their infants on their backs. Females are sometimes called to take the hardest part of the work. On some brick yards where I have been, the women have been selected as the *molders* of brick, instead of the men.

II. THE FOOD OF THE SLAVES

It was a general custom, wherever I have been, for the masters to give each of his slaves, male and female *one peck of corn per week* for their food. This at fifty cents per bushel, which was all that it was worth when I was there, would amount to twelve and a half cents per week for board per head.

It cost me upon an average, when at the south, one dollar per day for board. The price of fourteen bushels of corn per week. This would make my board equal in amount to the board of *forty-six slaves!* This is all that good or bad masters allow their slaves round about Savannah on the plantations. One peck of gourd-seed corn is to be measured out to each slave once every week. One man with whom I labored, however, being desirous to get all the work out of his hands he could, before I left, (about fifty in number,) bought for them every week, or twice a week, a beef's head from market. With this, they made a soup in a large iron kettle, around which the hands came at meal-time, and dipping out the soup, would mix it with their hominy Rev. Thomas P., and eat it as though it were a feast. This man permitted his slaves to eat twice a day while I was doing a job for him. He promised me a beaver hat and as good a suit of clothes as could be bought in the city, if I would accomplish so much for him before I returned to the north; giving me the entire control over his slaves. Thus you may see the temptations overseers sometimes have, to get all the work they can out of the poor slaves. The above is an exception to the general rule of feeding. For in all other places where I worked and visited; the slaves had *nothing from their masters but the corn,* or its equivalent in potatoes or rice, and to this, they were not permitted to come but *once a day.* The custom was to blow the horn early in the morning, as a signal for the hands to rise and go to work, when commenced, they continued work until about eleven o'clock, A. M., when, at the signal, all hands left off, and went into their huts, made their fires, made their corn-meal into hominy or cake, ate it, and went to work again at the signal of the horn, and worked until night, or until their tasks were done. Some cooked their breakfast in the field while at work. Each slave must grind his own corn in a hand-mill after he has done his work at night. There is generally one hand-mill on every plantation for the use of the slaves.

Some of the planters have no com, others often get out. The substitute for it is the equivalent of one peck of corn either in rice or sweet potatoes; neither of which is as good for the slaves as corn. They complain more of being faint, when fed on rice or potatoes, than when fed on corn. I was with one man a few weeks who gave me his hands to do a job of work, and to save time one cooked for all the rest. The following course was taken,— Two crotched sticks were driven down at one end of the yard, and a small pole being laid on the crotches, they swung a large iron kettle on the middle of the pole; then made up a fire under the kettle and boiled the hominy; when ready, the hands were called around this kettle with their wooden plates and spoons. They dipped out and ate standing around the kettle, or sitting upon the ground, as best suited their convenience. When they had potatoes they took them out with their hands, and ate them. As soon as it was thought they had had sufficient time to swallow their food they were called to their work again. *This was the only meal they ate through the day.* Now think of the little, almost naked and half-starved children, nibbling upon a piece of cold Indian cake, or a potato! Think of the poor female, just ready to be confined, without any thing that can be called convenient or comfortable! Think of the old toil-worn father and mother, without any thing to eat but the coarsest of food, and not half enough of that! Then think of *home.* When sick, their physicians are their masters and overseers, in most cases, whose skill consists in bleeding and in administering large portions of Epsom salts, when the whip and *cursing* will not start them from their cabins.

III. HOUSES

The huts of the slaves are mostly of the poorest kind. They are not as good as those temporary shanties which are thrown up beside railroads. They are erected with posts and crotches, with but little or no frame-work about them. They have no stoves or chimneys; some of them have something like a fireplace at one end, and a board or two off at that side, or on the roof, to let off the smoke. Others have nothing like a fireplace in them; in these the fire is sometimes made in the middle of the hut. These buildings have but one apartment in them; the places where they pass in and out, serve both for doors and windows; the sides and roofs are covered with coarse, and in many instances with refuse, boards. In warm weather, especially in the spring, the slaves keep up a smoke, or fire and smoke, all night, to drive away the gnats and musketoes, which are very troublesome in all the low country of the south; so much so that the whites sleep under frames with nets over them, knit so fine that the musketoes cannot fly through them.

Some of the slaves have rugs to cover them in the coldest weather, but I should think *more have not*. During driving storms they frequently have to run from one hut to another for shelter. In the coldest weather, where they can get wood or stumps, they keep up fires all night in their huts, and lay around them, with their feet towards the blaze. Men, women and children all lie down together, in most instances. There may be exceptions to the above statements in regard to their houses, but so far as my observations have extended, I have given a fair description, and I have been on a large number of plantations in Georgia and South Carolina up and down the Savannah River. Their huts are generally built compactly on the plantations, forming villages of huts, their size proportioned to the number of slaves on them. In these miserable huts the poor blacks are herded at night like swine, *without any conveniences of bedsteads, tables or chairs.* O misery to the full! To see the aged sire beating off the swarms of gnats and musketoes in the warm weather, and shivering in the straw, or bending over a few coals in the winter, clothed in rags. I should think males and females, both lie down at night with their working clothes on them. God alone knows how much the poor slaves suffer for the want of convenient houses to secure them from the piercing winds and howling storms of winter, especially the aged, sick and dying. Although it is much warmer there than here, yet I suffered for a number of weeks in the winter, almost as much in Georgia as I do in Massachusetts.

IV. CLOTHING

The masters [in Georgia] make a practice of getting two suits of clothes for each slave per year, a thick suit for winter, and a thin one for summer. They provide also one pair of northern made sale shoes for each slave in w*inter.* These shoes usually begin to rip in a few weeks. The negroes' mode of mending them is, to *wire* them together, in many instances. Do our northern shoemakers know that they are augmenting the sufferings of the poor slaves with their almost good for nothing sale shoes? Inasmuch as it is done unto one of those poor sufferers it is done unto our Saviour. The above practice of clothing the slave is customary to some extent. How many, however, fail of this, God only knows. The children and old slaves are, I should think, *exceptions* to the above rule. The males and females have their suits from the same cloth for their winter dresses. These winter garments appear to be made of a mixture of cotton and wool, very coarse and *sleazy.* The whole suit for the men consists of a pair of pantaloons and a short sailor-jacket, *without shirt, vest, hat, stockings, or any kind of loose garments!* These, if worn steadily when at work, would not probably last more than one or two months; therefore, for the sake of saving them, many of them work, especially in the summer, with no clothing on them except a cloth tied round their waist, and *almost all* with nothing more on them than pantaloons, and these frequently so torn that they do not serve the purposes of common decency. The women have for clothing a short petticoat, and a short loose gown, something like the male's sailor-jacket *without any under garment, stockings, bonnets, hoods, caps, or any kind of over-clothes.* When at work in warm weather, they usually strip off the loose gown, and have nothing on but a short petticoat with some kind of covering over their breasts. Many children may be seen in the summer months *as naked as they came into the world.* I think, as a whole, they suffer more for the want of comfortable bed-clothes, than they do for wearing apparel. It is true, that some by begging or buying, have more clothes than above described, but the *masters provide them with no more.* They are miserable objects of pity. It may be said of many of them, "I was *naked* and ye clothed me not." It is enough to melt the hardest heart to see the ragged mothers nursing their almost naked children, with but a morsel of the coarsest food to eat. The Southern horses and dogs have enough to eat and good care taken of them, but Southern negroes, who can describe their misery?

V. PUNISHMENTS

The ordinary mode of punishing the slaves is both cruel and barbarous. The masters seldom, if ever, try to govern their slaves by moral influence, but by whipping, kicking, beating, starving, branding, *cat-hauling,* loading with irons, imprisoning, or by some other cruel mode of torturing. They often boast of having invented some new mode of torture, by which they have "tamed the rascals." What is called a moderate flogging at the south is horribly cruel. Should we whip our horses for any offense as they whip their slaves for small offenses, we should expose ourselves to the penalty of the law. The masters whip for the smallest offenses, such as not performing their tasks, being caught by the guard or patrol by night, or for taking anything from the master's yard without leave. For these, and the like crimes, the slaves are whipped thirty-nine lashes, and sometimes seventy or a hundred, on the bare back. One slave, who was under my care, was whipped, I think, one hundred lashes, for getting a small handful of wood from his master's yard without leave. I heard an overseer boasting to this same master that he gave one of the boys seventy lashes, for not doing a job of work just as he thought it ought to be done. The owner of the slave appeared to be pleased that the overseer had been so faithful. The apology they make for whipping so cruelly is that it is to frighten the rest of the gang. The masters say, that what we call an ordinary flogging will not subdue the slaves; hence the most cruel and barbarous scourgings ever witnessed by man are daily and *hourly* inflicted upon the naked bodies of these miserable bondmen; not by masters and negro-drivers only, but by the constables in the common markets and jailors in their yards.

When the slaves are whipped, either in public or private, they have their hands fastened by the wrists, with a rope or cord prepared for the purpose: this being thrown over a beam, a limb of a tree, or something else, the culprit is drawn up and stretched by the arms as high as possible, without raising his feet from the ground or floor: and sometimes they are made to stand on tip-toe; then the feet are made fast to something prepared for them. In this distorted posture the monster flies at them, sometimes in great rage, with his implements of torture, and cuts on with all his might, over the shoulders, under the arms, and sometimes over the head and ears, or on parts of the body where he can inflict the greatest torment. Occasionally the whipper, especially if his victim does not beg enough to suit him while under the lash, will fly into a passion, uttering the most horrid oaths; while the victim of his rage is crying, at every stroke, "Lord have mercy! Lord have mercy!" The scenes exhibited at the whipping post are awfully terrific and frightful to one whose heart has not turned to stone; I never could look on but a moment. While under the lash, the bleeding victim writhes in agony, convulsed with torture. Thirty-nine lashes on the bare back, which tear the skin at almost every stroke, is what the South calls a very *moderate punishment!* Many masters whip until they are tired—until the back is a gore of blood—then rest upon it: after a short cessation, get up and go at it again; and after having satiated their revenge in the blood of their victims, they sometimes *leave them tied, for hours together, bleeding at every wound.*— Sometimes, after being whipped, they are bathed with a brine of salt and water. Now and then a master, but more frequently a mistress who has no husband, will send them to jail a few days, giving orders to have them whipped, so many lashes, once or twice a day. Sometimes, after being whipped, some have been shut up in a dark place and deprived of food, in order to increase their torments: and I have heard of some who have, in such circumstances, died of their wounds and starvation.

Such scenes of horror as above described are so common in Georgia that they attract no attention. To threaten them with death, with breaking in their teeth or jaws, or cracking their heads, is *common talk,* when scolding at the slaves. Those who run away from their masters and are caught again generally fare the worst. They are generally lodged in jail, with instructions from the owner to have them cruelly whipped. Some order the constables to whip them publicly in the market. Constables at the south are generally savage, brutal men. They have become so accustomed to catching and whipping negroes, that they are as fierce as tigers. Slaves who are absent from their yards, or plantations, after eight o'clock P. M., and are taken by the guard in the cities, or by the patrols in the country, are, if not called for before nine o'clock A. M. the next day, secured in prisons; and hardly ever escape, until their backs are torn up by the cow-hide. On plantations, the *evenings* usually present scenes of horror. Those slaves against whom charges are preferred for not having performed their tasks, and for various faults, must, after work-hours at night, undergo their torments. I have often heard the sound of the lash, the curses of the whipper, and the cries of the poor negro rending the air, late in the evening, and long before day-light in the morning.

It is very common for masters to say to the overseers or drivers, "put it on to them," "don't spare that fellow," "give that scoundrel one hundred lashes," &c. Whipping the women when in delicate circumstances, as they sometimes do, without any regard to their entreaties or the entreaties of their nearest friends, is truly barbarous. If negroes could testify, they would tell you of instances of women being whipped until they have miscarried at the whipping-post. I heard of such things at the south—they are undoubtedly facts. Children are whipped unmercifully for the smallest offenses and that before their mothers. A large proportion of the blacks have their shoulders, backs, and arms all scarred up, and not a few of them have had their heads laid open with clubs, stones, and brick-bats, and with the butt-end of whips and canes—some have had their jaws broken, others their teeth knocked in or out; while others have had their ears cropped and the sides of their cheeks gashed out. Some of the poor creatures have lost the sight of one of their eyes by the careless blows of the whipper, or by some other violence.

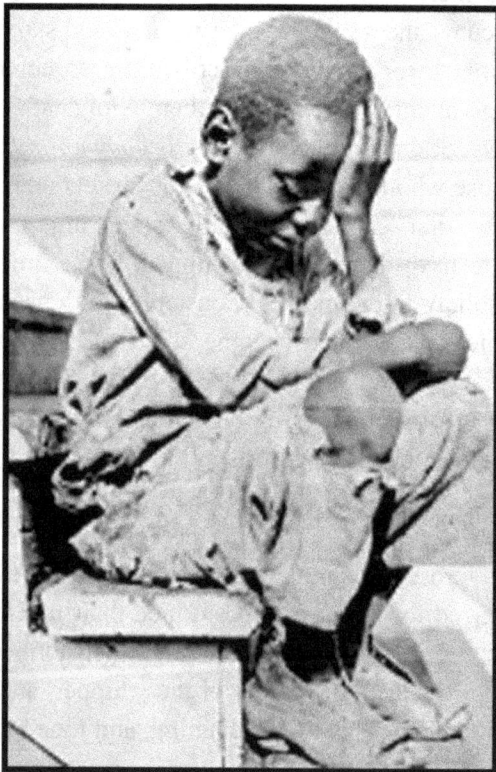

But punishing of slaves as above described, is not the only mode of torture. Some tie them up in a very uneasy posture, where they must stand *all night,* and they will then work them hard all day—that is, work them hard all day and torment them all night. Others punish by fastening them down on a log, or something else, and strike them on the bare skin with a board paddle full of holes. This breaks the skin, I should presume, at every hole where it comes in contact with it. Others, when other modes of punishment will not subdue them, *cat-haul* them —that is, take a cat by the nape of the neck and tail, or by the hind legs, and drag the claws across the back until satisfied. This kind of punishment poisons the flesh much worse than the whip, and is more dreaded by the slave. Some are branded by a hot iron; others have their flesh cut out in large gashes, to mark them. Some who are prone to run away, have iron fetters riveted around their ankles, sometimes they are put only on one foot, and are dragged on the ground.

Others have on large iron collars or yokes upon their necks, or clogs riveted upon their wrists or ankles. Some have bells put upon them, hung upon a sort of frame to an iron collar.

Some masters fly into a rage at trifles and knock down their negroes with their fists, or with the first thing that they can get hold of. The whip-lash-knots, or rawhide, have sometimes by a reckless stroke reached round to the front of the body and cut through to the bowels. One slaveholder with whom I lived, whipped one of his slaves one day, as many, I should think, as one hundred lashes, and then turned the *butt-end* and went to beating him over the head and ears, and truly I was amazed that the slave was not killed on the spot. Not a few slaveholders whip their slaves to death, and then say that they died under a "moderate correction." I wonder that ten are not killed where one is! Were they not much hardier than the whites many more of them must die than do. One young mulatto man, with whom I was well acquainted, was killed by his master in his yard with *impunity*. I boarded at the same time near the place where this glaring murder was committed, and knew the master well. He had a plantation, on which he enacted, almost daily, cruel barbarities, some of them, I was informed, more terrific, if possible, than death itself. Little notice was taken of this murder, and it all passed off without any action being taken against the murderer. The masters used to try to make me whip their negroes. They said I could not get along with them without flogging them—but I found I could get along better with them by coaxing and encouraging them than by beating and flogging them. I had not a heart to beat and kick about those beings; although I had not grace in my heart the three first years I was there, yet I sympathized with the slaves. I never was guilty of having but one whipped, and he was whipped but eight or nine blows. The circumstances were as follows: Several negroes were put under my care, one spring, *who were fresh from Congo and Guinea.* I could not understand them, neither could they me, in one word I spoke. I therefore pointed to them to go to work; all obeyed me willingly but one—he refused. I told the driver that he must tie him up and whip him. After he had tied him, by the help of some others, we struck him eight or nine blows, and he yielded. I told the driver not to strike him another blow. We untied him, and he went to work, and continued faithful all the time he was with me. This one was not a sample, however—many of them have such exalted views of freedom that it is hard work for the masters to whip them into brutes that is to subdue their noble spirits. The negroes being put under my care, did not prevent the masters from whipping them when they pleased. But they never whipped much in my presence. This work was usually left until I had dismissed the hands. On the plantations, the masters chose to have the slaves whipped in the presence of all the hands, to strike them with terror.

VI. RUNAWAYS

Numbers of poor slaves run away from their masters; some of whom doubtless perish in the swamps and other secret places, rather than return back again to their masters; others stay away until they almost famish with hunger, and then return home rather than die, while others who abscond are caught by the negro-hunters, in various ways. Sometimes the master will hire some of his most trusty negroes to secure any stray negroes, who come on to their plantations, for many come at night to beg food of their friends on the plantations. The slaves assist one another usually when they can, and not be found out in it. The master can now and then, however, get some of his hands to betray the runaways. Some obtain their living in hunting after lost slaves. The most common way is to train up young dogs to follow them. This can easily be done by obliging a slave to go out into the woods, and climb a tree, and then put the young dog on his track, and with a little assistance he can be taught to follow him to the tree, and when found, of course the dog would bark at such game as a poor negro on a tree. There was a man living in Savannah when I was there, who kept a large number of dogs for no other purpose than to hunt runaway negroes. And he always had enough of this work to do, for hundreds of runaways are never found, but could he get news soon after one had fled, he was almost sure to catch him. And this fear of the dogs restrains multitudes from running off.

When he went out on a hunting excursion, to be gone several days, he took several persons with him, armed generally with rifles and followed by the dogs. The dogs were as true to the track of a negro, if one had passed recently, as a hound is to the track of a fox when he has found it When the dogs draw near to their game, the slave must turn and fight them or climb a tree. If the latter, the dogs will stay and bark until the pursuers come. The blacks frequently deceive the dogs by crossing and re-crossing the creeks. Should the hunters who have no dogs, start a slave from his hiding place, and the slave not stop at the hunter's call, he will shoot at him, as soon as he would at a deer. Some masters advertise so much for a runaway slave, dead or alive. It undoubtedly gives such more satisfaction to know that their property is dead, than to know that it is alive without being able to get it. Some slaves run away who never mean to be taken alive. I will mention one. He run off and was pursued by the dogs, but having a weapon with him he succeeded in killing two or three of the dogs; but was afterwards shot. He had declared that he never would be taken alive. The people rejoiced at the death of the slave, but lamented the death of the dogs, they were such ravenous hunters. Poor fellow, he fought for life and liberty like a hero but the bullets brought him down. A negro can hardly walk unmolested at the south.—Every colored stranger that walks the streets is suspected of being a runaway slave, hence he must be interrogated by every negro hater whom he meets, and should he not have a pass, he must be arrested and hurried off to jail. Some masters boast that their slaves would not be free if they could. How little they know of their slaves! They are all sighing and groaning for freedom. May God hasten the time!

VII. CONFINEMENT AT NIGHT

When the slaves have done their day's work, they must be herded together like sheep in their yards, or on their plantations. They have not as much liberty as northern men have, who are sent to jail for debt, for they have liberty to walk a larger yard than the slaves have. The slaves must all be at their homes precisely at eight o'clock, P.M. At this hour the drums beat in the cities, as a signal for every slave to be in his den. In the country, the signal is given by firing guns, or some other way by which they may know the hour when to be at home. After this hour, the guard in the cities, and patrols in the country, being well armed are on duty until daylight in the morning. If they catch any negroes during the night without a pass, they are immediately seized and hurried away to the guard-house, or if in the country to some place of confinement, where they are kept until nine o'clock, A. M., the next day, if not called for by that time, they are hurried off to jail, and there remain until called for by their master and his jail and guard house fees paid. The guards and patrols receive one dollar extra for every one they can catch, who has not a pass from his master, or overseer, but few masters will give their slaves passes to be out at night unless on some special business : notwithstanding, many venture out, watching every step they take for the guard or patrol the consequence is, some are caught almost every night, and some nights many are taken; some, fleeing after being hailed by the watch, are shot down in attempting their escape, others are crippled for life. I find I shall not be able to write out more at present.

My ministerial duties are pressing, and if I delay this till the next mail, I fear it will not be in season. Your brother for those who are in bonds.

NARRATIVE AND TESTIMONY OF SARAH M. GRIMKE

Miss Grimke is a daughter of the late Judge Grimke, of the Supreme Court of South Carolina, and sister of the late Hon. Thomas S. Grimke.

"As I left my native state on account of slavery, and deserted the home of my fathers to escape the sound of the lash and the shrieks of tortured victims, I would gladly bury in oblivion the recollection of those scenes with which I have been familiar; but this may not, cannot be; they come over my memory like gory specters, and implore me with resistless power, in the name of a God of mercy, in the name of a crucified Savior, in the name of humanity; for the sake of the slaveholder, as well as the slave, to bear witness to the horrors of the southern prison house. I feel impelled by a sacred sense of duty, by my obligations to my country, by sympathy for the bleeding victims of tyranny and lust, to give my testimony respecting the system of American slavery,—to detail a few facts, most of which came under my *personal observation*. And here I may premise, that the actors in these tragedies were all men and women of the highest respectability, and of the first families in South Carolina, and, with one exception, citizens of Charleston; and that their cruelties did not in the slightest degree affect their standing in society.

A handsome mulatto woman, about 18 or 20 years of age, whose independent spirit could not brook the degradation of slavery, was in the habit of running away. For this offense she had been repeatedly sent by her master and mistress to be whipped by the keeper of the Charleston work-house. This had been done with such inhuman severity, as to lacerate her back in a most shocking manner; a finger could not be laid between the cuts. But the love of liberty was too strong to be annihilated by torture; and, as a last resort, she was whipped at several different times, and kept a close prisoner. A heavy iron collar, with three long prongs projecting from it, was placed round her neck, and a strong and sound front tooth was extracted, to serve as a mark to describe her, in case of escape. Her sufferings at this time were agonizing; she could lie in no position but on her back, which was sore from scourgings, as I can testify, from personal inspection, and her only place of rest was the floor, on a blanket. These outrages were committed in a family where the mistress daily read the scriptures, and assembled her children for family worship. She was accounted, and was really, so far as alms-giving was concerned, a charitable woman, and tender hearted to the poor; and yet this suffering slave, who was the seamstress of the family, was continually in her presence, sitting in her chamber to sew, or engaged in her other household work, with her lacerated and bleeding back, her mutilated mouth, and heavy iron collar, without, so far as appeared, exciting any feelings of compassion.

A highly intelligent slave, who panted after freedom with ceaseless longings, made many attempts to get possession of himself. For every offense he was punished with extreme severity. At one time he was tied up by his hands to a tree, and whipped until his back was one gore of blood. To this terrible infliction he was subjected at intervals for several weeks, and kept heavily ironed while at his work. His master one day accused him of a fault, in the usual terms dictated by passion and arbitrary power; the man protested his innocence, but was not credited. He again repelled the charge with honest indignation. His master's temper rose almost to frenzy; and seizing a fork, he made a deadly plunge at the breast of the slave. The man being far his superior in strength, caught his arm, and dashed the weapon on the floor. His master grasped at his throat, but the slave disengaged himself, and rushed from the apartment. Having made his escape, he fled to the woods; and after wandering about for many months, living on roots and berries, and enduring every hardship, he was arrested and committed to jail. Here he lay for a considerable time, allowed scarcely food enough to sustain life, whipped in the most shocking manner, and confined in a cell so loathsome, that when his master visited him, he said the stench was enough to knock a man down. The filth had never been removed from the apartment since the poor creature had been immured in it. Although a black man, such had been the effect of starvation and suffering, that his master declared he hardly recognized him—his complexion was so yellow, and his hair, naturally thick and black, had become red and scanty; an infallible sign of long continued living on bad and insufficient food. Stripes, imprisonment, and the gnawings of hunger, had broken his lofty spirit for a season; and, to use his master's own exulting expression, he was "as humble as a dog." After a time he made another attempt to escape, and was absent so long, that a reward was offered for him, *dead or alive.* He eluded every attempt to take him, and his master, despairing of ever getting him again, offered to pardon him if he would return home. It is always understood that such intelligence will reach the runaway; and accordingly, at the entreaties of his wife and mother, the fugitive once more consented to return to his bitter bondage. I believe this was the last effort to obtain his liberty. His heart became touched with the power of the gospel; and the spirit which no inflictions could subdue, bowed at the cross of Jesus, and with the language on his lips—"the cup that my father hath given me, shall I not drink it?," submitted to the yoke of the oppressor, and wore his chains in unmurmuring patience till death released him. The master, who perpetrated these wrongs upon his slave, was one of the most influential and honored citizens of South Carolina, and to his equals was bland, and courteous, and benevolent even to a proverb.

A slave, who had been separated from his wife, because it best suited the convenience of his owner, ran away. He was taken up on the plantation where his wife, to whom he was tenderly attached, then lived. His only object in running away was to return to her—no other fault was attributed to him. For this offense he was confined in the stocks *six weeks,* in a miserable hovel, not weather-tight. He received fifty lashes weekly during that time, was allowed food barely sufficient to sustain him, and when released from confinement, was not permitted to return to his wife. His master, although himself a husband and a father, was unmoved by the touching appeals of the slave, who entreated that he might only remain with his wife, promising to discharge his duties faithfully; his master continued inexorable, and he was torn from his wife and family. The owner of this slave was a professing Christian, in full membership with the church, and this circumstance occurred when he was confined to his chamber during his last illness.

A punishment dreaded more by the slaves than whipping, unless it is unusually severe, is one which was invented by a female acquaintance of mine in Charleston—I heard her say so with much satisfaction. It is standing on one foot and holding the other in the hand. Afterwards it was improved upon, and a strap was contrived to fasten around the ankle and pass around the neck; so that the least weight of the foot resting on the strap would choke the person. The pain occasioned by this unnatural position was great; and when continued, as it sometimes was, for an hour or more, produced intense agony. I heard this same woman say, that she had the ears of her waiting maid *slit* for some petty theft. This she told me in the presence of the girl, who was standing in the room. She often had the helpless victims of her cruelty severely whipped, not scrupling herself to wield the instrument of torture, and with her own hands inflict severe chastisement. Her husband was less inhuman than his wife, but he was often goaded on by her to acts of great severity. In his last illness I was sent for, and watched beside his death couch. The girl on whom he had so often inflicted punishment, haunted his dying hours; and when at length the king of terrors approached, he shrieked in utter agony of spirit, "Oh, the blackness of darkness, the black imps, I can see them all around me—take them away!" and amid such exclamations he expired. These persons were of one of the first families in Charleston.

A friend of mine, in whose veracity I have entire confidence, told me that about two years ago, a woman in Charleston with whom I was well acquainted, had starved a female slave to death. She was confined in a solitary apartment, kept constantly tied and condemned to the slow and horrible death of starvation. This woman was notoriously cruel. To those who have read the narrative of James Williams I need only say that the character of young Larimore's wife is an exact description of this female tyrant, whose countenance was ever dressed in smiles when in the presence of strangers, but whose heart was as the nether millstone toward her slaves.

As I was traveling in the lower country in South Carolina, a number of years since, my attention was suddenly arrested by an exclamation of horror from the coachman, who called out, "Look there, Miss Sarah, don't you see?" I looked in the direction he pointed, and saw a human head stuck up on a high pole. On inquiry, I found that a runaway slave, who was outlawed, had been shot there, his head severed from his body, and put upon the public highway, as a terror to deter slaves from running away.

On a plantation in North Carolina, where I was visiting, I happened one day, in my rambles, to step into a negro cabin; my compassion was instantly called forth by the object which presented itself. A slave, whose head was white with age, was lying in one corner of the hovel; he had under his head a few filthy rags, but the boards were his only bed, it was the depth of winter, and the wind whistled through every part of the dilapidated building—he opened his languid eyes when I spoke, and in reply to my question, "What is the matter?" he said, "I am dying of a cancer in my side."—As he removed the rags which covered the sore, I found that it extended half round the body, and was shockingly neglected. I inquired if he bad any nurse, "No, missey," was his answer, "but de people (the slaves) very kind to me, dey often steal time to run and see me and fetch me someting to eat; if dey did not, I might starve." The master and mistress of this man, who had been worn out in their service, were remarkable for their intelligence, and their hospitality knew no bounds towards those who were of their own grade in society: the master had for some time held the highest military office in North Carolina, and not long previous to the time of which I speak, was the Governor of the State.

On a plantation in South Carolina, I witnessed a similar case of suffering—an aged woman suffering under an incurable disease in the same miserably neglected situation. The "owner" of this slave was proverbially kind to her negroes; so much so, that the planters in the neighborhood said she spoiled them, and set a bad example, which might produce discontent among the surrounding slaves; yet I have seen this woman tremble with rage, when her slaves displeased her, and heard her use language to them which could only be expected from an inmate of Bridewell; and have known her in a gust of passion send a favorite slave to the workhouse to be severely whipped.

Another fact occurs to me. A young woman about eighteen stated some circumstances relative to her young master, which were thought derogatory to his character; whether true or false, I am unable to say; she was threatened with punishment, but persisted in affirming that she had only spoken the truth. Finding her incorrigible, it was concluded to send her to the Charleston workhouse and have her whipt; she pleaded in vain for a commutation of her sentence, not so much because she dreaded the actual suffering, as because her delicate mind shrunk from the shocking exposure of her person to the eyes of brutal and licentious men; she declared to me that death would be preferable; but her entreaties were vain, and as there was no means of escaping but by running away, she resorted to it as a desperate remedy, for her timid nature never could have braved the perils necessarily encountered by fugitive slaves, had not her mind been thrown into a state of despair.—She was apprehended after a few weeks, by two slave-catchers, in a deserted house, and as it was late in the evening they concluded to spend the night there. What inhuman treatment she received from them has never been revealed. They tied her with cords to their bodies, and supposing they had secured their victim, soon fell into a deep sleep, probably rendered more profound by intoxication and fatigue; but the miserable captive slumbered not; by some means she disengaged herself from her bonds, and again fled through the lone wilderness. After a few days she was discovered in a wretched hut, which seemed to have been long uninhabited; she was speechless; a raging fever consumed her vitals, and when a physician saw her, he said she was dying of a disease brought on by over fatigue; her mother was permitted to visit her, but ere she reached her, the damps of death stood upon her brow, and she had only the sad consolation of looking on the death-struck form and convulsive agonies of her child.

A beloved friend in South Carolina, the wife of a slaveholder, with whom I often mingled my tears, when helpless and hopeless we deplored together the horrors of slavery, related to me some years since the following circumstance.

On the plantation adjoining her husband's, there was a slave of pre-eminent piety. His master was not a professor of religion, but the superior excellence of this disciple of Christ was not unmarked by him, and I believe he was so sensible of the good influence of his piety that he did not deprive him of the few religious privileges within his reach. A planter was one day dining with the owner of this slave, and in the course of conversation observed, that all profession of religion among slaves was mere hypocrisy. The other asserted a contrary opinion, adding. I have a slave who I believe would rather die than deny his Saviour. This was ridiculed, and the master urged to prove the assertion. He accordingly sent for this man of God, and peremptorily ordered him to deny his belief in the Lord Jesus Christ. The slave pleaded to be excused; constantly affirming that he would rather die than deny the Redeemer, whose blood was shed for him. His master, after vainly trying to induce obedience by threats, had him terribly whipped. The fortitude of the sufferer was not to be shaken; he nobly rejected the offer of exemption from further chastisement at the expense of destroying his soul, and this blessed martyr *died in consequence of this severe infliction.* Oh, how bright a gem will this victim of irresponsible power be, in that crown which sparkles on the Redeemer's brow; and that many such will cluster there, I harbor not the shadow of a doubt.

Sarah M. Grimke. *Fort Lee, Bergen County, New Jersey, 3rd Month* 1830.

TESTIMONY OF THE LATE REV. JOHN GRAHAM

Of Townsend, Mass., who resided in S. Carolina, from 1831, to the latter part of 1833. Mr. Graham graduated at Amherst College in 1829, spent some time at the Theological Seminary, in New Haven, Ct., and went to South Carolina, for his health in 1830. He resided principally on the island of St. Helena, S. C, and most of the time in the family of James Tripp, Esq., a wealthy slave holding planter. During his residence at St. Helena, he was engaged as an instructor, and was most of the time the stated preacher on the island. Mr. G. was extensively known in Massachusetts; and his fellow students and instructors, at Amherst College, and at Yale Theological Seminary, can bear testimony to his integrity and moral worth. The following are extracts of letters, which he wrote while in South Carolina, to an intimate friend in Concord, Massachusetts, who has kindly furnished them for publication:

Springfield, St. Helena Isl., S.C., Oct 22, 1832. "Last night, about one o'clock, I was awakened by the report of a musket. I was out of bed almost instantly. On opening my window, I found the report proceeded from my host's chamber. He had let off his pistol, which he usually keeps by him night and day, at a slave, who had come into the yard, and as it appears, had been with one of his house servants. He did not hit him. The ball, taken from a pine tree the next morning, I will show you, should I be spared by Providence ever to return to you. The house servant was called to the master's chamber, where he received 75 lashes, very severe too; and I could not only hear every lash, but each groan which succeeded very distinctly as I lay in my bed. What was then done with the servant I know not. Nothing was said of this to me in the morning and I presume it will ever be kept from me with care, if I may judge of kindred acts. I shall make no comment."

In the same letter, Mr. Graham says: — "You ask me of my hostess"— then after giving an idea of her character says: "Today she has, I verily believe, laid in a very severe manner too, more than 300 *stripes,* upon the house servants," (17 in number.)

Darlington, Court House. S.C. March, 28th, 1838. "I walked up to the Court House today, where I heard one of the most interesting cases I ever heard. I say interesting, on account of its novelty to me, though it had no novelty for the people, as such cases are of frequent occurrence. The case was this: To know whether two ladies, present in court, were *white* or *black.* The ladies were dressed well, seemed modest, and were retiring and neat in their look, having blue eyes, black hair, and appeared to understand much of the etiquette of southern behavior.

"A man, more avaricious than humane, as is the case with most of the rich planters, laid a remote claim to those two modest, unassuming, innocent and free young ladies as his property, with the design of putting them into the field, and thus increasing his STOCK! As well as the people of Concord are known to be of a peaceful disposition, and for their love of good order, I verily believe if a similar trial should be brought forward there and conducted as this was, the good people would drive the lawyers out of the house. Such would be their indignation at their language, and at the mean under-handed manner of trying to ruin those young ladies, as to their standing in society in this district, if they could not succeed in dooming them for life to the degraded condition of slavery, and all its intolerable cruelties. Oh slavery! If statues of marble could curse you, they would speak. If bricks could speak, they would all surely thunder out their anathemas against you, accursed thing! How many white sons and daughters, have bled and groaned under the lash in this sultry climate," &c?

Under date of March, 1832, Mr. G. writes, "I have been doing what I hope never to be called to do again, and what I fear I have badly done, though performed to the best of my ability, namely, sewing up a very bad wound made by a wild hog. The slave was hunting wild hogs, when one, being closely pursued, turned upon his pursuer, who turning to run, was caught by the animal, thrown down, and badly wounded in the thigh. The wound is about five inches long and very deep. It was made by the tusk of the animal. The slaves brought him to one of the huts on Mr. Tripp's plantation and made every exertion to stop the blood by filling the wound with ashes, (their remedy for stopping blood) but finding this to fail they came to me (there being no other white person on the plantation, as it is now holidays) to know if I could stop the blood. I went and found that the poor creature must bleed to death unless it could be stopped soon. I called for a needle and succeeded in sewing it up as well as I could, and in stopping the blood. In a short time his master, who had been sent for came; and oh, you would have shuddered if you had heard the awful oaths that fell from his lips, threatening in the same breath "*to pay him for that.*'" I left him as soon as decency would permit, with his hearty thanks that I had saved him $500! Oh, may heaven protect the poor, suffering, fainting slave, and show his master his wanton cruelty—oh slavery! slavery!"

Under date of July, 1832, Mr. G. writes, "I wish you could have been at the breakfast table with me this morning to have seen and heard what I saw and heard, not that I wish your ear and heart and soul pained as mine is, 'with every day's' observation 'of wrong and outrage' with which this place is filled, but that you might have auricular and ocular evidence of the cruelty of slavery, of cruelties that mortal language can never describe—that you might see the tender mercies of a hardened slaveholder, one who bears the name of being *one of the mildest and most merciful masters of which this island can boast.* Oh, my friend, another is screaming under the lash, in the shed-room, but for what I know not. The scene this morning was truly distressing to me. It was this:—*After the blessing was asked* at the breakfast table, one of the servants, a woman grown, in giving one of the children some molasses, happened to pour out a little more than usual, though not more than the child usually eats. Her master was angry at the petty and indifferent mistake, or slip of the hand. He rose from the table, took both of her hands in one of his, and with the other began to beat her, first on one side of her head and then on the other, and repeating this, till, as he said on sitting down at table, it hurt his hand too much to continue it longer. He then took off his *shoe,* and with the heel began in the same manner as with his hand, till the poor creature could no longer endure it without screeches and raising her elbow as it is natural to ward off the blows. He then called a great overgrown negro *to hold her hands behind her* while he should wreak his vengeance upon the poor servant. In this position he began again to beat the poor suffering wretch. It now became intolerable to bear; she *fell, screaming to me for help.* After she fell, he beat her until I thought she would have died in his hands. She got up, however, went out and washed off the blood and came in before we rose from table, one of the most pitiable objects I ever saw till I came to the South. Her ears were almost as thick as my hand, her eyes awfully blood-shotten, her lips, nose, cheeks, chin, and whole head swollen so that no one would have known it was Etta—and for all this, she had to turn round as she was going out and *thank her master!* Now, all this was done while I was sitting at breakfast with the rest of the family. Think you not I wished myself sitting with the peaceful and happy circle around your table? Think of my feelings, but pity the poor negro slave, who not only fans his cruel master when he eats and sleeps, but bears the stripes his caprice may inflict. Think of this, and let heaven hear your prayers."

In a letter dated St. Helena Island, S. C, Dec. 3, 1832, Mr. G. writes, "If a slave here complains to his master, that his task is too great, his master at once calls him a scoundrel and tells him it is only because he has not enough to do, and orders the driver to increase his task, however unable he may be for the performance of it. I saw twenty-seven *whipped at one time* just because they did not do more, when the poor creatures were so tired that they could scarcely drag one foot after the other."

TESTIMONY OF MR. WILLIAM POE

Mr. Poe is a native of Richmond, Virginia, and was formerly a slaveholder. He was for several years a merchant in Richmond, and subsequently in Lynchburg, Virginia. A few years since, he emancipated his slaves, and removed to Hamilton County, Ohio, near Cincinnati; where he is a highly respected ruling elder in the Presbyterian Church. He says,—

I am pained exceedingly, and nothing but my duty to God, to the oppressors, and to the poor down-trodden slaves, who go mourning all their days, could move me to say a word. I will state to you a *few* cases of the abuse of the slaves, but time would fail, if I had language to tell how many and great are the inflictions of slavery, even in its mildest form.

Benjamin James Harris, a wealthy tobacconist of Richmond, Virginia, whipped a slave girl fifteen years old to death. While he was whipping her, his wife heated a smoothing iron, put it on her body in various places, and burned her severely. The verdict of the coroner's inquest was, "Died of excessive whipping." He was tried in Richmond, and acquitted. I attended the trial. Some years after, this same Harris whipped another slave to death. The man had not done so much work as was required of him. After a number of protracted and violent scourgings, with short intervals between, the slave died under the lash. Harris was tried, and again acquitted, because none but blacks saw it done. The same man afterwards whipped another slave severely, for not doing work to please him. After repeated and severe floggings in quick succession, for the same cause, the slave, in despair of pleasing him, cut off his own hand. Harris soon after became a bankrupt, went to New Orleans to recruit his finances, failed, removed to Kentucky, became a maniac, and died.

A captain in the United States' Navy, who married a daughter of the collector of the port of Richmond, and resided there, became offended with his negro boy, took him into the meat house, put him upon a stool, crossed his hands before him, tied a rope to them, threw it over a joist in the building, drew the boy up so that he could just stand on the stool with his toes, and kept him in that position, flogging him severely at intervals, until the boy became so exhausted that he reeled off the stool, and swung by his hands until he died. The master was tried and acquitted.

In Goochland County, Virginia, an overseer tied a slave to a tree, flogged him again and again with great severity, then piled brush around him, set it on fire, and burned him to death. The overseer was tried and imprisoned. The whole transaction may be found on the records of the court.

In traveling, one day, from Petersburg to Richmond, Virginia, I heard cries of distress at a distance, on the road. I rode up, and found two white men, beating a slave. One of them had hold of a rope, which was passed under the bottom of a fence; the other end was fastened around the neck of the slave, who was thrown flat on the ground, on his face, with his back bared. The other was beating him furiously with a large hickory.

A slaveholder in Henrico County, Virginia, had a slave who used frequently to work for my father. One morning he came into the field with his back completely *cut up*, and mangled from his head to his heels. The man was so stiff and sore he could scarcely walk. This same person got offended with another of his slaves, knocked him down, and struck out one of his eyes with a maul. The eyes of several of his slaves were injured by similar violence.

In Richmond, Virginia, a company occupied as a dwelling a large warehouse. They got angry with a negro lad, one of their slaves, took him into the cellar, tied his hands with a rope, bored a hole through the floor, and passed the rope up through it. Some of the family drew up the boy, while others whipped. This they continued until the boy died. The warehouse was owned by a Mr. Whitlock, on the site of one formerly owned by a Mr. Philpot.

Joseph Chilton, a resident of Campbell County, Virginia, purchased a quart of tanners' oil, for the purpose, as he said, of putting it on one of his negro's heads, that he had sometime previous pitched or tarred over, for running away.

In the town of Lynchburg, Virginia, there was a negro man put in prison, charged with having pillaged some packages of goods, which he, as head man of a boat, received at Richmond, to be delivered at Lynchburg. The goods belonged to A. B. Nichols, of Liberty, Bedford County, Virginia. He came to Lynchburg, and desired the jailor to permit him to whip the negro, to make him confess, as there was *no proof against him.* Mr. Williams, (I think that is his name,) a pious Methodist man, a great stickler for law and good order, professedly a great friend to the black man, delivered the negro into the hands of Nichols. Nichols told me that he took the slave, tied his wrists together then drew his arms down so far below his knees as to permit a staff to pass above the arms under the knees, thereby placing the slave in a situation that he could not move hand or foot. He then commenced his bloody work, and continued, at intervals, until 500 blows were inflicted. I received this statement from Nichols himself, who was, by the way, a *son of the land of steady habits*, where there are many like him, if we may judge from their writings, sayings, and doings.

PRIVATIONS OF THE SLAVES
I. FOOD

We begin with the *food* of the slaves, because if they are ill treated in this respect we may be sure that they will be ill treated in other respects, and generally in a greater degree. For a man habitually to stint his dependents in their food is the extreme of meanness and cruelty, and the greatest evidence he can give of utter indifference to their comfort. The father who stints his children or domestics, or the master his apprentices, or the employer his laborers, or the officer his soldiers, or the captain his crew, when able to furnish them with sufficient food, is everywhere looked upon as unfeeling and cruel. All mankind agree to call such a character inhuman. If anything can move a hard heart, it is the appeal of hunger. The Arab robber whose whole life is a prowl for plunder, will freely divide his camel's milk with the hungry stranger who halts at his tent door, though he may have just waylaid him and stripped him of his money. Even savages take pity on hunger. Who ever went famishing from an Indian's wigwam? As much as hunger craves, is the Indian's free gift even to an enemy. The necessity for food is such a universal want, so constant, manifest and imperative, that the heart is more touched with pity by the plea of hunger, and more ready to supply that want than any other. He, who can habitually inflict on others the pain of hunger by giving them insufficient food, can habitually inflict on them any other pain. He can kick and cuff and flog and brand them, put them in irons or the stocks, can overwork them, deprive them of sleep, lacerate their backs, make them work without clothing, and sleep without covering.

Other cruelties may be perpetrated in hot blood and the act regretted as soon as done—the feeling that prompts them is not a permanent state of mind, but a violent impulse stung up by sudden provocation. But he, who habitually withholds from his dependents sufficient sustenance, can plead no such palliation. The fact itself shows, that his permanent state of mind toward them is a brutal indifference to their wants and sufferings—A state of mind which will naturally, necessarily, show itself in innumerable privations and inflictions upon them, when it can be done with impunity.

If, therefore, we find upon examination, that the slaveholders do not furnish their slaves with sufficient food, and do thus habitually inflict upon them the pain of hunger, we have a clue furnished to their treatment in other respects, and may fairly infer habitual and severe privations and inflictions; not merely from the fact that men are quick to feel for those who suffer from hunger, and perhaps more ready to relieve that want than any other; but also, because it is more for the interest of the slaveholder to supply that want than any other; consequently, if the slave suffer in this respect, he must as the general rule, suffer *more* in other respects.

We now proceed to show that the slaves have insufficient food. This will be shown first from the express declarations of slaveholders, and other competent witnesses who are, or have been residents of slave states, that the slaves generally are *under-fed*. And then, by the laws of slave states, and by the testimony of slaveholders and others, the *kind, quantity,* and *quality,* of their allowance will be given, and the reader left to judge for himself whether the slave *must* not be a sufferer.

THE SLAVES SUFFER FROM HUNGER

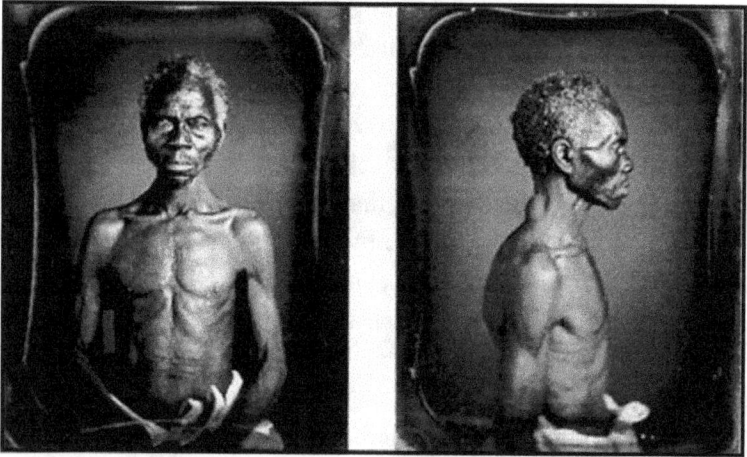

DECLARATIONS OF SLAVE-HOLDERS AND OTHERS

WITNESS

Hon. Alexander Smyth, a slave holder, and for ten years, Member of Congress from Virginia, in his speech on the Missouri question. Jan 28th, 1820

TESTIMONY

"By confining the slaves to the Southern states, where crops are raised for exportation, and bread and meat are purchased, you *doom them to scarcity and hunger.* It is proposed to hem in the blacks where they are ILL FED."

============

WITNESS
Rev. George Whitefield, in his letter, to the slave holders of Md. Va. N C., S.C. and Ga. published in Georgia, just one hundred years ago, 1739.

TESTIMONY
"My blood has frequently run cold within me, to think how many of your slaves *have not sufficient food to eat;* they are scarcely permitted to *pick up the crumbs that* fall from their master's table."

============

WITNESS
Rev. John Rankin, of Ripley, Ohio, a native of Tennessee, and for some year's a preacher in slave states.

TESTIMONY
"Thousands of the slaves are pressed with the gnawings of cruel hunger during their whole lives."

============

WITNESS
Report of the Gradual Emancipation Society of North Carolina, 1828. Signed Moses Swain, President, and William Swain, Secretary.

TESTIMONY
Speaking of the condition of slaves, in the eastern part of that state, the report says,—"The master puts the unfortunate wretches upon short allowances, scarcely sufficient for their sustenance, so that a *great part* of them go *half starved* much of the time."

============

WITNESS
Mr. Asa A. Stone, a Theological Student, who resided near Natchez, Miss., in 1834-5.

TESTIMONY
"On almost every plantation, the hands suffer more or less from hunger at some seasons of almost every year. There is always a *good deal of suffering* from hunger. On many plantations, and particularly in Louisiana, the slaves are in a condition of *almost utter famishment,* during a great portion of the year."

============

WITNESS

Thomas Clay, Esq., of Georgia, a Slaveholder.

TESTIMONY

"From various causes this [the slave's allowance of food] is *often* not adequate to the support of a laboring man."

==========

WITNESS

Mr. Tobias Boudinot, St. Albans, Ohio, a member of the Methodist Church. Mr. B. for some years navigated the Mississippi.

TESTIMONY

"The slaves down the Mississippi, are *half-starved,* the boats, when they stop at night, are constantly boarded by slaves, begging for something to eat."

==========

WITNESS

President Edwards, the younger, in a sermon before the Conn. Abolition Society, 1791.

TESTIMONY

"The slaves are supplied with barely enough to keep them from *starving.*"

==========

WITNESS

Rev. Horace Moulton, a Methodist Clergyman of Marlboro, Mass., who lived five years in Georgia.

TESTIMONY

"As a general thing on the plantations, the slaves suffer extremely for the want of food."

==========

WITNESS

Rev. George Bourne, late editor of the Protestant Vindicator, N. Y-, who was seven years pastor of a church in Virginia.

TESTIMONY

"The slaves are deprived of *needful* sustenance."

==========

1. KINDS OF FOOD

WITNESS

Hon. Robert Turnbull, a slaveholder of Charleston, South Carolina.

TESTIMONY

"The subsistence of the slaves consists, from March until August, of corn ground into grits, or meal, made into what is called *hominy,* or baked into corn bread. The other six months, they are fed upon the sweet potato. Meat, when given, is only by way of *indulgence or favor.*

===========

WITNESS

Mr. Eleazar Powell, Chippewa, Beaver Co., Penn. who resided in Mississippi, in 1836-7.

TESTIMONY

"The food of the slaves was generally corn bread, and *sometimes* meat or molasses."

===========

WITNESS

Reuben G. Macy, a member of the Society of Friends, Hudson, N. Y., who resided in South Carolina.

TESTIMONY

"The slaves had no food allowed them besides *corn,* excepting at Christmas, when they had beef."

===========

WITNESS

Mr. William Leftwich, a native of Virginia, and recently of Madison Co., Alabama, now member, of the Presbyterian Church, Delhi, Ohio.

TESTIMONY

"On my uncle's plantation, the food of the slaves was corn pone and a small allowance of meat."

===========

William Ladd, Esq., of Minot, Me., president of the American Peace Society, and formerly a slaveholder of Florida, gives the following testimony as to the allowance of food to slaves:

"The usual food of the slaves was *corn,* with a modicum of salt. In some cases the master allowed no salt, but the slaves boiled the sea water for salt in their little pots. For about eight days near Christmas, i.e., from the Saturday evening before, to the Monday evening after Christmas day, they were allowed some *meat*. They always with one single exception ground their corn in a hand-mill, and cooked their food themselves."

Extract of a letter from Rev. D. C. Eastman, a preacher of the Methodist Episcopal Church, in Fayette County, Ohio:.

"In March, 1838, Mr. Thomas Larrimer, a deacon of the Presbyterian Church in Bloomingburg, Fayette County, Ohio, Mr. G. S. Fullerton, merchant, and member of the same church, and Mr. William A. Ustick, an elder of the same church, spent a night with a Mr. Shepherd, about 30 miles North of Charleston, S. C, on the Monk's Corner road. He owned five families of negroes, who, he said, were fed from the same meal and meat tubs as himself, but that 99 out of a 100 of all the slaves in that county *saw meat but once a year,* which was on Christmas holidays."

As an illustration of the inhuman experiments sometimes tried upon slaves, in respect to the *kind* as well as the quality and quantity of their food, we solicit the attention of the reader to the testimony of the late General Wade Hampton, of South Carolina. General Hampton was for some time commander in chief of the army on the Canada frontier during the last war, and at the time of his death, about three years since, was the largest slaveholder in the United States. The General's testimony is contained in the following extract of a letter, just received from a distinguished clergyman in the west, extensively known both as a preacher and a writer. His name is with the executive committee of the American Anti-Slavery Society:

"You refer in your letter to a statement made to you while in this place, respecting the late General Wade Hampton, of South Carolina, and task me to write out for you the circumstances of the case—considering them well calculated to illustrate two points in the history of slavery: 1st, That the habit of slaveholding dreadfully blunts the feelings toward the slave, producing such insensibility that his sufferings and death are regarded with indifference. 2d, That the slave often has insufficient food, both in quantity and quality.

"I received my information from a lady in the west of high respectability and great moral worth, —but think it best to withhold her name, although the statement was not made in confidence.

"My informant stated that she sat at dinner once in company with General Wade Hampton, and several others; that the conversation turned upon the treatment of their servants, &c.; when the General undertook to entertain the company with the relation of an experiment he had made in the feeding of his slaves on cotton seed. He said that he first mingled one-fourth cotton seed with three-fourths corn, on which they seemed to thrive tolerably well; that he then had measured out to them equal quantities of each, which did not seem to produce any important change; afterwards he increased the quantity of cotton seed to three-fourths, mingled with one-fourth corn, and then he declared, with an oath, that' they died like rotten sheep!!' It is but justice to the lady to state that she spoke of his conduct with the utmost indignation; and she mentioned also that he received no countenance from the company present, but that all seemed to look at each other with astonishment. I give it to you just as I received it from one who was present, and whose character for veracity is unquestionable.

"It is proper to add that I had previously formed an acquaintance with Dr. Witherspoon, now of Alabama, if alive; whose former residence was in South Carolina; from whom I received a particular account of the manner of feeding and treating slaves on the plantations of General Wade Hampton, and others in the same part of the State; and certainly no one could listen to the recital without concluding that such masters and overseers as he described must have hearts like the nether millstone. The cotton seed experiment I had heard of before also, as having been made in other parts of the south; consequently, I was prepared to receive as true the above statement, even if I had not been so well acquainted with the high character of my informant."

2. QUANTITY OF FOOD

The legal allowance of food for slaves in North Carolina is, in the words of the law, "a quart of corn per day." See Haywood's Manual, 525. The legal allowance in Louisiana is more, a barrel [flour barrel] of corn, (in the ear,) or its equivalent in other grain, and a pint of salt a month. In the other slave states the amount of food for the slaves is left to the option of the master.

WITNESS

Thos. Clay, Esq., of Georgia, a slave holder, in his address before the Georgia Presbytery, 1833.

TESTIMONY

"The quantity allowed by custom is *a peck of corn a week!*"

==========

WITNESS

The Maryland Journal, and more Baltimore Advertiser, May 30, 1788.

TESTIMONY

"*A single peck of corn a week, or the like measure of rice,* is the *ordinary* quantity of provision for a *hard-working* slave; to which a small quantity of meat is occasionally, though *rarely,* added."

==========

WITNESS

W. C. Gildersleeve, Esq., a native of Georgia, and Elder in the Presbyterian Church, Wilkes-Barre, Perm.

TESTIMONY

The weekly allowance to grown slaves on this plantation, where I was best acquainted, was *one peck of* corn."

==========

WITNESS

Wm. Ladd, of Minot, Maine, formerly a slaveholder in Florida.

TESTIMONY

"The usual allowance of food was *one quart of corn a day,* to a full task hand, with a modicum of salt; kind masters allowed *a peck of corn a week;* some masters allowed no salt."

==========

WITNESS

Mr. Jarvis Brewster, in his "Exposition of the treatment of slaves in the Southern States," published in N. Jersey, 1815.

TESTIMONY

"The allowance of provisions for the slaves, is *one peck of corn, in the grain, per week.*"

==========

WITNESS

Rev. Horace Moulton, a Methodist Clergyman of Marlboro, Mass., who lived five years in Georgia.

TESTIMONY

"In Georgia the planters give each slave only *one peck of their gourd seed corn per week,* with a small quantity of salt."

===========

WITNESS

Mr. F. C. Macy, Nantucket, Mass., who resided in Georgia in 1830.

TESTIMONY

"The food of the slaves was three pecks of potatoes a week during the potato season, and one *peck of corn,* during the remainder of the year."

===========

WITNESS

Mr. Nehemiah Caulkins, a member of the Baptist Church in Waterford, Conn., who resided in North Carolina, eleven winters.

TESTIMONY

"The subsistence of the slaves consists of *seven quarts of meal* or *eight quarts of small rice for one week!*"

===========

WITNESS

William Savery, late of Philadelphia, an eminent Minister of the Society of Friends who traveled extensively in the slave states, on a Religious Visitation, speaking of the subsistence of the slaves, says, in his published Journal,

TESTIMONY

"*A peck of corn* is their (the slaves,) miserable subsistence *for a week.*"

===========

WITNESS

The late John Parrish, of Philadelphia, another highly respected Minister of the Society of Friends, who traversed the South, on a similar mission, in 1804 and 5, says in his "Remarks on the slavery of Blacks;"

TESTIMONY

"They allow them but *one peck of meal,* for a whole week, in some of the Southern states."

===========

WITNESS

Richard Macy, Hudson, N., Y. a Member of the Society of Friends who has resided in Georgia.

TESTIMONY

"Their usual allowance of food was one peck of corn per week, which was dealt out to them every first day of the week. They had nothing allowed them besides the corn, except one quarter of beef at Christmas."

============

WITNESS

Rev. C. S. Renshaw, of Quincy, Ill., (the testimony of a Virginian.)

TESTIMONY

"The slaves are generally allowanced: a pint of corn meal and a salt herring is the allowance, or in lieu of the herring a "dab" of fat meat of about the same value. I have known the sour milk, and clauber to be served out to the hands, when there was an abundance of milk on the plantation. This is a luxury not often afforded."

============

Testimony of Mr. George W. Westgate, member of the Congregational Church of Quincy, Illinois. Mr. W. has been engaged in the low country trade for twelve years, more than half of each year, principally on the Mississippi, and its tributary streams in the south-western slave states:

"Feeding is not sufficient,—let facts speak. On the coast, i.e. Natchez and the Gulf of Mexico, the allowance was one barrel of ears of corn, and a pint of salt per month. They may cook this in what manner they please, but it must be done after dark. They have no daylight to prepare it by. Some few planters, but only a few, let them prepare their corn on Saturday afternoon. Planters, overseers, and negroes, have told me, that in *pinching times,* i.e. when corn is high, they did not get near that quantity. In Miss., I know some planters who allowed their hands three and a half pounds of meat per week, when it was cheap. Many prepare their corn on the Sabbath, when they are not worked on that day, which however is frequently the case on sugar plantations. There are very many masters on "the coast" who will not suffer their slaves to come to the boats, because they steal molasses to barter for meat; indeed they generally trade more or less with stolen property. But it is impossible to find out what and when, as their articles of barter are of such trifling importance. They would often come on board our boats to beg a bone, and would tell how badly they were fed, that they were almost starved; many a time I have set up all night, to prevent them from stealing something to eat."

3. QUALITY OF FOOD

Having ascertained the kind and quantity of food allowed to the slaves, it is important to know something of its *quality that* we may judge of the amount of sustenance which it contains. For, if their provisions are of an inferior quality, or in a damaged state, then, power to sustain labor must be greatly diminished.

WITNESS

Thomas Clay, Esq. of Georgia, in an address to the Georgia Presbytery, 1834, speaking of the quality of the corn given to the slaves, says,

TESTIMONY

"There is *often a defect here.*"

==========

WITNESS

Rev. Horace Moulton, a Methodist clergyman at Marlboro', Mass. and rive years a resident of Georgia.

TESTIMONY

"The food, or 'feed' of slaves is generally of the *poorest* kind."

==========

WITNESS

The "Western Medical Reformer," in an article on the diseases peculiar to negroes, by a Kentucky physician, says of the diet of the slaves;

TESTIMONY

"They live on a coarse, *crude, unwholesome diet.*"

==========

WITNESS

Professor A. G. Smith, of the New York Medical College; formerly a physician in Louisville, Kentucky.

TESTIMONY

I have myself known numerous instances of large families of *badly-fed* negroes swept off by a prevailing epidemic; and it is well known to many intelligent planters in the south, that the best method of preventing that horrible malady, *Chachexia* Africana, is to feed the negroes with *nutritious* food.

==========

4. NUMBER AND TIME OF MEALS EACH DAY.

In determining whether or not the slaves suffer for want of food, the number of hours intervening, and the labor performed between their meals, and the number of meals each day, should be taken into consideration.

WITNESS
Philemon Bliss, Esq., a lawyer in Elyria, Ohio, and member of the Presbyterian Church who lived in Florida in 1834, and 1835.
TESTIMONY
"The slaves go to the field in the morning; they carry with them corn meal wet with water, and at *noon* build a fire on the ground and bake it in the ashes. After the labors of the day are over, they take their *second* meal of ash-cake."

===========

WITNESS
President Edwards, the younger.
TESTIMONY
"The slaves eat *twice* during the day."

===========

WITNESS
Mr. Eleazar Powell, Chippewa, Beaver County, Penn., who resided in Mississippi in 1836 and 1837.
TESTIMONY
"The slaves received *two* meals during the day. Those who have their food cooked for them get their breakfast about eleven o'clock, and their other meal *after night*."

===========

WITNESS
Mr. Nehemiah Caulkins, Waterford, Conn., who spent eleven winters in North Carolina.
TESTIMONY
"The *breakfast* of the slaves was generally about *ten or eleven* o'clock."

===========

WITNESS
Rev. Phineas Smith, Centreville, N. Y., who has lived at the south some years.

"The slaves have usually *two* meals a day, viz: at eleven o'clock and at night."

===========

WITNESS
Rev. C. S. Renshaw, Quincy, Illinois, —the testimony of a Virginian.
TESTIMONY
"The slaves have *two* meals a day. They breakfast at from ten to eleven, A. M., and eat their supper at from six to nine or ten at night, as the season and crops may be."

===========

The preceding testimony establishes the following points.

1st. That the slaves are allowed, in general, *no meat*. This appears from the fact, that in the *only* slave states which regulate the slaves' rations *by law,* (North Carolina and Louisiana,) the *legal ration* contains *no meat.* Besides, the late Hon. R. J. Turnbull, one of the largest planters in South Carolina, says expressly, "Meat, when given, is only by the way of indulgence or favor." It is shown also by the direct testimony recorded above, of slaveholders and others, in all parts of the slaveholding south and west that the *general* allowance on plantations is corn or meal and salt merely. To this there are doubtless many exceptions, but they are *only* exceptions; the number of slaveholders who furnish meat for their *field-hands,* is small, in comparison with the number of those who do not. The house slaves, that is, the cooks, chambermaids, waiters, &c., generally get some meat every day; the remainder bits and bones of their masters' tables. But that the great body of the slaves, those that compose the field gangs, whose labor and exposure, and consequent exhaustion, are vastly greater than those of house slaves, toiling as they do from day light till dark, in the fogs of the early morning, under the scorchings of midday, and amid the damps of evening, are *in general* provided with *no meat,* is abundantly established by the preceding testimony.

Now we do not say that meat *is necessary* to sustain men under hard and long continued labor, nor that it is *not.* This is not a treatise on dietetics; but it is a notorious fact, that the medical faculty in this country, with very few exceptions, do most strenuously insist that it is necessary;

and that working men in all parts of the country do *believe* that meat is indispensable to sustain them, even those who work within doors, and only ten hours a day, everyone knows. Further, it is notorious, that the slaveholders themselves *believe* the daily use of meat to be absolutely necessary to the comfort, not merely of those who labor, but of those who are idle, is proved by the fact of meat being a part of the daily ration of food provided for convicts in the prisons, in every one of the slave states, except in those rare cases where meat is expressly prohibited, and the convict is, by w*ay of extra punishment* confined to bread and water; he is occasionally, and for a little time only, confined to bread and water; that is, to the *ordinary diet* of slaves, with this difference in favor of the convict: his bread is made for him, whereas the slave is forced to pound or grind his own corn and make his own bread, when exhausted with toil.

The preceding testimony shows also, that *vegetables* form generally no part of the slaves' allowance. The *sole* food of the majority is *corn:* at every meal—from day to day—from week to week—from month to month, *corn.* In South Carolina, Georgia, and Florida, the sweet potato is, to a considerable extent, substituted for corn during a part of the year.

2d. The preceding testimony proves conclusively, that the *quantity of food* generally allowed to a full-grown field-hand, is a peck of corn a week, or a fraction over a quart and a gill of corn a day. The legal ration of North Carolina is *less*—in Louisiana it is *more.* Of the slaveholders and other witnesses, who give the foregoing testimony, the reader will perceive that no one testifies to a larger allowance of com than a peck for a week; though a number testify, that within the circle of their knowledge, *seven* quarts was the usual allowance. Frequently a small quantity of meat is added; but this, as has already been shown, is not the general rule for field-hands. We may add, also, that in the season of "pumpkins," "cimblins," "cabbages," "greens," &c., the slaves on small plantations are, to some extent, furnished with those articles.

Now, without entering upon the vexed question of how much food is necessary to sustain the human system, under severe toil and exposure, and without giving the opinions of physiologists as to the insufficiency or sufficiency of the slaves' allowance, we affirm that all civilized nations have, in all ages, and in the most emphatic manner, declared, that *eight quarts of corn a week,* (the usual allowance of our slaves,) is utterly insufficient to sustain the human body, under such toil and exposure as that to which the slaves are subjected.

To show this fully, it will be necessary to make some estimates, and present some statistics. And first, the northern reader must bear in mind, that the com furnished to the slaves at the south, is almost invariably the *white gourd seed* com, and that a quart of this kind of com weighs five or six ounces *less* than a quart of "flint com," the kind generally raised in the northern and eastern states; consequently a peck of the com generally given to the slaves, would be only equivalent to a fraction more than six quarts and a pint of the corn commonly raised in the New England States, New York, New Jersey, &c. Now, what would be said of the northern capitalist, who should allow his laborers but *six quarts and five gills of corn for a week's provisions*?

Further, it appears in evidence, that the com given to the slaves is often *defective*. This, the reader will recollect, is the voluntary testimony of Thomas Clay, Esq., the Georgia planter, whose testimony is given above. When this is the case, the amount of actual nutriment contained in a peck of the "gourd seed," may not be more than in five, or four, or even three quarts of "flint com."

As a quart of southern corn weighs at least five ounces less than a quart of northern corn, it requires little arithmetic to perceive, that the daily allowance of the slave fed upon that kind of com, would contain about one third of a pound less nutriment than though his daily ration were the same quantity of northern com, which would amount, in a year, to more than a hundred and twenty pounds of human sustenance! Which would furnish the slave with his full allowance of a peck of com a week for two months! It is unnecessary to add, that this difference in the weight of the two kinds of com, is an item too important to be overlooked. As one quart of the southern com weighs one pound and eleven-sixteenths of a pound, it follows that it would be about one pound and six-eighths of a pound. We now solicit the attention of the reader to the following unanimous testimony, of the civilized world, to the utter insufficiency of this amount of food to sustain human beings under labor. This testimony is to be found in the laws of all civilized nations, which regulate the rations of soldiers and sailors, disbursements made by governments for the support of citizens in times of public calamity, the allowance to convicts in prisons, &c. We will begin with the United States.

The daily ration for each United States' soldier, established by act of Congress, May 30, 1796, was the following: one pound of beef, one pound of bread, half a gill of spirits; and at the rate of one quart of salt, two quarts of vinegar, two pounds of soap, and one pound of candles to every hundred rations. To those soldiers "who were on the frontiers," (where the labor and exposure were greater,) the ration was one pound two ounces of beef and one pound two ounces of bread. Laws U. S. vol. 3d, sec. 10, p. 431.

After an experiment of two years, the preceding ration being found *insufficient,* it was increased, by act of Congress, July 16, 1798, and was as follows: beef one pound and a quarter, bread one pound two ounces; salt two quarts, vinegar four quarts, soap four pounds, and candles one and a half pounds to the hundred rations. The preceding allowance was afterwards still further increased.

The *present daily ration* for the United States' soldiers, is, as we learn from an advertisement of Captain Fulton, of the United States' army, in a late number of the Richmond (Va.) Enquirer, as follows: one and a quarter pounds of beef, one and three-sixteenths pounds of bread; and at the rate of *eight quarts of beans, eight pounds of sugar,* four pounds of coffee, two quarts of salt, four pounds of candles, and four pounds of soap, to every hundred rations.

We have before us the daily rations provided for the emigrating Ottawa Indians, two years since, and for the emigrating Cherokees last fall. They were the same—one pound of fresh beef, one pound of flour, &c.

The daily ration for the United States Navy is fourteen ounces of bread, half a pound of beef, six ounces of pork, three ounces of rice, three ounces of peas, one ounce of cheese, one ounce of sugar, half an ounce of tea, one-third of a gill molasses.

The daily ration in the British army is one and a quarter pounds of beef, one pound of bread, &c.

The daily ration in the French army is one pound of beef, one and a half pounds of bread, one pint of wine, &c.

The common daily ration for foot soldiers on the continent is one pound of meat, and one and a half pounds of bread.

The *sea ration* among the Portuguese has become the usual ration in the navies of European powers generally. It is as follows: "one and a half pounds of biscuit, one pound of salt meat, one pint of wine, with some dried fish and onions."

Prison Rations.—Before giving the usual daily rations of food allowed to convicts, in the principal prisons in the United States, we will quote the testimony of the "American Prison Discipline Society," which is as follows:

"The common allowance of food in the penitentiaries is equivalent to ONE POUND OF MEAT.

ONE POUND OF BREAD, AND ONE POUND OF VEGETABLES Per Day. It varies a little from this in some of them, but it is generally equivalent to it." First Report of American Prison Discipline Society, page 13.

The daily ration of food to each convict, in the principal prisons in this country, is as follows:

In the New Hampshire State Prison, one and a quarter pounds of meal, and fourteen ounces of beef, for *breakfast and dinner;* and for supper, a soup or porridge of potatoes and beans, or peas, the *quantity not limited.*

In the Vermont prison, the convicts are allowed to eat *as much as they wish.*

In the Massachusetts' penitentiary, one and a half pounds of bread, fourteen ounces of meat, half a pint of potatoes, and one gill of molasses, or one pint of milk.

In the Connecticut State Prison, one pound of beef, one pound of bread, two and a half pounds of potatoes, half a gill of molasses, with salt, pepper, and vinegar.

In the New York State Prison, at Auburn, one pound of beef, twenty-two ounces of flour and meal, half a gill of molasses; with two quarts of rye, four quarts of salt, two quarts of vinegar, one and a half ounces of pepper, and two and a half bushels of potatoes to every hundred rations.

In the New York State Prison at Sing Sing, one pound of beef, eighteen ounces of flour and meal, besides potatoes, rye coffee, and molasses.

In the New York City Prison, one pound of beef, one pound of flour; and three pecks of potatoes to every hundred rations, with other small articles.

In the New Jersey State Prison, one pound of bread, half a pound of beef, with potatoes and cabbage, (quantity not specified,) one gill of molasses, and a bowl of mush for supper.

In the late Walnut Street Prison, Philadelphia, one and a half pounds of bread and meal, half a pound of beef, one pint of potatoes, one gill of molasses, and half a gill of rye, for coffee. In the Baltimore prison, we believe the ration is the same with the preceding.

In the Pennsylvania Eastern Penitentiary, one pound of bread and one pint of coffee for breakfast, one pint of meat soup, with potatoes without limit, for dinner, and mush and molasses for supper.

In the Penitentiary for the District of Columbia, Washington city, one pound of beef, twelve ounces of Indian meal, ten ounces of wheat flour, half a gill of molasses; with two quarts of rye, four quarts of salt, four quarts of vinegar, and two and a half bushels of potatoes to every hundred rations.

Rations in English Prisons.—The daily ration of food in the Bedfordshire Penitentiary, is *two pounds of bread;* and if at hard labor, *a quart of soup for dinner.*

In the Cambridge County House of Correction, three pounds of bread, and one pint of beer.

In the Millbank General Penitentiary, one and a half pounds of bread, one pound of potatoes, six ounces of beef, with half a pint of broth therefrom.

In the Gloucestershire Penitentiary, one and a half pounds of bread, three-fourths of a pint of peas, made into soup, with beef, quantity not stated. Also gruel, made of vegetables, quantity not stated, and one and a half ounces of oatmeal mixed with it.

In the Leicestershire House of Correction, two pounds of bread, and three pints of gruel; and when at hard labor, one pint of milk in addition, and twice a week a pint of meat soup at dinner, instead of gruel.

In the Buxton House of Correction, one and a half pounds of bread, one and a half pints of gruel, one and a half pints of soup, four-fifths of a pound of potatoes, and two-sevenths of an ounce of beef.

Notwithstanding the preceding daily ration in the Buxton Prison is about double the usual daily allowance of our slaves, yet the visiting physicians decided, that for those prisoners who were required to work the tread-mill, it was *entirely insufficient.* This question was considered at length, and publicly discussed at the sessions of the Surry magistrates, with the benefit of medical advice; which resulted in "large additions" to the rations of those who worked on the tread-mill. See London Morning Chronicle, Jan. 13, 1830.

To the preceding we add the *ration of the Roman slaves*. The monthly allowance of food to slaves in Rome was called "Dimensum." The "Dimensum" was an allowance of wheat or of other grain, which consisted of five *modii* a month to each slave. Ainsworth, in his Latin Dictionary estimates the *modius,* when used for the measurement of grain, at *a peck and a half* our measure, which would make the Roman slave's allowance *two quarts of grain a day,* just double the allowance provided for the slave by *law* in North Carolina, and *six* quarts more per week than the ordinary allowance of slaves in the slave states generally, as already established by the testimony of slaveholders themselves. But it must by no means be overlooked that this "Dimensum," or *monthly* allowance, was far from being the sole allowance of food to Roman slaves. In *addition* to this, they had a stated *daily* allowance *(diarium)* besides a monthly allowance of *money,* amounting to about a cent a day.

Now without further trenching on the reader's time, we add, compare the preceding daily allowances of food to soldiers and sailors in this and other countries; to convicts in this and other countries; to bodies of emigrants rationed at public expense; and finally, with the fixed allowance given to Roman slaves, and we find the states of this Union, the *slave* states as well as the free, the United States' government, the different European governments, the old Roman empire, in fine, we may add, the *world,* ancient and modern, uniting in the testimony that to furnish men at hard labor from daylight till dark with but 1 7/8 lbs. of *corn* per day, their sole sustenance, is to MURDER THEM BY PIECE-MEAL. The reader will perceive by examining the preceding statistics that the *average daily ration* throughout this country and Europe exceeds the usual slave's allowance *at least a pound a day;* also that one third of this ration for soldiers and convicts in the United States, and for soldiers and sailors in Europe, is *meat,* generally beef; whereas the allowance of the mass of our slaves is corn, only. Further, the convicts in our prisons are sheltered from the heat of the sun, and from the damps of the early morning and evening, from cold, rain, &C; whereas, the great body of the slaves are exposed to all of these, in their season, from daylight till dark; besides this, they labor more hours in the day than convicts, as will be shown under another head, and are obliged to prepare and cook their own food after they have finished the labor of the day, while the convicts have theirs prepared for them. These, with other circumstances, necessarily make larger and longer draughts upon the strength of the slave, produce consequently greater exhaustion, and demand a larger amount of food to restore and sustain the laborer than is required by the convict in his briefer, less exposed, and less exhausting toils.

That the slaveholders themselves regard the usual allowance of food to slaves as insufficient, both in kind and quantity, for hard-working men, is shown by the fact, that in all the slave states, we believe without exception, *white* convicts at hard labor, have a much *larger* allowance of food than the usual one of slaves; and generally more than *one third* of this daily allowance is meat. This conviction of slaveholders shows itself in various forms. When persons wish to hire slaves to labor on public works, in addition to the inducement of high wages held out to masters to hire out their slaves, the contractors pledge themselves that a certain amount of food shall be given the slaves, taking care to specify a *larger* amount than the usual allowance, and a part of it *meat*.

The following advertisement is an illustration. We copy it from the "Daily Georgian" Savannah, Dec. 14, 1838:

NEGROES WANTED

The Contractors upon the Brunswick and Altamaha Canal are desirous to hire a number of prime Negro Men, from the 1st October next, for fifteen months, until the 1st January, 1840. They will pay at the rate of eighteen dollars per month for each prime hand.

These negroes will be employed in the excavation of the Canal. They will be provided with *three and a half pounds of pork or bacon, and ten quarts of gourd seed corn per week,* lodged in comfortable shanties, and attended constantly by a skilful physician.

J. H. Couper,
P. M. Nightingale.

But we have direct testimony to this point. The late Hon. John Taylor, of Caroline Co. Virginia, for many years Senator in Congress, and for many years president of the Agricultural Society of the State, says in his "Agricultural Essays," No. 30, page 97, "Bread Alone Ought NEVER TO BE CONSIDERED A SUFFICIENT DIET FOR SLAVES EXCEPT AS A PUNISHMENT." He urges upon the planters of Virginia to give their slaves, in addition to bread, "salt meat and vegetables," and adds, "we shall be astonished *to discover upon trial,* that this great comfort to them is a profit to the master."

The Managers of the American Prison Discipline Society, in their third Report, page 58, say, "In the Penitentiaries *generally,* in the United States, the *animal* food is equal to *one pound of meat per day* for each convict."

Most of the actual suffering from hunger on the part of the slaves is in the sugar and cotton-growing region, where the crops are exported and the corn generally purchased from the upper country. Where this is the case *there cannot but be suffering.* The contingencies of bad crops, difficult transportation, high prices, &.c. &c., naturally occasion short and often precarious allowances. The following extract from a New Orleans paper of April 26, 1837, affords an illustration. The writer in describing the effects of the *money pressure* in Mississippi, says:

"They, (the planters,) are now left without provisions and the means of living and using their industry, for the present year. In this dilemma, planters whose crops have been from 100 to 700 bales, find themselves forced to *sacrifice many of their slaves* in order to get the *common necessaries of life* for the support of themselves and the rest of their negroes. *In many places, heavy planters compel their slaves to fish for the means of subsistence, rather than sell them at such ruinous rates. There are at this moment* THOUSANDS OF SLAVES *in Mississippi that* KNOW NOT WHERE THE NEXT MORSEL IS TO COME FROM. *The master must be ruined to save the wretches from being* STARVED"

II. LABOR
THE SLAVES ARE OVERWORKED

This is abundantly proved by the number of hours that the slaves are obliged to be in the field. But before furnishing testimony as to their hours of labor and rest, we will present the express declarations of slaveholders and others, that the slaves are severely driven in the field.

WITNESS

The Senate and House of Representatives of *the* State of South Carolina.

TESTIMONY

"Many owners of slaves, and others who have the management of slaves, *do confine them so closely at hard labor* that *they have not sufficient time for natural rest.*—See 2 Brevard's Digest of the Laws of South Carolina, 243."

===========

WITNESS

History of Carolina —Vol. i, page 190

TESTIMONY

"So *laborious* is the task of raising, beating, and cleaning rice, that had it been possible to obtain European servants in sufficient numbers, *thousands and tens of thousands* must have PERISHED."

===========

WITNESS

Hon. Alexander Smyth, a slaveholder, and member of Congress from Virginia, in his speech on the "Missouri question," Jan. 28, 1820.

TESTIMONY

"Is it not obvious that the way to render their situation *more comfortable,* is to allow them to be taken where there is not the same motive to force the slave to Incessant Toil that there is in the country where cotton, sugar, and tobacco are raised for exportation. It is proposed to hem in the blacks *where they are* Hard Worked, that they may be rendered unproductive and the race be prevented from increasing. * * * The proposed measure would be Extreme Cruelty to the blacks. * * * You would * * * doom them to Hard Labor."

===========

WITNESS

"Travels in Louisiana," translated from the French by John Davies, Esq. —page 81.

TESTIMONY

"At the rolling of sugars, an interval of from two to three months, they *work both night and day.* Abridged of their sleep, they *scarce retire to rest during the whole period."*

===========

WITNESS

The Western Review, No. 2,—article "Agriculture of Louisiana."

TESTIMONY

"The work is admitted to be severe for the hands, (slaves,) requiring when the process is commenced to be *pushed night and day."*

===========

WITNESS

W. C. Gildersleeve, Esq., a native of Georgia, elder of the Presbyterian Church, Wilkes-Barre, Penn.

TESTIMONY

"Overworked? I know they (the slaves) are."

===========

WITNESS

Mr. Asa A. Stone, a theological student, near Natchez, Miss., in 1834 and 1835.

TESTIMONY

"Everybody here knows *overdriving* to be one of the most common occurrences, the planters do not deny it, except, perhaps, to northerners."

===========

WITNESS
Philemon Bliss, Esq., a lawyer of Elyria, Ohio, who lived in Florida in 1834 and 1835.

TESTIMONY
"During the cotton-picking season they usually labor in the field during the whole of the daylight, and then spend a good part of the night in ginning and baling. The labor required is very frequently *excessive,* and speedily impairs the constitution.

=============

WITNESS
Hon. R. J. Turnbull of South Carolina a slaveholder, speaking of the harvesting of cotton, says:

TESTIMONY
All the pregnant women even, on the plantation, and weak and *sickly* negroes incapable of other labor, are then *in requisition*

=============.

HOURS OF LABOR AND REST

WITNESS
Asa A Stone, theological student, a classical teacher near Natchez, Miss., 1835.

TESTIMONY
"It is a general rule on all regular plantations, that the slaves be in the field as *soon as it is light enough for them to see to work,* and remain there until it is *so dark that they cannot see."*

=============

WITNESS
Mr. Cornelius Johnson, of Farnrington, Ohio, who lived in Mississippi a part of 1837 and 1838.

TESTIMONY
"It is the common rule for the slaves to be kept at work *fifteen hours in the day,* and in the time of picking cotton a certain number of pounds is required of each. If this amount is not brought in at night, the slave is whipped, and the number of pounds lacking is added to the next day's job; this course is often repeated from day to day."

=============

WITNESS

W. C. Gildersleeve, Esq., Wilkes-Barre, Penn., a native of Georgia.

TESTIMONY

"It was customary for the overseers to call out the gangs *long before day,* say three o'clock, in the winter, while dressing out the crops; such work as could be done by fire light (pitch pine was abundant,) was provided."

===========

WITNESS

Mr. William Leftwich, a native of Virginia and son of a slaveholder— he has recently removed to Delhi, Hamilton county Ohio.

TESTIMONY

"*From dawn till dark,* the slaves are required to bend to their work."

===========

WITNESS

Mr. Nehemiah Caulkins, Waterford, Conn., a resident in North Carolina eleven winters.

TESTIMONY

"The slaves are obliged to work *from daylight till dark,* as long as they can see."

===========

WITNESS

Mr. Eleazar Powel, Chippewa, Beaver County, Penn., who lived in Mississippi in 1836 and 1837.

TESTIMONY

"The slaves had to cook and eat their breakfast and be in the field by *daylight, and continue there till dark.*"

===========

WITNESS

Philemon Bliss, Esq., a lawyer in Elyria, Ohio, who resided in Florida in 1834 and 1835.

TESTIMONY

"The slaves commence labor *by daylight* in the morning, and do not leave the field *till dark* in the evening."

===========

"Travels in Louisiana," page 87.

"Both in summer and winter the slave must *be in the field by the first dawning of day.*"

===========

Mr. Henry E. Knapp, member of a Christian church in Farmington, Ohio, who lived in Mississippi in 1837 and 1838.

"The slaves were made to work, from *as soon as they could see* in the morning, till as late as they could see at night. Sometimes they were made to work till nine o'clock at night, in such work as they could do, as burning cotton stalks, &c."

===========

A New Orleans paper, dated March 23, 1826, says: "To judge from the activity reigning in the cotton presses of the suburbs of St. Mary, and the *late* hours during which their slaves work, the cotton trade was never more brisk."

Mr. **George W. Westgate,** a member of the Congregational Church at Quincy, Illinois, who lived in the south western slave states a number of years, says, "The slaves are driven to the field in the morning *about four o'clock,* the general calculation is to get them at work by daylight. The time for breakfast is between nine and ten o'clock, this meal is sometimes eaten *bite* and *work,* others allow fifteen minutes, and this is the only rest the slave has while in the field. I have never known a case of stopping an hour, in Louisiana. In Mississippi the rule is milder, though entirely subject to the will of the master. On cotton plantations, in cotton picking time, that is from October to Christmas, each hand has a certain quantity to pick, and is flogged if his task is not accomplished; their tasks are such as to keep them all the while busy."

The preceding testimony under this head has sole reference to the actual labor of the slaves *in the field.* In order to determine how many hours are left for sleep, we must take into the account, the time spent in going to and from the field, which is often at a distance of one, two and sometimes three miles; also the time necessary for pounding, or grinding their corn, and preparing, over night, their food for the next day; also the preparation of tools, getting fuel and preparing it, making fires and cooking their suppers, if they have any, the occasional mending and washing of their clothes, &c. Besides this, as everyone knows who has lived on a southern plantation, many little errands and *chores* are to be done for their masters and mistresses, old and young, which have accumulated during the day and been kept in reserve till the slaves return from the field at night. To this we may add that the slaves are *social* beings, and that during the day, silence is generally enforced by the whip of the overseer or driver.* When they return at night, their pent up social feelings will seek vent, it is a law of nature, and though the body may be greatly worn with toil, this law cannot be wholly stifled. Sharers of the same woes, they are drawn together by strong affinities, and seek the society and sympathy of their fellows; even "*tired* nature" will joyfully forego for a time needful rest, to minister to a want of its being equally permanent and imperative as the want of sleep, and as much more profound, as the yearnings of the higher nature surpass the instincts of its animal appendage.

*We do not mean that they are not suffered to *speak*, but, that, as conversation would be a hindrance to labor, they are generally permitted to indulge in it but little.

All these things make drafts upon *time* to show how much of the slave's time, which is absolutely indispensable for rest and sleep, is necessarily spent in various labors after his return from the field at night, we subjoin a few testimonies:

Mr. **Cornelius Johnson**, Farmington, Ohio, who lived in Mississippi in the years 1837 and 38, says:

"On all the plantations where I was acquainted, the slaves were kept in the field till dark; after which, those who had to grind their own corn, had that to attend to, get their supper, attend to other family affairs of their own and of their master, such as bringing water, washing clothes, &c. &c., and be in the field as soon as it was sufficiently light to commence work in the morning."

Mr. **George W. Westgate**, of Quincy, Illinois, who has spent several years in the south western slave states, says:

"Their time, after full dark until four o'clock in the morning is their own; this fact alone would seem to say they have sufficient rest, but there are other things to be considered; much of their making, mending and washing of clothes, preparing and cooking food, hauling and chopping wood, fixing and preparing tools, and a variety of little nameless jobs must be done between those hours."

Philemon Bliss, Esq. of Elyria, Ohio, who resided in Florida in 1834 and 5, gives the following testimony:

"After having finished their field labors, they are occupied till nine or ten o'clock in doing *chores,* such as grinding corn, (as all the corn in the vicinity is ground by hand,) chopping wood, taking care of horses, mules, &c., and a thousand things necessary to be done on a large plantation. If any extra job is to be done, it must not hinder the 'niggers' from their work, but must be done in the night."

W. C. Gildersleeve, Esq., a native of Georgia, an elder of the Presbyterian Church at Wilkes-Barre, says:

"The corn is ground in a hand mill by the slave *after his task is done—*generally there is but one mill on a plantation, and as but one can grind at a time, the mill is going sometimes *very late at night."*

We now present another class of facts and testimony, showing that the slaves engaged in raising the large staples, are *overworked.*

In September, 1834, the writer of this had an interview with James G. Birney, Esq., who then resided in Kentucky, having removed with his family from Alabama the year before. A few hours before that interview, and on the morning of the same day, Mr. B. had spent a couple of hours with Hon. Henry Clay, at his residence, near Lexington. Mr. Birney remarked, that Mr. Clay had just told him, he had lately been led to mistrust certain estimates as to the increase of the slave population in the far southwest—estimates which he had presented, I think, in a speech before the Colonization Society. He now believed, that the births among the slaves in that quarter were *not equal to the deaths—*and that, of course, the slave population, independent of immigration from the slave-selling states, was *not sustaining itself.*

Among other facts stated by Mr. Clay, was the following, which we copy *verbatim* from the original memorandum, made at the time by Mr. Birney, with which he has kindly furnished us:

"Sept. 16, 1834.—Hon. H. Clay, in a conversation at his own house, on the subject of slavery, informed me, that Hon. Outerbridge Horsey, formerly a senator in Congress from the state of Delaware, and the owner of a sugar plantation in Louisiana, declared to him, that his overseer worked his hands so closely, that one of the women brought forth a child whilst engaged in the labors of the field.

"Also, that a few years since, he was at a brickyard in the environs of New Orleans, in which one hundred hands were employed; among them were from *twenty to thirty young women,* in the prime of life. He was told by the proprietor, that there had *not been a child born among them for the last two or three years, although they all had husbands."*

The preceding testimony of Mr. Clay, is strongly corroborated by advertisements of slaves, by Courts of Probate, and by executors administering upon the estates of deceased persons. Some of those advertisements for the sale of slaves, contain the names, ages, accustomed employment, &c., of all the slaves upon the plantation of the deceased. These catalogues show large numbers of young men and women, almost all of them between twenty and thirty-eight years old; and yet the number of young children is *astonishingly small.* We have laid aside many lists of this kind, in looking over the newspapers of the slaveholding states; but the two following are all we can lay our hands on at present. One is in the "Planter's Intelligencer," Alexandria, La., March 22, 1837, containing one hundred and thirty slaves; and the other in the New Orleans Bee, a few days later, April 8, 1837, containing fifty-one slaves. The former is a "Probate sale" of the slaves belonging to the estate of Mr. Charles S. Lee, deceased, and is advertised by G. W. Keeton, Judge of the Parish of Concordia, La. The sex, name, and age of each slave are contained in the advertisement, which fills two columns. The following are some of the particulars.

The whole number of slaves is *one hundred and thirty.* Of these, *only three are over forty years old.* There are *thirty-five females* between the ages of *sixteen and thirty-three,* and yet there are only thirteen children under the age of *thirteen years!*

It is impossible satisfactorily to account for such a fact, on any other supposition, than that these thirty-five females were so overworked, or underfed, or both, as to prevent child-bearing.

The other advertisement is that of a "Probate sale," ordered by the Court of the Parish of Jefferson—including the slaves of Mr. William Gormley. The whole number of slaves is fifty-one; the sex, age, and accustomed labors of each are given. The oldest of these slaves is but *thirty-nine years old:* of the females, *thirteen* are between the ages of sixteen and thirty-two, and the oldest female is but *thirty-eight*—and yet there are but *two children under eight years old!*

Another proof that the slaves in the southwestern states are over-worked is the fact, that so few of them live to old age. A large majority of them are *old* at middle age, and few live beyond fifty-five. In one of the preceding advertisements, out of one hundred and thirty slaves, only *three* are over forty years old! In the other, out of fifty-one slaves, only *two* are over *thirty-five;* the oldest is but thirty-nine, and the way in which he is designated in the advertisement, is an additional proof, that what to others is "middle age," is to the slaves in the southwest "old age:" he is advertised as "*Old* Jeffrey."

But the proof that the slave population of the southwest is so over-worked that it cannot *supply its own waste,* does not rest upon mere inferential evidence. The Agricultural Society of Baton Rouge, La., in its report, published in 1829, furnishes a labored estimate of the amount of expenditure necessarily incurred in conducting "a well-regulated sugar estate." In this estimate, the annual net loss of slaves, over and above the supply by propagation, is set down at TWO AND A HALF PERCENT! The late Hon. Josiah S. Johnson, a member of Congress from Louisiana, addressed a letter to the Secretary of the United States' Treasury, in 1830, containing a similar estimate, apparently made with great care, and going into minute details. Many items in this estimate differ from the preceding; but the estimate of the annual *decrease* of the slaves on a plantation was the same—TWO AND A HALF PERCENT!

The following testimony of Rev. Dr. Channing, of Boston, who resided some time in Virginia, shows that the over-working of slaves, to such an extent as to abridge life, and cause a decrease of population, is not confined to the far south and southwest.

"I heard of an estate managed by an individual who was considered as singularly successful, and who was able to govern the slaves without the use of the whip. I was anxious to see him, and trusted that some discovery had been made favorable to humanity. I asked him how he was able to dispense with corporal punishment. He replied to me, with a very determined look. 'The slaves know that the work *must* be done, and that it is better to do it without punishment than with it.' In other words, the certainty and dread of chastisement were so impressed on them, that they never incurred it.

"I then found that the slaves on this well-managed estate, *decreased* in number. I asked the cause. He replied, with perfect frankness and ease, 'The gang is not large enough for the estate.' In other words, they were not equal to the work of the plantation, and yet were *made to do it,* though with the certainty of abridging life.

"On this plantation the huts were uncommonly convenient. There was an unusual air of neatness. A superficial observer would have called the slaves happy. Yet they were living under a severe, subduing discipline, and were *over-worked* to a degree that *shortened life.*"— *Channing on Slavery,* page 162, first edition.

Philemon Bliss, Esq., a lawyer of Elyria, Ohio, who spent some time in Florida, gives the following testimony to the over-working of the slaves:

"It is not uncommon for hands, in hurrying times, besides working all day, to labor half the night. This is usually the case on sugar plantations, during the sugar-boiling season; and on cotton, during its gathering. Beside the regular task of picking cotton, averaging of the short staple, when the crop is good, 100 pounds a day to the hand, the ginning (extracting the seed,) and baling was done in the night. Said Mr. ____ to me, while conversing upon the customary labor of slaves, 'I work my niggers in a hurrying time till 11 or 12 o'clock at night, and have them up by four in the morning.'

"Beside the common inducement, the desire of gain, to make a large crop, the desire is increased by that spirit of gambling, so common at the south. It is very common to *bet* on the issue of a crop. A. lays a wager that, from a given number of hands, he will make more cotton than B. The wager is accepted, and then begins the contest; and who bears the burden of it? How many tears, yea, how many broken constitutions, and premature deaths, have been the effect of this spirit? From the desperate energy of purpose with which the gambler pursues his object, from the passions which the practice calls into exercise, we might conjecture many. Such is the fact. In Middle Florida, a *broken-winded* negro is more common than a *broken-winded* horse; though usually, when they are declared unsound, or when their constitution is so broken that their recovery is despaired of, they are exported to New Orleans, to drag out the remainder of their days in the cane-field and sugar house. I would not insinuate that all planters gamble upon their crops; but I mention the practice as one of the common inducements to 'push niggers.' Neither would I assert that all planters drive the hands to the injury of their health. I give it as a *general rule* in the district of Middle Florida, and I have no reason to think that negroes are driven worse there than in other fertile sections. People there told me that the situation of the slaves was far better than in Mississippi and Louisiana. And from comparing the crops with those made in the latter states, and for other reasons, I am convinced of the truth of their statements."

Dr. Demming, a gentleman of high respectability, residing in Ashland, Richland County, Ohio, stated to Professor Wright, of New York City, "That during a recent tour at the south, while ascending the Ohio River, on the steamboat Fame, he had an opportunity of conversing with a Mr. Dickinson, a resident of Pittsburg, in company with a number of cotton-planters and slave-dealers, from Louisiana, Alabama, and Mississippi. Mr. Dickinson stated as a fact, that the sugar planters upon the sugar coast in Louisiana had ascertained, that, as it was usually necessary to employ about *twice* the amount of labor during the boiling season, that was required during the season of raising, they could, by excessive driving, day and night, during the boiling season, accomplish the whole labor *with one set of hands. By* pursuing this plan, they could afford *to sacrifice a set of hands once in seven years!* He further stated that this horrible system was now practiced to a considerable extent! The correctness of this statement was substantially admitted by the slaveholders then on board."

The late Mr. **Samuel Blackwell**, a highly respected citizen of Jersey City, opposite the city of New York, and a member of the Presbyterian Church, visited many of the sugar plantations in Louisiana a few years since; and having for many years been the owner of an extensive sugar refinery in England, and subsequently in this country, he had not only every facility afforded him by the planters, for personal inspection of all parts of the process of sugar-making, but received from them the most unreserved communications, as to their management of their slaves. Mr. B., after his return, frequently made the following statement to gentlemen of his acquaintance,—"That the planters generally declared to him, that they were *obliged* so to over-work their slaves during the sugar-making season, (from eight to ten weeks,) as to *use them up* in seven or eight years. For, said they, after the process is commenced, it must be pushed without cessation, night and day; and we cannot afford to keep a sufficient number of slaves to do the *extra* work at the time of sugar-making, as we could not profitably employ them the rest of the year."

It is not only true of the sugar planters, but of the slaveholders generally throughout the far south and south west, that they believe it for their interest to wear out the slaves by excessive toil in eight or ten years after they put them into the field.*

*Alexander Jones, Esq., a large planter in West Feliciana, Louisiana, published a communication in the "North Carolina True American," Nov. 35, 1838, in which, speaking of the horses employed in the mills on the plantations for ginning cotton, he says, they " are much whipped and jaded;" and adds, "In fact, this service is so severe on horses, as to shorten their lives in many instances, if not actually kill them in gear."

Those who work *one* kind of their "live stock" so as to "shorten their lives," or "kill them in gear," would not stick at doing the same thing to another kind.

Rev. Doctor Reed, of London, who went through Kentucky, Virginia and Maryland in the summer of 1834, gives the following testimony:"I was told confidently and from *excellent authority* that recently at a meeting of planters in South Carolina, the question was seriously discussed whether the slave is more profitable to the owner, if well fed, well clothed, and worked lightly, or if made the most of *at once,* and exhausted in some eight years. The decision was in favor of the last alternative. That decision will perhaps make many shudder. But to my mind this is not the chief evil. The greater and original evil is considering the *slave as property.* If he is only property and my property, then I have some right to ask how I may make that property *most available."*

"Visit to the American Churches," by Rev. Drs. Reed and Mattheson. Vol. 2. p. 173.

Rev. John O. Choules, recently pastor of the Baptist Church at New Bedford, Massachusetts, now of Buffalo, New York, made substantially the following statement in a speech in Boston.

"While attending the Baptist Triennial Convention at Richmond, Virginia, in the spring of 1835, as a delegate from Massachusetts, I had a conversation on slavery, with an officer of the Baptist Church in that city, at whose house I was a guest. I asked my host if he did not apprehend that the slaves would eventually rise and exterminate their masters.

"Why," said the gentleman, "I used to apprehend such a catastrophe, but God has made a providential opening, *a merciful safety valve,* and now I do not feel alarmed in the *prospect* of what is coming. 'What do you mean, said Mr. Choules,' by providence opening a merciful safety valve?' Why, said the gentleman, I will tell you; the slave traders come from the cotton and sugar plantations of the South and are willing to buy up more slaves than we can part with. We must keep a stock for the purpose of *rearing* slaves, but we part with the most valuable, and at the same time, the most *dangerous,* and the demand is very constant and likely to be so, for when they go to these southern states, the average existence is ONLY FIVE YEARS!"

Monsieur C. C. Robin, a highly intelligent French gentleman, who resided in Louisiana from 1802 to 1806, and published a volume of travels, gives the following testimony to the overworking of the slaves there:

"I have been a witness, that after the fatigue of the day, their labors have been prolonged several hours by the light of the moon; and then, before they could think of rest, they must pound and cook their corn; and yet, long before day, an implacable scold, whip in hand, would arouse them from their slumbers. Thus, of more than twenty negroes, who in twenty years should have doubled, the number *was reduced to four or five."* In conclusion we add that slaveholders have in the most public and emphatic manner declared themselves guilty of barbarous inhumanity toward their slaves in exacting from them such *long continued daily labor.* The Legislatures of Maryland, Virginia and Georgia, have passed laws providing that convicts in their state prisons and penitentiaries, "shall be employed in work each day in the year except Sundays, not exceeding *eight* hours, in the months of November, December, and January; *nine* hours, in the months of February and October, and *ten* hours in the rest of the year." Now contrast this *legal* exaction of labor from convicts with the exaction from slaves as established by the preceding testimony. The reader perceives that the amount of time, in which by the preceding laws of Maryland, Virginia, and Georgia, the *convicts* in their prisons are required to labor, is on an average during the year but little more than Nine hours daily. Whereas, the laws of South Carolina permit the master to *compel* his slaves to work fifteen hours in the twenty-four, in summer, and fourteen in the winter—which would be in winter, from daybreak in the morning until *four hours* after sunset!—See 2 Brevard's Digest, 243

The other slave states, except Louisiana, have *no laws* respecting the labor of slaves, consequently if the master should work his slaves day and night without sleep till they drop dead, *he violates no law!*

The law of Louisiana provides for the slaves but TWO AND A HALF HOURS in the twenty-four for "rest!" See law of Louisiana, act of July 7. 1806, Martin's Digest 6. 10—12.

III. CLOTHING

We propose to show under this head, that the clothing of the slaves by day, and their covering by night, are inadequate, either for comfort or decency.

WITNESS

Hon. T. T. Bouldin, a slave-holder, and member of Congress from Virginia, in a speech in Congress, Feb. 16, 1835.

TESTIMONY

Mr. Bouldin said "he knew that many negroes had died from exposure to weather," and added, "they are clad in a flimsy fabric, that will turn neither wind nor water."

===========

WITNESS

George Buchanan, M. D., of Baltimore, member of the American Philosophical Society, in an oration at Baltimore, July 4, 1791.

TESTIMONY

"The slaves, naked and starved, often fall victims to the inclemencies of the weather."

===========

WITNESS

Wm. Savery of Philadelphia an eminent Minister of the Society of Friends, who went through the Southern states in 1791, on a religious visit: after leaving Savannah, Ga., we find the following entry in his journal, 6th, month, 28, 1791.

TESTIMONY

"We rode through many rice swamps, where the blacks were very numerous, great droves of these poor slaves, working up to the middle in water, men and women nearly naked."

===========

WITNESS

Rev. John Rankin, of Ripley, Ohio, a native of Tennessee.

TESTIMONY

"In every slave-holding state, many slaves suffer extremely, both while they labor and while they sleep, for want of clothing to keep them warm."

===========

WITNESS

John Parrish, late of Philadelphia, a highly esteemed minister in the Society of Friends, who travelled through the South in 1804

TESTIMONY

"It is shocking to the feelings of humanity, in travelling through some of those states, to see those poor objects, [slaves,] especially in the inclement season, in *rags* and *trembling with the cold.*"

"They suffer them, both male and female, *to go without clothing* at the age of ten and twelve years."

==========

WITNESS

Rev. Phineas Smith, Centreville, Allegany, Co., N. Y. Mr. S. has just returned from a residence of several years at the south, chiefly in Virginia, Louisiana, and among the American settlers in Texas.

TESTIMONY

"The apparel of the slaves, is of the coarsest sort and *exceedingly deficient* in quantity. I have been on many plantations, where children of eight and ten years old, were in a state of *perfect nudity.* Slaves are in *general wretchedly clad.*"

==========

WITNESS

Wm. Ladd, Esq., of Minot, Maine, recently a slaveholder in Florida.

TESTIMONY

"They were allowed two suits of clothes a year, viz. one pair of trowsers with a shirt or frock of osnaburgh* for summer; and for winter, one pair of trowsers, and a jacket of negro cloth, with a baize shirt and a pair of shoes. Some allowed hats, and some did not; and they were generally, I believe, allowed one blanket in two years. Garments of similar materials were allowed the women."

*Osnaburgh – a course cloth made from flax, tow or jute yarn.

==========

WITNESS

A Kentucky physician, writing in the Western Medical Reformer, in 1896, on the diseases peculiar to slaves, says,

TESTIMONY

"They are *imperfectly clothed* both summer and winter."

==========

WITNESS

Mr. Stephen E. Maltby, Inspector of provisions, Skaneateles, N. Y., who resided sometime in Alabama.

TESTIMONY

"I was at Huntsville, Alabama, in 1818-19, I frequently saw slaves on and around the public square, *with hardly a rag of clothing on them,* and in a *great many* instances with but a single garment both in summer and in winter; generally the only bedding of the slaves was a *blanket.*"

===========

WITNESS

Reuben G. Macy, Hudson, N. Y. member of the Society of Friends, who resided in South Carolina, in 1818 and 19.

TESTIMONY

"Their clothing consisted of a pair of trowsers and jacket, made of ' negro cloth. The women a petticoat, a very short 'short-gown,' and *nothing else,* the same kind of cloth; some of the women had an old pair of shoes, but they *generally went barefoot!'*

===========

WITNESS

Mr. Lemuel Sappington, of Lancaster, Pa., a native of Maryland, and formerly a slaveholder

TESTIMONY

"Their clothing is often made by themselves after night, though sometimes assisted by the old women, who are no longer able to do out-door work; consequently it is harsh and uncomfortable. And I have very frequently seen those who had not attained the age of twelve years *go naked.*"

===========

WITNESS

Philemon Bliss, Esq., a lawyer in Elyria, Ohio, who lived in Florida in 1834 and 35.

TESTIMONY

"It is very common to see the younger class of slaves up to eight or ten *without any clothing,* and most generally the laboring men wear *no shirts* in the warm season. The perfect nudity of the younger slaves is so familiar to the whites of both sexes that they seem to witness it with perfect indifference. I may add that the aged and feeble often *suffer from cold.*"

WITNESS
Richard Macy, a member of the Society of Friends, Hudson, N. Y., who has lived in Georgia.

TESTIMONY
"For *bedding* each slave was allowed *one blanket,* in which they rolled themselves up. I examined their houses, but could not find anything like *a bed.*"

WITNESS
W. C. Gildersleeve, Esq., Wilkes-Barre, Pa., a native of Georgia.

TESTIMONY
"It is an everyday sight to see women as well as men, with no other covering than a *few filthy rags fastened above the hips,* reaching midway to the ankles. *I never knew any kind of covering for the head* given. Children of both sexes, from infancy to ten years are seen in companies on the plantations, *in a state of perfect nudity.* This was so common that the most refined and delicate beheld them unmoved."

WITNESS
Mr. William Leftwich, a native of Virginia, now a member of the Presbyterian Church, in Delhi, Ohio.

TESTIMONY
"The only bedding of the slaves generally consists of *two old blankets.*"

Advertisements like the following from the "New Orleans Bee," May 31, 1837, are common in the southern papers:

"10 DOLLARS REWARD
Ranaway, the slave Solomon, about 28 years of age; Badly Clothed. The above reward will be paid on application to Fernandez & Whiting, No. 20, St. Louis St.

RANAWAY from the subscriber the negress Fanny, always badly dressed, she is about 25 or 26 years old. John Macoin, 117 S. Ann St.

The Darien (Ga.), Telegraph, of Jan. 24, 1837, in an editorial article, hitting off the aristocracy of the planters, incidentally lets out some secrets, about the usual *clothing* of the slaves. The editor says,—"The planter looks down, with the most sovereign contempt, on the merchant and the storekeeper. He deems himself a lord, because he gets his two or three RAGGED servants, to row him to his plantation every day, that he may inspect the labor of his hands."

The following is an extract from a letter lately received from **Rev. C. S. Renshaw**, of Quincy, Illinois:

"I am sorry to be obliged to give more testimony without the *name*. An individual, in whom I have great confidence, gave me the following facts. That I am not alone in placing confidence in him, I subjoin a testimonial from Dr. Richard Eells, Deacon of the Congregational Church, of Quincy, and Rev. Mr. Fisher, Baptist Minister of Quincy.

"We have been acquainted with the brother who has communicated to you some facts that fell under his observation, whilst in his native state; he is a professed follower of our Lord, and we have great confidence in him as a man of integrity, discretion, and strict Christian principle.

Richard Eells
Ezra Fisher
Quincy, Jan. 9th, 1839.

Testimony.—" I lived for thirty years in Virginia, and have travelled extensively through Fauquier, Culpepper, Jefferson, Stafford, Albemarle and Charlotte Counties; my remarks apply to these counties.

"The negro houses are miserably poor, generally they are a shelter from neither the wind, the rain, nor the snow, and the earth is the floor. There are exceptions to this rule, but they are only exceptions; you may sometimes see puncheon floor, but never, or almost never a plank floor. The slaves are generally without *beds or bedsteads;* some few have cribs that they fasten up for themselves in the corner of the hut. Their bed-clothes are a nest of rags thrown upon a crib, or in the corner; sometimes there are three or four families in one small cabin. Where the slaveholders have more than one family, they put them in the same quarter till it is filled, then build another. I have seen exceptions to this, when only one family would occupy a hut and where were tolerably comfortable bed-clothes.

"Most of the slaves in these counties are *miserably clad.* I have known slaves who went without shoes all winter, perfectly barefoot. The feet of many of them are frozen. As a general fact the planters do not serve out to their slaves, drawers, or any under clothing, or vests, or overcoats. Slaves sometimes, by working at night and on Sundays, get better things than their masters serve to them.

"Whilst these things are true of field-hands, it is also true that many slaveholders clothe their *waiters* and coachmen like gentlemen. I do not think there is any difference between the slaves of professing Christians and others; at all events, it is so small as to be scarcely noticeable.

"I have seen men and women at work in the field more than half naked: and more than once in passing, when the overseer was not near, they would stop and draw round them a tattered coat or some ribbons of a skirt to hide their nakedness and shame from the stranger's eye."

Mr. **George W. Westgate**, a member of the Congregational Church in Quincy, Illinois, who has spent the larger part of twelve years navigating the rivers of the south-western slave states with keel boats, as a trader, gives the following testimony as to the clothing and lodging of the slaves:

"In Lower Tennessee, Mississippi and Louisiana, the clothing of the slaves is wretchedly poor; and grows worse as you go south, in the order of the states I have named. The only material is cotton bagging, ie. bagging in which cotton is *baled,* not bagging made of cotton. In Louisiana, especially in the lower country, I have frequently seen them with nothing but a tattered coat, not sufficient to hide their nakedness. In winter their clothing seldom serves the purpose of comfort, and frequently not even of decent covering. In Louisiana *the planters never think of serving out shoes to slaves.* In Mississippi they give one pair a year generally. I never saw or heard of an instance of masters allowing them *stockings. A small poor blanket is generally the only bed-clothing,* and this they frequently wear in the field when they have not sufficient clothing to hide their nakedness or to keep them warm. Their manner of sleeping varies with the season. In hot weather they stretch themselves anywhere and sleep. As it becomes cool they roll themselves in their blankets, and lay scattered about the cabin. In cold weather they nestle together with their feet towards the fire, promiscuously. As a general fact the earth is their only floor and bed—not one in ten have anything like a bedstead, and then it is a mere bunk put up by themselves."

Mr. **George A. Avery**, an elder in the fourth Congregational Church, Rochester, N. Y., who spent four years in Virginia, says, "The slave children, very commonly of both sexes, up to the ages of eight and ten years, and I think in some instances beyond this age, go in a state of *disgusting* nudity. I have often seen them with their tow shirt (their only article of summer clothing) which, to all human appearance, had not been taken off from the time it was first put on, worn off from the bottom upwards, shred by shred, until nothing remained but the straps which passed over their shoulders, and the less exposed portions extending a very little way below the arms, leaving the principal part of the chest, as well as the limbs, entirely uncovered."

Samuel Ellison, a member of the Society of Friends, formerly of Southampton Co., Virginia, now of Marlborough, Stark Co., Ohio, says, "I knew a Methodist who was the owner of a number of slaves. The children of both sexes, belonging to him, under twelve years of age, were *entirely* destitute of clothing. I have seen an old man compelled to labor in the fields, not having rags enough to cover his nakedness."

Rev. H. Lyman, late pastor of the Free Presbyterian Church, in Buffalo, N. Y., in describing a tour down and up the Mississippi river in the winter of 1832-3, says, "At the wood yards where the boats stop, it is not uncommon to see female slaves employed in carrying wood. Their dress which was quite uniform was provided without any reference to comfort. They had no covering for their heads; the stuff which constituted the outer garment was sackcloth, similar to that in which brown domestic goods are done up. It was then December, and I thought that in such a dress, and being as they were, without *stockings,* they must suffer from the cold."

Mr. **Benjamin Anderson**, Colerain, Lancaster Co., Pa., a member of the Society of Friends, in a recent letter describing a short tour through the northern part of Maryland in the winter of 1836, thus speaks of a place a few miles from Chestertown. "About this place there were a number of slaves; very few, if any, had *either stockings or shoes;* the weather was intensely cold, and the ground covered with snow."

The late **Major Stoddard** of the United States' artillery, who took possession of Louisiana for the U. S. government, under the cession of 1804, published a book entitled "Sketches of Louisiana," in which, speaking of the planters of Lower Louisiana, he says, "*Few of them allow any clothing to their slaves.*"

The following is an extract from the Will of the late celebrated John Randolph of Virginia.

"To my old and faithful servants, Essex and his wife Hetty, I give and bequeath a pair of strong shoes, a suit of clothes and a blanket each, to be paid them annually; also an annual hat to Essex."

No Virginia slaveholder has ever had a better name as a "kind master," and "good provider" for his slaves, than John Randolph. Essex and Hetty were *favorite* servants, and the memory of the long uncompensated services of those "old and faithful servants," seems to have touched their master's heart. Now as this master was *John Randolph,* and as those servants were "faithful," and favorite servants, advanced in years, and worn out in his service, and as their allowance was, in their master's eyes, of sufficient moment to constitute a paragraph in his last *will and testament,* it is fair to infer that it would be *very liberal,* far better than the ordinary allowance for slaves.

Now we leave the reader to judge what must be the *usual* allowance of clothing to common field slaves in the hands of common masters, when Essex and Hetty, the "old" and "faithful" slaves of John Randolph, were provided, in his last will and testament, with but *one* suit of clothes annually, with but *one blanket* each for bedding, with no *stockings,* nor *socks,* nor *cloaks,* nor overcoats, nor *handkerchiefs,* nor *towels,* and with no *change* either of under or outside garments!

IV. DWELLINGS
THE SLAVES ARE WRETCHEDLY SHELTERED AND LODGED.

WITNESS

Mr. Stephen E. Maltby. Inspector of provisions, Skaneateles, N. Y. who has lived in Alabama.

TESTIMONY

"The huts where the slaves slept generally contained but *one* apartment, and that *without floor.*"

==========

WITNESS

Mr. George A. Avery, elder of the 4th Presbyterian Church, Rochester, N. Y. who lived four years in Virginia.

TESTIMONY

"Amongst all the negro cabins which I saw in Va., I *cannot call to mind one* in which there was any other floor than the *earth;* anything that a northern laborer, or mechanic, white or colored, would call a *bed,* nor a solitary *partition,* to separate the sexes."

==========

WITNESS

William Ladd, Esq., Minot, Maine. President of the American Peace Society, formerly a slaveholder in Florida.

TESTIMONY

"The dwellings of the slaves were palmetto huts, built by themselves of stakes and poles, thatched with the palmetto leaf. The door, when they had any, was generally of the same materials, sometimes boards found on the beach. They had *no floors,* no separate apartments, except the guinea negroes had sometimes a small enclosure for their 'god house.' These huts the slaves built themselves after task and on Sundays."

==========

WITNESS

Rev. Joseph M. Sadd, Pastor Pres. Church, Castile, Greene Co., N. Y., who lived in Missouri five years previous to 1837.

TESTIMONY

"The slaves live *generally* in *miserable huts,* which are *without floors,* and have a single apartment only, where both sexes are herded promiscuously together."

==========

WITNESS

Mr. George W. Westgate, member of the Congregational Church in Quincy, Illinois, who has spent a number of years in slave states.

TESTIMONY

"On old plantations, the negro quarters are of frame and clapboards, seldom affording a comfortable shelter from wind or rain; their size varies from 8 by 10, to 10 by 12, feet, and six or eight feet high; sometimes there is a hole cut for a window, but I never saw a sash, or glass in any. In the new country, and in the woods, the quarters are generally built of logs, of similar dimensions."

===========

WITNESS

Mr. Cornelius Johnson, a member of ri Christian Church in Farmington, Ohio. Mr. J. lived in Mississippi in 1837-8.

TESTIMONY

"Their houses were commonly built of logs, sometimes they were framed, often they had no floor, some of them have two apartments, commonly but one ; each of those apartments contained a family. Sometimes these families consisted of a man and his wife and children, while in other instances persons of both sexes, were thrown together without any regard to family relationship."

===========

WITNESS

The Western Medical Reformer, in an article on the Cachexia African by a Kentucky physician, thus speaks of the huts of the slaves.

TESTIMONY

"They are *crowded* together in a *small hut,* and sometimes having an imperfect, and sometimes no floor, and seldom raised from the ground, ill ventilated, and surrounded with filth."

===========

WITNESS

Mr. William Leftwich, a native of Virginia, but has resided most of his life in Madison, Co. Alabama.

TESTIMONY

"The dwellings of the slaves are log huts, from 10 to 12 feet square, often without windows, doors, or floors; they have neither chairs, table, or bedstead."

==========

WITNESS

Reuben L. Macy of Hudson, N. Y. a member of the Religious Society of Friends. He lived in South Carolina in 1818-19.

TESTIMONY

"The houses for the field slaves were about 14 feet square, built in the coarsest manner, with one room, *without any* chim*ney or flooring, with a hole in the roof to let the smoke out."*

==========

WITNESS

Mr. Lemuel Sapington of Lancaster, Pa. a native of Maryland, formerly a slaveholder.

TESTIMONY

"The descriptions generally given of negro quarters, are correct; the quarters are *without floors, and not sufficient to keep off the inclemency of the weather;* they are uncomfortable both in summer and winter."

==========

WITNESS

Rev. John Rankin, a native of Tennessee.

TESTIMONY

"When they return to their miserable huts at night, they find not there the means of comfortable rest; but *on the cold ground they must lie without covering and shiver while they slumber.*

==========

WITNESS

Philemon Bliss, Esq. Elyria, Ohio, who lived in Florida, in 1835.

TESTIMONY

"The dwellings of the slaves are usually small *open* log huts, with but one apartment and very generally *without floors."*

==========

WITNESS

Mr. W. C. Gildersleeve, Wilkes-Barre, Pa., a native of Georgia.

TESTIMONY

"Their huts were generally put up without a nail, frequently without floors, and with a single apartment."

==========

WITNESS

Hon. R. J. Turnbull, of South Carolina, a slaveholder.

TESTIMONY

"The slaves live in *clay cabins*."

V. TREATMENT OF THE SICK.

THE SLAVES SUFFER FROM INHUMAN NEGLECT WHEN SICK.

In proof of this we subjoin the following testimony:

Rev. Dr. Channing of Boston, who once resided in Virginia, relates the following fact in his work on slavery, page 163, 1st edition."I cannot forget my feelings on visiting a hospital belonging to the plantation of a gentleman *highly esteemed for his virtues, a*nd whose manners and conversation expressed much *benevolence and conscientiousness.* When I entered with him the hospital, the first object on which my eye fell was a young woman, very ill, probably approaching death. She was stretched on the floor. Her head rested on something like a pillow; but *her body and limbs were extended on the hard boards.* The owner, I doubt not, had at least as much kindness as myself; but he was so used to see the slaves living without common comforts, that the idea of unkindness in the present instance did not enter his mind."

This *dying* young woman "was *stretched on the floor*" "her body and limbs extended upon the hard boards,"—and yet her master "was highly esteemed for his virtues," and his general demeanor produced upon Dr. Channing the impression of "benevolence and conscientiousness." If the *sick and dying female* slaves of *such* a master, suffer such barbarous neglect, whose heart does not fail him, at the thought of that inhumanity, exercised by the *majority* of slaveholders, towards their aged, sick, and dying victims.

The following testimony is furnished by **Sarah M. Grimke,** a sister of the late Hon. Thomas S. Grimke, of Charleston, South Carolina:

"When the Ladies' Benevolent Society in Charleston, S. C, of which I was a visiting commissioner, first went into operation, we were applied to for the relief of several sick and aged colored persons; one case I particularly remember, of an aged woman who was dreadfully burnt from having fallen into the fire; she was living with some free blacks who had taken her in out of compassion. On inquiry, we found that *nearly all* the colored persons who had solicited aid, were *slaves,* who being no longer able to work for their "owners," were thus inhumanly cast out in their sickness and old age, and must have perished, but for the kindness of their friends.

"I was once visiting a sick slave in whose spiritual welfare peculiar circumstances had led me to be deeply interested. I knew that she had been early seduced from the path of virtue, as nearly all the female slaves are. I knew also that her mistress, though a professor of religion, had never taught her a single precept of Christianity, yet that she had had her severely punished for this departure from them, and that the poor girl was then ill of an incurable disease, occasioned partly by her own misconduct, and partly by the cruel treatment she had received, in a situation that called for tenderness and care. Her heart seemed truly touched with repentance for her sins, and she was inquiring, "What shall I do to be saved? I was sitting by her as she lay on the floor upon a blanket, and was trying to establish her trembling spirit in the fullness of Jesus, when I heard the voice of her mistress in loud and angry tones, as she approached the door. I read in the countenance of the prostrate sufferer, the terror which she felt at the prospect of seeing her mistress. I knew my presence would be very unwelcome, but staid, hoping that it might restrain, in some measure, the passions of the mistress. In this, however, I was mistaken; she passed me without apparently observing that I was there, and seated herself on the other side of the sick slave. She made no inquiry how she was, but in a tone of anger commenced a tirade of abuse, violently reproaching her with her past misconduct, and telling her in the most unfeeling manner, that eternal destruction awaited her. No word of kindness escaped her. What had then roused her temper I do not know. She continued in this strain several minutes, when I attempted to soften her by remarking, that she was very ill, and she ought not thus to torment her, and that I believed Jesus had granted her forgiveness. But I might as well have tried to stop the tempest in its career, as to calm the infuriated passions nurtured by the exercise of arbitrary power. She looked at me with ineffable scorn, and continued to pour forth a torrent of abuse and reproach. Her helpless victim listened in terrified silence, until nature could endure no more, when she uttered a wild shriek, and casting on her tormentor a look of unutterable agony, exclaimed, 'Oh, mistress, I am dying!' This appeal arrested her attention, and she soon left the room, but in the same spirit with which she entered it. The girl survived but a few days, and, I believe, saw her mistress *no more."*

Mr. **George A. Avery**, an elder of a Presbyterian Church in Rochester, N. Y., who lived some years in Virginia, gives the following:

"The manner of treating the sick slaves, and especially in *chronic* cases, was to my mind peculiarly revolting. My opportunities for observation in this department were better than in, perhaps, any other, as the friend under whose direction I commenced my medical studies, enjoyed a high reputation as a *surgeon.* I rode considerably with him in his practice, and assisted in the surgical operations and dressings from time to time. In confirmed cases of disease, it was common for the master to place the subject under the care of a physician or surgeon, at whose expense the patient should be kept, and if death ensued to the patient, or the disease was not cured, no compensation was to be made, but if cured a bonus of one, two, or three hundred dollars was to be given. No provision was made against the *barbarity* or *neglect* of the physician, &c. I have seen *fifteen or twenty of these helpless sufferers* crowded together in the true spirit of slaveholding inhumanity, like the "brutes that perish," and driven from time to time *like* brutes into a common yard, where they had to suffer any and every operation and experiment, which interest, caprice, or professional curiosity might prompt,—unrestrained by law, public sentiment, or the claims of common humanity."

Rev. William T. Allan, son of Rev. Dr. Allan, a slaveholder, of Huntsville, Alabama, says in a letter now before us:

"Colonel Robert H. Watkins, of Laurence County, Alabama, who owned about three hundred slaves, after employing a physician among them for some time, ceased to do so, alleging as the reason, that it was cheaper to lose a few negroes every year than to pay a physician. This Colonel Watkins was a Presidential elector in 1836."

A. A. Guthrie, Esq., elder in the Presbyterian Church at Putnam, Muskingum County, Ohio, furnishes the testimony which follows:

"A near female friend of mine in company with another young lady, in attempting to visit a sick woman on Washington's Bottom, Wood county, Virginia, missed the way, and stopping to ask directions of a group of colored children on the outskirts of the plantation of Francis Keen, Sen., they were told to ask 'aunty, in the house.' On entering the hut, says my informant, I beheld such a sight as I hope never to see again; its sole occupant was a female slave of the said Keen—her whole wearing apparel consisted of a frock, made of the coarsest tow cloth, and so scanty, that it could not have been made more tight around her person. In the hut there was neither table, chair, nor chest—a stool and a rude fixture in one corner, were all its furniture. On this last were a little straw and a few old remnants of what had been bedding—all exceedingly filthy.

"The woman thus situated *had been for more than a day in travail, without any assistance, any nurse, or any kind of proper provision*—during the night she said some fellow slave woman would stay with her, and the aforesaid children through the day. From a woman, who was a slave of Keen's at the same time, my informant learned, that this poor woman suffered for three days, and then died—when too late to save her life her master sent assistance. It was understood to be a rule of his, to neglect his women entirely in such times of trial, unless they previously came and informed him, and asked for aid."

Rev. Phineas Smith, of Centreville, N. Y., who has resided four years at the south, says: "Often when the slaves are sick, their accustomed toil is exacted from them. Physicians are rarely called for their benefit."

Rev. Horace Moulton, a minister of the Methodist Episcopal Church in Marlborough, Mass., who resided a number of years in Georgia, says:

"Another dark side of slavery is the neglect of the *aged* and *sick*. Many when sick, are suspected by their masters of *feigning* sickness, and are therefore whipped out to work after disease has got fast hold of them; when the masters learn, that they are really sick, they are in many instances left alone in their cabins during work hours; not a few of the slaves are left to die without having one friend to wipe off the sweat of death. When the slaves are sick, the masters do not, as a general thing, employ physicians, but "doctor" them themselves, and their mode of practice in almost all cases is to bleed and give salts. When women are confined they have no physician, but are committed to the care of slave midwives. Slaves complain very little when sick, when they die they are frequently buried at night without much ceremony, and in many instances without any; their coffins are made by nailing together rough boards, frequently with their feet sticking out at the end, and sometimes they are put into the ground without a coffin or box of any kind.

PERSONAL NARRATIVES-PART II

TESTIMONY OF THE REV. WILLIAM T. ALLAN, LATE OF ALABAMA

Mr. Allan is a son of the Rev. Dr. Allan, a slaveholder and pastor of the Presbyterian Church at Huntsville, Alabama. He has recently become the pastor of the Presbyterian Church in Chatham, Illinois.

"I was born and have lived most of my life in the slave states, mainly in the village of Huntsville, Alabama, where my parents still reside. I seldom went to a *plantation,* and as my visits were confined almost exclusively to the families of professing Christians, my *personal* knowledge of slavery, was consequently knowledge of its *fairest* side, (if fairest may be predicated of foul.)

"There was one plantation just opposite my father's house in the suburbs of Huntsville, belonging to Judge Smith, formerly a Senator in Congress from South Carolina, now of Huntsville. The name of his overseer was Tune. I have often seen him flogging the slaves in the field, and have often heard their cries. Sometimes, too, I have met them with the tears streaming down their faces, and the marks of the whip, ('whelks,') on their bare necks and shoulders. Tune was so severe in his treatment that his employer dismissed him after two or three years, lest, it was said, he should kill off all the slaves. But he was immediately employed by another planter in the neighborhood. The following fact was stated to me by my brother, James M. Allan, now residing at Richmond, Henry county, Illinois, and clerk of the circuit and county courts. Tune became displeased with one of the women who was pregnant, he made her lay down over a log, with her face towards the ground, and beat her so unmercifully, that she was soon after delivered of a *dead child.*

"My brother also stated to me the following, which occurred near my father's house, and within sight and hearing of the academy and public garden. Charles, a fine active negro, who belonged to a bricklayer in Huntsville, exchanged the burning sun of the brickyard to enjoy for a season the pleasant shade of an adjacent mountain. When his master got him back, he tied him by his hands so that his feet could just touch the ground—stripped off his clothes, took a paddle, bored full of holes, and paddled him leisurely all day long. It was two weeks before they could tell whether he would live or die. Neither of these cases attracted any particular notice in Huntsville.

"While I lived in Huntsville a slave was killed in the mountain nearby. The circumstances were these. A white man (James Helton) hunting in the woods, suddenly came upon a black man, and commanded him to stop. The slave kept on running, Helton fired his rifle and the negro was killed.*

* This murder was committed about twelve years since. At that time, James G. Birney, Esq., now Corresponding Secretary of the American Anti-Slavery Society was the Solicitor (prosecuting attorney) for that judicial district. His views and feelings upon the subject of slavery were, even at that period, in advance of the mass of slaveholders, and he determined if possible to bring the murderer to justice. He accordingly drew up an indictment and procured the finding of a true bill against Helton. Helton, meanwhile, moved over the line into the state of Tennessee, and such was the apathy of the community, individual effort proved unavailing; and though the murderer had gone no further than to an adjoining county (where perhaps he still resides) he was never brought to trial.—Ed.

"Mrs. Barr, wife of Rev. H. Barr of Carrollton, Illinois, formerly from Courtland, Alabama, told me last spring, that she has very often stopped her ears that she might not hear the screams of slaves who were under the lash, and that sometimes she has left her house, and retired to a place more distant, in order to get away from their agonizing cries.

"I have often seen groups of slaves on the public squares in Huntsville, who were to be sold at auction, and I have often seen their tears gush forth and their countenances distorted with anguish. A considerable number were generally sold publicly every month.

"The following facts I have just taken down from the lips of Mr. L. Turner, a regular and respectable member of the Second Presbyterian Church in Springfield, our county town. He was born and brought up in Caroline County, Virginia. He says that the slaves are neither considered nor treated as human beings. One of his neighbors whose name was Barr, he says, on one occasion stripped a slave and lacerated his back with a handcard (for cotton or wool) and then washed it with salt and water, with pepper in it. Mr. Turner saw this. He further remarked that he believed there were *many* slaves there in advanced life whose backs had *never* been well since they began to work.

"He stated that one of his uncles had killed a woman—broke her skull with an ax helve; she had insulted her mistress! No notice was taken of the affair. Mr. T. said, further, that slaves were *frequently murdered.*

"He mentioned the case of one slaveholder, whom he had seen lay his slaves on a large log, which he kept for the purpose, strip them, tie them with the face downward, then have a kettle of hot water brought—take the paddle, made of hard wood, and perforated with holes, dip it into the hot water and strike—before every blow dipping it into the water—every hole at every blow would raise a 'whelk.' This was the usual punishment for *running away.*

"Another slaveholder had a slave who had often run away, and often been severely whipped. After one of his floggings he burnt his master's barn; this so enraged the man, that when he caught him he took a pair of pincers and pulled his toenails out. The negro then murdered two of his master's children. He was taken after a desperate pursuit, (having been shot through the shoulder) and hung.

"One of Mr. Turner's cousins was employed as overseer on a large plantation in Mississippi. On a certain morning he called the slaves together, to give some orders. While doing it, a slave came running out of his cabin, having a knife in his hand and eating his breakfast. The overseer seeing him coming with the knife, was somewhat alarmed, and instantly raised his gun and shot him dead. He said afterwards, that he believed the slave was perfectly innocent of any evil intentions. He came out hastily to hear the orders whilst eating. No notice was taken of the killing.

"Mr. T. related the whipping habits of one of his uncles in Virginia. He was a wealthy man, had a splendid house and grounds. A tree in his *front yard* was used as a *whipping post.* When a slave was to be punished, he would frequently invite some of his friends, have a table, cards and wine set out under the shade; he would then flog his slave a little while, and then play cards and drink with his friends, occasionally taunting the slave, giving him the privilege of confessing such and such things, at his leisure, after a while flog him again, thus keeping it up for hours or half the day, and sometimes all day. This was his *habit*.

"*February* 4th.—Since writing the preceding. I have been to Carrollton, on a visit to my uncle, Rev. Hugh Barr, who was originally from Tennessee, lived 12 or 14 years in Courtland, Lawrence County, Alabama, and moved to Illinois in 1835. In conversation with the family, around the fireside, they stated a multitude of horrid facts that were perfectly notorious in the neighborhood of Courtland.

"William P. Barr, an intelligent young man, and member of his father's church in Carrollton, stated the following. Visiting at a Mr. Mosely's, near Courtland, William Mosely came in with a bloody knife in his hand, having just stabbed a negro man. The negro was sitting quietly in a house in the village, keeping a woman company who had been left in charge of the house,—when Mosely, passing along, went in and demanded his business there. Probably his answer was not as civil as slaveholding requires, and Mosely rushed upon him and stabbed him. The wound laid him up for a season. Mosely was called to no account for it. When he came in with the bloody knife, he said he wished he had killed him.

"John Brown, a slaveholder, and a member of the Presbyterian Church in Courtland, Alabama, stated the following a few weeks since, in Carrollton. A man near Courtland, of the name of Thompson, recently shot a negro *woman* through the head; and put the pistol so close that her hair was singed. He did it in consequence of some difficulty in his dealings with her as a concubine. He buried her in a log heap; she was discovered by the buzzards gathering around it."William P. Barr stated the following, as facts well known in the neighborhood of Courtland, but not witnessed by himself. Two men, by the name of Wilson, found a fine looking negro man at 'Dandridge's Quarter,' without a pass; and flogged him so that he died in a short time. They were not punished.

"Col. Blocker's overseer attempted to flog a negro—he refused to be flogged; whereupon the overseer seized an axe, and cleft his skull. The Colonel justified it.

"One Jones whipped a woman to death for 'grabbling' a potato hill. He owned 80 or 100 negroes. His own children could not live with him.

"A man in the neighborhood of Courtland, Alabama, by the name of Puryear, was so proverbially cruel that among the negroes he was usually called 'the Devil.' Mrs. Barr, wife of Rev. H. Barr, was at Puryear's house, and saw a negro girl about 13 years old, waiting around the table, with a single garment—and that in cold weather; arms and feet bare—feet wretchedly swollen— arms burnt, and full of sores from exposure. All the negroes under his care made a wretched appearance.

"Col. Robert H. Watkins had a runaway slave, who was called Jim Dragon. Before he was caught the last time, he had been out a year, within a few miles of his master's plantation. He never stole from anyone but his master, except when necessity compelled him. He said he had a right to take from his master; and when taken, that he had, whilst out, seen his master a hundred times. Having been whipped, clogged with irons, and yoked, he was set at work in the field. Col. Watkins worked about 300 hands—generally had one negro out hunting runaways. After employing a physician for some time among his negroes, he ceased to do so, alleging as the reason, that it was cheaper to lose a few negroes every year than to pay a physician. He was a Presidential elector in 1836.

"Col. Ben Sherrod, another large planter in that neighborhood, is remarkable for his kindness to his slaves. He said to Rev. Mr. Barr, that he had no doubt he should be rewarded in heaven for his kindness to his slaves; and yet his overseer, Walker, had to sleep with loaded pistols, for fear of assassination. Three of the slaves attempted to kill him once, because of his *treatment of their wives.*

"Old Major Billy Watkins was noted for his severity. I well remember, when he lived in Madison County, to have often heard him yell at his negroes with the most savage fury. He would stand at his house, and watch the slaves picking cotton; and if any of them straitened their backs for a moment, his savage yell would ring, 'bend your backs.'

"Mrs. Barr stated, that Mrs. H. of Courtland, a member of the Presbyterian Church, sent a little negro girl to jail, suspecting that she had attempted to put poison into the water pail. The fact was that the child had found a vial, and was playing in the water. This same woman (in high standing too,) told the Rev. Mr. McMillan, that she could 'cut Arthur Tappan's throat from ear to ear.'

"The clothing of slaves is in many cases comfortable, and in many it is far from being so. I have very often seen slaves, whose tattered rags were neither comfortable nor decent.

"Their *huts* are sometimes comfortable, but generally they are miserable *hovels,* where male and female are herded promiscuously together.

"As to the *usual* allowance of food on the plantations in North Alabama, I cannot speak confidently, from *personal* knowledge. There was a slave named Hadley, who was in the habit of visiting my father's slaves occasionally. He had run away several times. His reason was, as he stated, that they would not give him any meat— said he could not work without meat. The last time I saw him, he had quite a heavy iron yoke on his neck, the two prongs twelve or fifteen inches long, extending out over his shoulders and bending upwards.

"Legal marriage is unknown among the slaves, they sometimes have a marriage form—generally, however, *one at all.* The pastor of the Presbyterian Church in Huntsville, had two families of slaves when I left there. One couple were married by a negro preacher—the man was robbed of his wife a number of months afterwards, by her 'owner.' The other couple just 'took up together,' without any form of marriage. They are both members of churches—the man a Baptist deacon, sober and correct in his deportment. They have a large family of children—all children of concubinage—living in a minister's family.

"If these statements are deemed of any value by you, in forwarding your glorious enterprise, you are at liberty to use them as you please. The great wrong is *enslaving a man;* all other wrongs are pigmies, compared with that. Facts might be gathered abundantly, to show that it is *slavery itself,* and not cruelties merely, that make slaves unhappy. Even those that are most kindly treated, are generally far from being happy. The slaves in my father's family are almost as kindly treated as *slaves* can be, yet they pant for liberty.

"May the Lord guide you in this great movement. In behalf of the perishing,

Your friend and brother,

William T. Allan."

NARRATIVE OF MR. WILLIAM LEFTWICH, A NATIVE OF VIRGINIA.

Mr. Leftwich is a grandson of Gen. Jabez Leftwich, who was for some years a member of Congress from Virginia. Though born in Virginia, he has resided most of his life in Alabama, he now lives in Delhi, Hamilton County, Ohio, near Cincinnati.

As an introduction to his letter, the reader is furnished with the following testimonial to his character, from the Rev. Horace Bushnell, pastor of the Presbyterian Church in Delhi. Mr. B. says:

"Mr. Leftwich is a worthy member of this church, and is a young man of sterling integrity and veracity.

H. Bushnell"

The following is the letter of Mr. Leftwich, dated Dec. 26, 1838:

"Dear Brother—Though I am not ranked among the abolitionists, yet I cannot, as a friend of humanity, withhold from the public such facts in relation to the condition of the slaves, as have fallen under my own observation. That I am somewhat acquainted with slavery will be seen, as I narrate some incidents of my own life. My parents were slaveholders, and moved from Virginia to Madison County, Alabama, during my infancy. My mother soon fell a victim to the climate. Being the youngest of the children, I was left in the care of my aged grandfather, who never held a slave; though his sons owned from 90 to 100 during the time I resided with him. As soon as I could carry a hoe, my uncle, by the name of Neely, persuaded my grandfather that I should be placed in his hands, and brought up in habits of industry. I was accordingly placed under his tuition. I left the domestic circle, little dreaming of the horrors that awaited me. My mother's own brother took me to the cotton field, there to learn habits of industry, and to be benefited by his counsels. But the sequel proved that I was there to feel in my own person, and witness by experience many of the horrors of slavery. Instead of kind admonition, I was to endure the frowns of one, whose sympathies could neither be reached by the prayers and cries of his slaves, nor by the entreaties and sufferings of a sister's son. Let those who call slaveholders kind, hospitable and humane, mark the course the slaveholder pursues with one born free, whose ancestors fought and bled for liberty; and then say, if they can without a blush of shame, that he who robs the helpless of every *right,* can be truly kind and hospitable.

"In a short time after I was put upon the plantation, there was but little difference between me and the slaves, except being *white,* I ate at the master's table. The slaves were my companions in misery, and I well learned their condition, both in the house and field. Their dwellings are log huts, from ten to twelve feet square; often without windows, doors or floors. They have neither chairs, tables nor bedsteads. These huts are occupied by eight, ten or twelve persons each. Their bedding generally consists of two old blankets. Many of them sleep night after night sitting upon their blocks or stools; others sleep in the open air. Our task was appointed, and from dawn till dark all must bend to their work. Their meals were taken without knife or plate, dish or spoon. Their food was corn *pone,* prepared in the coarsest manner, with a small allowance of meat. Their meals in the field were taken from the hands of the carrier, wherever he found them, with no more ceremony than in the feeding of swine. My uncle was his own overseer. For punishing in the field, he preferred a large hickory stick; and woe to him whose work was not done to please him, for the hickory was used upon our heads as remorselessly as if we had been mad dogs. I was often the object of his fury, and shall bear the marks of it on my body till I die. Such was my suffering and degradation, that at the end of five years, I hardly dared to say I was free. When thinning cotton, we went mostly on our knees. One day, while thus engaged, my uncle found my row behind; and, by way of admonition, gave me a few blows with his hickory, the marks of which I carried for weeks. Often I followed the example of the fugitive slaves, and betook myself to the mountains; but hunger and fear drove me back, to share with the wretched slave his toil and stripes. But I have talked enough about my own bondage; I will now relate a few facts, showing the condition of the slaves *generally.*

"My uncle, wishing to purchase what is called a good 'house wench,' a *trader* in human flesh soon produced a woman, recommending her as highly as ever a jockey did a horse. She was purchased, but on trial was found wanting in the requisite qualifications. She then fell a victim to the disappointed rage of my uncle; innocent or guilty, she suffered greatly from his fury. He used to tie her to a peach tree in the yard, and whip her till there was no sound place to lay another stroke, and repeat it so often that her back was kept continually sore. Whipping the females around the legs was a favorite mode of punishment with him. They must stand and hold up their clothes, while he plied his hickory. He did not, like some of his neighbors, keep a pack of hounds for hunting runaway negroes, but he kept one dog for that purpose, and when he came up with a runaway, it would have been death to attempt to fly, and it was nearly so to stand. Sometimes, when my uncle attempted to whip the slaves, the dog would rush upon them and relieve them of their rags, if not of their flesh. One object of my uncle's special hate was "Jerry," a slave of a proud spirit. He defied all the curses, rage and stripes of his tyrant. Though he was often overpowered—for my uncle would frequently wear out his stick upon his head—yet he would never submit. As he was not expert in picking cotton, he would sometimes run away in the fall, to escape abuse. At one time, after an absence of some months, he was arrested and brought back. As is customary, he was stripped, tied to a log, and the cow-skin applied to his naked body till his master was exhausted. Then a large log chain was fastened around one ankle, passed up his back, over his shoulders, then across his breast, and fastened under his arm. In this condition he was forced to perform his daily task. Add to this he was chained each night, and compelled to chop wood every Sabbath, to make up lost time. After being thus manacled for some months, he was released—but his spirit was un-subdued. Soon after, his master, in a paroxysm of rage, fell upon him, wore out his staff upon his head, loaded him again with chains, and after a month, sold him farther south. Another slave, by the name of Mince, who was a man of great strength, purloined some bacon on a Christmas Eve. It was missed in the morning, and he being absent, was of course suspected. On returning home, my uncle commanded him to come to him, but he refused. The master strove in vain to lay hands on him; in vain he ordered his slaves to seize him—they dared not. At length the master hurled a stone at his head sufficient to have felled a bullock—but he did not heed it. At that instant my aunt sprang forward, and presenting the gun to my uncle, exclaimed, 'Shoot him! Shoot him!' He made the attempt, but the gun missed fire, and Mince fled. He was taken eight or ten months after that, while crossing the Ohio. When brought back, the master, and an overseer on another plantation, took him to the mountain and punished him to their satisfaction in secret; after which he was loaded with chains and set to his task.

"I have spent nearly all my life in the midst of slavery. From being the son of a slaveholder, I descended to the condition of a slave, and from that condition I rose (if you please to call it so,) to the station of a *driver* I have lived in Alabama, Tennessee, and Kentucky; and I *know* the condition of the slaves to be that of unmixed wretchedness and degradation. And on the part of slaveholders, there is cruelty *untold*. The labor of the slave is constant toil, wrung out by fear. Their food is scanty, and taken without comfort. Their clothes answer the purposes neither of comfort nor decency. They are not allowed to read or write. Whether they may worship God or not, depends on the will of the master. The young children, until they can work, often go naked during the warm weather. I could spend months in detailing the sufferings, degradation and cruelty inflicted upon slaves. But my soul sickens at the remembrance of these things."

TESTIMONY OF MR. LEMUEL SAPINGTON
A NATIVE OF MARYLAND

Mr. Sapington, is a repentant "soul driver" or slave trader, now a citizen of Lancaster, Pa. He gives the following testimony in a letter dated, Jan. 21, 1839.

"I was born in Maryland, afterwards moved to Virginia, where I commenced the business of farming and trafficking in slaves. In my neighborhood the slaves were 'quartered.' The description generally given of negro quarters is correct. The quarters are without floors, and not sufficient to keep off the inclemency of the weather, they are uncomfortable both in summer and winter. The food there consists of potatoes, pork, and corn, which were given to them daily, by weight and measure. The sexes were huddled together promiscuously. Their clothing is made by themselves after night, though sometimes assisted by the old women who are no longer able to do outdoor work. Consequently it is harsh and uncomfortable. I have frequently seen those of both sexes who have not attained the age of twelve years go naked. Their punishments are invariably cruel. For the slightest offense, such as taking a hen's egg, I have seen them stripped and suspended by their hands, their feet tied together, a fence rail of ordinary size placed between their ankles, and then most cruelly whipped, until, from head to foot, they were completely lacerated, a pickle made for the purpose of salt and water, would then be applied by a fellow-slave, for the purpose of healing the wounds as well as giving pain. Then taken down and without the least respite sent to work with their hoe.

Pursuing my assumed right of driving souls, I went to the Southern part of Virginia for the purpose of trafficking in slaves. In that part of the state, the cruelties practiced upon the slaves, are far greater than where I lived. The punishments there often resulted in death to the slave. There was no law for the negro, but that of the overseer's whip. In that part of the country, the slaves receive nothing for food, but corn in the ear, which has to be prepared for baking after working hours, by grinding it with a hand-mill. This they take to the fields with them, and prepare it for eating, by holding it on their hoes, over a fire made by a stump. Among the gangs, are often young women, who bring their children to the fields, and lay them in a fence corner, while they are at work, only being permitted to nurse them at the option of the overseer. When a child is three weeks old, a woman is considered in working order. I have seen a woman, with her young child strapped to her back, laboring the whole day, beside a man, perhaps the father of the child, and he not being permitted to give her any assistance, himself being under the whip. The uncommon humanity of the driver allowing her the comfort of doing so. I was then selling a drove of slaves, which I had brought by water from Baltimore, my conscience not allowing me to drive, as was generally the case uniting the slaves by collars and chains, and thus driving them under the whip. About that time an unaccountable something, which I now know was an interposition of Providence, prevented me from prosecuting any farther this unholy traffic; but though I had quitted it, I still continued to live in a slave state, witnessing every day its evil effects upon my fellow beings.

Among which was a heart-rending scene that took place in my father's house, which led me to leave a slave state, as well as all the imaginary comforts arising from slavery. On preparing for my removal to the state of Pennsylvania, it became necessary for me to go to Louisville, in Kentucky, where, if possible, I became more horrified with the impositions practiced upon the negro than before. There a slave was sold to go farther south, and was hand-cuffed for the purpose of keeping him secure. But choosing death rather than slavery, he jumped overboard and was drowned. When I returned four weeks afterwards his body, that had floated three miles below, was yet unburied. One fact; it is impossible for a person to pass through a slave state, if he has eyes open, without beholding every day cruelties repugnant to humanity. Respectfully Yours,

Lemuel Sapington.

TESTIMONY OF MRS. NANCY LOWRY, A NATIVE OF KENTUCKY

Mrs. Lowry, is a member of the non-conformist church in Onasburg, Stark County, Ohio. She is a native of Kentucky. We have received from her the following testimony:

"I resided in the family of Reuben Long, the principal part of the time, from seven to twenty-two years of age. Mr. Long had 16 slaves, among whom were three who were treated with severity, although Mr. Long was thought to be a very humane master. These three, namely John, Ned, and James, had wives; John and Ned had theirs at some distance, but James had his with him. All three died a premature death, and it was generally believed by his neighbors, that extreme whipping was the cause. I believe so too. Ned died about the age of 25 and John 34 or 35. The cause of their flogging was commonly staying a little over the time, with their wives. Mr. Long would tie them up by the wrist, so high that their toes would just touch the ground, and then with a cow-hide lay the lash upon the naked back, until he was exhausted, when he would sit down and rest. As soon as he had rested sufficiently, he would ply the cowhide again, thus he would continue until the whole back of the poor victim was lacerated into one uniform coat of blood. Yet he was a strict professor of the Christian religion, in the southern church. I frequently washed the wounds of John, with salt water, to prevent putrefaction. This was the usual course pursued after a severe flogging; their backs would be full of gashes, so deep that I could almost lay my finger in them. They were generally laid up after the flogging for several days. The last flogging Ned got, he was confined to the bed, which he never left till he was carried to his grave. During John's confinement in his last sickness on one occasion while attending on him, he exclaimed, 'Oh, Nancy, Miss Nancy, I haven't much longer in this world, I feel as if my whole body inside and all my bones were beaten into a jelly.' Soon after he died. John and Ned were both professors of religion.

"John Ruffner, a slaveholder, had one slave named Piney, whom he as well as Mrs. Ruffner would often flog very severely. I frequently saw Mrs. Ruffner flog her with the broom, shovel, or anything she could seize in her rage. She would knock her down and then kick and stamp her most unmercifully, until she would be apparently so lifeless, that I more than once thought she would never recover. Often Piney would try to shelter herself from the blows of her mistress, by creeping under the bed, from which Mrs. Ruffner would draw her by the feet, and then stamp and leap on her body, till her breath would be gone. Often Piney, would cry, 'Oh Missee, don't kill me!" "Oh Lord, don't kill me!' 'For God's sake don't kill me!' But Mrs. Ruffner would beat and stamp away, with all the venom of a demon. The cause of Piney's flogging was, not working enough, or making some mistake in baking, &c. &c. Many a night Piney had to lie on the bare floor, by the side of the cradle, rocking the baby of her mistress, and if she would fall asleep, and suffer the child to cry, so as to waken Mrs. Ruffner, she would be sure to receive a flogging."

TESTIMONY OF MR. WM. C. GILDERSLEEVE
A NATIVE OF GEORGIA

Mr. W. C. Gildersleeve, a native of Georgia, is an elder of the Presbyterian Church at Wilkes-Barre, Pa.

"*Acts of cruelty, without number, fell under my observation* while I lived in Georgia. I will mention but one. A slave of a Mr. Pinkney, on his way with a wagon to Savannah, 'camped' for the night by the road side. That night, the nearest hen-roost was robbed. On his return, the hen-roost was again visited, and the fowl counted one less in the morning. The oldest son, with some attendants made search, and came upon the poor fellow, in the act of dressing his spoil. He was too nimble for them, and made his retreat good into a dense swamp. When much effort to start him from his hiding place had proved unsuccessful, it was resolved to lay an ambush for him, some distance ahead. The wagon, meantime, was in charge of a lad, who accompanied the teamster as an assistant. The little boy lay still till nearly night, (in the hope probably that the teamster would return,) when he started with his wagon. After travelling some distance, the lost one made his appearance, when the ambush sprang upon him. The poor fellow was conducted back to the plantation. He expected little mercy. He begged for himself, in the most supplicating manner, 'pray massa give me 100 lashes and let me go.' He was then tied by the hands, to a limb of a large mulberry tree, which grew in the yard, so that his feet were raised a few inches from the ground, while a *sharpened stick* was driven underneath, that he might rest his weight on it, or swing by his hands. In this condition 100 lashes were laid on his bare body. I stood by and witnessed the whole, without as I recollect, feeling the least compassion. So hardening is the influence of slavery, that it very much destroys feeling for the slave."

TESTIMONY OF MR. HIRAM WHITE
A NATIVE OF NORTH CAROLINA

Mr. White resided thirty-two years in Chatham County, North Carolina, and is now a member of the Baptist Church, at Otter Creek Prairie, Illinois.

About the 20th December, 1830, a report was raised that the slaves in Chatham County, North Carolina, were going to rise on Christmas Day," in consequence of which a considerable commotion ensued among the inhabitants; orders were given by the Governor to the militia captains, to appoint patrolling captains in each district, and orders were given for every man subject to military duty to patrol as their captains should direct. I went two nights in succession, and after that refused to patrol at all. The reason why I refused was this, orders were given to search every negro house for books or prints of any kind, and *Bibles* and *Hymn books* were particularly mentioned. And should we find any, our orders were to inflict punishment by whipping the slave until he *informed who* gave them to him, or how they came by them.

As regards the comforts of the slaves in the vicinity of my residence, I can say they had nothing that would bear that name. It is true, the slaves in general, of a good crop year, were tolerably well fed, but of a bad crop year, they were, as a general thing, cut short of their allowance. Their houses were pole cabins, without loft or floor. Their beds were made of what is there called "broom-straw." The men more commonly sleep on benches. Their clothing would compare well with their lodging. Whipping was common. It was hardly possible for a man with a common pair of ears, if he was out of his house but a short time on Monday mornings, to miss of hearing the sound of the lash, and the cries of the sufferers pleading with their masters to desist. These scenes were more common throughout the time of my residence there, from 1799 to 1831.

Mr. Heddings of Chatham County held a slave woman. I traveled past Heddings as often as once in two weeks during the winter of 1828, and always saw her clad in a single cotton dress, sleeves came half way to the elbow, and in order to prevent her running away, a child, supposed to be about seven years of age, was connected with her by a long chain fastened round her neck, and in this situation she was compelled all the day to *grub* up the roots of shrubs and saplings to prepare ground for the plough. It is not uncommon for slaves to make up on Sundays what they are not able to perform through the week of their tasks.

At the time of the rumored insurrection above named, Chatham jail was filled with slaves who were said to have been concerned in the plot. Without the least evidence of it, they were punished in divers ways; some were whipped, some had their *thumbs screwed in a vice* to make them confess, but no proof satisfactory was ever obtained that the negroes had ever thought of an insurrection, nor did any so far as I could learn, acknowledge that an insurrection had ever been projected. From this time forth, the slaves were prohibited from assembling together for the worship of God, and many of those who had previously been authorized to preach the gospel were prohibited.

Amalgamation was common. There was scarce a family of slaves that had females of mature age where there were not some mulatto children.

Hiram White
Otter Creek Prairie, Jan. 22, 1839.

TESTIMONY OF MR. JOHN M. NELSON
A NATIVE OF VIRGINIA

Extract of a letter, dated January 3, 1839, from John M. Nelson, Esq., of Hillsborough. Mr. Nelson removed from Virginia to Highland County, Ohio, many years since, where he is extensively known and respected.

I was born and raised in Augusta County, Virginia; my father was an elder in the Presbyterian Church, and was "owner" of about twenty slaves; he was what was generally termed a "good master." His slaves were generally tolerably well fed and clothed, and not over worked; they were sometimes permitted to attend church, and called in to family worship. Few of them, however, availed themselves of these privileges. On *some occasions* I have seen him whip them severely, particularly for the crime of trying to obtain their liberty, or for what was called, "running away." For *this* they were scourged more severely than for anything else. After they have been retaken, I have seen them stripped naked and suspended by the hands, sometimes to a tree, sometimes to a post, until their toes barely touched the ground and whipped with a cowhide until the blood dripped from their backs. A boy named Jack, particularly, I have seen served in this way more than once. When I was quite a child, I recollect it grieved me very much to see one *tied up* to be whipped, and I used to intercede with tears in their behalf, and mingle my cries with theirs, and feel almost willing to take part of the punishment ; I have been severely rebuked by my father for this kind of sympathy. Yet, such is the hardening nature of such scenes, that from this kind of commiseration for the suffering slave, I became so blunted that I could not only witness their stripes with composure, but *myself* inflict them, and that without remorse. One case I have often looked back to with sorrow and contrition, particularly since I have been convinced that "negroes are men." When I was perhaps fourteen or fifteen years of age, I undertook to correct a young fellow named Ned, for some supposed offense; I think it was leaving a bridle out of its proper place; he being larger and stronger than myself took hold of my arms and held me, in order to prevent my striking him; this I considered the height of insolence, and cried for help, when my father and mother both came running to my rescue. My father stripped and tied him, and took him into the orchard, where switches were plenty, and directed me to whip him; when one switch wore out he supplied me with others. After I had whipped him a while, he fell on his knees to implore forgiveness, and I kicked him in the face; my father said, "don't kick him, but whip him". This I did until his back was literally covered with *welts*. I know I have repented, and trust I have obtained pardon for these things.

My father owned a woman, (we used to call Aunt Grace,) she was purchased in Old Virginia. She has told me that her old master, in his *will*, gave her her freedom, but at his death, his sons had sold her to my father: when he bought her she manifested some unwillingness to go with him, when she was put in irons and taken by force. This was before I was born; but I remember to have seen the irons, and was told that was what they had been used for. Aunt Grace is still living, and must be between seventy and eighty years of age; she has, for the last, forty years, been an exemplary Christian. When I was a youth I took some pains to learn her to read; this is now a great consolation to her. Since age and infirmity have rendered her of little value to her "owners," she is permitted to read as much as she pleases; this she can do, with the aid of glasses, in the old family Bible, which is almost the only book she has ever looked into. This with some little mending for the black children is all she does; she is still held as a slave. I well remember what *a heart-rending scene* there was in the family when *my father sold her husband*; this was, I suppose, thirty-five years ago. And yet my father was considered one of the best of masters. I know of few who were better, but of *many* who were worse.

The last time I saw my father, which was in the fall of 1832, he promised me that he would free all his slaves at his death. He died however without doing it; and I have understood since, that he omitted it, through the influence of Rev. Dr. Speece, a Presbyterian minister, who lived in the family, and was a *warm friend of the Colonization Society.*

About the year 1809 or 10, I became a student of Rev. George Bourne; he was the first abolitionist I had ever seen, and the first I had ever heard pray or plead for the oppressed, which gave me the first misgivings about the *innocence* of slaveholding. I received impressions from Mr. Bourne which I could not get rid of,* and determined in my own mind that when I settled in life, it should be in a free state; this determination I carried into effect in 1813, when I removed to this place, which 1 supposed at that time, to be all the opposition to slavery that was necessary, but the moment I became convinced that all slaveholding was in itself *sinful,* I became an abolitionist, which was about four years ago.

* Mr. Bourne resided seven years in Virginia, "in perils among false brethren," fiercely persecuted for his faithful testimony against slavery. More than twenty years since he published a work entitled "The Book and Slavery irreconcilable."

TESTIMONY OF ANGELINA GRIMKE WELD

Mrs. Weld is the youngest daughter of the late Judge Grimke, of the Supreme Court of South Carolina, and a sister of the late Hon. Thomas S. Grimke, of Charleston:

Fort Lee, Bergen Co., New Jersey, Fourth month 6th, 1839

I sit down to comply with thy request, preferred in the name of the Executive Committee of the American Anti-Slavery Society. The responsibility laid upon me by such a request, leaves me no option. While I live, and slavery lives, I *must* testify against it. If I should hold my peace, "the stone would cry out of the wall, and the beam out of the timber would answer it." But though I feel a necessity upon me, and "a woe unto me," if I withhold my testimony, I give it with a heavy heart. My flesh crieth out, "if it be possible, let *this* cup pass from me;" but, "Father, *thy* will be done," is, I trust, the breathing of my spirit. Oh, the slain of the daughter of my people! they lie in all the ways; their tears fall as the rain, and are their meat day and night; their blood runneth down like water; their plundered hearths are desolate; they weep for their husbands and children, because they are not; and the proud waves do continually go over them, while no eye pitieth, and no man careth for their souls.

But it is not alone for the sake of my poor brothers and sisters in bonds, or for the cause of truth, and righteousness, and humanity, that I testify; the deep yearnings of affection for the mother that bore me, who is still a slaveholder, both in fact and in heart; for my brothers and sisters, (a large family circle,) and for my numerous other slaveholding kindred in South Carolina, constrain me to speak: for even were slavery no curse to its victims, the exercise of arbitrary power works such fearful ruin upon the hearts of *slaveholders,* that I should feel impelled to labor and pray for its overthrow with my last energies and latest breath.

I think it important to premise, that I have seen almost nothing of slavery on *plantations.* My testimony will have respect exclusively to the treatment of *"house-servants"* and chiefly those belonging to the first families in the city of Charleston, both in the religious and in the fashionable world. And here let me say, that the treatment of *plantation* slaves cannot be fully known, except by the poor sufferers themselves, and their drivers and overseers. In a multitude of instances, even the master can know very little of the actual condition of his own field-slaves, and his wife and daughters far less. A few facts concerning my own family will show this. Our permanent residence was in Charleston; our country-seat (Bellemont,) was 200 miles distant, in the north-western part of the state; where, for some years, our family spent a few months annually. Our *plantation* was three miles from this family mansion. There, all the field-slaves lived and worked. Occasionally, once a month, perhaps, some of the family would ride over to the plantation, but I never visited the *fields where the slaves were at work,* and knew almost nothing of their condition; but this I do know, that the overseers who had charge of them, were generally unprincipled and intemperate men. But I rejoice to know, that the general treatment of slaves in that region of country, was far milder than on the plantations in the lower country.

Throughout all the eastern and middle portions of the state, the planters very rarely reside permanently on their plantations. They have almost invariably *two* residences, and spend less than half the year on their estates. Even while spending a few months on them, politics, field sports, races, speculations, journeys, visits, company, literary pursuits, &c., absorb so much of their time that they must, to a considerable extent, take the condition of their slaves on *trust,* from the reports of their overseers. I make this statement, because these slaveholders (the wealthier class,) are, I believe, almost the only ones who visit the north with their families;—and northern opinions of slavery are based chiefly on their testimony.

But not to dwell on preliminaries, I wish to record my testimony to the faithfulness and accuracy with which my beloved sister, Sarah M. Grimke, has, in her narrative and testimony, on a preceding page, described the condition of the slaves, and the effect upon the hearts of slaveholders, (even the best,) caused by the exercise of unlimited power over moral agents. Of the *particular acts* which she has stated, I have no personal knowledge, as they occurred before *my* remembrance; but of the spirit that prompted them, and that constantly displays itself in scenes of similar horror, the recollections of my childhood, and the effaceless imprint upon my riper years, with the breaking of my heart-strings, when, finding that I was powerless to shield the victims, I tore myself from my home and friends, and became an exile among strangers—all these throng around me as witnesses, and their testimony is graven on my memory with a pen of fire.

Why I did not become totally hardened, under the daily operation of this system, God only knows; in deep solemnity and gratitude, I say, it was the *Lord's* doing, and marvelous in mine eyes. Even before my heart was touched with the love of Christ, I used to say, "Oh that I had the wings of a dove, that I might flee away and be at rest;' for I felt that there could be no rest for me in the midst of such outrages and pollutions. And yet I saw *nothing* of slavery in its most vulgar and repulsive forms. I saw it in the *city,* among the fashionable and the honorable, where it was garnished by refinement, and decked out for show. A few *facts* will unfold the state of society in the circle with which I was familiar, far better than any general assertions I can make. I will first introduce the reader to a woman of the highest respectability—one who was foremost in every benevolent enterprise, and stood for many years, I may say, at the *head* of the fashionable elite of the city of Charleston, and afterwards at the head of the moral and religious female society there. It was after she had made a profession of religion, and retired from the fashionable world, that I knew her; therefore I will present her in her religious character. This lady used to keep cowhides, or small paddles, (called 'pancake sticks,') in four different apartments in her house; so that when she wished to punish, or to have punished, any of her slaves, she might not have the trouble of sending for an instrument of torture. For many years, one or other, and *often* more of her slaves, were flogged *every day;* particularly the young slaves about the house, whose faces were slapped, or their hands beat with the 'pancake stick,' for every trifling offense—and often for no fault at all. But the floggings were not all; the scoldings and abuse daily heaped upon them all, were worse: 'fools' and 'liars,' 'sluts' and 'husseys,' 'hypocrites' and 'good-for-nothing creatures,' were the *common* epithets with which her mouth was filled, when addressing her slaves, adults as well as children. Very often she would take a position at her window, in an upper story, and scold at her slaves while working in the garden, at some distance from the house, (a large yard intervening,) and occasionally order a flogging. I have known her thus on the watch, scolding for more than an hour at a time, in so loud a voice that the whole neighborhood could hear her; and this without the least apparent feeling of shame. Indeed, it was *no disgrace among slaveholders,* and did not in the least injure her standing, either as a lady or a Christian, in the aristocratic circle in which she moved. After the 'revival' in Charleston, in 1825, she opened her house to social prayer-meetings. The room in which they were held in the evening, and where the voice of prayer was heard around the family altar, and where she herself retired for private devotion thrice each day, was the very place in which, when her slaves were to be whipped with the cowhide, they were taken to receive the infliction; and the wail of the sufferer would be heard, where, perhaps only a few hours previous, rose the voices of prayer and praise. This mistress would occasionally send her slaves, male and female, to the Charleston work-house to be punished. One poor girl, whom she sent there to be flogged, and who was accordingly stripped *naked* and whipped, showed me the deep gashes on her back—I might have laid my whole finger in them---*large pieces of flesh had actually been cut out by the torturing lash.* She sent another female slave there, to be imprisoned and worked on the tread-mill. This girl was confined several days, and forced to work the mill while in a state of suffering from another cause. For ten days or two weeks after her return, she was lame, from the violent exertion necessary to enable her to keep the step on the machine. She spoke to me with intense feeling of this outrage upon her, as a *woman.* Her men servants were sometimes flogged there; and so exceedingly offensive has been the putrid flesh of their lacerated backs, for days after the infliction, that they would be kept out of the house—the smell arising from their wounds being too horrible to be endured. They were always stiff and sore for some days, and not in a condition to be seen by visitors.

This professedly Christian woman was a most awful illustration of the ruinous influence of arbitrary power upon the temper—her bursts of passion upon the heads of her victims were dreaded even by her own children, and very often, all the pleasure of social intercourse around the domestic board, was destroyed by her ordering the cook into her presence, and storming at him, when the dinner or breakfast was not prepared to her taste, and in the presence of all her children, commanding the waiter to slap his face. *Fault-finding*, was with her the constant accompaniment of every meal, and banished that peace which should hover around the social board, and smile on every face. It was common for her to order brothers to whip their own sisters, and sisters their own brothers, and yet no woman visited among the poor more than she did, or gave more liberally to relieve their wants. This may seem perfectly unaccountable to a northerner, but these seeming contradictions vanish when we consider that over *them* she possessed no arbitrary power, they were always presented to her mind as unfortunate sufferers, towards whom her sympathies most freely flowed; she was ever ready to wipe the tears from *their* eyes, and open wide her purse for *their* relief, but the others were her *vassals,* thrust down by public opinion beneath her feet, to be at her beck and call, ever ready to serve in all humility, her, whom God in his providence had set over them—it was their *duty* to abide in abject submission, and hers to *compel* them to do so—*it was thus that he reasoned.* Except at family prayers, none were permitted to *sit* in her presence, but the seamstresses and waiting maids, and they, however delicate might be their circumstances, were forced to sit upon low stools, without backs, that they might be constantly reminded of their inferiority. A slave who waited in the house, was guilty on a particular occasion of going to visit his wife, and kept dinner waiting a little, (his wife was the slave of a lady who lived at a little distance.) When the family sat down to the table, the mistress began to scold the waiter for the offense—he attempted to excuse himself—she ordered him to hold his tongue—he ventured another apology; her son then rose from the table in a rage, and beat the face and ears of the waiter so dreadfully that the blood gushed from his mouth, and nose, and ears. This mistress was *a professor of religion;* her daughter who related the circumstance, was a *fellow member* of the Presbyterian Church *with the poor outraged slave*—instead of feeling indignation at this outrageous abuse of her brother in the church, she justified the deed, and said "he got just what he deserved." I solemnly believe this to be a true picture of *slaveholding religion.*

The following is another illustration of it: A mistress in Charleston sent a grey headed female slave to the workhouse, and had her severely flogged. The poor old woman went to an acquaintance of mine and begged her to buy her, and told her how cruelly she had been whipped. My friend examined her *lacerated* back, and out of compassion did purchase her. The circumstance was mentioned to one of the former owner's relatives, who asked her if it were true. The mistress told her it was, and said that she had made the severe whipping of this aged woman a *subject of prayer,* and that she believed she had done right to have it inflicted upon her. The last owner of the poor old slave, said she, had no fault to find with her as a servant.

I remember very well that when I was a child, our next door neighbor whipped a young woman so brutally, that in order to escape his blows she rushed through the drawing-room window in the second story, and fell upon the street pavement below and broke her hip. This circumstance produced no excitement or inquiry.

The following circumstance occurred in Charleston, in 1828:

A slaveholder, after flogging a little girl about thirteen years old, set her on a table with her feet fastened in a pair of stocks. He then locked the door and took out the key. When the door was opened she was found dead, having fallen from the table. When I asked a prominent lawyer, who belonged to one of the first families in the State, whether the murderer of this helpless child could not be indicted, he coolly replied, that the slave was Mr.___ 's property, and if he chose to suffer the *loss,* no one else had anything to do with it. The loss of *human life,* the distress of the parents and other relatives of the little girl, seemed utterly out of his thoughts: it was the loss of *property* only that presented itself to his mind.

I knew a gentleman of great benevolence and generosity of character, so essentially to injure the eye of a little boy, about ten years old, as to destroy its sight, by the blow of a cowhide, inflicted whilst he was whipping him.* I have heard the same individual speak of " breaking down the spirit of a slave under the lash" as perfectly right.

~ 118 ~

I also know that an aged slave of his, (by marriage,) was allowed to get a scanty and precarious subsistence, by begging in the streets of Charleston—he was too old to work, and therefore *his allowance was stopped,* and he was turned out to make his living by begging.

When I was about thirteen years old, I attended a seminary, in Charleston, which was superintended by a man and his wife of superior education. They had under their instruction the daughters of nearly all the aristocracy. Their cruelty to their slaves, both male and female, I can never forget. I remember one day there was called into the school room to open a window, a boy whose head had been shaved in order to disgrace him, and he had been so dreadfully whipped that he could hardly walk. So horrible was the impression produced upon my mind by his heart-broken countenance and crippled person that I fainted away. The sad and ghastly countenance of one of their female mulatto slaves who used to sit on a low stool at her sewing in the piazza, is now fresh before me. She often told me, secretly, how cruelly she was whipped when they sent her to the work house. I had known so much of the terrible scourgings inflicted in that house of blood, that when I was once obliged to pass it, the very sight smote me with such horror that my limbs could hardly sustain me. I felt as if I was passing the precincts of hell. A friend of mine, who lived in the neighborhood, told me she often heard the screams of the slaves under their torture.

I once heard a physician of a high family, and of great respectability in his profession, say, that when he sent his slaves to the work-house to be flogged, he always went to *see* it done, that he might be sure they were properly, ie., *severely* whipped. He also related the following circumstance in my presence. He had sent a youth of about eighteen to this horrible place to be whipped and *afterwards* to be worked upon the treadmill. From not keeping the step, which probably he could not do, in consequence of the lacerated state of his body; his arm got terribly torn, from the shoulder to the wrist. This physician said, he went every day to attend to it himself, in order that he might use those restoratives, which *would inflict the greatest possible pain.* This poor boy, after being imprisoned there for some weeks, was then brought home, and compelled to wear iron clogs on his ankles for one or two months. I saw him with those irons on one day when I was at the house. This man was, when young, remarkable in the fashionable world for his elegant and fascinating manners, but the exercise of the slaveholder's power has thrown the fierce air of tyranny even over these.

I heard another man of equally high standing say that he believed he suffered far more than his waiter did, whenever he flogged him, for he felt the *exertion* for days afterward, but he could not let his servant go on in the neglect of his business, it was *his duty* to chastise him. "His duty" to flog this boy of seventeen so severely that he felt *the exertion* for days after! And yet he never felt it to be his duty to instruct him, or have him instructed, even in the common principles of morality. I heard the mother of this man say, it would be no surprise to her if he killed a slave some day, for, that, when transported with passion he did not seem to care what he did. He once broke a *large* stick over the back of a slave, and at another time the ivory butt-end of a long coach whip over the *head* of another. This last was attacked with epileptic fits some months after, and has ever since been subject to them, and occasionally to violent fits of insanity.

Southern mistresses sometimes flog their slaves themselves, though generally one slave is compelled to flog another. Whilst staying at a friend's house some years ago, I one day saw the mistress with a cow-hide in her hand, and heard her scolding in an under tone, her waiting man, who was about twenty-five years old. Whether she actually inflicted the blows I do not know, for I hastened out of sight and hearing. It was not the first time I had seen a mistress thus engaged. I knew she was a cruel mistress, and had heard her daughters disputing, whether their mother did right or wrong, to send the *slave children*, (whom she sent out to sweep chimneys) to the work house to be whipped if they did not bring in their wages regularly. This woman moved in the most fashionable circle in Charleston. The income of this family was derived mostly from the hire of their slaves, about one hundred in number. Their luxuries were blood-bought luxuries indeed. And yet what stranger would ever have inferred their cruelties from the courteous reception and bland manners of the parlor. Everything cruel and revolting is carefully concealed from strangers, especially those from the north. Take an instance. I have known the master and mistress of a family send to their friends to *borrow* servants to wait on company, because their own slaves had been so cruelly flogged in the work house, that they could not walk without limping at every step and their putrefied flesh emitted such an intolerable smell that they were not fit to be in the presence of company. How can northerners know these things when they are hospitably received at southern tables and firesides? I repeat it, no one who has not been an *integral part* of a slaveholding community, can have any idea of its abominations. It is a whited sepulchre full of dead men's bones and all uncleanness. Blessed be God, the Angel of *Truth* has descended and rolled away the stone from the mouth of the sepulchre, and *sits* upon it. The abominations so long hidden are now brought forth before all Israel and the sun. Yes, the Angel of Truth *sits upon this stone,* and it can never be rolled back again. The utter disregard of the comfort of the slaves, in *little* things, can scarcely be conceived by those who have not been a *component part* of slaveholding communities. Take a few particulars out of hundreds that might be named. In South Carolina musketoes swarm in myriads, more than half the year—they are so excessively annoying at night, that no family thinks of sleeping without nets or "musketoe-bars" hung over their bedsteads, yet slaves are never provided with them, unless it be the favorite old domestics who get the cast-off pavilions; and yet these very masters and mistresses will be so kind to their horses as to provide them with *fly nets.* Bedsteads and bedding too, are rarely provided for any of the slaves—if the waiters and coachmen, waiting maids, cooks, washers, &c., have beds at all, they must generally get them for themselves. Commonly they lie down at night on the bare floor, with a small blanket wrapped round them in winter, and in summer a coarse osnaburg sheet, or nothing. Old slaves generally have beds, but it is because when younger *they have provided them for themselves.*

Only two meals a day are allowed the house slaves—the *first at twelve* o'clock. If they eat before this time, it is by stealth, and I am sure there must be a good deal of suffering among them from *hunger,* and particularly by children. Besides this, they are often kept from their meals by way of punishment. No table is provided for them to eat from. They know nothing of the comfort and pleasure of gathering round the social board—each takes his plate or tin pan and iron spoon and holds it in the hand or on the lap. I *never* saw slaves seated round a *table* to partake of any meal.

As the general rule, no lights of any kind, no firewood—no towels, basins, or soap, no tables, chairs, or other furniture, are provided. Wood for cooking and washing *for the family* is found, but when the master's work is done, the slave must find wood for himself if he has a fire. I have repeatedly known slave children kept the whole winter's evening, sitting on the stair-case in a cold entry, just to be at hand to snuff candles or hand a tumbler of water from the side-board, or go on errands from one room to another. It may be asked why they were not permitted to stay in the parlor, when they would be still more at hand. I answer, because waiters are not allowed to *sit* in the presence of their owners, and as children who were kept running all day, would of course get very tired of standing for two or three hours, they were allowed to go into the entry and sit on the staircase until rung for. Another reason is, that even slaveholders at times find the presence of slaves very annoying; they cannot exercise entire freedom of speech before them on all subjects.

I have also known instances where seamstresses were kept in cold entries to work by the stair case lamps for one or two hours, every evening in winter—they could not see without standing up all the time, though the work was often too large and heavy for them to sew upon it in that position without great inconvenience, and yet they were expected to do their work as *well* with their cold fingers, and standing up, as if they had been sitting by a comfortable fire and provided with the necessary light. House slaves suffer a great deal also from not being allowed to leave the house without permission. If they wish to go even for a draught of water, they must *ask leave,* and if they stay longer than the mistress thinks necessary, they are liable to be punished, and often are scolded or slapped, or kept from going down to the next meal.

It frequently happens that relatives, among slaves, are separated for weeks or months, by the husband or brother being taken by the master on a journey, to attend on his horses and himself.— When they return, the white husband seeks the wife of his love ; but the black husband must wait to see *his* wife, until mistress pleases to let her chambermaid leave her room. Yes, such is the despotism of slavery, that wives and sisters dare not run to meet their husbands and brothers after such separations and hours sometimes elapse before they are allowed to meet; and, at times, a fiendish pleasure is taken in keeping them asunder—this furnishes an opportunity to vent feelings of spite for any little neglect of "duty."

The sufferings, to which slaves are subjected by separations of various kinds, cannot be imagined by those unacquainted with the working out of the system behind the curtain. Take the following instances. Chambermaids and seamstresses often sleep in their mistresses' apartments, but with no bedding at all. I know an instance of a woman who has been married eleven years, and yet has never been allowed to sleep out of her mistress's chamber

This is a *great* hardship to slaves. When we consider that house slaves are rarely allowed social intercourse during *the day,* as their work generally *separates* them; the barbarity of such an arrangement is obvious. It is peculiarly a hardship in the above case, as the husband of the woman does not "belong" to her "owner;" and because he is subject to dreadful attacks of illness, and can have but little attention from his wife in the *day.* And yet her mistress, who is an old lady, gives her the highest character as a faithful servant, and told a friend of mine, that she was " entirely dependent upon her for *all* her comforts; she dressed and undressed her, gave her all her food, and was so *necessary* to her that she could not do without her." I may add that this couple are tenderly attached to each other.

I also know an instance in which the husband was a slave and the wife was free; during the illness of the former, the latter was *allowed* to come and nurse him; she was obliged to leave the work by which she had made a living, and come to stay with her husband, and thus lost weeks of her time, or he would have suffered for want of proper attention; and yet his "owner" made her no compensation for her services. He had long been a faithful and a favorite slave, and his owner was a woman very benevolent to the poor whites. She went a great deal among these, as a visiting commissioner of the Ladies' Benevolent Society, and was in the constant habit of *paying* the *relatives of the poor whites* for nursing *their* husbands, fathers, and other relations; because she thought it very hard, when their time was taken up, so that they could not earn their daily bread, that they should be left to suffer. Now, such is the stupefying influence of the "*chattel* principle" on the minds of slaveholders that I do not suppose it ever occurred to her that this poor *colored* wife ought to be paid for her services, and particularly as she was spending her time and strength in taking care of *her* "*property.*" She no doubt only thought how kind she was, to *allow* her to come and stay so long in her yard; for, let it be kept in mind, that slaveholders have unlimited power to separate husbands and wives, parents and children, however and whenever they please; and if this mistress had chosen to do it, she could have debarred this woman from all intercourse with her husband, by forbidding her to enter her premises.

Persons, who own plantations and yet live in cities, often take children from their parents as soon as they are weaned, and send them into the country; because they do not want the time of the mother taken up by attendance upon her own children, it being too valuable to the mistress. As a *favor,* she is, in some cases, permitted to go to see them once a year. So, on the other hand, if field slaves happen to have children of an age suitable to the convenience of the master, they are taken from their parents and brought to the city. Parents are almost never consulted as to the disposition to be made of their children; they have as little control over them, as have domestic animals over the disposal of their young. Every natural and social feeling and affection are violated with indifference; slaves are treated as though they did not possess them.

Another way, in which the feelings of slaves are trifled with and often deeply wounded, is by changing their names; if, at the time they are brought into a family, there is another slave of the same name; or if the owner happens, for some other reason, not to like the name of the newcomer. I have known slaves very much grieved at having the names of their children thus changed, when they had been called after a dear relation. Indeed it would be utterly impossible to recount the multitude of ways in which the *heart* of the slave is continually lacerated by the total disregard of his feelings as a social being and a human creature.

The slave suffers also greatly from being continually *watched*. The system of espionage which is constantly kept up over slaves is the most worrying and intolerable that can be imagined. Many mistresses are, in fact, during the absence of their husbands, really their drivers; and the pleasure of returning to their families often, on the part of the husband, is entirely destroyed by the complaints preferred against the slaves when he comes home to his meals.

A mistress of my acquaintance asked her servant boy, one day, what was the reason she could not get him to do his work whilst his master was away, and said to him, "Your master works a great deal harder than you do; he is at his office all day, and often has to study his law cases at night." "Master," said the boy, "is working for himself, and for you, ma'am, but I am working for *him*" The mistress turned and remarked to a friend, that she was so struck with the truth of the remark, that she could not say a word to him.

But I forbear—the sufferings of the slaves are not only innumerable, but they are indescribable. I may paint the agony of kindred torn from each other's arms, to meet no more in time; I may depict the inflictions of the blood-stained lash, but I *cannot describe* the daily, hourly, ceaseless torture, endured by the heart that is constantly trampled under the foot of despotic power. This is a part of the horrors of slavery which, I believe, no one has ever attempted to delineate; I wonder not at it, it mocks all power of language. Who can describe the anguish of that mind which feels itself impaled upon the iron of arbitrary power—its living, writhing, helpless victim! Every human susceptibility tortured, its sympathies torn, and stung, and bleeding—always feeling the death-weapon in its heart, and yet not so deep as to *kill* that humanity which is made the curse of its existence.

In the course of my testimony I have entered somewhat into the *minutiae* of slavery, because this is a part of the subject often overlooked, and cannot be appreciated by any but those who have been witnesses, and entered into sympathy with the slaves as human beings. Slaveholders think nothing of them, because they regard their slaves as *property,* the mere instruments of their convenience and pleasure. *One who is a slaveholder at heart never recognizes a human being in a slave.*

As thou hast asked me to testify respecting the *physical condition* of the slaves merely, I say nothing of the awful neglect of their *minds* and *souls* and the systematic effort to imbrute them. A wrong and an impiety, in comparison with which all the other unutterable wrongs of slavery are but as the dust of the balance.

Angelina G. Weld.

GENERAL TESTIMONY TO THE CRUELTIES INFLICTED UPON SLAVES

Before presenting to the reader particular details of the cruelties inflicted upon American slaves, we will present in brief the well-weighed declarations of slaveholders and other residents of slave states, testifying that the slaves are treated with barbarous inhumanity. All *details* and particulars will be drawn out under their appropriate heads. We propose in this place to present testimony of a *general character*—the solemn declarations of slaveholders and others, that the slaves are treated with great cruelty.

To discredit the testimony of witnesses, who insist upon convicting themselves, would be an anomalous skepticism. .

To show that American slavery has *always* had one uniform character of diabolical cruelty, we will go back one hundred years, and prove it by unimpeachable witnesses, who have given their deliberate testimony to its horrid barbarity, from 1739 to 1839.

TESTIMONY OF REV. GEORGE WHITEFIELD

In a letter written by him in Georgia, and addressed to the slaveholders of Maryland, Virginia, North and South Carolina and Georgia, in 1739.— See Benezet's "Caution to Great Britain and her Colonies."

"As I lately passed through your provinces on my way hither, I was sensibly touched with a fellow-feeling of the miseries of the poor negroes.

"Sure I am, it is sinful to use them as bad, nay worse than if they were brutes; and whatever particular *exceptions* there may be, (as I would charitably hope there are *some,)* I fear the *generality* of you that own negroes, *are liable to such a charge.* Not to mention what numbers have been given up to the inhuman usage of cruel *taskmasters,* who by their unrelenting scourges, have ploughed their backs and made long furrows, and at length brought them to the grave!

"The blood of them, spilt for these many years, in your respective provinces, will ascend up to heaven against you!"

The following is the testimony of the celebrated John Woolman, an eminent minister of the Society of Friends, who traveled extensively in the slave states. We copy it from a "Memoir of John Woolman chiefly extracted from a Journal of his Life and Travels," It was published in Philadelphia, by the "Society of Friends."

"The following reflections were written in 1757, while he was traveling on a religious account among slaveholders."

"Many of the white people in these provinces, take little or no care of negro marriages; and when negroes marry, after their own way, some make so little account of those marriages, that, with views of outward interest, they often part men from their wives, by selling them far asunder; which is common when estates are sold by executors at vendue.

"Many whose labor is heavy, being followed at their business in the field by a man with a whip, hired for that purpose,—have, in common, little else allowed them but *one peck* of Indian corn and some salt for one week, with a few potatoes. (The potatoes they commonly raise by their labor on the first day of the week.) The correction ensuing on their disobedience to overseers, or slothfulness in business is often *very severe,* and sometimes *desperate.* Men and women have many times *scarce clothes enough to hide their nakedness*—and boys and girls, ten and twelve years old, are often *quite naked* among their masters' children. Some use endeavors to instruct those (negro children) they have in reading; but in common, this is not only neglected, but disapproved."—p. 12.

TESTIMONY OF THE
'MARYLAND JOURNAL AND BALTIMORE ADVERTISER'
OF MAY 30, 1788

"In the ordinary course of the business of the country, the punishment of relations frequently happens on the same farm, and in view of each other: the father often sees his beloved son—the son his venerable sire—the mother her much loved daughter—the daughter her affectionate parent—the husband sees the wife of his bosom, and she the husband of her affection, *cruelly bound up* without delicacy or mercy, and without daring to interpose in each other's behalf, and punished with all the *extremity of incensed rage, and all the rigor of unrelenting severity.* Let us reverse the case, and suppose it ours: ALL IS SILENT HORROR!"

TESTIMONY OF THE HON. WILLIAM PINCKNEY OF MARYLAND

In a speech before the Maryland House of Delegates, in 1789, Mr. P. calls slavery in that state, "a speaking picture of *abominable oppression*;" and adds: "It will not do thus to act like *unrelenting tyrants,* perpetually sermonizing it with liberty as our text, and actual *oppression* for our commentary. Is she [Maryland] not.... the foster mother of petty *despots,—* the patron of *wanton oppression?"*

EXTRACT FROM A SPEECH BY MR. RICE
in the Convention for forming the Constitution of Kentucky in 1790
"The master may, and *often does, inflict upon him all the severity of punishment the human body is capable of bearing."*

PRESIDENT EDWARDS, THE YOUNGER
In a sermon before the Connecticut Abolition Society, 1791, says: "From these drivers, for every imagined, as well as real neglect or want of exertion, they receive the lash—the smack of which is all day long in the ears of those who are on the plantation or in the vicinity; and it is used with such dexterity and severity, as not only to lacerate the skin, but to tear out small portions of the flesh at almost every stroke.

"This is the general treatment of the slaves. But many individuals suffer still more severely. *Many, many are knocked down; some have their eyes beaten out; some have an arm or a leg broken, or chopped off;* and many, for a very small, or for no crime at all, have been beaten to death, merely to gratify the fury of an enraged master or overseer."

GEORGE BUCHANAN, M. D.
Extract from an oration, delivered at Baltimore, July 4, 1791, by George Buchanan, M. D. A member of the American Philosophical Society:
Their situation (the slaves') is *insupportable;* misery inhabits their cabins, and pursues them in the field. Inhumanly beaten, they *often* fall sacrifices to the turbulent tempers of their masters! Who is there, unless inured to savage cruelties, that can hear of the inhuman punishments *daily inflicted* upon the unfortunate blacks, without feeling for them? Can a man who calls himself a Christian, coolly and deliberately tie up, *thumb screw, torture with pincers,* and beat unmercifully a poor slave, for perhaps a trifling neglect of duty?

TESTIMONY OF HON. JOHN RANDOLPH, OF ROANOKE
A SLAVEHOLDER
In one of his Congressional speeches, Mr. R. says: "Avarice alone can drive, as it does drive, this *infernal* traffic, and the wretched victims of it, like so many post-horses *whipped to death* in a mail coach. Ambition has

its cover-sluts in the pride, pomp, and circumstance of glorious war; but where are the trophies of avarice? *The hand-cuff, the manacle, the blood-stained cowhide.'"*

Major Stoddard, of the United States Army

He who took possession of Louisiana in behalf of the United States, under the cession of 1804, in his Sketches of Louisiana, page 332, says:

"The feelings of humanity are outraged—the most odious tyranny exercised in a land of freedom, and hunger and nakedness prevail amidst plenty. Cruel, and even unusual punishments are daily inflicted on these wretched creatures, enfeebled with hunger, labor and the lash. The scenes of misery and distress constantly witnessed along the coast of the Delta, [of the Mississippi,] the wounds and lacerations occasioned by demoralized masters and overseers, torture the feelings of the passing stranger, and wring blood from the heart."

Though only the third of the following series of resolutions is directly relevant to the subject now under consideration, we insert the other resolutions, both because they are explanatory of the third, and also serve to reveal the public sentiment of Indiana, at the date of the resolutions. As a large majority of the citizens of Indiana at that time, were *natives of slave states,* they well knew the actual condition of the slaves.

1. "Resolved Unanimously, by the Legislative Council and House of Representatives of Indiana Territory, that a suspension of the sixth article of compact between the United States and the territories and states north west of the river Ohio, passed the 13th day of January, 1783, for the term of ten years, would be highly advantageous to the territory, and meet the approbation of at least nine-tenths of the good citizens of the same.

2. "Resolved Unanimously, that the abstract question of liberty and slavery, is not considered as involved in a suspension of the said article, inasmuch as the number of slaves in the United States would not be augmented by the measure.

3. "Resolved Unanimously, that the suspension of the said article would be equally advantageous to the territory, to the states from whence the negroes would be brought, and *to the negroes themselves.* The states which are overburthened with negroes would be benefited by disposing of the negroes which they cannot comfortably support; and THE NEGRO HIMSELF WOULD EXCHANGE A SCANTY PITTANCE OF THE

COARSEST FOOD, for a plentiful and nourishing diet; and a situation which admits not the most distant prospect of emancipation, for one which presents no considerable obstacle to his wishes.

4. "Resolved Unanimously, that a copy of these resolutions be delivered to the delegate to Congress from this territory, and that he be, and he hereby is, instructed to use his best endeavors to obtain a suspension of the said article.

J. B. Thomas
Speaker of the House of Representatives
Pierre Minard
President pro tem. of the Legislative *Council*
Vincennes, Dec. 20, 1806

"Forwarded to the Speaker of the United States' Senate, by William Henry Harrison, Governor."

American State Papers, vol 1, p. 467.

MONSIEUR C. C. ROBIN

Who resided in Louisiana from 1802 to 1806, and published a volume containing the results of his observations there, thus speaks of the condition of the slaves:

"While they are at labor, the manager, the master, or the driver has commonly the whip in hand to strike the idle. But those of the negroes who are judged guilty of serious faults, are punished twenty, twenty-five, forty, fifty, or one hundred lashes. The manner of this cruel execution is as follows: four stakes are driven down, making a long square; the culprit is extended naked between these stakes, face downwards; his hands and his feet are bound separately, with strong cords, to each of the stakes, so far apart that his arms and legs, stretched in the form of St. Andrew's cross, give the poor wretch no chance of stirring. Then the executioner, who is ordinarily a negro armed with the long whip of a coachman, strikes upon the reins and thighs.

The crack of his whip resounds afar, like that of an angry cartman beating his horses. The blood flows, the long wounds cross each other; strips of skin are raised without softening either the hand of the executioner or the heart of the master, who cries 'sting him harder.'

"The reader is moved; so am I, my agitated hand refuses to trace the bloody picture, to recount how many times the piercing cry of pain has interrupted my silent occupations; how many times I have shuddered at the faces of those barbarous masters, where I saw inscribed the number of victims sacrificed to their ferocity.

"The women are subjected to these punishments as rigorously as the men—not even pregnancy exempts them; in that case, before binding them to the stakes, a hole is made in the ground to accommodate the enlarged form of the victim.

"It is remarkable that the white Creole women are ordinarily more inexorable than the men. Their slow and languid gait, and the trifling services which they impose, betoken only apathetic indolence; but should the slave not promptly obey, should he even fail to divine the meaning of their gestures, or looks, in an instant they are armed with a formidable whip; it is no longer the arm which cannot sustain the weight of a shawl or a reticule—it is no longer the form which but feebly sustains itself. They themselves order the punishment of one of these poor creatures, and with a dry eye see their victim bound to four stakes; they count the blows, and raise a voice of menace, if the arm that strikes relaxes, or if the blood does not flow in sufficient abundance. Their sensibility changed to fury must needs feed itself for a while on the hideous spectacle; they must, as if to revive themselves, hear the piercing shrieks, and see the flow of fresh blood; there are some of them who, in their frantic rage, pinch and bite their victims.

"It is by no means wonderful that the laws designed to protect the slave, should be little respected by the generality of such masters. I have seen some masters pay those unfortunate people the miserable overcoat which is their due; but others give them nothing at all, and do not even leave them the hours and Sundays granted to them by law. I have seen some of those barbarous masters leave them, during the winter, in a state of revolting nudity, even contrary to their own true interests, for they thus weaken and shorten the lives upon which repose the whole of their own fortunes. I have seen some of those negroes obliged to conceal their nakedness with the long moss of the country. The sad melancholy of these wretches, depicted upon their countenances, the flight of some, and the death of others, do not reclaim their masters; they wreak upon those who remain, the vengeance which they can no longer exercise upon the others."

WHITMAN MEAD. Esq.

Of New York, in his journal, published nearly a quarter of a century ago, under date of January 28, 1817.

"Savannah,

"To one not accustomed to such scenes as slavery presents, the condition of the slaves is *impressively shocking.* In the course of my walks, I was everywhere witness to their wretchedness. Like the brute creatures of the north, they are driven about at the pleasure of all who meet them; *half naked and half starved,* they drag out a pitiful existence, apparently almost unconscious of what they suffer. A threat accompanies every command, and a bastinado is the usual reward of disobedience."

TESTIMONY OF REV. JOHN RANKIN

A native of Tennessee, educated there, and for a number of years a preacher in slave states—now pastor of a church in Ripley, Ohio.

"Many poor slaves are stripped naked, stretched and tied across barrels, or large bags *and tortured with the lash during hours and even whole days, until their flesh is mangled to the very bones.* Others are stripped and hung up by the arms, their feet are tied together, and the end of a heavy piece of timber is put between their legs in order to stretch their bodies, and so prepare them for the torturing lash—and in this situation they are often whipped until their bodies are covered *with blood and mangled flesh*—and in order to add the greatest keenness to their sufferings, their wounds are washed with *liquid salt!* And some of the miserable creatures are permitted to hang in that position until they actually *expire;* some die under the lash, others linger about for a time, and at length die of their wounds, and many survive, and endure again similar torture. These bloody scenes are *constantly exhibiting in every slaveholding country—thousands of whips are every day stained in African blood!* Even the poor *females* are not permitted to escape these shocking cruelties."—*Rankin's Letters, pages* 57, 58.

These letters were published fifteen years ago.—They were addressed to a brother in Virginia, who was a slaveholder.

TESTIMONY OF THE AMERICAN COLONIZATION SOCIETY
"We have heard of slavery as it exists in Asia, and Africa, and Turkey—we have heard of the feudal slavery under which the peasantry of Europe have groaned from the days of Alaric until now, but excepting only the horrible system of the West India Islands, we have never heard of slavery in any country, ancient or modern, Pagan, Mohammedan, or *Christian! So terrible in its character,* as the slavery which exists in these United States."—*Seventh Report American Colonization Society,* 1824.

TESTIMONY OF THE
GRADUAL EMANCIPATION SOCIETY OF NORTH CAROLINA
Signed by Moses Swain, President, and William Swain, Secretary.

"In the eastern part of the state, the slaves considerably outnumber the free population. Their situation is there wretched beyond description. Impoverished by the mismanagement which we have already attempted to describe, the master, unable to support his own grandeur and maintain his slaves, puts the unfortunate wretches upon short allowances, scarcely sufficient for their sustenance, so that a great part of them go half naked and half starved much of the time. Generally, throughout the state, the African is an *abused, a monstrously outraged creature"*—See Minutes of the American Conven. Hon, convened in Baltimore, Oct. 25, 1826.

FROM NILES' BALTIMORE REGISTER FOR 1829, VOL. 35, p. 4.

"Dealing in slaves has become a *large business.* Establishments are made at several places in Maryland and Virginia, at which they are sold like cattle. These places of deposit are strongly built, and well supplied with *iron thumb-screws and gags* and ornamented with *cowskins and other whips—often times bloody."*

JUDGE RUFFIN, OF THE SUPREME COURT OF NORTH CAROLINA

In one of his judicial decisions, says:

"The slave, to remain a slave, must feel that there is NO APPEAL FROM HIS MASTER. No man can anticipate the provocations which the slave would give, nor the consequent wrath of the master, prompting him to BLOODY VENGEANCE on the turbulent traitor, a vengeance *generally* practiced with impunity, by reason of its Privacy."—See *Wheeler's Law of Slavery* p. 247.

MR. MOORE OF VIRGINIA

In his speech before the Legislature of that state, Jan. 15, 1832, says:

"It must be confessed, that although the treatment of our slaves is in the general, as mild and humane as it can be, that it must always happen, that there will be found hundreds of individuals, who, owing either to the natural ferocity of their dispositions, or to the effects of intemperance, will be guilty of cruelty and barbarity towards their slaves, which is *almost intolerable,* and at which humanity revolts."

TESTIMONY.OF B. SWAIN, ESQ., OF NORTH CAROLINA

"Let any man of spirit and feeling, for a moment cast his thoughts over this land of slavery— think of the *nakedness* of some, the *hungry yearnings* of others, the *flowing tears and heaving* sighs of parting relations, the *wailings and woe, the bloody cut of the keen lash, and the frightful scream that rends the very skies*—and all this to gratify ambition, lust, pride, avarice, vanity, and other depraved feelings of the human heart. *THE WORST IS NOT GENERALLY KNOWN.* Were all the miseries, the horrors of slavery, to burst at once into view, a peal of seven-fold thunder could scarce strike greater alarm."—*See "Swain's Address",* 1830.

TESTIMONY OF DR. JAMES C. FINLEY

Son of Dr. Finley, one of the founders of the Colonization Society, and brother of R. S. Finley, agent of the American Colonization Society. Dr. J. C. Finley was formerly one of the editors of the Western Medical Journal, at Cincinnati, and is well known in the west as utterly hostile to immediate abolition:

"In almost the last conversation I had with you before I left Cincinnati, I promised to give you some account of some scenes of atrocious cruelty towards slaves, which I witnessed while I lived at the south. I almost regret having made the promise, for not only are they *so atrocious* that you will with difficulty believe them, but I also fear that they will have the effect of driving you into that *abolitionism,* upon the borders of which you have been so long hesitating. The people of the north are *ignorant of the horrors of slavery*—of the *atrocities* which it commits upon the unprotected slave." I do not know that anything could be gained by particularizing the scenes of *horrible barbarity,* which fell under my observation during my *short* residence in one of the wealthiest, most intelligent, and most moral parts of Georgia. Their *number* and *atrocity* are such, that I am confident they would gain credit with none but *abolitionists.* Everything will be conveyed in the remark, that in a state of society calculated to foster the worst passions of our nature, the slave derives *no protection* either from *law* or *public opinion,* and that all the cruelties which the Russians are reported to have acted towards the Poles, after their late subjugation, Are scenes of EVERY DAY OCCURRENCE in the southern states. This statement, incredible as it may seem, falls short, very far short of the truth."

The foregoing is extracted from a letter written by Dr. Finley to Rev. Asa Mahan, his former pastor, then of Cincinnati, now President of Oberlin Seminary.

TESTIMONY OF REV. WILLIAM ALLAN, OF ILLINOIS

Son of a Slaveholder, Rev. Dr. Allan of Huntsville, Ala.

"At our house it is so common to hear their (the slaves') screams, that we think nothing of it: and lest anyone should think that in *general* the slaves are well treated, let me be distinctly understood:—*cruelty* is the *rule,* and *kindness* the *exception.* "

MR. NATHAN COLE OF ST. LOUIS, MISSOURI

Extract of a letter dated July 2d, 1834, to Arthur Tappan, Esq. of this city:

"I am not an advocate of the immediate and unconditional emancipation of the slaves of our country, yet *no man has ever yet depicted the wretchedness of the situation of the slaves in colors too dark for the truth.* I know that many good people are *not aware of the treatment to which slaves are usually subjected,* nor have they any just idea of the extent of the evil."

TESTIMONY OF REV. JAMES A. THOME

A native of Kentucky—Son of Arthur Thome Esq., till recently a Slaveholder:

Slavery is the parent of more suffering than has flowed from any one source since the date of its existence. Such sufferings too! *Sufferings inconceivable and innumerable—unmingled wretchedness* from the ties of nature rudely broken and destroyed, the *acutest bodily tortures, groans, tears and blood*—lying forever in weariness and painfulness, in watchings, in hunger and in thirst, in cold and nakedness."Brethren of the North, be not deceived. *These sufferings still exist,* and despite the efforts of their cruel authors to hush them down, and confine them within the precincts of their own plantations, they will ever and anon, struggle up and reach the ear of humanity."—*Mr. Thome's Speech at New York, May,* 1834.

TESTIMONY OF THE MARYVILLE (TENNESSEE) INTELLIGENCER, OF OCT. 4, 1835

The Editor, in speaking of the sufferings of the slaves which are taken by the internal trade to the South West, says:

"Place yourself in imagination, for a moment, in their condition. With *heavy galling chains,* riveted upon your person; *half-naked, half-starved;* your back *lacerated* with the 'knotted whip;' traveling to a region where your *condition through time will be second only to the wretched creatures in hell.* "This depicting is not visionary. Would to God that it was."

TESTIMONY OF THE PRESBYTERIAN SYNOD OF KENTUCKY

A large majority of whom are slaveholders:

"This system licenses and produces great cruelty.

"Mangling, imprisonment, starvation, every species of torture, may be inflicted upon him, (the slave,) and he has no redress.

"There are now in our whole land two millions of human beings, exposed, defenseless, to every insult, and every injury short of maiming or death, which their fellow-men may choose to inflict. *They suffer all* that can be inflicted by wanton caprice, by grasping avarice, by brutal lust, by malignant spite, and by insane anger. Their happiness is the sport of every whim, and the prey of every passion that may, occasionally, or habitually, infest the master's bosom. If we could calculate the amount of woe endured by ill-treated slaves, it would overwhelm every compassionate heart—it would move even the obdurate to sympathy. There is also a vast sum of suffering inflicted upon the slave by humane masters, as a punishment for that idleness and misconduct which slavery naturally produces. "*Brutal stripes* and all the varied kinds of personal indignities, are not the only species of cruelty which slavery licenses."

TESTIMONY OF THE REV. N. H. HARDING
Pastor of the Presbyterian Church, in Oxford, North Carolina, a slaveholder.

"I am greatly surprised that you should in any form have been the apologist of a system so full of deadly poison to all holiness and benevolence as slavery, the concocted essence of fraud, selfishness, and cold hearted tyranny, and the fruitful parent of unnumbered evils, both to the oppressor and the oppressed, THE ONE THOUSANDTH PART OF WHICH HAS NEVER BEEN BROUGHT TO LIGHT."

MR. ASA A. STONE

A theological student, who lived near Natchez, (Mi.,) in 1834 and 5, sent the following with other testimony, to be published under his own name, in the N. Y. Evangelist, while he was still residing there:

"Floggings for all offenses, including deficiencies in work, are *frightfully common,* and *most terribly severe.*

"Rubbing with salt and red pepper is very common after a severe whipping."

TESTIMONY OF REV. PHINEAS SMITH

Of Centreville, Allegany, Co., N.Y. who lived four years at the south.

"They are badly clothed, badly fed, wretchedly lodged and unmercifully whipped, from month to month, from year to year, from childhood to old age."

REV. JOSEPH M. SADD

Castile, Genessee Co. N.Y., who was till recently a preacher in Missouri, says:

"It is true that barbarous cruelties are inflicted upon them, such as terrible lacerations with the whip, and excruciating tortures are sometimes experienced from the thumb screw."

SARAH M. GRIMKE

Extract of a letter dated 4th Month, 2nd, 1839:

"If the following extracts from letters which I have received from South Carolina, will be of any use thou art at liberty to publish them. I need not say that the names of the writers are withheld of necessity, because such sentiments if uttered at the south would peril their lives.

Extracts: South Carolina, 4th Month, 5th, 1835.

'With regard to slavery I must confess, though we had heard a great deal on the subject, we found on coming South the *half,* the *worst* half too, had not been told us; not that we have ourselves *seen* much oppression, though truly we have felt its deadening influence, but the accounts we have received from every tongue that nobly dares to speak upon the subject, are indeed *deplorable* To quote the language of a lady, who with true Southern hospitality, received us at her mansion. "The *northern* people don't know anything of slavery at all, they think it is *perpetual bondage merely,* but of the *depth* of *degradation* that that word involves, they have no conception; if they had any just idea of it, they would I am sure use every effort until an end was put to such a shocking system.'

"Another friend writing from South Carolina, and who sustains herself the legal relation of slaveholder, in a letter dated April 4th, 1838, says—'I have some time since, given you my views on the subject of slavery, which so much engrosses your attention. I would most willingly forget what I have seen and heard in my own family, with regard to the slaves. *I shudder when I think of it,* and increasingly feel that slavery is a curse since it leads to such *cruelty.* "

PUNISHMENTS

I. FLOGGINGS

The slaves are terribly lacerated with whips, paddles, &c.; red pepper and salt are rubbed into their mangled flesh; hot brine and turpentine are poured into their gashes; and innumerable other tortures inflicted upon them.

We will in the first place, prove by a cloud of witnesses, that the slaves are whipped with such inhuman severity, as to lacerate and mangle their flesh in the most shocking manner, leaving permanent scars and ridges; after establishing this, we will present a mass of testimony, concerning a great variety of other tortures. The testimony, for the most part, will be that of the slaveholders themselves, and in their own chosen words. A large portion of it will be taken from the advertisements, which they have published in their own newspapers, describing by the scars on their bodies made by the whip, their own runaway slaves. To copy these advertisements *entire* would require a great amount of space, and flood the reader with a vast mass of matter irrelevant to the *point* before us; we shall therefore insert only so much of each, as will intelligibly set forth the precise point under consideration. Under the word "Witnesses," will be found the name of the individual, who signs the advertisement, or for whom it is signed, with his or her place of residence, and the name and date of the paper, in which it appeared, and generally the name of the place where it is published. Underneath the name of each witness, will be an extract, from the advertisement, containing his or her testimony.

WITNESS
Mr. D. Judd, jailor, Davidson Co., Tennessee, in the "Nashville Banner," Dec. 10th, 1838.

TESTIMONY
"Committed to jail as a runaway, a negro woman named Martha, 17 or 18" years of age, has *numerous scars o tike whip* on her back."

===========

WITNESS
Mr. Robert Nicoll, Dauphin St. between Emmanuel and Conception Sts, Mobile, Alabama, in the "Mobile Commercial Advertiser."

TESTIMONY
"Ten dollars reward for my woman Siby very *much scarred about the neck and ears by whipping.*"

===========

WITNESS
Mr. Bryant Johnson, Fort Valley, Houston Co., Georgia, in the "Standard of Union," Milledgeville Ga. Oct. 2, 1838.

TESTIMONY
"Ranaway, a negro woman, named Maria, *some scars on her back occasioned by the whip.*"

===========

WITNESS
Mr. James T. De Jarnett, Vernon, Autauga Co., Alabama, in the "Pensacola Gazette," July, 14, 1838.

TESTIMONY
"Stolen, a negro woman, named Celia. On examining her back you will find *marks caused by the whip.*"

===========

WITNESS
Maurice Y. Garcia, Sheriff of the County of Jefferson, La., in the "New Orleans Bee," August, 14, 1838.

TESTIMONY

"Lodged in jail, a mulatto boy, having *large marks of the whip* on his shoulders and other parts of his body."

==========

WITNESS

R. J. Bland, Sheriff of Claiborne Co, Miss., in the "Charleston (*S.C.)* Courier," August, 28, 1838.

TESTIMONY

"We committed a negro boy, named Tom, i*s much marked with the whip.*"

==========

WITNESS

Mr. James Noe, Red River Landing, La., in the "Sentinel," Vicksburg, Miss., August 22, 1837.

TESTIMONY

"Ranaway, a negro fellow named Dick---has *many scars on his back from being whipped.* "

==========

WITNESS

William Craze, jailor, Alexandria, La. in the "Planter's Intelligencer," Sept. 26, 1838.

TESTIMONY

"Committed to jail, a negro slave, his *back is very badly scarred.* "

==========

WITNESS

John A. Rowland, jailor, Lumberton, North Carolina, in the "Fayetteville (N. C.) Observer," June 20, 1838.

TESTIMONY

"Committed, a mulatto fellow---his back shows *lasting impressions of a whip*, and leaves no doubt of him being a slave."

==========

WITNESS

"J. K. Roberts, sheriff, Blount County, Ala., in the Huntsville Democrat," Dec. 9, 1838.

TESTIMONY

"Committed to jail, a negro man, his back *much marked by the whip.*"

==========

WITNESS

Mr. H. Varillat, No. 23 Girod Street, New Orleans—in the "Commercial Bulletin," August 27, 1838.

TESTIMONY

"Ranaway, the negro slave named Jupiter---has a fresh *mark of a cowskin* on one of his cheeks."

==========

WITNESS

Mr. Cornelius D. Tolin, Augusta, Ga., in the "Chronicle and Sentinel," Oct. 18, 1838.

TESTIMONY

"Ranaway, a negro man named Johnson---he has a *great many marks of the whip* on his back."

==========

WITNESS

W. H. Brasseale, sheriff, Blount County Ala., in the "Huntsville Democrat," June 9, 1838.

TESTIMONY

"Committed to jail, a negro slave name James---much scarred with a whip on his back."

==========

WITNESS

Mr. Robert Beasley, Macon, Ga., in the "Georgia Messenger," July 27, 1837.

TESTIMONY

"Ranaway, my man Fountain---he is marked on the back with the whip."

==========

WITNESS

Mr. John Wotton, Rockvllle, Montgomery County, Maryland, in the "Baltimore Republican," Jan. 13,1838.

TESTIMONY

"Ranaway, Bill---has several large scars on his back from a *severe whipping in early life.*"

==========

WITNESS

D. S. Bennett, sheriff, Natchitoches, La., in the "Herald," July 21,1838.

TESTIMONY

"Committed to jail, a negro boy who calls himself Joe---said negro bears *marks of the whip.*"

==========

WITNESS

Messrs. Whitehead, and R. A. Evans, Marion, Georgia, in the Milledgeville (Ga.) "Standard of Union," June26, 1838.

TESTIMONY

"Ranaway, negro fellow John---from being whipped, has *scars on his back arms and thighs.*"

==========

WITNESS

Mr. Samuel Stewart, Greensboro', Ala., in the "Southern Advocate," Huntsville, Jan. 6, 1838.

TESTIMONY

"Ranaway, a boy named Jim—with the marks of the *whip* on the small of the back, reaching round to the flank."

==========

WITNESS

Mr. John Walker, No. 6, Banks' Arcade, New Orleans, in the "Bulletin," August 11, 1838.

TESTIMONY

"Ranaway, the mulatto boy Quash—*considerably marked* on the back and other places with the lash.

==========

WITNESS

Mr. Jesse Beene, Cahawba, Ala., in the "State Intelligencer," Tuskaloosa, Dec. 25, 1837.

TESTIMONY

"Ranaway, my negro man Billy—he has the *marks of the* whip."

==========

WITNESS

Mr. John Turner, Thomaston, Upson County, Georgia—in the "Standard of Union," Milledgeville, June 26, 1838.

TESTIMONY

"Left, my negro man named George—has *marks of the whip very plain* on his thighs."

========

WITNESS

James Derrah, deputy sheriff, Claiborne County, Mi., in the "Port Gibson Correspondent," April 15, 1837.

TESTIMONY

"Committed to jail, negro man Toy—he has been *badly whipped.*"

========

WITNESS

S. B. Murphy, sheriff, Wilkinson County, Georgia—in the Milledgeville "Journal," May 15, 1838.

TESTIMONY

"Brought to jail, a negro man named George—he has a *great many scars from the lash.*"

========

WITNESS

Mr. L. E. Cooner, Branchville Orangeburgh District, South Carolina— in the Macon "Messenger," May 25, 1837.

TESTIMONY

"One hundred dollars reward, for my negro Glasgow, and Kate, his wife. Glasgow is 24 years old—has marks *of the whip* on his back. Kate is 26—has a *scar* on her cheek, *and several marks of a whip.*"

========

WITNESS

John H. Hand, jailor, parish of West Feliciana, in the St, "Francisville Journal," July 6, 1837.

TESTIMONY

"Committed to jail, a negro boy named John, about 17 years old—his back *badly marked* with the *whip,* his upper lip and chin *severely bruised.*"

========

The preceding are extracts from advertisements published in southern papers, mostly in the year 1838. They are mere samples of hundreds of similar ones published during the same period, with which, as the preceding are quite sufficient the commonness of inhuman floggings in the slave states, we need not burden the reader.

The foregoing testimony is, as the reader perceives, that of the slaveholders themselves, voluntarily certifying to the outrages which their own hands have committed upon defenseless and innocent men and women, over whom they have assumed authority. We have given to *their* testimony precedence over that of all other witnesses, for the reason that when men testify against *themselves* they are under no temptation to exaggerate.

We will now present the testimony of a large number of individuals, with their names and residences, of persons who witnessed the inflictions to which they testify. Many of them have been slave holders, and *all* residents for longer or shorter periods in slave states:

Rev. John H. Curtiss, a native of Keep Creek, Norfolk County, Virginia, now a local preacher of the Methodist Episcopal Church in Portage Co., Ohio, testifies as follows:

"In 1829 or 30, one of my father's slaves was accused of taking.the key to the office and stealing four or five dollars; he denied it. A constable by the name of Hull was called; he took the negro, very deliberately tied his hands, and whipped him till the blood ran freely down his legs. By this time Hull appeared tired, and stopped; he then took a rope, put a slip noose around his neck, and told the negro he was going to *kill* him, at the same time drew the rope and began whipping; the negro fell; his cheeks looked as though they would burst with strangulation. Hull whipped and kicked him, till I really thought he was going to kill him; when he ceased, the negro was in a complete gore of blood from head to foot."

Mr. David Hawley, a class-leader in the Methodist Church, at St. Alban's, Licking county, Ohio, who moved from Kentucky to Ohio in 1831, testifies as follows :

"In the year 1821 or 2, I saw a slave hung for killing his master. The master had whipped the slave's mother to Death, and, locking him in a room, threatened him with the same fate; and, cowhide in hand, had begun the work, when the slave joined battle and slew the master."

Samuel Ellison, a member of the Society of Friends, formerly of Southampton County, Virginia, now of Marlborough, Stark County, Ohio, gives the following testimony:

"While a resident of Southampton County, Virginia, I knew two men, after having been severely treated, endeavor to make their escape. In this they failed—were taken, tied to trees, and whipped to *death* by their overseer. I lived a mile from the negro quarters, and, at that distance, could frequently hear the screams of the poor creatures when beaten, and could also hear the blows given by the overseer with some heavy instrument."

Major Horace Nye, of Putnam, Ohio, gives the following testimony of Mr. Wm. Armstrong, of that place, a captain and supercargo of boats descending the Mississippi river:

"At Bayou Sarah, I saw a slave stak*ed out,* with his face to the ground, and whipped with a large whip, which laid open the flesh for about two and a half inches *every stroke.* 1 stayed about five minutes, but could stand it no longer, and left them whipping."

Mr. Stephen E. Maltby, inspector of provisions, Skaneateles, New York, who has resided in Alabama, speaking of the condition of the slaves, says:

"I have seen them cruelly whipped. I will relate one instance. One Sabbath morning, before I got out of my bed, I heard an outcry, and got up and went to the window, when I saw some six or eight boys, from eight to twelve years of age, near a rack (made for tying horses) on the public square. A man on horseback rode up, got off his horse, took a cord from his pocket, *tied one of the boys* by the *thumbs* to the rack, and with his horsewhip lashed him most severely. He then untied him and rode off without saying a word.

"It was a general practice, while I was at Huntsville, Alabama, to have a patrol every night; and, to my knowledge, this patrol was in the habit of traversing the streets with cow-skins, and, if they found any slaves out after eight o'clock without a pass, to whip them until they were out of reach, or to confine them until morning."

Mr. J. G. Baldwin of Middletown, Connecticut, a member of the Methodist Episcopal Church, gives the following testimony:

"I traveled at the south in 1827: when near Charlotte, N.C. a free colored man fell into the road just ahead of me, and went on peaceably. When passing a public-house, the landlord ran out with a large cudgel, and applied it to the head and shoulders of the man with such force as to shatter it in pieces. When the reason of his conduct was asked, he replied, that he owned slaves, and he would not permit free blacks to come into his neighborhood.

"Not long after, I stopped at a public-house near Halifax, N. C, between nine and ten o'clock P. M., to stay overnight, a slave sat upon a bench in the bar-room asleep. The master came in, seized a large horsewhip, and, without any warning or apparent provocation, laid it over the face and eyes of the slave. The master cursed, swore, and swung his lash—the slave cowered and trembled, but said not a word. Upon inquiry the next morning, I ascertained that the only offense was falling asleep and this too in consequence of having been up nearly all the previous night, in attendance upon company."

Rev. Joseph M. Sadd, of Castile, N. Y., who has lately left Missouri, where he was pastor of a church for some years, says:

"In one case, near where we lived, a runaway slave, when brought back, was most cruelly beaten—bathed in the *usual* liquid—laid in the sun, and a physician employed to heal his wounds — then the same process of punishment and healing was *repeated,* and *repeated again,* and then the poor creature was sold for the New Orleans market. This account we had from the *physician himself."*

Mr. Abraham Bell, of Poughkeepsie, New York, a member of the Scotch Presbyterian Church, was employed, in 1837 and 38, in leveling and grading for a railroad in the state of Georgia: he had under his direction, during the whole time, thirty slaves. Mr. B. gives the following testimony:

"All the slaves had their backs scarred, from the oft-repeated whippings they had received."

Mr. Alonzo Barnard, of Farmington, Ohio, who was in Mississippi in 1837 and 8, says:

"The slaves were often severely whipped. I saw one *woman* very severely whipped for accidentally cutting up a stalk of cotton.* When they were whipped they were commonly *held down by four men;* if these could not confine them, they were fastened by stakes driven firmly into the ground, and then lashed often so as to draw blood at each blow. I saw one woman who had lately been delivered of a child in consequence of cruel treatment."

*Mr. Cornelius Johnson, of Farmington, Ohio, was also a witness to this inhuman outrage upon an unprotected woman, for the unintentional destruction of a stalk of cotton!

In his testimony he is more particular, and says, that the number of lashes inflicted upon her by the overseer was ONE HUNDRED AND FIFTY!"

Rev. H. Lyman, late pastor of the Free Presbyterian Church at Buffalo, N. Y. says:

"There was a steam cotton press, in the vicinity of my boarding-house at New Orleans, which was driven night and day, without intermission. My curiosity led me to look at the interior of the establishment. There I saw several slaves engaged in rolling cotton bags, fastening ropes, lading carts, &c.

"The presiding genius of the place was a driver, who held a rope four feet long in his hand, which he wielded with cruel dexterity. He used it in single blows, just as the men were lifting to *tighten* the bale cords. It seemed to me that he was desirous to edify me with a specimen of his authority; at any rate the cruelty was horrible."

Mr. John Vance, a member of the Baptist Church, in St. Albans, Licking County, Ohio, who moved from Culpepper county, Va., his native state, in 1814, testifies as follows:

"In 1826, I saw a woman by the name of Mallix, flog her female slave with a horse-whip so horribly that she was washed in salt and water several days, to keep her bruises from mortifying.

"In 1811, I was returning from mill, in Shenandoah County, when I heard the cry of murder, in the field of a man named Painter. I rode to the place to see what was going on. Two men, by the names of John Morgan and Michael Siglar, had heard the cry and came running to the place. I saw Painter beating a negro with a tremendous club, or small handspike, swearing he would kill him; but he was rescued by Morgan and Siglar. I learned that Painter had commenced flogging the slave for not getting to work soon enough. He had escaped, and taken refuge under a pile of rails that were on some timbers up a little from the ground. The master had put fire to one end, and stood at the other with his club, to kill him as he came out. The pile was still burning. Painter said he was a turbulent fellow and he *would* kill him. The apprehension of Painter was talked about, but, as a compromise, the negro was sold to another man."

William Savery: Extract from the published Journal of the late Wm. Savery, of Philadelphia, an eminent minister of the religious Society of Friends :

"6th mo. 22d, 1791. We passed on to Augusta, Georgia. They can scarcely tolerate us, on account of our abhorrence of slavery. On the 28th we got to Savannah, and lodged at one Blount's, a hard-hearted slaveholder. One of his lads, aged about fourteen, was ordered to go and milk the cows: and falling asleep, through weariness, the master called out and ordered him a flogging. I asked him what he meant by a flogging. He replied, the way we serve them here is, we cut their backs until they are raw all over, and then salt them. Upon this my feelings were roused; I told him that was too bad; and queried if it were possible; he replied it was, with many curses upon the blacks. At supper this unfeeling wretch *craved a blessing!*

"Next morning I heard someone begging for mercy, and also the lash as of a whip. Not knowing whence the sound came, I rose, and presently found the poor boy tied up to a post, his toes scarcely touching the ground, and a negro whipper. He had already cut him in an unmerciful manner, and the blood ran to his heels. I stepped in between them, and ordered him untied immediately, which, with some reluctance and astonishment, was done. Returning to the house I saw the landlord, who then showed himself in his true colors, the most abominably wicked man I ever met with, full of horrid execrations and threatenings upon all northern people; but I did not spare him; which occasioned a bystander to say, with an oath, that I should be "popped over." We left them, and were in full expectation of their way-laying or coming after us, but the Lord restrained them. The next house we stopped at we found the same wicked spirit."

Col. Elijah Ellsworth, of Richfield, Ohio, gives the following testimony:

"Eight or ten years ago I was in Putnam County, in the state of Georgia, at a Mr. Slaughter's, the father of my brother's wife. A, negro, that belonged to Mr. Walker, (I believe,) was accused of stealing a pedlar's trunk. The negro denied, but, without ceremony, was lashed to a tree—the whipping commenced—six or eight men took turns—the poor fellow begged for mercy, but without effect, until he was literally cut *to pieces, from his shoulders to his hips,* and covered with a gore of blood. When he said the trunk was in a stack of fodder, he was unlashed. They proceeded to the stack, but found no trunk. They asked the poor fellow, what he lied about it for; he said, "Lord, Massa, to keep from being whipped to death; I know nothing about the trunk." They commenced the whipping with

~ 153 ~

redoubled vigor, until I really supposed he would be whipped to death on the spot; and such shrieks and crying for mercy! Again he acknowledged, and again they were defeated in finding, and the same reason given as before. Some were for whipping again, others thought he would not survive another, and they ceased. About two months after, the trunk was found, and it was then ascertained who the thief was: and the poor fellow, after being nearly beat to death, and twice made to lie about it, was as innocent as I was."

Major Horace Nye: The following statements are furnished by Major Horace Nye, of Putnam, Muskingum County, Ohio.

"In the summer of 1837, Mr. John H. Moorehead, a partner of mine, descended the Mississippi with several boat loads of flour. He told me that floating in a place in the Mississippi, where he could see for miles ahead, he perceived a concourse of people on the bank, that for at least a mile and a half above he saw them, and heard the screams of some person, and for a great distance, the crack of a whip, he run near the shore, and saw them whipping a black man, who was on the ground, and at that time nearly unable to scream, but the whip continued to be plied without intermission, as long as he was in sight, say from one mile and a half, to two miles below—he probably saw and heard them for one hour in all. He expressed the opinion that the man could not survive.

"About four weeks since I had a conversation with Mr. Porter, a respectable citizen of Morgan County, of this state, of about fifty years of age. He told me that he formerly traveled about five years in the southern states, and that on one occasion he stopped at a private house, to stay all night; (I think it was in Virginia,) while he was conversing with the man, his wife came in, and complained that the wench had broken some article in the kitchen, and that she must be whipped. He took the *woman* into the door yard, stripped her clothes down to her hips—tied her hands together, and drawing them up to a limb, so that she could just touch the ground, took a very large cowskin whip, and commenced flogging; he said that every stroke at first raised the skin, and immediately the blood came through; this he continued, until the blood stood in a puddle at her feet. He then turned to my informant and said, "Well, Yankee, what do you think of that?"

Mr. W. Dustin: Extract of a letter from Mr. W. Dustin, a member of the Methodist Episcopal Church, and, when the letter was written, 1835, a student of Marietta College, Ohio.

"I find by looking over my journal that the murdering, which I spoke of yesterday, took place about the first of June, 1834.

"Without commenting upon this act of cruelty, or giving vent to my own feelings, I will simply give you a statement of the fact, as known from *personal* observation.

"Dr. K. a man of wealth, and a practicing physician in the county of Yazoo, state of Mississippi, personally known to me, having lived in the same neighborhood more than twelve months, after having scourged one of his negroes for running away, declared with an oath, that if he ran away again, he would kill him. The negro, so soon as an opportunity offered, ran away again. He was caught and brought back. Again he was scourged, until his flesh, mangled and torn, and thick mingled with the clotted blood, rolled from his back. He became apparently insensible, and beneath the heaviest stroke would scarcely utter a groan. The master got tired, laid down his whip and nailed the negro's ear to a tree; in this condition, nailed fast to the rugged wood, he remained all night!

"Suffice it to say, in the conclusion, that the next day he was found dead!"

"Well, what did they do with the master? The sum total of it is this: He was taken before a magistrate and gave bonds, for his appearance at the next court. Well, to be sure he had plenty of cash, so he paid up his bonds and moved away, and there the matter ended.

"If the above fact will be of any service to you in exhibiting to the world the condition of the unfortunate negroes, you are at liberty to make use of it in any way you think best.

Yours, fraternally,

M. Dustin.

Mr. Alfred Wilkinson, a member of the Baptist Church in Skaneateles, N. Y. and the assessor of that town, has furnished the following:"I went down the Mississippi in December, 1808, and saw twelve or fourteen negroes punished, on one plantation, by stretching them on a ladder and tying them to it; then stripping off their clothes, and whipping them on the naked flesh with a heavy whip, the lash seven or eight feet long; most of the strokes cut the skin. I understood they were whipped for not doing the tasks allotted to them."

From **The Philanthropist**, Cincinnati, Ohio, Feb. 26, 1839:

"A very intelligent lady, the widow of a highly respectable preacher of the gospel, of the Presbyterian Church, formerly a resident of a free state, and a colonizationist, and a strong anti-abolitionist, who, although an enemy to slavery, was opposed to abolition on the ground that it was for carrying things too rapidly, and without regard to circumstances, and especially who believed that abolitionists exaggerated with regard to the evils of slavery, and used to say that such men ought to go to slave states and see for themselves, to be convinced that they did the slaveholders injustice, has gone and seen for herself. Hear her testament:.

Kentucky, Dec. 25, 1835.

"Dear Mrs. W.—I am still in the land of oppression and cruelty, but hope soon to breathe the air of a free state. My soul is sick of slavery, and I rejoice that my time is nearly expired; but the scenes that I have witnessed have made an impression that never can be effaced, and have inspired me with the determination to unite my feeble efforts with those who are laboring to suppress this horrid system. I am *now* an *abolitionist*. You will cease to be surprised at this, when I inform you, that I have just seen a poor slave who was beaten by his inhuman master until he could neither walk nor stand. I saw him from my window carried from the barn (where be bad been whipped) to the cabin, by two negro men; and he now lies there, and if he recovers, will be a sufferer for months, and probably for life. You will doubtless suppose that he committed some great crime; but it was not so. He was called upon by a young man (the son of his master,) to do something, and not moving as quickly as his young master wished him to, he drove him to the barn, knocked him down, and jumped upon him, stamped, and then cowhided him until he was almost dead. This is not the first act of cruelty that I have seen, though it is the *worst;* and I am convinced that those who have described the cruelties of slaveholders, have not exaggerated."

Gerrit Smith Esq.: Extract of a letter from Gerrit Smith, Esq., of Peterboro, N. Y. Peterboro, December 1, 1838. To the Editor of the Union Herald:

"My dear Sir:—You will be happy to hear, that the two fugitive slaves, to whom in the brotherly love of your heart, you gave the use of your horse, are still making undisturbed progress towards the *monarchical* land whither *republican* slaves escape for the enjoyment of liberty. They had eaten their breakfast, and were seated in my wagon, before day-dawn, this morning.

"Fugitive slaves have before taken my house in their way, but never any, whose lips and persons made so forcible an appeal to my sensibilities, and kindled in me so much abhorrence of the hell-concocted system of American slavery.

"The fugitives exhibited their bare backs to myself and a number of my neighbors. Williams' back is comparatively scarred. But, I speak within bounds, when I say, that one-third to one-half of the whole surface of the back and shoulders of poor Scott, *consists of scars and wales resulting from innumerable gashes.* His natural complexion being yellow and the callous places being nearly black, his back and shoulders remind you of a spotted animal."

The Louisville Reporter (Kentucky,) Jan. 15, 1839, contains the report of a trial for inhuman treatment of a female slave. The following is some of the testimony given in court:

"Dr. Constant testified that he saw Mrs. Maxwell at the kitchen door, whipping the negro severely, without being particular whether she struck her in the face or not. The negro was lacerated by the whip, and the blood flowing. Soon after, on going down the steps, he saw quantities of blood on them, and on returning, saw them again. She had been thinly clad—barefooted in very cold weather. Sometimes she had shoes—sometimes not. In the beginning of the winter she had linsey dresses, since then, calico ones. During the last four months, he had noticed many scars on her person. At one time had one of her eyes tied up for a week. During the last three months seemed declining, and had become stupified. Mr. Winters was passing along the street, heard cries, looked up through the window that was hoisted, saw the boy whipping her, as much as forty or fifty licks, while he staid. The girl was stripped down to the hips. The whip seemed to be a cow-hide. Whenever she turned her face to him, he would hit her across the face either with the butt end or small end of the whip to make her turn her back round square to the lash, that he might get a fair blow at her.

"Mr. Say had noticed several wounds on her person, chiefly bruises.

"Captain Porter, keeper of the work-house, into which Milly had been received, thought the injuries on her person very bad—some of them appeared to be burns—some bruises or stripes, as of a cow-hide."

Rev. John Rankin: Letter of Rev. John Rankin, of Ripley, Ohio, to the Editor of the Philanthropist:

Ripley, Feb. 20, 1839

"Some time since, a member of the Presbyterian Church of Ebenezer, Brown County, Ohio, landed his boat at a point on the Mississippi. He saw some disturbance among the colored people on the bank. He stepped up, to see what was the matter. A black man was stretched naked on the ground; his hands were tied to a stake, and one held each foot. He was doomed to receive fifty lashes; but by the time the overseer had given him twenty-five with his great whip, the blood was standing round the wretched victim in little puddles. It appeared just as if it had rained blood. Another observer stepped up, and advised to defer the other twenty-five to another time, lest the slave might die; and he was released, to receive the balance when he should have so recruited as to be able to bear it and live. The offense was, coming one hour too late to work."

Mr. Rankin, who is a native of Tennessee, in his letters on slavery, published fifteen years since, says:

"A respectable gentleman, who is now a citizen of Flemingsburg, Fleming County, Kentucky, when in the state of South Carolina, was invited by a slaveholder, to walk with him and take a view of his farm. He complied with the invitation thus given, and in their walk they came to the place where the slaves were at work, and found the overseer whipping one of them very severely for not keeping pace with his fellows— in vain the poor fellow alleged that he was sick, and could not work. The master seemed to think all was well enough, hence he and the gentleman passed on. In the space of an hour they returned by the same way, and found that the poor slave, who had been whipped as they first passed by the field of labor, was actually dead! This I have from unquestionable authority."

Member of Congress: Extract of a letter from a Member of Congress, to the Editor of the New York American, dated Washington, Feb. 18, 1839. The name of the writer is with the Executive Committee of the American Anti-Slavery Society.

"Three days ago, the inhabitants in the vicinity of the new Patent Building were alarmed by an outcry in the street, which proved to be that of a slave who had just been knocked down with a brick-bat by his pursuing master. Prostrate on the ground, with a large gash in his head, the poor slave was receiving the blows of his master on one side, and the kicks of his master's son on the other. His cries brought a few individuals to the spot; but no one dared to interfere, save to exclaim, "You will kill him!" which was met by the response, "He is mine, and I have a right to do what I please with him." The heart-rending scene was closed from *public* view by dragging the poor bruised and wounded slave from the public street into his master's stable. What followed is not known. The outcries were heard by members of Congress and others at the distance of near a quarter of a mile from the scene.

"And now, perhaps, you will ask, is not the city aroused by this flagrant cruelty and breach of the peace? I answer—not at all. Everything is quiet. If the occurrence is mentioned at all, it is spoken of in whispers."

From the **Mobile Examiner**, August 1, 1837. "Police Report—Mayor's Office. Saturday morning, August 12, 1837.

"His Honor the Mayor presiding.

"Mr. Miller, of the foundry, brought to the office this morning a small negro girl aged about eight or ten years, whom he had taken into his house some time during the previous night. She had crawled under the window of his bed room to screen herself from the night air, and to find a warmer shelter than the open canopy of heaven afforded. Of all objects of pity that have lately come to our view, this poor little girl most needs the protection of authority, and the sympathies of the charitable. From the cruelty of her master and mistress, she has been whipped, worked and starved, until she is now a breathing skeleton, hardly able to stand upon her feet.

"The back of the poor little sufferer, (which we ourselves saw,) *was actually cut into strings, and so perfectly was the flesh worn from her limbs,* by the wretched treatment she had received, that *every joint showed distinctly* its crevices and protuberances through the skin. Her little lips clung closely over her teeth—her cheeks were sunken and her head narrowed, and when her eyes were closed, the lids resembled film more than flesh or skin.

"We would desire of our northern friends such as choose to publish to the world their own version of the case we have related, not to forget to add, in conclusion, that the owner of this little girl is a foreigner, speaks against slavery as an institution, and reads his Bible to his wife, with the view of finding proofs for his opinions."

Rev. William Scales, of Lyndon, Vermont, gives the following testimony in a recent letter:

"I had a class-mate at the Andover Theological Seminary, who spent a season at the south,—in Georgia, I think—who related the following fact in an address before the Seminary. It occasioned very deep sensation on the part of opponents. The gentleman was Mr. Julius C. Anthony, of Taunton, Mass. He graduated at the Seminary in 1835. I do not know where he is now settled. I have no doubt of the fact, as he was an *eye-witness* of it. The man with whom he resided had a very athletic slave—a valuable fellow—a blacksmith. On a certain day a small strap of leather was missing. The man's little son accused this slave of stealing it. He denied the charge, while the boy most confidently asserted it. The slave was brought out into the yard and bound—his hands below his knees, and a stick crossing his knees, so that he would lie upon either side in form of the letter S. One of the overseers laid on fifty lashes—he still denied the theft—was turned over and fifty more put on. Sometimes the master and sometimes the overseers whipping as they relieved each other to take breath. Then he was for a time left to himself, and in the course of the day received four hundred lashes—still denying the charge. Next morning Mr. Anthony walked out—the sun was just rising—he saw the man greatly enfeebled, leaning against a stump. It was time to go to work—he attempted to rise, but fell back—again attempted, and again fell back—still making the attempt, and still falling back, Mr. Anthony thought, nearly *twenty times* before he succeeded in standing—he then staggered off to his shop. In course of the morning Mr. A. went to the door and looked in. Two overseers were standing by. The slave was feverish and sick— his skin and mouth dry and parched. He was very thirsty. One of the overseers, while Mr. A. was looking at him, inquired of the other whether it were not best to give him a little water. 'No. damn him, he will do well enough,' was the reply from the other overseer. This was all the relief gained by the poor slave. A few days after, the slaveholder's *son confessed that he stole the strap himself."*

Rev. D. C. Eastman, a minister of the Methodist Episcopal Church at Bloomingburg, Fayette County, Ohio, has just forwarded a letter, from which the following is an extract:

"George Roebuck, an old and respectable farmer, near Bloomingburg, Fayette County, Ohio, a member of the Methodist Episcopal Church, says, that almost forty-three years ago, he saw in Bath County, Virginia, a slave girl with a sore between the shoulders of the size and shape of a *smoothing iron*. The girl was "owned" by one M'Neil. A slaveholder who boarded at M'Neil's stated that Mrs. M'Neil had placed the aforesaid iron when hot, between the girl's shoulders, and produced the sore.

"Roebuck was once at this M'Neil's father's place, and whilst the old man was at morning prayer, he heard the son plying the whip upon a slave out of doors.

Eli West, of Concord Township, Fayette County, Ohio, formerly of North Carolina, a farmer and an exhorter in the Methodist Protestant Church, says, that many years since he went to live with an uncle who owned about fifty negroes. Soon after his arrival, his uncle ordered his waiting boy, who was *naked,* to be tied—his hands to a horse rack, and his feet together, with a rail passed between his legs, and held down by a person at each end. In this position he was whipped, from neck to feet, till covered with blood; after which he was *salted.*

"His uncle's slaves received one quart of corn each day, and that only, and were allowed one hour each day to cook and eat it. They had no meat but once in the year. Such was the general usage in that country.

"West, after this, lived one year with Esquire Starky and mother. They had two hundred slaves, who received the usual treatment of starvation, nakedness, and the cowhide. They had one likely negro woman who bore no children. For this neglect, her mistress had her back made naked and a severe whipping inflicted. But as she continued barren, she was sold to the 'negro buyers.'

Thomas Larrimer, a Deacon in the Presbyterian Church at Bloomingburg, Fayette County, Ohio, and a respectable farmer, says, that in April, 1837, as he was going down the Mississippi River, about fifty miles below Natchez, he saw ahead, on the left side of the river, a colored person tied to a post, and a man with a driver's whip, the lash about eight or ten feet long. With this the man commenced, with much deliberation, to whip, with much apparent force, and continued till he got out of sight.

"When coming up the river forty or fifty miles below Vicksburg, a Judge Owens came on board the steamboat. He was owner of a cotton plantation below there, and on being told of the above whipping, he said that slaves were often whipped to death for great offenses, such as *stealing,* &c.—but that when death followed, the overseers were generally severely *reproved.*

"About the same time, he spent a night at Mr. Casey's, three miles from Columbia, South Carolina. Whilst there they heard him giving orders as to what was to be done, and amongst other things, 'That nigger must be buried.' On inquiry, he learnt that a gentleman traveling with a servant, had a short time previous called there, and said his servant had just been taken ill, and he should be under the necessity of leaving him. He did so. The slave became worse, and Casey called in a physician, who pronounced it an old case, and said that he must shortly die. The slave said, if that was the case he would now tell the truth. He had been attacked, a long time since, with a difficulty in the side—his master swore he would 'have his own out of him,' and started off to sell him, with a threat to kill him if he told he had been sick, more than a few days. They saw them making a rough plank box to bury him in.

"In March, 1833, twenty-five or thirty miles south of Columbia, on the great road through Sumterville District, they saw a large company of female slaves carrying rails and building fence. Three of them were far advanced in pregnancy.

"In the month of January, 1838, he put up with a drove of mules and horses, at one Adams', on the Drovers' road, near the south border of Kentucky. His son-in-law, who had lived in the south, was there. In conversation about picking cotton, he said, 'some hands cannot get the sleight of it. I have a girl who today has done as good a day's work at grubbing as any *man,* but I could not make her a hand at cotton-picking. I whipped her, and if I did it once I did it five hundred times, but I found she *could* not; so I put her to carrying rails with the men. After a few days I found her shoulders were so raw that every rail was *bloody* as she laid it down. I asked her if she would not rather pick cotton than carry rails. 'No,' said she, 'I don't got whipped now.'"

William A. Ustick, an elder of the Presbyterian Church at Bloomingburg, and Mr. *G.* S. Fullerton, a merchant and member of the same Church, were with Deacon Larrimer on this journey, and are witnesses to the preceding facts.

Mr. Samuel Hall, a teacher in Marietta College, Ohio, and formerly secretary of the Colonization Society in that village, has recently communicated the facts which follow. We quote from his letter:

"The following horrid flagellation was witnessed in part, till his soul was sick, by Mr. Glidden, an inhabitant of Marietta, Ohio, who went down the Mississippi River, with a boat load of produce in the autumn of 1837; it took place at what is called 'Matthews' or 'Matheses Bend' in December, 1837. Mr. G. is worthy of credit:

"A negro was tied up, and flogged until the blood ran down and filled his shoes, so that when he raised either foot and set it down again, the blood would run over their tops. I could not look on any longer, but turned away in horror; the whipping was continued to the number of 500 lashes, as I understood; a quart of spirits of turpentine was then applied to his lacerated body. The same negro came down to my boat, to get some apples, and was so weak from his wounds and loss of blood, that he could not get up the bank, but fell to the ground. The crime for which the negro was whipped, was that of telling the other negroes, that *the overseer had lain with his wife."*

Mr. Hall adds :

"The following statement is made by a young man from Western Virginia. He is a member of the Presbyterian Church, and a student in Marietta College. All that prevents the introduction of his *name,* is the peril to his life, which would probably be the consequence, on his return to Virginia. His character for integrity and veracity is above suspicion.

'On the night of the great meteoric shower, in Nov. 1833. I was at Remley's Tavern, 12 miles west of Lewisburg, Greenbrier Co., Virginia. A drove of 50 or 60 negroes stopped at the same place that night. They usually 'camp out,' but as it was excessively muddy, they were permitted to come into the house. So far as my knowledge extends, 'droves,' on their way to the south, eat but twice a day, early in the morning and at night. Their supper was a compound of potatoes and meal, and was, without exception, *the dirtiest, blackest looking mess I ever saw.* I remarked at the time that the food was not as clean, in appearance, as that which was given to a *drove of hogs,* at the same place the night previous. Such as it was, however, a black woman brought it on her head, in a tray or trough two and a half feet long, where the men and women were promiscuously herded. The slaves rushed up and seized it from the trough in handfuls, before the woman could take it off her head. They jumped at it as if half-famished.

'They slept on the floor of the room which they were permitted to occupy, lying in every form imaginable, males and females, promiscuously. They were so thick on the floor, that in passing through the room it was necessary to step over them. There were three drivers, one of whom staid in the room to watch the drove, and the other two slept in an adjoining room. Each of the latter took a female from the drove to lodge

~ 164 ~

with him, as is the common practice of the drivers generally. There is no doubt about this particular instance, *for they were seen together.* The mud was so thick on the floor where this *drove* slept, that it was necessary to take a shovel, the next morning, and clear it out. Six or eight in this drove were chained; all were for the south.

A drove of slaves

'In the autumn of the same year, I saw a drove of upwards of a hundred, between 40 and 50 of them were fastened to one chain, the links being made of iron rods, as thick in diameter as a man's little finger. This drove was bound westward to the Ohio River, to be shipped to the south. I have seen many droves, and more or less in each, almost without exception, were chained. I never saw but one drove that went on their way making merry. In that one, they were blowing horns, singing, &c, and appeared as if they had been drinking whisky.

'They generally appear extremely dejected. I have seen in the course of five years, on the road near where I reside, 12 or 15 droves at least, passing to the south. They would average 40 in each drove. Near the first of January, 1834, I started about sunrise to go to Lewisburg. It was a bitter cold morning. I met a drove of negroes, 30 or 40 in number, remarkably ragged and destitute of clothing. One little boy particularly excited my sympathy. He was some distance behind the others, not being able to keep up with the rest. Although he was shivering with cold and crying, the driver was pushing him up in a trot to overtake the main gang. All of them looked as if they were half-frozen. There was one remarkable instance of tyranny, exhibited by a boy, not more than eight years old, that came under my observation, in a family by the name of D____n, six miles from Lewisburg. This youngster would swear at the slaves, and exert all the strength he possessed, to flog or beat them, with whatever instrument or weapon he could lay hands on, provided they did not obey him *instanter*. He was encouraged in this by his father, the master of the slaves. The slaves often fled from this young tyrant in terror."

Mr. Hall adds:

"The following extract is from a letter, to a student in Marietta College, by his friend in Alabama. With the writer, Mr. Isaac Knapp, I am perfectly acquainted. He was a student in the above College, for the space of one year, before going to Alabama, was formerly a resident of Dummerston, Vt. He is a professor of religion, and as worthy of belief as any member of the community. Mr. K. has returned from the South, and is now a member of the same college.

'In Jan. (1838) a negro of a widow Phillips, ran away, was taken up, and confined in Pulaski jail. One Gibbs, overseer for Mrs. P., mounted on horseback, took him from confinement, compelled him to run back to Elkton, a distance of fifteen miles, whipping him all the way. When he reached home, the negro, exhausted and worn out, exclaimed 'you have broke my heart,' i.e. you have killed me. For this, Gibbs flew into a violent passion, tied the negro to a stake, and, in the language of a witness 'cut *his back to mince-meat'* But the fiend was not satisfied with this. He burnt his legs to a blister, with hot embers, and then chained him *naked,* in the open air, weary with running, weak from the loss of blood, and smarting from his burns. It was a cold night—and *in the morning the negro was dead.* Yet this monster escaped without even *the shadow* of a trial. 'The negro,' said the doctor,' died, by he knew not what; anyhow, Gibbs did not kill him.'* A short time since, (the letter is dated, April, 1838,) 'Gibbs whipped another negro unmercifully because the horse, with which he was ploughing, broke the reins and ran. He then raised his whip against Mr. Bowers, (son of Mrs. P.) who shot him. Since I came here, (a period of about six months,) there have been eight white men and two negroes killed, within 30 miles of me.'

* Mr. Knapp, gives me some further verbal particulars about this affair. He says that his informant saw the negro dead the next morning, that his legs were blistered, and that the negroes affirmed that Gibbs compelled them to throw embers upon him. But Gibbs denied it, and said the blistering was the effect of frost, as the negro was much exposed to it before

~ 166 ~

being taken up. Mr. Bowers, a son of Mrs. Phillips by a former husband, attempted to have Gibbs brought to justice, but his mother justified Gibbs, and nothing was therefore done about it. The affair took place in Upper Elkton, Tennessee, near the Alabama line.

"The following is from Mr. Knapp's own lips, taken down a day or two since.

'Mr. Buster, with whom I boarded, in Limestone Co., Ala., related to me the following incident:

'George, a slave belonging to one of the estates in my neighborhood, was lurking about my residence without a pass. We were making preparations to give him a flogging, but he escaped from us. Not long afterwards, meeting a patrol which had just taken a negro in custody without a pass, I inquired, Who have you there? On learning that it was *George,* well, I rejoined, there is a small matter between him and myself, that needs adjustment, so give me the raw hide, which I accordingly took, and laid 60 strokes on his back, to the utmost of my strength.'

'I was speaking of this barbarity, afterwards, to Mr. Bradley, an overseer of the Rev. Mr. Donnell, who lives in the vicinity of Mooresville, Ala., 'Oh,' replied he,' we consider *that* a very light whipping here.' Mr. Bradley is a professor of religion, and is esteemed in that vicinity a very pious, exemplary Christian.'"

Rev. C. Stewart Renshaw Extract of a letter from Rev. C. Stewart Renshaw, of Quincy, Illinois, dated Jan. 1, 1839.

"I do not feel at liberty to disclose the name of the brother who has furnished the following facts. He is highly esteemed as a man of scrupulous veracity. I will confirm my own testimony by the certificate of Judge Snow and Mr. Keyes, two of the oldest and most respectable settlers in Quincy.

Quincy, Dec. 29, 1838.

"Dear Sir,—We have been long acquainted with the Christian brother who has named to you some facts that fell under his observation whilst a resident of slave states. He is a member of a Christian Church, in good standing; and is a man of strict integrity of character.

Henry H. Snow
Willard Keyes
Rev. C. Stewart Renshaw.

"My informant spent thirty years of his life in Kentucky and Missouri. Whilst in Kentucky he resided in Hardin Co. I noted down his testimony very nearly in his own words, which will account for their *evidence-like* form. On the general condition of the slaves in Kentucky, through Hardin Co., he said, their houses were very uncomfortable, generally without floors, other than the earth: many had puncheon floors, but he never remembers to have seen a plank floor. In regard to clothing they were very badly off. In summer they cared little for thing; but in winter they almost froze. Their rags might hide their nakedness from the sun in summer, but would not protect them from the cold in winter. Their bed-clothes were tattered rags, thrown into a corner by day, and drawn before the fire by night. 'The only thing,' said he, 'to which I can compare them, in winter, is *stock without a shelter.'*

"He made the following comparison between the condition of slaves in Kentucky and Missouri. So far as he was able to compare them, he said, that in Missouri the slaves had better *quarters*—but are not so well clad, and are more severely punished than in Kentucky. In both states, the slaves are huddled together, without distinction of sex, into the same quarter, till it is filled, then another is built; often two or three families in a log hovel, twelve feet square.

"It is proper to state, that the sphere of my informant's observation was mainly in the region of Hardin Co., Kentucky, and the eastern part of Missouri, and not through those states generally."Whilst at St. Louis, a number of years ago, as he was going to work with Mr. Henry Males, and another carpenter, they heard groans from a barn by the road-side: they stopped, and looking through the cracks of the barn, saw a negro bound hand and foot to a post, so that his toes just touched the ground; and his master, Captain Thorpe, was inflicting punishment; he had whipped him till exhausted,—rested himself, and returned again to the punishment. The wretched sufferer was in a most pitiable condition, and the warm blood and dry dust of the barn had formed a mortar up to his instep. Mr. Males jumped the fence, and remonstrated so effectually with Capt. Thorpe, that he ceased the punishment. It was six weeks before that slave could put on his shirt!"

John Mackey, a rich slaveholder, lived near Clarksville, Pike co., Missouri, some years since. He whipped his slave Billy, a boy fourteen years old, till he was sick and stupid; he then sent him home. Then, for his stupidity, whipped him again, and fractured his skull with an axe-helve. He buried him away in the woods; dark words were whispered, and the body was disinterred. A coroner's inquest was held, and Mr. R. Anderson, the coroner, brought in a verdict of death from fractured skull, occasioned by blows from an axe handle, inflicted by John Mackey. The case was brought into court, but Mackey was rich, and his murdered victim was his Slave; after expending about $500 he walked free.

"One Mrs. Mann, living near ____, in_____ Co., Missouri, was known to be very cruel to her slaves. She had a bench made purposely to whip them upon; and what she called her "six pound paddle," an instrument of prodigious torture, bored through with holes; this she would wield with both hands as she stood over her prostrate victim.

"She thus punished a hired slave woman named Fanny, belonging to Mr. Charles Trabue, who lives near Palmyra, Marion Co., Missouri; on the morning after the punishment Fanny was a corpse; she was silently and quickly buried, but rumor was not so easily stopped. Mr. Trabue heard of it, and commenced suit for his *property*. The murdered slave was disinterred, and an inquest held; her back was a mass of jellied muscle; and the coroner brought in a verdict of "Death by the six pound paddle".' Mrs. Mann fled for a few months, but returned again, and her friends found means to protract the suit.

"This same Mrs. Mann had another hired slave woman living with her, called Patterson's Fanny, she belonged to a Mr. Patterson; she had a young babe with her, just beginning to creep. One day, after washing, whilst a tub of rinsing water yet stood in the kitchen, Mrs. Mann came out in haste, and sent Fanny to do something out of doors. Fanny tried to beg off—she was afraid to leave her babe, lest it should creep to the tub and get hurt—Mrs. M. said she would watch the babe, and sent her off. She went with much reluctance, and heard the child struggle as she went out the door. Fearing lest Mrs. M. should leave the babe alone, she watched the room, and soon saw her pass out of the opposite door. Immediately Fanny hurried in, and looked around for her babe, she could not see it, she looked at the tub—there her babe was floating, a strangled corpse. The poor woman gave a dreadful scream; and Mrs. M. rushed into the room, with her hands raised, and exclaimed, 'Heavens, Fanny! Have you drowned your child? It was vain for the poor bereaved one to attempt to vindicate herself; in vain she attempted to convince them that the babe had not been alone a moment, and could not have drowned itself; and that she had not been in the house a moment, before she screamed at discovering her drowned babe. All was false! Mrs. Mann declared it was all pretence— that Fanny had drowned her own babe and now wanted to lay the blame upon her, and Mrs. Mann was a white woman!—of course her word was more valuable than the oaths of all the slaves of Missouri. No evidence but that of slaves could be obtained, or Mr. Patterson would have prosecuted for his 'loss of property.' As it was, every one believed Mrs. M. guilty, though the affair was soon hushed up."

Thomas Rogers: Extract of a letter from Col. Thomas Rogers, a native of Kentucky, now an Elder in the Presbyterian Church at New Petersburg, Highland Co., Ohio.

"When a boy, in Bourbon Co., Kentucky, my father lived near a slaveholder of the name of Clay, who had a large number of slaves; I remember being often at their quarters; not one of their shanties, or hovels, had any floor but the earth. Their clothing was truly neither fit for covering nor decency. We could distinctly, of a still morning, hear this man whipping his blacks, and hear their screams from my father's farm; this could be heard almost any still morning about the dawn of day. It was said to be his usual custom to repair, about the break of day, to their cabin doors, and, as the blacks passed out, to give them as many strokes of his cowskin as opportunity afforded; and he would proceed in this manner from cabin to cabin until they were all out. Occasionally some of his slaves would abscond, and upon being retaken they were punished severely; and some of them, it is believed, died in consequence of the cruelty of their usage. I saw one of this man's slaves, about seventeen years old, wearing a collar, with long iron horns extending from his shoulders far above his head.

"In the winter of 1828-29 I traveled through part of the states of Maryland and Virginia to Baltimore. At Frost Town, on the national road, I put up for the night. Soon after, there came in a slaver with his drove of slaves; among them were two young men, chained together. The bar room was assigned to them for their place of lodging—those in chains were guarded when they had to go out. I asked the 'owner' why he kept these men chained; he replied, that they were stout young fellows, and should they rebel, he and his son would not be able to manage them. I then left the room, and shortly after heard a *scream,* and when the landlady inquired the cause, the slaver coolly told her not to trouble herself, he was only chastising one of his women. It appeared that three days previously her child had died on the road, and been thrown into a hole or crevice in the mountain, and a few stones thrown over it; and the mother weeping for her child was chastised by her master, and told by him, she 'should have something to cry for.' The name of this man I can give if called for.

"When engaged in this journey I spent about one month with my relations in Virginia. It being shortly after New Year, *the* time *of hiring* was over; but I saw the pounds, and the scaffolds which remained of the pounds, in which the slaves had been penned up."

Mr. George W. Westgate, of Quincy, Illinois, who lived in the southwestern slave states a number of years, has furnished the following statement:

"The great mass of the slaves are under drivers and overseers. I never saw an overseer without a whip; the whip usually carried is a short handled stock, with a heavy lash from five to six feet long. When they whip a slave they make him pull off his shirt, if he has one, then make him lie down on his face, and taking their stand at the length of the lash, they inflict the punishment. Whippings are so *universal* that a negro that has not been whipped is talked of in all the region as a wonder. By whipping I do not mean a few lashes across the shoulders, but a set flogging, and generally *lying down.*

"On sugar plantations generally, and on some cotton plantations, they have negro drivers, who are in such a degree responsible for their gang, that if they are at fault, the driver is whipped. The result is, the gang are constantly driven by him to the extent of the influence of the lash; and it is uniformly the case that gangs dread a negro driver more than a white overseer.

"I spent a winter on Widow Calvert's plantation, near Rodney, Mississippi, but was not in a situation to see extraordinary punishments. Bellows, the overseer, for a trifling offense, took one of the slaves, stripped him, and with a piece of burning wood applied to his posteriors, burned him cruelly; while the poor wretch screamed in the greatest agony. The principal preparation for punishment that Bellows had was single handcuffs made of iron, with chains, by which the offender could be chained to four stakes on the ground. These are very common in all the lower country. I noticed one slave on Widow Calvert's plantation, who was whipped from twenty-five to fifty lashes every fortnight during the whole winter. The expression 'whipped to death,' as applied to slaves, is common at the south.

"Several years ago I was going below New-Orleans, in what is called the Plaquemine Country, and a planter sent down in my boat a runaway he had found in New-Orleans, to his plantation at Orange 5 Points. As we came near the Points he told me, with deep feeling, that he expected to be whipped almost to death; pointing to a graveyard, he said, 'There lie five who were whipped to death.' Overseers generally keep some of the women on the plantation; I scarce know an exception to this. Indeed, their intercourse with them is very much promiscuous,—they show them not much, if any favor. Masters frequently follow the example of their overseers in this thing."George W. Westgate."

II. TORTURES, IRON COLLARS, CHAINS, FETTERS, HANDCUFFS, &c.

The slaves are often tortured by iron collars, with long prongs or horns." and sometimes bells attached to them—they are made to wear chains, handcuffs, fetters, iron clogs, bars, rings, and bands of iron upon their limbs, iron marks upon their faces, iron gags in their mouths, &c.

In proof of this, we give the testimony of slaveholders themselves, under their own names; it will be mostly in the form of extracts from their own advertisements, in southern newspapers, in which, describing their runaway slaves, they specify the iron collars, handcuffs, chains, fetters &c, which they wore upon their necks, wrists, ankles, and other parts of their bodies. To publish the *whole* of each advertisement, would needlessly occupy space and tax the reader; we shall consequently, as heretofore, give merely the name of the advertiser, the name and date of the newspaper containing the advertisement, with the place of publication, and only so much of the advertisement as will give the particular *fact,* proving the truth of the assertion contained in the *general head.*

WITNESS
William Toler, Sheriff of Simpson County, Mississippi, in the "Southern Sun," Jackson, Mississippi, September 22,1838.
TESTIMONY
"Was committed to jail, a yellow boy named Jim—had on a large lock chain around his neck."

==========

WITNESS

Mr. James R. Green, in the "Beacon," Greensborough, Alabama, August 23, 1838.

TESTIMONY

Ranaway, a negro man named Squire—had on a *chain locked with a house-lock, around his neck.*"

==========

WITNESS

Mr. Hazlet Lofiano, in the "Spectator," Staunton, Virginia, Sept. 27, 1833.

TESTIMONY

"Ranaway, a negro named David—with some *iron hobbles around each ankle.*"

==========

WITNESS

Mr. T. Enggy, New Orleans, Gallatin street, between Hospital and Barracks, N. O. "Bee," Oct. 27, 1837.

TESTIMONY

"Ranaway, negress Caroline—had on a *collar with one prong turned down.*"

==========

WITNESS

Mr. John Henderson, Washington, County, Mi., in the "Grand Gulf Advertiser," August 2D, 1833.

TESTIMONY

"Ranaway, a black woman, Betsey—had an *iron bar on her right leg.*"

==========

WITNESS

William Dyer, Sheriff, Claiborne, Louisiana, in the "Herald," Natchitoches, (La.) July 26, 1837.

TESTIMONY

"Was committed to jail, a negro named Ambrose—has a *ring of iron around his neck.*"

==========

WITNESS

Mr. Owen Cooke, Mary Street, between Common and Jackson Streets," New Orleans, in the N. O. "Bee," September 12, 1837.

TESTIMONY

"Ranaway, my slave Amos, had *a chain* attached to one of his legs."

===========

WITNESS

H. W. Rice, Sheriff, Colleton District, South Carolina, in the "Charleston Mercury," September 1, 1838.

TESTIMONY

"Committed to jail, a negro named Patrick, about forty-five years old, and is *handcuffed*."

===========

WITNESS

W. P. Reeves, jailor, Shelby County, Tennessee, in the "Memphis Enquirer, June 17, 1837

TESTIMONY

"Committed to jail, a negro—had on his right leg an *iron band* with one link of a chain.'

===========

WITNESS

Mr. Francis Durett, Lexington, Lauderdale County, Ala., in the "Huntsville Democrat," August 29, 1837.

TESTIMONY

"Ranaway, a negro man named Charles—had on a *drawing chain,* fastened around his ankle with a house lock."

===========

WITNESS

Mr. A. Murat, Baton Rouge, in the New Orleans "Bee," June 20, 1837.

TESTIMONY

"Ranaway, the negro Manuel, *much marked with irons* ."

===========

WITNESS

Mr. Jordan Abbott, in the "Huntsville Democrat," Nov. 17, 1838.

TESTIMONY

"Ranaway, a negro boy named Daniel, about nineteen years old, and was *handcuffed*."

===========

WITNESS

Mr. J. Macoin, No. 177 Ann Street, New Orleans, in the "Bee," August 11, 1838.

TESTIMONY

"Ranaway, the negress Fanny—had on an *iron band about her neck.*"

==========

WITNESS

Menard Brothers, Parish of Bernard, Louisiana, in the N. O. "Bee," August 18, 1838.

TESTIMONY

"Ranaway, a negro named John—having an *iron around his right foot.*"

==========

WITNESS

Messrs. J. L. and W. H. Bolton, Shelby County, Tennessee, in the "Memphis Enquirer," June 7, 1837.

TESTIMONY

"Absconded, a colored boy named Peter—had an *iron round his neck* when he went away."

==========

WITNESS

H. Gridly, Sheriff of Adams County, Mi., in the "Memphis (Tenn.) Times," September, 1834.

TESTIMONY

"Was committed to jail, a negro boy—had on a *large neck iron* with a *huge pair of horns and a large bar or band of iron* on his left leg."

==========

WITNESS

Mr. Lambre, in the "Natchitoches (La.) Herald," March 29, 1837.

TESTIMONY

"Ranaway, the negro boy Teams—he had on his neck *an iron collar.*"

==========

WITNESS

Mr. Ferdinand Lemos, New Orleans, in the "Bee," January 29, 1838.

TESTIMONY

"Ranaway, the negro George—he had on *his neck an iron collar,* the branches of which had been taken off."

==========

WITNESS

Mr. T. J. De Yampert, merchant, Mobile, Alabama, of the firm of De Yampert, King & Co., in the "Mobile Chronicle," June 15, 1838.

TESTIMONY

"Ranaway, a negro boy about *twelve* years old—had round his neck *a chain dog-collar,* with 'De Yampert engraved on it."

==========

WITNESS

J. H. Hand, jailor, St. Francisville, La., in the "Louisiana Chronicle", July 20, 1837.

TESTIMONY

"Committed to jail, slave John—has several scars on his wrists, occasioned, as he says, by *handcuffs.*"

==========

WITNESS

Mr. Charles Curener, New Orleans, in the "Bee," July 2, 1838.

TESTIMONY

"Ranaway, the negro, Hown—has a ring of iron on his left foot. Also, Grisee, his *wife,* having a *ring and chain on the left leg.*"

==========

WITNESS

Mr. P. T. Manning, Huntsville, Alabama, in the "Huntsville Advocate," Oct 23, 1838.

TESTIMONY

"Ranaway, a negro boy named James—said boy was *ironed* when he left me."

==========

WITNESS

Mr. William L. Lambeth, Lynchburg, Virginia, in the "Moulton [Ala.l Whig," January 30, 1830.

TESTIMONY

"Ranaway, Jim—had on when he escaped a pair of *chain hand. cuffs*

==========

WITNESS

Mr. D. F. Guex, Secretary of the Steam Cotton Press Company, New Orleans, in the "Commercial Bulletin," May 27, 1837.

TESTIMONY

"Ranaway, Edmund Coleman—it is supposed he must have *iron shackles on his ankles.*"

═══════════

WITNESS

Mr. Francis Durett, Lexington, Alabama, in the "Huntsville Democrat," March 8, 1833.

TESTIMONY

"Ranaway,_____, a mulatto, had on when he left, a *pair of handcuffs* and a *pair of drawing chains.*"

═══════════

WITNESS

B. W. Hodges, jailor, Pike County, Alabama, in the "Montgomery Advertiser," Sept. 29, 1837.

TESTIMONY

"Committed to jail, a man who calls his name John—he has a *clog of iron on his right foot which will weigh four or five pounds.*"

═══════════

WITNESS

P. Bayhi, captain of police, in the N. O."Bee," June9, 1838.

TESTIMONY

"Detained at the police jail, the negro wench Myra—has several marks of *lashing,* and has *irons on her feet.*"

═══════════

WITNESS

Mr. Charles Kernin, parish of Jefferson, Louisiana, in the N. O. "Bee," August 11, 1837.

TESTIMONY

"Ranaway, Betsey—when she left she had on her *neck an iron collar.*"

═══════════

The foregoing advertisements are sufficient for our purpose. Scores of similar ones may be gathered from the newspapers of the slave states every month.

To the preceding testimony of slaveholders, published by themselves, and vouched for by their own signatures, we subjoin the following testimony of other witnesses to the same point.

John M. Nelson, Esq., a native of Virginia, now a highly respected citizen of Highland county, Ohio, and member of the Presbyterian Church in Hillsborough, in a recent letter states the following:

"In Staunton, Va., at the house of Mr. Robert McDowell, a merchant of that place, I once saw a colored woman, of intelligent and dignified appearance, who appeared to be attending to the business of the house, with an *iron collar* around her neck, with horns or prongs extending out on either side, and up, until they met at something like a foot above her head, at which point there was a bell attached. This *yoke*, as they called it, I understood was to prevent her from running away, or to punish her for having done so. I had frequently seen *men* with iron collars, but this was the first instance that I recollect to have seen a *female* thus degraded."

Major Horace Nye, an elder in the Presbyterian Church at Putnam, Muskingum County, Ohio, in a letter, dated Dec. 5, 1838, makes the following statement:

"Mr. Wm. Armstrong, of this place, who is frequently employed by our citizens as captain and supercargo of descending boats, whose word maybe relied on, has just made tome the following statement:

"While laying at Alexandria, on Red River, Louisiana, he saw a slave brought to a blacksmith's shop and a collar of iron fastened round his neck, with two pieces riveted to the sides, meeting some distance above his head. At the top of the arch, thus formed, was attached a large cow-bell, the motion of which, while walking the streets, made it necessary for the slave to hold his hand to one of its sides, to steady it.

"In New Orleans he saw several with iron collars, with horns attached to them. The first he saw had three prongs projecting from the collar ten or twelve inches, with the letter S on the end of each. He says iron collars are quite frequent there.

To the preceding Major Nye adds:

"When I was about twelve years of age I lived at Marietta, in this state: I knew little of slaves, as there were few or none, at that time, in the part of Virginia opposite that place. But I remember seeing a slave who had run away from some place beyond my knowledge at that time; he had an iron collar round his neck, to which was a strap of iron riveted to the collar, on each side, passing over the top of the head; and another strap, from the back side to the top of the first—thus inclosing the head on three sides. I looked on while the blacksmith severed the collar with a file, which, I think, took him more than an hour."

Rev. John Dudley, Mount Morris, Michigan, resided as a teacher at the missionary station, among the Choctaws, in Mississippi, during the years 1830 and 31. In a letter just received Mr. Dudley says:

"During the time I was on missionary ground, which was in 1830 and 31, I was frequently at the residence of the agent, who was a slaveholder. I never knew of his treating his own slaves with cruelty; but the poor fellows who were escaping, and lodged with him when detected, found no clemency. I once saw there a fetter for '*the d—d runaways,* the weight of which can be judged by its size. It was at least three inches wide, half an inch thick, and something over a foot long. At this time I saw a poor fellow compelled to work in the field, at 'logging,' with such a galling fetter on his ankles. To prevent it from wearing his ankles, a string was tied to the centre, by which the victim suspended it when he walked, with one hand, and with the other carried his burden. Whenever he lifted, the fetter rested

~ 180 ~

on his bare ankles. If he lost his balance and made a misstep, which must very often occur in lifting and rolling logs, the torture of his fetter was severe. Thus he was doomed to work while wearing the torturing iron, day after day, and at night he was confined in the runaways' jail. Sometime after this, I saw the same dejected, heart-broken creature obliged to wait on the other hands, who were husking corn. The privilege of sitting with the others was too much for him to enjoy; he was made to hobble from house to barn and barn to house, to carry food and drink for the rest. He passed round the end of the house where I was sitting with the agent: he seemed to take no notice of me, but fixed his eyes on his tormentor till he passed quite by us."

Mr. Alfred Wilkinson, member of the Baptist Church in Skaneateles, N. Y. and an assessor of that town, testifies as follows:

"I stayed in New Orleans three weeks: during that time there used to pass by where I stayed a number of slaves, each with an iron band around his ankle, a chain attached to it, and an eighteen pound ball at the end. They were employed in wheeling dirt with a wheelbarrow; they would put the ball into the barrow when they moved.— I recollect one day, that I counted nineteen of them, sometimes there were not as many; they were driven by a slave, with a long lash, as if they were beasts. These, I learned, were runaway slaves from the plantations above New Orleans.

"There was also a negro woman, that used daily to come to the market with milk; she had an iron band around her neck, with three rods projecting from it, about sixteen inches long, crooked at the ends."

For the fact which follows we are indebted to **Mr. Samuel Hall**, a teacher in Marietta College, Ohio. We quote his letter:

"Mr. Curtis, a journeyman cabinet-maker, of Marietta, relates the following, of which he was an eye witness. Mr. Curtis is every way worthy of credit.

"In September, 1837, at Milligan's Bend, in the Mississippi River, I saw a negro with an iron band around his head, locked behind with a padlock. In the front, where it passed the mouth, there was a projection inward of an inch and a half, which entered the mouth.

"The overseer told me, he was so addicted to running away, it did not do any good to whip him for it. He said he kept this gag constantly on him, and intended to do so as long as he was on the plantation so that, if he ran away, he could not eat, and would starve to death. The slave asked for drink in my presence and the overseer made him lie down on his back, and turned water on his face two or three feet high, in order to torment him, as he could not swallow a drop.

The slave then asked permission to go to the river, which being granted, he thrust his face and head entirely under the water that being the only way he could drink with his gag on. The gag was taken off when he took his food, and then replaced afterwards."

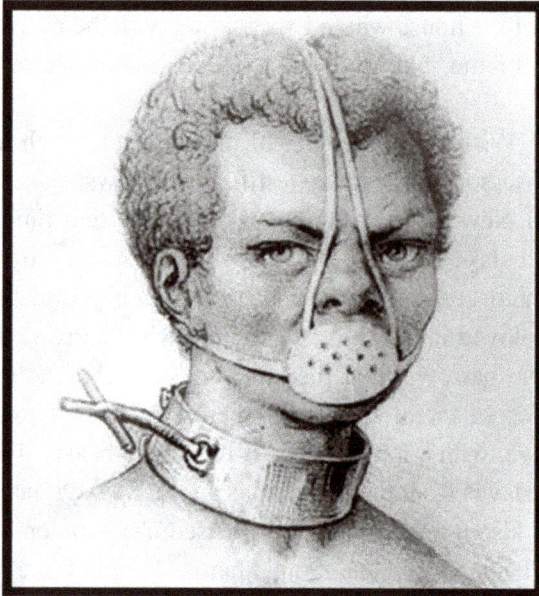

Extract of a letter from **Mrs. Sophia Little**, of Newport, Rhode Island, daughter of Hon. Asher Robbins, senator in Congress for that state."There was lately found, in the hold of a vessel engaged in the southern trade, by a person who was clearing it out, an iron collar, with three horns projecting from it. It seems that a young female slave, on whose slender neck was riveted this fiendish instrument of torture, ran away from her tyrant, and begged the captain to bring her off with him. This, the captain, refused to do; but un-riveted the collar from her neck, and threw it away in the hold of the vessel. The collar is now at the anti-slavery office, Providence. To the truth of these facts Mr. William H. Reed, a gentleman of the highest moral character, is ready to vouch.

"Mr. Reed is in possession of many facts of cruelty witnessed by persons of veracity; but these witnesses are not willing to give their names.

One case in particular he mentioned. Speaking with a certain captain, of the state of the slaves at the south, the captain contended that their punishments were often very *lenient;* and, as an instance of their excellent clemency, mentioned, that in one instance, not wishing to whip a slave, they sent him to a blacksmith, and had an iron band fastened around him, with three long projections reaching above his head; and this he wore some time."

Extract of a letter from **Mr. Jonathan F. Baldwin**, of Lorain County, Ohio. Mr. B. was formerly a merchant in Massillon, Ohio, and an Elder in the Presbyterian Church there.

"Dear Brother,—In conversation with Judge Lyman, of Litchfield County, Connecticut, last June, he stated to me, that several years since he was in Columbia, South Carolina, and observing a colored man lying on the floor of a blacksmith's shop, as he was passing it, his curiosity led him in. He learned the man was a slave and rather unmanageable. Several men were attempting to detach from his ankle an iron which had been bent around it.

"The iron was a piece of a flat bar of the ordinary size from the forge hammer, and bent around the ankle, the ends meeting, and forming a hoop of about the diameter of the leg. There was one or more strings attached to the iron and extending up around his neck, evidently so to suspend it as to prevent its galling by its weight when at work, yet it had galled or gripped till the leg had swollen out beyond the iron and inflamed and suppurated, so that the leg for a considerable distance above and below the iron, was a mass of putrefaction, the most loathsome of any wound he had ever witnessed on any living creature. The slave lay on his back on the floor, with his leg on an anvil which sat also on the floor, one man had a chisel used for splitting iron, and another struck it with a sledge, to drive it between the ends of the hoop and separate it so that it might be taken off. Mr. Lyman said that the man swung the sledge over his shoulders as if splitting iron, and struck many blows before he succeeded in parting the ends of the iron at all, the bar was so large and stubborn—at length they spread it as far as they could without driving the chisel so low as to ruin the leg. The slave, a man of twenty-five years, perhaps, whose countenance was the index of a mind ill-adapted to the degradations of slavery, never uttered a word or a groan in all the process, but the copious flow of sweat from every pore, the dreadful contractions and distortions of every muscle in his body, showed clearly the great amount of his sufferings; and all this while, such was the diseased state of the limb, that at every blow, the bloody, corrupted matter gushed out in all directions several feet, in such profusion as literally to cover a large area around the anvil. After various other fruitless attempts to spread the iron, they concluded it was necessary to weaken by filing before it could be got off, which he left them attempting to do."

Mr. William Drown, a well known citizen of Rhode Island, formerly of Providence, who has traveled in nearly all the slave states, thus testifies in a recent letter:

"I recollect seeing large gangs of slaves, generally a considerable number in each gang, being chained, passing westward over the mountains from Maryland, Virginia, &c. to the Ohio. On that river I have frequently seen flat boats loaded with them, and their keepers armed with pistols and dirks to guard them.

"At New Orleans I recollect seeing gangs of slaves that were driven out every day, the Sabbath not excepted, to work on the streets. These had heavy chains to connect two or more together, and some had iron collars and yokes, &c. The noise as they walked, or worked in their chains, was truly dreadful."

Rev. Thomas Savage, pastor of the Congregational Church at Bedford, New Hampshire, who was for some years a resident of Mississippi and Louisiana, gives the following fact, in a letter dated January 9, 1839.

"In 1819, while employed as an instructor at Second Creek, near Natchez, Mississippi, I resided on a plantation where I witnessed the following circumstance. One of the slaves was in the habit of running away. He had been repeatedly taken, and repeatedly whipped, with great severity, but to no purpose. He would still seize the first opportunity to escape from the plantation. At last his owner declared, "I'll fix him, I'll put a stop to his running away". He accordingly took him to a blacksmith, and had an *iron head-frame* made for him, which may be called lock-jaw, from the use that was made of it. It had a lock and key, and was so constructed, that when on the head and locked, the slave could not open his mouth to take food, and the design was to prevent his running away. But the device proved unavailing. He was soon missing, and whether by his own desperate effort, or the aid of others, contrived to sustain himself with food; but he was at last taken, and if my memory serves me, his life was soon terminated by the cruel treatment to which he was subjected."

The Western Luminary, a religious paper published at Lexington, Kentucky, in an editorial article, in the summer of 1833, says:

"A few weeks since, we gave an account of a company of men, women and children, part of whom were manacled, passing through our streets. Last week, a number of slaves were driven through the main street of our city, among whom were a number manacled together, two abreast, all connected by, and supporting a *heavy iron chain,* which extended the whole length of the line."

TESTIMONY OF A VIRGINIAN:.

The *name* of this witness cannot be published, as it would put him in peril; but his *credibility* is vouched for by the Rev. Ezra Fisher, Pastor of the Baptist Church, Quincy, Illinois, and Dr. Richard Eels, of the same place. These gentlemen say of him, "We have great confidence in his integrity, discretion, and strict Christian principle."

He says:

"About five years ago, I remember to have in *a single day,* four droves of slaves for the south west; the largest drove had 350 slaves in it, and the smallest upwards of 200. I counted 68 or 70 in a single *coffle.* The '*coffle chain'* is a chain fastened at one end to the centre of the bar of a pair of hand cuffs, which are fastened to the right wrist of one, and the left wrist of another slave, they standing abreast, and the chain between them. These are the head of the coffle. The other end is passed through a ring in the bolt of the next handcuffs, and the slaves being manacled thus, two and two together, walk up, and the coffle chain is passed, and they go up towards the head of the coffle. Of course they are closer or wider apart in the coffle, according to the number to be coffled, and to the length of the chain. I *have seen* hundreds *of droves and chain-coffles of this description,* and every coffle was a scene of misery and woe, of tears and brokenness of heart."

Mr. Samuel Hall, a teacher in Marietta College, Ohio, gives, in a late letter, the following statement of a fellow student, from Kentucky, of whom he says, "he is a professor of religion, and worthy of entire confidence."

"I have seen at least *fifteen* droves of 'human cattle,' passing by us on their way to the south; and I do not recollect an exception, where there were not more or less of them *chained* together."

Mr. George P. C. Hussey, of Fayetteville, Franklin County, Pennsylvania, writes thus:

"I was born and raised in Hagerstown, Washington County, Maryland, where slavery is perhaps milder than in any other part of the slave states; and yet I have seen *hundreds* of colored men and women chained together, two by two, and driven to the south. I have seen slaves tied up and lashed till the blood ran down to their heels."

Mr. Giddings, member of Congress from Ohio, in his speech in the House of Representatives, Feb. 13, 1839, made the following statement:

"On the beautiful avenue in front of the Capitol, members of Congress, during this session, have been compelled to turn aside from their path, to permit a coffle of slaves, males and females, *chained to each other by their necks,* to pass on their way to this *national slave market".*

Testimony of **James K. Paulding, Esq.** the present Secretary of the United States Navy. In 1817, Mr. Paulding published a work, entitled 'Letters from the South, written during an excursion in the summer of 1816.' In the first volume of that work, page 128, Mr. P. gives the following description:

"The sun was shining out very hot and in turning the angle of the road, we encountered the following group: first, a little cart drawn by one horse, in which five or six half naked black children were tumbled like pigs together. The cart had no covering, and they seemed to have been broiled to sleep. Behind the cart marched three black women, with head, neck and breasts uncovered, and without shoes or stockings; next came three men, bare-headed, and *chained together with an* ox-chain. Last of all, came a white man on horseback, carrying his pistols in his belt, and who, as we passed him, had the impudence to look us in the face without blushing. At a house where we stopped a little further on, we learned that he had bought these miserable beings in Maryland, and was marching them in this manner to one of the more southern states. Shame on the State of Maryland! And I say shame on the State of Virginia! And every state through which this wretched cavalcade was permitted to pass! I do say, that when they (the slaveholders) permit such flagrant and indecent outrages upon humanity as that I have described; when they sanction a villain in thus marching half naked women and men, loaded with chains, without being charged with any crime but that of being *black,* from one section of the United States to another, hundreds of miles in the face of day, they disgrace themselves, and the country to which they belong."*

* The fact that Mr. Paulding, in the reprint of these "Letters," in 1835, *struck out this passage* with all others disparaging to slavery and its supporters, does not impair the force of his testimony, however much it may sink the man. Nor will the next generation regard with any more reverence, his character as a *prophet,* because in the edition of 1835, two years after the American Anti-Slavery Society was formed, and when its auxiliaries were numbered by hundreds, he inserted a *prediction,* that such movements would be made at the North, with most disastrous results. "Wot ye not that such a man as I can certainly divine!" Mr. Paulding has already been taught by Judge Jay, that he who aspires to the fame of an oracle, without its inspiration, must resort to other expedients to prevent detection, than the clumsy one of *antedating* his responses.

III. BRANDINGS, MAIMINGS, GUN-SHOT WOUNDS, &c.

The slaves are often branded with hot irons, pursued with fire arms and *shot,* hunted with dogs and torn by them, shockingly maimed with knives, dirks, &.c.; have their ears cut off, their eyes knocked out, their bones dislocated and broken with bludgeons, their fingers and toes cut off, their faces and other parts of their persons disfigured with scars and gashes, *besides* those made with the lash.

We shall adopt, under this head, the same course as that pursued under previous ones,—first give the testimony of the slaveholders themselves, to the mutilations, &c. by copying their own graphic descriptions of them, in advertisements published under their own names, and in newspapers published in the slave states, and, generally, in their own immediate vicinity. We shall, as heretofore, insert only so much of each advertisement as will be necessary to make the point intelligible.

WITNESS

Mr. Micajah Ricks, Nash County, North Carolina, in the Raleigh "Standard," July 18, 1838.

TESTIMONY

Ranaway, a negro woman and two children; a few days before she went off, I *burnt her with a hot iron,* on the left side of her face, *I tried to make the letter M.*

============

WITNESS

Mr. Asa B. Metcalf, Kingston, Adams Co. Mi. in the "Natchez Courier," June 15, 1832.

TESTIMONY

"Ranaway Mary, a black woman, has a *scar* on her back and right arm near the shoulder, *caused by a rifle ball.*"

============

WITNESS

Mr. William Overstreet, Benton, Yazoo Co. Mi. in the "Lexington (Kentucky) Observer," July 22, 1838.

TESTIMONY

"Ranaway a negro man named Henry, *his left eye out,* some scars from a *dirk* on and under his left arm, and *much scarred* with the whip."

============

WITNESS

Mr. R. P. Carney, Clark Go. Ala., In the Mobile Register, Dec. 22, 1832.

TESTIMONY

One hundred dollars reward for a negro fellow Pompey, 40 years old, he is *branded* on the *left jaw.*

============

WITNESS

Mr. J. Guyler, Savannah Georgia, in the "Republican", April 12, 1837.

TESTIMONY

"Ranaway Laman, an old negro man, grey, has *only one eye.*'"

=========

WITNESS

J. A. Brown, jailor, Charleston, South Carolina, in the "Mercury," Jan. 12, 1837.

TESTIMONY

"Committed to jail a negro man, has *no toes* on his left foot."

=========

WITNESS

Mr. J. Scrivener, Herring Bay, Anne Arundel Co. Maryland, in the Annapolis Republican, April 18, 1837.

TESTIMONY

"Ranaway negro man Elijah, has a scar on his left cheek, apparently occasioned by *a shot.*"

=========

WITNESS

Madame Burvant, corner of Chartres and Toulouse Streets, New Orleans, in the "Bee," Dec. 21, 1838.

TESTIMONY

"Ranaway a negro woman named Rachel, has *lost all her toes* except the large one."

=========

WITNESS

Mr. O. W. Lains, in the "Helena, (Ark.) Journal," June 1, 1833.

TESTIMONY

Ranaway Sam, he was *shot* a short time since, through the hand, and has *several shots in his left arm and side.*"

=========

WITNESS

Mr. R. W. Sizer, in the "Grand Gulf, [Mi.] Advertiser," July 8, 1837.

TESTIMONY

"Ranaway my negro man Dennis, said negro has been *shot* in the left arm between the shoulders and elbow, which has [paralyzed the left hand."

=========

WITNESS

Mr. Nicholas Edmunds, in the "Petersburg [Va.] Intelligencer," May 22, 1838.

TESTIMONY

Ranaway, my negro man named Simon, he *has been shot badly* in his back and right arm

===========

WITNESS

Mr. J. Bishop, Bishopville, Sumpter District, South Carolina, in the "Camden [S.C.] Journal," March 4, 1837.

TESTIMONY

"Ranaway a negro named Arthur, has a considerable *scar* across his *breast* and *each arm,* made by a knife; loves to talk much of the goodness of God."

===========

WITNESS

Mr. S. Neyle, Little Ogeechee, Georgia, in the "Savannah Republican," July 3, 1837.

TESTIMONY

"Ranaway George, he has a *sword cut* lately received on his left arm."

===========

WITNESS

Mrs. Sarah Walsh, Mobile, Ala in the "Georgia Journal," March 27, 1837,

TESTIMONY

"Twenty five dollars reward for my man Isaac, he has a scar on his forehead caused by a *blow,* and one on his back made by *a shot from a pistol.*"

===========

WITNESS

Mr. J. P. Ashford, Adams Co. Mi. in the "Natchez Courier," August 24, 1838.

TESTIMONY

"Ranaway a negro girl called Mary, has a small scar over her eye, a *good many teeth missing,* the letter A. *is branded on her cheek and forehead.*"

===========

WITNESS

Mr. Ely Townsend, Pike Co. Ala, in the "Pensacola Gazette," Sep. 16, 1837.

TESTIMONY

"Ranaway negro Ben, has a scar on his right hand, his thumb and fore finger being injured by being *shot* last fall, a part of *the bone came out,* he has also one or two *large scars* on his back and hips."

==========

WITNESS

S. B. Murphy, jailer, Irvington, Ga. in the "Milledgeville Journal," May 29, 1838.

TESTIMONY

"Committed a negro man, is *very badly shot in the right side* and right hand."

==========

WITNESS

Mr. A. Luminais, Parish of St. John, Louisiana, in the New Orleans "Bee," March 3, 1838.

TESTIMONY

"Detained at the jail, a mulatto named Tom, has a *scar* on the right cheek and appears to have been *burned with powder* on the face."

==========

WITNESS

Mr. Isaac Johnson, Pulaski Co. Georgia, in the "Milledgeville Journal," June 19, 1838.

TESTIMONY

"Ranaway a negro man named Ned, *three of his fingers* are drawn into the palm of his hand by a *cut,* has a *scar* on the back of his neck nearly half round, done by a *knife*."

==========

WITNESS

Mr. Thomas Hudnall, Madison Co. Mi. in the "Vicksburg Register," September 5, 1838.

TESTIMONY

"Ranaway a negro named Hambleton, *limps* on his left foot where he was *shot* a few weeks ago, while runaway."

==========

WITNESS

Mr. John McMurrain, Columbus, Ga. in the "Southern Sun," August 7, 1838.

TESTIMONY

"Ranaway a negro boy named Mose, he has a *wound* in the right shoulder near the back bone, which was occasioned by *a rifle shot.*"

==========

WITNESS

Mr. Moses Orme, Annapolis, Maryland, in the "Annapolis Republican," June 20, 1837.

TESTIMONY

"Ranaway my negro man Bill, he has a *fresh wound in his head* above his ear."

==========

WITNESS

William Strickland, Jailor, Kershaw District, S.C. in the "Camden [S.C.] Courier," July 8, 1837.

TESTIMONY

"Committed to jail a negro, says his name is Cuffee, he is lame in one knee, occasioned *by a shot.*"

==========

WITNESS

The Editor of the "Grand Gulf Advertiser," Dec. 7, 1838.

TESTIMONY

"Ranaway Joshua, his thumb is off of his left hand."

==========

WITNESS

Mr. William Bateman, in the "Grand Gulf Advertiser," Dec. 7, 1838.

TESTIMONY

"Ranaway William, *scar* over his left eye, one between his eye brows, one on his breast, and his right leg has been *broken.*"

==========

WITNESS

Mr. B. G. Simmons, in the "Southern Argus," May 30, 1837.

TESTIMONY

"Ranaway Mark, his left arm has been *broken,* right *leg also.*"

==========

WITNESS

Mr. James Artop, in the "Macon [Ga.] Messenger, May 25, 1837.

TESTIMONY

"Ranaway, Caleb, 50 years old, has an awkward gait occasioned by his being *shot* in the thigh."

==========

WITNESS

J. L. Jolley, Sheriff of Clinton, Co. Mi., in the "Clinton Gazette," July 23, 1836.

TESTIMONY

"Was committed to jail a negro man, says his name is Josiah, his back very much scarred by the whip, and *branded on the thigh and hips, in three or four places,* thus (J. M.) the *rim of his right ear has been bit or cut off.*"

==========

WITNESS

Mr. Thomas Ledwith, Jacksonville East Florida, in the "Charleston [S.C.] Courier, Sept. 1, 1838.

TESTIMONY

"Fifty dollars reward, for my fellow Edward, he has a *scar* on the corner of his mouth, two *cuts* on and under his arm, and the *letter E on his arm.*"

==========

WITNESS

Mr. Joseph James, Sen., Pleasant Ridge, Paulding Co. Ga., in the "Milledgeville Union," Nov. 7, 1837.

TESTIMONY

"Ranaway, negro boy Ellic, has a *scar* on one of his arms *from the bite of a dog.*'

==========

WITNESS

Mr. W. Riley, Orangeburg District, South Carolina, in the "Columbia [S.C.] Telescope," Nov. 11, 1837.

TESTIMONY

"Ranaway a negro man, has a *scar* on the ankle produced by a *burn* and a *mark on his arm* resembling the letter S."

==========

WITNESS

Mr. Samuel Mason, Warren Co, Mi., in the "Vicksburg Register," July 18, 1838.

TESTIMONY

Ranaway, a negro man named Allen, he has a scar on his breast, also a scar under the left eye, and has *two buck shot in his right arm.*"

==========

WITNESS

Mr. F. L. C. Edwards, in the "Southern Telegraph," Sept. 25, 1837

TESTIMONY

"Ranaway from the plantation of James Surgette, the following negroes, Randal, *has one ear cropped;* Bob, *has lost one eye,* Kentucky Tom, *has one jaw broken* ."

==========

WITNESS

Mr. Stephen M. Jackson, in the "Vicksburg Register," March 10, 1837.

TESTIMONY

"Ranaway, Anthony, one of his *ears cut off,* and his left hand cut with an axe."

==========

WITNESS

Philip Honerton, deputy sheriff of Halifax Co. Virginia, Jan. 1837.

TESTIMONY

"Was committed, a negro man, has a *scar* on his right side by a burn, one on his knee, and one on the calf of his leg *by the bite of a dog.*"

==========

WITNESS

Stearns & Co. No. 28, New Levee, New Orleans, in the "Bee," March 22, 1837.

TESTIMONY

"Absconded, the mulatto boy Tom, his fingers *scarred* on his right hand, and has a *scar* on his right cheek."

==========

WITNESS

Mr. John W. Walton, Greensboro, Ala. in the "Alabama Beacon," Dec. 13, 1838.

TESTIMONY

"Ranaway my black boy Frazier, with a *scar* below and one above his right ear."

==========

WITNESS
Mr. R. Furman, Charleston, S.C. in the "Charleston Mercury," Jan. 12, 1839.
TESTIMONY
"Ranaway, Dick, about 19, has lost the small toe of one foot."

===========

WITNESS
Mr. John Tart, Sen. in the "Fayetteville [N. C.] Observer," Dec. 26, 1838.
TESTIMONY
"Stolen a mulatto boy, *ten* years old, he has a *scar* over his eye which was made by an axe."

===========

WITNESS
Mr. Richard Overstreet, Brook Neal, Campbell Co. Virginia, in the "Danville [Va.] Reporter," Dec, 21, 1838.
TESTIMONY
"Absconded my negro man Coleman, has a *very large scar* on one of his legs, also one on *each* arm, by a burn, and his heels have been frosted."

===========

WITNESS
The editor of the New Orleans "Bee," in that paper, August 27, 1837.
TESTIMONY
"Fifty dollars reward, for the negro Jim Blake—has a *piece cut out of each ear,* and the middle finger of the left hand *cut off* to the second joint."

===========

WITNESS
Mr. Bryant Johnson, Fort Valley, Houston county, Georgia, in the Milledgeville "Union," Oct. 2, 1838.
TESTIMONY
"Ranaway, a negro woman named Maria—has a scar on one side of her cheek, by a *cut*—some scars on her back."

===========

WITNESS
Mr. Lemuel Miles, Steen's Creek, Rankin County, Mi. in the "Southern Sun" Sept. 22, 1838.

TESTIMONY

"Ranaway, Gabriel—has *two or three scars across his neck* made with a knife."

==========

WITNESS

Mr. Bezou, New Orleans, in the "Bee" May 23, 1838.

TESTIMONY

"Ranaway, the mulatto wench Mary—has a *cut on the left arm, a scar on the shoulder, and two upper teeth missing.*"

==========

WITNESS

Mr. James Kimborough, Memphis, Tenn. in the "Memphis Enquirer," July 13, 1838.

TESTIMONY

"Ranaway, a negro boy, named Jerry—has a *scar* on his right cheek two inches long, from the cut of a knife."

==========

WITNESS

Mr. Robert Beasley, Macon, Georgia, in the "Georgia Messenger," July 27, 1837.

TESTIMONY

"Ranaway, my man Fountain—has *holes in his ears, a scar* on the right side of his forehead—has been *shot in the hind parts of his legs*—is marked on the back with the whip."

==========

WITNESS

Mr. B. G. Barrer, St. Louis, Missouri, in the "Republican," Sept. 6, 1837.

TESTIMONY

"Ranaway, a negro man named Jarrett—*has a scar* on the under part of one of his arms, occasioned by a wound from a knife."

==========

WITNESS

Mr. John D. Turner, near Norfolk, Virginia, in the "Norfolk Herald," June 27, 1838.

TESTIMONY

"Ranaway, a negro by the name of Joshua—he has a cut across one of his ears, which he will conceal as much as possible—one of his ankles is *enlarged by an ulcer.*"

==========

WITNESS

Mr. William Stansell, Picksville, Ala. in the "Huntsville Democrat," August 29, 1837.

TESTIMONY

"Ranaway, negro boy Harper—*has a scar* on one of his hips in the form of a G."

==========

WITNESS

Hon. Ambrose H. Sevier, Senator in Congress, from Arkansas, in the "Vicksburg Register," of Oct. 13.

TESTIMONY

"Ranaway, Bob, a slave—has a *scar across his breast,* another on the *right side of his head*—his back is *much scarred* with the whip."

==========

WITNESS

Mr. R. A. Greene, Milledgeville, Georgia, in the "Macon Messenger," July 27, 1837.

TESTIMONY

"Two hundred and fifty dollars reward, for my negro man Jim—he is much marked with *shot* in his right thigh,—the shot entered on the outside, half way between the hip and knee joints."

==========

WITNESS

Benjamin Russel, deputy sheriff, Bibb County, Ga. in the "Macon Telegraph," December 25, 1837.

TESTIMONY

"Brought to jail, John—*left ear cropt.*"

==========

WITNESS

Hon. H. Hitchcock, Mobile, judge of the Supreme Court, in the "Commercial Register," Oct. 27, 1837.

TESTIMONY

"Ranaway, the slave Ellis—he has *lost one of his ears*."

==========

WITNESS

Mrs. Elizabeth L. Carter, near Groveton, Prince William County, Virginia, in the "National Intelligencer," Washington, D.C. June 10, 1837.

TESTIMONY

"Ranaway, a negro man, Moses—he has *lost a part* of one of his ears."

==========

WITNESS

Mr. William D. Buckels, Natchez, Mi. in the "Natchez Courier," July 28, 1838.

TESTIMONY

"Taken up, a negro man—is *very much scarred* about the face and body, and has the left *ear bit off*."

==========

WITNESS

Mr. Walter R. English, Monroe County, Ala. in the "Mobile Chronicle," Sept. 2, 1837.

TESTIMONY

"Ranaway, my slave Lewis—he has lost a *piece of one ear,* and a *part of one of his fingers,* a *part of one of his toes* is also lost."

==========

WITNESS

Mr. James Saunders, Grany Spring, Hawkins County, Tenn. in the "Knoxville Register," June 6, 1838.

TESTIMONY

"Ranaway, a black girl named Mary—has a *scar* on her cheek, and the end of one of her toes *cut off*."

==========

WITNESS

Mr. John Jenkins, St. Joseph's, Florida, captain of the steamboat Ellen, "Apalachicola Gazette," June 7, 1838.

TESTIMONY

"Ranaway, the negro boy Caesar—he has *but one eye* ."

==========

WITNESS

Mr. Peter Hanson, Lafayette city, La., in the New Orleans "Bee," July 28, 1838.

TESTIMONY

"Ranaway, the negress Martha—she has *lost her right eye*."

==========

WITNESS

Mr. Orren Ellis, Georgeville, Mi. in the "North Alabamian," Sept. 15, 1837.

TESTIMONY

"Ranaway, George—has had the lower part of *one of his ears bit off*."

==========

WITNESS

Mr. Zadock Sawyer, Cuthbert, Randolph County, Georgia, in the "Milledgeville Union," Oct. 9, 1838.

TESTIMONY

"Ranaway, my negro Tom—has a piece *bit off the top of his right ear, and his little finger is stiff*."

==========

WITNESS

Mr. Abraham Gray, Mount Morino, Pike County, Ga. in the "Milledgeville Union," Oct. 9, 1838.

TESTIMONY

"Ranaway, my mulatto woman Judy—she has had her *right arm broke*."

==========

WITNESS

S. B. Tuston, jailer, Adams County, Mi. in the "Natchez Courier," June 15, 1838.

TESTIMONY

"Was committed to jail, a negro man named Bill—has had the *thumb of his left hand split*."

==========

WITNESS

Mr. Joshua Antrim, Nineveh, Warren County, Virginia, in the "Winchester Virginian," July 11, 1837.

TESTIMONY

"Ranaway, a mulatto man named Joe—his fingers on the left hand are *partly amputated.*"

==========

WITNESS

J. B. Randall, jailor, Marietta, Cobb County, Ga., in the "Southern Recorder," Nov. 6, 1838.

TESTIMONY

"Lodged in jail, a negro man named Jupiter—is very *lame in his left hip,* so that he can hardly walk—has lost a joint of the middle finger of his left hand."

==========

WITNESS

Mr. John N. Dillahunty, Woodville, Mi., in the "N. O. Commercial Bulletin," July 21, 1837.

TESTIMONY

"Ranaway, Bill—has a scar over one eye, also one on his leg, from *the bite of a dog*—has a *burn on his buttock, from a piece of hot iron in shape of a T.*"

==========

WITNESS

William K. Ratcliffe, sheriff, Franklin County, Mi. in the "Natchez Free Trader," August 23, 1838.

TESTIMONY

"Committed to jail, a negro named Mike—*his left ear off.*"

==========

WITNESS

Mr. Preston Halley, Barnwell, South Carolina, in the "Augusta [Ga.] Chronicle," July 27, 1838.

TESTIMONY

"Ranaway, my negro man Levi—his left hand has been *burnt,* and I think the end of his fore finger is *off.*"

==========

WITNESS

Mr. Welcome H. Robbins, St. Charles County, Mo. in the "St. Louis Republican," June 30, 1838.

TESTIMONY

"Ranaway, a negro named Washington—has *lost a part of his middle finger and the end of his little finger.*"

==========

WITNESS

G. Gourdon & Co. druggists, corner of Rampart and Hospital streets, New Orleans, in the "Commercial Bulletin," Sept. 18, 1838.

TESTIMONY

"Ranaway, a negro named David Drier—has *two toes cut.*"

==========

WITNESS

Mr. William Brown, in the "Grand Gulf Advertiser," August 29, 1838.

TESTIMONY

"Ranaway, Edmund—has a *scar* on his right temple, and under his right eye, and *holes in both ears.*"

==========

WITNESS

Mr. James McDonnell Talbot County, Georgia, in the "Columbus Enquirer," Jan. 18, 1838.

TESTIMONY

"Runaway, a negro boy *twelve or thirteen* years old—has a scar on his left cheek *from the bite of a dog.*"

==========

WITNESS

Mr. John W. Cherry, Marengo County, Ala. in the "Mobile Register," June 15, 1838.

TESTIMONY

"Fifty dollars reward, for my negro man John—he has a considerable scar on his *throat,* done with a *knife.*"

==========

WITNESS

Mr. Thos. Brown, Roane Co. Tenn. in the "Knoxville Register," Sept. 12, 1838.

TESTIMONY

"Twenty-five dollars reward, for my man John—the *tip* of his nose is b*it off.*"

==========

WITNESS

Messrs. Taylor, Lawton & Co., Charleston, South Carolina, in the "Mercury," Nov. 1838.

TESTIMONY

"Ranaway, a negro fellow called Hover—has a *cut* above the right eye."

==========

WITNESS

Mr. Louis Schmidt, Taubourg, Sivaudais, La. in the New Orleans "Bee," Sept. 5, 1837.

TESTIMONY

"Ranaway, the negro man Hardy—has a *scar* on the upper lip, and another made with a *knife* on his neck."

==========

WITNESS

W. M. Whitehead, Natchez, in the "New Orleans Bulletin," July 21, 1837.

TESTIMONY

"Ranaway, Henry—has half of one *ear bit off.*"

==========

WITNESS

Mr. Conrad Salvo, Charleston, South Carolina, in the "Mercury, August 10, 1837.

TESTIMONY

"Ranaway, my negro man Jacob—he has but *one eye.*"

==========

WITNESS

William Baker, jailer, Shelby County, Ala., in the "Montgomery (Ala.) Advertiser," Oct. 5, 1838.

TESTIMONY

"Committed to jail, Ben—his *left thumb off* at the first joint."

==========

WITNESS

Mr. S. N. Hite, Camp Street, New Orleans, in the "Bee," Feb. 19, 1838.

TESTIMONY

"Twenty-five dollars reward for the negro slave Sally—walks as though *crippled* in the back."

==========

WITNESS

Mr. Stephen M. Richards, Whitesburg, Madison County, Alabama, in the "Huntsville Democrat," Sept. 8, 1838.

TESTIMONY

"Ranaway, a negro man named Dick—has a *little finger off* the right hand."

========

WITNESS

Mr. A. Brove, parish of St. Charles, La. in the "New Orleans Bee," Feb. 19, 1838.

TESTIMONY

"Ranaway, the negro Patrick—has his little finger of the right hand *cut close to the hand.*"

========

WITNESS

Mr. Needham Whitefield, Aberdeen, Mi. in the "Memphis (Tenn.) Enquirer," June 15, 1838.

TESTIMONY

"Ranaway, Joe Dennis—has a small *notch* in one of his ears."

========

WITNESS

Col. M. J. Sheith, Charleston, South Carolina, in the "Mercury," Nov. 27, 1837.

TESTIMONY

"Ranaway, Dick—has *lost the little toe* of one of his feet."

========

WITNESS

Mr. R. Lancette, Haywood, North Carolina, in the "Raleigh Register," April 30, 1838.

TESTIMONY

"Escaped, my negro man Eaton—his *little finger* of the right hand has been *broke.*"

========

WITNESS

Mr. G. C. Richardson, Owen Station, Mo., in the St. Louis "Republican," May 5, 1838.

TESTIMONY

"Ranaway, my negro man named Top—has had one of his *legs broken*."

==========

WITNESS

Mr. E. Han, La Grange, Fayette County, Tenn. in the Gallatin "Union," June 23, 1837.

TESTIMONY

"Ranaway, negro boy Jack—has a small *crop out of his left ear*."

==========

WITNESS

D. Herring, warden of Baltimore city jail, in the "Marylander," Oct. 6, 1837.

TESTIMONY

"Was committed to jail, a negro man—has *two scars* on his forehead, and the *top of his left ear cut off*."

==========

WITNESS

Mr. James Marks, near Natchitoches, La. in the "Natchitoches Herald," July 21, 1838.

TESTIMONY

"Stolen, a negro man named Winter—has a *notch* cut out of the left ear, and the mark of *four or five buck shot* on his legs."

==========

WITNESS

Mr. James Barr, Amelia Court House, Virginia, in the "Norfolk Herald," Sept. 12, 1838.

TESTIMONY

"Ranaway, a negro man—*scar back of his left eye,* as if from the *cut* of a knife."

==========

WITNESS

Mr. Isaac Mitchell, Wilkinson County, Georgia, in the "Augusta Chronicle," Sept. 21, 1837

TESTIMONY

"Ranaway, negro man Buck—has a very *plain mark* under his ear on his jaw, about the size of a dollar, having been *inflicted by a knife*."

==========

WITNESS

Mr. P. Bayhi, captain of the police, Suburb Washington, third municipality, New Orleans, in the "Bee," Oct. 13, 1837.

TESTIMONY

"Detained at the jail, the negro boy Hermon—has a scar below his left ear, from the *wound of a knife*."

==========

WITNESS

Mr. Willie Paterson, Clinton, Jones County, Ga. in the "Darien Telegraph," Dec. 5, 1837.

TESTIMONY

"Ranaway, a negro man by the name of John—he has a *scar* across his cheek, and one on his right arm, apparently done with a *knife*."

==========

WITNESS

Mr. Samuel Ragland, Triana, Madison County, Alabama, in the "Huntsville Advocate," Dec. 23, 1837.

TESTIMONY

"Ranaway, Isham—has a *scar* upon the breast and upon the under lip, from the *bite of a dog*."

==========

WITNESS

Mr. Moses E. Bush, near Clayton, Ala. in the "Columbus [Ga.] Enquirer," July 5, 1838.

TESTIMONY

"Ranaway, a negro man—has a *scar* on his hip and on his breast, and *two front teeth out*."

==========

WITNESS

C. W. Wilkins, sheriff Baldwin Co, Ala. in the "Mobile Advertiser," Sept. 22, 1837:

TESTIMONY

"Committed to jail, a negro man, he is *crippled* in the right leg."

==========

WITNESS

Mr. James H. Taylor, Charleston South Carolina, in the "Courier," August 7, 1837.

TESTIMONY

"Absconded, a colored boy, named Peter, *lame* in the right leg."

============

WITNESS

N. M. C. Robinson, jailer, Columbus, Georgia, in the "Columbus (Ga.) Enquirer," August 2, 1838.

TESTIMONY

"Brought to jail, a negro man, his left ankle has been *broke*."

============

WITNESS

Mr. Littlejohn Rynes, Hinds Co. Mi. in the "Natchez Courier," August, 17, 1838.

TESTIMONY

"Ranaway, a negro man named Jerry, has a small piece *cut out of the top of each ear*."

============

WITNESS

The Heirs of J. A. Alston, near Georgetown, South Carolina, in the "Georgetown, [S.C.] Union," June 17, 1837:

TESTIMONY

"Absconded a negro named Cuffee, has *lost one finger;* has an *enlarged leg*."

============

WITNESS

A. S. Ballinger, Sheriff, Johnston Co, North Carolina, in the "Raleigh Standard," Oct. 18, 1838.

TESTIMONY

"Committed to jail, a negro man; has a *very sore leg*."

============

WITNESS

Mr. Thomas Crutchfield, Atkins, Ten. In the "Tennessee Journal," Oct. 17, 1838.

TESTIMONY

"Ranaway, my mulatto boy Cy, has but *one hand,* all the fingers of his right hand were *burnt* off when young."

============

WITNESS

J. A. Brown, jailer, Orangeburg, South Carolina, in the "Charleston Mercury," July 18, 1838.

TESTIMONY

"Was committed to jail, a negro named Bob, appears to be *crippled* in the right leg."

==========

WITNESS

S. B. Turton, jailer, Adams Co. Miss. in the "Natchez Courier," Sept. 28, 1828.

TESTIMONY

"Was committed to jail, a negro man, has his *left thigh broke.*"

==========

WITNESS

"Mr. John H. King, High street, Georgetown, in the "National Intelligencer," August 1, 1837.

TESTIMONY

"Ranaway, my negro man, he has the *end of one* of his fingers *broken.*"

==========

WITNESS

Mr. John B. Fox, Vicksburg, Miss. in the "Register," March 29, 1837.

TESTIMONY

"Ranaway, a yellowish negro boy named Tom, has a *notch* in the back of one of his ears."

==========

WITNESS

Messrs. Fernandez and Whiting, auctioneers, New Orleans, in the "Bee," April 8, 1837.

TESTIMONY

"Will be sold Martha, aged nineteen, *has one eye out.*"

==========

WITNESS

Mr. Marshall Jett, Farrowsville, Fauquier Co. Virginia, in the "National Intelligencer," May 30, 1837.

TESTIMONY

"Ranaway, negro man Ephraim, has a *mark* over one of his eyes, occasioned by a *blow.*"

========

WITNESS

S. B. Turton, jailer Adams Co. Miss. in the "Natches Courier," Oct. 12, 1838.

TESTIMONY

"Was committed a negro, calls himself Jacob, has been *crippled* in his right leg."

========

WITNESS

John Ford, sheriff of Mobile County, in the "Mississippian," Jackson Mi. Dec. 28, 1838.

TESTIMONY

"Committed to jail, a negro man, Cary, a *large scar on his forehead.*"

========

WITNESS

E. W. Morris, sheriff of Warren County, in the "Vicksburg " [Mi.] Register," March 28, 1838.

TESTIMONY

"Committed as a runaway, a negro man Jack, he has *several scars* on his face."

========

WITNESS

Mr. John P. Holcombe, in the Charleston Mercury," April 17, 1828.

TESTIMONY

"Absented himself, his negro man Ben, *has scars* on his throat, occasioned by the *cut of a knife.*"

========

WITNESS

Mr. Willis Patterson, in the "Charleston Mercury," December 11, 1837.

TESTIMONY

"Ranaway, a negro man, John, a *scar* across his cheek, and one on his right arm, apparently done *with a knife.*"

========

WITNESS

Wm. Magee, sheriff, Mobile Co. in the "Mobile Register," Dec. 27, 1837.

TESTIMONY

"Committed to jail, a runaway slave, Alexander, a *scar* on his left cheek."

==========

WITNESS

Mr. Henry M. McGregor, Prince George County, Maryland, in the "Alexandria [D. C.] Gazette," Feb. 6, 1838.

TESTIMONY

"Ranaway, negro Phil, *scar through the right eye brow,* part of the *middle toe* on the right foot *cut off.*"

==========

WITNESS

Green B. Jourdan, Baldwin County Ga. in the "Georgia Journal," April 18, 1837.

TESTIMONY

"Ranaway, John, has a *scar* on one of his hands extending from the wrist joint to the little finger, also a *scar* on one of his legs."

==========

WITNESS

Messrs. Daniel and Goodman, New Orleans, in the "N. O. Bee," Feb. 2, 1838.

TESTIMONY

"Absconded, mulatto slave Alick, has a *large scar over* one of his cheeks."

==========

WITNESS

Jeremiah Woodward, Goochland, Co. Va. in the "Richmond Va.Whig," Jan. 30, 1838.

TESTIMONY

"200 DOLLARS REWARD for Nelson, has a *scar* on his forehead occasioned by a *burn,* and one on his lower lip and one about the knee."

==========

WITNESS

Samuel Rawlins, Gwinnet Co. Ga. in the "Columbus Sentinel," Nov. 29, 1838.

TESTIMONY

"Ranaway, a negro man and his wife, named Nat and Priscilla, he has a small *scar* on his left cheek, *two stiff fingers* on his right hand with a *running sore* on them; his wife has a *scar* on her left arm, and one *upper tooth out.*"

===========

The reader perceives that we have under this head, as under previous ones, given to the testimony of the slaveholders themselves, under their own names, precedence over that of all other witnesses. We now ask the reader's attention to the testimonies which follow. They are endorsed by responsible names—men who 'speak what they know, and testify what they have seen—testimonies which show, that the slaveholders who wrote the preceding advertisements, describing the work of their own hands, in branding with hot irons, maiming, mutilating, cropping, shooting, knocking out the teeth and *eyes* of their slaves, breaking their bones, &c, have manifested, *as far as they have gone* in the description, a commendable fidelity to truth.

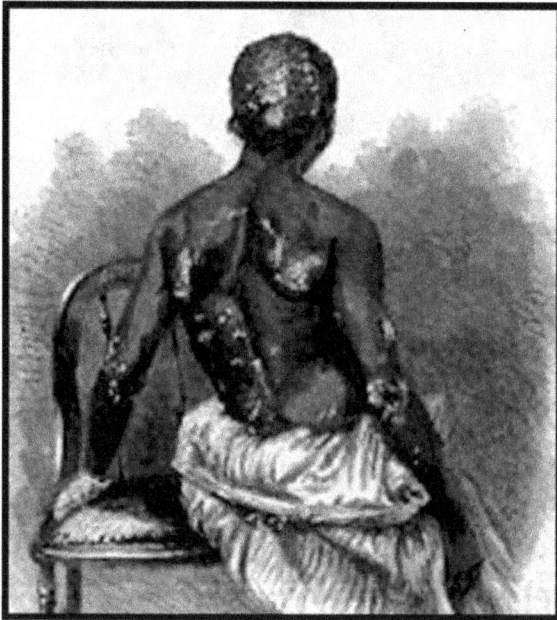

13 year old girl burned for running away

It is probable that some of the scars and maiming in the preceding advertisements were the result of accidents; and some *may be* the result of violence inflicted by the slaves upon each other. Without arguing that point, we say, these are the *facts;* whoever reads and ponders them, will need no argument to convince him, that the proposition which they have seen employed to sustain, *cannot be shaken.* That any considerable portion of them were *accidental,* is totally improbable, from the nature of the case; and is in most instances disproved by the advertisements themselves. That they have not been produced by assaults of the slaves upon each other, is manifest from the fact, that injuries of that character inflicted by the slaves upon each other, are, as all who are familiar with the habits and condition of slaves well know, exceedingly rare; and of necessity must be so, from the constant action upon them of the strongest dissuasive from such acts that can operate on human nature.

Advertisements similar to the preceding may at any time be gathered by scores from the daily and weekly newspapers of the slave states. Before presenting the reader with further testimony in proof of the proposition at the head of this part of our subject, we remark, that some of the tortures enumerated under this and the preceding heads, are not in all cases inflicted by slaveholders as *punishments,* but sometimes merely as preventives of escape, for the greater security of their 'property.' Iron collars, chains, &c. are put upon slaves when they are driven or transported from one part of the country to another, in order to keep them from running away. Similar measures are often resorted to upon plantations. When the master or owner suspects a slave of plotting an escape, an iron collar with long 'horns,' or a bar of iron, or a ball and chain, are often fastened upon him, for the double purpose of retarding his flight, should he attempt it, and of serving as an easy means of detection.

Another inhuman method of *marking* slaves, so that they may be easily described and detected when they escape, is called cropping. In the preceding advertisements, the reader will perceive a number of cases, in which the runaway is described as '*croft*' or a '*notch cut* in the ear, or a part or the whole of the ear *cut off,* &c.

Two years and a half since, the writer of this saw a letter, then just received by Mr. Lewis Tappan, of New York, containing a negro's ear cut off close to the head. The writer of the letter, who signed himself Thomas

Aylethorpe, Montgomery, Alabama, sent it to Mr. Tappan as 'a specimen of a negro's ears', and desired him to add it to his 'collection.'

Another method of *marking* slaves is by drawing out or breaking off one or two *front teeth* commonly the upper ones, as the mark would in that case be the more obvious. An instance of this kind the reader will recall in the testimony of Sarah M. Grimke, and of which she had *personal* knowledge; being well acquainted both with the inhuman master, (a distinguished citizen of South Carolina,) by whose order the brutal deed was done, and with the poor young girl whose mouth was thus barbarously mutilated, to furnish a convenient mark by which to describe her in case of her elopement, as she had frequently run away.

The case stated by Miss G. serves to unravel what, to one uninitiated, seems quite a mystery: i.e. the frequency with which, in the advertisements of runaway slaves published in southern papers, they are described as having *one or* two *front teeth out.* Scores of such advertisements are in southern papers now on our table. We will furnish the reader with a dozen or two.

WITNESS
Jesse Debruhl, sheriff, Richland District, "Columbia (S.C.) Telescope," Feb. 24, 1838.

TESTIMONY
"Committed to jail, Ned, about 25 years of age, has lost his *two upper front teeth.*"

==========

WITNESS
Mr. John Hunt, Black Water Bay, "Pensacola (Ga.) Gazette," October 14, 1837.

TESTIMONY
"100 DOLLARS REWARD, for Perry, *one under front tooth* missing, aged 23 years."

==========

WITNESS
Mr. John Frederick, Branchville, Orangeburgh District, S.C. "Charleston [S.C.] Courier," June 12, 1837.

TESTIMONY
10 DOLLARS REWARD, for Mary, *one or two upper teeth* out, about 25 years old."

==========

WITNESS

Mr. Egbert A. Raworth, eight miles west of Nashville on the Charlotte Road, "Daily Republican Banner," Nashville, Tennessee, April 30, 1838.

TESTIMONY

"Ranaway, Myal, 23 years old, one of his *fore teeth out*."

==========

WITNESS

Benjamin Russel, Deputy sheriff, Bibb Co. Ga. "Macon (Ga.) Telegraph," Dec. 25, 1837.

TESTIMONY

"Brought to jail John, 23 years old, *one fore tooth out*."

==========

WITNESS

F. Wisner, Master of the Work House, "Charleston (S.C.) Courier." Oct. 17, 1837.

TESTIMONY

"Committed to the Charleston Work House Tom, *two of his upper front teeth out,* about 30 years of age."

==========

WITNESS

Mr. S. Neyle, "Savannah (Ga.) Republican," July 3, 1837.

TESTIMONY

"Ranaway Peter, has lost *two front teeth* in the upper jaw."

==========

WITNESS

Mr. John McMurrain, near Columbus, "Georgia Messenger," Aug. 2, 1838.

TESTIMONY

"Ranaway, a boy named Moses, some of his *front teeth out*.

==========

WITNESS

Mr. John Kennedy, Stewart Co. La. "New Orleans Bee," April 7, 1837

TESTIMONY

"Ranaway, Sally, her *fore teeth out*."

==========

WITNESS

Mr. A. J. Hutchings, near Florence, Ala. "North Alabamian," August 25, 1838.

TESTIMONY

"Ranaway, George Winston, two of his *upper fore teeth out* immediately in front."

==========

WITNESS

Mr. James Purdon, 33 Common Street, N. O. "New Orleans Bee," Feb. 13, 1838.

TESTIMONY

"Ranaway, Jackson, has lost *one of his front teeth* ."

==========

WITNESS

Mr. Robert Calvert, in the "Arkansas State Gazette," August 22, 1838.

TESTIMONY

"Ranaway, Jack, 25 years old, has lost *one of his fore teeth.*"

==========

WITNESS

Mr. A. G. A. Beazley, in the Memphis Gazette," March 18, 1338.

TESTIMONY

"Ranaway, Abraham, 20 or 22 years of age, *his front teeth out.*"

==========

WITNESS

Mr. Samuel Townsend, in the "Huntsville [Ala.] Democrat," May 24, 1837.

TESTIMONY

"Ranaway, Dick, 18 or 20 years of age, *has one front tooth out.*"

==========

WITNESS

Mr. Philip A. Dew, in the "Virginia Herald," of May 24, 1837.

TESTIMONY

"Ranaway, Washington, about 25 years of age, has *an upper front tooth out.*"

==========

WITNESS

Mr. John Frederick, in the "Charleston Mercury," August 10, 1837.

TESTIMONY

"50 DOLLARS REWARD, for Mary, 25 or 26 years old, *one or two upper teeth out.*"

============

WITNESS

Jesse Debruhl, sheriff of Richland District, in the "Columbia [S.C.] "Telegraph," Sept. 2, 1837.

TESTIMONY

"Committed to jail, Ned, 25 or 26 years old, has lost his *two upper front teeth.*"

============

WITNESS

M. E. W. Gilbert, in the "Columbus [Ga.] Enquirer," Oct. 5. 1837.

TESTIMONY

"50 DOLLARS REWARD, for Prince, 25 or 26 years old, *one or two teeth out* in front on the upper jaw."

============

WITNESS

Publisher of the "Charleston Mercury," Aug. 31, 1838.

TESTIMONY

"Ranaway, Seller Saunders, one *fore tooth out,* about 22 years of age."

============

WITNESS

Mr. Byrd M. Grace, in the "Macon [Ga.] Telegraph," Oct. 16, 1838.

TESTIMONY

"Ranaway, Warren, about 25 or 26 years old, has lost *some of his front teeth.*"

============

WITNESS

Mr. George W. Barnes, in the "Milledgeville [Ga.] journal," May 22, 1837.

TESTIMONY

"Ranaway, Henry, about 23 years old, has one of his *upper front teeth out.*"

============

D. Herring, Warden of Baltimore Jail, in "Baltimore Chronicle," Oct. 6, 1837.

TESTIMONY
"Committed to jail Elizabeth Steward, 17 or 18 years old, has *one of her front teeth out.*"

======================

WITNESS
Mr. J. L. Colborn, in the "Huntsville [Ala.] Democrat," July 4, 1837.

TESTIMONY
"Ranaway Liley, 26 years of age, *one fore tooth gone* ."

======================

WITNESS
Samuel Harman Jr. in the "New Orleans Bee," Oct. 12, 1838.

TESTIMONY
"50 DOLLARS REWARD, for Adolphe, 28 years old, *two of his front teeth* are missing."

======================

Were it necessary, we might easily add to the preceding list, *hundreds.* The reader will remark that all the slaves, whose ages are given, are *young*—not one has arrived at middle age; consequently it can hardly be supposed that they have lost their teeth either from age or decay. The probability that their teeth were taken out by force, is increased by the fact of their being front teeth in almost every case, and from the fact that the loss of no *other* is mentioned in the advertisements. It is well known that the front teeth are not generally the first to fail. Further, it is notorious that the teeth of the slaves are remarkably sound and serviceable, that they decay far less, and at a much later period of life than the teeth of the whites: owing partly, no doubt, to original constitution; but more probably to their diet, habits, and mode of life.

As an illustration of the horrible mutilations *sometimes* suffered by them in the breaking and tearing out of their teeth, we insert the following, from the New-Orleans Bee of May 31, 1837:

$10 REWARD

Ranaway, Friday, May 12, Julia, a negress, EIGHTEEN OR TWENTY YEARS OLD. SHE HAS LOST HER UPPER TEETH AND THE UNDER ONES ARE ALL BROKEN. Said reward will be paid to whoever will bring her to her master, No. 172 Barracks-street, or lodge her in the jail.

The following is contained in the same paper:

Ranaway, Nelson, 27 years old,—"ALL HIS TEETH ARE MISSING." This advertisement is signed by "SELFER," Faubourg Marigny.

We now call the attention of the reader to a mass of testimony in support of our general proposition.

George B. Ripley, Esq. of Norwich, Connecticut, has furnished the following statement, in a letter dated Dec. 12, 1838:

"Gurdon Chapman, Esq., a respectable merchant of our city, one of our county commissioners,—last spring a member of our state legislature,— and whose character for veracity is above suspicion, about a year since visited the county of Nansemond, Virginia, for the purpose of buying a cargo of corn. He purchased a large quantity of Mr.____, with whose family he spent a week or ten days; after he returned, he related to me and several other citizens the following facts:

In order to prepare the corn for market by the time agreed upon, the slaves were worked as hard as they would bear, from daybreak until 9 or 10 o'clock at night. They were called directly from their bunks in the morning to their work, without a morsel of food until noon, when they took their breakfast and dinner, consisting of bacon and corn bread. The quantity of meat was not one tenth of what the same number of northern laborers usually have at a meal. They were allowed but fifteen minutes to take this meal, at the expiration of this time the horn was blown. The rigor, with which they enforce punctuality to its call, may be imagined from the fact, that a little boy only nine years old was whipped so severely by the driver, that in many places the whip cut through his clothes (which were of cotton,) for tardiness of not over three minutes. They then worked without intermission until 9 or 10 at night; after which they prepared and ate their second meal, as scanty as the first. An aged slave, who was remarkable for his industry and fidelity, was working with all his might on the threshing floor; amidst the clatter of the shelling and winnowing machines the master spoke to him, but he did not hear; he presently gave him several severe cuts with the raw hide, saying, at the same time, 'damn you, if you cannot hear I'll see if you can feel.' One morning the master rose from breakfast and whipped most cruelly, with a raw hide, a nice girl who was waiting on the table, for not opening a *west* window when he had told her to open an east one. The number of slaves was only forty, and yet the lash was in constant use. The bodies of all of them were literally covered with old scars.

"Not one of the slaves attended church on the Sabbath. The social relations were scarcely recognized among them, and they lived in a state of promiscuous concubinage. The master said he took pains to breed from his best stock—the whiter the progeny the higher they would sell for house servants. When asked by Mr. C. if he did not fear his slaves would run away if he whipped them so much, he replied, they know too well what they must suffer if they are taken—and then said, 'I'll tell you how I treat my runaway niggers. I had a big nigger that ran away the second time; as soon as I got track of him I took three good fellows and went in pursuit, and found him in the night, some miles distant, in a corn house; we took him and ironed him hand and foot, and carted him home. The next morning we tied him to a tree, and whipped him until there was not a sound place on his back. I then tied his ankles and hoisted him up to a *limb*—feet up and head down—we then whipped him, until the damned nigger smoked so that I thought he would take fire and burn up. We then took him down; and to make sure that he should not run away the third time, I run my knife in back of the ankles, and *cut off the large cords,*—and then I ought to have put some lead into the wounds, but I forgot it.'

"The truth of the above is from unquestionable authority; and you may publish or suppress it, as shall best subserve the cause of God and humanity."

Extract of a letter from **Stephen Sewall, Esq.**, Winthrop, Maine, dated Jan. 12th, 1839. Mr. S. is a member of the Congregational Church in Winthrop, and late agent of the Winthrop Manufacturing company.

"Being somewhat acquainted with slavery, by a residence of about five years in Alabama, and having witnessed many acts of slaveholding cruelty, I will mention one or two that came under my eye; and one of excessive cruelty mentioned to me at the time, by the gentleman (now dead,) that interfered in behalf of the slave.

"I was witness to such cruelties by an overseer to a slave that he twice attempted to drown himself, to get out of his power; this was on a raft of staves, in the Mobile River. I saw an owner take his runaway slave, tie a rope round him, then get on his horse, give the slave and horse a cut with the whip, and run the poor creature barefooted, very fast, over rough ground, where small black jack oaks had been cut up, leaving the sharp stumps, on which the slave would frequently fall; then the master would drag him as long as he could himself hold out; then stop, and whip him up on his feet again—then proceed as before. This continued until he got out of my sight, which was about half a mile. But what further cruelties this wretched man, (whose passion was so excited that he could scarcely utter a word when he took the slave into his own power,) inflicted upon his poor victim, the Day of Judgment will unfold.

"I have seen slaves severely whipped on plantations, but this *is an everyday occurrence,* and comes under the head of general treatment.

"I have known the case of a husband compelled to whip his wife. This I did not witness, though not two rods from the cabin at the time.

"I will now mention the case of cruelty before referred to. In 1820 or 21, while the public works were going forward on Dauphin Island, Mobile Bay, a contractor, engaged on the works, beat one of his slaves so severely that the poor creature had no longer power to writhe under his suffering: he then took out his knife, and began to *cut his flesh in strips, from his hips down.* At this moment, the gentleman referred to, who was also a contractor, shocked at such inhumanity, stepped forward, between the wretch and his victim, and exclaimed, "If you touch that slave again you do it at the peril of your life!." The slaveholder raved at him for interfering between him and his slave; but he was obliged to drop his victim, fearing the arm of my friend—whose stature and physical powers were extraordinary."

Extract of a letter from **Mrs. Mary Cowles**, a member of the Protestant Church at Geneva, Ashtabula County, Ohio, dated 12th, mo. 18th, 1838. Mrs. Cowles is a daughter of Mr. James Colwell of Brook County, Virginia, near West Liberty:

"In the year 1809, I think, when I was twenty-one years old, a man in the vicinity where I resided, in Brooke Co. Va. near West Liberty, by the name of Morgan, had a little slave girl about six years old, who had a habit or rather a natural infirmity common to children of that age. On this account her master and mistress would pinch her ears with hot tongs, and throw hot embers on her legs. Not being able to accomplish their object by these means, they at last resorted to a method too indelicate, and too horrible to describe in detail. Suffice it to say, it soon put an end to her life in the most excruciating manner. If further testimony to authenticate what I have stated is necessary, I refer you to Dr. Robert Mitchel who then resided in the vicinity, but now lives at Indiana, Pennsylvania, above Pittsburgh."

Mary Cowles.

Testimony of **William Ladd, Esq.**, now of Minot, Maine, formerly a slaveholder in Florida. Mr. Ladd is now the President of the American Peace Society. In a letter dated November 29, 1838, Mr. Ladd says:

"While I lived in Florida I knew a slaveholder whose name was Hutchinson, he had been a preacher and a member of the Senate of Georgia. He told me that he dared not keep a gun in his house, because he was so passionate; and that he had *been the death of three or four men.* I understood him to mean *slaves.* One of his slaves, a girl, once came to my house. She had run away from him at Indian River. The cords of one of her hands were so much contracted that her hand was useless. It was said that he had thrust her hand into the fire while he was in a fit of passion, and held it there, and this was the effect. My wife had hid the girl, when Hutchinson came for her. Out of compassion for the poor slave, I offered him more than she was worth, which he refused. We afterward let the girl escape, and I do not know what became of her, but I believe he never got her again. It was currently reported of Hutchinson, that he once knocked down a *new* negro (one recently from Africa) who was clearing up land, and who complained of the cold, as it was mid-winter. The slave was stunned with the blow. Hutchinson, supposing he had the 'sulks,' applied fire to the side of the slave until it was so roasted that he said the slave was not worth curing, and ordered the other slaves to pile on brush, and he was consumed.

"A murder occurred at the settlement, (Musquito) while I lived there. An overseer from Georgia, who was employed by a Mr. Cormick, in a fit of jealousy shot a slave of Samuel Williams, the owner of the next plantation. He was apprehended, but afterward suffered to escape. This man told me that he had rather whip a negro than sit down to the best dinner. This man had, near his house, a contrivance like that which is used in armies where soldiers are punished with the picket; by this the slave was drawn up from the earth, by a cord passing round his wrists, so that his feet could just touch the ground. It somewhat resembled a New England well sweep, and was used when the slaves were flogged.

"The treatment of slaves at Musquito I consider much milder than that which I have witnessed in the United States. Florida was under the Spanish government while I lived there. There were about fifteen or twenty plantations at Musquito. I have an indistinct recollection of four or five slaves dying of the cold in Amelia Island. They belonged to Mr. Runer of Musquito. The compensation of the overseers was a certain portion of the crop."

Gerrit Smith, Esq. of Peterboro, in a letter, dated Dec. 15, 1838, says:

"I have just been conversing with an inhabitant of this town, on the subject of the cruelties of slavery. My neighbors inform me that he is a man of veracity. The candid manner of his communication utterly forbade the suspicion that he was attempting to deceive me.

"My informant says that he resided in Louisiana and Alabama during a great part of the years 1819 and 1820;—that he frequently saw slaves whipped, never saw any killed; but often heard of their being killed;—that in several instances he had seen a slave receive, in the space of two hours, five hundred lashes—each stroke drawing blood. He adds that this severe whipping was always followed by the application of strong brine to the lacerated parts.

"My informant further says, that in the spring of 1819, he steered a boat from Louisville to New Orleans. Whilst stopping at a plantation on the east bank of the Mississippi, between Natchez and New Orleans, for the purpose of making sale of some of the articles with which the boat was freighted, he and his fellow boatmen saw a shockingly cruel punishment inflicted on a couple of slaves for the repeated offense of running away. Straw was spread over the whole of their backs, and, after being fastened by a band of the same material, was ignited, and left to burn, until entirely consumed. The agonies and screams of the sufferers he can never forget."

Dr. David Nelson, late president of Marion College, Missouri, a native of Tennessee, and till forty years old a slaveholder, said in an Anti-Slavery address at Northampton, Mass. Jan. 1839:

"I have not attempted to harrow your feelings with stories of cruelty. I will, however, mention one or two among the many incidents that came under my observation as family physician. I was one day dressing a blister, and the mistress of the house sent a little black girl into the kitchen to bring me some warm water. She probably mistook her message; for she returned with a bowl full of boiling water; which her mistress no sooner perceived, than she thrust her hand into it, and held it there till it was half cooked."

Mr. Henry H. Loomis, a member of the Presbyterian Theological Seminary in the city of New York, says, in a recent letter:

"The Rev. Mr. Hart, recently my pastor, in Otsego County, New York, and who has spent some time at the south as a teacher, stated to me that in the neighborhood in which he resided a slave was set to watch a turnip patch near an academy, in order to keep off the boys who occasionally trespassed on it. Attempting to repeat the trespass in presence of the slave, they were told that his 'master forbad it.' At this the boys were enraged, and hurled brickbats at the slave until his face and other parts were much injured and wounded—but nothing was said or done about it as an injury to the slave.

"He also said, that a slave from the same neighborhood was found out in the woods, with his arms and legs burned almost to a cinder, up as far as the elbow and knee joints; and there appeared to be but little more said or thought about it than if he had been a brute. It was supposed that his master was the cause of it—making him an example of punishment to the rest of the gang!"

The following is an extract of a letter dated March 5, 1839, from **Mr. John Clarke**, a highly respected citizen of Scriba, Oswego County, New York, and a member of the Presbyterian Church.

The 'Mrs. Turner' spoken of in Mr. C.'s letter, is the wife of Hon. Fielding S. Turner, who in 1803 resided at Lexington, Kentucky, and was the attorney for the Commonwealth. Soon after that, he removed to New Orleans, and was for many years Judge of the Criminal Court of that city. Having amassed an immense fortune, he returned to Lexington a few years since, and still resides there. Mr. C., the writer, spent the winter of 1836-7 in Lexington. He says:

"Yours of the 27th ult. is received, and I hasten to state the facts which came to my knowledge while in Lexington, respecting the occurrences about which you inquire. Mrs. Turner was originally a Boston lady. She is from 35 to 40 years of age, and the wife of Judge Turner, formerly of New Orleans, and worth a large fortune in slaves and plantations. I repeatedly heard, while in Lexington, Kentucky, during the winter of 1836-7, of the wanton cruelty practiced by this woman upon her slaves, and that she had caused several to be *whipped to death;* but I never heard that she was suspected of being deranged, otherwise than by the indulgence of an ungoverned temper, until I heard that her husband was attempting to incarcerate her in the Lunatic Asylum. The citizens of Lexington, believing the charge to be a false one, rose and prevented the accomplishment for a time, until, lulled by the fair promises of his friends, they left his domicile, and in the dead of night she was taken by force, and conveyed to the asylum. This proceeding being judged illegal by her friends, a suit was instituted to liberate her. I heard the testimony on the trial, which related only to proceedings had in order to getting her admitted into the asylum; and no facts came out relative to her treatment of her slaves, other than of a general character.

"Some days after the above trial, (which by the way did not come to an ultimate decision, as I believe) I was present in my brother's office, when Judge Turner, in a long conversation with my brother on the subject of his trials with his wife, said, *"That woman has been the immediate cause of the death of six of my servants, by her severities."* '

"I was repeatedly told, while I was there, that she drove a colored boy from the second story window, a distance of 15 to 18 feet, onto the pavement, which made him a cripple for a time.

"I heard the trial of a man for the murder of his slave, by whipping, where the evidence was to my mind perfectly conclusive of his guilt; but the jury were two of them for convicting him of manslaughter, and the rest for acquitting him; and as they could not agree were discharged—and on a subsequent trial, as I learned by the papers, the culprit was acquitted."

Rev. Thomas Savage, of Bedford, New Hampshire, in a recent letter, states the following fact:

"The following circumstance was related to me last summer, by my brother, now residing as a physician, at Rodney, Mississippi; and who, though a pro-slavery man, spoke of it in terms of reprobation, as an act of capricious, wanton cruelty. The planter who was the actor in it, I myself knew; and the whole transaction is so characteristic of the man, that, independent of the strong authority I have, I should entertain but little doubt of its authenticity. He is a wealthy planter, residing near Natchez, eccentric, capricious and intemperate. On one occasion he invited a number of guests to an elegant entertainment, prepared in the true style of southern luxury. From some cause, none of the guests appeared. In a moody humor, and under the influence, probably, of mortified pride, he ordered the overseer to call the people (a term by which the field hands are generally designated,) on to the piazza. The order was obeyed, and the people came. 'Now,' said he, 'have them seated at the table. Accordingly they were seated at the well-furnished, glittering table, while he and his overseer waited on them, and helped them to the various dainties of the feast. 'Now,' said he, after a while, raising his voice, 'take these rascals, and give them twenty lashes a piece. I'll show them how to eat at my table.' The overseer, in relating it, said he had to comply, though reluctantly, with this brutal command."

Mr. Henry P. Thompson, a native and still a resident of Nicholasville, Kentucky, made the following statement at a public meeting in Lane Seminary, Ohio, in 1833. He was at that time a slaveholder:

"*Cruelties,* said he, *are so common,* I hardly know what to relate. But one fact occurs to me just at this time that happened in the village where I live. The circumstances are these. A colored man, a slave, ran away;. As he was crossing Kentucky River, a white man, who suspected him, attempted to stop him. The negro resisted. The white man procured help, and finally succeeded in securing him. He then wreaked his vengeance on him for resisting—flogging him till he was not able to walk. They then put him on a horse, and came on with him ten miles to Nicholasville. When they entered the village, it was noticed that he sat upon his horse like a drunken man. It was a very hot day; and whilst they were taking some refreshment, the negro sat down upon the ground, under the shade. When they ordered him to go, he made several efforts before he could get up; and when he attempted to mount the horse, his strength was entirely insufficient. One of the men struck him, and with an oath ordered him to get on the horse without any more fuss. The negro staggered back a few steps, fell down, and died. I do not know that any notice was ever taken of it."

Rev. Coleman S. Hodges, a native and still a resident of Western Virginia, gave the following testimony at the same meeting:

"I have frequently seen the mistress of a family in Virginia, with whom I was well acquainted, beat the woman who performed the kitchen work, with a stick two feet and a half long, and nearly as thick as my wrist; striking her over the head, and across the small of the back, as she was bent over at her work, with as much spite as you would a snake, and for what I should consider no offense at all. There lived in this same family a young man, a slave, who was in the habit of running away. He returned one time after a week's absence. The master took him into the barn, stripped him entirely naked, tied him up by his hands so high that he could not reach the floor, tied his feet together, and put a small rail between his legs, so that he could not avoid the blows, and commenced whipping him. He told me that he gave him five hundred lashes. At any rate, he was covered with wounds from head to foot. Not a place as big as my hand but what was cut. Such things as these are perfectly common all over Virginia; at least so far as I am acquainted. Generally, planters avoid punishing their slaves before strangers."

Mr. Calvin H. Tate, of Missouri, whose father and brother were slaveholders, related the following at the same meeting. The plantation on which it occurred, was in the immediate neighborhood of his father's:

"A young woman, who was generally very badly treated, after receiving a more severe whipping than usual, ran away. In a few days she came back, and was sent into the field to work. At this time the garment next her skin was stiff like a scab, from the running of the sores made by the whipping. Towards night, she told her master that she was sick, and wished to go to the house. She went, and as soon as she reached it, laid down on the floor exhausted. The mistress asked her what the matter was? She made no reply. She asked again; but received no answer. 'I'll see,' said she, 'if I can't make you speak.' So taking the tongs, she heated them red hot, and put them upon the bottoms of her feet; then upon her legs and body; and, finally, in a rage, took hold of her throat. This had the desired effect. The poor girl faintly whispered, 'Oh, misse, don't—I am most gone;' and expired."

Extract of a letter from **Rev. C. S. Renshaw**, pastor of the Congregational Church, Quincy, Illinois.

"Judge Menzies of Boone County, Kentucky, an elder in the Presbyterian Church, and a slaveholder, told me that *he knew* some overseers in the tobacco growing region of Virginia, who, to make their slaves careful in picking the tobacco, that is taking the worms off, (you know what a loathsome thing the tobacco worm is) would make them *eat* some of the worms, and others who made them eat every worm they missed in picking."

"Mrs. Nancy Judd, a member of the Non-Conformist Church in Osnaburg, Stark County, Ohio, and formerly a resident of Kentucky, testifies that she knew a slaveholder:

"Mr. Brubecker, who had a number of slaves, among whom was one who would frequently avoid labor by hiding himself; for which he would get severe floggings without the desired effect, and that at last Mr. B. would tie large cats on his naked body and whip them to make them tear his back, in order to break him of his habit of hiding."

Rev. Horace Moulton, a minister of the Methodist Episcopal Church in Marlborough, Massachusetts, says:

"Some, when other modes of punishment will not subdue them, *cat-haul* them ; that is, take a cat by the nap of the neck and tail, or by its hind legs, and drag the claws across the back until satisfied; this kind of punishment, as 1 have understood, poisons the flesh much worse than the whip, and is more dreaded by the slave."

Rev. Abel Brown, Jr. late pastor of the first Baptist Church, Beaver, Pennsylvania, in a communication to Rev. C. P. Grosvenor, Editor of the Christian Reflector, says:

"I almost daily see the poor heart-broken slave making his way to a land of freedom. A short time since, I saw a noble, pious, distressed, spirit crushed slave, a member of the Baptist Church, escaping from a (professed Christian) bloodhound, to a land where he could enjoy that of which he had been robbed during forty years. His prayers would have made us all feel. I saw a Baptist sister of about the same age, her children had been torn from her, her head was covered with fresh wounds, while her upper lip had scarcely ceased to bleed, in consequence of a blow with the poker, which knocked out her teeth; she too, was going to a land of freedom. Only a very few days since, I saw a girl of about eighteen, with a child as white as myself, aged ten months; a Christian master was raising her child (as well his own perhaps) to sell to a southern market. She had heard of the intention, and at midnight took her only treasure and traveled twenty miles on foot through a land of strangers— she found friends."

Rev. Henry T. Hopkins, pastor of the Primitive Methodist Church in New York City, who resided in Virginia from 1821 to 1826, relates the following fact:

"An old colored man, the slave of Mr. Emerson, of Portsmouth, Virginia, being under deep conviction for sin, went into the back part of his master's garden to pour out his soul in prayer to God. For this offense he was whipped thirty-nine lashes."

Extract of a letter from **Doctor F. Julius LeMoyne,** of Washington, Pennsylvania, dated Jan. 9, 1839:

"Lest you should not have seen the statement to which I am going to allude, I subjoin a brief outline of the facts of a transaction which occurred in Western Virginia, adjacent to this county, a number of years ago—a full account of which was published in the "Witness" about two years since by Dr. Mitchell, who now resides in Indiana County, Pennsylvania. A slave boy ran away in cold weather, and during his concealment had his legs frozen; he returned, or was retaken. After some time the flesh decayed and *sloughed*—of course was offensive—he was carried out to a field and left there without bed, or shelter, *deserted to die.* His only companions were the house dogs which he called to him. After several days and nights spent in suffering and exposure, he was visited by Drs. McKitchen and Mitchell in the field, of their own accord, having heard by report of his lamentable condition; they remonstrated with the master; brought the boy to the house, amputated both legs, and he finally recovered."

Hon. James K. Paulding, the Secretary of the Navy of the U. States, in his "Letters from the South" published in 1817, relates the following:

"At one of the taverns along the road we were set down in the same room with an elderly man and a youth who seemed to be well acquainted with him, for they conversed familiarly and with true republican independence—for they did not mind who heard them. From the tenor of his conversation I was induced to look particularly at the elder. He was telling the youth something like the following detested tale. He was going, it seems, to Richmond, to inquire about a draft for seven thousand dollars, which he had sent by mail, but which, not having been acknowledged by his correspondent, he was afraid had been stolen, and the money received by the thief. 'I should not like to lose it,' said he, 'for I worked hard for it, and sold many a poor devil of a black to Carolina and Georgia, to scrape it together.' He then went on to tell many a perfidious tale. All along the road it seems he made it his business to inquire where lived a man who might be tempted to become a party in this accursed traffic, and when he had got some half dozen of these poor creatures, *he tied their hands behind their backs,* and drove them three or four hundred miles or more, bareheaded and half naked through the burning southern sun. Fearful that *even southern humanity* would revolt at such an exhibition of human misery and human barbarity, he gave out that they were runaway slaves he was carrying home to their masters. On one occasion a poor black woman exposed this fallacy, and told the story of her *being kidnapped,* and when he got her into a wood out of hearing, he beat her, to use his own expression, 'till her back was white.' It seems he married all the men and women he bought, himself, because they would sell better for being man and wife! But, asked the youth, were you not afraid, in traveling through the wild country and sleeping in lone houses, these slaves would rise and kill you?' To be sure I was,' said the other, 'but I always fastened my door, put a chair on a table before it, so that it might wake me in falling, and slept with a loaded pistol in each hand. It was a bad life, and I left it off as soon as I could live without it; for many is the time I have separated wives from husbands, and husbands from wives, and parents from children, but then I made them amends by marrying them again as soon as I had a chance, that is to say, I made them call each other man and wife, and sleep together, which is quite enough for negroes. I made one bad purchase though,' continued he. 'I bought a young mulatto girl, a lively creature, a great bargain. She had been the favorite of her master, who had lately married. The difficulty was to get her to go, for the poor creature loved her master. However, I swore most bitterly I was only going to take her to her mother's at _____ and she went with me, though she seemed to doubt me very much. But when she discovered, at last, that we were out of the state, I thought she would go mad, and in fact, the next night she drowned herself in the river close by. I lost a good five hundred dollars by this foolish trick.'" Vol. I. p. 121. .

Mr. Spillman, a native, and till recently a resident of Virginia, now a member of the Presbyterian Church in Delhi, Hamilton Co., Ohio, has furnished the two following facts, of which he had personal knowledge:

"David Stallard, of Shenandoah Co., Virginia, had a slave, who ran away; he was taken up and lodged in Woodstock jail. Stallard went with another man and took him out of the jail, tied him to their horses and started for home. The day was excessively hot, and they rode so fast, dragging the man by the rope behind them, that he became perfectly exhausted—fainted—dropped down, and died.

"Henry Jones, of Culpepper Co., Virginia, owned a slave, who ran away. Jones caught him, tied him up, and for two days, at intervals, continued to flog him, and rub salt into his mangled flesh, until his back was literally cut up. The slave sunk under the torture; and for some days it was supposed he must die. He, however, slowly recovered; though it was some weeks before he could walk."

Mr. Nathan Cole, of St. Louis, Missouri, in a letter to Mr. Arthur Tappan, of New-York, dated July 2, 1834, says:

"You will find enclosed an account of the proceedings of an inquest lately held in this city upon the body of a slave, the details of which, if published, not one in ten could be induced to believe true.* It appears that the master or mistress, or both, suspected the unfortunate wretch of hiding a bunch of keys which were missing; and to extort some explanation, which, it is more than probable, the slave was as unable to do as her mistress, or any other person, her master, Major Harney, an officer of our army, had whipped her for three successive days, and it is supposed by some, that she was kept tied during the time, until her flesh was so lacerated and torn that it was impossible for the jury to say whether it had been done with a whip or hot iron; some think both—but she was tortured to death. It appears also that the husband of the said slave had become suspected of telling some neighbor of what was going on, for which Major Harney commenced torturing him, until the man broke from him, and ran into the Mississippi and drowned himself. The man was a pious and very industrious slave, perhaps not surpassed by any in this place. The woman has been in the family of John Shackford, Esq., the present doorkeeper of the Senate of the United States, for many years; was considered an excellent servant—was the mother of a number of children—and I believe was sold into the family where she met her fate, as matter of conscience, to keep her from being sent below."

* The following is the newspaper notice referred to: An inquest was held at the dwelling house of Major Harney, in this city, on the 27th inst. by the coroner, on the body of Hannah, a slave. The jury, on their oaths, and after hearing the testimony of physicians and several other witnesses, found, that said slave "came to her death by wounds inflicted by William S. Harney."

Mr. Ezekiel Birdseye, a highly respected citizen of Cornwall, Litchfield Co., Connecticut, who resided for many years at the south, furnished to the Rev. E. R. Tyler, editor of the Connecticut Observer, the following personal testimony:

"While I lived in Limestone Co., Alabama, in 1826-7, a tavern-keeper of the village of Mooresville discovered a negro carrying away a piece of old carpet. It was during the Christmas holidays, when the slaves are allowed to visit their friends. The negro stated that one of the servants of the tavern owed him some twelve and a half or twenty-five cents, and that he had taken the carpet in payment. This the servant denied. The innkeeper took the negro to a field nearby, and whipped him cruelly. He then struck him with a stake, and punched him in the face and mouth, knocking out some of his teeth. After this, he took him back to the house, and committed him to the care of his son, who had just then come home with another young man. This was at evening. They whipped him by turns, with heavy cowskins, and made the *dogs shake him.* A Mr. Phillips, who lodged at the house, heard the cruelty during the night. On getting up he found the negro in the bar-room, terribly mangled with the whip, and his flesh so torn by the dogs, that the cords were bare. He remarked to the landlord that he was dangerously hurt, and needed care. The landlord replied that he deserved none. Mr. Phillips went to a neighboring magistrate, who took the slave home with him, where he soon died. The father and son were both tried, and acquitted!! A suit was brought, however, for damages in behalf of the owner of the slave, a young lady by the name of Agnes Jones. I *was on the jury when these facts were stated on oath.* Two men testified, one that he would have given $1000 for him, the other $900 or $950. The jury found the latter sum.

"At Union Court House, S. C, a tavern-keeper, by the name of Samuel Davis, procured the conviction and execution of his own slave, for stealing a cake of gingerbread from a grog shop. The slave raised the latch of the back door, and took the cake, doing no other injury. The shop keeper, whose name was Charles Gordon, was willing to forgive him, but his master procured his conviction and execution by hanging. The slave had but one arm; and an order on the state treasury by the court that tried him, which also assessed his value, brought him more money than he could have obtained for the slave in market."

Mr._____, an elder of the Presbyterian Church in one of the slave states, lately wrote a letter to an agent of the Anti-Slavery Society, in which he states the following fact. The name of the writer is with the Executive Committee of the American Anti-Slavery Society:

"I was passing through a piece of timbered land, and on a sudden I heard a sound as of murder; I rode in that direction, and at some distance discovered a naked black man, hung to the limb of a tree by his hands, his feet chained together, and a pine rail laid with one end on the chain between his legs, and the other upon the ground, to steady him; and in this condition the overseer gave him *four hundred lashes.* The miserably lacerated slave was then taken down, and put to the care of a physician. And what do you suppose was the offense for which all this was done? Simply this: his owner, observing that he laid off corn rows too crooked, he replied, 'Massa, much corn grow on crooked row as on straight one.' This was it—this was enough. His overseer, boasting of his skill in managing a *nigger,* he was submitted to him, and treated as above."

David L. Child, Esq., of Northampton, Massachusetts, Secretary of the United States minister at the Court of Lisbon during the administration of President Monroe, stated the following fact in an oration delivered by him in Boston, in 1834: (See Child's "Despotism of Freedom," p. 30.)

"An honorable friend, who stands high in the state and in the nation,* was *present at the* burial of a female slave in Mississippi, who *had been whipped to death* at the stake by her master, because she was gone longer of an errand to the neighboring town than her master thought necessary. Under the lash she protested that she was ill, and was obliged to rest in the fields. To complete the climax of horror, she was delivered of a dead infant while undergoing the punishment."

*The narrator of this fact is now absent from the United States, and I do not feel at liberty to mention his name."

The same fact is stated by Mrs. Child in her "Appeal." In answer to a recent letter, inquiring of Mr. and Mrs. Child if they were now at liberty to disclose the name of their informant, Mr. C. says, "The witness who stated to us the fact was John James Appleton, Esq., of Cambridge, Mass. He is now in Europe, and it is not without some hesitation that I give his name. He, however, has openly embraced our cause, and taken a conspicuous part in some anti-slavery public meetings since the time that I felt a scruple at publishing his name. Mr. Appleton is a gentleman of high talents and accomplishments. He has been Secretary of Legation at Rio Janeiro, Madrid, and The Hague; Commissioner at Naples, and Charge d' Affaires at Stockholm."

The two following facts are stated upon the authority of the **Rev. Joseph G. Wilson,** pastor of the Presbyterian Church in Salem, Washington Co., Indiana:

"In Bath Co., Kentucky, Mr. L., in the year '32 or '33, while intoxicated, in a fit of rage whipped a female slave until she fainted and fell on the floor. Then he whipped her to get up; then with red hot tongs he burned off her ears, and whipped her again! But all in vain. He then ordered his negro men to carry her to the cabin. There she was found dead next morning.

"One Wall, in Chester district, S. C, owned a slave, whom he hired to his brother-in-law, Wm. Beckman, for whom the slave worked eighteen months, and worked well. Two weeks after returning to his master he ran away on account of bad treatment. To induce him to return, the master sold him *nominally* to his neighbor, to whom the slave gave himself up, and by whom he was returned to his master:—Punishment: *stripes.* To prevent escape a bar of iron was fastened with three bands, at the waist, knee, and ankle. That night he broke the bands and bar, and escaped. Next day he was taken and whipped to death, by three men, the master, Thorn, and the overseer. First, he was whipped and driven towards home; on the way he attempted to escape, and was shot at by the master, caught, and knocked down with the butt of the gun by Thorn. In attempting to cross a ditch he fell, with his feet down, and face on the bank; they whipped in vain to get him up—he died. His soul ascended to God, to be a swift witness against his oppressors. This took place at 12 o'clock. Next evening an inquest was held. Of thirteen jurors, summoned by the coroner, nine said it was murder; two said it was manslaughter, and two said it was JUSTIFIABLE! He was bound over to court, tried, and acquitted—not even fined!"

The following fact is stated on the authority of **Mr. Wm. Willis**, of Green Plains, Clark Co. Ohio; formerly of Caroline Co. on the eastern shore of Maryland:

"Mr. W. knew a slave called Peter White, who was sold to be taken to Georgia; he escaped, and lived a long time in the woods—was finally taken. When he found himself surrounded, he surrendered himself quietly. When his pursuers had him in their possession, they shot him in the leg, and broke it, out of mere wantonness. The next day a Methodist minister set his leg, and bound it up with splints. The man who took him, then went into his place of confinement, wantonly jumped upon his leg and crushed it. His name was William Sparks."

Most of our readers are familiar with the horrible atrocities perpetrated in New Orleans, in 1834, by a certain Madame La Laurie, upon her slaves. They were published extensively in northern newspapers at the time. The following are extracts from the accounts as published in the New Orleans papers immediately after the occurrence.

The New Orleans Bee says:

"Upon entering one of the apartments, the most appalling spectacle met their eyes. Seven slaves, more or less horribly mutilated, were seen suspended by the neck, with their limbs apparently stretched and torn, from one extremity to the other. They had been confined for several months in the situation from which they had thus providentially been rescued; and had been merely kept in existence to prolong their sufferings, and to make them taste all that a most refined cruelty could inflict."

The New Orleans Mercantile Advertiser says:

"A negro woman was found chained, covered with bruises and wounds from severe flogging. All the apartments were then forced open. In a room on the ground floor, two more were found chained, and in a deplorable condition. Upstairs and in the garret, four more were found chained; some so weak as to be unable to walk, and all covered with wounds and sores. One mulatto boy declares himself to have been chained for five months, being fed daily with only a handful of meal, and receiving every morning the most cruel treatment."

The New Orleans Courier says:

"We saw one of these miserable beings.—He had a large hole in his head—his body, from head to foot, was covered with scars and filled with worms."

The New Orleans Mercantile Advertiser says:

"Seven poor unfortunate slaves were found— some chained to the floor, others with chains around their necks, fastened to the ceiling; and one poor old man, upwards of sixty years of age, chained hand and foot, and made fast to the floor, in a *kneeling position*. His head bore the appearance of having been beaten until it was broken, and the worms were actually to be seen making a feast of his brains!! A woman had her back literally cooked (if the expression may be used) with the lash; *the very bones might be seen projecting through the skin!"*

The New York Sun, of Feb. 21, 1837, contains the following: "Two negroes, runaways from Virginia, were overtaken a few days since near

~ 233 ~

Johnstown, Columbia Co. N. Y. when the persons in pursuit called out for them to stop or they would shoot them.— One of the negroes turned around and said, he would die before he would be taken, and at the moment received a rifle ball through his knee: the other started to run, but was brought to the ground by a ball being shot in his back. After receiving the above wounds they made battle with their pursuers, but were captured and brought into Johnstown. It is said that the young men who shot them had orders to take them dead or alive."

Mr. M. M. Shafter, of Townsend, Vermont, recently a graduate of the Wesleyan University at Middletown, Connecticut, makes the following statement:

"Some of the events of the Southampton, Va. insurrection were narrated to me by Mr. Benjamin W. Britt, from Riddicksville, N.C. Mr. Britt claimed the honor of having shot a black on that occasion, for the crime of disobeying Mr. Britt's imperative 'Stop!' And Mr. Ashurst, of Edenton, Georgia, told me that a neighbor of his "fired at a likely negro boy of his mother," because the said boy encroached upon his premises."

Mr. David Hawley, a class leader in the Methodist Episcopal Church at St. Albans, Licking County, Ohio, who moved from Kentucky to Ohio in 1831, certifies as follows:

"About the year 1825, a slave had escaped for Canada, but was arrested in Hardin County. On his return, I saw him in Hart County—his wrists tied together before, his arms tied close to his body, the rope then passing behind his body, thence to the neck of a horse on which rode the master, with a club about three feet long, and of the size of a hoe handle; which, by the appearance of the slave, had been used on his head, so as to wear off the hair and skin in several places, and the blood was running freely from his mouth and nose; his heels very much bruised by the horse's feet, as his master had rode on him because he *would* not go fast enough. Such was the slave's appearance when passing through where I resided. Such cases were not un-frequent."

The following is furnished by **Mr. F. A. Hart,** of Middletown, Connecticut, a manufacturer, and an influential member of the Methodist Episcopal Church. It occurred in 1824, about twenty-five miles this side of Baltimore, Maryland:

"I had spent the night with a Methodist brother; and while at breakfast, a person came in and called for help. We went out and found a crowd collected around a carriage. Upon approaching we discovered that a slave-trader was endeavoring to force a woman into his carriage. He had already put in three children, the youngest apparently about eight years of age. The woman was strong, and whenever he brought her to the side of the carriage, she resisted so effectually with her feet that he could not get her in. The woman becoming exhausted, at length, by her frantic efforts, he thrust her in with great violence, *stamped her down upon the bottom with his feet!* Shouted to the driver to go on; and away they rolled, the miserable captives moaning and shrieking, until their voices were lost in the distance."

Mr. Samuel Hall, a teacher in Marietta College, Ohio, writes as follows:

"Mr. Isaac C. Fuller is a member of the Methodist Episcopal Church in Marietta. He was a fellow student of mine while in college, and now resides in this place. He says: In 1832, as I was descending the Ohio with a flat boat, near the 'French Islands,' so called, below Cincinnati, I saw two negroes on horseback. The horses apparently took fright at something and ran. Both jumped over a rail fence; and one of the horses, in so doing, broke one of his fore-legs, falling at the same time and throwing the negro who was upon his back. A white man came out of a house not over two hundred yards distant, and came to the spot. Seizing a stake from the fence, he knocked the negro down five or six times in succession.

"In the same year I worked for a Mr. Nowland, eleven miles above Baton Rouge, La. at a place called 'Thomas' Bend.' He had an overseer who was accustomed to flog more or less of the slaves every morning. I heard the blows and screams as regularly as we used to hear the college bell that summoned us to any duty when we went to school. This overseer was a nephew of Nowland, and there were about fifty slaves on his plantation. Nowland himself related the following to me: One of his slaves ran away, and came to the Homo Chitto River, where he found no means of crossing. Here he fell in with a white man who knew his master, being on a journey from that vicinity. He induced the slave to return to Baton Rouge, under the promise of giving him a pass, by which he might escape, but, in reality, to betray him to his master. This he did, instead of fulfilling his promise. Nowland said that he took the slave and inflicted five hundred lashes upon him, cutting his back all to pieces, and then threw on hot embers. The slave was on the plantation at the time, and told me the same story. He also rolled up his sleeves, and showed me the scars on his arms, which, in consequence, appeared in places to be callous to the bone. I was with Nowland between five and six months."

Rev. John Rankin, formerly of Tennessee, now pastor of the Presbyterian Church of Ripley, Ohio, has furnished the following statement:

"The Rev. Ludwell G. Gaines, now pastor of the Presbyterian Church of Goshen, Clermont County, Ohio, stated to me, that while a resident of a slave state, he was summoned to assist in taking a man who had made his black woman work naked several days, and afterwards murdered her. The murderer armed himself, and threatened to shoot the officer who went to take him; and although there was ample assistance at hand, the officer declined further interference."

Mr. Rankin adds the following:

"A Presbyterian preacher, now resident in a slave state, and therefore it is not expedient to give his name, stated, that he saw on board of a steamboat at Louisville, Kentucky, a woman who had been forced on board, to be carried off from all she counted dear on earth. She ran across the boat and threw herself into the river, in order to end a life of intolerable sorrows. She was drawn back to the boat and taken up. The brutal driver beat her severely, and she immediately threw herself again into the river. She was hooked up again, chained, and carried off."

Testimony of **Mr. William Hansborough,** of Culpepper County, Virginia, the "owner" of sixty slaves:

"I saw a slave taken out of prison by his master, on a hot summer's day, and driven, by said master, on the road before him, till he dropped down dead."

The above statement was made by Mr. Hansborough to Lindley Coates, of Lancaster County, Pa. a distinguished member of the Society of Friends, and a member of the late Convention in Pa. for altering the State Constitution. The letter from Mr. C. containing this testimony of Mr. H. is now before us.

Mr. Tobias Boudinot, a member of the Methodist Church in St. Albans, Licking County, Ohio, says:

"In Nicholasville, Ky. in the year 1823, he saw a slave fleeing before the patrol, but he was overtaken near where he stood, and a man with a knotted cane, as large as his wrist, struck the slave a number of times on his head, until the club was broken and he made tame; the blood was thrown in every direction by the violence of the blows."

The **Rev. William Dickey**, of Bloomingburg, Fayette County, Ohio, wrote a letter to the Rev. John Rankin, of Ripley, Ohio, thirteen years since, containing a description of the *cutting up of a slave* with a broad axe; beginning at the feet and gradually cutting the legs, arms, and body into pieces! This diabolical atrocity was committed in the state of Kentucky, in the year 1807. The perpetrators of the deed were two brothers, Lilburn and Isham Lewis, NEPHEWS OF PRESIDENT JEFFERSON. The writer of this having been informed by Mr. Dickey, that some of the facts connected with this murder were not contained in his letter published by Mr. Rankin, requested him to write the account *anew,* and furnish the additional facts. This he did, and the letter containing it was published in the "Human Rights" for August, 1837. We insert it here, slightly abridged, with the introductory remarks which appeared in that paper:

"Mr. Dickey's first letter has been scattered all over the country, south and north; and though multitudes have affected to disbelieve its statements, *Kentuckians* know the truth of them quite too well to call them in question. The story is fiction or fact—if *fiction,* why has it not been nailed to the wall? Hundreds of people around the mouth of Cumberland River are personally knowing to these facts. *There* are the records of the court that tried the wretches.—*There* their acquaintances and kindred still live. All over that region of country, the brutal butchery of George is a matter of public notoriety. It is quite needless, perhaps, to add, that the Rev. Wm. Dickey is a Presbyterian clergyman, one of the oldest members of the Chillicothe Presbytery, and greatly respected and beloved by the churches in Southern Ohio. He was born in South Carolina, and was for many years pastor of a church in Kentucky.

Rev. Wm. Dickey's Letter

"In the county of Livingston, Ky. near the mouth of Cumberland River lived Lilburn Lewis, a sister's son of the celebrated Jefferson. He was the wealthy owner of a considerable gang of negroes, whom he drove constantly, fed sparingly, and lashed severely. The consequence was that they would run away. Among the rest was an ill-thrived boy of about seventeen, who, having just returned from a skulking spell, was sent to the spring for water, and in returning let fall an elegant pitcher; it was dashed to shivers upon the rocks. This was made the occasion for reckoning with him. It was night, and the slaves were all at home. The master had them all collected in the most roomy negro-house, and a rousing fire put on. When the door was secured, that none might escape, either through *fear of him* or *sympathy with George,* he opened to them the design of the interview, namely, that they might be effectually advised to *stay at home and obey his orders.* All things now in train, he called up George, who approached his master with unreserved submission. He bound him with cords; and by the assistance of Isham Lewis, his youngest brother, laid him on a broad bench, the *meatblock.* He then proceeded to *hack off George at the ankles.* It was with the *broad axe!* In vain did the unhappy victim *scream and roar!* For he was completely in his master's power; not a hand among so many durst interfere; casting the feet into the fire, he lectured them at some length.— He next *chopped him* off *below the knees!* George *roaring out* and praying his master to begin at the *other end!* He admonished them again, throwing the legs into the fire—then, above the knees, tossing the joints into the fire—the next stroke severed the thighs from the body; these were also committed to the flames—and so it may be said of the arms, head, and trunk, until all was in the fire! He threatened any of them with similar punishment who should in future disobey, run away, or disclose the proceedings of that evening. Nothing now remained but to consume the flesh and bones; and for this purpose the fire was brightly stirred until two hours after midnight; when a coarse and heavy back-wall, composed of rock and clay, covered the fire and the remains of George. It was the Sabbath—this put an end to the *amusements* of the evening. The negroes were now permitted to disperse, with charges to keep this matter among themselves, and never to whisper it in the neighborhood, under the penalty of a like punishment.

"When he returned home and retired, his wife exclaimed, 'Why, Mr. Lewis, where have you been, and what were you doing?' She had heard a strange *pounding* and dreadful *screams,* and had smelled something like fresh meat *burning.* The answer he returned was, that he had never enjoyed himself at a ball so well as he had enjoyed himself that night.

"Next morning he ordered the hands to rebuild the back-wall, and he himself superintended the work, throwing the pieces of flesh that still remained, with the bones, behind, as it went up—thus hoping to conceal the matter. But it *could not be* hid—much as the negroes seemed to hazard, they did *whisper the horrid deed.* The neighbors came, and in his presence tore down the wall; and finding the *remains* of the boy, they apprehended Lewis and his brother, and testified against them. They were committed to jail, that they might answer at the coming court for this shocking outrage; but finding security for their appearance at court, THEY WERE ADMITTED TO BAIL!

"In the interim, other articles of evidence leaked out. That of Mrs. Lewis hearing a pounding, and screaming and her smelling fresh meat burning, for not till now had this come out. He was offended with her for disclosing these things, alleging that they might have some weight against him at the pending trial.

"In connection with this is another item, full of horror. Mrs. Lewis, or her girl, in making her bed one morning after this, found, under her bolster, *a keen* BUTCHER KNIFE! The appalling discovery forced from her the confession that she considered her life in jeopardy. Messrs. Rice and Philips, whose wives were her sisters, went to see her and to bring her away if she wished it. Mr. Lewis received them with all the expressions of *Virginia hospitality.* As soon as they were seated they said, 'Well, Letitia, we supposed that you might be unhappy here, and afraid for your life; and we have come today to take you to your father's, if you desire it.' She said,' Thank you, kind brothers, I am indeed afraid for my life.'— We need not interrupt the story to tell how much surprised he affected to be with this strange procedure of his brothers-in-law, and with this declaration of his wife. But all his professions of fondness for her, to the contrary notwithstanding, they rode off with her before his eyes. He followed and overtook, and went with them to her father's; but she was locked up from him, with her own consent, and he returned home.

"Now he saw that his character was gone, his respectable friends believed that he had massacred George; but, worst of all, he saw that they considered the life of the harmless Letitia was in danger from his perfidious hands. It was too much for his chivalry to sustain. The proud Virginian sunk under the accumulated load of public odium. He proposed to his brother Isham, who had been his accomplice in the George affair, that they should finish the play of life with a still deeper tragedy. The plan was that they should shoot one another. Having made the hot-brained bargain, they repaired with their guns to the graveyard, which was on an

~ 239 ~

eminence in the midst of his plantation. It was enclosed with a railing, say thirty feet square. One was to stand at one railing and the other over against him at the other. They were to make ready, take aim, and count deliberately 1, 2, 3, and then fire. Lilburn's will was written, and thrown down open beside him. They cocked their guns and raised them to their faces; but the peradventure occurring that one of the guns might miss fire, Isham was sent for a rod, and when it was brought, Lilburn cut it off at about the length of two feet, and was showing his brother how the survivor might do provided one of the guns should fail; (for they were determined upon going together;) but forgetting, perhaps, in the perturbation of the moment that the gun was cocked, when he touched the trigger with the rod the gun fired, and he fell, and died in a few minutes—and was with George in the eternal world, where *the slave is free from his master.* But poor Isham was so terrified with this unexpected occurrence, and so confounded by the awful contortions of his brother's face, that he had not nerve enough to follow up the play and finish the plan as was intended, but suffered Lilburn to go alone. The negroes came running to see what it meant that a gun should be fired in the graveyard. There lay their master, dead! They ran for the neighbors. Isham still remained on the spot. The neighbors at the first charged him with the murder of his brother. But he, though as if he had lost more than half his mind, told the whole story; and the course or range of the ball in the dead man's body agreeing with his statement, Isham was not farther charged with Lilburn's death.

"The Court sat—Isham was judged to be guilty of a capital crime in the affair of George He was to be hanged at Salem. The day was set. My good old father visited him in the prison—two or three times talked and prayed with him; I visited him once myself. We fondly hoped that he was a sincere penitent. Before the day of execution came, by some means, I never knew what, Isham was *missing.* About two years after, we learned that he had gone down to Natchez, and had married a lady of some refinement and piety. I saw her letters to his sisters, who were worthy members of the church of which I was pastor. The last letter told of his death. He was in Jackson's army, and fell in the famous battle of New Orleans. "I am, sir, your friend,   Wm. Dickey."

PERSONAL NARRATIVES-PART III

Mr. Hawley is the pastor of the Baptist Church in Colebrook, Litchfield County, Connecticut. He has resided fourteen years in the slave states, North and South Carolina. His character and standing with his own denomination at the south, may be inferred from the fact, that the Baptist State Convention of North Carolina appointed him, a few years since, their general agent to visit the Baptist churches within their bounds, and to secure their co-operation in the objects of the Convention. Mr. H. accepted the appointment, and for some time traveled in that capacity.

"I rejoice that the Executive Committee of the American Anti-Slavery Society has resolved to publish a volume of facts and testimony relative to the character and workings of American slavery. Having resided fourteen years at the south, I cheerfully comply with your request, to give the result of my observation and experience.

And I would here remark, that one may reside at the south for years, and not witness extreme cruelties; a northern man, and one who is not a slaveholder, would be the last to have an opportunity of witnessing the infliction of cruel punishments.

PLANTATIONS

"A majority of the large plantations are on the banks of rivers, far from the public eye. A great deal of low marshy ground lies in the vicinity of most of the rivers at the south; consequently the main roads are several miles from the rivers, and generally no *public* road passes the plantations. A stranger traveling on the *ridge,* would think himself in a miserably poor country; but every two or three miles he will see a road turning off, and leading into the swamp; taking one of those roads, and traveling from two to six miles, he will come to a large gate; passing which, he will find himself in a clearing of several hundred acres of the first quality of land; passing on, he will see 30, or 40, or more slaves—men, women, boys and girls, at their task, every one with a hoe; or, if in cotton picking season, with their baskets. The overseer, with his whip, either riding or standing about among them; or if the weather is hot, sitting under a shade. At a distance, on a little rising ground, if such there be, he will see a cluster of huts, with a tolerable house in the midst, for the overseer. Those huts are from ten to fifteen feet square, built of logs, and covered, not with shingles, but with boards, about four feet long, split out of pine timber with a *'frow'* The floors are very commonly made in this way. Clay is first worked until it is soft; it is then spread upon the ground, about four or five inches thick; when it dries, it becomes nearly as hard as a brick. The crevices between the logs are sometimes filled with the same. These huts generally cost the master nothing—they are commonly built by the negroes at night, and on Sundays. When a slave of a neighboring plantation takes a wife, or to use the phrase common at the south, 'takes up' with one of the women, he builds a hut, and it is called her house. Upon entering these huts, (not as comfortable in many instances as the horse stable,) generally, you will find no chairs, but benches and stools; no table, no bedstead, and no bed, except a blanket or two, and a few rags or moss; in some instances a knife or two, but very rarely a fork. You may also find a pot or skillet, and generally a number of gourds, which serve them instead of bowls and plates. The cruelties practiced on those secluded plantations, the judgment day alone can reveal. Oh, brother, could I summon ten slaves from ten plantations that I could name, and have them give but one year's history of their bondage, it would thrill the land with horror. Those overseers, who follow the business of overseeing for a livelihood, are generally the most unprincipled and abandoned of men. Their wages are regulated according to their skill in extorting labor. The one who can make the most bags of cotton, with a given number of hands, is the one generally sought after; and there is a competition among them to see who shall make the largest crop, according to the hands he works. I ask, what must be the condition of the poor slaves, under the unlimited power of such men, in whom, by the long-continued practice of the most heart-rending cruelties, every feeling of humanity has been obliterated? But it may be asked, cannot the slaves have redress by appealing to their masters? In many instances it is impossible, as their masters live hundreds of miles off. There are perhaps thousands in the northern slave states, [and many in the free states,] who own plantations in the southern slave states, and many more spend their summers at the north, or at the various watering places. But what would the slaves gain, if they should appeal to the master? He has placed the overseer over them, with the understanding that he will make as large a crop as possible, and that he is to have entire control, and manage them according to his own judgment. Now, suppose that in the midst of the season, the slaves make complaint of cruel treatment. The master cannot get along without an overseer—it is perhaps very sickly on the plantation—he dare not risk his own life there. Overseers are all engaged at that season, and if he takes part with his slaves against the overseer, he would destroy his authority, and very likely provoke him to leave his service— which would of course be a very great injury to him. Thus, in nineteen cases out of twenty, self-interest would prevent the master from paying any attention to the complaints of his slaves. And, if any should complain, it would of course come to the ears of the overseer, and the complainant would be inhumanly punished for it.

CLOTHING

"The rule, where slaves are hired out, is two suits of clothes per year, one pair of shoes, and one blanket; but as it relates to the great body of the slaves, this cannot be called a general rule. On many plantations, the children under ten or twelve years old, go *entirely naked*—or, if clothed at all, they have nothing more than a shirt. The cloth is of the coarsest kind, far from being durable or warm; and their shoes frequently come to pieces in a few weeks. I have never known any provision made, or time allowed for the washing of clothes. If they wish to wash, as they have generally but one suit, they go after their day's toil to some stream, build a fire, pull off their clothes and wash them in the stream, and dry them by the fire; and in some instances they wear their clothes until they are worn off, without washing. I have never known an instance of a slaveholder putting himself to any expense, that his slaves might have decent clothes for the Sabbath. If, by making baskets, brooms, mats, &c. at night or on Sundays, the slaves can get money enough to buy a Sunday suit, very well. I have never known an instance of a slaveholder furnishing his slaves with stockings or mittens. I *know* that the slaves suffer much, and no doubt many die in consequence of not being well clothed.

FOOD

"In the grain-growing part of the south, the slaves, as it relates to food, fare tolerably well; but in the cotton, and rice growing, and sugar-making portion, some of them fare badly. I have been on plantations where, from the appearance of the slaves, I should judge they were half-starved. They receive their allowance very commonly on Sunday morning. They are left to cook it as they please, and when they please. Many slaveholders rarely give their slaves meat, and very few give them more food than will keep them in a working condition. They rarely ever have a *change* of food. I have never known an instance of slaves on plantations being furnished either with sugar, butter, cheese, or milk.

WORK

"If the slaves on plantations were well fed and clothed, and had the stimulus of wages, they could perhaps in general perform their tasks without injury. The horn is blown soon after the dawn of day, when all the hands destined for the field must be 'on the march.' If the field is far from their huts, they take their breakfast with them. They toil till about ten o'clock, when they eat it. They then continue their toil till the sun is set.

"A neighbor of mine, who has been an overseer in Alabama, informs me, that there, they ascertain how much labor a slave can perform in a day, in the following manner. When they commence a new cotton field, the overseer takes his watch, and marks how long it takes them to hoe one row, and then lays off the task accordingly. My neighbor also informs me, that the slaves in Alabama are worked very hard; that the lash is almost universally applied at the close of the day, if they fail to perform their task in the cotton picking season. You will see them, with their baskets of cotton, slowly bending their way to the cotton house, where each one's basket is weighed. They have no means of knowing accurately, in the course of the day, how they make progress; so that they are in suspense, until their basket is weighed. Here comes the mother, with her children; she does not know whether herself, or children, or all of them, must take the lash; they cannot weigh the cotton themselves—the whole must be trusted to the overseer. While the weighing goes on, all is still. So many pounds short, cries the overseer, and takes up his whip, exclaiming, 'Step this way, you d—n lazy scoundrel,' or 'bitch.' The poor slave begs, and promises, but to no purpose. The lash is applied until the overseer is satisfied. Sometimes the whipping is deferred until the weighing is all over. I have said that all must be *trusted* to the overseer. If he owes any one a grudge, or wishes to enjoy the fiendish pleasure of whipping a little, (for some overseers really delight in it,) they have only to tell a falsehood relative to the weight of their basket; they can then have a pretext to gratify their diabolical disposition; and from the character of overseers, I have no doubt that it is frequently done. On all plantations, the male and female slaves fare pretty much alike; those who are with child are driven to their task till within a few days of the time of their delivery; and when the child is a few weeks old, the mother must again go to the field. If it is far from her hut, she must take her babe with her, and leave it in the care of some of the children—perhaps of one not more than four or five years old, If the child cries, she cannot go to its relief; the eye of the overseer is upon her; and if, when she goes to nurse it, she stays a little longer than the overseer thinks necessary, he commands her back to her task, and perhaps a husband and father must hear and witness it all. Brother, you cannot begin to know what the poor slave mothers suffer, on thousands of plantations at the south!

"I will now give a few facts, showing the workings of the system. Some years since, a Presbyterian minister moved from North Carolina to Georgia. He had a negro man of an uncommon mind. For some cause, I know not what, this minister whipped him most unmercifully. He next nearly *drowned* him; he then put him *in the fence;* this is done by lifting up the corner of a 'worm' fence, and then putting the feet through; the rails serve as *stocks.* He kept him there some time, how long I was not informed, but the poor slave *died* in a few days; and, if I was rightly informed, nothing was done about it, either in church or state. After some time, he moved back to North Carolina, and is now a member of

~ 245 ~

Presbytery. I have heard him preach, and have been in the pulpit with him. May God forgive me!

"At Laurel Hill, Richmond County, North Carolina, it was reported that a runaway slave was in the neighborhood. A number of young men took their guns, and went in pursuit. Some of them took their station near the stage road, and kept on the look-out. It was early in the evening—the poor slave came along, when the ambush rushed upon him, and ordered him to surrender. He refused, and kept them off with his club. They still pressed upon him with their guns presented to his breast. Without seeming to be daunted, he caught hold of the muzzle of one of the guns, and came near getting possession of it. At length, retreating to a fence on one side of the road, he sprang over into a cornfield, and started to run in one of the rows. One of the young men stepped to the fence, fired, and lodged the whole charge between his shoulders; he fell, and died in a short time. He died without telling who his master was, or whether he had any, or what his own name was, or where he was from. A hole was dug by the side of the road his body tumbled into it, and thus ended the whole matter.

"The Rev. Mr. C. a Methodist minister, held as his slave a negro man, who was a member of his own church. The slave was considered a very pious man, had the confidence of his master, and all who knew him, and if I recollect right, he sometimes attempted to preach. Just before the Nat Turner insurrection, in Southampton County, Virginia, by which the whole south was thrown into a panic, this worthy slave obtained permission to visit his relatives, who resided either in Southampton, or the county adjoining. This was the only instance that ever came to my knowledge, of a slave being permitted to go so far to visit his relatives. He went and returned according to agreement. A few weeks after his return, the insurrection took place, and the whole country was deeply agitated. Suspicion soon fixed on this slave. Nat Turner was a Baptist minister, and the south became exceedingly jealous of all negro preachers. It seemed as if the whole community was impressed with the belief that he knew all about it; that he and Nat Turner had concerted an extensive insurrection; and so confident were they in this belief, that they took the poor slave, tried him, and hung him. It was all done in a few days. He protested his innocence to the last. After the excitement was over, many were ready to acknowledge that they believed him innocent. He was hung upon *suspicion!*

"In R____ County, North Carolina, lived a Mr. B. who had the name of being a cruel master. Three or four winters since, his slaves were engaged in clearing a piece of new land. He had a negro girl, about 14 years old, whom he had severely whipped a few days before, for not performing her task. She again failed. The hands left the field for home; she went with them a part of the way, and fell behind; but the negroes thought she would soon be along; the evening passed away, and she did not come. They finally concluded that she had gone back to the new ground to lie by the log heaps that were on fire. But they were mistaken: she had sat down by the foot of a large pine. She was thinly clad—the night was cold and rainy. In the morning the poor girl was found, but she was speechless and died in a short time.

"One of my neighbors sold to a speculator, a negro boy, about 14 years old. It was more than his poor mother could bear. Her reason fled, and she became a perfect *maniac*, and had to be kept in close confinement. She would occasionally get out and run off to the neighbors. On one of these occasions she came to my house. She was indeed a pitiable object. With tears rolling down her cheeks, and her frame shaking with agony, she would cry out, '*don't you hear him—they are whipping him now, and he is calling for me.*" This neighbor of mine, who tore the boy away from his poor mother, and thus broke her heart, was a *member of the Presbyterian Church.*

"Mr. S____, of Marion District, South Carolina, informed me that a boy was killed by the overseer on Mr. P____ 's plantation. The boy was engaged in driving the horses in a cotton gin. The driver generally sits on the end of the sweep. Not driving to suit the overseer, he knocked him off with the butt of his whip, his skull was fractured. He died in a short time.

"A man of my acquaintance in South Carolina, and of considerable wealth, had an only son, whom he educated for the bar; but not succeeding in his profession, he soon returned home. His father having a small plantation three or four miles off, placed his son on it as an overseer. Following the example of his father, as I have good reason to believe, he took the wife of one of the negro men. The poor slave felt himself greatly injured, and expostulated with him. The wretch took his gun, and deliberately shot him. Providentially he only wounded him badly. When the father came, and undertook to remonstrate with his son about his conduct, he threatened to shoot him also! And finally, took the negro woman, and went to Alabama, where he still resided when I left the south.

"An elder in the Presbyterian Church related to me the following: 'A speculator with his drove of negroes was passing my house, and I bought a little girl, nine or ten years old. After a few months, I concluded that I would rather have a plough-boy. Another speculator was passing, and I sold the girl. She was much distressed, and was very unwilling to leave.' She had been with him long enough to become attached to his own and his negro children, and he concluded by saying, that in view of the little girl's tears and cries, he had determined never to do the like again. I would not trust him, for I know him to be a very avaricious man.

"While traveling in Anson County, North Carolina, I put up for a night at a private house. The man of the house was not at home when I stopped, but came in the course of the evening, and was noisy and profane, and nearly drunk. I retired to rest, but not to sleep; his cursing and swearing were enough to keep a regiment awake. About midnight he went to his kitchen, and called out his two slaves, a man and woman. His object, he said, was to whip them. They both begged and promised, but to no purpose. The whipping began, and continued for some time. Their cries might have been heard at a distance.

"I was acquainted with a very wealthy planter, on the Pedee River, in South Carolina, who has since died in consequence of intemperance. It was said that he had occasioned the death of twelve of his slaves, by compelling them to work in water, opening a ditch in the midst of winter. The disease with which they died was pleurisy.

"In crossing Pedee River, at Cashway Ferry, I observed that the ferryman had no hair on either side of his head. I asked him the cause. He informed me that it was caused by his master's cane. I said, you have a very bad master. 'Yes, a very bad master.' I understood that he was once a member of Congress from South Carolina.

"While traveling as agent for the North Carolina Baptist State Convention, I attended a three days' meeting in Gates County. Friday, the first day, passed off. Saturday morning came, and the pastor of the church, who lived a few miles off, did not make his appearance. The day passed off, and no news from the pastor. On Sabbath morning, he came hobbling along, having but little use of one foot. He soon explained; said he had a hired negro man, who, on Saturday morning, gave him a 'little slack jaw.' Not having a stick at hand, he fell upon him with his fist and foot, and in kicking him, he injured his foot so seriously, that he could not attend meeting on Saturday.

"Some of the slaveholding ministers at the south, put their slaves under overseers, or hire them out, and then take the pastoral care of churches. The Rev. Mr. B____, formerly of Pennsylvania, had a plantation in Marlborough District, South Carolina, and was the pastor of a church in Darlington District. The Rev. Mr. T___, of Johnson County, North Carolina, has a plantation in Alabama.

"I was present, and saw the Rev. J____ W____, of Mecklenburg County, North Carolina, hire out four slaves to work in the gold mines in Burke County. The Rev. H____M____ of Orange County sold for $900, a negro man to a speculator, on a Monday of a camp meeting.

"Runaway slaves are frequently hunted with guns and dogs. I was once out on such an excursion, with my rifle and two dogs. I trust the Lord has forgiven me this heinous wickedness! We did not take the runaways.

"Slaves are sometimes most unmercifully punished for trifling offenses, or mere mistakes.

"As it relates to amalgamation, I can say, that I have been in respectable families, (so called,) where I could distinguish the family resemblance in

~ 249 ~

the slaves who waited upon the table. I once hired a slave who belonged to his own uncle. It is so common for the female slaves to have white children, that little or nothing is ever said about it. Very few inquiries are made as to who the father is.

"Thus, brother—, I have given you very briefly, the result, in part, of my observations and experience relative to slavery. You can make what disposition of it you please. I am willing that my name should go to the world with what I have now written.

"Yours affectionately, for the oppressed,
"FRANCIS HAWLEY."
Colebrook, Connecticut, March 18, 1839.

TESTIMONY OF REUBEN G. MACY AND RICHARD MACY

The following is an extract of a letter recently received from Charles Marriott of Hudson, New York. Mr. Marriott is an elder in the Religious Society of Friends, and is extensively known and respected:

"The two following brief statements, are furnished by Richard Macy and Reuben G. Macy, brothers, both of Hudson, New York. They are head carpenters by trade, and have been well known to me for more than thirty years, as esteemed members of the Religious Society of Friends. They inform me that during their stay in South Carolina, a number more similar cases to those here related, came under their notice, which to avoid repetition they omit.

C. Marriott.

TESTIMONY OF REUBEN G. MACY

"During the winter of 1818 and 19, I resided on an island near the mouth of the Savannah River, on the South Carolina side. Most of the slaves that came under my particular notice, belonged to a widow and her daughter, in whose family I lived. No white man belonged to the plantation. Her slaves were under the care of an overseer who came once a week to give orders, and settled the score laid up against such as their mistress thought deserved punishment, which was from twenty-five to thirty lashes on their naked backs with a whip which the overseer generally brought with him. This whip had a stout handle about two feet long, and a lash about four and a half feet. From two to four received the above, I believe nearly every week during the winter, sometimes in my presence, and always in my hearing. I examined the backs and shoulders of a number of the men, which were mostly naked while they were about their labor, and found them covered with hard ridges in every direction. One day, while busy in the cotton house, hearing a noise, I ran to the door and saw a colored woman pleading with the overseer, who paid no attention to her cries, but tied her hands together, and passed the rope over a beam, over head, where was a platform for spreading cotton, he then drew the rope as tight as he could, so as to let her toes touch the ground; then stripped her body naked to the waist, and went deliberately to work with his whip, and put on twenty-five or thirty lashes, she pleading in vain all the time. I inquired, the cause of such treatment, and was informed it was for answering her mistress rather '*short.* '"

"A woman from a neighboring plantation came where I was, on a visit; she came in a boat rowed by six slaves, who, according to the common practice, were left to take care of themselves, and having laid them down in the boat and fallen asleep, the tide fell, and the water filling the stern of the boat, wet their mistresses trunk of clothes. When she discovered it, she called them up near where I was, and compelled them to whip each other, till they all had received a severe flogging. She was standing by with a whip in her hand to see that they did not spare each other. Their usual allowance of food was one peck of corn per week, which was dealt out to them every first day of the week and such as was not there to receive their portion at the appointed time, had to live as they could during the coming week. Each one had the privilege of planting a small piece of ground, and raising poultry for their own use which they generally sold, that is, such as did improve the privilege which were but few. They had nothing allowed them besides the corn, except one quarter of beef at Christmas which a slave brought three miles on his head. They were allowed three days rest at Christmas. Their clothing consisted of a pair of trowsers and jacket, made of whitish woolen cloth called negro cloth. The women had nothing but a petticoat, and a very short short-gown, made of the same kind of cloth. Some of the women had an old pair of shoes, but they generally went *barefoot.* The houses for the field slaves were about fourteen feet square, built in the coarsest manner, having but one room, without any chimney, or flooring, with a hole at the roof at one end to let the smoke out."Each one was allowed one blanket in which they rolled themselves up. I examined their houses but could not discover anything like a bed. I was informed that when they had a sufficiency of potatoes the slaves were allowed some; but the season that I was there they did not raise more than were wanted for seed. All their corn was ground in one hand-mill, every night just as much as was necessary for the family, then each one his daily portion, which took considerable time in the night. I often awoke and heard the sound of the mill. Grinding the corn in the night, and in the dark, after their day's labor, and the want of other food, were great hardships.

"The traveling in those parts, among the islands, was altogether with boats, rowed by from four to ten slaves, which often stopped at our plantation, and staid through the night, when the slaves, after rowing through the day, were left to shift for themselves; and when they went to Savannah with a load of cotton they were obliged to sleep in the open boats, as the law did not allow a colored person to be out after eight o'clock in the evening, without a pass from his master."

TESTIMONY OF RICHARD MACY

"The above account is from my brother. I was at work on Hilton Head about twenty miles north of my brother, during the same winter. The same allowance of one peck of corn for a week, the same kind of houses to live in, and the same method of grinding their corn, and always in the night, and in the dark, was practiced there.

"A number of instances of severe whipping came under my notice. The first was this:—two men were sent out to saw some blocks out of large live oak timber on which to raise my building. Their saw was in poor order, and they sawed them badly, for which their master stripped them naked and flogged them.

"The next instance was a boy about sixteen years of age. He had crept into the coach to sleep; after two or three nights he was caught by the coach driver, a *northern man,* and stripped *entirely naked, and whipped without mercy, his master looking on.*

"Another instance: The overseer, a young white man, had ordered several negroes, a boat's crew, to be on the spot at a given time. One man did not appear until the boat had gone. The overseer was very angry and told him to *strip and be flogged;* he being slow, was told if he did not instantly strip off his jacket, he, the overseer, would whip it off, which he did in shreds, whipping him cruelly.

"The man ran into the barrens and it was about a month before they caught him. He was *nearly starved*, and at last stole a turkey; then another, and was caught.

"Having occasion to pass a plantation very early one foggy morning, in a boat, we heard the sound of the *whip*, before we could see, but as we drew up in front of the plantation, we could see the negroes at work in the field. The overseer was going from one to the other causing them to lay down their hoe, strip off their garment, hold up their hands and receive their number of *lashes*. Thus he went on from one to the other until we were out of sight. In the course of the winter a family came where I was, on a visit from a neighboring island; of course, in a boat with negroes to row them—one of these a barber, told me that he ran away about two years before, and joined a company of negroes who had fled to the swamps. He said they suffered a great deal—were at last discovered by a party of hunters, who fired among them, and caused them to scatter. Himself and one more fled to the coast, took a boat and put off to sea, a storm came on and swamped or upset them, and his partner was drowned, he was taken up by a passing vessel and returned to his master.

Richard Macy.

Hudson, 12 mo. 29th, 1838

TESTIMONY OF MR. ELEAZAR POWELL

EXTRACT OF A LETTER FROM Mr. WILLIAM SCOTT, a highly respectable citizen of Beaver Co. Pennsylvania, dated Jan. 7, 1839:

Chippewa Township, Beaver Co. Pa.

Jan. 7, 1839.

"I send you the statement of Mr. Eleazar Powell, who was born, and has mostly resided in this township from his birth. His character for sobriety and truth stands above impeachment. With sentiments of esteem, I am your friend,   WILLIAM SCOTT

"In the month of December, 1836, I went to the State of Mississippi to work at my trade, (masonry and bricklaying,) and continued to work in the counties of Adams and Jefferson, between four and five months. In following my business I had an opportunity of seeing the treatment of slaves in several places.

"In Adams County I built a chimney for a man named Joseph Gwatney; he had forty-five field hands of both sexes. The field in which they worked at that time, lay about two miles from the house; the hands had to cook and eat their breakfast, prepare their dinner, and be in the field at daylight, and continue there till dark. In the evening the cotton they had picked was weighed, and if they fell short of their task they were whipped. One night I attended the weighing—two women fell short of their task, and the master ordered the black driver to take them to the quarters and flog them; one of them was to receive twenty-five lashes and pick a peck of cotton seed. I have been with the overseer several times through the negro quarters. The huts are generally built of split timber, some larger than rails, twelve and a half feet wide and fourteen feet long—some with and some without chimneys, and generally without floors; they were generally without daubing, and mostly had split clapboards nailed on the cracks on the outside, though some were without even that; in some there was a kind of rough bedstead, made from rails, polished with the axe, and put together in a very rough manner, the bottom covered with clapboards, and over that a bundle of worn out clothes. In some huts there was no bedstead at all. The above description applies to the places generally with which I was acquainted, and they were mostly *old settlements*.

"In the east part of Jefferson County I built a chimney for a man named____M'Coy. He had forty-seven laboring hands. Near where I was at work, M'Coy had ordered one of his slaves to set a post for a gate. When he came to look at it, he said the slave had not set it in the right place; and ordered him to strip, and lie down on his face; telling him that if he struggled, or attempted to get up, two men, who had been called to the spot, should seize and hold him fast. The slave agreed to be quiet, and M'Coy commenced flogging him on the bare back, with the wagon whip. After some time the sufferer attempted to get up; one of the slaves standing by, seized him by the feet and held him fast; upon which he yielded, and M'Coy continued to flog him ten or fifteen minutes. When he was up, and had put on his trowsers, the blood came through them.

"About half a mile from M'Coy's was a plantation owned by his stepdaughter. The overseer's name was James Farr, of whom it appears Mrs. M'Coy's waiting woman was enamored. One night, while I lived there, M'Coy came from Natchez, about 10 o'clock at night. He said that Dinah was gone, and wished his overseer to go with him to Farr's lodgings.

They went accordingly, one to each door, and caught Dinah as she ran out, she was partly dressed in her mistress's clothes; M'Coy whipped her unmercifully, and she afterwards made her escape. On the next day, (Sabbath), M'Coy came to the overseer's, where I lodged, and requested him and me to look for her, as he was afraid that she had hanged herself. He then gave me the particulars of the flogging. He stated that near Farr's he had made her strip and lie down, and had flogged her until he was tired; that before he reached home he had a second time made her strip, and again flogged her until he was tired; that when he reached home he had tied her to a peach-tree, and after getting a drink had flogged her until he was thirsty again; and while he went to get a drink the woman made her escape. He stated that he knew, from the whipping he had given her, there must be in her back cuts an inch deep. He showed the place where she had been tied to the tree; there appeared to be as much blood as if a hog had been stuck there. The woman was found on Sabbath evening, near the spring, and had to be carried into the house.

"While I lived there I heard M'Coy say, if the slaves did not raise him three hundred bales of cotton the ensuing season, he would kill every negro he had.

"Another case of flogging came under my notice:—Philip O. Hughes, sheriff of Jefferson County, had hired a slave to a man, whose name I do not recollect. On a Sabbath day the slave had drank somewhat freely; he was ordered by the tavern keeper, (where his present master had left his horse and the negro,) to stay in the kitchen; the negro wished to be out. In persisting to go out he was knocked down three times; and afterwards flogged until another young man and myself ran about half a mile, having been drawn by the cries of the negro and the sound of the whip. When we came up, a number of men that had been about the tavern, were whipping him, and at intervals would ask him if he would take off his clothes. At seeing them drive down the stakes for a regular flogging he yielded, and took them off. They then flogged him until satisfied. On the next morning I saw him, and his pantaloons were all in a gore of blood.

"During my stay in Jefferson County, Philip O. Hughes was out one day with his gun—he saw a negro at some distance, with a club in one hand and an ear of corn in the other—Hughes stepped behind a tree, and waited his approach; he supposed the negro to be a runaway, who had escaped about nine months before from his master, living not very far distant. The negro discovered Hughs before he came up, and started to run; he refusing to stop, Hughes fired, and shot him through the arm. Through loss of blood the negro was soon taken and put in jail. I saw his wound twice dressed, and heard Hughes make the above statement.

"When in Jefferson County I boarded six weeks in Fayette, the county town, with a tavern keeper named James Truly. He had a slave named Lucy, who occupied the station of chamber maid and table waiter. One day, just after dinner, Mrs. Truly took Lucy and bound her arms round a pine sapling behind the house, and commenced flogging her with a riding-whip; and when tired would take her chair and rest. She continued thus, alternately flogging and resting, for at least an hour and a half. I afterwards learned from the barkeeper, and others, that the woman's offense was that she had bought two candles to set on the table the evening before, not knowing there were yet some in the box. I did not see the act of flogging above related; but it was commenced before I left the house after dinner; and my work not being more than twenty rods from the house, I distinctly heard the cries of the woman all the time, and the manner of tying I had from those who did see it.

"While I boarded at Truly's, an overseer shot a negro about two miles northwest of Fayette, belonging to a man named Hinds Stuart. I heard Stuart himself state the particulars. It appeared that the negro's wife fell under the overseer's displeasure, and he went to whip her. The negro said she should not be whipped. The overseer then let her go, and ordered him to be seized. The negro, having been a driver, rolled the lash of his whip round his hand, and said he would not be whipped at that time. The overseer repeated his orders. The negro took up a hoe, and none dared to take hold of him. The overseer then went to his coat, that he had laid off to whip the negro's wife, and took out his pistol and shot him dead. His master ordered him to be buried in a hole without a coffin. Stuart stated that he would not have taken two thousand dollars for him. No punishment was inflicted on the overseer. ELEAZAR POWELL, Jr."

TESTIMONY ON THE AUTHORITY OF REV. WM. SCALES
LYNDON, VT.

The following is an extract of a letter from two professional gentlemen and their wives, who have lived for some years in a small village in one of the slave states. They are all persons of the highest respectability, and are well known in at least one of the New England states. Their names are with the Executive Committee of the American Anti-Slavery Society; but as the individuals would doubtless be murdered by the slaveholders, if they were published, the Committee feel sacredly bound to withhold them. The letter was addressed to a respected clergyman in New England. The writers say:

"A man near us owned a valuable slave—his best—most faithful servant. In a gust of passion, he struck him dead with a lever, or stick of wood.

"During the years '36 and '37, the following transpired. A slave in our neighborhood ran away and went to a place about thirty miles distant. There he was found by his pursuers on horseback, and compelled by the whip to *run* the distance of thirty miles. It was an exceedingly hot day— and within a few hours after he arrived at the end of his journey the slave was dead.

"Another slave ran away, but concluded to return. He had proceeded some distance on his return, when he was met by accompany of two or three drivers, who raced, whipped and abused him until he fell down and expired. This took place on the Sabbath."

The writer after speaking of another murder of a slave in the neighborhood, without giving the circumstances, says:

"There is a powerful New England influence at____ the village where they reside. We may therefore suppose that there would be as little of barbarian cruelty practiced there as anywhere;—at least we might suppose that the average amount of cruelty in that vicinity would be sufficiently favorable to the side of slavery.—Describe a circle, the centre of which shall be____, the residence of the writers, and the radius fifteen miles, and in about one year, three, and I think four slaves have been *murdered*, within that circle, under circumstances of horrid cruelty.—What must have been the amount of murder in the whole slave territory? The whole south is rife with the crime of separating husbands and wives, parents and children."

TESTIMONY OF JOSEPH IDE, ESQ.

Mr. Ide is a respected member of the Baptist Church in Sheffield, Caledonia County, Vt.; and recently the Postmaster in that town. He spent a few months at the south in the years 1837 and 8. In a letter to the Rev.

Wm. Scales of Lyndon, Vt. written a few weeks since, Mr. Ide writes as follows:

"In answering the proposed inquiries, I will say first, that although there are various other modes resorted to, whipping with the cowskin is the usual mode of inflicting punishment on the poor slave. I have never actually witnessed a whipping scene, for they are usually taken into some back place for that purpose; but I have often heard their groans and screams while writhing under the lash; and have seen the blood flow from their torn and lacerated skins after the vengeance of the inhuman master or mistress had been glutted. You ask if the woman where I boarded whipped a slave to death. I can give you the particulars of the transaction as they were related to me. My informant was a gentleman—a member of the Presbyterian Church in Massachusetts—who the winter before boarded where I did. He said that Mrs. T_____ had a female slave, whom she used to whip unmercifully, and on one occasion, she whipped her as long as she had strength, and after the poor creature was suffered to go, she crawled off into a cellar. As she did not immediately return, search was made, and she was found dead in the cellar, and the horrid deed was kept a secret in the family, and it was reported that she died of sickness. This wretch at the same time was a member of a Presbyterian Church. Towards her slaves she was certainly the most cruel wretch of any woman with whom I was ever acquainted—yet she was nothing more than a slaveholder. She would deplore slavery as much as I did, and often told me she was much of an abolitionist as I was. She was constant in the declaration that her kind treatment to her slaves was proverbial. Thought I, then the Lord have mercy on the rest. She has often told me of the cruel treatment of the slaves on a plantation adjoining her father's in the low country of South Carolina. She says she has often seen them driven to the necessity of eating frogs and lizards to sustain life. As to the mode of living generally, my information is rather limited, being with few exceptions confined to the different families where I have boarded. My stopping places at the south have mostly been in cities. In them the slaves are better fed and clothed than on plantations. The house servants are fed on what the families leave. But they are kept short, and I think are oftener whipped for stealing something to eat than any other crime. On plantations their food is principally hominy, as the southerners call it. It is simply cracked com boiled. This probably constitutes seven eights of their living. The house-servants in cities are generally decently clothed, and some favorite ones are richly dressed, but those on the plantations, especially in their dress, if it can be called dress, exhibit the most haggard and squalid appearance. I have frequently seen those of both sexes more than two-thirds naked. I have seen from forty to sixty, male and female, at work in a field, many of both sexes with their bodies entirely naked—who did not exhibit signs of shame more than cattle. As I did not go among them much on the plantations, I have had but few opportunities for examining the backs of slaves—but have frequently passed where they were at work, and been occasionally present with them, and in almost every case there were marks of violence on some parts of them—every age, sex and condition being liable to the whip. A son of the gentleman with whom I boarded, a young man about twenty-one years of age, had a plantation and eight or ten slaves. He used to boast almost every night of whipping some of them. One day he related to me a case of whipping an old negro I should judge sixty years of age. He said he called him up to flog him for some real or supposed offense, and the poor old man, being pious, asked the privilege of praying before he received his punishment. He said he granted him the favor, and to use his own expression, 'The old nigger knelt down and prayed for me, and then got up and took his whipping.' In relation to negro huts, I will say that planters usually own large tracts of land. They have extensive clearings and a beautiful mansion house and generally some forty or fifty rods from the dwelling are situated the negro cabins, or huts, built of logs in the rudest manner. Some consist of poles rolled up together and covered with mud or clay—many of them not as comfortable as northern pig-sties."

TESTIMONY OF REV. PHINEAS SMITH

MR. SMITH is now pastor of the Presbyterian Church in Centreville, Allegany County, N.Y. He has recently returned from a residence in the slave states, and the American slave holding settlements in Texas. The following is an extract of a letter lately received from him:

"You inquire respecting instances of cruelty that have come within my knowledge. I reply.

Avarice and cruelty constitute the very gist of the whole slave system. Many of the enormities committed upon the plantations will not be described till God brings to light the hidden things of darkness, then the tears and groans and blood of innocent men, women and children will be revealed, and the oppressor's spirit must confront that of his victim.

"I will relate a case of *torture* which occurred on the Brassos while I resided a few miles distant upon the Chocolate Bayou. The case should be remembered as a true illustration of the nature of slavery, as it exists at the south. The facts are these: An overseer by the name of Alexander, notorious for his cruelty, was found dead in the timbered lands of the Brassos. It was supposed that he was murdered, but who perpetrated the act was unknown. Two black men were however seized, taken into the Prairie and put to the torture. A physician by the name of Parrott from Tennessee, and another from New England by the name of Anson Jones, were present on this occasion. The latter gentleman is now the Texan minister plenipotentiary to the United States, and resides at Washington. The unfortunate slaves being stripped, and all things arranged, the torture commenced by whipping upon their bare backs. Six athletic men were employed in this scene of inhumanity, the names of some of whom I well remember. There was one of the name of Brown, and one or two of the name of Patton. Those six executioners were successively employed in cutting up the bodies of these defenseless slaves, who persisted to the last in the avowal of their innocence. The bloody whip was however kept in motion till savage barbarity itself was glutted. When this was accomplished, the bleeding victims were re-conveyed to the enclosure of the mansion house where they were deposited for a few moments. '*The dying groans however incommoding the ladies, they were taken to a back shed where one of them soon expired.* *'The life of the other slave was for a time despaired of, but after hanging over the grave for months, he at length so far recovered as to walk about and labor at light work. These facts *cannot be controverted.* They were disclosed under the solemnity of an oath, at Columbia, in a court of justice. I was present, and shall never forget them. The testimony of Drs. Parrott and Jones was most appalling. I seem to hear the death-groans of that murdered man. His cries for mercy and protestations of innocence fell upon adamantine hearts.

* The words of Dr. Parrott, a witness on the trial hereafter referred to.

The facts above stated, and others in relation to this scene of cruelty came to light in the following manner. The master of the murdered man commenced legal process against the actors in this tragedy for the *recovery of the value of the chattel,* as one would institute a suit for a horse or an ox that had been unlawfully killed. It was a suit for the recovery of *damages* merely. No *indictment was* even dreamed of. Among the witnesses brought upon the stand in the progress of this cause were the physicians, Parrott and Jones above named. The part which they were called to act in this affair was, it is said, to examine the pulse of the victims during the process of *torture.* But they were mistaken as to the quantum of torture which a human being can undergo and not die under it. Can it be believed that one of these physicians was born and educated in the land of the pilgrims? Yes, in my own native New England. It is even so! The stone-like apathy manifested at the trial of the above cause, and the screams and the death-groans of an innocent man, as developed by the testimony of the witnesses, can never be obliterated from my memory. They form an era in my life, a point to which I look back with horror.

"Another case of cruelty occurred on the San Bernard near Chance Prairie, where I resided for some time. The facts were these. A slave man fled from his master, (Mr. Sweeny) and being closely *pursued* by the overseer and a son of the owner, he stepped a few yards in the Bernard and placed himself upon a root, from which there was no possibility of his escape, for he could not swim. In this situation he was fired upon with a blunderbuss loaded heavily with ball and grape shot. The overseer who shot the gun was at a distance of a few feet only. The charge entered the body of the negro near the groin. He was conveyed to the plantation, lingered in inexpressible agony a few days and expired. A physician was called, but medical and surgical skill was unavailing. No notice whatever was taken of this murder by the public authorities, and the murderer was not discharged from the service of his employer.

"When slaves flee, as they not un-frequently do, to the timbered lands of Texas, they are hunted with guns and dogs.

"The sufferings of the slave not un-frequently drive him to despair and suicide. At a plantation on the San Bernard, where there were but five slaves, two during the same year committed suicide by drowning."

TESTIMONY OF PHILEMON BLISS, ESQ.

Mr. Bliss is a highly respectable member of the bar, in Elyria, Lorain Co. Ohio, and member of the Presbyterian Church, in that place. He resided in Florida, during the years 1834 and 5.

The following extracts are from letters, written by Mr. B. in 1835, while residing on a plantation near Tallahassee, and published soon after in the Ohio Atlas; also from letters written in 1836, and published in the New York Evangelist:

"In speaking of slavery as it is, I hardly know where to begin. The physical condition of the slave is far from being accurately known at the north. Gentlemen *traveling* in the south can know nothing of it. They must make the south their residence; they must live on plantations, before they can have any opportunity of judging of the slave. I resided in Augustine five months, and had I not made *particular* inquiries, which most northern visitors very seldom or never do, I should have left there with the impression that the slaves were generally very *well* treated, and were a happy people. Such is the report of many northern travelers who have no more opportunity of knowing their real condition than if they had remained at home. What confidence could we place in the reports of the traveler, relative to the condition of the Irish peasantry, who formed his opinion from the appearance of the waiters at a Dublin hotel, or the household servants of a country gentleman? And it is not often on plantations even, that *strangers* can witness the punishment of the slave. I was conversing the other day with a neighboring planter, upon the brutal treatment of the slaves which I had witnessed; he remarked that had I been with him I should not have seen this. "When I whip niggers, I take them out of sight and hearing." Such being the difficulties in the way of a stranger's ascertaining the treatment of the slaves, it is not to be wondered at that gentlemen, of undoubted veracity, should give directly false statements relative to it. But facts cannot lie, and in giving these I confine myself to what has come under my own personal observation.

"The negroes commence labor by daylight in the morning, and, excepting the plowboys, who must feed and rest their horses, do not leave the field till dark in the evening. There is a good deal of contention among planters, who shall make the most cotton to the hand, or, who shall drive their negroes the hardest; and I have heard bets made and staked upon the issue of the crops. Col. W. was boasting of his large crops, and swore that 'he made for his force, the largest crops in the country.' He was disputed of course. On riding home in company with Mr. C. the conversation turned upon Col. W. My companion remarked that though Col. W. had the reputation of making a large crop, yet he could beat him himself, and did

~ 262 ~

do it the last year. I remarked that I considered it no honor to *Col. W.* to drive his slaves to death to make a large crop. I have heard no more about large crops from him since. Drivers or overseers usually drive the slaves worse than masters. Their reputation for good overseers depends in a great measure upon the crops they make, and the death of a slave is no loss to them.

"Of the extent and cruelty of the punishment of the slave, the northern public knows nothing. From the nature of the case they can know little, as I have before mentioned, "I *have seen* a woman, a mother, compelled, in the presence of her master and mistress, *to hold* up *her clothes,* and endure the whip of the driver on the naked body for more than *twenty minutes,* and while her cries would have rent the heart of anyone, who had not hardened himself to human suffering. Her master and mistress were conversing with apparent indifference. What was her crime? She had a task given her of sewing which she *must finish* that day. Late at night she finished it; but *the stitches were too long,* and she must be whipped. The same was repeated three or four nights for the same offense. I *have seen* a man tied to a tree, hands and feet, and receive 305 blows with the paddle* on the fleshy parts of the body. Two others received the same kind of punishment at the time, though I did not count the blows. One received 230 lashes. Their crime was stealing mutton. I have *frequently* heard the shrieks of the slaves, male and female, accompanied by the strokes of the paddle or whip, when I have not gone near the scene of horror. I knew not their crimes, excepting of one woman, which was stealing *four potatoes* to eat with her bread!

* A piece of oak timber two and a half feet long, flat and wide at one end.

The more common number of lashes inflicted was fifty or eighty; and this I saw not once or twice, but so frequently that I cannot tell the number of times I have seen it. So frequently, that my own heart was becoming so hardened that I could witness with comparative indifference, the female writhe under the lash, and her shrieks and cries for mercy ceased to pierce my heart with that keenness, or give me that anguish which they first caused. It was not always that I could learn their crimes; but of those I did learn, the most common was non-performance of tasks. I have seen men strip and receive from one to three hundred strokes of the whip and paddle. My studies and meditations were almost nightly interrupted by the cries of the victims of cruelty and avarice. Tom, a slave of Col. N. obtained permission of his overseer on Sunday, to visit his son, on a neighboring plantation, belonging in part to his master, but neglected to take a "pass." Upon its being demanded by the other overseer, he replied that he had permission to come, and that his having a mule was sufficient evidence of it, and if he did not consider it as such, he could take him up. The overseer replied he would take him up; giving him at the same time a blow on the arm with a stick he held in his hand, sufficient to lame it for some time. The negro collared him, and threw him; and on the overseer's commanding him to submit to be tied and whipped, he said he would not be whipped by *him* but would leave it to massa J. They came to massa J.'s. I was there. After the overseer had related the case as above, he was blamed for not shooting or stabbing him at once. After dinner the negro was tied, and the whip given to the overseer, and he used it with a severity that was shocking. I know not how many lashes were given, but from his shoulders to his heels there was not a spot un-ridged! And at almost every stroke the blood flowed. He could not have received less than 300, *well laid on.* But his offense was great, almost the greatest known, laying hands on a *white* man! Had he struck the overseer, under any provocation, he would have been in some way disfigured, perhaps by the loss of his ears, in addition to a whipping: or he might have been hung.

The most common cause of punishments is, not finishing tasks."But it would be tedious mentioning further particulars. The negro has no other inducement to work but the *lash;* and as man never acts without motive, the lash must be used so long as all other motives are withheld. Hence corporeal punishment is a necessary part of slavery."Punishments for runaways are usually severe.

Once whipping is not sufficient. I have known runaways to be whipped for six or seven nights in succession for one offense. I have known others who, with pinioned hands, and a chain extending from an iron collar on their neck, to the saddle of their master's horse, have been driven at a smart trot, one or two hundred miles, being compelled to ford water courses, their drivers, according to their own confession, not abating a whit in the rapidity of their for the ease of the slave. One tied a kettle of sand to his slave to render his journey more arduous.

"Various are the instruments of torture devised to keep the slave in subjection. The stocks are sometimes used. Sometimes blocks are filled with pegs and nails, and the slave compelled to stand upon them.

"While stopping on the plantation of a Mr. C. I saw a whip with a knotted lash lying on the table, and inquired of my companion, who was also an acquaintance of Mr. C.'s, if he used that to whip his negroes ? "Oh," says he," Mr. C. is not severe with his hands. He never whips very hard. The *knots in the lash are* so *large* that he does not usually draw blood in whipping them."

"It was principally from hearing the conversation of southern men on the subject that I judge of the cruelty that is generally practiced toward slaves. They will deny that slaves are generally ill treated; but ask them if they are not whipped for certain offenses, which either a freeman would have no temptation to commit, or which would not be an offense in any but a slave, and for non-performance of tasks, they will answer promptly in the affirmative. And frequently have I heard them excuse their cruelty by citing Mr. A. or Mr. B. who is a Christian, or Mr. C. a preacher, or Mr. D. from the *north,* who "drives his hands tighter, and whips them harder, than we ever do." Driving negroes to the utmost extent of their ability, with occasionally a hundred lashes or more, and a few switchings in the field if they hang back in the driving seasons, viz: in the hoeing and picking months, is perfectly consistent with good treatment!

"While traveling across the Peninsula in a stage, in company with a northern gentleman, and southern lady, of great worth and piety, a dispute arose respecting the general treatment of slaves, the gentleman contending that their treatment was generally good—'O, no!' interrupted the lady, 'You can know nothing of the treatment they receive on the plantations. People here do whip the poor negroes most cruelly, and many half starve them. You have, neither of you, had opportunity to know scarcely anything of the cruelties that are practiced in this country! And more to the same effect. I met with several others, besides this lady, who appeared to feel for the sins of the land, but they are few and scattered, and not usually of sufficiently stern mould to withstand the popular wave.

"Masters are not forward to publish their "domestic regulations," and as neighbors are usually several miles apart, one's observation must be limited. Hence the few instances of cruelty which break out can be but a fraction of what is practiced. A planter, a professor of religion, in conversation upon the universality of whipping remarked that a planter in G_____ , who had whipped a great deal, at length got tired of it, and invented the following *excellent* method of punishment, which I saw practiced while I was paying him a visit. The negro was placed in a sitting position, with his hands made fast above his head, and feet in the stocks, so that he could not move any part of the body.

"The master retired, intending to leave him till morning, but we were awakened in the night by the groans of the negro, which were so doleful that we feared he was dying. We went to him, and found him covered with a cold sweat, and almost gone. He could not have lived an hour longer. Mr.____found the 'stocks' such an effective punishment, that it almost superseded the whip."

"How much do you give your niggers for a task while hoeing cotton," inquired Mr. C. of his neighbor Mr. H .

H. "I give my men an acre and a quarter, and my women an acre."*

*Cotton is planted in drills about three feet apart, and is hilled like corn.

C. "Well, that is a fair task. Niggers do a heap better if they are drove pretty tight."

H. "O yes, I have driven mine into complete subordination. When I first bought them they were discontented and wished me to sell them, but I soon whipped *that* out of them; and they now work very contentedly!"

C. "Does Mary keep up with the rest?

H. "No, she doesn't often finish the task alone; she has to get Sam to help her out after he has done his, *to save her a whipping.* There's no other way but to be severe with them."

C. "No other, sir, if you favor a nigger you spoil him."

"The whip is considered as necessary on a plantation as the plough ; and its use is almost as common. The negro whip is the common teamster's whip with a black leather stock, and a short, fine, knotted lash. The paddle is also frequently used, sometimes with holes bored in the flattened end. The ladies (!) in chastising their domestic servants generally use the cowhide. I have known some use shovel and tongs. It is, however, more common to commit them to the driver to be whipped. The manner of whipping is as follows: The negro is tied by his hands, and sometimes feet, to a post or tree, and stripped to the skin. The female slave is not always tied. The number of lashes depends upon the character for severity of the master or overseer.

"Another instrument of torture is sometimes used, how extensively I know not. The negro, or, in the case which came to my knowledge, the negress was compelled to stand barefoot upon a block filled with sharp pegs and nails for two or three hours.

In case of sickness, if the master or overseer thinks them seriously ill, they are taken care of, but their complaints are usually not much heeded. A physician told me that he was employed by a planter last winter to *go* to a plantation of his in the country, as many if the negroes were sick. Says he—"I found them in a most miserable condition. The weather was cold, and the negroes were barefoot, with hardly enough of *cotton* clothing to cover their nakedness. Those who had huts to shelter them were obliged to build them nights and Sundays. Many were sick and some had died. I had the sick taken to an older plantation of their masters, where they could be made comfortable, and they recovered. I directed that they should not go to work till after sunrise, and should not work in the rain till their health became established. But the overseer refusing to permit it, I declined attending on them farther. "I was called", continued he, "by the overseer of another plantation to see one of the men. I found him lying by the side of a log in great pain. I asked him how he did.

"'O,'" says he, "'I'm most dead, can live but little longer.'"

"How long have you been sick?"

"I've felt for more than six weeks as though I could hardly stir."

"Why didn't you tell your master, you was sick?"

"I couldn't see my master, and the overseer always whips us when we complain, I could not stand a whipping."

I did all I could for the poor fellow, but his *lungs were rotten.* He died in three days from the time he left off work. The cruelty of that overseer is such that the negroes almost tremble at his name. Yet he gets a high salary, for he makes the largest crop of any other man in the neighborhood, though none but the hardiest negroes can stand it under him. "That man," says the Doctor, "would be hung in my country." He was a German.

TESTIMONY OF REV. WILLIAM A. CHAPIN

Rev. William Scales, of Lyndon, Vermont, has furnished the following testimony, under date of Dec. 15, 1838:

"I send you an extract from a letter that I have just received, which you may use *ad libitum.* The letter is from Rev. Wm. A. Chapin, Greensborough, Vermont. To one who is acquainted with Mr. C. his opinion and statements must carry conviction even to the most obstinate and incredulous. He observes:

"I resided, as a teacher, nearly two years in the family of Carroll Webb, Esq., of Hampstead, New Kent Co. about twenty miles from Richmond, Virginia. Mr. Webb had three or four plantations, and was considered one of the two wealthiest men in the county: it was supposed he owned about two hundred slaves. He was a member of the Presbyterian Church, and was elected an elder while I was with him. He was a native of Virginia, but a graduate of a New England college."

"The slaves were called in the morning before daylight, I believe at all seasons of the year, that they might prepare their food, and be ready to go to work as soon as it was light enough to see. I know that at the season of husking corn, October and November, they were usually compelled to work late—till 12 or 1 o'clock at night. I know this fact because they accompanied their work with a loud singing of their own sort. I usually retired to rest between 11 and 12 o'clock, and generally heard them at their work as long as I was awake. The slaves lived in wretched log cabins, of one room each, without floors or windows. I believe the slaves sometimes suffer for want of food. One evening, as I was sitting in the parlor with Mr. W. one of the most resolute of the slaves came to the door, and said, "Master, I am willing to work for you, but I want something to eat." The only reply was, "Clear yourself." I learned that the slaves had been without food all day, because the man who was sent to mill could not obtain his grinding. He went again the next day, and obtained his grist, and the slaves had no food till he returned. He had to go about five miles.*

* To this. Rev. Mr. Scales adds, "In familiar language, and in more detail, as I have learned it in conversation with Mr. Chapin, the fact is as follows:

"Mr. W. kept what he called a 'boy,' i.e. a *man*, to go to mill. It was his custom not to give his slaves anything to eat while he was gone to mill—let him have been gone longer or shorter—for this reason, if he was lazy, and delayed, the slaves would become hungry; hence indignant, and abuse him—this was his punishment. On that occasion he went to mill in the morning. The slaves came up at noon, and returned to work without food. At night, after having worked hard all day, without food, went to bed without supper. About 10 o'clock the next day, they came up in a company, to their master's door, (that master an elder in the church), and deputed one more resolute than the rest to address him. This he did in the most respectful tones and terms. "We are willing to work for you, master, but we can't work without food; we want something to eat."Clear yourself," was the answer. The slaves retired; and in the morning were driven away to work without food. At noon, I think, or somewhat after, they were fed."

"I know the slaves were sometimes severely whipped. I saw the backs of several which had numerous scars, evidently caused by long and deep lacerations of the whip; and I have good reason to believe that the slaves were generally in that condition; for I never saw the back of one exposed that was not thus marked,—and from their tattered and scanty clothing their backs were often exposed."

TESTIMONY OF MESSRS. T. D. M. AND F. C. MACY

This testimony is communicated in a letter from Mr. Cyrus Pierce, a respectable and well known citizen of Nantucket, Mass. Of the witnesses, Messrs. T. D. M. and F. C. Macy, Mr. Pierce says, "They are both inhabitants of this island, and have resided at the south; they are both worthy men, for whose integrity and intelligence I can vouch unqualifiedly; the former has furnished me with the following statement:

"During the winter of 1832—3, I resided on the island of St. Simon, Glynn County, Georgia. There are several extensive cotton plantations on the island. The overseer of the plantation on that part of the island where I resided was a Georgian—a man of stern character, and at times-*cruelly abusive to* his slaves. I have often been witness of the *abuse* of his power. In South Carolina and Georgia, on the low lands, the cultivation is chiefly of rice. The land where it is raised is often inundated, and the labor of preparing it, and raising a crop, is very arduous. Men and women are in the field from earliest dawn to dark—often *without hats,* and up to their armpits in mud and water. At St. Simon's, cotton was the staple article. Ocra, the driver, usually waited on the overseer to receive orders for the succeeding day. If any slave was insolent, or negligent, the driver was authorized to punish him with the whip, with as many blows as the magnitude of the crime justified. He was frequently cautioned, upon the peril of his skin, to see that all the negroes were off to the field in the morning. 'Ocra,' said the overseer, one evening, to the driver, 'if any pretend to be sick, send me word—allow no lazy wench or fellow to skulk in the negro house.' Next morning, a few minutes after the departure of the hands to the field, Ocra was seen hastening to the house of the overseer. He was soon in his presence. 'Well, Ocra, what now?' Nothing, sir, only Rachel says she sick—can't go to de field to-day.' 'Ah, sick, is she? I'll see to her; you may be off. She shall see if I am longer to be fooled with in this way. Here, Christmas, mix these salts—bring them to me at the negro house.' And seizing his whip, he made off to the negro settlement. Having a strong desire to see what would be the result, I followed him. As I approached the negro house, I heard high words. Rachel was stating her complaint—children were crying from fright—and the overseer threatening. Rachel.—'I can't work to-day—I'm sick.' Overseer.—' But you shall work, if you die for it. Here, take these salts. Now move off— quick— let me see your face again before night, and, by G—d, you shall smart for it. Be off—no begging—not a word;'—and he dragged her from the house, and followed her 20 or 30 rods, threatening. The woman did not reach the field. Overcome by the exertion of walking, and by agitation, she sunk down exhausted by the road side—was taken up, and carried back to the house, where an *abortion* occurred, and her life was greatly jeopardized.

"It was *no uncommon* sight to see a whole family, father, mother, and from two to five children, collected together around their piggin of hominy, or pail of potatoes, watched by the overseer. One meal was always eaten in the field. No time was allowed for relaxation.

"It was not unusual for a child of five or six years to perform the office of nurse—because the mother worked in a remote part of the field, and was not allowed to leave her employment to take care of her infant. Want of proper nutriment induces sickness of the worst type.

"No matter what the nature of the service, a peck of corn dealt out on Sunday, must supply the demands of nature for a week.

"The Sabbath, on a southern plantation, is a mere nominal holiday. The slaves are liable to be called upon at all times, by those who have authority over them.

"When it rained, the slaves were allowed to collect under a tree until the shower had passed. Seldom, on a week day, were they permitted to go to their huts during rain; and even had this privilege been granted, many of those miserable habitations were in so dilapidated a condition, that they would afford little or no protection. Negro huts are built of logs, covered with boards or thatch, having *no flooring,* and but one apartment, serving all the purposes of sleeping, cooking, &c. Some are furnished with a temporary loft. I have seen a whole family herded together in a loft ten feet by twelve. In cold weather, they gather around the fire, spread their blankets *on the ground,* and keep as comfortable as they can. Their supply of clothing is scanty—each slave being allowed a Holland coat and pantaloons, of the coarsest manufacture, and one pair of cowhide shoes. The women, enough of the same kind of cloth for one frock. They have also one pair of shoes. Shoes are given to the slaves in the winter only. In summer, their clothing is composed of osnaburg. Slaves on different plantations are not allowed without a written permission, to visit their fellow bondsmen, under penalty of severe chastisement. I witnessed the chastisement of a young male slave, who was found lurking about the plantation, and could give no other account of himself, than that he wanted to visit some of his acquaintance. Fifty lashes was the penalty for this offense. I could not endure the dreadful shrieks of the tortured slave, and rushed away from the scene." I

The remainder of this testimony is furnished by Mr. F. C. Macy:

"I went to Savannah in 1820. Sailing up the river, I had my first view of slavery. A large number of men and women, with *a piece of board on their heads, carrying mud,* for the purpose of dyking near the river. After tarrying a while in Savannah, I went down to the sea islands of De Fuskee and Hilton Head, where I spent six months. Negro houses are small, built of rough materials, *and no floor.* Their clothing, (one suit,) coarse; which they received on Christmas day. Their food was three pecks of potatoes per week, in the potato season, and one peck of corn the remainder of the year. The slaves carried with them into the field their meal, and a gourd of water. They cooked their hominy in the field, and ate it with a wooden paddle Their treatment was little better than that of brutes. *Whipping* was nearly an every-day practice. On Mr. M___ 's plantation, at the island De Fuskee, I saw an old man whipped; he was about 60. He had no clothing on, except a shirt. The man that inflicted the blows was Flim, a tall and stout man. The whipping was *very severe.* I inquired into the cause. Some vegetables had been stolen from his master's garden, of which he could give no account.

I saw several women whipped, some of whom were in very *delicate* circumstances. The case of one I will relate. She had been purchased in Charleston, and separated from her husband. On her passage to Savannah, or rather to the island, she was delivered of a child; and in about three weeks after this, she appeared to be deranged. She would leave her work, go into the woods, and sing.

Her master sent for her, and ordered the driver to whip her. I was near enough to hear the strokes."I have known negro boys, partly by persuasion, and partly by force, made to strip off their clothing and fight for *the amusement of their masters.* They would fight until both got to crying.

"One of the planters told me that his boat had been used without permission. A number of his negroes were called up, and put in a building that was lathed and shingled. The covering could be easily removed from the inside. He called one out for examination. While examining this one, he discovered another negro, coming out of the roof He ordered him back; he obeyed. In a few moments he attempted it again. The master took deliberate aim at his head, but his gun missed fire. He told me he should probably have killed him, had his gun gone off. The negro jumped and run. The master took aim again, and fired; but he was so far distant, that he received only a few shots in the calf of his leg. After several days he returned, and received a severe whipping.

"Mr. B , planter at Hilton Head, freely confessed, that he kept one of his slaves as a mistress. She slept in the same room with him. This, I think, is a very common practice."

TESTIMONY OF A CLERGYMAN

The following letter was written to Mr. Arthur Tappan, of New York, in the summer of 1833. As the name of the writer cannot be published with safety to himself, it is withheld. The following testimonials, from Mr. Tappan, Professor Wright, and Thomas Ritter, M. D. of New York, establish the trust-worthiness and high respectability of the writer:

"I received the following letters from the south during the year 1833. They were written by a gentleman who had then resided some years in the slave states. Not being at liberty to give the writer's name, I cheerfully certify that he is a gentleman of established character, a graduate of Yale College, and a respected minister of the gospel.   "Arthur Tappan."

"My acquaintance with the writer of the following letter commenced, I believe, in 1823, from which time we were fellow students in Yale College till 1826. I have occasionally seen him since. His character, so far as it has come within my knowledge, has been that of an upright and remarkably *candid* man. I place great confidence both in his habits of careful and unprejudiced observation and his veracity. "E. Wright, Jun. "New York, April 13, 1839."

"I have been acquainted with the writer of the following letter about twelve years, and know him to be a gentleman of high respectability, integrity, and piety. We were fellow students in Yale College, and my opportunities for judging of his character, both at that time and since our graduation, have been such, that I feel myself fully warranted in making the above unequivocal declaration. "Thomas Ritter, 104, Cherry-street, New York."

"Natchez, 1833

"It has been almost four years since I came to the south-west; and although I have been told, from month to month, that I should soon wear off my northern prejudices, and probably have slaves of my own, yet my judgment in regard to oppression, or my prejudices, if they are pleased so to call them, remain with me still. I judge still from those principles which were fixed in my mind at the north; and a residence at the south has not enabled me so to pervert truth, as to make injustice appear justice.

"I have studied the state of things here, now for years, coolly and deliberately, with the eye of an uninterested looker on; and hence I may not be altogether unprepared to state to you some facts, and to draw conclusions from them.

"Permit me then to relate what I have seen; and do not imagine that these are all exceptions to the general treatment, but rather believe that thousands of cruelties are practiced in this Christian land, every year, which no eye that ever shed a tear of pity could look upon.

"Soon after my arrival I made an excursion into the country, to the distance of some twenty miles. And as I was passing by a cotton field, where about fifty negroes were at work, I was inclined to stop by the road side to view a scene which was then new to me. While I was, in my mind, comparing this mode of labor with that of my own native place, I heard the driver, with a rough oath, order one that was near him, who seemed to be laboring to the extent of his power, to "lie down." In a moment he was obeyed; and he commenced whipping the offender upon his naked back, and continued, to the amount of about twenty lashes, with a heavy raw-hide whip, the crack of which might have been heard more than half a mile. Nor did the females escape; for although I stopped scarcely fifteen minutes, no less than three were whipped in the same manner, and that so severely, I was strongly inclined to interfere.

"You may be assured, sir, that I remained not unmoved: I could no longer look on such cruelty, but turned away and rode on, while the echoes of the lash were reverberating in the woods around me. Such scenes have long since become familiar to me. But then the full effect was not lost; and I shall never forget, to my latest day, the mingled feelings of pity, horror, and indignation that took possession of my mind. I involuntarily exclaimed, O God of my fathers, how dost thou permit such things to defile our land! Be merciful to us! And visit us not in justice, for all our iniquities and the iniquities of our fathers!

"As I passed on I soon found that I had escaped from one horrible scene only to witness another. A planter with whom I was well acquainted, had caught a negro without a pass. And at the moment I was passing by, he was in the act of fastening his feet and hands to the trees, having previously made him take off all his clothing except his trowsers. When he had sufficiently secured this poor creature, he beat him for several minutes with a green switch more than six feet long; while he was writhing with anguish, endeavoring in vain to break the cords with which he was bound, and incessantly crying out, "Lord, master! Do pardon me this time! do, master, have mercy!" These expressions have recurred to me a thousand times since; and although they came from one that is not considered among the sons of men, yet I think they are well worthy of remembrance, as they might lead a wise man to consider whether such shall receive mercy from the righteous Judge, as never showed mercy to their fellow men.

"At length I arrived at the dwelling of a planter of my acquaintance, with whom I passed the night. At about eight o'clock in the evening I heard the barking of several dogs, mingled with the most agonizing cries that I ever heard from any human being. Soon after the gentleman came in, and began to apologize, by saying that two of his runaway slaves had just been brought home; and as he had previously tried every species of punishment upon them without effect, he knew not what else to add, except to set his blood hounds upon them. 'And,' continued he, 'one of them has been so badly bitten that he has been trying to die. I am only sorry that he did not; for then I should not have been further troubled with him. If he lives I intend to send him to Natchez or to New Orleans, to work with the ball and chain.'

"From this last remark I understood that private individuals have the right of thus subjecting their unmanageable slaves. I have since seen numbers of these 'ball and chain' men, both in Natchez and New Orleans, but I do not know whether there were any among them except the state convicts.

"As the summer was drawing towards a close, and the yellow fever beginning to prevail in town, I went to reside some months in the country. This was the cotton picking season, during which, the planters say, there is a greater necessity for flogging than at any other time. And I can assure you, that as I have sat in my window night after night, while the cotton was being weighed, I have heard the crack of the whip, without much intermission, for a whole hour, from no less than three plantations, some of which were a full mile distant.

"I found that the slaves were kept in the field from daylight until dark; and then, if they had not gathered what the master or overseer thought sufficient, they were subjected to the lash.

"Many by such treatment are induced to run away and take up their lodging in the woods. I do not say that all who run away are thus closely pressed, but I do know that many are; and I have known no less than a dozen desert at a time from the same plantation, in consequence of the overseer's forcing them to work to the extent of their power, and then whipping them for not having done more.

"But suppose that they run away—what is to become of them in the forest? If they cannot steal they must perish of hunger—if the nights are cold, their feet will be frozen; for if they make a fire they may be discovered, and be shot at. If they attempt to leave the country, their chance of success is about nothing. They must return, be whipped—if old offenders, wear the collar, perhaps be branded, and fare worse than before.

"Do you believe it, sir, not six months since, I saw a number of my *Christian* neighbors packing up provisions, as I supposed for a deer hunt; but as I was about offering myself to the party, I learned that their powder and balls were destined to a very different purpose: it was, in short, the design of the party to bring home a number of runaway slaves, or to shoot them if they should not be able to get possession of them in any other way.

"You will ask, is not this murder? Call it, sir, by what name you please, such are the facts: Many are shot every year, and that too while the masters say they treat their slaves well.

"But let me turn your attention to another species of cruelty. About a year since I knew a certain slave who had deserted his master, to be caught, and for the first time fastened to the stocks. In those same stocks, from which at midnight I have heard cries of distress, while the master slept, and was dreaming, perhaps, of drinking wine and of discussing the price of cotton. On the next morning he was chained in an immovable posture, and branded in both cheeks with red hot stamps of iron. Such are the tender mercies of men who love wealth, and are determined to obtain it at any price.

"Suffer me to add another to the list of enormities, and I will not offend you with more.

"There was, some time since, brought to trial in this town a planter residing about fifteen miles distant, for whipping his slave to death. You will suppose, of course, that he was punished. No, sir, he was acquitted, although there could be no doubt of the fact. I heard the tale of murder from a man who was acquainted with all the circumstances. 'I was,' said he, 'passing along the road near the burying-ground of the plantation, about nine o'clock at night, when I saw several lights gleaming through the woods; and as I approached, in order to see what was doing, I beheld the coroner of Natchez, with a number of men, standing around the body of a young female, which by the torches seemed almost perfectly white. On inquiry I learned that the master had so unmercifully beaten this girl that she died under the operation and that also he had so severely punished another of his slaves that he was but just alive.'"

We here rest the case for the present, so far as respects the presentation of facts showing the condition of the slaves, and proceed to consider the main objections which are usually employed to weaken such testimony, or wholly to set it aside. But before we enter upon the examination of specific objections, and introductory to them, we remark,—

1. That the system of slavery must be a system of horrible cruelty follows of necessity, from the fact that two millions seven hundred thousand human beings *are held by force,* and used as articles of property. Nothing but a heavy yoke, and an iron one, could possibly keep so many necks in the dust. That must be a constant and mighty pressure which holds so still such a vast army; nothing could do it but the daily experience of severities and the ceaseless dread and certainty of the most terrible inflictions if they should dare to toss in their chains.

2. Were there nothing else to prove it a system of monstrous cruelty, the fact that FEAR is the only motive with which the slave is plied during his whole existence, would be sufficient to brand it with execration as the grand tormentor of man. The slave's *susceptibility of pain* is the sole fulcrum on which slavery works the lever that moves him. In this it plants all its stings; here it sinks its hot irons; cuts its deep gashes; flings its burning embers, and dashes its boiling brine and liquid fire; into this it strikes its cold flesh hooks, grappling irons, and instruments of nameless torture; and by it drags him shrieking to the end of his pilgrimage. The fact that the master inflicts pain upon the slave not merely as an *end* to gratify passion, but constantly as a *means* of extorting labor, is enough of itself to show that the system of slavery is unmixed cruelty.

3. That the slaves must suffer frequent and terrible inflictions follows inevitably from the *character of those who direct their labor.* Whatever may be the character of the slaveholders themselves, all agree that the overseers are, as a class, most abandoned, brutal, and desperate men. This is so well known and believed that any testimony to prove it seems needless. The testimony of Mr. Wirt, late Attorney General of the United

States, a Virginian and a slaveholder, is as follows. In his life of Patrick Henry, p. 36, speaking of the different classes of society in Virginia, he says,—" Last and lowest a feculum, of beings called 'overseers'—*the most abject, degraded,* un*principled race,* always cap in hand to the dons who employ them, and furnishing materials for the exercise of their *pride, insolence, and spirit of domination."*

Rev. Phineas Smith, of Centreville, New-York, who has resided some years at the south, says of overseers—"It need hardly be added that overseers are in general ignorant, *unprincipled and cruel,* and in such low repute that they are not permitted to come to the tables of their employers; yet they have the constant control of all the human cattle that belong to the master.

"These men are continually advancing from their low station to the higher one of masters. These changes bring into the possession of power a class of men of whose mental and moral qualities I have already spoken."

Rev. Horace Moulton, of Marlboro, Massachusetts, who lived in Georgia several years, says of them,—

"The overseers are *generally loose in their* mo*rals;* it is the object of masters to employ those whom they think will get the most work out of their hands,—hence those who *whip and torment the slaves the most* are in many instances called the best overseers. The masters think those whom the slaves fear the most are the best. Quite a portion of the masters employ their own slaves as overseers, or rather they are called drivers; these are more subject to the will of the masters than the white overseers are; some of them are as lordly as an Austrian prince, and sometimes more cruel even than the whites."

That the overseers are, as a body, sensual, brutal, and violent men is *proverbial.* The tender mercies of such men *must be cruel.*

4. The *ownership* of human beings necessarily presupposes an utter disregard of their happiness. He who assumes it monopolizes their *whole capital,* leaves them no stock on which to trade, and out of which to *make* happiness. Whatever is the master's gain is the slave's loss, a loss wrested from him by the master, for the express purpose of making it *his own gain;* this is the master's constant employment—forcing the slave to toil— violently wringing from him all he has and all he gets, and using it as his own;—like the vile bird that never builds its nest from materials of its own gathering, but either drives other birds from theirs and takes possession of

them, or tears them in pieces to get the means of constructing their own. This daily practice of forcibly robbing others, and habitually living on the plunder, cannot but beget in the mind the *habit* of regarding the interests and happiness of those whom it robs, as of no sort of consequence in comparison with its own; consequently whenever those interests and this happiness are in the way of its own gratification, they will be sacrificed without scruple. He who cannot see this would be unable to *feel* it, if it were seen.

OBJECTIONS CONSIDERED

Objection I—"SUCH CRUELTIES ARE INCREDIBLE."

The enormities inflicted by slaveholders upon their slaves will never be discredited except by those who overlook the simple fact, that he who holds human beings as his bona fide property, *regards* them as property, and not as *persons;* this is his permanent state of mind toward them. He does not contemplate slaves as human beings, consequently does not *treat* them as such; and with entire indifference sees them suffer privations and writhe under blows, which, if inflicted upon whites, would fill him with horror and indignation. He regards that as good treatment of slaves, which would seem to him insufferable abuse if practiced upon others; and would denounce that as a monstrous outrage and horrible cruelty, if perpetrated upon white men and women, which he sees every day meted out to black slaves, without perhaps ever thinking it cruel. Accustomed all his life to regard them rather as domestic animals, to hear them stormed at, and to see them cuffed and caned; and being himself in the constant habit of treating them thus, such practices have become to him a mere matter of course, and make no impression on his mind. True, it is incredible that men should treat as *chattels* those whom they truly regard as *human beings;* but that they should treat as chattels and working animals those whom they *regard* as such is no marvel. The common treatment of dogs, when they are in the way, is to kick them out of it; we see them every day kicked off the sidewalks, and out of shops, and on Sabbaths out of churches,—yet, as they are but *dogs,* these do not strike us as outrages; yet, if we were to see men, women, and children—our neighbors and friends, kicked out of stores by merchants, or out of churches by the deacons and sexton, we should call the perpetrators inhuman wretches.

We have said that slaveholders regard their slaves not as human beings, but as mere working animals, or merchandise. The whole vocabulary of slaveholders, their laws, their usages, and their entire treatment of their slaves fully establish this. The same terms are applied to slaves that are given to cattle. They are called "stock." So when the children of slaves are spoken of prospectively, they are called their "increase;" the same term that is applied to flocks and herds. So the female slaves that are mothers, are called "breeders" till past child bearing; and often the same terms are applied to the different sexes that are applied to the males and females among cattle. Those who compel the labor of slaves and cattle have the same appellation, "drivers:" the names which they call them are the same and similar to those given to their horses and oxen. The laws of slave states make them property, equally with goats and swine; they are levied upon for debt in the same way; they are included in the same advertisements of public sales with cattle, swine, and asses; when moved from one part of the country to another, they are herded in droves like cattle, and like them urged on by drivers; their labor is compelled in the same way. They are bought and sold, and separated like cattle; when exposed for sale, their good qualities are described as jockeys show off the good points of their horses; their strength, activity, skill, power of endurance, &c. are lauded,— and those who bid upon them examine their persons, just as purchasers inspect horses and oxen; they open their mouths to see if their teeth are sound; strip their backs to see if they are badly scarred, and handle their limbs and muscles to see if they are firmly knit. Like horses, they are warranted to be "sound," or to be returned to the owner if "unsound." A father gives his son a horse and a *slave*; by his will he distributes among them his race-horses, hounds, game-cocks, and *slaves*. We leave the reader to carry out the parallel which we have only begun. Its details would cover many pages.

That slaveholders do not practically regard slaves as *human beings* is abundantly shown by their own voluntary testimony. In a recent work entitled, "The South Vindicated from the Treason and Fanaticism of Northern Abolitionists," which was written, we are informed, by **Colonel Dayton**, late member of Congress from South Carolina; the writer, speaking of the awe with which the slaves regard the whites, says,—

"The northerner looks upon a band of negroes as upon so many *men,* but the planter or southerner *views them in a very different light."*

Extract from the speech of **Mr. Summers,** of Virginia, in the legislature of that state, Jan. 26, 1832. See the Richmond Whig:

"When, in the sublime lessons of Christianity, he (the slaveholder) is taught to 'do unto others as he would have others do unto him, 'HE NEVER DREAMS THAT THE DEGRADED NEGRO IS WITHIN THE PALE OF THAT HOLY CANON."

President Jefferson, in his letter to Governor Coles, of Illinois, dated Aug. 25, 1814, asserts that slaveholders regard their slaves as brutes, in the following remarkable language:

"Nursed and educated in the daily habit of seeing the degraded condition, both bodily and mental, of these unfortunate beings [the slaves], FEW MINDS HAVE YET DOUBTED BUT THAT THEY WERE AS LEGITIMATE SUBJECTS OF PROPERTY AS THEIR HORSES OR CATTLE."

Having shown that slaveholders regard their slaves as mere working animals and cattle, we now proceed to show that their actual treatment of them is *worse* than it would be if they were brutes. We repeat it, SLAVEHOLDERS TREAT THEIR SLAVES WORSE THAN THEY DO THEIR BRUTES.

Whoever heard of cows or sheep being deliberately tied up and beaten and lacerated till they died? or horses coolly tortured by the hour, till covered with mangled flesh, or of swine having their legs tied and being suspended from a tree and lacerated with thongs for hours, or of hounds stretched and made fast at full length, flayed with whips, red pepper rubbed into their bleeding gashes, and hot brine dashed on to aggravate the torture? Yet just such forms and degrees of torture are *daily* perpetrated upon the slaves. Now no man that knows human nature will marvel at this. Though great cruelties have always been inflicted by men upon brutes, yet incomparably the most horrid ever perpetrated, have been those of men upon *their own species.* Any leaf of history turned over at random has proof enough of this. Every reflecting mind perceives that when men hold *human beings* as *property,* they must, from the nature of the case, treat them worse than they treat their horses and oxen. It is impossible for *cattle* to excite in men such tempests of fury as men excite in each other. Men are often provoked if their horses or hounds refuse to do, or their pigs refuse to go where they wish to drive them, but the feeling is rarely intense and never permanent. It is vexation and impatience, rather than settled rage, malignity, or revenge. If horses and dogs were intelligent beings, and still held as property, their opposition to the wishes of their owners, would exasperate them immeasurably more than it would be possible for them to do, with the minds of brutes. None but little children and idiots get angry at sticks and stones that lie in their way or hurt them; but put into sticks and stones intelligence, and will, and power of feeling and motion, while they remain as now, articles of property, and what a towering rage would men be in, if bushes whipped them in the face when they walked among them, or stones rolled over their toes when they climbed hills! And what exemplary vengeance would be inflicted upon door-steps and hearth-stones, if they were to move out of their places, instead of lying still where they were put for their owners to tread upon. The greatest provocation to human nature is *opposition to its will*. If a man's will be resisted by one far *below* him, the provocation is vastly greater, than when it is resisted by an acknowledged superior. In the former case, it inflames strong passions, which in the latter, lie dormant. The rage of proud Hainan knew no bounds against the poor Jew who would not do as he wished, and so he built a gallows for him. If the person opposing the will of another, be so far below him as to be on a level with chattels, and be actually held and used as an article of property; pride, scorn, lust of power, rage and revenge explode together upon the hapless victim. The idea of *property* having a will, and that too in opposition to the will of its *owner,* and counteracting it, is a stimulant of terrible power to the most relentless human passions; and from the nature of slavery, and the constitution of the human mind, this fierce stimulant must, with various degrees of strength, act upon slaveholders almost without ceasing. The slave, however abject and crushed, is an intelligent being: he has a *will,* and that will cannot be annihilated, *it will show itself;* if for a moment it is smothered, like pent up fires when vent is found, it flames the fiercer. Make intelligence *property,* and its manager will have his match; he is met at every turn by an *opposing will,* not in the form of down-right rebellion and defiance, but yet, visibly, an *ever-opposing will.* He sees it in the dissatisfied look, and reluctant air and unwilling movement; the constrained strokes of labor, the drawling tones, the slow hearing, the feigned stupidity, the sham pains and sickness, the short memory; and he *feels* it every hour, in innumerable forms, frustrating his designs by a ceaseless though perhaps invisible countermining. This unceasing opposition to the will of its 'owner,' on the part of his rational 'property,' is to the slaveholder as the hot iron to the nerve. He raves under it, and storms, and gnashes, and smites; but the more he smites, the hotter it gets, and the more it burns him. Further, this opposition of the slave's will to his owner's, not only excites him to severity, that he may gratify his rage, but makes it necessary for him to use violence in breaking down this resistance—thus subjecting the slave to additional tortures.

There is another inducement to cruel inflictions upon the slave, and a necessity for it, which does not exist in the case of brutes. Offenders must be made an example to others, to strike them with terror. If a slave runs away and is caught, his master flogs him with terrible severity, not merely to gratify his resentment, and to keep him from running away again, but as a warning to others. So in every case of disobedience, neglect, stubbornness, unfaithfulness, indolence, insolence, theft, feigned sickness, when his directions are forgotten, or slighted, or supposed to be, or his wishes crossed, or his property injured, or left exposed, or his work ill-executed, the master is tempted to inflict cruelties, not merely to wreak his own vengeance upon him, and to make the slave more circumspect in future, but to sustain his authority over the other slaves, to restrain them from like practices, and to preserve his own property.

A multitude of facts, illustrating the position that slaveholders treat their slaves *worse* than they do their cattle, will occur to all who are familiar with slavery. When cattle break through their owners' enclosures and escape, if found, they are driven back and fastened in again; and even slaveholders would execrate as a wretch, the man who should tie them up, and bruise and lacerate them for straying away; but when *slaves* that have escaped are caught, they are flogged with the most terrible severity. When herds of cattle are driven to market, they are suffered to go in the easiest way, each by himself; but when slaves are driven to market, they are fastened together with handcuffs, galled by iron collars and chains, and thus forced to travel on foot hundreds of miles, sleeping at night in their chains. Sheep, and sometimes horned cattle are marked with their owners' initials—but this is generally done with paint, and of course produces no pain. Slaves, too, are often marked with their owners' initials, but the letters are stamped into their flesh with a hot iron. Cattle are suffered to graze their pastures without stint; but the slaves are restrained in their food to a fixed allowance. The slaveholders' horses are notoriously far better fed, more moderately worked, have fewer hours of labor, and longer intervals of rest than their slaves; and their valuable horses are far more comfortably housed and lodged, and their stables more effectually defended from the weather, than the slaves' huts. We have here merely *begun* a comparison, which the reader can easily carry out at length, from the materials furnished in this work.

We will, however, subjoin a few testimonies of slaveholders, and others who have resided in slave states, expressly asserting that slaves are treated *worse than brutes.*

The late **Dr. George Buchanan**, of Baltimore, Maryland, a member of the American Philosophical Society, in an oration delivered in Baltimore, July 4, 1791, page 10, says:

"The Africans whom you despise, whom you *more inhumanly treat than brutes,* are equally capable of improvement with yourselves."

The **Rev. George Whitefield**, in his celebrated letter to the slaveholders of Maryland, Virginia, North and South Carolina, and Georgia, written one hundred years ago, (See Benezet's "Caution to Great Britain and her Colonies", page 13), says:

"Sure I am, it is sinful to use them as bad, nay worse than if they were brutes; and whatever particular *exceptions* there may be, (as I would charitably hope there are some) I fear the *generality* of you that own negroes, *are liable to such a charge."*

Mr. Rice, of Kentucky in his speech in the Convention that formed the Constitution of that state, in 1790, says:

"He [the slave] is a rational creature, reduced by the power of legislation to the *state of a brute,* and thereby deprived of every privilege of humanity. The brute may steal or rob, to supply his hunger; but the slave, though in the most starving condition, *dare not do either, on 'penalty of death, or some severe punishment."*

Rev. Horace Moulton, a minister of the Methodist Episcopal Church, in Marlborough, Mass. who lived some years in Georgia, says:

"The southern horses and dogs have enough to eat, and good care is taken of them; but southern negroes—who can describe their misery and their wretchedness, their nakedness and their cruel scourgings! None but God. Should we *whip our horses* as they whip their slaves, even for small offenses, we should expose ourselves to the penalty of the law."

Rev. Phineas Smith, Centreville, Allegany County, New York, who has resided four years in the midst of southern slavery:

"Avarice and cruelty are twin sisters; and I do not hesitate to declare before the world, as my deliberate opinion, that there is *less compassion* for working slaves at the south, than for working oxen at the north."

Stephen Sewall, Esq. Winthrop, Maine, a member of the Congregational Church, and late agent of the Winthrop Manufacturing Company, who resided five years in Alabama, says:

"I do not think that brutes, not even horses, are treated with *so much cruelty* as American slaves.

If the preceding considerations are insufficient to remove incredulity respecting the cruelties suffered by slaves, and if northern objectors still say, 'We might believe such things of savages, but that civilized men, and republicans, in this Christian country, can openly and by system perpetrate such enormities, is impossible;'—to such we reply, that this incredulity of the people of the free states, is not only discreditable to their intelligence, but to their consistency.

Who is so ignorant as not to know, or so incredulous as to disbelieve, that the early Baptists of New England were fined, imprisoned, scourged, and finally banished by our puritan forefathers? And that the Quakers were confined in dungeons, publicly whipped at the cart-tail, had their ears cut off, cleft sticks put upon their tongues, and that five of them, four men and one woman, were hung on Boston Common, for propagating the sentiments of the Society of Friends? Who discredits the fact, that the civil authorities in Massachusetts, less than a hundred and fifty years ago, confined in the public jail a little girl of four years old, and publicly hung the Rev. Mr. Burroughs, and eighteen other persons, mostly women, and killed another, (Giles Corey,) by extending him upon his back, and piling weights upon his breast till he was crushed to death*—and this for no other reason than that these men and women, and this little child, were accused by others of *bewitching* them.

* Judge Sewall, of Mass. in his diary, describing this horrible scene, says that when the tongue of the poor sufferer had, in the extremity of his dying agony, protruded from his mouth, a person in attendance took his cane and thrust it back into his mouth.

Even the children in Connecticut, know that the following was once a law of that state:

"No food or lodging shall be allowed to a Quaker. If any person turns Quaker, he shall be banished, and not be suffered to return on pain of death."

These objectors can readily believe the fact, that in the city of New York, less than a hundred years since, thirteen persons were publicly burned to death, over a slow fire: and that the legislature of the same State took under its paternal care the African slave-trade, and declared that "all encouragement should be given to the *direct* importation of slaves; that all *smuggling* of slaves should be condemned, as *an eminent discouragement to the fair trader.*"

They do not call in question the fact that the African slave-trade was carried on from the ports of the free states till within thirty years; that even members of the Society of Friends were actively engaged in it, shortly before the revolutionary war.* That as late as 1807, no less than fifty-nine of the vessels engaged in that trade, were sent out from the little state of Rhode Island, which had then only about seventy thousand inhabitants; that among those most largely engaged in these foul crimes, are the men whom the people of Rhode Island delight to honor: that the man who dipped most deeply in that trade of blood (James De Wolf,) and amassed a most princely fortune by it, was not long since their senator in Congress; and another, who was captain of one of his vessels, was recently Lieutenant Governor of the state.

*See "Life and Travels of John Woolman", page 92.

They can believe, too, all the horrors of the middle passage, the chains, suffocation, maiming, strangling, starvation, drowning, and cold blooded murders, atrocities perpetrated on board these slave-ships by their own citizens, perhaps by their own townsmen and neighbors—possibly by their own *fathers;* but oh! They can't believe that the slaveholders can be so hard-hearted towards their slaves as to treat them with great cruelty.' They can believe that His Holiness the Pope, with his cardinals, bishops and priests, have tortured, broken on the wheel, and burned to death thousands of Protestants—that eighty thousand of the Anabaptists were slaughtered in Germany—that hundreds of thousands of the blameless Waldenses, Huguenots and Lollards, were torn in pieces by the most titled dignitaries of church and state, and that *almost every professedly Christian sect, has, at some period of its history, persecuted unto blood* those who dissented from their creed. They can believe, also, that in Boston, New York, Utica, Philadelphia, Cincinnati, Alton, and in scores of other cities and villages of the free states, 'gentlemen of property and standing,' led on by civil officers, by members of state legislatures, and of Congress, by judges and attorneys-general, by editors of newspapers, and by professed ministers of the gospel, have organized mobs, broken up lawful meetings of peaceable citizens, committed assault and battery upon their persons, knocked them down with stones, led them about with ropes, dragged them from their beds at midnight, gagged and forced them into vehicles, and driven them into unfrequented places, and there tormented and disfigured them—that they have rifled their houses, made bonfires of their furniture in the streets, burned to the ground, or torn in pieces the halls or churches in which they were assembled—attacked them with deadly weapons, stabbed some, shot others, and killed ONE. They can believe all this—and further, that a majority of the citizens in the places where these outrages have been committed, connived at them; and by refusing to indict the perpetrators, or, if they were indicted, by combining to secure their acquittal, and rejoicing in it, have publicly adopted these felonies as their own. All these things they can believe without hesitation, and that they have even been done by their own acquaintances, neighbors, relatives; perhaps those with whom they interchange courtesies, those for whom they *vote*, or to whose *salaries they contribute*—but yet, oh! They can never believe that slaveholders inflict cruelties upon their slaves!

They can give full credence to the kidnapping, imprisonment, and deliberate murder of William Morgan, and that by men of high standing in society; they can believe that this deed was aided and abetted, and the murderers screened from justice, by a large number of influential persons, who were virtually accomplices, either before or after the fact; and that this combination was so effectual, as successfully to defy and triumph over the combined powers of the government;—yet that those who constantly rob men of their time, liberty, and wages, and all their *rights,* should rob them of bits of flesh, and occasionally of a tooth, make their backs bleed, and put fetters on their legs, is too monstrous to be credited! Further these same persons, who 'can't believe' that slaveholders are so iron-hearted as to ill-treat their slaves, believe that the very *elite* of these slaveholders, those most highly esteemed and honored among them, are continually daring each other to mortal conflict, and in the presence of mutual friends, taking deadly aim at each other's hearts, with settled purpose to *kill,* if possible. That among the most distinguished governors of slave states, among their most celebrated judges, senators, and representatives in Congress, there is hardly *one,* who has not either killed, or tried to kill, or aided and abetted his friends in trying to kill, one or more individuals. That pistols, dirks, bowie knives, or other instruments of death. are generally carried throughout the slave states—and that deadly affrays with them, in the streets of their cities and villages, are matters of daily occurrence; that the sons of slaveholders in southern colleges, bully, threaten, and fire upon their teachers, and their teachers upon them; that during the last summer, in the most celebrated seat of science and literature in the south, the University of Virginia, the professors were attacked by more than seventy armed students, and, in the words of a Virginia paper, were obliged 'to conceal themselves from their fury;' also that almost all the riots and violence that occur in northern colleges, are produced by the turbulence and lawless passions of southern students. That such are the furious passions of slaveholders, no considerations of personal respect, none for the proprieties of life, none for the honor of our national legislature, none for the character of our country abroad, can restrain the slaveholding members of Congress from the most disgraceful personal encounters on the floor of our nation's legislature—smiting their fists in each other's faces, throttling, and even *kicking* and trying to *gouge* each other —that even during the session of the Congress just closed, no less than six slaveholders, taking fire at words spoken in debate, have either rushed at each other's throats, or kicked, or struck, or attempted to knock each other down; and that in all these instances, they would doubtless have killed each other, if their friends had not separated them. Further, they know full well, these were not insignificant, vulgar blackguards, elected because they were the head bullies and bottle-holders in a boxing ring, or because their constituents went drunk to the ballot box; but they were some of the most conspicuous members of the House—one of them a former speaker.

Our newspapers are full of these and similar daily occurrences among slaveholders, copied verbatim from their own accounts of them in their own papers, and all this we fully credit; no man is simpleton enough to cry out, 'Oh, I can't believe that slaveholders do such things,'—and yet when we turn to the treatment which these men mete out to their *slaves,* and show that they are in the habitual practice of striking, kicking, knocking down and shooting *them* as well as each other—the look of blank incredulity that comes over northern dough-faces, is a study for a painter: and then the sentimental outcry, with eyes and hands uplifted, 'Oh, indeed, I can't believe the slaveholders are so cruel to their slaves.' Most amiable and touching charity! Truly, of all Yankee notions and Free State products, there is nothing like a *'doughface'*—the great northern staple for the southern market—'made to order,' in any quantity, and *always on hand.* 'Doughfaces!' Thanks to a slaveholder's contempt for the name, with its immortality of truth, infamy and scorn.*

*"Doe face," which owes its paternity to John Randolph, age has mellowed into "*dough*face"—a cognomen quite as expressive and appropriate, if not as classical.

Though the people of the free states affect to disbelieve the cruelties perpetrated upon the slaves, yet slaveholders believe *each other* guilty of them, and speak of them with the utmost freedom. If slaveholders disbelieve any statement of cruelty inflicted upon a slave, it is not on account of its *enormity.* The traveler at the south will hear in Delaware, and in all parts of Maryland and Virginia, from the lips of slaveholders, statements of the most horrible cruelties suffered by the slaves farther south, in the Carolinas and Georgia; when he finds himself in those states he will hear similar accounts about the treatment of the slaves in *Florida* and *Louisiana;* and in Missouri, Kentucky, and Tennessee he will hear of the tragedies enacted on the plantations in Arkansas, Alabama and Mississippi. Since Anti-Slavery Societies have been in operation, and slaveholders have found themselves on trial before the world, and put upon their good behavior, northern slaveholders have grown cautious, and now often substitute denials and set defenses, for the voluntary testimony about cruelty in the far south, which, before that period, was given with entire freedom. Still, however, occasionally the 'truth will out,' as the reader will see by the following testimony of an East Tennessee newspaper, in which, speaking of the droves of slaves taken from the upper country to Alabama, Mississippi, Louisiana, &c., the editor says, they are 'traveling to a region where their condition through time WILL BE SECOND ONLY TO THAT OF THE WRETCHED CREATURES IN HELL. See "Maryville Intelligencer," of Oct. 4, 1835.

Distant cruelties and cruelties *long past,* have been till recently, favorite topics with slaveholders. They have not only been ready to acknowledge that their *fathers* have exercised great cruelty toward their slaves, but have voluntarily, in their official acts, made proclamation of it and entered it on their public records. The Legislature of North Carolina, in 1798, branded the successive legislatures of that state for more than thirty years previous, with the infamy of treatment towards their slaves, which they pronounce to be 'disgraceful to humanity, and degrading in the highest degree to the laws and principles of a free, Christian, and enlightened country.' This treatment was the enactment and perpetuation of a most barbarous and cruel law. But enough! As the objector can and does believe all the preceding facts, if he still 'can't believe' as to the cruelties of slaveholders, it would be barbarous to tantalize his incapacity either with evidence or argument. Let him have the benefit of the act in such case made and provided.

Having shown that the incredulity of the objector respecting the cruelty inflicted upon the slaves, is discreditable to his consistency, we now proceed to show that it is equally so to his *intelligence.*

Whoever disbelieves the foregoing statements of cruelties, on the ground of their enormity, proclaims his own ignorance of the nature and history of man. What! incredulous about the atrocities perpetrated by those who hold human beings as property, to be used for their pleasure, when history herself has done little else in recording human deeds, than to dip her blank chart in the bloodshed by arbitrary power, and unfold to human gaze the great red scroll? That cruelty is the natural effect of arbitrary power, has been the result of all experience, and the voice of universal testimony since the world began. Shall human nature's axioms, six thousand years old, go for nothing? Are the combined product of human experience, and the concurrent records of human character, to be set down as 'old wives' fables*?* To disbelieve that arbitrary power naturally and habitually perpetrates cruelties, where it can do it with impunity, is not only ignorance of man, but of *things.* It is to be blind to innumerable proofs which are before every man's eyes; proofs that are stereotyped in the very words and phrases that are on every one's lips. Take for example the words *despot* and *despotic.* Despot signifies etymologically, merely one who possesses arbitrary power, and at first, it was used to designate those alone who *possessed* unlimited power over human beings, entirely irrespective of the way in which they exercised it, whether mercifully or cruelly. But the fact, that those who possessed such power, made their subjects their *victims,* has wrought a total change in the popular meaning of the word. It now signifies, in common parlance, not one who *possesses* unlimited power over others, but one who exercises the power that he has, whether little or much, *cruelly.* So *despotic,* instead of meaning what it once did, something pertaining to the *possession* of unlimited power, signifies something pertaining to the *capricious, unmerciful and relentless exercise* of such power.

The word *tyrant* is another example—formerly it implied merely a *possession* of arbitrary power, but from the invariable abuse of such power by its possessors, the proper and entire meaning of the word is lost, and it now signifies merely one who *exercises power to the injury of others.* The words tyrannical and tyranny follow the same analogy. So the word arbitrary; which formerly implied that which pertains to the will of one, independently of others; but from the fact that those who had no restraint upon their wills, were invariably capricious, unreasonable and oppressive, these words convey accurately the present sense of *arbitrary,* when applied to a person.

How can the objector persist in disbelieving that cruelty is the natural effect of arbitrary power, when the very words of every day, rise up on his lips in testimony against him—words which once signified the *mere possession* of arbitrary power, but have lost their meaning, and now signify merely its cruel *exercise;* because such a use of it has been proved by the experience of the world, to be inseparable from its *possession*—words now frigid with horror, and never used even by the objector without feeling a cold chill run over him.

Arbitrary power is to the mind what alcohol is to the body; it intoxicates. Man loves power. It is perhaps the strongest human passion; and the more absolute the power, the stronger the desire for it; and the more it is desired, the more its exercise is enjoyed: this enjoyment is to human nature a fearful temptation,—generally an overmatch for it. Hence it is true, with hardly an exception, that arbitrary power is abused in proportion as it is *desired.* The fact that a person intensely desires power over others, *without restraint,* shows the absolute necessity of restraint. What woman would marry a man who made it a condition that he should have the power to divorce her whenever he pleased? Oh! He might never wish to exercise it, but the *power* he would have! No woman, not stark mad, would trust her happiness in such hands.

Would a father apprentice his son to a master, who insisted that his power over the lad should be *absolute?* The master might perhaps, never *wish* to commit a battery upon the boy, but if he should, he insists upon having full swing! He, who would leave his son in the clutches of such a wretch, would be bled and blistered for a lunatic as soon as his friends could get their hands upon him.

The possession of power, even when greatly restrained, is such a fiery stimulant, that its lodgment in human hands is always perilous. Give men the handling of immense sums of money, and all the eyes of Argus and the hands of Briareus can hardly prevent embezzlement.

The mutual and ceaseless accusations of the two great political parties in this country, show the universal belief that this tendency of human nature to abuse power, is so strong, that even the most powerful legal restraints are insufficient for its safe custody. From congress and state legislatures down to grog-shop caucuses and street wrangling, each party keeps up an incessant din about *abuses of power.* Hardly an officer, either of the general or state governments, from the President down to the ten thousand postmasters, and from governors to the fifty thousand constables, escapes the charge of *'abuse of power.'* 'Oppression,' 'Extortion,' 'Venality,' 'Bribery,' 'Corruption,' 'Perjury,' 'Misrule,' 'Spoils,' 'Defalcation,' stand on every newspaper. Now without any estimate of the lies told in these mutual charges, there is truth enough to make each party ready to believe of the other and *of their best men too,* any abuse of power, however monstrous. As is the State, so is the Church. From General Conferences to circuit preachers; and from General Assemblies to church sessions, abuses of power spring up as weeds from the dunghill.

All legal restraints are framed upon the presumption, that men will abuse their power if not hemmed in by them. This lies at the bottom of all those checks and balances contrived for keeping governments upon their centers. If there is among human convictions one that is invariable and universal, it is, that when men possess unrestrained power over others, over their time, choice, conscience, persons, votes, or means of subsistence, they are under great temptations to abuse it; and that the intensity with which such power is desired, generally measures the certainty and the degree of its abuse.

That American slaveholders possess a power over their slaves which is virtually absolute, none will deny.* That they *desire* this absolute power, is shown from the fact of their holding and exercising it, and making laws to confirm and enlarge it. That the desire to possess this power, every tittle of it, is *intense,* is proved by the fact that slaveholders cling to it with such obstinate tenacity, as well as by all their, doings and sayings, their threats, cursings and gnashings against all who denounce the exercise of each power as usurpation and outrage, and counsel its immediate abrogation.

* The following extracts from the laws of slave-states are proofs sufficient:
"The slave is ENTIRELY subject to the WILL of his master."—Louisiana Civil Code, Art. 273.
"Slaves shall be deemed, sold, taken, reputed, and adjudged in law to be *chattels personal,* in the hands of their owners and possessors, and their executors, administrators

and assigns, TO ALL INTENTS, CONSTRUCTIONS AND PURPOSES WHATSOEVER"—Laws of South Carolina, 2 Brev. Dig. 229; Prince's Digest, 446, &c.

From the nature of the case—from the laws of mind, such power, so intensely desired, gripped with such a death-clutch, and with such fierce spurning of all curtailment or restraint, *cannot but be abused.* Privations and inflictions must be its natural, habitual products, with ever and anon, terror, torture, and despair let loose to do their worst upon the helpless victims.

Though power over others is in every case liable to be used to their injury, yet, in almost all cases, the subject individual is shielded from great outrages by strong safeguards. If he have talents, or learning, or wealth, or office, or personal respectability, or influential friends, these, with the protection of law and the rights of citizenship, stand round him as a body guard; and even if he lacked all these, yet, had he the same color, features, form, dialect, habits, and associations with the privileged caste of society, he would find in *them* a shield from many injuries, which would be *invited,* if in these respects he differed widely from the rest of the community, and was on that account regarded with disgust and aversion. This is the condition of the slave; not only is he deprived of the artificial safeguards of the law, but has none of those *natural* safeguards enumerated above, which are a protection to others. But not only is the slave destitute of those peculiarities, habits, tastes, and acquisitions, which by as simulating the possessor to the rest of the community, excite their interest in him, and thus, in a measure, secure for him their protection; but he possesses those peculiarities of bodily organization which are looked upon with deep disgust, contempt, prejudice, and aversion. Besides this, constant contact with the ignorance and stupidity of the slaves, their filth, rags, and nakedness; their cowering air, servile employments, repulsive food, and squalid hovels, their purchase and sale, and use as brutes—all these associations, constantly mingling and circulating in the minds of slaveholders, and inveterated by the hourly irritations which must assail all who use human beings as things, produce in them a permanent state of feeling toward the slave, made up of repulsion and settled ill-will. When we add to this the corrosions produced by the petty thefts of slaves, the necessity of constant watching, their reluctant service, and indifference to their master's interests, their ill-concealed aversion to him, and spurning of his authority; and finally, that fact, as old as human nature, that men always hate those whom they oppress, and oppress those whom they hate, thus oppression and hatred mutually begetting and perpetuating each other—and we have a raging compound of fiery elements and disturbing forces, stimulating and inflaming the mind of the slaveholder against the slave, that *it cannot but break forth upon him with desolating fury.*

To deny that cruelty is the spontaneous and uniform product of arbitrary power, and that the natural and controlling tendency of such power is to make its possessor cruel, oppressive, and revengeful towards those who are subjected to his control, is, we repeat, to set at naught, the combined experience of the human race, to invalidate its testimony, and to reverse its decisions from time immemorial.

A volume might be filled with the testimony of American slaveholders alone, to the truth of the preceding position. We subjoin a few illustrations, and first, the memorable declaration of **President Jefferson**, who lived and died a slaveholder. It has been published a thousand times, and will live forever. In his "Notes on Virginia," sixth Philadelphia edition, p. 251, he says,—

"The WHOLE COMMERCE between master and slave, is a PERPETUAL EXERCISE of the most *boisterous passions,* the most unremitting DESPOTISM on the one part, and degrading submission on the other......The parent *storms,* the child looks on, catches the lineaments of *wrath,* puts on the same airs in the circle of smaller slaves, GIVES LOOSE TO THE WORST OF PASSIONS; and thus *nursed, educated, and daily exercised in tyranny,* cannot but be stamped by it with odious peculiarities."

Hon. Lewis Summers, Judge of the General Court of Virginia, and a slaveholder, said in a speech before the Virginia legislature in 1832; (see Richmond Whig of Jan. 26, 1832,):

"A slave population exercises *the most pernicious influence* upon the manners, habits an character, of those among whom it exists. Lisping infancy learns the vocabulary of abusive epithets, and struts the *embryo tyrant* of its little domain. The consciousness of superior destiny takes possession of his mind at its earliest dawning, and love of power and rule, 'grows with his growth, and strengthens with his strength.' Unless enabled to rise above the operation of those powerful causes, he enters the world with miserable notions of self-importance, and under the government of an unbridled temper."

The late **Judge Tucker of Virginia**, a slaveholder, and Professor of Law in the University of William and Mary, in his "Letter to a Member of the Virginia Legislature," 1801, says,—

"I say nothing of the baneful effects of slavery on our *moral character,* because I know you have been long sensible of this point."

The **Presbyterian Synod** of South Carolina and Georgia, consisting of all the clergy of that denomination in those states, with a lay representation from the churches, most, if not all of whom are slaveholders, published a report on slavery in 1834, from which the following is an extract:

"Those only, who have the management of servants, know what the *hardening effect* of it is upon *their own feelings towards them.* There is no necessity to dwell on this point, as all *owners* and *managers* fully understand it. He who commences to manage them with tenderness and with a willingness to favor them in every way, must be watchful, otherwise he will settle down in *indifference, if not severity.* "

General William H. Harrison, now of Ohio, son of the late Governor Harrison of Virginia, a slaveholder, while minister from the United States to the Republic of Colombia, wrote a letter to General Simon Bolivar, then President of that Republic, just as he was about assuming despotic power. The letter is dated Bogota, Sept. 22, 1826. The following is an extract:

"From knowledge of your own disposition and present feelings, your Excellency will not be willing to believe that you could ever be brought to an act of tyranny, or even to execute justice with unnecessary rigor. But trust me, sir; there is nothing more corrupting, nothing more *destructive of the noblest and finest feelings of our nature than the exercise of unlimited power.* The man, who in the beginning of such a career, might shudder at the idea of taking away the life of a fellow-being, might soon have his conscience so seared by the repetition of crime, that the agonies of his murdered victims might become music to his soul, and the drippings of the scaffold afford blood to swim in. History is full of such excesses."

William H. Fitzhugh, Esq. of Virginia, a slaveholder, says,—
"Slavery, in its mildest form, is cruel and unnatural; *its injurious effects on our morals and habits are mutually felt.* "

Hon. Samuel S. Nicholas, late Judge of the Court of Appeals of Kentucky, and a slaveholder, in a speech before the legislature of that state, Jan. 1837, says,—

"The deliberate convictions of the most matured consideration I can give the subject, are, that the institution of slavery is a *most serious injury to the habits, manners and morals* of our white population—that it leads to sloth, indolence, dissipation, and vice."

Dr. Thomas Cooper, late President of the College of South Carolina, in a note to his edition of the "Institutes of Justinian," page 413, says,—

"All absolute power has a direct tendency, not only to detract from the happiness of the persons who are subject to it, but to DEPRAVE THE GOOD QUALITIES OF THOSE WHO POSSESS IT" The whole history of human nature, in the present and every former age, will justify me in saying that *such is the tendency of power* on the one hand and slavery on the other."

A **South Carolina slaveholder**, whose name is with the executive committee of the Am. A. S. Society, says, in a letter, dated April 4, 1838:

"I think it (slavery) *ruinous to the temper* and to our spiritual life; it is a thorn in the flesh, forever and forever goading us on to say and to do what the Eternal God cannot but be displeased with. I speak from experience, and oh! My desire is to be delivered from it."

Monsieur C. C. Robin, who was a resident of Louisiana from 1802 to 1806, published a work on that country; in which, speaking of the effect of slaveholding on masters and their children, he says:

"The young creoles make the negroes who surround them, the play-things of their whims; they flog, for pastime, those of their own age, just as their fathers flog the others at their will. These young creoles, arrived at the age in which the passions are impetuous, *do not know how to bear contradiction;* they will have everything done which they command, *possible or not;* and in default of this, they avenge their offended pride by multiplied punishments."

Dr. George Buchanan, of Baltimore, Maryland, member of the American Philosophical Society, in an oration at Baltimore, July 4, 1791, said:

"For such are the effects of subjecting man to slavery, that *it destroys every humane principle,* vitiates the mind, instills ideas of unlawful cruelties, and eventually subverts the springs of government."— *Buchanan's Oration,* p. 12.

President Edwards the younger, in a sermon before the Connecticut Abolition Society, in 1791, page 8, says:

"Slavery has a most direct tendency to haughtiness, and a *domineering spirit* and conduct in the proprietors of the slaves, in their children, and in all who have the control of them. A man who has been bred up in domineering over negroes, can scarcely avoid contracting such a habit of haughtiness and domination as will express itself in his general treatment of mankind, whether in his private capacity, or in any office, civil or military, with which he may be invested."

The celebrated **Montesquieu**, in his "Spirit of the Laws," thus describes the effect of slaveholding upon the master:

"The master contracts all sorts of bad habits; and becomes *haughty, passionate, obdurate, vindictive, voluptuous, and cruel.*"

Wilberforce, in his speech at the anniversary of the London Anti-Slavery Society, in March, 1828, said:

"It is *utterly impossible* that they who live in the administration of the petty despotism of a slave community, whose minds have been *warped* and *polluted* by that contamination, should not *lose that respect* for their fellow creatures over whom they tyrannize, which is essential in the nature and moral being of man, to rescue them from the abuse of power over their prostrate fellow creatures."

In the great debate, in the British Parliament, on the African slave-trade, **Mr. Whitbread** said:

"Arbitrary power would spoil the hearts of the best."

But we need not multiply proofs to establish our position: it is sustained by the concurrent testimony of sages, philosophers, poets, statesmen, and moralists, in every period of the world; and who can marvel that those in all ages who have wisely pondered men and things, should be unanimous in such testimony, when the history of arbitrary power has come down to us from the beginning of time, struggling through heaps of slain, and trailing her parchments in blood.

Time would fail to begin with the first despot and track down the carnage step by step. All nations, all ages, ail climes crowd forward as witnesses, with their scars, and wounds, and dying agonies.

But to survey a multitude bewilders; let us look at a single nation. We instance Rome; both because its history is more generally known, and because it furnishes a larger proportion of instances, in which arbitrary power was exercised with comparative mildness, than any other nation ancient or modern. And yet, her whole existence was a tragedy, every actor was an executioner, the curtain rose amidst shrieks and fell upon corpses, and the only shifting of the scenes was from blood to blood. The whole world stood aghast, as under sentence of death, awaiting execution, and all nations and tongues were driven, with its own citizens, as sheep to the slaughter. Of her seven kings, her hundreds of consuls, tribunes, decemvirs, and dictators, and her fifty emperors, there is hardly one whose name has come down to us unstained by horrible abuses of power; and that too, notwithstanding we have mere shreds of the history of many of them, owing to their antiquity, or to the perturbed times in which they lived; and these shreds gathered from the records of their own partial countrymen, who wrote and sung their praises. What does this prove? Not that the Romans were worse than other men, nor that their rulers were worse than other Romans, for history does not furnish nobler models of natural character than many of those same rulers, when first invested with arbitrary power. Neither was it mainly because the martial enterprise of the earlier Romans and the gross sensuality of the later hardened their hearts to human suffering. In both periods of Roman history, and in both these classes, we find men, the keen sympathies, generosity, and benevolence of whose general character embalmed their names in the grateful memories of multitudes. *They were human beings and possessed power without restraint*—this unravels the mystery.

Who has not heard of the Emperor Trajan, of his moderation, his clemency, his gushing sympathies, his forgiveness of injuries and forgetfulness of self, his tearing in pieces his own robe, to furnish bandages for the wounded—called by the whole world in his day, "the best emperor of Rome;" and so affectionately regarded by his subjects, that, ever afterwards, in blessing his successors upon their accession to power, they always said, "May you have the virtue and goodness of Trajan!" yet the deadly conflict of gladiators who are trained to kill each other, to make sport for the spectators, furnished his chief pastime. At one time he kept up those spectacles for 123 days in succession. In the tortures which he inflicted on Christians, fire and poison, daggers and dungeons, wild beasts and serpents, and the rack, did their worst. He threw into the sea, Clemens, the venerable bishop of Rome, with an anchor about his neck; and tossed to the famishing lions in the amphitheatre the aged Ignatius.

Pliny the younger, who was proconsul under Trajan, may well be mentioned in connection with the emperor, as a striking illustration of the truth, that goodness and amiableness towards one class of men is often turned into cruelty towards another. History can hardly show a more gentle and lovely character than Pliny. While pleading at the bar, he always sought out the grievances of the poorest and most despised persons, entered into their wrongs with his whole soul, and never took a fee. Who can read his admirable letters without being touched by their tenderness and warmed by their benignity and philanthropy; and yet, this tender-hearted Pliny coolly plied with excruciating torture two spotless females, who had served as deaconesses in the Christian church, hoping to extort from them matter of accusation against the Christians. He commanded Christians to abjure their faith, invoke the gods, pour out libations to the statues of the emperor, burn incense to idols, and curse Christ. If they refused, he ordered them to execution.

Who has not heard of the Emperor Titus—so beloved for his mild virtues and compassionate regard for the suffering, that he was named " The Delight of Mankind;" so tender of the lives of his subjects that he took the office of high priest, that his hands might never be defiled with blood; and was heard to declare, with tears, that he had rather die than put another to death. So intent upon making others happy, that when once about to retire to sleep, and not being able to recall any particular act of beneficence performed during the day, he cried out in anguish, "Alas! I have lost a day!" And, finally, whom the learned Kennet, in his Roman Antiquities, characterizes as "the only prince in the world that has the character of *never doing an ill action."* Yet, witnessing the mortal combats of the captives taken in war, killing each other in the amphitheatre, amidst the acclamations of the populace, was a favorite amusement with Titus. At one time he exhibited shows of gladiators, which lasted one hundred days, during which the amphitheatre was flooded with human blood. At another of his public exhibitions he caused five thousand wild beasts to be baited in the amphitheatre. During the siege of Jerusalem, he set ambushes to seize the famishing Jews, who stole out of the city by night to glean food in the valleys: these he would first dreadfully scourge, then torment them with all conceivable tortures, and, at last, crucify them before the wall of the city. According to Josephus, not less than five hundred a day were thus tormented. And when many of the Jews, frantic with famine, deserted to the Romans, Titus cut off their hands and drove them back. After the destruction of Jerusalem, he dragged to Rome one hundred thousand captives, sold them as slaves, and scattered them through every province of the empire.

The kindness, condescension, and forbearance of Adrian were proverbial; he was one of the most eloquent orators of his age; and when pleading the cause of injured innocence, would melt and overwhelm the auditors by the pathos of his appeals. It was his constant maxim, that he was an Emperor, not for his own good, but for the benefit of his fellow creatures. He stooped to relieve the wants of the meanest of his subjects, and would peril his life by visiting them when sick of infectious diseases; he prohibited, by law, masters from killing their slaves, gave to slaves legal trial, and exempted them from torture; yet towards certain individuals and classes, he showed himself a monster of cruelty. He prided himself on his knowledge of architecture, and ordered to execution the most celebrated architect of Rome, because he had criticized one of the Emperor's designs. He banished all the Jews from their native land, and drove them to the ends of the earth; and unloosed the bloodhounds of persecution to rend in pieces his Christian subjects.

The gentleness and benignity of the Emperor Aurelius have been celebrated in story and song. History says of him, 'Nothing could quench his desire of being a blessing to mankind;' and Pope's eulogy of him is in the mouth of every schoolboy—'Like good Aurelius, let him reign;' and yet, 'good Aurelius,' lifted the flood gates of the fourth, and one of the most terrible persecutions against Christians that ever raged. He sent orders into different parts of his empire, to have the Christians murdered who would not deny Christ. The blameless Polycarp, trembling under the weight of a hundred years, was dragged to the stake and burned to ashes. Pothinus, Bishop of Lyons, at the age of ninety, was dragged through the streets, beaten, stoned, trampled upon by the soldiers, and left to perish. Tender virgins were put into nets, and thrown to infuriated wild bulls; others were fastened in red hot iron chairs; and venerable matrons were thrown to be devoured by dogs.

Constantine the Great has been the admiration of Christendom for his virtues. The early Christian writers adorn his justice, benevolence and piety with the most exalted eulogy. He was baptized, and admitted to the Christian church. He abrogated Paganism, and made Christianity the religion of his empire; he attended the councils of the early fathers of the church, consulted with the bishops, and devoted himself with the most untiring zeal to the propagation of Christianity, and to the promotion of peace and love among its professors; he convened the Council of Nice, to settle disputes which had long distracted the church, appeared in the assembly with admirable modesty and temper, moderated the heats of the contending parties, implored them to exercise mutual forbearance, and exhorted them to love unfeigned, to forgive one another, as they hoped to be forgiven by Christ. Who would not think it uncharitable to accuse such a man of barbarity in the exercise of power?—and yet he drove Arius and his associates into banishment, for opinion's sake, denounced death against all with whom his books should afterwards be found, and prohibited, on pain of death, the exercise, however peaceably, of the functions of any other religion than Christianity. In a fit of jealousy and rage, he ordered his innocent son, Crispus, to execution, without granting him a hearing; and upon finding him innocent, killed his own wife, who had falsely accused him.

To the preceding may be added Theodosius the Great, the last Roman emperor before the division of the empire. He was a member of the Christian church, and in his zeal against paganism, and what he deemed heresy, surpassed all who were before him. The Christian writers of his time speak of him as a most illustrious model of justice, generosity, magnanimity, benevolence, and every virtue. And yet Theodosius denounced capital punishments against those who held ' heretical' opinions, and commanded inter-marriage between cousins to be punished by burning the parties alive. On hearing that the people of Antioch had demolished the statues set up in that city, in honor of himself, and had threatened the governor, he flew into a transport of fury, ordered the city to be laid in ashes, and all the inhabitants to be slaughtered; and upon hearing of a resistance to his authority in Thessalonica, in which one of his lieutenants was killed, he instantly ordered a *general massacre* of the inhabitants; and in obedience to his command, seven thousand men, women and children were butchered in the space of three hours.

The foregoing are a few of many instances in the history of Rome, and of a countless multitude in the history of the world, illustrating the truth, that the lodgment of arbitrary power, in the best human hands, is always a fearfully perilous experiment; that the mildest tempers, the most humane and benevolent dispositions, the most blameless and conscientious previous life, with the most rigorous habits of justice, are no security, that, in a moment of temptation, the possessors of such power will not make their subjects their victims; illustrating also the truth, that, while men may exhibit nothing but honor, honesty, mildness, justice, and generosity, in their intercourse with those of their own grade, or language, or nation, or hue, they may practice towards others, for whom they have contempt and aversion, the most revolting meanness, perpetrate robbery unceasingly, and inflict the severest privations, and the most barbarous cruelties. But this is not all; history is full of examples, showing not only the effects of arbitrary power on its victims, but its terrible reaction on those who exercise it; blunting their sympathies, and hardening to adamant their hearts toward *them*, at least, if not toward the human race generally. This is shown in the fact that almost every tyrant in the history of the world, has entered upon the exercise of absolute power with comparative moderation; multitudes of them with marked forbearance and mildness, and not a few with the most signal condescension, magnanimity, gentleness and compassion. Among these last are included those who afterwards became the bloodiest monsters that ever cursed the earth. Of the Roman Emperors, almost every one of whom perpetrated the most barbarous atrocities, Vitellius seems to have been the only one who cruelly exercised his power from the *outset*. Most of the other emperors, sprung up into fiends in the hot-bed of arbitrary power. If they had not been plied with its fiery stimulants, but had lived under the legal restraints of other men, instead of going to the grave under the curses of their generation, multitudes might have called them blessed.

The moderation which has generally distinguished absolute monarchs at the commencement of their reigns, was doubtless in some cases assumed from policy; in the greater number, however, as is manifest from their history, it has been the natural workings of minds held in check by previous associations, and not yet hardened into habits of cruelty, by being accustomed to the exercise of power without restraint. But as those associations have weakened, and the wielding of uncontrolled sway has become a habit, like other evil doers, they have, in the expressive language of Scripture, 'waxed worse and worse.'

For eighteen hundred years an involuntary shudder has run over the human race, at the mention of the name of Nero; yet, at the commencement of his reign, he burst into tears when called upon to sign the death-warrant of a criminal, and exclaimed, 'Oh, that I had never learned to write!' His mildness and magnanimity won the affections of his subjects; and it was not till the poison of absolute power had worked within his nature for years, that it swelled him into a monster.

Tiberius, Claudius, and Caligula, began the exercise of their power with singular forbearance, and each grew into a prodigy of cruelty. So averse was Caligula to bloodshed, that he refused to look at a list of conspirators against his own life, which was handed to him; yet afterwards, a more cruel wretch never wielded a scepter. In his thirst for slaughter, he wished all the necks in Rome *one that* he might cut it off at a blow.

Domitian, at the commencement of his reign, carried his abhorrence of cruelty to such lengths, that he forbad the sacrificing of oxen, and would sit whole days on the judgment-seat, reversing the unjust decisions of corrupt judges; yet afterwards, he surpassed even Nero in cruelty. The latter was content to torture and kill by proxy, and without being a spectator; but Domitian could not be denied the luxury of seeing his victims writhe, and hearing them shriek; and often with his own hand directed the instrument of torture, especially when some illustrious senator or patrician was to be killed by piece-meal. Commodus began with gentleness and condescension, but soon became a terror and a scourge, outstripping in his atrocities most of his predecessors. Maximin too, was just and generous when first invested with power, but afterwards rioted in slaughter with the relish of a fiend. History has well said of this monarch, 'the change in his disposition may readily serve to show how dangerous a thing is power that could transform a person of such rigid virtues into such a monster.'

Instances almost innumerable might be furnished in the history of every age, illustrating the blunting of sympathies, and the total transformations of character wrought in individuals by the exercise of arbitrary power. Not to detain the reader with long details, let a single instance suffice.

Perhaps no man has lived in modern times, whose name excites such horror as that of Robespierre. Yet it is notorious that he was naturally of a benevolent disposition, and tender sympathies.

"Before the revolution, when as a judge in his native city of Arras he had to pronounce judgment on an assassin, he took no food for two days afterwards, but was heard frequently exclaiming, 'I am sure he was guilty; he is a villain; but yet, to put a human being to death!!' He could not support the idea; and that the same necessity might not recur, he relinquished his judicial office.—(See Laponneray's Life of Robespierre, p. 8.)

~ 305 ~

Afterwards, in the Convention of 1791, he urged strongly the abolition of the punishment of death; and yet, for sixteen months, in 1793 and 1794, till he perished himself by the same guillotine which he had so mercilessly used on others, no one at Paris consigned and caused so many fellow-creatures to be put to death by it, with more ruthless insensibility."— *Turner's Sacred History of the World,* vol. 2. p. 119.

But it is time we had done with the objection, "such cruelties are Incredible." If the objector still reiterates it, he shall have the last word without farther molestation.

An objection kindred to the preceding now claims notice. It is the profound induction that slaves *must* be well treated because *slaveholders say they are!*

Objection II—"SLAVEHOLDERS PROTEST THAT THEY TREAT THEIR SLAVES WELL."

Self-justification is human nature; self-condemnation is a sublime triumph over it, and as rare as sublime. What culprits would be convicted, if their own testimony were taken by juries as good evidence? Slaveholders are on trial, charged with cruel treatment to their slaves, and though in their own courts they can clear themselves *by their own oaths** they need not think to do it at the bar of the world. The denial of crimes, by men accused of them, goes for nothing as evidence in all *civilized* courts; while the voluntary confession of them is the best evidence possible, as it is testimony *against themselves,* and in the face of the strongest motives to conceal the truth. On the preceding pages, are hundreds of just such testimonies; the voluntary and explicit testimony of slaveholders against themselves, their families and ancestors, their constituents and their rulers; against their characters and their memories; against their justice, their honesty, their honor and their benevolence. Now let candor decide between those two classes of slaveholders, which is most entitled to credit; that which testifies in its own favor, just as self-love would dictate, or that which testifies against all selfish motives and in spite of them; and though it has nothing to gain, but everything to lose by such testimony, still utters it.

* The law of which the following is an extract, exists in South Carolina: "If any slave shall suffer in life, limb or member, when no white person shall be present, or being present, shall refuse to give evidence, the owner or other person, who shall have the care of such slave, and in whose power such slave shall be, shall be deemed guilty of such offense, *unless* such owner or other person shall make the contrary appear by good and sufficient evidence, or shall BY HIS OWN OATH CLEAR AND EXCULPATE HIMSELF. Which oath every court where such offense shall be tried, is hereby empowered to administer, and to *acquit the offender,* if clear proof of the offense be not made by *two* witnesses at least."— 2 Brevard's Digest, 242. The state of Louisiana has a similar law.

But if there were no counter testimony, if all slaveholders were unanimous in the declaration that the treatment of the slaves is *good,* such a declaration would not be entitled to a feather's weight as testimony; it is not *testimony* but *opinion.* Testimony respects matters of *fact,* not matters of opinion; it is the declaration of a witness as to *facts,* not the giving of an opinion as to the nature or qualities of actions, or the *character* of a course of conduct. Slaveholders organize themselves into a tribunal to adjudicate upon their own conduct, and give us in their decisions, their estimate of their own character; informing us with characteristic modesty, that they have a high opinion of themselves; that in their own judgment they are very mild, kind, and merciful gentlemen! In these conceptions of their own merits, and of the eminent propriety of their bearing towards their slaves, slaveholders remind us of the Spaniard, who always took off his hat whenever he spoke of himself, and of the Governor of Schiraz, who, from a sense of justice to his own character added to his other titles, those of, 'Flower of Courtesy,' 'Nutmeg of Consolation,' and Rose of Delight.'

The *sincerity* of those worthies, no one calls in question; their real notions of their own merits doubtless ascended into the sublime: but for aught that appears, they had not the arrogance to demand that their own notions of their personal excellence, should be taken as the *proof* of it. Not so with our slaveholders. Not content with offering incense at the shrine of their own virtues, they have the effrontery to demand, that the rest of the world shall offer it, because *they* do; and shall implicitly believe the presiding divinity to be a good Spirit rather than a Devil, because *they* call him so! In other words, since slaveholders profoundly appreciate their own gentle dispositions toward their slaves, and their kind treatment of them, and everywhere protest that they do truly show forth these rare excellencies, they demand that the rest of the world shall not only believe that they *think* so, but that they think *rightly;* that these notions of themselves are *true,* that their taking off their hats to themselves proves them worthy of homage, and that their assumption of the titles of, 'Flower of Kindness,' and 'Nutmeg of Consolation,' is conclusive evidence that they deserve such appellations!

Was there ever a more ridiculous doctrine, than that a man's opinion of his own actions is the true standard for measuring them, and the certificate of their real qualities!—that his own estimate of his treatment of others is to be taken as the true one, and such treatment be set down as *good* treatment upon the strength of his judgment. He who argues the good treatment of the slave, from the slaveholder's *good opinion* of such treatment, not only argues against human nature and all history, his own common sense, and even the testimony of his senses, but refutes his own arguments by his daily practice. Everybody acts on the presumption that men's feelings will vary with their *practices;* that the light in which they view individuals and classes, and their feelings towards them, will modify their opinions of the treatment which they receive. In any case of treatment that affects himself, his church, or his political party, no man so stultifies himself as to argue that such treatment must be good, because the *author* of it thinks so.

Who would argue that the American Colonies were well treated by the mother country, because parliament thought so? Or that Poland was well treated by Russia, because Nicholas thought so? Or that the treatment of the Cherokees by Georgia is proved good by Georgia notions of it? Or that of the Greeks by the Turks, by Turkish opinions of it? Or that of the Jews by almost all nations, by the judgment of their persecutors? Or that of the victims of the Inquisition, by the opinions of the Inquisitor general, or of the Pope and his cardinals? Or that of the Quakers and Baptists, at the hands of the Puritans,—to be judged of by the opinions of the legislatures that authorized, and the courts that carried it into effect. All those classes of persons did not, in their own opinion, abuse their victims. If charged with perpetrating outrageous cruelty upon them, all those oppressors would have repelled the charge with indignation.

Our slaveholders chime lustily the same song, and no man with human nature within him, and human history before him, and with sense enough to keep him out of the fire, will be gulled by such professions, unless his itch to be humbugged has put on the type of a downright chronic incurable. We repeat it—when men speak of the treatment of others as being either good or bad, their declarations are not generally to be taken as testimony to matters of *fact,* so much as expressions of *their own feelings* towards those persons or classes who are the subjects of such treatment. If those persons are their fellow citizens; if they are in the same class of society with themselves; of the same language, creed, and color; similar in their habits, pursuits, and sympathies; they will keenly feel any wrong done to them, and denounce it as base, outrageous treatment; but let the same wrongs be done to persons of a condition in all respects the reverse, persons whom they habitually despise, and regard only in the light of mere conveniences, to be used for their pleasure, and the idea that such treatment is barbarous will be laughed at as ridiculous. When we hear slaveholders say that their slaves are *well treated*, we have only to remember that they are not speaking of *persons*, but of *property*; not of men and women, but of *chattels* and *things*; not of friends and associates, but of *vassals* and *victims*; not of those whom they respect and honor, but of those whom they *scorn* and trample on; not of those with whom they sympathize, and co-operate, and interchange courtesies, but of those whom they regard with contempt and aversion, and disdainfully set with the dogs of their flock. Reader, keep this fact in your mind, and you will have a clue to the slaveholder's definition *of "good treatment."* Remember also, that a part of this "good treatment" of which slaveholders boast, is plundering the slaves of all their inalienable rights, of the ownership of their own bodies, of the use of their own limbs and muscles, of all their time, liberty, and earnings, of the free exercise of choice, of the rights of marriage and parental authority, of legal protection, of the right to be, to do, to go, to stay, to think, to feel, to work, to rest, to eat, to sleep, to learn, to teach, to earn money, and to expend it, to visit, and to be visited, to speak, to be silent, to worship according to conscience, in fine, their right to be protected by just and equal laws, and to be *amenable to such only*. Of *all these rights the slaves are plundered;* and this is a *part* of that "good treatment" of which their plunderers boast! What then is the rest of it? The above is enough for a sample, at least a specimen-brick from the kiln. Reader, we ask you no questions, but merely tell you what you *know*, when we say that men and women who can habitually do such things to human beings, can *do* ANYTHING *to them.*

The declarations of slaveholders, that they treat their slaves well, will put no man in a quandary, who keeps in mind this simple principle, that the state of mind towards others, which leads one to inflict cruelties on them, *blinds the inflictor* to the real nature of his own acts. To him, they do not *seem* to be cruelties; consequently, when speaking of such treatment toward such persons, he will protest that it is not cruelty; though, if inflicted upon himself or his friends, he would indignantly stigmatize it as atrocious barbarity. The objector equally overlooks another every-day fact of human nature, which is this...that cruelties invariably cease to *seem* cruelties when the *habit* is formed, though previously the mind regarded them as such, and shrunk from them with horror.

The following fact, related by the late lamented **Thomas Pringle**, whose Life and Poems have recently been published in England, is an appropriate illustration. Mr. Pringle states it on the authority of Captain W. F. Owen, of the Royal Navy:

"When his Majesty's ships, the Leven and the Barraconta, employed in surveying the coast of Africa, were at Mozambique, in 1823, the officers were introduced to the family of Senor Manuel Pedro d'Almeydra, a native of Portugal, who was a considerable merchant settled on that coast; and it was an opinion agreed in by all, that Donna Sophia d'Almeydra was the most superior woman they had seen since they left England. Captain Owen, the leader of the expedition, expressing to Senor d'Almeydra his detestation of slavery, the Senor replied, 'You will not be long here before you change your sentiments. Look at my Sophia there. Before she would marry me, she made me promise that I should give up the slave trade. When we first settled at Mozambique, she was continually interceding for the slaves, and she *constantly wept when I punished them;* and now she is among the slaves from morning to night; she regulates the whole of my slave establishment; she inquires into every offense committed by them, pronounces sentence upon the offender, and *stands by and sees them punished.'*

"To this, Mr. Pringle, who was himself for six years a resident of the English settlement at the Cape of Good Hope, adds, 'The writer of this article has seen, in the course of five or six years, as great a change upon English ladies and gentlemen of respectability, as that described to have taken place in Donna Sophia d'Almeydra; and one of the individuals whom he has in his eye, while he writes this passage, lately confessed to him this melancholy change, remarking at the same time, 'how altered I am in my feelings with regard to slavery. I do not appear to myself the same person I was on my arrival in this colony, and if I would give the world for the feelings I then had, I could not recall them.'"

Slaveholders know full well that familiarity with slavery produces indifference to its cruelties and reconciles the mind to them. The late

Judge Tucker, a Virginia slaveholder and professor of law in the University of William and Mary, in the appendix to his edition of Blackstone's Commentaries, part 2, pp. 56, 57, commenting on the law of Virginia previous to 1792, which outlawed fugitive slaves, says:

"Such are the cruelties to which slavery gives rise, such the horrors to which the mind becomes *reconciled* by its adoption."

The following facts from the pen of **Charles Stuart**, happily illustrate the same principle:

"A young lady, the daughter of a Jamaica planter, was sent at an early age to school in England, and after completing her education, returned to her native country.

"She is now settled with her husband and family in England. I visited her near Bath, early last spring, (1834.) Conversing on the above subject, the paralyzing effects of slaveholding on the heart, she said:

"While at school in England, I often thought with peculiar tenderness of the kindness of a slave who had nursed and carried me about. Upon returning to my father's, one of my first inquiries was about him. I was deeply afflicted to find that he was on the point of undergoing a "law flogging for having run away." I threw myself at my father's feet and implored with tears, his pardon; but my father steadily replied, that it would ruin the discipline of the plantation, and that the punishment must take place. I wept in vain, and retired so grieved and disgusted, that for some days after, I could scarcely bear with patience, the sight of my own father. But many months had not elapsed ere I *was as ready as anybody* to seize the domestic whip, *and flog my slaves without hesitation.*"

"This lady is one of the most Christian and noble minds of my acquaintance. She and her husband distinguished themselves several years ago, in Jamaica, by immediately emancipating their slaves."

"A lady, now in the West Indies, was sent in her infancy, to her friends, near Belfast, in Ireland, for education. She remained under their charge from five to fifteen years of age, and grew up everything which her friends could wish. At fifteen, she returned to the West Indies—was married—and after some years paid her friends near Belfast, a second visit. Towards white people, she was the same elegant, and interesting woman as before; apparently full of every virtuous and tender feeling; but towards the colored people she was like a tigress. If Wilberforce's name was mentioned, she would say, 'Oh, I wish we had the wretch in the West

Indies, I would be one of the first to help to tear his heart out!'—and then she would tell of the manner in which the West Indian ladies used to treat their slaves. 'I have often,' she said, 'when my women have displeased me, snatched their baby from their bosom, and running with it to a well, have tied my shawl round its shoulders and pretended to be drowning it: oh, it was so funny to hear the mother's screams!!'—and then she laughed almost convulsively at the recollection."

Mr. John M. Nelson, a native of Virginia, whose testimony is on a preceding page, furnishes a striking illustration of the principle in his own case. He says: "When I was quite a child, I recollect it grieved me very much to see one tied up to be whipped, and I used to intercede *with tears in their behalf,* and *mingle my cries with theirs,* and feel almost willing to take part of the punishment. Yet such is the hardening nature of such scenes, that from this kind of commiseration for the suffering slave, I became so blunted that I could not only witness their stripes with composure, but *myself* inflict them, and that without remorse. When I was perhaps fourteen or fifteen years of age, I undertook to correct a young fellow named Ned, for some supposed offense, I think it was leaving a bridle out of its proper place; he being larger and stronger than myself took hold of my arms and held me, in order to prevent my striking him ; this I considered the height of insolence, and cried for help, when my father and mother both came running to my rescue. My father stripped and tied him, and took him into the orchard, where switches were plenty, and directed me to whip him; when one switch wore out he supplied me with others. After I had whipped him a while, he fell on his knees to implore forgiveness, and I kicked him in the face; my father said, 'don't kick him but whip him,' this I did until his back was literally covered with *wells."*

W. C. Gildersleeve, Esq., a native of Georgia, now elder of the Presbyterian Church, Wilkes-Barre, Penn. after describing the flogging of a slave, in which his hands were tied together, and the slave hoisted by a rope, so that his feet could not touch the ground; in which condition one hundred lashes were inflicted, says:

"I stood by and witnessed the whole without feeling the least compassion; so *hardening* is the influence of slavery that it *very much destroys feeling for the slave."*

Mrs. Child, in her admirable "Appeal," has the following remarks:

"The ladies who remove from the free States into the slaveholding ones almost invariably write that the sight of slavery was at first exceedingly painful; but that they soon become habituated to it; and after a while, they are very apt to vindicate the system, upon the ground that it is extremely convenient to have such submissive servants. This reason was actually given by a lady of my acquaintance, who is considered an unusually fervent Christian. Yet Christianity expressly teaches us to love our neighbor as ourselves. This shows how dangerous it is, for even the best of us, to become *accustomed* to what is wrong.

"A judicious and benevolent friend lately told me the story of one of her relatives, who married a slave owner, and removed to his plantation. The lady in question was considered very amiable, and had a serene, affectionate expression of countenance. After several years residence among her slaves, she visited New England. 'Her history was written in her face,' said my friend; 'its expression had changed into that of a fiend. She brought but few slaves with her; and those few were of course compelled to perform additional labor. One faithful negro woman nursed the twins of her mistress, and did all the washing, ironing, and scouring. If, after a sleepless night with the restless babes, (driven from the bosom of their mother,) she performed her toilsome avocations with diminished activity, her mistress, with her own lady-like hands, applied the cowskin, and the neighborhood resounded with the cries of her victim. The instrument of punishment was actually kept hanging in the entry, to the no small disgust of her New England visitors. For my part,' continued my friend, 'I did not try to be polite to her; for I was not hypocrite enough to conceal my indignation.'"

The fact that the greatest cruelties may be exercised quite unconsciously when cruelty has become a habit and that at the same time, the mind may feel great sympathy and commiseration towards other persons and even towards irrational animals, is illustrated in the case of Tamerlane the Great. In his Life, written by himself, he speaks with the greatest sincerity and tenderness of his grief at having accidentally crushed an ant; and yet he ordered melted lead to be poured down the throats of certain persons who drank wine contrary to his commands. He was manifestly sincere in thinking himself humane, and when speaking of the most atrocious cruelties perpetrated by himself, it does not seem to ruffle in the least the self-complacency with which he regards his own humanity and piety. In one place he says, "I never undertook anything but I commenced it placing my faith on God"—and he adds soon after, "the people of Shiraz took part with Shah Mansur, and put my governor to death; I therefore ordered *a general massacre of all the inhabitants.*"

It is one of the most common caprices of human nature, for the heart to become by habit, not only totally insensible to certain forms of cruelty, which at first gave it inexpressible pain, but even to find its chief amusement in such cruelties, till utterly intoxicated by their stimulation; while at the same time the mind seems to be pained as keenly as ever, at forms of cruelty to which it has not become accustomed, thus retaining *apparently* the same general susceptibilities. Illustrations of this are to be found everywhere; one happens to lie before us. Bourgoing, in his history of modern Spain, speaking of the bull fights, the barbarous national amusement of the Spaniards, says:

"Young ladies, old men, people of all ages and of all characters, are present, and yet the habit of attending these bloody festivals does not correct their weakness or their timidity, nor injure the sweetness of their manners. I have moreover known foreigners, distinguished by the gentleness of their manners, who experienced at first seeing a bull-fight such very violent emotions as made them turn pale, and they became ill; but, notwithstanding, this entertainment became afterwards an irresistible attraction, without operating any revolution in their characters."

Modern State of Spain, by J. F. Bourgoing, Minister Plenipotentiary from France to the Court of Madrid, Vol. ii., page 342.

It is the *novelty* of cruelty, rather than the *degree,* which repels most minds. Cruelty in a *new* form, however slight, will often pain a mind that is totally unmoved by the most horrible cruelties in a form to which it is *accustomed.* When Pompey was at the zenith of his popularity in Rome, he ordered some elephants to be tortured in the amphitheatre for the amusement of the populace; this was the first time they had witnessed the torture of those animals, and though for years accustomed to witness in the same place, the torture of lions, tigers, leopards, and almost all sorts of wild beasts, as well as that of men of all nations, and to shout acclamations over their agonies, yet, this *novel form* of cruelty so shocked the beholders, that the most popular man in Rome was execrated as a cruel monster, and came near falling a victim to the fury of those who just before were ready to adore him.

We will now briefly notice another objection, somewhat akin to the preceding, and based mainly upon the same and similar fallacies

Objection III—"SLAVEHOLDERS ARE PROVERBIAL FOR THEIR KINDNESS, HOSPITALITY, BENEVOLENCE, AND GENEROSITY."

Multitudes scout as fictions the cruelties inflicted upon slaves, because slaveholders are famed for their courtesy and hospitality. They tell us that their generous and kind attentions to their guests, and their well-known sympathy for the suffering, sufficiently prove the charges of cruelty brought against them to be calumnies, of which their uniform character is a triumphant refutation.

Now that slaveholders are proverbially hospitable to their guests, and spare neither pains nor expense in ministering to their accommodation and pleasure, is freely admitted and easily accounted for. That those who make their inferiors work for them, without pay, should be courteous and hospitable to those of their equals and superiors whose good opinions they desire, is human nature in its everyday dress. The objection consists of a fact and an inference; the fact, that slaveholders have a special care to the accommodation of their *guests;* the inference, that therefore they must seek the comfort of their *slaves*—that as they are bland and obliging to their equals, they must be mild and condescending to their inferiors—that as the wrongs of their own grade excite their indignation, and their woes move their sympathies, they must be touched by those of their chattels— that as they are full of pains-taking toward those whose good opinions and good offices they seek, they will, of course, show special attention to those to whose good opinions they are indifferent, and whose good offices they can *compel*—that as they honor the literary and scientific, they must treat with high consideration those to whom they deny the alphabet—that as they are courteous to certain *persons,* they must be so to "property"— eager to anticipate the wishes of visitors, they cannot but gratify those of their vassals—jealous for the rights of the Texans, quick to feel at the disfranchisement of Canadians and of Irishmen, alive to the oppressions of the Greeks and the Poles, they must feel keenly for their *negroes!* Such conclusions from such premises do not call for serious refutation. Even a half-grown boy, who should argue, that because men have certain feelings toward certain persons in certain circumstances, they must have the same feelings toward all persons in all circumstances, or toward persons in opposite circumstances, of totally different grades, habits, and personal peculiarities, might fairly be set down as a hopeless simpleton: and yet, men of sense and reflection on other subjects, seem bent upon stultifying themselves by just such shallow inferences from the fact, that slaveholders are hospitable and generous to certain persons in certain grades of society belonging to their own caste. On the ground of this reasoning, all the crimes ever committed may be disproved, by showing that their perpetrators were hospitable and generous to those who sympathized and co-operated with them. To prove that a man does not hate one of his neighbors, it is only necessary to show that he loves another; to make it appear that he does not treat contemptuously the ignorant, he has only to show that he bows respectfully to the learned; to demonstrate that he does not disdain his inferiors, lord it over his dependents, and grind the faces of the poor, he need only show that he is polite to the rich, pays deference to titles and office, and fawns for favor upon those above him! The fact that a man always smiles on his customers, proves that he never scowls at those who dun him! and since he has always a melodious "good morning!" for "gentlemen of property and standing," it is certain that he never snarls at beggars. He who is quick to make room for a doctor of divinity, will, of course, see to it that he never runs against a porter; and he who clears the way for a lady, will be sure never to rush against a market-woman, or jostle an apple-seller's board. If accused of beating down his laundress to the lowest fraction, of making his boot-black call a dozen times for his pay, of higgling and screwing a fish boy till he takes off two cents, or of threatening to discharge his seamstress unless she will work for a shilling a day! How easy to brand it all as slander, by showing that he pays his minister in advance, is generous in Christmas presents, gives a splendid new-year's party, expends hundreds on elections, and puts his name with a round sum on the subscription paper of the missionary society.

Who can forget the hospitality of King Herod, that model of generosity "beyond all ancient fame," who offered half his kingdom to a guest, as a compensation for an hour's amusement. Could such a noble spirit have murdered John the Baptist? Incredible! Joab too! How his soft heart was pierced at the exile of Absalom! And how his bowels yearned to restore him to his home! Of course, it is all fiction about his assassinating his nephew, Amasa, and Abner the captain of the host! Since David twice spared the life of Saul when he came to murder him, wept on the neck of

Jonathan, threw himself upon the ground in anguish when his child sickened, and bewailed, with a broken heart, the loss of Absalom—it proves that he did not coolly plot and deliberately consummate the murder of Uriah! As the Government of the United States generously gave a township of land to General Lafayette, it proves that they have never defrauded the Indians of theirs! So the fact, that the slaveholders of the present Congress are, to a man, favorable to recognizing the independence of Texas, with her fifty or sixty thousand inhabitants, *before she has achieved it,* and before it is recognized by any other government, proves that these same slaveholders do *not oppose* the recognition of Haiti, with her million of inhabitants, whose independence was achieved nearly half a century ago, and which is recognized by the most powerful governments on earth!

But, seriously, no man is so slightly versed in human nature as not to know that men habitually exercise the most opposite feelings, and indulge in the most opposite practices toward different persons or different classes of persons around them. No man has ever lived who was more celebrated for his scrupulous observance of the most exact justice, and for the illustration furnished in his life of the noblest natural virtues, than the Roman Cato. His strict adherence to the nicest rules of equity—his integrity, honor, and incorruptible faith—his jealous watchfulness over the rights of his fellow citizens, and his generous devotion to their interest, procured for him the sublime appellation of "The Just." Towards free *men* his life was a model of everything just and noble; but to his slaves he was a monster. At his meals, when the dishes were not done to his liking, or when his slaves were careless or inattentive in serving, he would seize a thong and violently beat them, in presence of his guests. When they grew old or diseased, and *were* no longer serviceable, however long and faithfully they might have served him, he either turned them adrift and left them to perish, or starved them to death in his own family. No facts in his history are better authenticated than these.

No people were ever more hospitable and munificent than the Romans, and none more touched with the sufferings of others. Their public theatres often rung with loud weeping, thousands sobbing convulsively at once over fictitious woes and imaginary sufferers: and yet these same multitudes would shout amidst the groans of a thousand dying gladiators, forced by their conquerors to kill each other in the amphitheatre for the *amusement* of the public.*

* Dr. Leland, in his " Necessity of a Divine Revelation," thus describes the prevalence of these shows among the Romans:—" They were exhibited at the funerals of great and rich men, and on many other occasions, by the Roman consuls, praetors, aediles, senators, knights, priests, and almost all that bore great offices in the state, as well as by the emperors; and in general, by all that had a mind to make an interest with the people, who were extravagantly fond of those kinds of shows. Not only the men, but the women, ran eagerly after them; who were, by the prevalence of custom, so far divested of that compassion and softness which is natural to the sex, that they took a pleasure in seeing them kill one another, and only desired that they should fall genteelly, and in an agreeable attitude. Such was the frequency of those shows, and so great the number of men that were killed on those occasions, that Lipedus says, no war caused such slaughter of mankind, as did these sports of pleasure, throughout the several provinces of the vast Roman Empire."— *Leland's Neces. of Div. Rev.* vol. II. p. 51.

Alexander, the tyrant of Pheraes, sobbed like a child over the misfortunes of the Trojan queens, when the tragedy of Andromache and Hecuba was played before him; yet he used to murder his subjects every day for no crime, and without even setting up the pretence of any, but merely *to make himself sport.*

The fact that slaveholders may be full of benevolence and kindness toward their equals and toward whites generally, even so much so as to attract the esteem and admiration of all, while they treat with the most inhuman neglect their own slaves, is well illustrated by a circumstance mentioned by the **Rev. Dr. Channing**, of Boston, (who once lived in Virginia,) in his work on slavery, p. 162, 1st edition:

"I cannot," says the doctor, "forget my feelings on visiting a hospital belonging to the plantation of a gentleman *highly esteemed for his virtues,* and whose manners and conversation expressed much *benevolence* and *conscientiousness.* When I entered with him the hospital, the first object on which my eye fell was a young woman very ill, probably approaching death. She was stretched on the floor. Her head rested on something like a pillow, but her body and limbs were extended on the hard boards. The owner, I doubt not, had, at least, as much kindness as myself; but he was so used to see the slaves living with, out common comforts, that the idea of unkindness in the present instance did not enter his mind."

Mr. **George A. Avery**, an elder of a Presbyterian Church in Rochester, N. Y. who resided some years in Virginia, says:

"On one occasion I was crossing the plantation and approaching the house of a friend, when I met him, *rifle in hand,* in pursuit of one of his negroes, declaring he would shoot him in a moment if he got his eye upon him. It appeared that the slave had refused to be flogged, and ran off to avoid the consequences; *and yet the generous hospitality of this man to myself, and white friends generally, scarcely knew any bounds.*

"There were amongst my slaveholding friends and acquaintances, persons who were as *humane* and *conscientious* as men can be, and persist in the impious claim of *property* in a fellow being. Still I can recollect but *one instance* of corporal punishment, whether the subject were male or female, in which the infliction was not on the *bare back* with the *rawhide,* or a similar instrument, the subject being *tied* during the operation to a post or tree. The *exception* was under the following circumstances. I had taken a walk with a friend on his plantation, and approaching his gang of slaves, I sat down whilst he proceeded to the spot where they were at work; and addressing himself somewhat earnestly to a female who was wielding the hoe, in a moment caught up what I supposed a *tobacco stick,* (a stick some three feet in length, on which the tobacco, when cut, is suspended to dry,) about the size of a *man's wrist,* and laid on a number of blows furiously over her head. The woman crouched, and seemed stunned with the blows, but presently recommenced the motion of her hoe".

Dr. David Nelson, a native of Tennessee, and late president of Marion College, Missouri, in a lecture at Northampton, Mass. in January, 1839, made the following statement:

"I remember a young lady who played well on the piano, and was very ready to weep over any fictitious tale of suffering. I was present when one of her slaves lay on the floor in a high fever, and we feared she might not recover. I saw that young lady *stamp upon her with her feet;* and the only remark her mother made was, 'I am afraid Evelina is too *much* prejudiced against poor Mary.'"

General William Eaton, for some years U. S. Consul at Tunis, and commander of the expedition against Tripoli, in 1805, thus gives vent to his feelings at the sight of many hundreds of Sardinians who had been enslaved by the Tunisians:

"Many have died of grief, and the others linger out a life less tolerable than death. Alas! Remorse seizes my whole soul when I reflect, that this is indeed but a copy of the very barbarity which *my eyes have seen* in my own native country. *How frequently,* in the southern states of my own country, have I seen *weeping mothers* leading the guiltless infant to the sales with as *deep anguish* as if they led them to the slaughter; and *yet felt my bosom tranquil* in the view of these aggressions on defenseless humanity. But when I see the same enormities practiced upon beings whose complexions and blood claim kindred with my own, *I curse the perpetrators, and weep over the wretched victims of their rapacity.* Indeed, truth and justice demand from me the confession, that the Christian slaves among the barbarians of Africa are treated with more humanity than the African slaves among professing Christians of civilized America; and yet *here* [in Tunis] sensibility *bleeds at every pore* for the wretches whom fate has doomed to slavery."

Rev. H. Lyman, late pastor of the free Presbyterian Church, Buffalo, N. Y. who spent the winter of 1832-3 at the south, says:

"In the interior of Mississippi I was invited to the house of a planter, where I was received with great cordiality, and entertained with marked hospitality.

"There I saw a master in the midst of his household slaves. The evening passed most pleasantly, as indeed it must, where assiduous hospitalities are exercised towards the guest.

"Late in the morning, when I had gained the tardy consent of my host to go on my way, as a final act of kindness, he called a slave to show me across the fields by a nearer route to the main road. 'David,' said he, 'go and show this gentleman as far as the post-office. Do you know the big bay tree?' 'Yes sir.' 'Do you know where the cotton mill is?' 'Yes sir.' 'Where Squire Malcolm's old field is?' 'Y-e-s, sir,' said David, (beginning to be bewildered). "Do you know where Squire Malcolm's cotton field is?' 'No sir.' 'No sir? said the enraged master, *leveling his gun at him.* 'What do you stand here, saying, Yes, yes, yes, for, when you don't know?' All this was accompanied with *threats* and *imprecations,* and a manner that contrasted strangely with the *religious conversation and gentle manners* of the previous evening."

The , formerly a slaveholder in South Carolina, now pastor of the Presbyterian Church in Hennepin, Ill. in his "Review of Nevins' Biblical Antiquities," after asserting that slaveholding tends to beget "a spirit of cruelty and tyranny, and to destroy every generous and noble feeling," he adds the following as a note:

"It may be that this will be considered censorious, and the proverbial generosity and hospitality of the south will be appealed to as a full confutation of it. The writer thinks he can appreciate southern kindness and hospitality. Having been born in Virginia, raised and educated in South Carolina and Kentucky, he is altogether southern in his feelings, and habits, and modes of familiar conversation. He can say of the south as Cowper said of England, 'With all thy faults I love thee still, my country.' And nothing but the abominations of slavery could have induced him willingly to forsake a land endeared to him by all the associations of childhood and youth.

"Yet it is candid to admit that it is not all gold that glitters. There is a fictitious kindness and hospitality. The famous Robin Hood was kind and generous—no man more hospitable—he robbed the rich to supply the necessities of the poor. Others rob the poor to bestow gifts and lavish kindness and hospitality on their rich friends and neighbors. It is an easy matter for a man to appear kind and generous, when he bestows that which others have earned.

"I said, there is a fictitious kindness and hospitality. I once knew a man who left his wife and children three days, without firewood, without bread-stuff, and without shoes, while the ground was covered with snow—that he might indulge in his cups. And when I attempted to expostulate with him, he took the subject out of my hands, and expatiating on the evils of intemperance more eloquently than I could, concluded by warning me *with tears,* to avoid the snares of the latter. He had tender feelings, yet a hard heart. I once knew a young lady of polished manners and accomplished education, who would weep with sympathy over the fictitious woes exhibited in a novel. And waking from her reverie of grief, while her eye was yet wet with tears, would call her little waiter, and if she did not appear at the first call, would rap her head with her thimble till my head ached." I knew a man who was famed for kindly sympathies. He once took off his shirt and gave it to a poor white man. The same man hired a black man, and gave him for his *daily task,* through the winter, to feed the beasts, keep fires, and make one hundred rails: and in case of failure the lash was applied so freely, that, in the spring, his back was *one continued sore, from his shoulders to his waist.* Yet this man was a professor of religion, and famous for his tender sympathies to white men!"

~ 321 ~

Objection IV—"NORTHERN VISITORS AT THE SOUTH TESTIFY THAT THE SLAVES ARE NOT CRUELLY TREATED."

Answer:—Their knowledge on this point must have been derived, either from the slaveholders and overseers themselves, or from the slaves, or from their own observation. If from the slaveholders, *their* testimony has already been weighed and found wanting; if they derived it from the slaves, they can hardly be so simple as to suppose that the *guest, associate and friend of the master,* would be likely to draw from his *slaves* any other testimony respecting his treatment of them, than such as would please *him.* The great shrewdness and tact exhibited by slaves in *keeping themselves out of difficulty,* when close questioned by strangers as to their treatment, cannot fail to strike every accurate observer. The following remarks of **Chief Justice Henderson,** a North Carolina slaveholder, in his decision (in 1830,) in the case of the State *versus* Charity, 2 Devereaux's North Carolina Reports, 543, illustrate the folly of arguing the good treatment of slaves from their own declarations, *while in the power of their masters.* In the case above cited, the Chief Justice, in refusing to permit a master to give in evidence, declarations made to him by his slave, says of masters and slaves generally:

"The master has an almost *absolute control* over the body and *mind* of his slave. The master's *will* is the slave's *will.* All his acts, *all his sayings,* are made with a view to propitiate his master. His confessions are made, not from a love of truth, not from a sense of duty, not to speak a falsehood, but *to please his master*—and it is in vain that his master tells him to speak the truth, and conceals from him how he wishes the question answered. The slave *will* ascertain, or, which is the same thing, think that he has ascertained *the wishes of his master,* and MOULD HIS ANSWER ACCORDINGLY. We therefore more often get the wishes of the master, or the slave's belief of his wishes, than the truth."

The following extract of a letter from the **Hon. Seth M. Gates,** member elect of the next Congress, furnishes a clue by which to interpret the looks, actions, and protestations of slaves, when in the presence of their masters' guests, and the pains sometimes taken by slaveholders, in teaching their slaves the art of *pretending* that they are treated well, love their masters, are happy, &c. The letter is dated Leroy, Jan. 4, 1839.

"I have sent your letter to Rev. Joseph M. Sadd, Castile, Genesee county, who resided five years in a slave state, and left, disgusted with slavery. I trust he will give you some facts. I remember one fact, which his wife witnessed. A relative, where she boarded, returning to his plantation after a temporary absence, was not met by his servants with such demonstrations of joy as was their wont. He ordered his horse put out, took down his whip, ordered his servants to the barn, and gave them a most cruel beating, because they did not run out to meet him, and pretend great attachment to him. Mrs. Sadd had overheard the servants agreeing not to go out, before his return, as they said *they did not love him*—and this led her to watch his conduct to them. This man was a professor of religion!"

If these northern visitors derived their information that the slaves are *not* cruelly treated from *their own observation,* it amounts to this, *they did not see* cruelties inflicted on the slaves. To which we reply, that the preceding pages contain testimony from hundreds of witnesses, who testily that they *did see* the cruelties whereof they affirm. Besides this, they contain the solemn declarations of scores of slaveholders themselves, in all parts of the slave states, that the slaves are cruelly treated. These declarations are moreover fully corroborated, by the laws of slave states, by a multitude of advertisements in their newspapers, describing runaway slaves, by their scars, brands, gashes, maiming, cropped ears, iron collars, chains, &c. &e.

Truly, after the foregoing array of facts and testimony, and after the objectors' forces have one after another filed off before them, now to march up a phalanx of northern *visitors,* is to beat a retreat. 'Visitors!' What insight do casual visitors get into the tempers and daily practices of those whom they visit, or of the treatment that their slaves receive at their hands, especially if these visitors are strangers, and from a region where there are no slaves, and which claims to be opposed to slavery? What opportunity has a stranger, and a temporary guest, to learn the every-day habits and caprices of his host? Oh, these northern visitors tell us they have visited scores of families at the south, and never saw a master or mistress whip their slaves. Indeed! They have, doubtless, visited hundreds of families at the north—did they ever see, on such occasions, the father or mother whip their children? If so, they must associate with very ill-bred persons. Because well-bred parents do not whip their children in the presence, or within the hearing of their guests, are we to infer that they never do it *out* of their sight and hearing? But perhaps the fact that these visitors do not *remember* seeing slaveholders strike their slaves, merely proves, that they had so little feeling for them, that though they might be struck every day in their presence, yet as they were only slaves and 'niggers,' it produced no effect upon them; consequently they have no impressions to recall. These visitors have also doubtless *rode* with scores of slaveholders. Are they quite certain they ever saw them whip their *horses?* And can they recall the persons, times, places, and circumstances? But even if these visitors regarded the slaves with some kind feelings, when they first went to the south, yet being constantly with their oppressors, seeing them used as articles of property, accustomed to hear them charged with all kinds of misdemeanors, their ears filled with complaints of their laziness, carelessness, insolence, obstinacy, stupidity, thefts, elopements, &c. and at the same time, receiving themselves the most gratifying attentions and caresses from the same persons, who, while they make to them these representations of their slaves, are giving them airings in their coaches, making parties for them, taking them on excursions of pleasure, lavishing upon them their choicest hospitalities, and urging them to protract indefinitely their stay—what more natural than for the flattered guest to admire such hospitable people, catch their spirit, and fully sympathize with their feelings toward their slaves, regarding with increased disgust and aversion those who can habitually tease and worry such loveliness and generosity.*

* Well saith the Scripture, "A gift blindeth the eyes". The slaves understand this, though the guest may not; they know very well that they have no sympathy to expect from their master's guests; that the good cheer of the "big house," and the attentions shown them, will generally commit them in their master's favor, and against themselves. Messrs. Thome and Kimball, in their late work, state the following fact, in illustration of this feeling among the negro apprentices in Jamaica.

"The governor of one of the islands, shortly after his arrival, dined with one of the wealthiest proprietors. The next day one of the negroes of the estate said to another, "De new gubner been *poisoned.*" "What dat you say? inquired the other in astonishment, "De gubner been *poison'd!* Dah, now!—How him poisoned?" *"Him eat massa's turtle soup last night"* said the shrewd negro. The other took his meaning at once; and his sympathy for the governor was turned into concern for himself when he perceived that the poison was one from which he was likely to suffer more than his Excellency."—*Emancipation in the West Indies, p.* 334.

After the visitor had been in contact with the slaveholding spirit long enough to have imbibed it, (no very tedious process,) a cuff, or even a kick administered to a slave, would not be likely to give him such a shock that his memory would long retain the traces of it. But lest we do these visitors injustice, we will suppose that they carried with them to the south humane feelings for the slave, and that those feelings remained un-blunted; still, what opportunity could they have to witness the actual condition of the slaves? They come in contact with the house-servants only, and as a general thing, with none but the select ones of these, the parlor-servants; who generally differ as widely in their appearance and treatment from the cooks and scullions in the kitchen, as parlor furniture does from the kitchen utensils. Certain servants are assigned to the parlor, just as certain articles of furniture are selected for it, *to be seen*—and it is no less ridiculous to infer that the kitchen scullions are clothed and treated like those servants who wait at the table, and are in the presence of guests, than to infer that the kitchen is set out with sofas, ottomans, piano-fortes, and full-length mirrors, because the parlor is. But the house-slaves are only a fraction of the whole number. The *field-hands* constitute the great mass of the slaves, and these the visitors rarely get a glimpse at. They are away at their work by day-break, and do not return to their huts till dark. Their huts are commonly at some distance from the master's mansion, and the fields in which they labor, generally much farther, and out of sight. If the visitor traverses the plantation, care is taken that he does not go alone; if he expresses a wish to see it, the horses are saddled, and the master or his son gallops the rounds with him; if he expresses a desire to see the slaves at work, his conductor will know *where* to take him, and when, and *which* of them to show; the overseer, too, knows quite too well the part he has to act on such occasions, to shock the uninitiated ears of the visitors with the shrieks of his victims. It is manifest that visitors can see only the least repulsive parts of slavery, inasmuch as it is wholly at the option of the master, what parts to show them; as a matter of necessity, he can see only the *outside*—and that, like the outside of doorknobs and andirons, is furbished up to be *looked at.* So long as it is human nature to wear *the best side out,* so long the northern guests of southern slaveholders will see next to nothing of the reality of slavery. Those visitors may still keep up their autumnal migrations to the slave states, and, after a hasty survey of the tinsel hung before the curtain of slavery, without a single glance behind it, and at the paint and varnish that *cover up* dead men's bones, and while those who have hoaxed them with their smooth stories, and white-washed specimens of slavery, are tittering at their gullibility, they return in the spring on the same fool's-errand with their predecessors, retailing their lesson, and mouthing the praises of the masters, and the comforts of the slaves. They now become village umpires in all disputes about the condition of the slaves, and each thenceforward ends all controversies with his oracular, "I've *seen,* and sure I ought to know."

But all northern visitors at the south are not thus easily gulled. Many of them, as the preceding pages show, have too much sense to be caught with chaff.

We may add here, that those classes of visitors whose representations of the treatment of slaves are most influential in molding the opinions of the free states, are ministers of the gospel, agents of benevolent societies, and teachers who have traveled and temporarily resided in the slave states— classes of persons less likely than any others to witness cruelties, because slaveholders generally take more pains to keep such visitors in ignorance than others, because their vocations would furnish them fewer opportunities for witnessing them, and because they come in contact with a class of society in which fewer atrocities are committed than in any other, and that too, under circumstances which make it almost impossible for them to witness those which are actually committed.

Of the numerous classes of persons from the north who temporarily reside in the slave states, the mechanics who find employment on the *plantations* are the only persons who are in circumstances to look "behind the scenes." Merchants, peddlers, venders of patents, drovers, speculators, and almost all descriptions of persons who go from the free states to the south to make money, see little of slavery, except *upon the road,* at public inns, and in villages and cities.

Let not the reader infer from what has been said, that the parlor-slaves, chamber-maids, &c. in the slave states are not treated with cruelty— far from it. They often experience terrible inflictions; not generally so terrible or so frequent as the field-hands, and very rarely in the presence of guests.* House-slaves are for the most part treated far better than plantation-slaves, and those under the immediate direction of the master and mistress, than those under overseers and drivers. It is quite worthy of remark, that of the thousands of northern men who have visited the south, and are always lauding the kindness of slaveholders and the comfort of the slaves, protesting that they have never seen cruelties inflicted on them, &c. each perhaps, without exception, has some story to tell which reveals, better perhaps than the most barbarous butchery could do, a public sentiment toward slaves, showing that the most cruel inflictions must of necessity be the constant portion of the slaves.

* Rev. Joseph M. Sadd, a Presbyterian clergyman, in Castile, Genesee County, N. Y. recently from Missouri, where he has preached five years, in the midst of slaveholders, says, in a letter just received, speaking of the pains taken by slaveholders to conceal from the eyes of strangers and visitors, the cruelties which they inflict upon their slaves—

"It is difficult to be an eye-witness of these things; the master and mistress almost invariably punish their slaves, only in the presence of other slaves, or before other members of their own family, and often at the dead of night"

Though facts of this kind lie thick in every corner, the reader will, we are sure, tolerate even a *needless* illustration, if told that it is from the pen of **N. P. Rogers, Esq.** of Concord, N. H. who, whatever he writes, though it be, as in this case, a mere hasty letter, always finds readers to the end:

"At a court session at Guilford, Stafford County, N. H. in August, 1837, the Hon. Daniel M. Durell, of Dover, formerly Chief Justice of the Common Pleas for that state, and a member of Congress, was charging the abolitionists, in presence of several gentlemen of the bar, at their boarding house, with exaggerations and misrepresentations of slave treatment at the south. 'One instance in particular,' he witnessed, he said, where he 'knew they misrepresented. It was in the Congregational meeting house at Dover. He was passing by, and saw a crowd entering and about the door; and on inquiry, found that *abolition was going on in there.* He stood in the entry for a moment, and found the Englishman, Thompson, was holding forth. The fellow was speaking of the treatment of slaves; and he said it was no uncommon thing for masters, when exasperated with the slave, to hang him up by the two thumbs, and flog him. 'I knew the fellow lied *there,'* said the judge, 'for I had traveled through the south, from Georgia north, and I never saw a single instance of the kind. The fellow said it was a common thing.' 'Did you see any *exasperated masters,* Judge,' said I, 'in your journey?' 'No sir,' said he, 'not an individual instance.' 'You hardly are able to convict Mr. Thompson of falsehood, then, Judge,' said I, 'if I understood you right. He spoke, as I understood you, of *exasperated masters*—and you say you did not see any. Mr. Thompson did not say it was common for masters in *good humor* to hang up their slaves.' The Judge did not perceive the materiality of the distinction. 'Oh, they misrepresent and lie about this treatment of the niggers,' he continued. 'In going through all the states I visited, I do not now remember a single instance of cruel treatment. Indeed, I remember of seeing but one nigger struck, during my whole journey. There was one instance. We were riding in the stage, pretty early one morning, and we met a black fellow, driving a span of horses, and a load (I think he said) of hay. The fellow turned out before we got to him, clean down into the ditch, as far as he could get. He knew, you see, what to depend on, if he did not give the road. Our driver, as we passed the fellow, fetched him a smart crack with his whip across the chops. He did not make any noise, though I guess it hurt him some—he grinned.—Oh, no! These fellows exaggerate. The niggers, as a general thing, are kindly treated. There may be exceptions, but I saw nothing of it.' (By the way, the Judge did not know there were any abolitionists present.) 'What did you *do* to the driver, Judge,' said I, 'for striking that man? 'Do!' said he, 'I did nothing to him, to be sure.' 'What did you *say* to him, sir?' said I. 'Nothing,' he replied: 'I said nothing to him.' 'What did the other passengers do?' said I. 'Nothing, sir,' said the Judge. 'The fellow turned out the white of his eye, but he did not make any noise.' 'Did the driver say anything, Judge, when he struck the man?' 'Nothing,' said the Judge, 'only he *damned him,* and told him he'd learn him to keep out of the reach of his whip' 'Sir,' said I, 'if George Thompson had told this story, in the warmth of an anti-slavery speech, I should scarcely have credited it. I have attended many anti-slavery meetings, and I never heard an instance of such *cold-blooded, wanton, insolent,* diabolical cruelty as this; and, sir, if I live to attend another meeting, I shall relate this, and give Judge Durell's name as the witness of it.' An infliction of the most insolent character, entirely unprovoked, on a perfect stranger, who had showed the utmost civility, in giving all the road, and only could not get beyond the long reach of the driver's whip—and he a stage driver, a class *generous* next to the sailor, in the sober hour of morning—and *borne in silence*—and *told to show that the colored man of the south was kindly treated*—all evincing, to an unutterable extent, that the temper of the south toward the slave is merciless, even to *diabolism*—and that the north regards him with, if possible, a more fiendish indifference still!"

It seems but an act of simple justice to say, in conclusion, that many of the slaveholders from whom our northern visitors derive their information of the "good treatment" of the slave, may not *design* to deceive them. Such visitors are often, perhaps, generally brought in contact with the better class of slaveholders, whose slaves are really better fed, clothed, lodged, and housed; more moderately worked; more seldom whipped, and with less severity, than the slaves generally. Those masters in speaking of the *good* condition of their slaves, and asserting that they are treated *well,* use terms that are not *absolute* but *comparative* and it may be, and doubtless often is *true* that their slaves are treated well *as slaves,* in comparison with the treatment received by slaves generally. So the overseers of such slaves, and the slaves themselves, may, without lying or designing to mislead, honestly give the same testimony. As the great body of slaves within their knowledge *fare worse,* it is not strange that, when speaking of the treatment on their own plantation, they should call it *good.*

Objection V—"IT IS FOR THE INTEREST OF THE MASTERS TO TREAT THEIR SLAVES WELL."

So it is for the interest of the drunkard to quit his cups; for the glutton to curb his appetite; for the debauchee to bridle his lust; for the sluggard to be up betimes; for the spendthrift to be economical, and for all sinners to stop sinning. Even if it were for the interest of masters to treat their slaves well, he must be a novice who thinks *that* a proof that the slaves are well treated. The whole history of man is a record of real interests sacrificed to present gratification. If all men's actions were consistent with their best interests, folly and sin would be words without meaning.

If the objector means that it is for the *pecuniary* interests of masters to treat their slaves well, and thence infers their good treatment, we reply, that though the love of money is strong, yet appetite and lust, pride, anger and revenge, the love of power and honor, are each an overmatch for it; and when either of them is roused by a sudden stimulant, the love of money is worsted in the grapple with it. Look at the hourly lavish outlays of money to procure a momentary gratification for those passions and appetites. As the desire for money is, in the main, merely a desire for the means of gratifying *other* desires, or rather for one of the means, it must be the *servant* not the sovereign of those desires, to whose gratification its only use is to minister. But even if the love of money were the strongest human passion, who is simple enough to believe that it is all the time so powerfully excited, that no other passion or appetite can get the mastery over it? Who does not know that gusts of rage, revenge, jealousy and lust drive it before them as a tempest tosses a feather?

The objector has forgotten his first lessons; they taught him that it is human nature to gratify the *uppermost* passion: and is *prudence* the uppermost passion with slaveholders, and self-restraint their great characteristic? The strongest feeling of any moment is the sovereign of that moment, and rules. Is a propensity to practice *economy* the predominant feeling with slaveholders? Ridiculous! Every northerner knows that slaveholders are proverbial for lavish expenditures, never higgling about the *price* of a gratification. Human passions have not, like the tides, regular ebbs and flows, with their stationary, high and low water marks. They are a dominion convulsed with revolutions; coronations and dethronements in ceaseless succession—each ruler a usurper and a despot. Love of money gets a snatch at the scepter as well as the rest, not by hereditary right, but because, in the fluctuations of human feelings, a chance wave washes him up to the throne and the next perhaps washes him off, without time to nominate his successor. Since, then, as a matter of fact, a host of appetites and passions do hourly get the better of love of money, what protection does the slave find in his master's *interest,* against the sweep of his passions and appetites? Besides, a master can inflict upon his slave horrible cruelties without perceptibly injuring his health, or taking time from his labor, or lessening his value as property. Blows with a small stick give more acute pain, than with a large one. A club bruises, and benumbs the nerves, while a *switch,* neither breaking nor bruising the flesh, instead of blunting the sense of feeling, wakes up and stings to torture all the susceptibilities of pain. By this kind of infliction, more actual cruelty can be perpetrated in the giving of pain at the instant, than by the most horrible bruisings and lacerations; and that, too, with little comparative hazard to the slave's health, or to his value as property, and without loss of time from labor. Even giving to the objection all the force claimed for it, what protection is it to the slave? It *professes* to shield the slave from such treatment alone, as would either lay him aside from labor, or injure his health, and thus lessen his value as a working animal, making him a *damaged article* in the market. Now, is nothing *bad treatment* of a human being except that which produces these effects? Does the fact that a man's constitution is not actually shattered, and his life shortened by his treatment, prove that he is treated well? Is no treatment cruel except what sprains muscles, or cuts sinews, or bursts blood vessels, or breaks bones, and thus lessens a man's value as a working animal?

A slave may get blows and kicks every hour in the day, without having his constitution broken, or without suffering sensibly in his health, or flesh, or appetite, or power to labor. Therefore, beaten and kicked as he is, he must be treated *well,* according to the objector, since the master's *interest* does not suffer thereby.

Finally, the objector virtually maintains that all possible privations and inflictions suffered by slaves, that do not actually cripple their power to labor, and make them 'damaged merchandize,' are to be set down as 'good treatment,' and that nothing is *bad* treatment except what produces these effects.

Thus we see that even if the slave were effectually shielded from all those inflictions, which, by lessening his value as property, would injure the interests of his master, he would still have no protection against numberless and terrible cruelties. But we go further, and maintain that in respect to large classes of slaves; it is for the interest of their masters to treat them with barbarous inhumanity.

1. *Old slaves.* It would be for the interest of the masters to shorten their days.

2. *Worn out slaves.* Multitudes of slaves by being overworked have their constitutions broken in middle life. It would be *economical* for masters to starve or flog such to death.

3. *The incurably diseased and maimed.* In all such cases it would be *cheaper* for masters to buy poison than medicine.

4. *The blind, lunatics, and idiots.* As all such would be a tax on him, it would be for his interest to shorten their days.

5. *The deaf and dumb, and persons greatly deformed.* Such might or might not be serviceable to him; many of them at least would be a burden, and few men carry burdens when they can throw them off.

6. *Feeble infants.* As such would require much nursing, the time, trouble and expense necessary to raise them, would generally be more than they would be worth as *working animals.* How many such infants would be likely to be 'raised,' from *disinterested* benevolence? To this it may be added that in the far south and south west, it is notoriously for the interest of the master not to 'raise' slaves at all. To buy slaves when nearly grown, from the northern slave states, would be *cheaper* than to raise them. This is shown in the fact that mothers with infants sell for less in those states than those without them. And when slave traders purchase such in the upper country, it is notorious that they not un-frequently either sell their infants,

or give them away. Therefore it would be for the *interest* of the masters, throughout that region, to have all the new-born children left to perish. It would also be for his interest to make such arrangements as effectually to separate the sexes, or if that were not done, so to overwork the females as to prevent childbearing.

7. *Incorrigible slaves.* On most of the large plantations, there are, more or less, incorrigible slaves,—that is, slaves who *will not* be profitable to their masters—and from whom torture can extort little but defiance.* These are frequently slaves of uncommon minds, who feel so keenly the wrongs of slavery that their proud spirits spurn their chains and defy their tormentors.

* Advertisements like the following are not un-frequent in the southern papers:
From the Elizabeth (N.C.) *Phenix, Jan.*5, 1839.
"The subscriber offers for sale his blacksmith Nat, 28 years of age, and *remarkably large and likely.* The only cause of my selling him is I CANNOT CONTROL HIM. *Hertford, Dec.*5, 1838. J. Gordon."

They have commonly great sway over the other slaves, their example is contagious, and their influence subversive of 'plantation discipline.' Consequently they must be made a warning to others. It is for the *interest* of the masters (at least they believe it to be) to put upon such slaves iron collars and chains, to brand and crop them; to disfigure, lacerate, starve and torture them—in a word, to inflict upon them such vengeance as shall strike terror into the other slaves. To this class may be added the incorrigibly thievish and indolent; it would be for the interest of the masters to treat them with such severity as would deter others from following their example.

7. *Runaways.* When a slave has once runaway from his master and is caught, he is thenceforward treated with severity. It is for the interest of the master to make an example of him, by the greatest privations and inflictions.

8. *Hired slaves.* It is for the interest of those who hire slaves to get as much out of them as they can; the temptation to overwork them is powerful. If it be said that the master could, in that case, recover damages, the answer is, that damages would not be recoverable in law unless actual injury—enough to impair the power of the slave to labor be *proved.* And this ordinarily would be impossible, unless the slave has been worked so greatly beyond his strength as to produce some fatal derangement of the vital functions. Indeed, as all who are familiar with such cases in southern

courts well know, the proof of actual injury to the slave, so as to lessen his value, is exceedingly difficult to make out, and every hirer of slaves can overwork them, give them insufficient food, clothing, and shelter, and inflict upon them nameless cruelties with entire impunity. We repeat then that it is for the *interest* of the hirer to push his slaves to their utmost strength, provided he does not drive them to such an extreme, that their constitutions actually give way under it, while in his hands. The supreme court of Maryland has decided that, 'There must be *at least a diminution of the faculty of the slave for bodily labor* to warrant an action by the master.'—1 *Harris and Johnson's Reports*, 4.

9. *Slaves under overseers whose wages are proportioned to the crop which they raise.* This is an arrangement common in the slave states, and in its practical operation is equivalent to a bounty on *hard driving*—a virtual premium offered to overseers to keep the slaves whipped up to the top of their strength. Even where the overseer has a fixed salary, irrespective of the value of the crop which he takes off, he is strongly tempted to overwork the slaves, as those overseers get the highest wages who can draw the largest income from a plantation with a given number of slaves; so that we may include in this last class of slaves, the majority of all those who are under overseers, whatever the terms on which those overseers are employed.

Another class of slaves maybe mentioned; we refer to the slaves of masters who *bet* upon their crops. In the cotton and sugar region there is a fearful amount of this desperate gambling, in which, though money is the ostensible stake and forfeit, *human life* is the real one. The length to which this rivalry is carried at the south and south west, the multitude of planters who engage in it, and the recklessness of human life exhibited in driving the murderous game to its issue, cannot well be imagined by one who has not lived in the midst of it. Desire of gain is only one of the motives that stimulate them; — the *eclat* of having made the largest crop with a given number of hands, is also a powerful stimulant; the southern newspapers, at the crop season, chronicle carefully the "cotton brag," and the "crack cotton picking," and "unparalleled driving," &c. Even the editor of professedly religious papers, cheer on the *melee* and sing the triumphs of the victor. Among these we recollect the celebrated Rev. J. N. Maffit, recently editor of a religious paper at Natchez, Miss, in which he took care to assign a prominent place, and capitals to 'The Cotton Brag." The testimony of Mr.

Bliss, page 38, details some of the particulars of this *betting* upon crops. All the preceding classes of slaves are in circumstances which make it "for the *interest* of their masters," or those who have the management of them, to treat them cruelly.

Besides the operation of the causes already specified, which make it for the interest of masters and overseers to treat cruelly *certain classes* of their slaves, a variety of others exist, which make it for their interest to treat cruelly *the great body* of their slaves. These causes are the nature of certain kinds of products, the kind of labor required in cultivating and preparing them for market, the best times for such labor, the state of the market, fluctuations in prices, facilities for transportation, the weather, seasons, &c. &c. Some of the causes which operate to produce this are:

1. *The early market.* If the planter can get his crop into market early, he may save thousands which might be lost if it arrived later.

2. *Changes in the market.* A sudden rise in the market with the probability that it will be short, or a gradual fall with a probability that it will be long, is a strong temptation to the master to push his slaves to the utmost, that he may in the one case make all he can, by taking the tide at the flood, and in the other lose as little as may be, by taking it as early as possible in the ebb.

3. *High prices.* Whenever the slave-grown staples bring a high price, as is now the case with cotton, every slaveholder is tempted to overwork his slaves. By forcing them to do double work for a few weeks or months, while the price is up, he can *afford* to lose a number of them and to lessen the value of all by overdriving. A cotton planter with a hundred vigorous slaves would have made a profitable speculation, if, during the years '34, 5, and 6, when the average price of cotton was 17 cents a pound, he had so overworked his slaves that half of them died upon his hands in '37, when cotton had fallen to six and eight cents. No wonder that the poor slaves pray that cotton and sugar may be cheap. The writer has frequently heard it declared by planters in the lower country, that, it is more profitable to drive the slaves to such over exertion as to *use them up,* in seven or eight years, than to give them only ordinary tasks and protract their lives to the ordinary period.

4. *Untimely seasons.* When the winter encroaches on the spring, and makes late seed time, the first favorable weather is a temptation to overwork the slaves, too strong to be resisted by those who hold men as

mere working animals. So when frosts set in early, and a great amount of work is to be done in a little time, or great loss suffered. So also after a long storm either in seed or crop time, when the weather becomes favorable, the same temptation presses, and in all these cases the master would *save money* by overdriving his slaves.

5. *Periodical pressure of certain kinds of labor.* The manufacture of sugar is an illustration.

In a work entitled "Travels in Louisiana in 1802," translated from the French, by John Davis, is the following testimony under this head:

"At the rolling of sugars, an interval of from two to three months, they (the slaves in Louisiana,) work *both night and day.* Abridged of their sleep, they scarcely retire to rest during the whole period."

In an article on the agriculture of Louisiana, published in the second number of the "**Western Review**," is the following: "The work is admitted to be severe for the hands, (slaves) requiring, when the process of making sugar is commenced, TO BE PRESSED NIGHT AND DAY."

It would be for the interest of the sugar planter greatly to overwork his slaves, during the annual process of sugar-making.

The severity of this periodical pressure, in preparing for market other staples of the slave states besides sugar, may be inferred from the following. **Mr. Hammond**, of South Carolina, in his speech in Congress, Feb. 1. 1836, (See National Intelligencer) said:

"In the heat of the crop, the loss of one or two days, would inevitably ruin it."

6. *Times of scarcity.* Drought, long rain, frost, &c. are liable to cut off the corn crop, upon which the slaves are fed. If this happens when the staple which they raise is at a low price, it is for the interest of the master to put the slave on short rations, thus forcing him to suffer from hunger.

7. *The raising of crops for exportation.* In all those states where cotton and sugar are raised for exportation, it is, for the most part, more profitable to buy provisions for the slaves than to raise them. Where this is the case the slaveholders believe it to be for their interest to give their slaves less food, than their hunger craves, and they do generally give them insufficient sustenance.*

* Hear the testimony of a slaveholder, on this subject, a member of Congress from Virginia, from 1817 to 1830, Hon. Alexander Smyth:

In the debate on the Missouri question in the U. S. Congress, 1819-30, the admission of Missouri to the Union, as a slave state, was urged, among other grounds, as a measure of humanity to the slaves of the south. Mr. Smyth, of Virginia said, 'The plan of our opponents seems to be to confine the slave population to the southern states, to the countries where *sugar, cotton, and tobacco* are cultivated. But, sir, by confining the slaves to a part of the country where crops are raised for exportation, and the bread and meat are *purchased, you doom them to scarcity and hunger.* Is it not obvious that the way to render their situation more comfortable is to allow them to be taken where there is not the same motive to force the slave to INCESSANT TOIL, that there is in the country where cotton, sugar, and tobacco, are raised for exportation. It is proposed to hem in the blacks *where they are* HARD WORKED AND ILL FED that they may be rendered unproductive and the race be prevented from increasing. . . . The proposed measure would be EXTREME CRUELTY to the blacks. . . . You would doom them to SCARCITY AND HARD LABOR"—[Speech of Mr. Smyth, Jan. 38, 1820.]—See National Intelligencer.

Those states where the crops are raised for exportation, and a large part of the provisions purchased, are, Louisiana, Mississippi, Alabama, Arkansas, Western Tennessee, Georgia, Florida, and, to a considerable extent, South Carolina. That this is the case in Louisiana is shown by the following. "Corn, flour, and bread stud's, generally are obtained from Kentucky, Ohio," &c. See "Emigrant's Guide through the Valley of the Mississippi," Page 275. That it is the case with Alabama appears from the testimony of W. Jefferson Jones, Esq. a lawyer of high standing in Mobile. In a series of articles published by him in the Mobile Morning Chronicle, he says: (See that paper for Aug. 26, 1837.)

"The people of Alabama *export* what they raise, and *import* nearly all they consume. But it seems quite unnecessary to prove, what all persons of much intelligence well know, that the states mentioned export the larger part of what they raise, and import the larger part of what they consume. Now more than *one million of slaves* are held in those states, and parts of states, where provisions are mainly imported, and consequently they are "*doomed to scarcity and hunger.*"

Now let us make some estimate of the proportion which the slaves, included in the foregoing *nine classes,* sustain to the whole number, and then of the proportion affected by the operation of the *seven* causes just enumerated.

It would be nearly impossible to form an estimate of the proportion of the slaves included in a number of these classes, such as the old, the worn out, the incurably diseased, maimed and deformed, idiots, feeble infants, incorrigible slaves, &c. More or less of this description are to be found on all the considerable plantations, and often, many on the same plantation; though we have no accurate data for an estimate, the proportion cannot be less than one in twenty-five of the whole number of slaves, which would give a total of more than *one hundred thousand.* Of some of the remaining classes we have data for a pretty accurate estimate.

1st. *Lunatics.*—Various estimates have been made, founded upon the data procured by actual investigation, prosecuted under the direction of the Legislatures of different States; but the returns have been so imperfect and erroneous, that little reliance can be placed upon them. The Legislature of New Hampshire recently ordered investigations to be made in every town in the state, and the number of insane persons to be reported. A committee of the legislature, who had the subject in charge say, in their report—" From many towns no returns have been received, from others the accounts are erroneous, there being cases *known to the committee* which escaped the notice of the 'selectmen.' The actual number of insane persons is therefore much larger than appears by the documents submitted to the committee.

"The Medical Society of Connecticut appointed a committee of their number, composed of some of the most eminent physicians in the state, to ascertain and report the whole number of insane persons in that state. The committee says, in their report: "The number of towns from which returns have been received is seventy, and the cases of insanity which have been noticed in them are five hundred and ten." The committee adds, "fifty more towns remain to be heard from, and if insanity should be found equally prevalent in them, the entire number will scarcely fall short of *one thousand* in the state." This investigation was made in 1821, when the population of the state was less than two hundred and eighty thousand. If the estimate of the Medical Society be correct, the proportion of the insane to the whole population would be about one in two hundred and eighty. This strikes us as a large estimate, and yet a committee of the legislature of that state in 1837, reported seven hundred and seven insane persons in the state, who were either wholly or in part supported as *town paupers, or by charity.* It can hardly be supposed that more than *two-thirds* of the insane in Connecticut belong to families *unable to support them.* On this supposition, the whole number would be greater than the estimate of the Medical Society sixteen years previous, when the population was perhaps thirty thousand less. But to avoid the possibility of an over-estimate, let us suppose the present number of insane persons in Connecticut to be only seven hundred.

The population of the state is now probably about three hundred and twenty thousand; according to this estimate, the proportion of the insane to the whole population would be one to about four hundred and sixty. Making this the basis of our calculation, and estimating the slaves in the United States at two millions, seven hundred thousand, their present probable number, and we come to this result, that there are about six thousand insane persons among the slaves of the United States. We have no adequate data by which to judge whether the proportion of lunatics among slaves is greater or less than among the whites; some considerations favor the supposition that it is. But the dreadful physical violence to which the slaves are subjected, and the constant sundering of their tenderest ties, might lead us to suppose that it would be more. The only data in our possession is the official census of Chatham County, Georgia, for 1838, containing the number of lunatics among the whites and the slaves.—(See the Savannah Georgian, July 24, 1838.) According to this census, the number of lunatics among eight thousand three hundred and seventy three whites in the country, is only *two,* whereas, the number among ten thousand eight hundred and ninety-one slaves, is *fourteen.*

2d. *The Deaf and Dumb.*—The proportion of deaf and dumb persons to the other classes of the community, is about one in two thousand. This is the testimony of the directors of the 'American Asylum for the Deaf and Dumb,' located at Hartford, Connecticut. Making this the basis of our estimate, there would be one thousand six hundred deaf and dumb persons among the slaves of the United States.

3d. *The Blind.*—*We* have before us the last United States census, from which it appears, that in 1830, the number of blind persons in New Hampshire was one hundred and seventeen, out of a population of two hundred and sixty-nine thousand five hundred and thirty-three. Adopting this as our basis, the number of blind slaves in the United States would be nearly one thousand three hundred.

4th. *Runaways.*—Of the proportion of the slaves that run away, to those that do not, and of the proportion of the runaways that are *taken* to those that escape entirely, it would be difficult to make a probable estimate. Something, however, can be done towards such an estimate. We have before us, in the Grand Gulf (Miss.) Advertiser, for August 2, 1838, a list of runaways that were then in the jails of the two counties of Adams and Warren, in that State; the names, ages, &c. of each one given; and their owners are called upon to take them away. The number of runaways thus taken up and committed in these *two* counties is forty-six. The whole number of *counties* in Mississippi is *fifty-six.* Many of them, however, are thinly populated. Now, without making this the basis of our estimate for the whole slave population in all the state—which would doubtless make the number much too large—we are sure no one who has any knowledge of facts as they are in the south, will charge upon us an over-statement, when we say, that of the present generation of slaves, probably *one in thirty* is of that class ie., has at some time, perhaps often, runaway and been retaken;

on that supposition the whole number would be not far from NINETY THOUSAND.

5th. *Hired Slaves.*—It is impossible to estimate with accuracy the proportion which the hired Slaves bear to the whole number. That it is very large all who have resided at the south, or travelled there; with their eyes open well know. Some of the largest slaveholders in the country, instead of purchasing plantations and working their slaves themselves, hire them out to others. This practice is very common.

Rev. Horace Moulton, a minister of the Methodist Episcopal church in Marlborough, Mass., who lived some years in Georgia, says: "A *large proportion* of the slaves are owned by masters who keep them on purpose to hire out."

Large numbers of slaves, especially in Mississippi, Louisiana, Arkansas, Alabama, and Florida, are owned by *non-residents;* thousands of them by northern capitalists, who hire *them out.* These capitalists in many cases own large plantations, which are often leased for a term of years with a 'stock' of slaves sufficient to work them.

Multitudes of slaves 'belonging' to *heirs,* are hired out by their guardians till such heirs become of age, or by the executors or trustees of persons deceased.

That the reader may form some idea of the large number of slaves that are hired out, we insert below a few advertisements, as a specimen of hundreds in the newspapers of the slave states.

From the "Pensacola Gazette" May 27

"**Notice To Slaveholders**. Wanted upon my contract, on the Alabama, Florida and Georgia Rail Road, FOUR HUNDRED BLACK LABORERS, *for which* a liberal price will be paid.　　　R. LORING, *Contractor."*

The same paper has the following, signed by an officer of the United States:

"**Wanted At The Navy Yard, Pensacola, Sixty Laborers.** The Owners to subsist and quarter them beyond the limits of the yard. Persons having laborers to hire will apply to the Commanding Officer.

W. K. LATIMER."

From the "Richmond (Va.) Enquirer" April 10, 1838

"**Laborers Wanted.**—The James River, and Kenawha Company, are in immediate want of several hundred good laborers,. Gentlemen wishing to send negroes from the country, are assured that the very best care shall be taken of them. RICHARD REINS, *Agent of* the *James River, and Kenawha* Co."

From the "Vicksburg (Miss.) Register," Dec. 27, 1838
"**60 Negroes, males and females,** *for hire* for the year 1839. Apply to H. HENDREN."

From the "Georgia Messenger" Dec. 27, 1838
"**Negroes To Hire.** On the first Tuesday next. Including CARPENTERS, BLACKSMITHS, SHOEMAKERS, SEAMSTRESSES, COOKS, &c. &c. For information Apply to OSSIAN GREGORY."

From the "Alexandria (D.C.) Gazette," Dec. 30, 1837
"**THE subscriber** wishes to *employ* by the month or year, **One Hundred Able Bodied Men, And Thirty Boys.** Persons having servants will do well to give him a call.   PHILIP ROACH, near Alexandria.

From the "Columbia (S.C.) Telescope" May 19, 1838
"**Wanted To Hire,** twelve or fifteen NEGRO GIRLS, from ten to fourteen years of age. They are wanted for the term of two or three years.
E. H. &. J. FISHER."
"**Negroes Wanted.** The Subscriber is desirous of hiring 50 or 60 *first rate Negro Men.*   WILSON NESBITT."

From the "Norfolk (Va.) Beacon" March 21, 1838
"**Laborers Wanted.** One hundred able bodied men are wanted. The hands will be required to be delivered in Halifax by the *owners.*
Apply to SHIELD & WALKE."

From the "Lynchburg Virginian" Dec. 13, 1838
"**40 Negro Men.** The subscribers wish to hire for the next year, 40 NEGRO MEN.   LANGHORNE, SCRUGGS & COOK."
"**Hiring Of Negroes.** On Saturday, the 29th day of December, 1838, at Mrs. Tayloe's tavern, in Amherst county, there will be *hired* thirty or forty valuable Negroes.

In addition to the above, I have for *hire,* 20 men, women, boys, and girls—several of them excellent house servants.

MAURICE H. GARLAND."

From the "Savannah Georgian" Feb. 5, 1838
"Wanted To Hire, One Hundred prime negroes, by the year.

J. V. REDDEN."

From the "North Carolina Standard" Feb. 31, 1838
"Negroes Wanted.—W. & A. STITH, will give twelve dollars per month for *FIFTY* strong Negro fellows, to commence work immediately; and for *FIFTY* more on the first day of February, and for *FIFTY* on the first day of March."

From the "Lexington (Ky.) Reporter" Dec. 26, 1838
"Will Be Hired, for one year, on the first day of January, 1839, on the farm of the late Mrs. Meredith, a number of valuable NEGROES. R. S. TODD, Sheriff of Fayette Co. and Curator for James and Elizabeth Breckenridge."

"Negroes To Hire. On Wednesday, the 26th inst. I will hire to the highest bidder, the NEGROES belonging to Charles and Robert Innes.

GEO. W. WILLIAMS. *Guardian."*

The following *nine* advertisements were published in one column of the "Winchester Virginian," Dec. 20, 1838.

"NEGRO HIRINGS.' "Will be offered for hire, at Captain Long's Hotel, a number of SLAVES—men, women, boys and girls—belonging to the orphans of George Ash, deceased.

RICHARD W. BARTON, *Guardian.*

"Will be offered for hire, at my Hotel, a number of SLAVES, consisting of men, women, boys and girls.

JOSEPH LONG, *Exr. of Edmund Shackleford, dec'd."*

"Will be offered for hire, for the ensuing year, at Capt. Long's Hotel, a number of SLAVES.

MOSES R. RICHARDS."

"Will be offered for hire, the slaves belonging to the estate of James Bowen, deceased, and consisting of men, and women, boys and girls.

GILES COOK. *One of the Exrs. of James Bowen dec'd."*

"The *hiring* at Millwood will take place on Friday, the 28th day of December, 1838. BURWELL."

"N. B. We are desired to say that other valuable NEGROES will also be *hired* at Millwood on the same day, besides those offered by Mr. B."

"The SLAVES of the late John Jolliffe, about twenty in number, and of all ages and both sexes, will be offered for hire at Cain's Depot.

DAVID W. BARTON. *Administrator."*

"I Will hire at public hiring before the tavern door of Dr. Lacy, about 30 NEGROES, consisting of men, and women. JAMES R. RICHARDS."

"Will be hired, at Carter's Tavern, on 31st of December, a number of NEGROES. JOHN J. H. GUNNELL."

"Negroes For Hire, (privately.) About twelve servants, consisting of men, women, boys, and girls, for hire privately. Apply to the subscriber at Col. Smith's in Battletown. JOHN W. OWEN."

A volume might easily be filled with advertisements like the preceding, showing conclusively that *hired* slaves must be a large proportion of the whole number. The actual proportion has been variously estimated, at 1/2, 1/3, 1/4, 1/5 &c. if we adopt the last as our basis, it will make the number of hired slaves, in the United States, FIVE HUNDRED AND FORTY THOUSAND!

6th. *Slaves under overseers whose wages are a part of the crop.*—That this is a common usage appears from the following testimony:

The late **Hon. John Taylor**, of Caroline Co. Virginia, one of the largest slaveholders in the state, President of the State Agricultural Society, and three times elected to the Senate of the United States, says, in his "Agricultural Essays," No. 15. P. 57:

"This necessary class of men, (overseers,) are bribed by agriculturalists, not to improve, but to impoverish their land, *by a share of the crop for one year.* The *greatest* annual crop, and not the most judicious culture, advances his interest, and establishes his character; and the fees of these land-doctors, are much higher for killing than for curing. The most which the land can yield, and seldom or never improvement with a view to future profit, is a point of common consent, and mutual need between the agriculturist and his overseer. Must the practice of hiring a man for one year, by a share of the crop, to lay out all his skill and industry in killing land, and as little as possible in improving it, be kept up to commemorate the pious leaning of man to his primitive state of ignorance and barbarity? Unless this *is abolished,* the attempt to fertilize our lands is needless."

Philemon Bliss, Esq. of Elyria, Ohio, who lived in Florida, in 1834-5, says:

"It is common for owners of plantations and slaves, to hire overseers to take charge of them, while they themselves reside at a distance. *Their wages depend principally upon the amount of labor which they can exact from the slave.* The term "good overseer," signifies one who can make the greatest amount of the staple, cotton for instance, from a given number of hands, besides raising sufficient provisions for their consumption. He has no interest in the life of the slave. Hence the fact, so notorious at the south, that negroes are driven harder and fare worse under overseers than under their owners.

William Ladd, Esq. of Minot, Maine, formerly a slaveholder in Florida, speaking, in a recent letter of the system of labor adopted there, says:

The compensation of the overseers *was a certain portion of the crop."*

Rev. Phineas Smith, of Centreville, Allegany Co. N. Y. who has recently returned from a four years' residence, in the Southern slave states and Texas, says:

"The mode in which *many* plantations are managed, is calculated and *designed,* as an inducement to the slave driver, to lay upon the slave the *greatest possible burden, the overseer being entitled by contract, to a certain share of the crop."*

We leave the reader to form his own opinion, as to the proportion of slaves under overseers, whose wages are in proportion to the crop, raised by them. We have little doubt that we shall escape the charge of wishing to make out a "strong case" when we put the proportion at one-*eighth* of the whole number of slaves, which would be *three hundred and fifty thousand.*

Without drawing out upon the page, a sum in addition for the reader to "run up," it is easily seen that the slaves in the preceding classes, amount to more than Eleven Hundred Thousand, exclusive of the deaf and dumb, and the blind, many of whom, especially the former, might be profitable to their "owners."

Now it is plainly for the *interest* of the "owners" of these slaves, or of those who have the charge of them, to *treat them cruelly,* to overwork, under-feed, half-clothe, half-shelter, poison, or kill outright, the aged, the broken down, the incurably diseased, idiots, feeble infants, most of the blind, some deaf and dumb &c. It is besides a part of the slave-holder's creed that it is *for his interest* to treat with terrible severity, all runaways and the incorrigibly stubborn, thievish, lazy, &c.; also for those who hire slaves, to *overwork* them; also for overseers to overwork the slaves under them, when their own wages are increased by it.

We have thus shown that it would be *"for the interest"* of masters and overseers to treat with *habitual* cruelty *more than one million* of the slaves in the United States. But this is not all; as we have said already, it is for the interest of overseers generally, whether their wages are proportioned to the crop or not, to overwork the slaves; we need not repeat the reasons.

Neither is it necessary to re-state the arguments, going to show that it is for the interest of slaveholders, who cultivate the great southern staples, especially cotton, and the sugar cane, to overwork periodically *all* their slaves, and *habitually* the majority of them, when the demand for those staples creates high prices, as has been the case with cotton for many years, with little exception. Instead of entering into a labored estimate to get at the proportion of the slaves, affected by the operation of these and the other causes enumerated, we may say, that they operate *directly* on the "field hands," employed in raising the southern staples, and indirectly upon all classes of the slaves.

Finally, we conclude this head by turning the objector's negative proposition into an affirmative one, and state formally what has been already proved.

It is for the interest of slaveholders, upon their own principles, and by their own showing, TO TREAT CRUELLY *the great body of their slaves.*

Objection VI—"THE FACT THAT THE SLAVES MULTIPLY SO RAPIDLY PROVES THAT THEY ARE NOT INHUMANLY TREATED, BUT ARE IN A COMFORTABLE CONDITION."

To this we reply in brief, 1st. It has been already shown under a previous head, that, m considerable sections of the slave states, especially in the South West, the births among slaves are fewer than the deaths, which would exhibit a fearful decrease of the slave population in those sections, if the deficiency were not made up by the slave trade from the upper country.

2d. The fact that all children born of slave *mothers,* whether their fathers are whites or free colored persons, are included in the census with the slaves, and further that all children born of white mothers, whose fathers are mulattos or blacks, are also included in the census with colored persons and almost invariably with *slaves,* shows that it is impossible to ascertain with any accuracy, *what is the actual increase of the slaves alone.*

3d. The fact that thousands of slaves, generally in the prime of life, are annually smuggled into the United States from Africa, Cuba, and elsewhere, makes it manifest that all inferences drawn from the increase of the slave population, which do not make large deductions, for constant importations, must be fallacious. **Mr. Middleton of South Carolina**, in a speech in Congress in 1819, declared that "THIRTEEN THOUSAND AFRICANS ARE ANNUALLY SMUGGLED INTO THE SOUTHERN STATES." **Mr. Mercer of Virginia**, in a speech in Congress about the same time declared that *"Cargoes,"* of African slaves were smuggled into the South to a deplorable extent.

Mr. Wright, of Maryland, in a speech in Congress, estimated the number annually at FIFTEEN THOUSAND.

Miss Martineau, in her recent work, (Society in America,) informs us that a large slaveholder in Louisiana assured her in 1835 that the annual importation of native Africans was from thirteen to fifteen thousand.

The **President of the United States**, in his message to Congress, December, 1837, says: "The large force under Commodore Dallas, [on the West India station,] has been most actively and efficiently employed in protecting our commerce, IN PREVENTING THE IMPORTATION OF SLAVES," &c. &c.

The New Orleans Courier of 15th February, 1839, has these remarks:

~ 345 ~

"It is believed that African negroes have been *repeatedly* introduced into the United States. The number and the proximity of the Florida ports to the island of Cuba, make it no difficult matter; nor is our extended frontier on the Sabine and Red Rivers, at all unfavorable to the smuggler. Human laws have, in all countries and ages, been violated whenever the inducements to do so afforded hopes of great profit.

"The United States' law against the importation of Africans, *could it be strictly enforced,* might in a few years give the sugar and cotton planters of Texas advantage over those of this state; as it would, we apprehend, enable the former, under a stable government, to furnish cotton and sugar at a lower price than we can do. When giving publicity to such reflections as the subject seems to suggest, we protest against being considered advocates for any violation of the laws of our country. Every good citizen must respect those laws, notwithstanding we may deem them *likely to be evaded* by men less scrupulous."

That both the south and north swarm with men 'less scrupulous,' everyone knows.

The Norfolk (Va.) Beacon, of June 8, 1837, has the following:

"*Slave. Trade.—Eight African negroes* have been taken into custody, at Apalachicola, by the U. S. Deputy Marshal, alleged to have been imported from Cuba, on board the schooner Emperor, Captain Cox. Indictments for piracy, under the acts for the suppression of the slave trade, have been found against Captain Cox, and other parties implicated. The negroes were bought in Cuba by a Frenchman named Malherbe, formerly a resident of Tallahassee, who was drowned soon after the arrival of the schooner."

The following testimony of **Rev. Horace Moulton**, now a minister of the Methodist Episcopal Church, in Marlborough, Mass. who resided some years in Georgia, reveals some of the secrets of the slave-smugglers, and the connivance of the Georgia authorities at their doings. It is contained in a letter dated February 24, 1839:

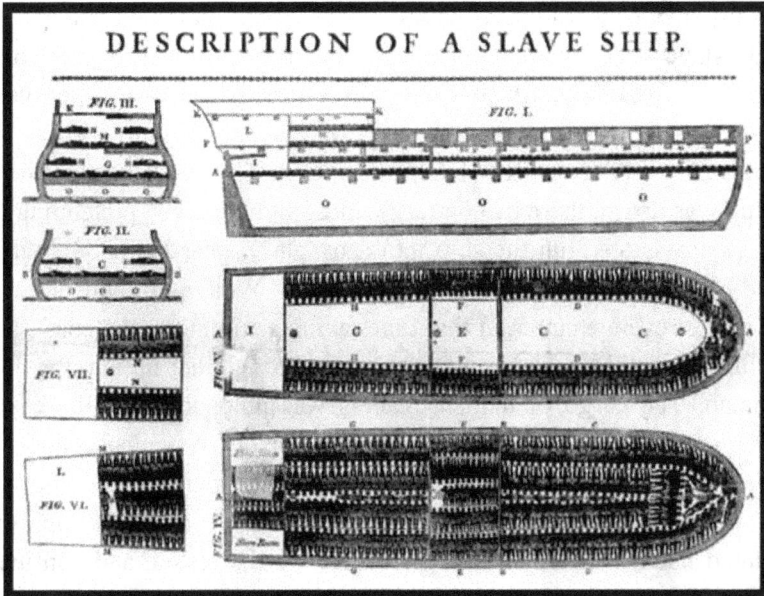

DESCRIPTION OF A SLAVE SHIP.

"The foreign slave-trade was carried on to some considerable extent when I was at the south, notwithstanding a law had been made some ten years previous to this, making this traffic piracy on the high seas. I was somewhat acquainted with the secrets of this traffic, and, I suppose, I might have engaged in it, had I so desired. Were you to visit all the plantations in South Carolina, Georgia, Alabama, and Mississippi, I think you would be convinced that the horrors of the traffic in human flesh have not yet ceased. I was *surprised to find so many that could not speak English among the slaves,* until the mystery was explained. This was done, when I learned that slave-cargoes were landed on the coast of Florida, not a thousand miles from St. Augustine. They could, and can still, in my opinion, be landed as safely on this coast as in any port of this continent. You can imagine for yourself how easy it was to carry on the traffic between this place and the West Indies. When landed on the coast of Florida, it is an easy matter to distribute them throughout the more southern states. The law which makes it piracy to traffic in the foreign slave trade is a dead letter; and I doubt not it has been so in the more southern states ever since it was enacted. For you can perceive at once, that interested men, who believe the colored man is so much better off here than he possibly can be in Africa, will not hesitate to kidnap the blacks whenever an opportunity presents itself. I will notice one fact that came under my own observation, which will convince you that the horrors of the foreign slave trade have not yet ceased among our southern gentry. It is as follows. A slave ship, which I have reason to believe was employed by southern men, came near the port of Savannah with about FIVE HUNDRED SLAVES, FROM GUINEA AND CONGO. It was said that the ship was driven there by contrary winds; and the crew, pretending to be short of provisions, run the ship into a by place, near the shore, between Tybee Light and Darien, to recruit their stores. Well, as Providence would have it, the revenue cutter, at that time taking a trip along the coast, fell in with this slave ship, took her as a prize, and brought her up into the port of Savannah. The cargo of human chattels was unloaded, and the captives were placed in an old barracks, in the fort of Savannah, under the protection of the city authorities, they pretending that they should return them all to their native country again, as soon as a convenient opportunity presented itself. The ship's crew of course were arrested, and confined in jail. Now for the sequel of this history: About one third part of the negroes died in a few weeks after they were landed, in seasoning, so called, or in becoming acclimated—or, as I should think, a distemper broke out among them, and they died like the Israelites, when smitten with the plague. Those who did not die in seasoning must be hired out a little while, to be sure, as the city authorities could not afford to keep them on expense doing nothing. As it happened, the man in whose employ I was when the cargo of human beings arrived, hired some twenty or thirty of them, and put them under my care. They continued with me until the sickly season drove me off to the north. I soon returned, but could not hear a word about the crew of pirates. They had something like a mock trial, as I should think, for no one, as I ever learned, was condemned, fined, or censured. But where were the poor captives, who were going to be returned to Africa by the city authorities, as soon as they could make it convenient? Oh, forsooth, those of whom I spoke, being under my care, were tugging away for the same man; the remainder were scattered about among different planters. When I returned to the north again, the next year, the city authorities had not, down to that time, made it convenient to return these poor victims. The fact is, they belonged there; and, in my opinion, they were designed to be landed near by the place where the revenue cutter seized them. Probably those very planters for whom they were originally designed received them; and still there was a pretence kept up that they would be returned to Africa.

This must have been done, that the consciences of those might be quieted, who were looking for justice to be administered to these poor captives. It is easy for a company of slaveholders, who desire to traffic in human flesh, to fit out a vessel, under Spanish colors, and then go prowling about the African coast for the victims of their lusts. If all the facts with relation to the African slave-trade, now secretly carried on at the south, could be disclosed, the people of the free states would be filled with amazement."

It is plain, from the nature of this trade, and the circumstances under which it is carried on, that the number of slaves imported would be likely to be estimated far *below* the truth. There can be little doubt that the estimate of Mr. Wright, of Maryland, (fifteen thousand annually,) is some thousands too small. But even according to his estimate, the African slave-trade adds ONE HUNDRED AND FIFTY THOUSAND SLAVES TO Each United States' Census. These are in the prime of life, and their children would swell the slave population many thousands annually—thus making a great addition to each census.

4. It is a notorious fact, that large numbers of free colored persons are kidnapped every year in the free states, taken to the south, and sold as slaves.

Hon. George M. Stroud, Judge of the Criminal Court of Philadelphia, in his sketch of the slave laws, speaking of the kidnapping of free colored persons in the northern states, says:

"Remote as is the city of Philadelphia from those slaveholding states in which the introduction of slaves from places within the territory of the United States is freely permitted, and where also the market is tempting, *it has been* ascertained, that MORE THAN THIRTY FREE COLORED PERSONS, MOSTLY CHILDREN, HAVE BEEN KIDNAPPED HERE, AND CARRIED AWAY, WITHIN THE LAST TWO YEARS. Five of these, through the kind interposition of several humane gentlemen, have been restored to their friends, though not without *great expense and difficulty;* the others *are still retained in bondage,* and if rescued at all, it must be by sending white witnesses a journey of more than a thousand miles. The costs attendant upon lawsuits, under such circumstances, will probably fall but little short of the estimated value, as slaves, of the individuals kidnapped."

The following is an extract from **Mrs. Child's** Appeal, pp. 64-6:

"I know the names of four colored citizens of Massachusetts, who went to Georgia on board a vessel, were seized under the laws of that state, and sold as slaves. They have sent the most earnest exhortations to their families and friends, to do something for their relief; but the attendant expenses require more money than the friends of negroes are apt to have, and the poor fellows, as yet, remain unassisted.

"A New York paper, of November, 1829, contains the following caution:

"*Beware of Kidnappers!*—It is well understood, that there is at present in this city, a gang of kidnappers, busily engaged in their vocation, of stealing colored children for the southern market. It is believed that three or four have been stolen within as many days. There are suspicions of a foul nature connected with some who serve the police in subordinate capacities. It is hinted that there may be those in some authority, not altogether ignorant of these diabolical practices. Let the public be on their guard! It is still fresh in the memories of all, that a cargo, or rather drove of negroes, was made up from this city and Philadelphia, about the time that the emancipation of all the negroes in this state took place, under our present constitution, and were taken through Virginia, the Carolinas, and Tennessee, and disposed of in the state of Mississippi. Some of those who were taken from Philadelphia were persons of intelligence; and after they had been driven through the country in chains, and disposed of by sale on the Mississippi, wrote back to their friends, and were rescued from bondage.* The persons who were guilty of this abominable transaction are known, and now reside in North Carolina. They may very probably be engaged in similar enterprises at the present time—at least there is reason to believe, that the system of kidnapping free persons of color from the northern cities, has been carried on more extensively than the public are generally aware of."

*Read the book "Twelve Years a Slave" written by Solomon Northrup, a free man who was kidnapped approximately 5 years after this book was published. He suffered 12 long years in Louisiana before he was finally freed. BPC

George Bradburn, Esq. of Nantucket, Mass. a member of the Legislature of that state, at its last session, made a report to that body, March 6, 1839, 'On the deliverance of citizens liable to be sold as slaves.' That report contains the following facts and testimony.

"The following facts are a few out of a VAST MULTITUDE, to which the attention of the undersigned has been directed:

"On the 27th of February last, the undersigned had an interview with the Rev. Samuel Snowden, a respectable and intelligent clergyman of the city of Boston. This gentleman stated, and he is now ready to make oath, that during the last six years, he has himself, by the aid of various benevolent individuals, procured the deliverance from jail of six citizens of Massachusetts, who had been arrested and imprisoned as runaway slaves, and who, but for his timely interposition, would have been sold into perpetual bondage. The names and the places of imprisonment of those persons, as stated by Mr. S. were as follows: "James Hight, imprisoned at Mobile; William Adams, at Norfolk; William Holmes, also at Norfolk; James Oxford, at Wilmington; James Smith, at Baton Rouge; John Tidd, at New Orleans.

"In 1836, Mary Smith, a native of this state, returning from New Orleans, whither she had been in the capacity of a servant, was cast upon the shores of North Carolina. She was there seized and sold as a slave. Information of the fact reached her friends at Boston. Those friends made an effort to obtain her liberation. They invoked the assistance of the Governor of this Commonwealth. A correspondence ensued between His Excellency and the Governor of North Carolina, copies of which were offered for the inspection of your committee. Soon afterwards, by permission of the authorities of North Carolina, 'Mary Smith' returned to Boston. But it turned out, that this was not *the* Mary Smith, whom our worthy Governor, and other excellent individuals of Boston, had taken so unwearied pains to redeem from slavery. It was another woman, of the same name, who was also a native of Massachusetts, and had been seized in North Carolina as a runaway slave. *The* Mary Smith has not yet been heard of. If alive, she is now, in all probability, wearing the chains of slavery."About a year and a half since, several citizens of different free states were rescued from slavery at New Orleans, by the direct personal efforts of an acquaintance of the undersigned. The benevolent individual alluded to is **Jacob Barker, Esq.** a name not unknown to the commercial world. Mr. Barker is a resident of New Orleans. A statement of the cases in reference is contained in a letter addressed by him to the Hon. Samuel H. Jenks, of Nantucket."

The letter of Mr. Barker, referred to in this report to the Legislature of Massachusetts, bears date August 19, 1837. The following are extracts from it:

"A free man, belonging to Baltimore, by the name of Ephraim Larkin, who came here as cook of the William Tell, was arrested and thrown into prison a few weeks since and sent in chains to work on the road. I heard of it, and with difficulty found him; and after the most diligent and active exertions, got him released—in effecting which, I traveled in the heat of the day, thermometer ranging in the shade from 94 to 100, more than twenty times to and from prison, the place of his labor, and the different courts, a distance of near three miles from my residence; and after I had established his freedom, had to pay for his arrest, maintenance, and the advertising of him as a runaway slave, $29.89, as per copy of bill herewith—the allowance for work not equaling the expenses, the amount augments with every day of confinement.

"In pursuing the cook of the William Tell, I found three other free men, confined in the same prison; one belonged also to Baltimore, by the name of Leaven Dogerty. He was also released, on my paying $28 expenses; one was a descendant of the Indians who once inhabited Nantucket —his name is Eral Lonnon. Lonnon had been six weeks in prison; he was released without difficulty, on my paying $20.38 expenses—and no one seemed to know why he had been confined or arrested, as the law does not presume persons of mixed blood to be slaves. But for the others, I had great difficulty in procuring what was considered competent witnesses to prove them free. No complaint of improper conduct had been made against either of them. At one time, the Recorder said the witness must be white; at another, that one respectable witness was insufficient; at another, that a person who had been (improperly) confined and released, was not a competent witness, &c. &c. Lonnon has been employed in the South Sea fishery from Nantucket and New Bedford, nearly all his life; has sailed on those voyages in the ships Eagle, Maryland, Gideon, Triton, and Samuel. He was born at Marshpee, Plymouth [Barnstable] County, Mass. and prefers to encounter the leviathan of the deep, rather than the turnkeys of New Orleans.

"The other was born in St. Johns, Nova Scotia, and bears the name of William Smith, a seaman by profession.

"Immediately after these men were released, two others were arrested. They attempted to escape, and being pursued, ran for the river, in the vain hope of being able to swim across the Mississippi, a distance of a mile, with a current of four knots. One soon gave out, and made for a boat which had been dispatched for their recovery, and was saved; the other being a better swimmer, continued on until much exhausted, then also made for the boat—it was too late; he sank before the boat could reach him, and was drowned. They claimed to be freemen.

"On Sunday last I was called to the prison of the Municipality in which I reside, to serve on an inquest on the body of a drowned man. There I saw one other free man confined, by the name of Henry Tier, a yellow man, born in New York, and formerly in my employ. He had been confined as a supposed runaway, near six months, without a particle of testimony; although from his color, the laws of Louisiana presume him to be free. I applied immediately for his release, which was promptly granted. At first, expenses similar to those exacted in the third Municipality were required; but on my demonstrating to the recorder that the law imposed no such burthen on free men, he was released without any charge whatever. How free men can obtain satisfaction for having been thus wrongfully imprisoned, and made to work in chains on the highway, is not for me to decide. I apprehend no satisfaction can be had without more active friends, willing to espouse their cause, than can be found in this quarter. Therefore I repeat...that no person of color should come here without a certificate of freedom from the governor of the state to which he belongs.

"Very respectfully, Your assured friend,

Jacob Barker."

"N.B.—Since writing the preceding, I have procured the release of another free man from the prison of the third Municipality, on the payment of $39.65, as per bill, copy herewith. His name is William Lockman—he was born in New Jersey, of free parents, and resides at Philadelphia. A greater sum was required which was reduced by the allowance of his maintenance (written *labor,*) while at work on the road, which the law requires the Municipality to pay; but it had not before been so expounded in the third Municipality. I hope to get it back in the case of the other three. The allowance for labor, in addition to their maintenance, is twenty-five cents per day; but they require those illiterate men to advance the whole before they can leave the prison, and then to take a certificate for their labor, and go for it to another department—to collect which, is ten times more trouble than the money when received is worth. While these free men, without having committed any fault, were compelled to work in chains, on the roads, in the burning sun, for 25 cents per day, and pay in advance 18 3/4 cents per day for maintenance, doctor's, and other bills, and not able to work half their time, I paid others, working on ship-board, in sight, two dollars per day. J. B."

The preceding letter of Mr. Barker, furnishes grounds for the belief, that *hundreds,* if not thou*sands* of free colored persons, from the different states of this Union, both slave and free from the West Indies, South America, Mexico, and the British possessions in North America, and from other parts of the world, are reduced to slavery *every year* in our slave states. If a single individual, in the course of a few days, *accidentally* discovered *six* colored free men, working in irons, and soon to be sold as slaves, in a *single* southern city, is it not fair to infer, that in all the slave states, there must be *multitudes* of such persons, now in slavery, and that this number is rapidly increasing, by ceaseless accessions?

The letter of Mr. Barker is valuable, also, as a graphic delineation of the 'public opinion' of the south. The great difficulty with which the release of these free men was procured, notwithstanding the personal efforts of Mr. Jacob Barker, who is a gentleman of influence, and has, we believe, been an alderman of New Orleans, reveals a 'public opinion,' insensible as adamant to the liberty of colored men.

It would be easy to fill scores of pages with details similar to the preceding. We have furnished enough, however, to show, that, in all probability, each United States' census of the *slave* population, is increased by the addition to it of *thousands* of free colored persons, kidnapped and sold as slaves.

5th. To argue that the rapid multiplication of any class in the community, is proof that such a class is well-clothed, well-housed, abundantly fed, and very *comfortable,* is as absurd as to argue that those who have *few children,* must, of course, be ill-clothed, ill-housed, badly lodged, overworked, ill-fed, &c. &c. True, privations and inflictions may be carried to such an extent as to occasion a fearful diminishment of population. That was the case generally with the slave population in the West Indies, and, as has been shown, is true of certain portions of the southern states. But the fact that such an effect is *not* produced, does not prove that the slaves do not experience great privations and severe inflictions. They may suffer much hardship, and great cruelties, without experiencing so great a derangement of the vital functions as to prevent child-bearing. The Israelites multiplied with astonishing rapidity, under the task-masters and burdens of Egypt. Does this falsify the declarations of Scripture, that 'they sighed by reason of their bondage,' and that the Egyptians 'made them serve *with rigor,*' and made 'their lives bitter with *hard bondage.*' 'I have seen,' said God,' their *afflictions.* I have heard their groan*ing,*' &c. The history of the human race shows, that great *privations and much suffering* may be experienced, without materially checking the rapid increase of population.

Besides, if we should give to the objection all it claims, it would merely prove, that the female slaves, or rather a portion of them, are in a comfortable condition; and that, so far as the absolute necessities of life are concerned, the females of *child-bearing age,* in Delaware, Maryland, northern, western, and middle Virginia, the upper parts of Kentucky and Missouri, and among the mountains of east Tennessee and western North Carolina, are in general tolerably well supplied. The same remark, with some qualifications, may be made of the slaves generally, in those parts of the country where the people are slaveholders, mainly, that they may enjoy the privilege and profit of being *slave-breeders.*

Objection VIII.—"PUBLIC OPINION IS A PROTECTION TO THE SLAVE."

Answer. It was public opinion that *made man a slave.* In a republican government the people make the laws, and those laws are merely public opinion *in legal forms.* We repeat it,—public opinion made them slaves, and keeps them slaves; in other words, it sunk them from men to chattels, and now, forsooth, this same public opinion will see to it, that these *chattels* are treated like *men!*

By looking a little into this matter, and finding out how this 'public opinion' (law) protects the slaves in some particulars, we can judge of the amount of its protection in others. 1. It protects the slaves from *robbery,* by declaring that those who robbed their mothers may rob them and their children. "All negroes, mulatoes, or mestizoes who now are, or shall hereafter be in this province, and all their offspring, are hereby declared to be, and shall remain, forever, hereafter, absolute slaves, and shall follow the condition of the mother."—Law of South Carolina, 2 Brevard's Digest, 229. Others of the slave states have similar laws.

2. It protects their *persons,* by giving their master a right to flog, wound, and beat them when he pleases. See Devereaux's North Carolina Reports, 263.—Case of the State vs. Mann, 1829; in which the Supreme Court decided, that a master who *shot* at a female slave and wounded her, because she got loose from him when he was flogging her, and started to run from him, had violated *no law,* AND COULD NOT BE INDICTED. It has been decided by the highest courts of the slave states generally, that assault and battery upon a slave is not indictable as a criminal offense.

The following decision on this point was made by the Supreme Court of South Carolina in the case of the State vs. Cheetwood, 2 Hill's Reports, 459.

Protection of slaves: "The criminal offense of assault and battery *cannot, at common law, be committed on the person of a slave.* For, notwithstanding for some purposes a slave is regarded in law as a person, yet generally he is a mere chattel personal, and his right of personal protection belongs to his master, who can maintain an action of trespass for the battery of his slave.

"There can be therefore no offense against the state for a mere beating of a slave, unaccompanied by any circumstances of cruelty, or an attempt to kill and murder. The peace of the state is not thereby broken; for a slave is not generally regarded as legally capable of being within the peace of the state. He is not a citizen, and *is not in that character entitled to her protection."*

This 'public opinion' protects the *persons* of the slaves by depriving them of Jury trial;* their *consciences,* by forbidding them to assemble for worship, unless their oppressors are present;** their *characters,* by branding them as liars, in denying them their oath in law;*** their *modesty,* by leaving their master to clothe, or let them go naked, as he pleases **** and their *health,* by leaving him to feed or starve them, to work them, wet or dry, with or without sleep, to lodge them, with or without covering, as the whim takes him;***** and their *liberty,* marriage relations, parental authority, and filial obligations, by *annihilating* the whole.****** This is the protection which 'Public Opinion,' in the form of *law,* affords to the slaves; this is the chivalrous knight, always in stirrups, with lance in rest, to champion the cause of the slaves.

*Law of South Carolina. James' Digest, 392-3. Law of Louisiana. Martin's Digest, 642. Law of Virginia. Rev. Code, 429.

**Miss. Rev. Code, 390. Similar laws exist in the slave states generally.

***A slave cannot be a witness against a white person, either in a civil or criminal cause." Stroud's Sketch of the Laws of Slavery, 65.

**** Stroud's Sketch of the Slave Laws, 132.

***** Stroud's Sketch, 26—38.

******Stroud's Sketch, 22—24.

Public opinion, protection to the slave! Brazen effrontery, hypocrisy, and falsehood! We have, in the laws cited and referred to above, the formal testimony of the Legislatures of the slave states, that,' public opinion' does pertinaciously *refuse* to protect the slaves; not only so, but that it does itself persecute and plunder them all; that it originally planned, and now presides over, sanctions, executes and perpetuates the whole system of robbery, torture, and outrage under which they groan.

In all the slave states, this 'public opinion' has taken away from the slave his *liberty;* it has robbed him of his right to his own body, of his right to improve his mind, of his right to read the Bible, of his right to worship God according to his conscience, of his right to receive and enjoy what he earns, of his right to live with his wife and children, of his right to better his condition, of his right to eat when he is hungry, to rest when he is tired, to sleep when he needs it, and to cover his nakedness with clothing: this 'public opinion' makes the slave a prisoner for life on the plantation, except when his jailor pleases to let him out with a 'pass,' or sells him, and transfers him in irons to another jail-yard; this 'public opinion' traverses the country, buying up men, women, children—chaining them in coffles, and driving them forever from their nearest friends; it sets them on the auction table, to be handled, scrutinized, knocked off to the highest bidder; it proclaims that they shall not have their liberty; and, if their masters give it them, 'public opinion' seizes and throws them back into slavery. This same 'public opinion' has formally attached the following legal penalties to the following acts of slaves:

If more than seven slaves are found together in any road, without a white person, *twenty lashes apiece;* for visiting a plantation without a written pass, *ten lashes;* for letting loose a boat from where it is made fast, *thirty-nine lashes for the first offense;* and for the second, '*shall have cut off from his head one ear;* for keeping or carrying a *club, thirty-nine lashes;* for having any article for sale, without a ticket from his master, *ten lashes;* for traveling in any other than 'the most usual and accustomed road,' when going alone to any place, *forty lashes;* for traveling in the night, without a pass, *forty lashes;* for being found in another person's negro-quarters, *forty lashes;* for hunting with dogs in the woods, *thirty lashes;* for being on *horseback* without the written permission of his master, *twenty-five lashes;* for riding or going abroad in the night, or riding horses in the day time, without leave, a slave may be whipped, *cropped,* or *branded in the cheek* with the letter R, or otherwise punished, *not extending to life,* or so as to render him *unfit for labor.*

The laws referred to may be found by consulting 2 Brevard's Digest, 228, 243, 246; Haywood's Manual, 78, chap. 13, pp. 518, 529; 1 Virginia Revised Code, 722-3; Prince's Digest, 454; 2 Missouri Laws, 741; Mississippi Revised Code, 371. Laws similar to these exist throughout the southern slave code. Extracts enough to fill a volume might be made from these laws, showing that the protection which 'public opinion' grants to the slaves, is hunger, nakedness, terror, bereavements, robbery, imprisonment, the stocks, iron collars, hunting and worrying them with dogs and guns, mutilating their bodies, and murdering them.

A few specimens of the laws and the judicial decisions on them will show what is the state of 'public opinion' among slaveholders towards their slaves. Let the following suffice:

"Any person may lawfully kill a slave, who has been outlawed for running away and lurking in swamps, &c.'—Law of North Carolina; Judge Stroud's Sketch of the Slave Laws, 103; Haywood's Manual, 524."

"A slave *endeavoring* to entice another slave to runaway, if provisions, &c. be prepared for the purpose of aiding in such running away, shall be punished with DEATH. And a slave who shall aid the slave so endeavoring to entice another slave to run away, shall also suffer DEATH.'—Law of South Carolina; Stroud's Sketch of Slave Laws, 103-4; 2 Brevard's Digest, 233, 244."

Another law of South Carolina provides that if a slave shall, when absent from the plantation, refuse to be examined by '*any white* person,' (no matter how crazy or drunk,) 'such white person may seize and chastise him; and if the slave shall *strike* such white person, such slave may be lawfully killed.'—2 Brevard's Digest, 231.

The following is a law of Georgia: 'If any slave shall presume to strike any white person, such slave shall, upon trial and conviction before the justice or justices, suffer such punishment for the first offense as they shall think fit, not extending to life or limb; and for the second offense, DEATH.'—Prince's Digest, 450. The same law exists in South Carolina, with this difference, that death is made the punishment for the *third* offense. In both states, the law contains this remarkable proviso: 'Provided always, that such strikings be not done by the command and in the defense of the person or property of the owner, or other person having the government of such slave, in which case the slave shall be wholly excused.' According to this law, if a slave, by the direction of his Overseer, strike a white man who is beating said overseer's *dog*, 'the slave shall be wholly excused;' but if the white man has rushed upon the slave himself, instead of the *dog*, and is furiously beating him, if the slave strike back but a single blow, the legal penalty is 'Any *punishment* not extending to life or limb;' and if the tortured slave has a second onset made upon him, and, after suffering all but death, again strike back in self-defense, the law KILLS him for it. So, if a female slave, in obedience to her mistress, and in defense of her property, strike a white man who is kicking her mistress' pet kitten, she 'shall be wholly excused,' saith the considerate law; but if the unprotected girl, when beaten and kicked *herself,* raise her hand against her brutal assailant, the law condemns her to '*any* punishment, not extending to life or limb;' and if a wretch assail her again, and attempt to violate her chastity, and the trembling girl, in her anguish and terror, instinctively raise her hand against him in self-defense, she shall, saith the law, 'suffer death.'

Reader, this diabolical law is the 'public opinion' of Georgia and South Carolina toward the slaves. This is the vaunted 'protection' afforded them by their 'high-souled chivalry.' To show that the 'public opinion' of the slave states far more effectually protects the *property* of the master than the *person* of the slave, the reader is referred to two laws of Louisiana, passed in 1819. The one attaches a penalty 'not exceeding one thousand dollars, and imprisonment not exceeding two years,' to the crime of 'cutting or breaking any iron chain or collar,' which any master of slaves has used to prevent their running away; the other, a penalty 'not exceeding five hundred dollars,' to 'wilfully cutting out the tongue, putting out the eye, *cruelly* burning, or depriving any slave of *any limb!* Look at it—the most horrible dismemberment conceivable cannot be punished by a fine of *more* than five hundred dollars. The law expressly fixes that, as the utmost limit, and it *may* not be half that sum; not a single moment's imprisonment stays the wretch in his career, and the next hour he may cut out another slave's tongue, or burn his hand off. But let the same man break a chain put upon a slave, to keep him from running away, and, besides paying double the penalty that could be exacted from him for cutting off a slave's leg, the law imprisons him not exceeding two years!

This law reveals the *heart* of slaveholders towards their slaves, their diabolical indifference to the most excruciating and protracted torments inflicted on them by '*any* person;' it reveals, too, the *relative* protection afforded by 'public opinion' to the *person* of the slave, in appalling contrast with the vastly surer protection which it affords to the master's *property* in the slave. The wretch who cuts out the tongue, tears out the eyes, shoots off the arms, or burns off the feet of a slave, over a slow fire, *cannot* legally be fined more than five hundred dollars; but if he should in pity loose a chain from his galled neck, placed there by the master to keep him from escaping, and thus put his property in some jeopardy, he may be fined *one thousand dollars,* and thrust into a dungeon for two years! And this, be it remembered, not for *stealing* the slave from the master, nor for *enticing* or even advising him to run away, or giving him any information how he can effect his escape; but merely, because, touched with sympathy for the bleeding victim, as he sees the rough iron chafe the torn flesh at every turn, he removes it; and, as escape without this encumbrance would be easier than with it, the master's property in the slave is put at some risk. For having caused this slight risk, the law provides a punishment—fine not exceeding one thousand dollars, and imprisonment not exceeding *two years.* We say 'slight risk,' because the slave may not be disposed to encounter the dangers, and hunger, and other sufferings of the woods, and the certainty of terrible inflictions if caught; and if he should attempt it, the risk of losing him is small. An advertisement of five lines will set the whole community howling on his track; and the trembling and famished fugitive is soon scented out in his retreat, and dragged back and delivered over to his tormentors.

The preceding law is another illustration of the 'protection' afforded to the limbs and members of slaves, by 'public opinion' among slaveholders.

Here follow two other illustrations of the brutal indifference of' public opinion' to the *torments* of the slave, while it is full of zeal to compensate the master, if any one disables his slave so as to lessen his market value:

The first is a law of South Carolina. It provides, that if a slave, engaged in his owner's service, be attacked by a person 'not having sufficient cause for so doing,' and if the slave shall be '*maimed or disabled*' by him, so that the owner suffers a loss from his inability to labor, the person maiming him shall pay for his 'lost time,' and 'also the charges for the cure of the slave!' This Vandal law does not deign to take the least notice of the anguish of the '*maimed*' slave, made, perhaps, a groaning cripple for life; the horrible wrong and injury done to *him,* is passed over in utter silence. It is thus declared to be *not a criminal act.* But the pecuniary interests of the master are not to be thus neglected by 'public opinion.' Oh no! its tender bowels run over with sympathy at the master's injury in the 'lost *time'* of his slave, and it carefully provides that he shall have pay for the whole of it.—See 2 *Brevard's Digest,* 231, 2.

A law similar to the above has been passed in Louisiana, which contains an additional provision for the benefit of the *master* ordaining, that 'if the slave' (thus *maimed and* disabled,) 'be forever rendered unable to work,' the person maiming, shall pay the master the appraised value of the slave before the injury, and shall, in addition, *take* the slave, and maintain him during life.' Thus 'public opinion' transfers the helpless cripple from the hand of his master, who, as he has always had the benefit of his services, might possibly feel some tenderness for him, and puts him in the sole power of the wretch who has disabled him for life—protecting the victim from the fury of his tormentor, by putting him into his hands! What but butchery by piecemeal can, under such circumstances, be expected from a man brutal enough at first to 'maim' and 'disable' him, and now exasperated by being obliged to pay his full value to the master, and to have, in addition, the daily care and expense of his maintenance. Since writing the above, we have seen the following judicial decision, in the case of Jourdan, vs. Patton—5 Martin's Louisiana Reports, 615:

A slave of the plaintiff had been deprived of his *only eye,* and thus rendered *useless,* on which account the court adjudged that the defendant should pay the plaintiff his full value. The case went up, by appeal, to the Supreme Court. Judge Mathews, in his decision said, that 'when the defendant had paid the sum decreed, the slave ought to be placed in his possession,'—adding, that 'the judgment making full compensation to the owner *operates a change of property.'* He adds, 'The principle of humanity which would lead us to suppose, that the mistress whom he had long served, would treat her miserable blind slave with more kindness than the defendant to whom the judgment ought to transfer him, CANNOT BE TAKEN INTO CONSIDERATION!' The full compensation of the mistress for the loss of the services of the slave, is worthy of all 'consideration,' even to the uttermost farthing; 'public opinion' is omnipotent for *her* protection; but when the food, clothing, shelter, fire and lodging, medicine and nursery, comfort and entire condition and treatment of her poor blind slave, throughout his dreary pilgrimage, is the question —ah! That, says the mouth-piece of the law, and the representative of 'public opinion,' CANNOT BE TAKEN INTO CONSIDERATION! Protection of slaves by 'public opinion' among slaveholders!!

The foregoing illustrations of southern 'public opinion,' from the laws made by it and embodying it, are sufficient to show, that, so far from being an efficient protection to the slaves, it is their deadliest foe, persecutor and tormentor.

But here we shall probably be met by the legal lore of some 'Justice Shallow,' instructing us that the *life* of the slave is fully protected by law, however unprotected he may be in other respects. This assertion we meet with a point blank denial. The law does not, in reality, protect the life of the slave. But even if the *letter* of the law would fully protect the life of the slave, 'public opinion' in the slave states would make it a *dead* letter. The letter of the law would have been all-sufficient for the protection of the lives of the miserable gamblers in Vicksburg, and other places in Mississippi, from the rage of those whose money they had won; but 'gentlemen of property and standing' laughed the law to scorn, rushed to the gamblers' house, put ropes round their necks, dragged them through the streets, hanged them in the public square, and thus saved the sum they had not yet paid. Thousands witnessed this wholesale murder, yet of the scores of legal officers present not a soul raised a finger to prevent it, the whole city consented to it, and thus aided and abetted it. How many hundreds of them helped to commit the murders, *with their own hands,* does not appear, but not one of them has been indicted for it, and no one made the least effort to bring them to trial. Thus, up to the present hour, the blood of those murdered men rests on that whole city, and it will continue to be a CITY OF MURDERERS, so long as its citizens agree together to shield those felons from punishment; and they do thus agree together so long as they encourage each other in refusing to bring them to justice. Now, the *laws* of

Mississippi were not in fault that those men were murdered; nor are they now in fault, that their murderers are not punished; the laws demand it, but the people of Mississippi, the legal officers, the grand juries and legislature of the state, with one consent agree, that the law *shall be a dead letter,* and thus the whole state assumes the guilt of those murders, and in bravado, flourishes her reeking hands in the face of the world.*

* We have just learned from Mississippi papers, that the citizens of Vicksburg are erecting a public monument in honor of Dr. H. S. Bodley, who was the ring-leader of the lynchers, in their attack upon their miserable victims. To give to crime the cold encouragement of impunity alone, or such slight tokens of favor as a home and a sanctuary, is beneath the chivalry and hospitality of Mississippians; so they tender it incense, an altar, and a crown of glory. Let the marble rise till it be seen from afar, a beacon marking the spot where law lies lifeless by the hand of felons; and murderers, with chaplets on their heads, dance and shout upon its grave, while 'all the people say, amen.'

The letter of the law on the statute book is one thing, the practice of the community under that law often a totally different thing. Each of the slave states has laws providing that the life of no *white* man shall be taken without his having first been indicted by a grand jury, allowed an impartial trial by a petit jury, with the right of counsel, cross-examination of witnesses, &c.; but who does not know that if Arthur Tappan were pointed out in the streets of New Orleans, Mobile, Savannah, Charleston, Natchez, or St. Louis, he would be torn in pieces by the citizens with one accord, and that if anyone should attempt to bring his murderers to punishment, he would be torn in pieces also. The editors of southern newspapers openly vaunt, that every abolitionist who sets foot in their soil, shall, if he be discovered, be hung at once, without judge or jury. What mockery to quote the *letter of the law* in those states, to show that abolitionists would have secured to them the legal protection of an impartial trial!

Before the objector can make out his case, that the life of the slave is protected by the law, he must not only show that *the words of the law* grant him such protection, but that such a state of public sentiment exists as will carry out the provisions of the law in their true spirit. Anything short of this will be set down as mere prating by every man of common sense. It has been already abundantly shown in the preceding pages, that the public sentiment of the slaveholding states toward the slaves is diabolical. Now, if there were laws in those states, the *words* of which granted to the life of the slave the same protection granted to that of the master, what would they avail? Acts constitute protection; and is that public sentiment which makes the slave 'property,' and perpetrates hourly robbery and batteries upon him, so penetrated with a sense of the sacredness of his right to life, that it will protect it at all hazards, and drag to the gallows his owner, if he take the life of his own *property?* If it be asked, why the penalty for killing a slave is not a mere *fine* then, if his life is not really regarded as sacred by public sentiment—we answer, that formerly in most, if not in all the slave states, the murder of a slave *was* punished by a mere fine. This was the case in South Carolina till a few years since. Yes, as late as 1821, in the state of South Carolina, which boasts of its chivalry and honor, at least as loudly as any state in the Union, a slaveholder might butcher his slave in the most deliberate manner—with the most barbarous and protracted torments, and yet not be subjected to a single hour's imprisonment—pay his fine, stride out of the court and kill another—pay his fine again and butcher another, and so long as he paid to the state, cash down, its own assessment of damages, without putting it to the trouble of prosecuting for it, he might strut 'a gentleman.'—Sec 2 *Brevard's Digest,* 241.

The reason assigned by the legislature for enacting a law which punished the willful murder of a human being by a *fine,* was that CRUELTY *is* HIGHLY UNBECOMING,' and 'odious.' It was doubtless the same reason that induced the legislature in 1821, to make a show of giving *more* protection to the life of the slave. Their fathers, when they gave *some* protection, did it because the time had come when, not to do it would make them 'Odious.' So the legislature of 1821 made a show of giving still greater protection, because, not to do it would make them '*odious.'* Fitly did they wear the mantles of their ascending fathers! In giving to the life of a slave the miserable protection of a fine, their fathers did not even pretend to do it out of any regard to the sacredness of his life as a human being, but merely because cruelty is 'unbecoming' and 'odious.' The legislature of 1821 *nominally* increased this protection; not that they cared more for the slave's rights, or for the inviolabity of his life as a human being, but the civilized world had advanced since the date of the first law. The slave-trade which was then honorable merchandise, and plied by lords, governors, judges, and doctors of divinity, raising them to immense wealth, had grown 'unbecoming,' and only raised its votaries by a rope to the yard arm; besides this, the barbarity of the slave codes throughout the world was fast becoming 'odious' to civilized nations, and slaveholders found that the only conditions on which they could prevent themselves from being thrust out of the pale of civilization, was to meliorate the iron rigor of their slave code, and thus *seem* to secure to their slaves some protection. Further, the northern states had passed laws for the abolition of slavery—all the South American states were acting in the matter; and Colombia and Chili passed acts of abolition that very year. In addition to all this the Missouri question had been for two years previous under discussion in Congress, in State legislatures, and in every village and stage coach; and this law of South Carolina had been held up to execration by northern members of Congress, and in newspapers throughout the free states—in a word, the legislature of South Carolina found that they were becoming 'odious;' and while in their sense of justice and humanity they did not surpass their fathers, they winced with equal sensitiveness under the sting of the world's scorn, and with equal promptitude sued for a truce by modifying the law.

The legislature of South Carolina modified another law at the same session. Previously, the killing of a slave 'on a sudden heat or passion, or by undue correction,' was punished by a fine of three hundred and fifty pounds. In 1821 an act was passed diminishing the fine to five hundred dollars, but authorizing an imprisonment 'not exceeding six months.' Just before the American Revolution, the Legislature of North Carolina passed a law making *imprisonment* the penalty for the willful and malicious murder of a slave. About twenty years after the revolution, the state found itself becoming 'odious' as the spirit of abolition was pervading the nations. The legislature, perceiving that Christendom would before long rank them with barbarians if they so cheapened human life, repealed the law, candidly assigning in the preamble of the new one the reason for repealing the old— that it was 'DISGRACEFUL' and 'DEGRADING.' As this preamble expressly recognizes the slave as 'a human creature,' and as it is couched in a phraseology which indicates some sense of justice, we would gladly give the legislature credit for sincerity, and believe them really touched with humane movings towards the slave, were it not for a proviso in the law clearly revealing that the show of humanity and regard for their rights, indicated by the words, is nothing more than a hollow pretence— a hypocritical flourish to produce an impression favorable to their justice and magnanimity. After declaring that he who is 'guilty of willfully and maliciously killing a slave, shall suffer the same punishment as if he had killed a freeman;' the act concludes thus: 'Provided, always, this act shall not extend to the person killing a slave outlawed by virtue of any act of Assembly of this state; or to any slave in the act of resistance to his lawful overseer, or master, or to any slave dying under their *moderate correction.'* Reader, look at this proviso. 1. It gives free license to all persons to kill *outlawed slaves.* Well, what is an outlawed slave? A slave who runs away, lurks in swamps, &c., and kills a *hog* or any other domestic animal to keep himself from starving, is subject to a proclamation of *outlawry;* (Haywood's Manual, 521,) and then whoever finds him may shoot him, tear him in pieces with dogs, burn him to death over a slow fire, or kill him by any other tortures. 2. The proviso grants full license to a master to kill his slave, if the slave *resist* him. The North Carolina Bench has decided that this law contemplates not only actual resistance to punishment, &c., but also *offering* to resist. If, for example, a slave undergoing the process of branding should resist by pushing aside the burning stamp; or if wrought up to frenzy by the torture of the lash, he should catch and hold it fast; or if he break loose from his master and run, refusing to stop at his command; or if he *refuse* to be flogged; or struggle to keep his clothes on while his master is trying to strip him; if, in all these, or any one of the hundred other ways he *resist,* or offer, or *threaten* to resist the infliction; or, if the master attempt the violation of the slave's wife, and the husband resist his attempts without the least effort to injure him, but merely to shield his wife from his assaults, this law does not merely permit, but it *authorizes* the master to murder the slave on the spot.

The brutality of these two provisos brands its authors as barbarians. But the third cause of exemption could not be outdone by the legislation of fiends; "Dying under "Moderate *correction!"* Moderate *correction* and death—cause and effect! 'PROVIDED ALWAYS,' says the law, 'this act shall not extend to *any* slave dying under *MODERATE CORRECTION!"* Here is a formal proclamation of impunity to murder—an express pledge of *acquittal* to all slaveholders who wish to murder their slaves, a legal absolution—an indulgence granted before the commission of the crime! Look at the phraseology. Nothing is said of maiming, dismemberment, skull fractures, of severe bruising, or lacerations, or even of floggings; but a word is used, the common-parlance import of which is, *slight chastisement;* it is not even *whipping,* but '*correction'.* And as if hypocrisy and malignity were on the rack to outwit each other, even that weak word must be still farther diluted; so *'moderate'* is added: and, to crown the climax, compounded of absurdity, hypocrisy, and COLD BLOODED MURDER, the *legal definition* of 'moderate correction' is covertly given; which is, *any punishment* that KILLS the victim. All inflictions are either *moderate* or *immoderate;* and the design of this law was manifestly to shield the murderer from conviction, *by carrying on its face the rule for its own interpretation;* thus advertising, beforehand, courts and juries, that the fact of any infliction *producing death,* was no evidence that it was *immoderate,* and that beating a man to death came within the legal meaning of 'moderate correction!' The *design* of the-legislature of North Carolina in framing this law is manifest; it was to produce the impression upon the world that they had so high a sense of justice as voluntarily to grant adequate protection to the lives of their slaves. This is ostentatiously set forth in the preamble, and in the body of the law. That this was the most despicable hypocrisy, and that they had predetermined to grant no such protection, notwithstanding the pains taken to get the *credit* of it, is fully revealed by the *proviso,* which was framed in such a way as to nullify the law, for the express accommodation of slaveholding gentlemen murdering their slaves. All such find in this proviso a convenient accomplice before the fact, and a packed jury, with a ready-made verdict of 'not guilty,' both gratuitously furnished by the government! The preceding law and proviso are to be found in Haywood's Manual, 530; also in Laws of Tennessee, Act of October 23, 1791; and in Stroud's Sketch, 37.

Enough has been said already to show, that though the laws of the slave states profess to grant adequate protection to the life of the slave, such professions are mere empty pretence, no such protection being in reality afforded by them. But there is still another fact, showing that all laws which profess to protect the slaves from injury by the whites are a mockery. It is this—that the testimony, neither of a slave nor of a free colored person, is *legal* testimony against a white. To this rule there is *no exception* in any of the slave states: and this, were there no other evidence, would be sufficient to stamp, as hypocritical, all the provisions of the codes which *profess* to protect the slaves. Professing to grant *protection,* while, at the same time, it strips them of the only *means* by which they can make that protection available! Injuries must be legally *proved* before they can be legally *redressed;* to deprive men of the power of *proving* their injuries, is itself the greatest of all injuries; for it not only exposes to all, but invites them, by a virtual guarantee of impunity, and is thus the *author* of all injuries. It matters not what other laws exist, professing to throw safeguards round the slave—*this* makes them blank paper. How can a slave prove outrages perpetrated upon him by his master or overseer, when his own testimony and that of all his fellow-slaves, his kindred, associates, and acquaintances, are ruled out of court? And when he is entirely in the *power* of those who injure him, and when the only care necessary, on their part, is, to see that no *white* witness is looking on. Ordinarily, but *one* white man, the overseer, is with the slaves while they are at labor; indeed, on most plantations, to commit an outrage in the *presence* of a white witness would be more difficult than in their absence. He who wished to commit an illegal act upon a slave, instead of being obliged to *take pains* and watch for an opportunity to do it unobserved by a white, would find it difficult to do it in the presence of a white if he wished to do so. The supreme court of Louisiana, in their decision, in the case of Crawford vs. Cherry, 15, *(Martin's La. Rep.* 142; also *"Law of Slavery"* 49,) where the defendant was sued for the value of a slave whom he had shot and killed, say, "The act charged here, is one *rarely* committed in the presence of *witnesses"*(whites). So in the case of the State vs. Mann, *(Devereux, N.C. Rep.* 263; and *"Law of Slavery"* 247;) in which the defendant was charged with shooting a slave girl 'belonging' to the plaintiff; the Supreme Court of North Carolina, in their decision, speaking of the provocations of the master by the slave, and the consequent wrath of the master prompting him to *bloody vengeance,* add, *a vengeance generally practiced with impunity, by reason of its privacy.'*

Laws excluding the testimony of slaves and free colored persons, where a white is concerned, do not exist in all the slave slates. One or two of them have no legal enactment on the subject; but, in those, *'public opinion'* acts with the force of law, and the courts *invariably reject it.* This brings us back to the potency of that oft-quoted 'public opinion,' so ready, according to our objector, to do battle for the *protection* of the slave!

Another proof that 'public opinion,' in the slave states, plunders, tortures, and murders the slaves, instead of *protecting* them, is found in the fact, that the laws of slave states inflict *capital* punishment on slaves for a variety of crimes, for which, if their masters commit them, the legal penalty is merely *imprisonment.* Judge Stroud, in his Sketch of the Laws of Slavery, says, that, by the laws of Virginia, there are 'seventy-one crimes for which slaves are capitally punished, though in none of these are whites punished in a manner more severe than by imprisonment in the penitentiary.' It should be added, however, that though the penalty for each of these seventy-one crimes is 'death,' yet a majority of them are, in the words of the law, 'death within clergy;' and in Virginia, *clergyable* offenses, though *technically* capital, are not so in fact. In Mississippi, slaves are punished capitally for more than *thirty* crimes, for which whites are punished only by fine or imprisonment, or both. Eight of these are not *recognized as crimes,* either by common law or by statute, when committed by whites. In South Carolina slaves are punished capitally for *nine* more crimes than the whites—in Georgia, for *six*—and in Kentucky, for *seven* more than whites, &c. We surely need not detain the reader by comments on this monstrous inequality with which the penal codes of slave states treat slaves and their masters. When we consider that guilt is in proportion to intelligence, and that these masters have by law doomed their slaves to ignorance, and then, as they darkle and grope along their blind way, inflict penalties upon them for a variety of acts regarded as praiseworthy in whites; killing them for crimes, when whites are only fined or imprisoned—to call such a 'public opinion' inhuman, savage, murderous, diabolical, would be to use tame words, if the English vocabulary could supply others of more horrible import.

But slaveholding brutality does not stop here. While punishing the slaves for crimes with vastly greater severity than it does their masters for the same crimes, and making a variety of acts *crimes* in law, which are right, and often *duties,* it persists in refusing to make known to the slaves that complicated and barbarous penal code which loads them with such fearful liabilities. The slave is left to get knowledge of these laws as he can, and cases must be of constant occurrence at the south, in which slaves get their first knowledge of the existence of a law by suffering its penalty. Indeed, this is probably the way in which they commonly learn what the laws are; for how else can the slave get knowledge of the laws? He cannot *read*—he cannot *learn* to read; if he try to master the alphabet, so that he may spell out the words of the law, and thus avoid its penalties, the law shakes its terrors at him; while, at the same time, those who made the laws refuse to make them known to those for whom they are designed. The memory of Caligula will blacken with execration while time lasts, because he hung up his laws so high that people could not read them, and then punished them because they did not keep them. Our slaveholders aspire to blanker infamy. Caligula was content with hanging up his laws where his subjects could *see* them; and if they could not read them, they knew where they were, and might get at them, if, in their zeal to learn his will, they had used the same means to get up to them that those did who hung them there. Even Caligula, wretch as he was, would have shuddered at cutting their legs off, to prevent their climbing to them; or, if they had got there, at boring their eyes out, to prevent their reading them. Our slaveholders virtually do both; for they prohibit their slaves acquiring that knowledge of letters which would enable them to read the laws; and if, by stealth, they get it in spite of them, they prohibit them books and papers, and flog them if they are caught at them. Further—Caligula merely hung his laws so high that they could not be *read*—our slaveholders have hung theirs so high above the slave that they cannot be *seen*—they are utterly out of sight, and he finds out that they are there only by the falling of the penalties on his head.* Thus the "public opinion" of slave states protects the defenseless slave by arming a host of legal penalties and setting them in ambush at every thicket along his path, to spring upon him unawares.

* The following extract from the Alexandria (D. C.) Gazette is an illustration:

"**Criminals Condemned.**—On Monday last the Court of the borough of Norfolk, Va. sat on the trial of four negro boys arraigned for burglary. The first indictment charged them with breaking into the hardware store of Mr. E. P. Tabb, upon which two of them were found guilty by the Court, and condemned to suffer the penalty of the law, which, in the case of a slave, is death. The second Friday in April is appointed for the execution of their awful sentence. *Their ages do not exceed sixteen.* The first, a fine active boy, belongs to a widow lady in Alexandria; the latter, a house servant, is owned by a gentleman in the borough. The value of one was fixed at $1000, and the other at $800; which sums are to be reimbursed to their respective owners out of the state treasury." In all probability these poor boys, who are to be hung for stealing, never dreamed that death was the legal penalty of the crime.

Here is another, from the "New Orleans Bee" of _____14, 1837:

"The slave who Struck some citizens in Canal Street, some weeks since, has been tried and found guilty, and is sentenced to be HUNG on the 24th.

Stroud, in his Sketch of the Laws of Slavery, page 100, thus comments on this monstrous barbarity:

"The hardened convict moves their sympathy, and is to be taught the laws before he is expected to obey them, yet the guiltless slave is subjected to an extensive system of cruel enactments, of no part of which, probably, has he ever heard."*

"It shall be the duty of the keeper [of the penitentiary] on the receipt of each prisoner, to *read* to him or her such parts of the penal laws of this state as impose penalties for escape, and to make all the prisoners in the penitentiary acquainted with the same. It shall also be his duty, on the discharge of such prisoner, to read to him or her such parts of the said laws as impose additional punishments for the repetition of offenses."—*Rule 12th, for the internal government of the Penitentiary of Georgia. Sec.* 26 *of the Penitentiary Act of* 1816—*Prince's Digest,* 386.

Having already drawn so largely on the reader's patience, in illustrating southern 'public opinion' by the slave laws, instead of additional illustrations of the same point from another class of those laws, as was our design, we will group together a few particulars, which the reader can take in at a glance, showing that the "public opinion" of slaveholders towards their slaves, which exists at the south, in the form of law, tramples on all those fundamental principles of right, justice, and equity, which are recognized as sacred by all civilized nations, and receive the homage even of barbarians. 1. One of these principles is, that the *benefits* of law to the subject should overbalance its burdens—its protection more than compensate for its restraints and exactions—and its blessings altogether outweigh its inconveniences and evils—the former being numerous, positive, and permanent, the latter few, negative, and incidental. Totally the reverse of all this is true in the case of the slave. Law is to him all exaction and no protection; instead of lightening his *natural* burdens, it crushes him under a multitude of artificial ones; instead of a friend to succor him, it is his deadliest foe, transfixing him at every step from the cradle to the grave. Law has been beautifully defined to be "benevolence acting by rule;" to the American slave it is malevolence torturing by system. It is an old truth, that *responsibility* increases with *capacity;* but those same laws which make the slave a "*chattel,*" require of him *more* than of *men.* The same law which makes him a *thing* incapable of obligation loads him with obligations superhuman—while sinking him below the level of a brute in dispensing its *benefits,* he lays upon him burdens which would break down an angel.

2. *Innocence is entitled to the protection of law.* Slaveholders make innocence free plunder; this is their daily employment; their laws assail it, make it their victim, inflict upon it all, and, in some respects, more than all the penalties of the greatest guilt. To other innocent persons, law is a blessing, to the slave it is a curse, only a curse and that continually.

3. *Deprivation of liberty is one of the highest punishments of crime;* and in proportion to its justice when inflicted on the guilty, is its injustice when inflicted on the innocent; this terrible penalty is inflicted on two million seven hundred thousand, innocent persons in the Southern states.

4. *Self-preservation and self-defense,* are universally regarded as the most sacred of human rights, yet the laws of slave states punish the slave with *death* for exercising these rights in that way, which in others is pronounced worthy of the highest praise.

5. *The safe-guards of law are most needed where natural safe-guards are weakest.* Every principle of justice and equity requires, that, those who are totally unprotected by birth, station, wealth, friends, influence, and popular favor, and especially those who are the innocent objects of public contempt and prejudice, should be more vigilantly protected by law, than those who are so fortified by defense, that they have far less need of *legal* protection; yet the poor slave who is fortified by none of these *personal* bulwarks, is denied the protection of law, while the master, surrounded by them all, is panoplied in the mail of legal protection, even to the hair of his head; yea, his very shoe-tie and coat-button are legal protégées.

6. The grand object of law is to *protect men's natural rights,* but instead of protecting the natural rights of the slaves, it gives slaveholders license to wrest them from the weak by violence, protects them in holding their plunder, and *kills* the rightful owner if he attempt to recover it.

This is the *protection* thrown around the rights of American slaves by the 'public opinion,' of slaveholders; these restraints that hold back their masters, overseers, and *drivers,* from inflicting injuries upon them!

In a Republican government, *law* is the pulse of its *heart*—as the heart beats the pulse beats, except that it often beats *weaker* than the heart, never stronger—or to drop the figure, laws are never *worse* than those who make them, very often better. If human history proves anything, cruelty of practice will always go beyond cruelty of law.

Law-making is a formal, deliberate act, performed by persons of mature age, embodying the intelligence, wisdom, justice and humanity, of the community; performed, too, at leisure, after full opportunity had for a comprehensive survey of all the relations to be affected, after careful investigation and protracted discussion. Consequently laws must, in the main, be a true index of the permanent feelings, the settled *frame of mind,* cherished by the community upon those subjects, and towards those persons and classes whose condition the laws are designed to establish. If the laws are in a high degree cruel and inhuman, towards any class of persons, it proves that the feelings habitually exercised towards that class of persons, by those who make and perpetuate those laws, are at least *equally* cruel and inhuman. We say *at least equally* so; for if the *habitual* state of feeling towards that class be unmerciful, it must be unspeakably cruel, relentless and malignant when *provoked;* if its *ordinary* action is inhuman, its contortions and spasms must be tragedies; if the waves run high when there has been no wind, where will they not break when the tempest heaves them!

Further, when cruelty is the *spirit* of the law towards a proscribed class, when it *legalizes great outrages* upon them, it connives at, and abets *greater* outrages, and is virtually an accomplice of all who perpetrate them. Hence, in such cases, though the *degree* of the outrage is illegal, the perpetrator will rarely be convicted, and, even if convicted, will be almost sure to escape punishment. This is not *theory* but *history.* Every judge and lawyer in the slave states *knows,* that the legal conviction and *punishment* of masters and mistresses, for illegal outrages upon their slaves, is an event which has rarely, if ever, occurred in the slave states; they know, also, that although *hundreds* of slaves have been *murdered* by their masters and mistresses in the slave states, within the last twenty-five years, and though the fact of their having committed those murders has been established beyond a *doubt* in the minds of the surrounding community, yet that the murderers have not, in a single instance, suffered the penalty of the law. Finally, since slaveholders have deliberately legalized the perpetration of the most cold-blooded atrocities upon their slaves, and do pertinaciously refuse to make these atrocities *illegal,* and to punish those w ho perpetrate them, they stand convicted before the world, upon their own testimony, of the most barbarous, brutal, and habitual inhumanity. If this be slander and falsehood, their own lips have uttered it, their own fingers have written it, their own acts have proclaimed it; and however it may be with their *morality,* they have too much human nature to perjure themselves for the sake of publishing their own infamy.

Having dwelt at such length on the legal code of the slave states, that unerring index of the public opinion of slaveholders towards their slaves; and having shown that it does not protect the slaves from cruelty, and that even in the few instances in which the letter of the law, if *executed,* would afford some protection, it is virtually nullified by the connivance of courts and juries, or by popular clamor; we might safely rest the case here, assured that every honest reader would spurn the absurd falsehood, that the 'public opinion' of the slave states protects the slaves and restrains the master. But, as the assertion is made so often by slaveholders, and with so much confidence, notwithstanding its absurdity is fully revealed by their own legal code, we propose to show its falsehood by applying other tests.

We lay it down as a truth that can be made no plainer by reasoning, that the same 'public opinion,' which restrains men from *committing* outrages, will restrain them from *publishing* such outrages, if they do commit them;—in other words, if a man is restrained from certain acts through fear of losing his character, should they become known, he will not voluntarily destroy his character by *making them known,* should he be guilty of them. Let us look at this. It is assumed by slaveholders, that 'public opinion' at the south so frowns on cruelty to the slaves, that *fear of disgrace* would restrain from the infliction of it, were there no other consideration.

Now, that this is sheer fiction is shown by the fact, that the newspapers in the slaveholding states, teem with advertisements for runaway slaves, in which the masters and *mistresses* describe their men and women, as having been 'branded with a hot iron,' on their 'cheeks,' 'jaws,' 'breasts,' 'arms,' 'legs,' and 'thighs;' also as 'scarred,' ' very much scarred,' 'cut up,' 'marked,' etc. ' with the whip,' also with ' iron collars on,' 'chains,' 'bars of iron,' 'fetters,' 'bells,' 'horns,'' shackles,' &c. They, also, describe them as having been wounded by 'buck-shot,' 'rifle-balls,' &c. fired at them by their 'owners,' and others when in pursuit; also, as having ' notches,' cut in their ears, the tops or bottoms of their ears 'cut off,' or 'slit,' or 'one ear cut off,' or 'both ears cut off,' &c. &c. The masters and mistresses who thus advertise their runaway slaves, coolly sign their names to their advertisements, giving the street and number of their residences, if in cities, their post office address, &c. if in the country ; thus making public proclamation as widely as possible that *they* 'brand', 'scar', 'gash', 'cut up', &c. the flesh of their slaves; load them with irons, cut off their ears, &c.; they speak of these things with the utmost *sang froid,* not seeming to think it possible, that any one will esteem them at all the less because of these outrages upon their slaves; further, these advertisements swarm in many of the largest and most widely circulated political and commercial papers that are published in the slave states. The editors of those papers constitute the main body of the literati of the slave states; they move in the highest circle of society, are among the 'popular' men in the community, and *as a class,* are more influential than any other; yet these editors publish these advertisements with iron indifference. So far from proclaiming to such felons, homicides, and murderers, that they will not be their blood-hounds, to hunt down the innocent and mutilated victims who have escaped from their torture, they freely furnish them with every facility, become their accomplices and share their spoils; and instead of outraging 'public opinion,' by doing it, they are the men after its own heart, its organs, its representatives, its *self.*

To show that the 'public opinion' of the slave states, towards the slaves, is absolutely *diabolical,* we will insert a few, out of a multitude, of similar advertisements from a variety of southern papers now before us:

The North Carolina Standard, of July 18, 1838, contains the following:

"**TWENTY DOLLARS REWARD.** Ranaway from the subscriber, a negro woman and two children ; the woman is tall and black, and *a few days before she went off,* I BURNT HER WITH A HOT IRON ON THE LEFT SIDE OF HER FACE; I TRIED TO MAKE THE LETTER M, *and she kept a cloth over her head and face, and a fly bonnet on her head so as to cover the burn;* her children are both boys, the oldest is in his seventh year; he is a *mulatto* and has blue eyes; the youngest is black and is in his fifth year. The woman's name is Betty, commonly called Bet.

Micajah Ricks. Nash County, July 7, 1838

Hear the wretch tell his story, with as much indifference as if he were describing the cutting of his initials in the bark of a tree. "*I burnt her with a hot iron on the left side of her face,*"—" *I tried to make the letter M,"* and this he says in a newspaper, and puts his name to it, and the editor of the paper who is, also, its proprietor, publishes it for him and pockets his fee. Perhaps the reader will say, 'Oh, it must have been published in an insignificant sheet printed in some obscure corner of the state; perhaps by a gang of 'squatters,' in the Dismal Swamp, universally regarded as a pest, and edited by some "scape-gallows", who is detested by the whole community. To this I reply that the "North Carolina Standard," the paper which contains it, is a large six columned weekly paper, handsomely printed and ably edited; it is the leading Democratic paper in that state, and is published at Raleigh, the Capital of the state, Thomas Loring, Esq. Editor and Proprietor. The motto in capitals under the head of the paper is, "THE CONSTITUTION AND THE UNION OF THE STATES THEY MUST BE PRESERVED."

The same Editor and Proprietor, who exhibits such brutality of feeling towards the slaves, by giving the preceding advertisement a conspicuous place in his columns, and taking his pay for it, has apparently a keen sense of the proprieties of life, where *whites* are concerned, and a high regard for the rights, character and feelings of those whose skin is colored like his own. As proof of this, we copy from the number of the paper containing the foregoing advertisement, the following *Editorial* on the pending political canvass:

"We cannot refrain from expressing the hope that the Gubernatorial canvass will be conducted with a *due regard to the character,* and *feelings* of the distinguished individuals who are candidates for that office; and that the press of North Carolina will *set an example* in this respect, worthy of *imitation and of praise."*

What is this but chivalrous and honorable feeling? The good name of North Carolina is dear to him—on the comfort, 'character and feelings,' of her *white* citizens he sets a high value; he feels too, most deeply for the *character of the Press* of North Carolina, sees that it is a city set on a hill, and implores his brethren of the editorial corps to 'set an example' of courtesy and magnanimity worthy of imitation and praise. Now, reader, put all these things together and con them over, and then read again the preceding advertisement contained in the same number of the paper, and you have the true "North Carolina Standard," by which to measure the protection extended to slaves by the 'public opinion' of that state.

J. P. Ashford advertises as follows in the "Natchez Courier," August 24, 1838:

"**Ranaway**, a negro girl called Mary, has a small scar over her eye, a *good many teeth missing,* the letter A. is *branded on her cheek and forehead."*

A. B. Metcalf thus advertises a woman in the same paper, June 15, 1838:

"**Ranaway,** Mary, a black woman, has a *scar* on her back and right arm near the shoulder, *caused by a rifle ball."*

John Henderson, in the "Grand Gulf Advertiser," August 29, 1838, advertises Betsey:

"**Ranaway**, a black woman Betsey, has an *iron bar on her right leg."*

Robert Nicoll, whose residence is in Mobile, in Dauphin Street, between Emmanuel and Conception streets, thus advertises a woman in the "Mobile Commercial Advertiser:

"TEN DOLLARS REWARD will be given for my negro woman Liby. The said Liby is about 30 years old, and VERY MUCH SCARRED ABOUT THE NECK AND EARS, occasioned by whipping, had on a handkerchief tied round her ears, as she COMMONLY WEARS IT TO HIDE THE SCARS."

To show that slaveholding brutality now is the same that it was the eighth of a century ago, we publish the following advertisement from the "Charleston (S.C.) Courier," of 1825:

"TWENTY DOLLARS REWARD—Ranaway from the subscriber, on the 14th instant, a negro girl named Molly.

"The said girl was sold by Messrs. Wm. Payne & Sons, as the property of an estate of a Mr. Gearrall, and purchased by a Mr. Moses, and sold by him to a Thomas Prisley, of Edgefield District, of whom I bought her on the 17th of April, 1819. She is 16 or 17 years of age, slim made, LATELY BRANDED ON THE LEFT CHEEK. THUS, R, AND A PIECE TAKEN OFF OF HER EAR ON THE SAME SIDE; THE SAME LETTER ON THE INSIDE OF BOTH HER LEGS.

"Abner Ross, Fairfield District."

But instead of filling pages with similar advertisements, illustrating the horrible brutality of slaveholders towards their slaves, the reader is referred to the preceding pages of this work, to the scores of advertisements written by slaveholders, printed by slaveholders, published by slaveholders, in newspapers edited by slaveholders, and patronized by slaveholders; advertisements describing not only men and boys, but women, aged and middle-aged, matrons and girls of tender years, their necks chafed with iron collars with prongs, their limbs galled with iron rings, and chains, and bars of iron, iron hobbles and shackles, all parts of their persons scarred with the lash, and branded with hot irons, and torn with rifle bullets, pistol balls and buck shot, and gashed with knives, their eyes out, their ears cut off, their teeth drawn out, and their bones broken. He is referred also to the cool and shocking indifference with which these slaveholders, 'gentlemen' and 'ladies,' Reverends, and Honorables, and Excellencies, write and print, and publish and pay, and take money for, and read and circulate, and sanction, such infernal barbarity. Let the reader ponder all this, and then lay it to heart, that this is that 'public opinion' of the slaveholder, which protects their slaves from all injury, and is an effectual guarantee of personal security.

However far gone a community may be in brutality, something of protection may yet be hoped for from its 'public opinion,' if *respect for woman* survives the general wreck; that gone, protection perishes; public opinion becomes universal rapine; outrages, once occasional, become habitual; the torture, which was before inflicted only by passion, becomes the constant product of a *system,* and, instead of being the index of sudden and fierce impulses, is coolly plied as the permanent means to an end. When *women* are branded with hot irons on their faces; when iron collars, with prongs, are riveted about their necks; when iron rings are fastened upon their limbs, and they are forced to drag after them chains and fetters; when their flesh is torn with whips, and mangled with bullets and shot, and lacerated with knives; and when those who do such things, are regarded in the community, and associated with as 'gentlemen' and 'ladies;' to say that the 'public opinion' of *such* a community is a protection to *its* victims, is to blaspheme God, whose creatures they are, cast in his own sacred image, and dear to him as the apple of his eye.

But we are not yet quite ready to dismiss this protector, 'Public Opinion.' To illustrate the hardened brutality with which slaveholders regard their slaves, the shameless and apparently unconscious indecency with which they speak of their female slaves, examine their persons, and describe them, under their own signatures, in newspapers, hand-bills, &c. just as they would describe the marks of cattle and swine, on all parts of their bodies; we will make a few extracts from southern papers. Reader, as we proceed to these extracts, remember our motto—'True humanity consists *not* in a squeamish ear':

Mr. P. Abdie of New Orleans advertises in the New Orleans Bee, of January 29, 1838, for one of his female slaves, as follows:

"**Ranaway,** the negro wench named Betsey, aged about 22 years, handsome-faced, and good countenance; having the marks of the whip behind her neck, and SEVERAL OTHERS ON HER RUMP

The above reward, ($10,) will be given to whoever will bring that wench to P. Abdie."

The New Orleans Bee, in which the advertisement of this Vandal appears, is the 'Official Gazette of the State—of the General Council—and of the first and third Municipalities of New Orleans.' It is the largest and the most influential paper in the south-western states, and perhaps the most ably edited—and has undoubtedly a larger circulation than any other. It is a daily paper, of $12 a year, and its circulation being mainly among the larger merchants, planters, and professional men, it is a fair index of the 'public opinion' of Louisiana, so far as represented by those classes of persons. Advertisements equally gross, indecent, and abominable, or nearly so, can be found in almost every number of that paper.

Mr. William Robinson, Georgetown, District of Columbia, advertised for his slave in the National Intelligencer, of Washington City, Oct. 2, 1837, as follows:

"Eloped from my residence a young negress, 22 years old, of a chesnut, or brown color. She has a very singular mark—this mark, to the best of my recollection, covers a part of her *breasts, body,* and *limbs* and when her neck and arms are uncovered, is very perceptible; she has been frequently seen east and south of the Capitol Square, and is harbored by ill-disposed persons, of every complexion, for her services."

Mr. John C. Beasley, near Huntsville, Alabama, thus advertises a young girl of eighteen, in the Huntsville Democrat, of August 1st, 1837. **"Ranaway** Maria, about 18 years old, *very far advanced with child."* He then offers a reward to anyone who will commit this young girl, in this condition, *to jail.*

Mr. James T. De Jarnett, Vemon, Antauga Co. Alabama, thus advertises a woman in the Pensacola Gazette, July 14, 1838. "Celia is a *bright* copper-colored negress, *fine figure* and *very smart. On* Examining Her Back, you will find marks caused by the whip." He closes the advertisement, by offering a reward *of five hundred dollars* to any person who will lodge her in *jail,* so that he can get her.

A person who lives at 124 Chartres Street, New Orleans, advertises in the 'Bee,' of May 31, for "the negress Patience, about 28 years old, has *large hips,* and is *bow-legged."*

A Mr. T. Cuggy, in the same paper, thus describes "the negress Caroline." "*She has awkward feet, clumsy ankles, turns out her toes greatly in walking, and has a sore on her left shin."* In another, of June 22, Mr. P. Bahi advertises "Maria, with a clear white complexion, and *double nipple on her right breast."*

Mr. Charles Craiqe, of Federal Point, New Hanover Co. North Carolina, in the Wilmington Advertiser, August 11, 1837, offers a reward for his slave Jane, and says "*she is far advanced in pregnancy."*

The New Orleans Bulletin, August 18, 1838, advertises "the negress Mary, aged nineteen, has a scar on her face, walks parrot-toed, and is *pregnant."*

Mr. J. G. Muir, of Grand Gulf, Mississippi, thus advertises a woman in the Vicksburg Register, December 5, 1838. "**Ranaway** a negro girl—has a number of *black lumps on her breasts, and is in a state of pregnancy."*

Mr. Jacob Besson, Donaldsonville, Louisiana, advertises in the New Orleans Bee, August 7, 1838, "the negro woman Victorine—she is *advanced in pregnancy."*

Mr. J. H. Leverich & Co. No. 10, Old Levee, New Orleans, advertises in the 'Bulletin,' January 22, 1839, as follows:
"**$50 Reward.**—**Ranaway** a negro girl named Caroline about 18 years of age, is *far advanced in child-bearing.* The above reward will be paid for her delivery at either of the jails of the city."

Mr. John Duggan, thus advertises a woman in the New Orleans Bee, of Sept. 7:
"**Ranaway** from the subscriber a mulatto woman, named Esther, about thirty years of age, *large stomach,* wants her upper front teeth, and walks pigeon-toed—supposed to be about the lower fauxbourg.

Mr. Francis Foster, of Troup Co. Georgia, advertises in the Columbus (Ga.) Enquirer of June 22, 1837—" My negro woman Patsey, has a stoop in her walking, occasioned by a *severe bum on her abdomen.*"

The above are a few specimens of the gross details, in describing the persons of females, of all ages, and the marks upon all parts of their bodies; proving incontestably, that slaveholders are in the habit not only of stripping their female slaves of their clothing, and inflicting punishment upon their 'shrinking flesh,' but of subjecting their naked persons to the most minute and revolting inspection, and then of publishing to the world the results of their examination, as well as the scars left by their own inflictions upon them, their length, size, and exact position on the body; and all this without impairing in the least, the standing in the community of the shameless wretches who thus proclaim their own abominations. That such things should not at all affect the standing of such persons in society, is certainly no marvel: how could they affect it, when the same communities enact laws *requiring* their own legal officers to inspect minutely the persons and bodily marks of all slaves taken up as runaways, and to publish in the newspapers a particular description of all such marks and peculiarities of their persons, their size, appearance, position on the body, &c. Yea, verily, when the 'public opinion' of the community, in the solemn form of law, commands jailors, sheriffs, captains of police, &c. to divest of their clothing aged matrons and young girls, minutely examine their naked persons, and publish the results of their examination—who can marvel, that the same 'public opinion' should tolerate the slaveholders themselves, in doing the same things to their own property, which they have appointed legal officers to do as their proxies.*

* As a sample of these laws, we give the following extract from one of the laws of Maryland, where slaveholding 'public opinion' exists in its mildest form:

"It shall be the duty of the sheriffs of the several counties of this state, upon any runaway servant or slave being committed to his custody, to cause the same to be advertised, &c. and to make particular and minute descriptions of the person *and bodily marks* of such runaway."—*Laws of Maryland of* 1802, Chap. 96, Sec. 1 and 2.

That the sheriffs, jailors, &c. do not neglect this part of their official 'duty,' is plain from the minute description which they give in the advertisements of marks upon all parts of the persons of females, as well as males; and also from the occasional declaration, 'no scars discoverable on any part,' or 'no marks discoverable *about* her;" which last is taken from an advertisement in the Milledgeville Geo..) Journal, June 26, 1838, signed T. S. Densler, Jailor."

The zeal with which slaveholding *'public opinion'* protects the lives of the slaves, may be illustrated by the following advertisements, taken from a multitude of similar ones in southern papers. To show that slaveholding' public opinion' is the same *now,* that it was half a century ago, we will insert, in the first place, an advertisement published in a North Carolina newspaper, Oct. 29, 1785, by W. Skinner, the Clerk of the County of Perquimans, North Carolina:

"Ten silver dollars reward will be paid for apprehending and delivering to me my man Moses, who ran away this morning; or I will give five times the sum to any person who will make due proof of his *being killed,* and never ask a question to know by whom it was done."
W. Skinner. *Perquimans County, N.C. Oct.* 29, 1785.

The late **John Parrish**, of Philadelphia, an eminent minister of the religious Society of Friends, who traveled through the slave states about *thirty-five years* since, on a religious mission, published on his return a pamphlet of forty pages, entitled 'Remarks on the Slavery of the Black People.' From this work we extract the following illustrations of 'public opinion' in North and South Carolina and Virginia at that period:

"When I was traveling through North Carolina, a black man, who was outlawed, being shot by one of his pursuers, and left wounded in the woods, they came to an ordinary where I had stopped, to feed my horse, in order to procure a cart to bring the poor wretched object in. Another, I was credibly informed, was shot, his head cut off, and carried in a bag by the perpetrators of the murder, who received the reward, which was said to be $200, continental currency, and that his head was stuck on a coal house at an iron works in Virginia—and this for going to visit his wife at a distance. Crawford gives an account of a man being gibbeted alive in South Carolina, and the buzzards came and picked out his eyes. Another was burnt to death at a stake in Charleston, surrounded by a multitude of spectators, some of whom were people of the *first rank;* the poor object was heard to cry, as long as he could breathe, 'not guilty—not guilty.'"

The following is an illustration of the 'public opinion' of South Carolina about fifty years ago. It is taken from **Judge Stroud's Sketch of the Slave Laws,** page 39:

"I find in the case of 'the State vs. M'Gee,' 1 Bay's Reports, 164, it is said incidentally by Messrs. Pinckney and Ford, counsel for the state (of S.C.), 'that the *frequency* of the offense *(willful* murder of a slave) was owing to the *nature of the punishment',* &c....This remark was made in 1791, when the above trial took place. It was made in a public place—a court-house—and by men of great personal respectability. There can be, therefore, no question as to its *truth,* and as little of its *notoriety. "*

In 1791 the **Grand Jury for the district of Cheraw, S.C.** made a *presentment,* from which the following is an extract:

"We, the Grand Jurors of and for the district of Cheraw, do present the inefficacy of the present punishment for killing negroes, as a great defect in the legal system of this state: and we do earnestly recommend to the attention of the legislature, that clause of the negro act, which confines the penalty for killing slaves to fine and imprisonment only in full confidence, that they will provide some other *more effectual* measures to prevent the frequency of crimes of this nature."—*Matthew Carey's American Museum, for Feb.* 1791.—Appendix, p. 10.

The following is a specimen of the 'public opinion' of Georgia twelve years since. We give it in the strong words of **Colonel Stone**, Editor of the New-York Commercial Advertiser. We take it from that paper of June 8, 1827:

"Hunting Men With Dogs—A negro who had absconded from his master, and for whom a reward of $100 was offered, has been apprehended and committed to prison in Savannah. The editor, who states the fact, adds, with as much coolness as though there were no barbarity in the matter, that he did not surrender till *he was considerably* MAIMED BY THE DOGS that had been set on him—desperately fighting them—one of which he badly cut with a sword."

Twelve days after the publication of the preceding fact, the following horrible transaction took place in Perry County, Alabama. We extract it from the **African Observer**, a monthly periodical, published in Philadelphia, by the Society of Friends. See No. for August, 1827.

"Tuscaloosa, Ala. June 20, 1827.

"Some time during the last week a Mr. M'Neilly having lost some clothing, or other property of no great value, the slave of a neighboring planter was charged with the theft. M'Neilly, in company with his brother, found the negro driving his master's wagon; they seized him, and either did, or were about to chastise him, when the negro stabbed M'Neilly, so that he died in an hour afterwards. The negro was taken before a justice of the peace, who *waved his authority,* perhaps through fear, as a crowd of persons had collected to the number of seventy or eighty, near Mr. People's (the justice) house. *He acted as president of the mob,* and put the vote, when it was decided he should be immediately executed by *being burnt to death.* The sable culprit was led to a tree, and tied to it, and a large quantity of pine knots collected and placed around him, and the fatal torch applied to the pile, even against the remonstrance of several gentlemen who were present; and the miserable being was in a short time burned to ashes.

"This is the SECOND negro who has been THUS put to death, without judge or jury, in this county."

The following advertisements, testimony, &c. will show that the slaveholders of *today* are the *children* of those who shot, and hunted with bloodhounds, and burned over slow fires, the slaves of half a century ago; the worthy inheritors of their civilization, chivalry, and tender mercies:

The "Wilmington (North Carolina) Advertiser" of July 13, 1838, contains the following advertisement:

$100 will be paid to any person who may apprehend and safely confine in any jail in this state, a certain negro man, named Alfred. And the same reward will be paid, if satisfactory evidence is given of *his having been* killed. He has one or more scars on one of his hands, caused by his having been shot.   "THE CITIZENS OF ONSLOW
                            "Richlands, Onslow Co. May 16th, 1838."

In the same column with the above and directly under it is the following:

"Ranaway my negro man Richard. A reward of $25 will be paid for his apprehension DEAD or ALIVE. Satisfactory proof will only be required of his being KILLED. He has with him, in all probability, his wife Eliza, who ran away from Col. Thompson, now a resident of Alabama, about the time he commenced his journey to that state. Durant H. Rhodes."

In the "Macon (Georgia) Telegraph" May 28, is the following:
"About the 1st of March last the negro man Ransom left me without the least provocation whatever; I will give a reward of twenty dollars for said

negro, if taken DEAD OR ALIVE—and if killed in any attempt, an advance of five dollars will be paid. Bryant Johnson.

"Crawford Co. Georgia."

See the "Newbern (N.C.) Spectator" Jan. 5, 1838, for the following:

"**RANAWAY**, from the subscriber, a negro man named SAMPSON. Fifty dollars reward will be given for the delivery of him to me, or his confinement in any jail so that I get him, and should he resist in being taken, so that violence is necessary to arrest him, I will not hold any person liable for damages should the slave be Killed. Enoch Foy.

"Jones County, N.C."

From the "Macon (Ga.) Messenger" June 14, 1838:

"**To The Owners of Runaway Negroes**. A large mulatto Negro man, between thirty-five and forty years old, about six feet in height, having a high forehead, and hair slightly grey, was killed, near my plantation, on the 9th inst. *He would not surrender,* but assaulted Mr. Bowen, who killed him in self-defense. If the owner desires further information relative to the death of his negro, he can obtain it by letter, or by calling on the subscriber ten miles south of Perry, Houston County. Edm'd. Jas. Mcgehee."

From the 'Charleston (S.C.) Courier,' Feb. 20, 1836:

"**$300 REWARD.** Ranaway from the subscriber, in November last, his two negro men, named Billy and Pompey.

"Billy is 25 years old, and is known as the patroon of my boat for many years; in all probability he may resist; in that event 50 dollars will be paid for his HEAD."

From the 'Newbern (N.C.) Spectator,' Dec. 2. 1836.

"**$200 REWARD.** Ranaway from the subscriber, about three years ago, a certain negro man named Ben, commonly known by the name of Ben Fox. He had but one eye. Also, one other negro, by the name of Rigdon, who ran away on the 8th of this month.

"I will give the reward of one hundred dollars for each of the above negroes, to be delivered to me or confined in the jail of Lenoir or Jones County, or FOR THE KILLING OF THEM SO THAT I CAN SEE THEM. W. D. COBB."

"In the same number of the Spectator two Justices of the Peace advertise the same runaways, and give notice that if they do not immediately return to W. D. Cobb, their master, they will be considered as outlaws, and any body may kill them. The following is an extract from the proclamation of the Justices:

"And we do hereby, by virtue of an act of the assembly of this state, concerning servants and slaves, intimate and declare, if the said slaves do not surrender themselves and return home to their master immediately after the publication of these presents, *that any person may kill and destroy said slaves by such means as he or* they *think fit, without accusation or impeachment of any crime or offense for so doing, or without incurring any penalty or forfeiture thereby.*

"Given under our hands and seals, this 12th November, 1836.

"B. Coleman, J. P. [Seal.]
"Jas. Jones, J. P. [Seal.]"

On the 28th, of April 1836, in the city of St. Louis, Missouri, a black man, named McIntosh, who had stabbed an officer, that had arrested him, was seized by the multitude, fastened to a tree *in the midst of the city,* wood piled around him, and in open day and in the presence of an immense throng of citizens, he was burned to death. The Alton (Ill.) Telegraph, in its account of the scene says:

"All was silent as death while the executioners were piling wood around their victim. He said not a word, until feeling that the flames had seized upon him. He then uttered an awful howl, attempting to sing and pray, then hung his head, and suffered in silence, except in the following instance:

After the flames had surrounded their prey, his eyes burnt out of his head, and his mouth seemingly parched to a cinder, someone in the crowd, more compassionate than the rest, proposed to put an end to his misery by shooting him, when it was replied, 'that would be of no use, since he was already out of pain.' 'No, no,' said the wretch, 'I am not, I am suffering as much as ever; shoot me, shoot me!' 'No, no!' said one of the fiends who was standing about the sacrifice they were roasting, 'he shall not be shot. I *would sooner slacken the fire, if that would increase his misery,'* and the man who said this was, as we understand, an OFFICER of JUSTICE!"

The St. Louis correspondent of a New York paper adds:

"The shrieks and groans of the victim were loud and piercing, and to observe one limb after another drop into the fire was awful indeed. He was about fifteen minutes in dying. I visited the place this morning, and saw his body, or the remains of it, at the place of execution. He was burnt to a crump. His legs and arms were gone, and only a part of his head and body were left."

Lest this demonstration of 'public opinion' should be regarded as a sudden impulse merely, not an index of the settled tone of feeling in that community, it is important to add, that the Hon. Luke E. Lawless, Judge of the Circuit Court of Missouri, at a session of that Court in the city of St. Louis, some months after the burning of this man, decided officially that since the burning of McIntosh was the act, either directly or by countenance of a *majority* of the citizens, it is 'a case which transcends the jurisdiction,' of the Grand Jury! Thus the state of Missouri has proclaimed to the world, that the wretches who perpetrated that unspeakably diabolical murder, and the thousands that stood by consenting to it, were *her representatives,* and the Bench sanctifies it with the solemnity of a judicial decision.

The 'New Orleans Post,' of June 7, 1836, publishes the following:

"We understand, that a negro man was lately condemned, by the mob, to be BURNED OVER A SLOW FIRE, which was put into execution at Grand Gulf, Mississippi, for murdering a black woman, and her master."

Mr. Henry Bradley, of Pennyan, N.Y., has furnished us with an extract of a letter written by a gentleman in Mississippi to his brother in that village, detailing the particulars of the preceding transaction. The letter is dated Grand Gulf, Miss. August 15, 1836. The extract is as follows:

I left Vicksburg and came to Grand Gulf. This is a fine place immediately on the banks of the Mississippi, of something like fifteen hundred inhabitants in the winter, and at this time, I suppose, there are not over two hundred white inhabitants, but in the town and its vicinity there are negroes by thousands. The day I arrived at this place there was a man by the name of G_____ murdered by a negro man that belonged to him.

G____ was born and brought up in A_____ , state of New York. His father and mother now live south of A____ . He has left a property here, it is supposed, of forty thousand dollars, and no family.

"They took the negro, mounted him on a horse, led the horse under a tree, put a rope around his neck, raised him up by throwing the rope over a limb; they then got into a quarrel among themselves; some swore that he should be burnt alive; the rope was cut and the negro dropped to the ground. He immediately jumped to his feet; they then made him walk a short distance to a tree; he was then tied fast and a fire kindled, when another quarrel took place; the fire was pulled away from him when about half dead, and a committee of twelve appointed to say in what manner he should be disposed of. They brought in that he should then be cut down, his head cutoff, his body burned, and his head stuck on a pole at the corner of the road in the edge of the town. That was done and all parties satisfied!

"G____ *owned the negro's wife, and was in the habit of sleeping with her!* The negro said he had killed him, and he believed he should be rewarded in heaven for it.

"This is but one instance among many of a similar nature.   S. S."

We have received a more detailed account of this transaction from Mr. **William Armstrong**, of Putnam, Ohio, through Maj. Horace Nye, of that place. Mr. A. who has been for some years employed as captain and supercargo of boats descending the river, was at Grand Gulf at the time of the tragedy, and *witnessed* it. It was on the Sabbath. From Mr. Armstrong's statement, it appears that the slave was a man of uncommon intelligence; had the over-sight of a large business—superintended the purchase of supplies for his master, &c.—that exasperated by the intercourse of his master with his wife, he was upbraiding her one evening, when his master overhearing him, went out to quell him, was attacked by the infuriated man and killed on the spot. The name of the master was Green; he was a native of Auburn, New York, and had been at the south but a few years.

Mr. Ezekiel Birdseye, of Cornwall, Conn., a gentleman well known and highly respected in Litchfield County, who resided a number of years in South Carolina, gives the following testimony:

"A man by the name of Waters was killed by his slaves, in Newberry District. Three of them were tried before the court, and ordered to be burnt. I was but a few miles distant at the time, and conversed with those who saw the execution. The slaves were tied to a stake, and pitch pine wood piled around them, to which the fire was communicated. *thousands were collected to witness this barbarous transaction. *Other executions of this kind took place in various parts of the state, during my residence in it, from* 1818 *to* 1824. About three or four years ago, a young negro was burnt in Abbeville District, for an attempt at rape."

In the fall of 1837, there was a rumor of a projected insurrection on the Red River, in Louisiana. The citizens forthwith seized and hanged NINE SLAVES, AND THREE FREE COLORED MEN WITHOUT TRIAL. A few months previous to that transaction, a slave was seized in a similar manner and publicly burned to death, in Arkansas. In July, 1835, the citizens of Madison County, Mississippi, were alarmed by rumors of an insurrection; arrested five slaves and publicly executed them without trial.

The **Missouri Republican**, April 30, 1838, gives the particulars of the deliberate murder of a negro man named Tom, a cook on board the steamboat Pawnee, on her passage up from New Orleans to St. Louis. Some of the facts stated by the Republican are the following:

"On Friday night, about 10 o'clock, a deaf and dumb German girl was found in the storeroom with Tom. The door was locked, and at first Tom denied she was there. The girl's father came. Tom unlocked the door, and the girl was found secreted in the room behind a barrel. The next morning some four or five of the deck passengers spoke to the captain about it. This was about breakfast time. Immediately after he left the deck, a number of the deck passengers rushed upon the negro, bound his arms behind his back and carried him forward to the bow of the boat. A voice cried out ' throw him overboard!' and was responded to from every quarter of the deck—and in an instant he was plunged into the river. The whole scene of tying him and throwing him overboard scarcely occupied *ten minutes,* and was so precipitate that the officers were unable to interfere in time to save him.

"There were between two hundred and fifty and three hundred passengers on board."

The whole process of seizing Tom, dragging him upon deck, binding his arms behind his back, forcing him to the bow of the boat, and throwing him overboard, occupied, the editor informs us, about TEN MINUTES and of the two hundred and fifty or three hundred deck passengers, with perhaps as many cabin passengers, it does not appear that *a single individual raised a finger to prevent this deliberate murder;* and the cry "throw him overboard," was it seems, "responded to from every quarter of the deck!"

Rev. **James A. Thome**, of Augusta, Ky., son of Arthur Thome, Esq., till recently a slaveholder, published five years since the following description of a scene witnessed by him in New Orleans:

"In December of 1833, I landed at New Orleans, in the steamer W____. It was after night, dark and rainy. The passengers were called out of the cabin, from the enjoyment of a fire, which the cold, damp atmosphere rendered very comfortable, by a sudden shout of, 'catch him—catch him—catch the negro!' The cry was answered by a hundred voices—'Catch him—*kill* him!' and a rush from every direction toward our boat, indicated that the object of pursuit was near. The next moment we heard a man plunge into the river, a few paces above us. A crowd gathered upon the shore, with lamps and stones, and clubs, still crying, 'catch him—kill him—catch him— shoot him!'

"I soon discovered the poor man. He had taken refuge under the prow of another boat, and was standing in the water up to his waist. The angry vociferation of his pursuers, did not intimidate him. He defied them all. 'Don't you *dare* to come near me, or I will sink you in the river.' He was armed with despair. For a moment the mob was palsied by the energy of his threatenings. They were afraid to go to him with a skiff, but a number of them went on to the boat and tried to seize him. They threw a noose rope down repeatedly, *that they might pull him up by the neck!* But he planted his hand firmly against the boat and dashed the rope away with his arms. One of them took a long bar of wood, and leaning over the prow, endeavored to strike him on the head. The blow must have shattered the skull, but it did not reach low enough. The monster raised up the heavy club again and said, 'Come out now, you old rascal, or die!' 'Strike,' said the negro; 'strike— shiver my brains *now;* I want to die;' and down went the club again, without striking. This was repeated several times. The mob, seeing their efforts fruitless, became more enraged and threatened to stone him, if he did not surrender himself into their hands. He again defied then and declared that he would drown himself in the river, before they should have him. They then resorted to persuasion, and promised they would not hurt him. 'I'll die first;' was his only reply. Even the furious mob was awed, and for a while stood dumb.

"After standing in the cold water for an hour, the miserable being began to fail. We observed him gradually sinking—his voice grew weak and tremulous—yet he continued to *curse!* In the midst of his oaths he uttered broken sentences—'I didn't steal the meat—I didn't steal—my master lives—master—master lives up the river—(his voice began to gurgle in his throat, and he was so chilled that his teeth chattered audibly)—I didn't — steal—I didn't steal—my—my master—my— I want to see my master—I didn't—no—my mas—you want—you want to kill me—I didn't steal the'—His last words could just be heard as he sunk under the water.

"During this indescribable scene, *not one of the hundred that stood around made any effort to save the man until he was apparently drowned.* He was then dragged out and stretched on the bow of the boat, and soon sufficient means were used for his recovery. The brutal captain ordered him to be taken off his boat—declaring, with an oath, that he would throw him into the river again, if he was not immediately removed. I withdrew, sick and horrified with this appalling exhibition of wickedness.

"Upon inquiry, I learned that the colored man lived some fifty miles up the Mississippi; that he had been charged with stealing some article from the wharf; was fired upon with a pistol, and pursued by the mob.

"In reflecting upon this unmingled cruelty—this insensibility to suffering and disregard of life—I exclaimed, "Is there no flesh in man's obdurate heart?"

One poor man, chased like a wolf by a hundred blood hounds, yelling, howling, and gnashing their teeth upon him—plunges into the cold river to seek protection! A crowd of spectators witness the scene, with all the composure with which a Roman populace would look upon a gladiatorial show. Not a voice heard in the sufferer's behalf. At length the powers of nature give way; the blood flows back to the heart—the teeth chatter—the voice trembles and dies, while the victim drops down into his grave.

"What an atrocious system is that which leaves two millions of souls, friendless and powerless—hunted and chased—afflicted and tortured and driven to death, without the means of redress.—Yet such is the system of slavery."

The 'public opinion' of slaveholders is illustrated by scores of announcements in southern papers, like the following, from the **Raleigh, (N.C.) Register**, August 20, 1838. Joseph Gales and Son, editors and proprietors—the father and brother of the editor of the National Intelligencer, Washington city, D.C:

"On Saturday night, Mr. George Holmes, of this county, and some of his friends, were in pursuit of a runaway slave (the property of Mr.

Holmes) and fell in with him in attempting to make his escape. Mr. H. discharged a gun at his legs, for the purpose of disabling him; but unfortunately, the slave stumbled, and the shot struck him near the small of the back, of which wound he died in a short time. The slave continued to run some distance after he was shot, until overtaken by one of the party. We are satisfied, from all that we can learn, that Mr. H. had no intention of inflicting a mortal wound."

Oh! The *gentleman,* it seems, only shot at his legs, merely to 'disable'— and it must be expected that every *gentleman* will amuse himself in shooting at his own property whenever the notion takes him, and if he should happen to hit a little higher and go through the small of the back instead of the legs, why everybody says it is 'unfortunate,' and the whole of the editorial corps, instead of branding him as a barbarous wretch for shooting at his slave, whatever part he aimed at, join with the oldest editor in North Carolina, in complacently exonerating Mr. Holmes by saying, "We are satisfied that Mr. H. had no intention of inflicting a mortal wound." And so 'public opinion' wraps it up!

The Franklin (La.) Republican, August 19, 1837, has the following:

"**Negroes Taken.**—Four gentlemen of this vicinity, went out yesterday for the purpose of finding the camp of some noted runaways, supposed to be near this place; the camp was discovered about 11 o'clock, the negroes four in number, three men and one woman, finding they were discovered, tried to make their escape through the cane; two of them were fired on, one of which made his escape; the other one fell after running a short distance, his wounds are not supposed to be dangerous; the other man was taken without any hurt; the woman also made her escape."

Thus terminated the morning's amusement of the *'four gentlemen,'* whose exploits are so complacently chronicled by the editor of the Franklin Republican. The three men and one woman were all fired upon, it seems, though only one of them was shot down. The half famished runaways made not the least resistance, they merely rushed in panic among the canes, at the sight of their pursuers, and the bullets whistled after them and brought to the ground one poor fellow, who was carried back by his captors as a trophy of the 'public opinion' among slaveholders.

In the **Macon (Ga.) Telegraph**, Nov. 27, 1838, we find the following account of a runaway's den, and of the good luck of a 'Mr. Adams,' in running down one of them with his excellent dogs:'

"**A runaway's den was discovered** on Sunday near the Washington Spring, in a little patch of woods, where it had been for several months, so artfully concealed underground, that it was detected only by accident, though in sight of two or three houses, and near the road and fields where there has been constant daily passing. The entrance was concealed by a pile of pine straw, representing a hog bed—which being removed, discovered a trap door and steps that led to a room about six feet square, comfortably ceiled with plank, containing a small fire-place the flue of which was ingeniously conducted above ground and concealed by the straw. The inmates took the alarm and made their escape; but Mr. Adams and his excellent dogs being put upon the trail, soon run down and secured one of them, which proved to be a negro fellow who had been out about a year. He stated that the other occupant was a woman, who had been a runaway a still longer time. In the den was found a quantity of meal, bacon, corn, potatoes, &c., and various cooking utensils and wearing apparel."

Yes, Mr. Adams 'Excellent Dogs' did the work! They were well trained, swift, fresh, keen-scented, 'excellent' men-hunters, and though the poor fugitive in his frenzied rush for liberty, strained every muscle, yet they gained upon him, and after dashing through fens, brier beds, and the tangled undergrowth till faint and torn, he sinks, and the blood-hounds are upon him. What blood-vessels the poor straggler burst in his desperate push for life—how much he was bruised and lacerated in his plunge through the forest, or how much the dogs tore him, the Macon editor has not chronicled—they are matters of no moment—but his heart is touched with the merits of Mr. Adams "Excellent Dogs", that soon '*run down* and *secured*' a guiltless and trembling human creature!

The Georgia Constitutionalist, of Jan. 1837, contains the following letter from the coroner of Barnwell District, South Carolina, dated Aiken, S.C. Dec. 20, 1836:

"*To the Editor of the Constitutionalist:*

"I have just returned from an inquest I held over the body of a negro man, a runaway, that was shot near the South Edisto, in this District, (Barnwell,) on Saturday last. He came to his death by his own recklessness. He refused to be taken alive—and said that other attempts to take him had been made, and he was determined that he would not be taken. He was at first, (when those in pursuit of him found it absolutely necessary,) shot at with small shot, with the intention of merely crippling him. He was shot at several times, and at last he was so disabled as to be compelled to surrender. He kept in the run of a creek in a very dense swamp all the time that the neighbors were in pursuit of him. As soon as the negro was taken, the best medical aid was procured, but he died on the same evening. One of the witnesses at the inquisition, stated that the negro boy said he was from Mississippi, and belonged to so many persons, that he did not know who his master was, but again he said his master's name was Brown. He said his name was Sam, and when asked by another witness, who his master was, he muttered something like Augusta or Augustine. The boy was apparently above thirty-five or forty years of age, about six feet high, slightly yellow in the face, very long beard or whiskers, and very stout built, and a stern countenance; and appeared to have been a runaway for a long time.

"William H. Pritchard,

Coroner Ex-officio, Barnwell Dist. S.C.

The Norfolk (Va.) Herald, of Feb. 1837 the following:

"Three negroes in a ship's yawl, came on shore yesterday evening, near New Point Comfort, and were soon after apprehended and lodged in jail. Their story is, that they belonged to a brig from New York bound to Havana, which was cast away to the southward of Cape Henry, some day last week; that the brig was called the Maria, Captain Whittemore. I have no doubt they are deserters from some vessel in the bay, as their statements are very confused and inconsistent. One of these fellows is a mulatto, and calls himself Isaac Turner; the other two are quite black, the one passing by the name of James Jones and the other John Murray. They have all their clothing with them, and are dressed in sea-faring apparel. They attempted to make their escape, and *it was not till a musket was fired at them, and one of them slightly wounded,* that they surrendered. They will be kept in jail till something further is discovered respecting them."

The **'St. Francisville (La.) Chronicle'** of Feb. 1, 1839. Gives the following account of a 'negro hunt' in that Parish:

"Two or three days since a gentleman of this parish, in *hunting runaway negroes,* came upon a camp of them in the swamp on Cat Island. He succeeded in arresting two of them, but the third made fight; and upon *being shot in the shoulder,* fled to a sluice, where the *dogs succeeded* in drowning him before assistance could arrive."

"The dogs *succeeded* in drowning him"! Poor fellow! He tried hard for his life, plunged into the sluice, and, with a bullet in his shoulder, and the blood hounds un-fleshing his bones, he bore up for a moment with feeble stroke as best he might, but 'public opinion,' '*succeeded'* in drowning him,' and the same 'public opinion,' calls the man who fired and crippled him, and cheered on the dogs, 'a gentleman,' and the editor who celebrates the exploit is a 'gentleman' also!"

A large number of extracts similar to the above might here be inserted from Southern newspapers in our possession, but the foregoing are more than sufficient for our purpose, and we bring to a close the testimony on this point, with the following. Extract of a letter, from the **Rev. Samuel J. May,** of South Scituate, Mass. dated Dec. 20, 1838.

"You doubtless recollect the narrative given in the Oasis, of a slave in Georgia, who having ran away from his master, (accounted a very hospitable and even humane gentleman,) was hunted by his master and his retainers with horses, dogs, and rifles, and having been driven into a tree by the hounds, was shot down by his more cruel pursuers. All the facts there given, and some others equally shocking, connected with the same case, were first communicated to me in 1833, by Mr. W. Russell, a highly respectable teacher of youth in Boston. He is doubtless ready to vouch for them. The same gentleman informed me that he was keeping school on or near the plantation of the monster who perpetrated the above outrage upon humanity, that he was even invited by him to join in the hunt, and when he expressed abhorrence at the thought, the planter holding up the rifle which he had in his hand said with an oath, "damn that rascal, this is the third time he has runaway, and he shall never run again. I'd rather put a ball into his side, than into the best buck in the land!"

Mr. Russell, in the account given by him of this tragedy in the 'Oasis,' page 267, thus describes the slaveholder who made the above expression, and was the leader of the 'hunt,' and in whose family he resided at the time as an instructor; he says of him—He was "an opulent planter, in whose family the evils of slaveholding were palliated by every expedient that a humane and generous disposition could suggest. He was a man of noble and elevated character, and distinguished for his generosity, and kindness of heart."

In a letter to Mr. May, dated Feb. 3, 1839, Mr. Russell, speaking of the hunting of runaways with dogs and guns, says: "Occurrences of a nature similar to the one related in the 'Oasis,' were not un-frequent in the interior of Georgia and South Carolina twenty years ago. *Several* such fell under my notice within the space of fifteen months. In two such 'hunts,' I was solicited to join."

The following was written by a sister-in-law of **Gerrit Smith, Esq.**, Peterboro. She is married to the son of a North Carolinian:

"In North Carolina, some years ago, several slaves were arrested for committing serious crimes and depredations, in the neighborhood of Wilmington, among other things, burning houses, and, in one or more instances, murder.

"It happened that the wife of one of these slaves resided in one of the most respectable families in Wilmington in the capacity of nurse. Mr. J. *the first lawyer in the place,* came into the room, where the lady of the house was sitting, with the nurse, who held a child in her arms, and, addressing the nurse, said, "Hannah! Would you know your husband if you should see him?—"Oh, yes, sir", she replied—WHEN HE DREW FROM BENEATH HIS CLOAK THE HEAD OF THE SLAVE at the sight of which the poor woman immediately fainted. The heads of the others were placed upon poles, in some part of the town, afterwards known as 'Negro Head Point.'"

We have just received the above testimony, enclosed in a letter from Mr Smith, in which he says, "that the fact stated by my sister-in-law, actually occurred, there can be no doubt."

The following extract from the Diary of the **Rev. Elias Cornelius,** we insert here, having neglected to do it under a preceding head, to which it more appropriately belongs.

"New Orleans, Sabbath, February 15, 1818. Early this morning accompanied A. H. Esq. to the *hospital,* with the view of making arrangements to preach to such of the sick as could understand English. The first room we entered presented a scene of human misery, such as I had never before witnessed. A poor negro man was lying upon a couch, apparently in great distress; a more miserable object can hardly be conceived. His face was much d*isfigured,* an IRON COLLAR, TWO INCHES WIDE AND HALF AN INCH THICK, WAS CLASPED ABOUT HIS NECK, while one of his feet and part of the leg were in a state of putrefaction. We inquired the cause of his being in this distressing condition, and he answered us in a faltering voice, that he was willing to tell us all the truth.

"He belonged to Mr.____, a Frenchman, ran away, was caught, and punished with one hundred lashes! This happened about Christmas; and during the cold weather at that time, he was confined in the *Cane-house, with a scanty portion of clothing, and without fire.* In this situation his foot had frozen, and mortified, and having been removed from place to place, he was yesterday brought here by order of his new master, who was an American. I had no time to protract my conversation with him then, but resolved to return in a few hours and pray with him.

"Having returned home, I again visited the hospital at half past eleven o'clock, and concluded first of all [he was to preach at 12,] to pray with the poor lacerated negro. I entered the apartment in which he lay, and observed an old man sitting upon a couch; but, without saying anything went up to the bed-side of the negro, who appeared to be asleep. I spoke to him, but he gave no answer. I spoke again, and moved his head, still he said nothing. My apprehensions were immediately excited, and I felt for his pulse, but it was gone. Said I to the old man, 'surely this negro is dead.' 'No,' he answered, 'he has fallen asleep, for he had a very restless season last night.' I again examined and called the old gentleman to the bed, and alas, it was found true, that he was dead. Not an eye had witnessed his last struggle, and I was the first, as it should happen, to discover the fact. I called several men into the room, and without ceremony they wrapped him in a sheet, and carried him to the dead-house, as it is called."—*Edwards' Life of Rev. Elias Cornelius*, pp. 101, 2,3.

THE PROTECTION EXTENDED BY 'PUBLIC OPINION,' TO THE HEALTH* OF THE SLAVES

This may be judged of from the fact that it is perfectly notorious among slaveholders, both North and South, that of the tens of thousands of slaves sold annually in the northern slave states to be transported to the south, large numbers of them die under the severe process of acclimation, *all* suffer more or less, and multitudes *much,* in their health and strength, during their first years in the far south and south west. That such is the case is sufficiently proved by the care taken by all who advertise for sale or hire in Louisiana, Mississippi, Alabama, Arkansas, &c. &c. to inform the reader, that their slaves are ' Creoles,' 'southern born,' 'country born,' &c.

or if they are from the north, that they are 'acclimated,' and the importance attached to their *acclimation,* is shown in the fact, that it is generally distinguished from the rest of the advertisements either by *italics* or Capitals. Almost every newspaper published in the states far south contains advertisements like the following:.

From the **"Vicksburg (Mi.) Register"** Dec 27, 1838:
"I Offer my plantation for sale. Also seventy-live *acclimated Negroes.* O. B. Cobb."

From the **"Southerner"** June 7, 1837:
"I Will sell my Old-River plantation near Columbia in Arkansas;—also ONE HUNDRED AND THIRTY ACCLIMATED SLAVES. Benj. Hughes." *Port Gibson, Jan.* 14, 1837.

From the **"Planters"(La.) Intelligencer"** March 22:
"Probate sale—Will be offered for sale at Public Auction, to the highest bidder, ONE HUNDRED AND THIRTY *acclimated* slaves."

G. W. Keeton. Judge of the Parish of Concordia. From the **"Arkansas Advocate"** May 22, 1837:
"By virtue of a Deed of Trust, executed to me, I will sell at public auction at Fisher's Prairie, Arkansas, sixty *LIKELY NEGROES,* consisting of Men, Women, Boys and Girls, the most of whom are Well Acclimated.
Grandison D. Royston, *Trustee."*

From the "New Orleans Bee" Feb. 9, 1838:
"VALUABLE ACCLIMATED NEGROES will be sold on Saturday, 10th inst. at 12 o'clock, at the city exchange, St. Louis street."
Then follows a description of the slaves, closing with the same assertion, which forms the caption of the advertisement "All Acclimated."

General Felix Houston, of Natchez, advertises in the **"Natchez Courier"** April 6, 1838:
"Thirty five very fine *acclimated* Negroes."

Without inserting more advertisements, suffice it to say, that when slaves are advertised for sale or hire, in the lower southern country, if they

~ 398 ~

are *natives*, or have lived in that region long enough to become acclimated, it is *invariably* stated.

But we are not left to *conjecture* the amount of suffering experienced by slaves from the north in undergoing the severe process of 'seasoning' to the climate, or '*acclimation*'. A writer in the New Orleans Argus, September, 1830, in an article on the culture of the sugar cane, says: 'The loss by *death* in bringing slaves from a northern climate, which our planters are under the necessity of doing, is not less than Twenty-five per cent.'

Nothwithstanding the immense amount of suffering endured in the process of acclimation, and the fearful waste of life, and the *notoriety* of this fact, still the 'public opinion' of Virginia, Maryland, Delaware, Kentucky, Missouri, *&c.* annually drives to the far south, thousands of their slaves to undergo these sufferings, and the ' public opinion,' of the far south buys them, and forces the helpless victims to endure them.

THE 'PROTECTION' VOUCHSAFED BY 'PUBLIC OPINION,' TO LIBERTY.

This is shown by hundreds of advertisements in southern papers, like the following:

From the "Mobile Register" July 21, 1837:

"WILL BE SOLD CHEAP FOR CASH, in front of the Court House of Mobile County, on the 22d day of July next, one mulatto man named HENRY HALL, WHO SAYS HE IS FREE; his owner or owners, *if any*, having failed to demand him, he is to be sold according to the statute in such cases made and provided, *to pay Jail fees.* Wm. Magee, Sh'ff M.C."

From the "Grand Gulf (Miss.) Advertiser" Dec. 7, 1838:

"COMMITTED to the jail of Chickasaw Co. Edmund, Martha, John and Louisa; the man 50, the woman 35, John 3 years old, and Louisa 14 months. They say they are FREE and were decoyed to this state."

The "Southern Argus" of July 25, 1837, contains the following:

"RANAWAY from my plantation, a negro boy named William. Said boy was taken up by Thomas Walton, and says *he was free,* and that his parents live near Shawneetown, Illinois, and that he was *taken* from that place in July 1836; says his father's name is William, and his mother's Sally Brown, and that they moved from Fredericksburg, Virginia. I will give twenty dollars to any person who will deliver said boy to me or Col. Byrn, Columbus.   SAMUEL H. BYRN."

The first of the following advertisements was a standing one, in the "Vicksburg Register" from Dec. 1835 till Aug. 1836. The second advertises the same Free man for sale.

"SHERIFF'S SALE"
"COMMITTED, to the jail of Warren County, as a Runaway, on the 23d inst. a Negro man, who calls himself John J. Robinson; *says* that *he is free,* says that he kept a baker's shop in Columbus, Miss, and that he peddled through the Chickasaw nation to Pontotoc, and came to Memphis, where he sold his horse, took water, and came to this place. The owner of said boy is requested to come forward, prove property, pay charges, and take him away, or he will be dealt with as the law directs.
                                        Wm. Everett, Jailer.
                                        Dec. 24, 1835

"NOTICE is hereby given, that the above described boy, who calls himself John J. Robinson, having been confined in the Jail of Warren County as a Runaway, for six months—and having been regularly advertised during this period, I shall proceed to sell said Negro boy at public auction, to the highest bidder for cash, at the door of the Court House in Vicksburg, on Monday, 1st day of August, 1836, in pursuance of the statute in such cases made and provided.   E. W. Morris, Sheriff.
                                        Vicksburg, July 2, 1836."
See "Newbern (N.C.) Spectator," of Jan. 5, 1838, for the following advertisement:
"RANAWAY, from the subscriber a negro man known as Frank Pilot. He is five feet eight inches high, dark complexion, and about 50 years old, HAS BEEN FREE SINCE 1829—is now my property, as heir at law of his last owner, *Samuel Ralston,* dec. I will give the above reward if he is taken and confined in any jail so that I can get him.   Samuel Ralston.
                                        Pactolus, Pitt County."

From the Tuscaloosa (Ala.) "Flag of the Union" June 7.

COMMITTED to the Jail of Tuscaloosa County, a negro man, who says his name is Robert Winfield, and *says he is free.*

R. W. Barber, *Jailer."*

That "public opinion," in the slave states affords no protection to the liberty of colored persons, even after those persons become legally free, by the operation of their own laws, is declared by Governor Comegys, of Delaware, in his recent address to the Legislature of that state, Jan. 1839. The Governor, commenting upon the law of the state which provides that persons convicted of certain crimes shall be sold as servants for a limited time, says:

"The case is widely different with the negro (!) Although ordered to be disposed of as a servant for a term of years, *perpetual slavery in the south. is his inevitable doom*; unless, peradventure, age or disease may have rendered him *worthless,* or some resident of the State, from motives of benevo*lence,* will pay for him three or four times his intrinsic *value.* It matters not for how short a time he is ordered to be sold, so that he can be carried from the State. Once beyond its limits, *all chance of restored freedom is gone*—for he is removed far from the reach of any testimony to aid him in an effort to be released from bondage, when his *legal* term of servitude has expired. *Of the many colored convicts sold out of the State, it is believed none ever return.* Of course they are purchased *with the express view to their transportation for life,* and bring such enormous prices as to prevent all *competition on* the part of those of our citizens who *require* their services, and *would keep them in the State."*

From the "Memphis (Ten.) Enquirer" Dec. 28, 1838:

"$50 Reward. Ranaway, from the subscriber, on Thursday last, a negro man named Isaac, 22 years old, about 5 feet 10 or 11 inches high, dark complexion, well made, full face, speaks quick, and very correctly for a negro. *He was originally from New-York,* and no doubt will attempt to pass himself as free. I will give the above reward for his apprehension and delivery, or confinement, so that I obtain him, if taken out of the state, or $30 if taken within the state.   Jno. Simpson.

Memphis, Dec. 28."

Mark, with what shameless hardihood this Jno. Simpson, tells the public that *he knew* Isaac Wright was a free man!' HE WAS

~ 401 ~

ORIGINALLY FROM NEW YORK,' he tells us. And yet he adds with brazen effrontery, '*he will attempt to pass himself as free.*' This Isaac Wright, was shipped by a man named Lewis, of New Bedford, Massachusetts, and sold as a slave in New Orleans. After passing through several hands, and being flogged nearly to death, he made his escape, and five days ago, (March 5,) returned to his friends in Philadelphia.

From the "Baltimore Sun" Dec. 23, 1838:

"Free Negroes.—Merry Ewall, a Free negro, from Virginia, was committed to jail, at Snow Hill, Md. last week, for remaining in the State longer than is allowed by the law of 1831. The fine in his case amounts to $225. Capril Purnell, a negro from Delaware, is now in jail in the same place, for a violation of the same act. His fine amounts to FOUR THOUSAND DOLLARS AND HE WILL BE SOLD IN A SHORT TIME."

The following is the decision of the Supreme Court, of Louisiana, in the case of Gomez *vs.* Bonneval, Martin's La. Reports, 656, and Wheeler's " Law of Slavery" p. 380-1.

Marginal remark of the Compiler.—"*A slave does not become free on his being illegally imported into the state.*"

"*Per Cur. Derbigny,* J. The petitioner is a negro in actual state of slavery; he claims his freedom, and is bound to prove it. In his attempt, however, to show that he was free before he was introduced into this country, he has failed, so that his claim rests entirely on the laws prohibiting the introduction of slaves in the United States. That the plaintiff was imported since that prohibition does exist is a fact sufficiently established by the evidence. What right he has acquired under the laws forbidding such importation is the only question which we have to examine. Formerly, while the act dividing Louisiana into two territories was in force in this country, slaves introduced here in contravention to it, were freed by operation of law; but that act was merged in the legislative provisions which were subsequently enacted on the subject of importation of slaves into the United States generally. Under the now existing laws, the individuals thus imported acquire *no personal right,* they are mere passive beings, who are disposed of *according to the* will of the different state legislatures. In this country they are to *remain slaves,* and TO BE SOLD

FOR THE BENEFIT OF THE STATE. The plaintiff, therefore, has nothing to claim as a freeman; and as to a mere change of master, should such be his wish, *he cannot be listened to in a court of justice. "*

Extract from a speech of **Mr. Thomson of Penn.** in Congress, March 1, 1826, on the prisons in the District of Columbia:

"I visited the prisons twice that I might myself ascertain the truth. In one of these cells (but eight feet square,) were confined at that time, seven persons, three women and four children. The children were confined under a strange system of law in this District, by which a colored person who *alleges* He IS FEE, and appeals to the tribunals of the country, to have the matter tried, is COMMITTED TO PRISON, till the decision takes place. They were almost naked, one of them was sick, lying on the damp brick, floor, *without bed, pillow, or covering.* In this abominable cell, seven human beings were confined day by day, and night after night, without a bed, chair, or stool, or any other of the most common necessaries of life."—*Gales 'Congressional Debates',* v. 2, p. 1480.

The following facts serve to show, that the present generation of slaveholders do but follow in the footsteps of their fathers, in their *zeal for* LIBERTY:

Extract from a document submitted by the Committee of the yearly meeting of Friends in Philadelphia, to the Committee of Congress, to whom was referred the memorial of the people called Quakers, in 1797:

"In the latter part of the year 1776, several of the people called Quakers, residing in the counties of Perquimans and Pasquotank, in the state of North Carolina, liberated their negroes, as it was then clear there was no existing law to prevent their so doing; for the law of 1741 could not at that time be carried into effect; and they were suffered to remain free, until a law passed, in the spring of 1777, under which they were taken up and sold, contrary to the Bill of Rights, recognized in the constitution of that state, as a part thereof, and to which it was annexed.

"In the spring of 1777, when the General Assembly met for the first time, a law was enacted to prevent slaves from being emancipated, except for meritorious services, &c. to be judged of by the county courts or the general assembly; and ordering, that if any should be manumitted in any other way, they be taken up, and the county courts within whose

~ 403 ~

jurisdictions they are apprehended should order them to be sold. Under this law the county courts of Perquimans and Pasquotank, in the year 1777, ordered A LARGE NUMBER OF PERSONS TO BE SOLD, WHO WERE FREE AT THE TIME THE LAW WAS MADE.

In the year 1778 several of those cases were, by certiorari, brought before the superior court for the district of Edenton, where the decisions of the county courts were reversed, the superior court declaring, that said county courts, in such their proceedings, have exceeded their jurisdiction, violated the rights of the subject, and acted in direct opposition to the Bill of Rights of this state, considered justly as part of the constitution thereof; by giving to a law, not intended to affect this case, a retrospective operation, thereby to deprive freemen of this state of their liberty, contrary to the laws of the land. In consequence of this decree several of the negroes were again set at liberty; but the next General Assembly, early in 1779, passed a law, wherein they mention, that doubts have arisen, whether the purchasers of such slaves have a good and legal title thereto, and confirm the same; under which they were again taken up by the purchasers and reduced to slavery." [The number of persons thus re-enslaved was 134.]

The following are the decrees of the Courts, ordering the sale of those freemen:

"Perquimans County, July term, at Hartford, A. D. 1777.

"These may certify, that it was then and there ordered, that the sheriff of the county, tomorrow morning, at ten o'clock, expose to sale, to the highest bidder, for ready money at the court-house door, the several negroes taken up as free, and in his custody, agreeable to law.

"Test. Wm. Skinner, Clerk.
"A true copy, 25th August, 1791.
"Test. J. Harvet, Clerk."

"Pasquotank County, September Court, &c. &c.

1777. "Present, the Worshipful Thomas Boyd, Timothy Hickson, John Paclin, Edmund Chancey, Joseph Reading, and Thomas Rees, Esqrs. Justices.

"It was then and there ordered, that Thomas Reading, Esq. take the Free negroes taken up under an act to prevent domestic insurrections and other purposes, and expose the same to *the best bidder,* at public vendue, for ready money, and be accountable for the same, agreeable to the aforesaid act; and make return to this or the next succeeding court of his proceedings.

"A copy"   "Enoch Reese, C.C."

THE PROTECTION OF "PUBLIC OPINION" TO DOMESTIC TIES.

The barbarous indifference with which slaveholders regard the forcible sundering of husbands and wives, parents and children, brothers and sisters, and the unfeeling brutality indicated by the language in which they describe the efforts made by the slaves, in their yearnings after those from whom they have been torn away, reveals a 'public opinion' towards them as dead to their agony as if they were cattle. It is well nigh impossible to open a southern paper without finding evidence of this. Though the truth of this assertion can hardly be called in question, we subjoin a few illustrations, and could easily give hundreds:

From the "Savannah Georgian" Jan. 17, 1839:

"$100 reward will be given for my two fellows, Abram and Frank. Abram has a *wife* at Colonel Stewart's, in Liberty County, and a *sister* in Savannah, at Capt. Grovenstine's. Frank has a *wife* at Mr. LeCont's, Liberty County; a *mother* at Thunderbolt, and a *sister* in Savannah.

Wm. Robarts, Wallhourville, 5th Jan. 1839"

From the "Lexington (Ky.) Intelligencer' July 7, 1838:

"$160 Reward.—Ranaway from the subscribers, living in this city, on Saturday 16th inst. a negro man, named Dick, about 37 years of age. It is highly probable said boy will make for New Orleans, as *he has a wife living in that city*, and he has been heard to say frequently that *he was determined to go to New Orleans.*

"Drake & Thompson."Lexington, June 17, 1838."

From the "Southern Argus" Oct. 31, 1837:

"Runaway—my negro man, Frederick, about 20 years of age. He is no doubt near the plantation of G. W. Corprew, Esq. of Noxubbee County, Mississippi, As *his wife belongs to that gentleman, and he followed her from my residence.* The above reward will be paid to anyone who will confine him in jail and inform me of it at Athens, Ala.

"Athens, Alabama, Kerkman Lewis.'"

~ 405 ~

From the "Savannah Georgian" July 8, 1837:

"Ran away from the subscriber, his man Joe. He visits the city occasionally, where he has been harbored by his *mother* and *sister.* I will give one hundred dollars for proof sufficient to *convict his harborers.*

R. P. T. Mongin."

The "Macon (Georgia) Messenger" Nov. 23, 1837, has the following:

"$25 Reward.—Ran away, a negro man, named Cain. He was brought from Florida, and *has a wife near Mariana,* and probably will attempt to make his way there.

H. L. Cook."From the "Richmond (Va.) Whig" July 25, 1837:

"Absconded from the subscriber, a negro man, by the name of Wilson. He was born in the county of New Kent, and raised by a gentleman named Ratliff, and by him sold to a gentleman named Taylor, on whose farm he had a *wife* and several *children.* Mr. Taylor sold him to a Mr. Slater, who, in consequence of removing to Alabama, Wilson left; and when retaken was sold, and afterwards purchased, by his present owner, from T. McCargo and Co. of Richmond."

From the "Savannah (Ga.) Republican" Sept. 3, 1838:

"$20 Reward for my negro man Jim. Jim is about 50 or 55 years of age. It is probable he will aim for Savannah, as he said *he had children* in that vicinity. J. G. Owens, Barnwell District, S.C."

From the "Staunton (Va.) Spectator" Jan. 3, 1839:

"Ranaway, Jesse.—He has a *wife,* who belongs to Mr. John Ruff, of Lexington, Rockbridge County, and he may probably be lurking in that neighborhood. Moses McCue."

From the "Augusta (Georgia) Chronicle" July 10, 1837:

"$120 Reward for my negro Charlotte. She is about 20 years old. She was purchased some months past from Mr. Thomas J. Walton, of Augusta, by Thomas W. Oliver; and, as her *mother* and acquaintances live in that city, it is very likely she is *harbored* by some of them. Martha Oliver."

From the "Raleigh (N.C.) Register" July 18, 1837:

"**Ranaway** from the subscriber, a negro man named Jim, the property of Mrs. Elizabeth Whitfield. He *has a wife* at the late Hardy Jones', and may probably be lurking in that neighborhood.   John O'Rorke."

From the "Richmond (Va.) Compiler" Sept. 8, 1837:

"**Ranaway** from the subscriber, Ben. He ran off without any known cause, and *I suppose he is aiming to go to his wife, who was carried from the neighborhood last winter.*   John Hunt."

From the "Charleston (S.C.) Mercury" Aug. 1, 1837:

"**Absconded** from Mr. E. D. Bailey, on Wadmalaw, his negro man, named Saby. Said fellow was purchased in January, from Francis Dickinson, of St. Paul's parish, and is probably now in that neighborhood, *where he has a wife.*   Thomas N. Gadsden."

From the "Portsmouth (Va.) Times" August 3, 1838:

"**$50 dollars Reward** will be given for the apprehension of my negro man Isaac. He *has a wife* at James M. Riddick's, of Gates County, N.C. where he may probably be lurking.   C. Miller."

From the "Savannah (Georgia) Republican" May 24, 1838:

"**$40 Reward.**—Ran away from the subscriber in Savannah, his negro girl Patsey. She was purchased among the gang of negroes, known as the Hargreave's estate. She is no doubt lurking about Liberty County, at which place *she has relatives.*   Edward Houstoun, of Florida."

From the "Charleston (S.C.) Courier" June 29, 1837:

"**$20 Reward** will be paid for the apprehension and delivery, at the work-house in Charleston, of a mulatto woman, named Ida. It is probable she may have made her way into Georgia, where she has *connections.*
                Matthew Muggridge."

From the "Norfolk (Va.) Beacon" March 31, 1838:

"**The subscriber will give $20** for the apprehension of his negro woman, Maria, who ran away about twelve months since. She is known to be lurking in or about Chuckatuch, in the county of Nansemond, where *she has a husband,* and *formerly belonged.*   Peter Oneill."

From the "Macon (Georgia) Messenger" Jan. 16, 1839:

"**Ranaway from the subscriber**, two negroes, Davis, a man about 45 years old; also Peggy, his wife, near the same age. Said negroes will probably make their way to Columbia County, as *they have children* living in that county. I will liberally reward any person who may deliver them to me.   Nehemiah King."

From the "Petersburg (Va.) Constellation" June 27, 1837:
"**Ranaway**, a negro man, named Peter. *He has a wife* at the plantation of Mr. C. Haws, near Suffolk, where it is supposed he is still lurking.
                                             John L.Dunn."

From the "Richmond (Va.) Whig" Dec. 7, 1839:
"**Ranaway from the subscriber**, a negro man, named John Lewis. It is supposed that he is lurking about in New Kent County, where he professes to have *a wife*.   Hill Jones, "Agent for R. F. & P. Railroad Co."

From the "Red River (La.) Whig" June 2d, 1838:
"**Ran away from the subscriber**, a mulatto woman, named Maria. It is probable she may be found in the neighborhood of Mr. Jesse Bynum's plantation, where *she has relations, &c.*   Thomas J. Wells."

From the "Lexington (Ky.) Observer and Re porter" Sept. 28, 1838:
"**$50 Reward.**—Ran away from the subscriber, a negro girl, named Maria. She is of a copper color, between 13 and 14 years of age—*bare headed* and *bare footed.* She is small of her age—very sprightly and very likely. She stated she was *going to see her mother* at Maysville.
                                             Sanford Thomson."

From the "Jackson (Tenn.) Telegraph" Sept. 14, 1838:
"**Committed to the jail of Madison County**, a negro woman, who calls her name Fanny, and says she belongs to William Miller, of Mobile. She formerly belonged to John Givins, of this county, who now owns *several of her children.*   David Shropshire, Jailor."

From the "Norfolk (Va.) Beacon" July 3d, 1838:
"**Runaway** from my plantation below Edenton, my negro man, Nelson. *He has a mother living* at Mr. James Goodwin's, in Ballahack, Perquimans

County; and *two brothers,* one belonging to Job Parker, and the other to Josiah Coffield. Wm. D. Rascoe."

From the "Charleston (S.C.) Courier" Jan. 12, 1838:
"$100 Reward.—Run away from the subscriber, his negro fellow, John. He is well known about the city as one of my bread carriers; *has a wife* living at Mrs. Weston's, on Hempstead. John formerly belonged to Mrs. Moor, near St. Paul's church, where his *mother* still lives, and *has been harbored by her* before. John T. Marshall, 60 Tradd-Street."

From the "Newbern (N.C.) Sentinel" March 17, 1837:
"Ranaway, Moses, a black fellow, about 40 years of age—has a *wife* in Washington. Thomas Bragg, Sen. Warrenton, N.C."

From the "Richmond (Va.) Whig" June 30, 1837:
"Ranaway, my man Peter.—He has a *sister* and *mother* in New Kent, and a *wife* about fifteen or eighteen miles above Richmond, at or about Taylorsville. Theo. A. Lacy."

From the "New Orleans Bulletin," Feb. 7, 1838:
"Ranaway, my negro Philip, aged about 40 years.—He may have gone to St. Louis, as *he has a wife there.* W. G. Clark, 70 New Levee.
"From the "Georgian" Jan. 29, 1838:
"A Reward of $5 will be paid for the apprehension of his negro woman, Diana. Diana is from 45 to 50 age. She formerly belonged to Mr. Nath. Law, of Liberty County, *where her husband still lives.* She will endeavor to go there perhaps. D. O'Byrne."

From the "Richmond (Va.) Enquirer" Feb. 20, 1838:
"$10 Reward for a negro woman, named Sally, 40 years old. We have just reason to believe the said negro to be now lurking on the James River Canal, or in the Green Spring neighborhood, where, we are informed, *her husband resides.* The above reward will be given to any person *securing* her. Polly C. Shields. Mount Elba, Feb. 19, 1838."

"$50 Reward.—Ran away from the subscriber, his negro man Pauladore, commonly called Paul. I understand Gen. R. Y. Hayne *has purchased his wife and children* from H. L. Pinckney, Esq. and has them now on his plantation at Goosecreek, where, no doubt, the fellow is frequently *lurking.*   T.Davis."

"**$25 Reward.**—Ran away from the subscriber, a negro woman, named Matilda. It is thought she may be somewhere up James River, as she was claimed as *a wife* by some boatman in Goochland.   J. Alvis."

"**Stop the Runaway!!—$25 Reward**. Ranaway from the Eagle Tavern, a negro fellow, named Nat. He is no doubt attempting to *follow his wife, who was lately sold to a speculator* named Redmond. The above reward will be paid by Mrs. Lucy M. Downman, of Sussex County, Va."

Multitudes of advertisements like the above appear annually in the southern papers. Reader, look at the preceding list—mark the unfeeling barbarity with which their masters and *mistresses* describe the struggles and perils of sundered husbands and wives, parents and children, in their weary midnight travels through forests and rivers, with torn limbs and breaking hearts, seeking the embraces of each other's love. In one instance, a mother torn from all her children and taken to a remote part of another state, presses her way back through the wilderness, hundreds of miles, to clasp once more her children to her heart: but, when she has arrived within a few miles of them, in the same county, is discovered, seized, dragged to jail, and her purchaser told, through an advertisement, that she awaits his order. But we need not trace out the harrowing details already before the reader.

Rev. C. S. Renshaw, of Quincy, Illinois, who resided some time in Kentucky, says:

I was told the following fact by a young lady, daughter of a slaveholder in Boone County, Kentucky, who lived within half a mile of Mr. Hughes' farm. Hughes and Neil traded in slaves down the river: they had bought up a part of their stock in the upper counties of Kentucky, and brought them down to Louisville, where the remainder of their drove was in jail, waiting their arrival. Just before the steamboat put off for the lower country, two negro women were offered for sale, each of them having a young child at the breast. The traders bought them, took their babes from their arms, and offered them to the highest bidder; and they were sold for one dollar apiece, whilst the stricken parents were driven on board the boat, and in an hour were on their way to the New Orleans market. You are aware that a young babe *decreases* the value of a field hand in the lower country, whilst it increases her value in the 'breeding states.'"

The following is an extract from an address, published by the **Presbyterian Synod of Kentucky**, to the churches under their care, in 1835

"Brothers and sisters, parents and children, husbands and wives, are *torn asunder,* and permitted to see each other no more. These acts are daily occurring in the midst of us. The *shrieks* and the *agony, often* witnessed on such occasions, proclaim, with a trumpet tongue, the iniquity of our system. *There is not a neighborhood* where these heart-rending scenes are not displayed. *There is not a village or road* that does not behold the sad procession of manacled outcasts, whose mournful countenances tell that they are exiled by *force* from all THAT THEIR HEARTS HOLD DEAR." *Address,* p. 12.

Professor Andrews, late of the University of North Carolina, in his recent work on Slavery and the Slave Trade, page 147, in relating a conversation with a slave-trader, whom he met near Washington City, says, he inquired:

"Do you *often* buy the wife without the husband?'

'Yes, Very Often; and FREQUENTLY, too, they *sell me the mother while they keep her children I have often known them take away the infant from its mother's breast, and keep it, while they sold her.* "

The following sale is advertised in the "Georgia Journal" Jan. 2, 1838:

"Will be sold, the following Property, to wit:

One Child, by the name of James, *about eight months old,* levied on as the property of Gabriel Gunn."

The following is a standing advertisement in the Charleston (S.C.) papers:

"120 Negroes for Sale.—The subscriber has *just arrived from Petersburg, Virginia,* with one hundred and twenty *likely young* negroes of both sexes and every description, which he offers for sale on the most reasonable terms.

"The lot now on hand consists of plough boys, several likely and well-qualified house servants of both sexes, several *women with children, small girls* suitable for nurses, and several SMALL BOYS WITHOUT THEIR

MOTHERS. Planters and traders are earnestly requested to give the subscriber a call previously to making purchases elsewhere, as he is enabled and will sell as cheap, or cheaper, than can be sold by any other person in the trade.   Benjamin Davis, Hamburg, S.C. Sept. 28, 1838."

Extract of a letter to a member of Congress, from a friend in Mississippi, published in the **"Washington Globe"** June, 1837:

"The times are truly alarming here. Many plantations *are entirely stripped of negroes* (protection!) and horses, by the marshal or sheriff.— Suits are multiplying—two thousand five hundred in the United States Circuit Court, and three thousand in Hinds County Court."

Testimony of **Mr. Silas Stone**, of Hudson, New York. Mr. Stone is a member of the Episcopal Church, has several times been elected an Assessor of the city of Hudson, and for three years has filled the office of Treasurer of the County. In the fall of 1807, Mr. Stone witnessed a sale of slaves, in Charleston, South Carolina, which he thus describes in a communication recently received from him:

"I saw droves of the poor fellows driven to the slave markets kept in different parts of the city, one of which I visited. The arrangements of this place appeared something like our northern horse-markets, having sheds, or barns, in the rear of a public house, where alcohol was a handy ingredient to stimulate the spirit of jockeying. As the traders appeared, lots of negroes were brought from the stables into the bar room, and by a flourish of the whip were made to assume an active appearance. 'What will you give for these fellows? 'How old are they? 'Are they healthy?' 'Are they quick? &c; at the same time the owner would give them a cut with a cowhide, and tell them to dance and jump, cursing and swearing at them if they did not move quick. In fact all the transactions in buying and selling slaves, partakes of jockeyship, as much as buying and selling horses. There was as little regard paid to the feelings of the former as we witness in the latter.

"From these scenes I turn to another, which took place in front of the noble 'Exchange Buildings,' in the heart of the city. On the left side of the steps, as you leave the main hall, immediately under the windows of that proud building, was a stage built, on which a mother with eight children were placed, and sold at auction. I watched their emotions closely, and saw their feelings were in accordance to human nature. The sale began with the

~ 412 ~

eldest child, who, being struck off to the highest bidder, was taken from the stage or platform by the purchaser, and led to his wagon and stowed away, to be carried into the country; the second, and third were also sold, and so until seven of the children were torn from their mother, while her discernment told her they were to be separated probably forever, causing in that mother the most agonizing sobs and cries, in which the children seemed to share. The scene beggars description; suffice it to say, it was sufficient to cause tears from one at least 'whose skin was not colored like their own,' and I was not ashamed to give vent to them."

**THE "PROTECTION" AFFORDED BY 'PUBLIC OPINION'
TO CHILDHOOD AND OLD AGE.**

In the "New Orleans Bee" May 31, 1837, Mr. P. Bahi, gives notice that he has *committed to ja*il, as a runaway, a *little* negro AGED ABOUT SEVEN YEARS.'

In the "Mobile Advertiser" Sept. 13, 1838, William Magee, Sheriff, gives notice that George Walton, Esq. Mayor of the city has *committed to j*ail as a runaway slave, Jordan, ABOUT TWELVE YEARS OLD and the Sheriff proceeds to give notice that if no one claims him the boy will be *sold as a slave* to pay jail fees.

In the "Memphis (Tenn.) Gazette" May 2, 1837, W. H. Montgomery advertises that he will sell at auction a BOY AGED 14, ANOTHER AGED 12, AND A GIRL 10, to pay the debts of their deceased master.

B. F. Chapman, Sheriff, Natchitoches (La.) advertises in the 'Herald' of May 17, 1837, that he has " *committed to* jail, as a runaway a negro boy BETWEEN 11 AND 12 YEARS OF AGE."

In the "Augusta (Ga.) Chronicle" Feb. 13, 1838. R. H. Jones, jailor, says, "Brought *to jail* a negro *woman* Sarah, she is about 60 *or* 65 *years old."*

In the "Winchester Virginian" August 8, 1837, Mr. R. H. Menifee, offers ten dollars reward to anyone who will catch and lodge in jail, Abram and Nelly, *about* 60 *years old,* so that he can get them again.

J. Snowden, Jailor, Columbia, S.C. gives notice in the "Telescope" Nov, 18,1837, that he has committed to jail as a runaway slave, *"Caroline fifty years of age."*

Y. S. Pickard, Jailor, Savannah, Georgia, gives notice in the "Georgian" June 22, 1837, that he has taken up for a runaway and lodged in jail Charles, 60 *years of age.*

In the Savannah "Georgian" April 12, 1837, Mr. J. Cuyler, says he will give five dollars, to anyone who will catch and bring back to him Saman, *an old negro man, and grey, and has only one eye."*

In the "Macon (Ga.) Telegraph" Jan. 15, 1839, Messrs. T. and L. Napier, advertise for sale Nancy, a woman 65 *years of age,* and Peggy, a woman 65 *years of age.*

The following is from the "Columbian (Ga.) Enquirer" March 8, 1838:
"$25 Reward.—Ranaway, a Negro Woman named MATILDA, aged about 30 or 35 years. Also, on the same night, a Negro fellow of small size, very aged, *stoop-shouldered,* who walks VERY DECREPIDLY, is supposed to have gone off. His name is DAVE, and he has claimed Matilda for wife. It may be they have gone off together. I will give twenty

five dollars for the woman, delivered to me in Muscogee County, or confined in any jail so that I can get her.   Moses Butt."

J. B. Randall, Jailor, Cobb (Co.) Georgia, advertises an old negro man, in the "Milledgeville Recorder" Nov. 6, 1838.

"A NEGRO MAN, has been lodged in the common jail of this county, who says his name is Jupiter. He *has lost all his front teeth above and below—speaks very indistinctly, is very lame, so that he can hardly walk.*"

Rev. Charles Stewart Renshaw, of Quincy, Illinois, who spent some time in slave states, speaking of his residence in Kentucky, says:"One Sabbath morning, whilst riding to meeting near Burlington, Boone Co. Kentucky, in company with Mr. Willis, a teacher of sacred music and a member of the Presbyterian Church, I was startled at mingled shouts and screams, proceeding from an old log house, some, distance from the road side. As we passed it, some five or six boys from 12 to 15 years of age, came out, some of them cracking whips, followed by two colored boys crying. I asked Mr. W. what the scene meant. 'Oh,' he replied, 'those boys have been whipping the niggers; that is the way we bring slaves into subjection in Kentucky—we let the children beat them.' The boys returned again into the house, and again their shouting and stamping was heard, but ever and anon a scream of agony that would not be drowned, rose above the uproar; thus they continued till the sounds were lost in the distance."

Well did Jefferson say, that the children of slaveholders are 'NURSED EDUCATED AND DAILY EXERCISED IN TYRANNY.'

The 'protection' thrown around a mother's yearnings, and the helplessness of childhood by the 'public opinion' of slaveholders, is shown by *thousands* of advertisements of which the following are samples:

From the "New Orleans Bulletin" June 2:

"NEGROES FOR SALE.—A negro woman 24 years of age, and has two children, one eight and the other three years. Said negroes will be sold SEPARATELY or together *as desired.* The woman is a good seamstress. She will be sold low for cash, or *exchanged for* Groceries. For terms apply to Mayhew Bliss, & Co. 1 Front Levee.

"From the "Georgia Journal" Nov. 7.

"**TO BE SOLD**—One negro girl about 18 *months old,* belonging to the estate of William Chambers, dec'd. Sold for the purpose of *distribution!!*
Jethro Dean & Samuel Beall, Ex'ors."

From the "Natchez Courier" April 2, 1838:

"**NOTICE**—Is hereby given that the undersigned, pursuant to a certain Deed of Trust, will on Thursday the 12th day of April next, expose to sale at the Court House, to the highest bidder for cash, the following Negro slaves, to wit; Fanny, aged about 28 years; Mary, aged about 7 years; Amanda, aged about 3 months; Wilson, aged about 9 months.

"Said slaves, to be sold for the satisfaction of the debt secured in said Deed of Trust.   W. J. Minor."

From the "Milledgeville Journal" Dec. 26, 1837:

"**EXECUTOR'S SALE.**"Agreeable to an order of the court of Wilkinson County, will be sold on the first Tuesday in April next, before the Court-house door in the town of Irwington, ONE NEGRO GIRL *about two years old,* named Rachel, belonging to the estate of William Chambers dec'd. Sold *for the benefit* of the heirs and creditors of said estate.
Samuel Belt, Jesse Peacock, *Ex'ors."*

From the "Alexandria (D. C.) Gazette" Dec. 19:

"I will give the highest cash price for likely negroes, *from* 10 *to* 25 *years of age.*   Geo. Kephart."

From the "Southern Whig" March 2, 1838:

"**WILL BE SOLD** in La Grange, Troup County, one negro girl, by the name of Charity, aged about 10 or 12 years; as the property of Littleton L. Burk, to satisfy a mortgage fi. fa. from Troup Inferior Court, in favor of Daniel S. Robertson vs. said Burk."

From the "Petersburgh (Va.) Constellation" March 18, 1837:

"**50** *Negroes wanted immediately.*—The subscriber will give a good market price for fifty likely negroes, *from* 10 *to* 30 *years of age.*
Henry Davis."

The following is an extract of a letter from a gentleman, a native and still a resident of one of the slave states, and *still a slaveholder.* He is an elder in the Presbyterian Church, his letter is now before us, and his name is with the Executive Committee of the Am. Anti-slavery Society:

"Permit me to say, that around this very place where I reside, slaves are brought almost constantly, and sold to Miss, and Orleans; that *it is usual* to part families forever by such sales—the parents from the children and the children from the parents, of every size and age. A mother was taken not long since, in this town, from a *sucking child,* and sold to the lower country. Three young men I saw some time ago taken from this place in chains—while the mother of one of them, old and decrepit, *followed with tears and prayers her son,* 18 *or* 20 *miles, and bid him a final farewell!* O, thou Great Eternal, is this justice! Is this equity !!—Equal Rights!!"

We subjoin a few miscellaneous facts illustrating the inhumanity of slaveholding 'public opinion:.'

The shocking indifference manifested at the death of slaves as *human beings,* contrasted with the grief at their loss *as property,* is a true index to the public opinion of slaveholders.

Colonel Oliver of Louisville lost a valuable race-horse by the explosion of the steamer Oronoko, a few months since in the Mississippi River. Eight human beings whom he held as slaves were also killed by the explosion. They were the-riders and grooms of his race-horses. A Louisville paper thus speaks of the occurrence:

"Colonel Oliver suffered severely by the explosion of the Oronoko. He lost *eight* of his rubbers and riders, and his horse, Joe Kearney, which he had sold the night before for $3,000."

Mr. King, of the New York American, makes the following just comment on the barbarity of the above paragraph:

"Would anyone, in reading this paragraph from an evening paper, conjecture that these *'eight* rubbers and riders,' that together with a horse, are merely mentioned as a 'loss' to their owner, were human beings—immortal as the writer who thus brutalizes them, and perhaps cherishing life as much? In this view, perhaps, the 'eight' lost as much as Colonel Oliver."

The following is from the "Charleston (S.C.) Patriot" Oct. 18:

"Loss of Property!—Since I have been here, (Rice Hope, N. Santee,) I have seen much misery, and much of human suffering. The loss of Property has been immense, not only on South Santee, but also on this

river. Mr. Shoolbred has lost, (according to the statement of the physician,) forty-six negroes—the majority lost being the *primest hands* he had—bricklayers, carpenters, blacksmiths and Coopers. Mr. Wm. Mazyck has lost 35 negroes. Col. Thomas Pinkney, in the neighborhood of 40, and many other planters, 10 to 20 on each plantation. Mrs. Elias Harry, adjoining the plantation of Mr. Lucas, has lost up to date, 32 negroes—the *best part of her primest* negroes on her plantation."

From the "Natchez (Miss.) Daily Free Trader" Feb. 12, 1838:

"*Found.*—**A Negro's Head Was Picked Up On** THE RAIL-ROAD YESTERDAY, WHICH THE OWNER CAN HAVE BY CALLING AT THIS OFFICE AND PAYINGFOR THE ADVERTISEMENT."

The way in which slaveholding 'public opinion' protects a poor female lunatic is illustrated in the following advertisement in the "Fayetteville (N.C.) Observer" June 27, 1838:

"Taken and committed to jail, a negro girl named Nancy, who is supposed to belong to Spencer P. Wright, of the State of Georgia. She is about 30 years of age, and is a lunatic. The owner is requested to come forward, prove property, pay charges, and take her away, Or SHE WILL BE SOLD TO PAY HER JAIL FEES.   FRED'K. HOME, Jailor."

A late Prospectus of the South Carolina Medical College, located in Charleston, contains the following passage:

"Some advantages of a *peculiar* character are connected with this Institution, which it may be proper to point out. No place in the United States offers as great opportunities for the acquisition of anatomical knowledge, subjects being OBTAINED FROM AMONG THE COLORED POPULATION IN SUFFICIENT NUMBER FOR EVERY PURPOSE, AND PROPER DISSECTIONS CARRIED ON WITHOUT OFFENDING ANY INDIVIDUALS IN THE COMMUNITY!!"

Without offending any individuals in the community! More than half the population of Charleston, we believe, is 'colored;' *their* graves may be ravaged, their dead may be dug up, dragged into the dissecting room, exposed to the gaze, heartless gibes, and experimenting knives, of a crowd of inexperienced operators, who are given to understand in the prospectus, that, if they do not acquire manual dexterity in dissection, it will be wholly their own fault, in neglecting to improve the unrivalled advantages afforded by the institution—since each can have as many human bodies as he pleases to experiment upon—and as to the fathers, mothers, husbands, wives, brothers, and sisters, of those whom they cut to pieces from day to day, why, they are not 'individuals in the community,' but 'property' and however *their* feelings may be tortured, the 'public opinion' of slaveholders is entirely too 'chivalrous' to degrade itself by caring for them!

The following which has been for some time a standing advertisement of the South Carolina Medical College, in the Charleston papers, is another index of the same 'public opinion' toward slaves. We give an extract:

"Surgery of the Medical College of South Carolina, Queen St.—The Faculty inform their professional brethren, and the public, that they have established a *Surgery,* at the Old College, Queen Street, for THE TREATMENT OF NEGROES, which will continue in operation, during the session of the College, say from first November, to the fifteenth of March ensuing.

"The *object* of the faculty, in opening this Surgery, is to collect as *many interesting cases,* as possible, for the *benefit* and *instruction* of their pupils—at the same time, they indulge the hope, that it may not only prove an *accommodation,* but also a matter of economy to the public. They would respectfully call the attention of planters, living in the vicinity of the city, to this subject; particularly such as may have servants laboring under Surgical diseases. Such persons *of color as* may not be able to pay for medical advice, will be attended to gratis, at stated hours, as often as may be necessary.

"The faculty takes this opportunity of soliciting the co-operation of such of their professional brethren, as are favorable to their objects."

"The first thing that strikes the reader of the advertisement is, that this *Surgery* is established exclusively 'for the treatment of *negroes'* and if he knows little of the hearts of slaveholders towards their slaves, he charitably supposes, that they 'feel the dint of pity,' for the poor sufferers and have founded this institution as a special charity for their relief. But the delusion vanishes as he reads on; the professors take special care that no such derogatory inference shall be drawn from their advertisement. They give us the *three* reasons which have induced them to open this 'Surgery for the treatment of negroes'. The first and main one is, 'to collect as many *interesting cases* as possible for the benefit and instruction of their *pupils'*—another is, 'the hope that it may prove an *accommodation,'*—and the third, that it may be 'a matter of economy to the *public'*. Another reason, doubtless, and a controlling one, though the professors are silent about it, is that a large collection of 'interesting surgical cases' always on hand, would prove a powerful attraction to students, and greatly increase the popularity of the institution. In brief, then, the motives of its founders, the professors, were these, the accommodation of their *students*—the accommodation of the *public* (which means, *the whites)*—and the accommodation of slaveholders who have on their hands disabled slaves, that would make 'interesting cases,' for surgical operation in the presence of the pupils—to these reasons we may add the accommodation of the Medical Institution and the accommodation of *themselves!* Not a syllable about the *accommodation* of the hopeless sufferers, writhing with the agony of those gunshot wounds, fractured sculls, broken limbs and ulcerated backs which constitute the 'interesting cases' for the professors to 'show off' before their pupils, and, as practice makes perfect, for the students themselves to try their hands at by way of experiment.

Why, we ask, was this surgery established 'for the treatment of *negroes'* alone? Why were these 'interesting cases' selected from that class exclusively? No man who knows the feeling of slaveholders towards slaves will be at a loss for the reason. 'Public opinion' would tolerate surgical experiments, operations, processes, performed upon them, which it would execrate if performed upon their master or other whites. As the great object in collecting the disabled negroes is to have 'interesting cases' for the students, the professors who perform the operations will of course endeavor to make them as 'interesting' as possible. The in*struction of the student* is the immediate object, and if the professors can accomplish it best by *protracting* the operation, pausing to explain the different processes, &c. the subject is only a negro, and what is his protracted agony, that it should restrain the professor from making the case as 'interesting' as possible to the students by so using his knife as will give them the best knowledge of the parts, and the process, however it may protract or augment the pain of the subject. The *end* to be accomplished is the *instruction* of the student, operations upon the negroes are the *means* to the end; *that* tells the whole story—and he who knows the hearts of slaveholders and has common sense, however short the allowance, can find the way to his conclusions without a lantern.

By an advertisement of the same Medical Institution, dated November 12, 1838, and published in the Charleston papers, it appears that an 'infirmary has been opened in connection with the college' The professors manifest a great desire that the masters of servants should send in their disabled slaves, and as an inducement to the furnishing of such *interesting cases* say, all medical and surgical aid will be offered *without making them liable to any professional charges.* Disinterested bounty, pity, sympathy, philanthropy! However difficult or numerous the surgical cases of slaves thus put into their hands by the masters, they charge not a cent for their *professional services.* Their yearnings over human distress are so intense, that they beg the privilege of performing all operations, and furnishing all the medical attention needed, *gratis,* feeling that the relief of misery is its own reward!!! But we have put down our exclamation points too soon— upon reading the whole of the advertisement we find the professors conclude it with the following paragraph:

"**The Sole Object** of the faculty in the establishment of such an institution being to promote the interest of Medical Education within their native State and City."

In the "Charleston (South Carolina) Mercury" of October 12, 1838, we find an advertisement of half a column, by a Dr. T. Stillman, setting forth the merits of another 'Medical Infirmary' under his own special supervision, at No. 110 Church Street, Charleston. The doctor, after inveighing loudly against 'men totally ignorant of medical science,' who flood the country with quack nostrums backed up by 'fabricated proofs of miraculous cures,' proceeds to enumerate the diseases to which his 'Infirmary' is open, and to which his practice will be mainly confined. Appreciating the importance of 'interesting cases,' as a stock in trade, on which to commence his experiments, he copies the example of the medical professors, and advertises for them. But, either from a keener sense of justice, or more generosity, or greater confidence in his skill, or for some other reason, he proposes to *buy up* an assortment of *damaged* negroes, given over, as incurable, by others, and to make such his 'interesting cases,' instead of experimenting on those who are the 'property' of others.

Dr. Stillman closes his advertisement with the following notice :

"**To Planters and Others.**—**Wanted** *fifty negroes.* Any person having sick negroes, considered incurable by their respective physicians, and wishing to dispose of them, Dr. S. will pay cash for negroes affected with scrofula or king's evil, confirmed hypocondriasm, apoplexy, diseases of the liver, kidneys, spleen, stomach and intestines, bladder and its appendages, diarrhea, dysentery, &c. The highest cash price will be paid on application as above."

The absolute barbarism of a 'public opinion' which not only tolerates, but *produces* such advertisements as this, was outdone by nothing in the dark ages. If the reader has a heart of flesh, he can feel it without help, and if he has not, comment will not create it. The total indifference of slaveholders to such a cold blooded proposition, their utter unconsciousness of the paralysis of heart, and death of sympathy, and every feeling of common humanity for the slave, which it reveals, is enough, of itself, to show that the tendency of the spirit of slaveholding is, to kill in the soul whatever it touches. It has no eyes to see, nor ears to hear, nor mind to understand, nor heart to feel for its victims as *human beings.* To show that the above indication of the savage state is not an index of individual feeling, but of 'public opinion,' it is sufficient to say, that it appears to be a standing advertisement in the Charleston Mercury, the leading political paper of South Carolina, the organ of the Honorables John C. Calhoun, Robert Barnwell Rhett, Hugh S. Legare, and others regarded as the elite of her statesmen and literati. Besides, candidates for popular favor, like the doctor who advertises for the fifty 'incurables,' take special care to conciliate, rather than outrage, 'public opinion.' Is the doctor so ignorant of 'public opinion' in his own city, that he has unwittingly committed violence upon it in his advertisement? We trow not. The same 'public opinion' which gave birth to the advertisement of doctor Stillman, and to those of the professors in both the medical institutions, founded the Charleston 'Work House'—a soft name for a Moloch temple dedicated to torture, and reeking with blood, in the midst of the city; to which masters and mistresses send their slaves of both sexes to be stripped, tied up, and cut with the lash till the blood and mangled flesh flow to their feet, or to be beaten and bruised with the terrible paddle, or forced to climb the tread-mill till nature sinks, or to experience other nameless torments.

The "Vicksburg (Miss.) Register" Dec. 27, 1838, contains the following item of information:

"Ardor in Betting.—Two gentlemen, at a tavern, having summoned the waiter, the poor fellow had scarcely entered, when he fell down in a fit of apoplexy. 'He's dead!' exclaimed one. 'He'll come to!' replied the other.

'Dead, for five hundred!' 'Done!' retorted the second. The noise of the fall, and the confusion which followed, brought up the landlord, who called out to fetch a doctor. 'No! no! We must have no interference—there's a bet depending!' 'But, sir, I shall lose a valuable servant!' 'Never mind! You can put him down in the bill!"

About the time the Vicksburg paper containing the above came to hand, we received a letter from **N. P. Rogers, Esq**. of Concord, N. H. the editor of the 'Herald of Freedom,' from which the following is an extract:

"Some thirty years ago, I think it was, Col. Thatcher, of Maine, a lawyer, was in Virginia, on business, and was there invited to dine at a public house, with a company of the gentry of the south. *The place* I forget—the fact was told me by George Kimball, Esq. now of Alton, Illinois, who had the story from Col. Thatcher himself. Among the servants waiting was a young negro man, whose beautiful person, obliging and assiduous temper, and his activity and grace in serving, made him a favorite with the company. The dinner lasted into the evening, and the wine passed freely about the table. At length, one of the gentlemen, who was pretty highly excited with wine, became unfortunately incensed, either at some trip of the young slave, in waiting, or at some other cause happening when the slave was within his reach. He seized the long-necked wine bottle, and struck the young man suddenly in the temple, and felled him dead upon the floor. The fall arrested, for a moment, the festivities of the table. 'Devilish unlucky,' exclaimed one. 'The gentleman is very unfortunate,' cried another. 'Really a loss,' said a third, &c. &c. The body was dragged from the dining hall, and the feast went on; and at the close, one of the gentlemen, and the very one, I believe, whose hand had done the homicide, shouted, in bacchanalian bravery, and *southern generosity* amid the broken glasses and fragments of chairs, 'LANDLORD! PUT THE NIGGER INTO THE BILL! This was that murdered young man's *requiem and funeral service.*"

Mr. **George A. Avery**, a merchant in Rochester, New York, and an elder in the Fourth Presbyterian Church in that city, who resided four years in Virginia, gives the following testimony:"I knew a young man who had been out hunting, and returning with some of his friends, seeing a negro man in the road, at a little distance, deliberately drew up his rifle, and shot him dead. This was done without the slightest provocation, or a word passing. This young man passed through the *form* of a trial, and, although it was not even *pretended* by his counsel that he was not guilty of the act, deliberately and wantonly perpetrated, *he was acquitted.* It was urged by his counsel, that he was a *young* man, (about 20 years of age,) had no *malicious* intention, his mother was a widow, &c. &c."

Mr. Benjamin Clendenon, of Colerain, Lancaster County, Pennsylvania, a member of the Society of Friends, gives the following testimony:

"Three years ago the coming month, I took a journey of about seventy-five miles from home, through the eastern shore of Maryland, and a small part of Delaware. Calling one day, near noon, at Georgetown Cross-Roads, I found myself surrounded in the tavern by slaveholders. Among other subjects of conversation, their human cattle came in for a share. One of the company, a middle-aged man, then living with a second wife, acknowledged, that after the death of his first wife, he lived in a state of concubinage with a female slave; but when the time drew near for the taking of a second wife, he found it expedient to remove the slave from the premises. The same person gave an account of a female slave he formerly held, who had a propensity for some one pursuit, I think the attendance of religious meetings. On a certain occasion, she presented her petition to him, asking for this indulgence; he refused—she importuned—and he, with sovereign indignation, seized a chair, and with a blow upon the head, knocked her senseless upon the floor. The same person, for some act of disobedience, on the part, I think, of the same slave, when employed in stacking straw, felled her to the earth with the handle of a pitch fork. All these transactions were related with the *utmost composure,* in a bar-room within thirty miles of the Pennsylvania line." The two following advertisements are illustrations of the regard paid to the marriage relations by slaveholding judges, governors, senators in Congress, and mayors of cities:

From the "Montgomery, (Ala.) Advertiser" Sept. 29, 1837:

"**$20 Reward.**—Ranaway from the subscriber, a negro man named Moses. He is of common size, about 28 years old. He formerly belonged to Judge Benson, of Montgomery, and it is said, has a wife in that county.

John Gayle."

The John Gayle who signs this advertisement, is an Ex-Governor of Alabama.

From the "Charleston Courier" Nov. 28:"

Ranaway from the subscriber, about twelve months since, his negro man Paulladore. His complexion is dark—about 50 years old. I understand Gen. R. Y. Hayne has purchased his wife and children from H. L. Pinckney, Esq. and has them now on his plantation, at Goose Creek, where, no doubt, the fellow is frequently lurking.   Thomas Davis."

It is hardly necessary to say, that the General R. Y. Hayne, and H. L. Pinckney, Esq. named in the advertisement, are Ex-Governor Hayne, formerly U. S. Senator from South Carolina, and Hon. Henry L. Pinckney, late member of Congress from Charleston District, and now Intendant (Mayor) of that city.

It is no difficult matter to get at the 'public opinion' of a community, when *ladies* of property and standing publish, under their own names, such advertisements as the following:

Mrs. Elizabeth L. Carter, of Groveton, Prince William County, Virginia, thus advertises her negro man Moses:

"Ranaway from the subscriber, a negro man named Moses, aged about 40 years, about six feet high, well made, and possessing a good address, and HAS LOST A PART OF ONE OF HIS EARS. "

Mrs. B. Newman, of the same place, and in the same paper, advertises:

"Penny, the wife of Moses, aged about 30 years, brown complexion, tall and likely, *no particular marks of person recollected."*

Both of the above advertisements appear in the National Intelligencer, (Washington City,) June 10, 1837.

In the Mobile Mercantile Advertiser, of Feb. 13, 1838, is an advertisement signed Sarah Walsh, of which the following is an extract:

"Twenty-five dollars reward will be paid to anyone who may apprehend and deliver to me, or confine in any jail, so that I can get him, my man Isaac, who ran away sometime in September last. He is 26 years of age, 5 feet 10 inches high, has a *scar on his forehead, caused by a blow,* and one on his back, MADE BY A SHOT FROM A PISTOL. "

In the "New Orleans Bee" Dec. 21, 1838, Mrs. Burvant, whose residence is at the corner of Chartres and Toulouse streets, advertises a woman as follows:

"Ranaway, a negro woman named Rachel—*has lost all her toes except the large one."*

From the "Huntsville (Ala.) Democrat" June 16, 1838:

"Ten Dollars Reward.—Ranaway from the subscriber, a negro woman named Sally, about 21 years of age, taking along her two children— one three years, and the other seven months old. These negroes were PURCHASED BY ME at the sale of George Mason's negroes, on the first Monday in May, and left *a few days* thereafter. Any person delivering them to the jailor in Huntsville, or to me, at my plantation, five miles above Triana, on the Tennessee River, shall receive the above reward.

Charity Cooper."

From the "Mississippian" May 13, 1838:

"Ten Dollars Reward.—Ranaway from the subscriber, a man named Aaron, yellow complexion, blue eyes, &c. I have no doubt he is lurking about Jackson and its vicinity, probably harbored by some of the negroes sold as the property of *my late husband,* Harry Long, deceased. Some of them are about Richland, in Madison Co. I will give the above reward when brought to me, about six miles north-west of Jackson, *or put* in *jail, so that I can get him.* Lucy Long."

If the reader, after perusing the preceding facts, testimony, and arguments, still insists that the 'public opinion' of the slave states protects the slave from outrages, and alleges, as proof of it, that *cruel* masters are frowned upon and shunned by the community generally, and regarded as monsters, we reply by presenting the following facts and testimony:

"Col. Means, of Manchester, Ohio, says that when he resided in South Carolina, *his neighbor,* a physician, became enraged with his slave, and sentenced him to receive two hundred lashes. After having received one hundred and forty, he fainted. After inflicting the full number of lashes, the cords with which he was bound were loosed. When he revived, he staggered to the house, and sat down in the sun. Being faint and thirsty, he *begged* for some water to drink. The master went to the well, and procured some water—but instead of giving him to drink, he threw the whole bucket-full in his face. Nature could not stand the shock—he sunk to rise no more. For this crime, the physician was bound over to Court, and tried, and *acquitted*—and THE NEXT YEAR HE WAS ELECTED TO THE LEGISLATURE!"

Testimony of **Hon. John Randolph**, of Virginia:

~ 426 ~

"In one of his Congressional speeches, Mr. R. says: Avarice alone can drive, as it does drive, this *infernal* traffic, and the wretched victims of it, like so many post-horses, *whipped to death* in a mail coach. Ambition has its cover-sluts in the pride, pomp, and circumstance of glorious war; but where are the trophies of avarice? *The hand-cuff, the manacle, the blood-stained cowhide! WHAT MANS IS WORSE RECEIVED IN SOCIETY* FOR BEING A HARD MASTER? WHO DENIES THE HAND OF A SISTER OR DAUGHTER TO SUCH MONSTERS?"

Mr. **George A. Avery,** of Rochester, New York, who resided four years in Virginia, testifies as follows:

"I know a local Methodist minister, a man of talents, and popular as a preacher, who took his negro girl into his barn, in order to whip her— and *she was brought out a corpse!* His friends seemed to think this of *so little importance to his ministerial standing,* that although I lived near him about three years, I do not recollect to have heard them apologize for the deed, though I recollect having heard one of his neighbors allege this fact as a reason why he did not wish to hear him preach."

Notwithstanding the mass of testimony which has been presented establishing the fact that in the 'public opinion' of the South the slaves find no protection, some may still claim that the 'public opinion' exhibited by the preceding facts is not that of the *highest class of society at the South,* and in proof of this assertion, refer to the fact, that 'Negro Brokers,' Negro Speculators, Negro Auctioneers, and Negro Breeders, &c., are by that class universally despised and avoided, as are all who treat their slaves with cruelty.

To this we reply, that, if all claimed by the objector were true, it could avail him nothing for '*public* opinion' is neither made nor unmade by 'the first class of society.' That class produces in it, at most, but slight modifications; those who belong to it have generally a 'public opinion,' within their own circle which has rarely more, either of morality or mercy than the public opinion of the mass, and is, at least, equally heartless and more intolerant. As to the estimation in which 'speculators,' 'soul drivers,' &c. are held, we remark, that, they are not despised because they *trade in slaves* but because they are *working* men, all such are despised by slaveholders. White drovers who go with droves of swine and cattle from the free states to the slave states, and Yankee peddlers who traverse the south, and white day-laborers are, in the main, equally despised, or, if negro-traders excite more contempt than drovers, peddlers, and day-laborers, it is because, they are, as a class more ignorant and vulgar, men from low families and are boors in their manners. Ridiculous! to suppose, that a people, who have, *by law,* made men articles of trade equally with swine, should despise men drovers and traders, more than hog-drovers and traders. That they are not despised because it is their business to trade in *human beings* and bring them to market, is plain from the fact that when some 'gentleman of property and standing' and of a 'good family' embarks in a negro speculation, and employs a dozen 'soul drivers' to traverse the upper country, and drive to the south coffles of slaves, expending hundreds of thousands in his wholesale purchases, he does not lose caste. It is known in Alabama, that Mr. Erwin, son-in-law of the Hon. Henry Clay, and brother of J. P. Erwin, formerly postmaster, and late mayor of the city of Nashville, laid the foundation of a princely fortune in the slave-trade, carried on from the Northern Slave States to the Planting South ; that the Hon. H. Hitchcock, brother-in-law of Mr. E., and since one of the judges of the Supreme Court of Alabama, was interested with him in the traffic; and that a late member of the Kentucky Senate (Col. Wall) not only carried on the same business, a few years ago, but accompanied his droves in person down the Mississippi. Not as the *driver,* for that would be vulgar drudgery, beneath a gentleman, but as a nabob in state, ordering his understrappers.

It is also well known that President Jackson was a 'soul driver,' and that even so late as the year before the commencement of the last war, he bought up a coffle of slaves and drove them down to Louisiana for sale.

Thomas N. Gadsden, Esq. the principal slave auctioneer in Charleston, S.C. is of one of the first families in the state, and moves in the very highest class of society there. He is a descendant of the distinguished General Gadsden of revolutionary memory, the most prominent southern member in the Continental Congress of 1765, and afterwards elected lieutenant governor and then governor of the state. The Rev. Dr. Gadsden, rector of St. Philip's Church, Charleston, and the Rev. Phillip Gadsden, both prominent Episcopal clergymen in South Carolina, and Colonel James Gadsden of the United States Army, after whom a county in Florida was recently named, are all brothers of this Thomas N. Gadsden, Esq. the largest slave auctioneer in the state, under whose hammer, men, women and children go off by thousands; its stroke probably sunders *daily,* husbands and wives, parents and children, brothers and sisters, perhaps to see each other's faces no more. Now who supply the auction table of this Thomas N. Gadsden, Esq. with its loads of human merchandize? These same detested 'soul drivers' forsooth! They prowl through the country, buy, catch, and fetter them, and drive their chained coffles up to his stand, where Thomas N. Gadsden, Esq. knocks them off to the highest bidder, to Ex-Governor Butler perhaps, or to Ex-Governor Hayne, or to Hon. Robert Barnwell Rhett, or to his own reverend brother, Dr. Gadsden. Now this high born, wholesale *soul-seller* doubtless despises the retail 'soul-drivers' who give him their custom, and so does the wholesale grocer, the drizzling tapster who sneaks up to his counter for a keg of whiskey to dole out under a shanty in two cent glasses; and both for the same reason.

The plea that the 'public opinion' among the highest classes of society at the south is mild and considerate towards the slaves, that *they* do not overwork, underfeed, neglect when old and sick, scantily clothe, badly lodge, and half shelter their slaves; that *they* do not barbarously flog, load with irons, imprison in the stocks, brand and maim them; hunt them when runaways with dogs and guns, and sunder by force and forever the nearest kindred—is shown, by almost every page of this work, to be an assumption, not only utterly groundless, but directly opposed to masses of irrefragable evidence. If the reader will be at the pains to review the testimony recorded on the foregoing pages he will find that a very large proportion of the atrocities detailed were committed, not by the most ignorant and lowest classes of society, but by persons 'of property and standing,' by masters and mistresses belonging to the 'upper classes,' by persons in the learned professions, by civil, judicial, and military officers, by the *literati,* by the fashionable elite and persons of more than ordinary 'respectability' and *external* morality—large numbers of whom are professors of religion.

It will be recollected that the testimony of Sarah M. Grimke and Angelina G. Weld, was confined *exclusively* to the details of slavery as exhibited in the *highest classes of society,* mainly in Charleston, S.C. The former has furnished us with the following testimony in addition to that already given:

"Nathaniel Heyward of Combahee, S. C, one of the wealthiest planters in the state, stated, in conversation with some other planters who were complaining of the idle and lazy habits of their slaves, and the difficulty of ascertaining whether their sickness was real or pretended, and the loss they suffered from their frequent absence on this account from their work, said, 'I NEVER LOSE A DAYS WORK; it is an *established rule* on my plantations that the tasks of all the sick negroes *shall be done by those who are well in addition to their own.* By this means a vigilant supervision is kept up by the slaves over each other, and they take care that nothing but real sickness keeps any one out of the field.' I spent several winters in the neighborhood of Nathaniel Heyward's plantations, and well remember his character as a severe task master. *I was present when the above statement was made."*

The cool barbarity of such a regulation is hardly surpassed by the worst edicts of the Roman Caligula—especially when we consider that the plantations of this man were in the neighborhood of the Combahee river, one of the most unhealthy districts in the low country of South Carolina; further, that large numbers of his slaves worked in the *rice marshes,* or 'swamps' as they are called in that state—and that during six months of the year, so fatal to health is the malaria of the swamps in that region that the planters and their families invariably abandon their plantations, regarding it as downright presumption to spend a single day upon them 'between the frosts' of the early spring and the last of November.

The reader may infer the high standing of Mr. Heyward in South Carolina, from the fact that he was selected with four other freeholders to constitute a Court for the trial of the conspirators in the insurrection plot at Charleston, in 1822. Another of the individuals chosen to constitute that court was Colonel Henry Deas, now president of the Board of Trustees of Charleston College, and a few years since a member of the Senate of South Carolina. From a late correspondence in the "Greenville (S.C.) Mountaineer" between Rev. William M. Wightman, a professor in Randolph, Macon, College, and a number of the citizens of Lodi, South Carolina, it appears that the cruelty of this Colonel Deas to his slaves, is proverbial in South Carolina, so much that Professor Wightman, in the sermon which occasioned the correspondence, spoke of the Colonel's inhumanity to his slaves as a matter of perfect notoriety.

Another South Carolina slaveholder, Hon. Whitmarsh B. Seabrook, recently, we believe, Lieut. Governor of the state, gives the following testimony to his own inhumanity, and his certificate of the 'public opinion' among South Carolina slaveholders 'of high degree.'

In an essay on the management of slaves, read before the Agricultural Society of St. Johns, S.C. and published by the Society, Charleston, 1834, Mr. S. remarks:

"I consider *imprisonment in the stocks at night,* with or without hard labor in the day, as a powerful auxiliary in the cause of *good* government. To the correctness of this opinion *many* can bear testimony. Experience has convinced me that there is no punishment to which the slave looks with more horror."

The advertisements of the Professors in the Medical Colleges of South Carolina, published with comments—on pp. 169, 170, are additional illustrations of the 'public opinion' of the *literati.*

That the 'public opinion' of *the highest class of society* in South Carolina, regards slaves as mere *cattle,* is shown by the following advertisement, which we copy from the "Charleston (S.C.) Mercury" of May 16:

"Negroes For Sale.—A Girl about twenty years of age, (raised in Virginia) and her two female children, one four and the other two years old—is remarkably strong and healthy—never having had a day's sickness, with the exception of the small pox, in her life. The children are fine and healthy. She is very prolific in her generating qualities, *and affords a rare opportunity to any person who wishes to raise a family of strong and healthy servants for their own use."*Any person wishing to purchase, will please leave their address at the Mercury office."

The Charleston Mercury, in which this advertisement appears, is the *leading political paper in South Carolina,* and is well known to be the political organ of Messrs. Calhoun, Rhett, Pickens, and others of the most prominent politicians in the state. Its editor, John Stewart, Esq., is a lawyer of Charleston, and of a highly respectable family. He is a brother-in-law of Hon. Robert Barnwell Rhett, the late Attorney-General, now a Member of Congress, and Hon. James Rhett, a leading member of the Senate of South Carolina; his wife is a niece of the late Governor Smith, of North Carolina, and of the late Hon. Peter Smith, Intendant (Mayor) of the city of Charleston; and a cousin of the late Hon. Thomas S. Grimke.

The circulation of the 'Mercury' among the wealthy, the literary, and the fashionable, is probably much larger than that of any other paper in the state.

These facts in connection with the preceding advertisement are a sufficient exposition of the 'public opinion' towards slaves, prevalent in these classes of society.

The following scrap of 'public opinion' in Florida is instructive. We take it from the Florida Herald, June 23, 1838:

Ranaway from my plantation, on Monday night, the 13th instant, a negro fellow named Ben; eighteen years of age, polite when spoken to, and speaks very good English for a negro. As I have traced him out in several places in town, I am certain he is harbored. This notice is given that I am determined, that whenever he is taken, *to punish him till he informs me* who has given him food and protection, and I *shall apply the law of "Judge Lynch" to my own satisfaction,* on those concerned in his concealment. A. Watson, June 16, 1838."

Now, who is this A. Watson, who proclaims through a newspaper, his determination to *put to the torture* this youth of eighteen, and to Lynch to his ' satisfaction' whoever has given a cup of cold water to the panting fugitive. Is he some low miscreant beneath public contempt? Nay, verily, he is a ' gentleman of property and standing,' one of the wealthiest planters and largest slaveholders in Florida. He resides in the vicinity of St. Augustine, and married the daughter of the late Thomas C. Morton, Esq. one of the first merchants in New York.

We may mention in this connection the well known fact, that many wealthy planters make it a rule *never to employ a physician among their slaves.* Hon. William Smith, Senator in Congress, from South Carolina, from 1816 to 1823, and afterwards from 1826 to 1831, is one of this number. He owns a number of large plantations in the south western states. One of these borders upon the village of Huntsville, Alabama. The people of that village can testify that it is a part of Judge Smith's *system* never to employ a physician *even in the most extreme cases.* If the medical skill of the overseer, or of the slaves themselves, can contend successfully with the disease, they live, if not, *they die.* At all events, a physician is *not to be called.* Judge Smith was appointed a judge of the Supreme Court of the United States three years since.

The reader will recall a similar fact in the testimony of Rev. W. T. Allan, son of Rev. Dr. Allan, of Huntsville, who says that Colonel Robert H. Watkins, a wealthy planter, in Alabama, and a Presidential Elector in 1836, who works on his plantations three hundred slaves; After employing a physician for some time among his negroes, he ceased to do so, alleging as the reason, that it was *cheaper to lose a few negroes every year than to pay a physician.'*

It is a fact perfectly notorious, that the late General Wade Hampton, of South Carolina, who was the largest slaveholder in the United States, and probably the wealthiest man south of the Potomac, was *excessively cruel* in the treatment of his slaves.

The preceding are but a few of a large number of similar cases contained in the foregoing testimonies. The slaveholder mentioned by Mr. Ladd, who knocked down a slave and afterwards piled brush upon his body, and consumed it, held the hand of a female slave in the fire till it was burned so as to be useless for life, and confessed to Mr. Ladd, that he had killed *four* slaves, had been a *member of the Senate of Georgia* and a *clergyman.*

The slaveholder who whipped a female slave to death in St. Louis, in 1837, as stated by Mr. Cole, was a *Major in the United States Army.* One of the physicians who was an abettor of the tragedy on the Brassos, in which a slave was tortured to death, and another so that he barely lived, (see Rev. Mr. Smith's testimony) was Dr. Anson Jones, a native of Connecticut, who was soon after appointed minister plenipotentiary from Texas to this government, and now resides at Washington City. The slave mistress at Lexington, Ky., who, as her husband testifies, has killed six of his slaves, (see testimony of Mr. Clarke) is the wife of Hon. Fielding S. Turner, late judge of the criminal court of New Orleans, and one of the wealthiest slaveholders in Kentucky. Lilburn Lewis, who deliberately chopped in pieces his slave George, with a broad-axe, (see testimony of Rev. Mr. Dickey) was a wealthy slaveholder, and a nephew of President Jefferson. Rev. Francis Hawley, who was a general agent of the Baptist State Convention of North Carolina, confesses that while residing in that state he once went out with his hounds and rifle, to hunt fugitive slaves. But instead of making further reference to testimony already before the reader, we will furnish additional instances of the barbarous cruelty which is tolerated and sanctioned by the 'upper classes' of society at the south; we begin with clergymen, and other officers and members of churches.

That the reader may judge of the degree of 'protection' which slaves receive from 'public opinion,' and among the members and ministers of professed Christian churches, we insert the following illustrations:

Extract from an editorial article in the "Lowell (Mass.) Observer" a religious paper edited at the time (1833) by the **Rev. Daniel S. Southmayd**, who recently died in Texas:

"We have been among the slaves at the south. We took pains to make discoveries in respect to the evils of slavery. We formed our sentiments on the subject of the cruelties exercised towards the slave from having witnessed them. We now affirm that we never saw a man, who had never been at the south, who thought as much of the cruelties practiced on the slaves, as we *know* to be a fact.

"A slave whom I loved for his kindness and the amiableness of his disposition, and who belonged to the family where I resided, happened to stay out *fifteen minutes longer* than he had permission to stay. It was a mistake—it was *unintentional*. But what was the penalty? He was sent to the house of correction with the order that he should have *thirty lashes upon his naked body with a knotted rope!!!* He was brought home and laid down in the stoop, in the back of the house, in *the sun, upon the floor*. And there he lay, with more the appearance of a rotten carcass than a living man, for four days before he could do more calling; God's property his own, and using it as he would not have dared to use a beast? You may say he was a tiger—one of the more wicked sort, and that we must not judge others by him. *He was a professor of that religion which will pour upon the willing slaveholder the retribution due to his sin.*

"We wish to mention another fact, which our own eyes saw and our own ears heard. We were called to evening prayers. The family assembled around the altar of their accustomed devotions. There was one female *slave* present, who belonged to another master, but who had been hired for the day and tarried to attend family worship. The precious Bible was opened, and nearly half a chapter had been road, when the eye of the master, who was reading, observed that the new female servant, instead of being seated like his own slaves, flat *upon the floor,* was standing in a stooping posture upon her feet. He told her to sit down on the floor. She said it was not her custom at home. He ordered her again to do it. She replied that her master did not require it. Irritated by this answer, he repeatedly struck *her upon the head with the very Bible he held in his hand.* And not content with this, he seized his cane and *caned her down stairs most unmercifully.* He then returned to resume his profane work, but we need not say that *all* the family were not there. Do you ask again, who was this wicked man? *He was a professor of religion!"*

Rev. Huntington Lyman, late pastor of the Free Church in Buffalo, New York, says:

"Walking one day in New Orleans with a professional gentleman, who was educated in Connecticut, we were met by a black man; the gentleman was greatly incensed with the black man for passing so *near* him, and turning upon him *he pushed him with violence off the walk into the street.* This man was a professor of religion."

[And *we* add, a member, and if we mistake not an *officer* of the Presbyterian Church which was established there by Rev. Joel Parker, and which was then under his teachings.—Ed.]

Mr. Ezekiel Birdseye, a gentleman of known probity, in Cornwall, Litchfield County, Conn. gives the testimony which follows:

"A Baptist Clergyman in Laurens District, S.C. WHIPPED HIS SLAVE TO DEATH, whom he *suspected* of having stolen about sixty dollars. The slave was in the prime of life and was purchased a few weeks before for $800 of a slave trader from Virginia or Maryland. The coroner, Wm. Irby, at whose house I was then boarding, *told me,* that on reviewing the dead body, he found it *beat to a jelly from head to foot.* The master's wife discovered the money a day or two after the death of the slave. She had herself removed it from where it was placed; not knowing what it was, as it was tied up in a thick envelope. I happened to be present when the trial of this man took place, at Laurens Court House. His daughter testified that her father untied the slave, when he appeared to be failing, and gave him cold water to drink, of which he took freely. His counsel pleaded that his death *might* have been caused by drinking cold water in a state of excitement. The Judge charged the jury, that it would be their duty to find the defendant guilty, if they believed the death was caused by the whipping; but if they were of opinion that *drinking cold water* caused the death, they would find him not guilty! The jury found him—Not Guilty!"

Dr. Jeremiah S. Waugh, a physician in Somerville, Butler County, Ohio, testifies as follows:

"In the year 1825, I boarded with the Rev. John Mushat, a Seceder minister, and principal of an academy in Iredell County, N.C. He had slaves, and was in the habit of restricting them on the Sabbath. One of his slaves, however, ventured to disobey his injunctions. The offense was, he went away on Sabbath evening, and did not return till Monday morning. About the time we were called to breakfast, the Rev. gentleman was engaged in chastising him *for breaking the Sabbath.* He determined not to submit—attempted to escape by flight. The master immediately took down his gun and pursued him—leveled his instrument of death, and told him. if he did not stop instantly *he would blow him through.* The poor slave returned to the house and submitted himself to the lash; and the good master, while YET PALE WITH RAGE, *sat down to the table, and with a trembling voice* ASKED GOD'S BLESSING!"

The following letter was sent by **Capt. Jacob Dunham**, of New York City, to a slaveholder in Georgetown, D.C. more than twenty years since:

"Georgetown, June 13, 1815.

"Dear sir—Passing your house yesterday, I beheld a scene of cruelty seldom witnessed; that was the brutal chastisement of your negro girl, *lashed to a ladder and beaten in an inhuman manner, too bad to describe.* My blood chills while I contemplate the subject. This has led me to investigate your character from your neighbors; who inform me that you have *caused the death* of one negro man, whom you struck with a sledge for some trivial fault—that you have beaten another black girl with such severity that the *splinters* remained in her back for some weeks after you sold her—and many other acts of barbarity, too lengthy to enumerate. And to my great surprise, I find you are a *professor of the Christian religion!*

"You will naturally inquire why I meddle with your family affairs. My answer is, the cause of humanity and a sense of my duty requires it.— With these hasty remarks I leave you to reflect on the subject; but wish you to remember, that there is an all-seeing eye who knows all our faults and will reward us according to our deeds. I remain, sir, yours, &c.

Jacob Dunham, Master of the brig Cyrus, of N.Y."

Rev. Sylvester Cowles, pastor of the Presbyterian Church in Fredonia, N. Y. says:

"A young man, a member of the church in Cohnewago, went to Alabama last year, to reside as a clerk in an uncle's store. When he had been there about nine months, he wrote his father that he must return home. To see members of the same church sit at the communion table of our Lord one day, and the next to see one seize any weapon and knock the other down, *as he had seen,* he *could not* live there. His good father forthwith gave him permission to return home."

The following is a specimen of the shameless hardihood with which a professed minister of the Gospel and editor of a religious paper assumes the right to hold God's image as a chattel. It is from the **Southern Christian Herald:**

"It is stated in the Georgetown Union, that a negro, supposed to have died of cholera, when that disease prevailed in Charleston, was carried to the public burying ground to be interred; but before interment signs of life appeared, and, by the use of proper means, he was restored to health. And now the man who first perceived the signs of life in the slave, and that led to his preservation, claims the property as his own, and is about bringing suit for its recovery. As well might a man who rescued his neighbor's slave or his *horse,* from drowning, or who extinguished the flames that would otherwise soon have burnt down his neighbor's house, claim the *property* as his own."

Rev. George Bourne, of New-York City, late Editor of the "Protestant Vindicator" who was a preacher seven years in Virginia, gives the following testimony:

"Benjamin Lewis, who was an elder in the Presbyterian Church, engaged a carpenter to repair and enlarge his house. After some time had elapsed, Kyle, the builder, was awakened very early in the morning by a most piteous moaning and shrieking. He arose, and following the sound, discovered a colored woman nearly naked, tied to a fence, while Lewis was lacerating her. Kyle instantly commanded the slave driver to desist. Lewis maintained his jurisdiction over his slaves, and threatened Kyle that he would punish him for his interference. Finally Kyle obtained the release of the victim.

"A second and a third scene of the same kind occurred, and on the third occasion the altercation almost produced a battle between the elder and the carpenter.

"Kyle immediately arranged his affairs, packed up his tools and prepared to depart. 'Where are you going?' demanded Lewis. 'I am going home;' said Kyle. 'Then I will pay you nothing for what you have done,' retorted the slave driver, 'unless you complete your contract.' The carpenter went away with this edifying declaration, "I will not stay here a day longer;

for I expect the fire of God will come down and burn you up altogether, and I do not choose to go to hell with you!" Through hush-money and promises not to whip the women any more, I believe Kyle returned and completed his engagement.

"James Kyle of Harrisonburg, Virginia, frequently narrated that circumstance, and his son, the carpenter, confirmed it with all the minute particulars combined with his temporary residence on the Shenandoah River.

A few years since Mr. Bourne published a work entitled, "Picture of slavery in the United States" in which he describes a variety of horrid atrocities perpetrated upon slaves; such as brutal scourging and lacerations with the application of pepper, mustard, salt, vinegar, &c, to the bleeding gashes; also maiming, cat-hauling, burnings, and other tortures similar to hundreds described on the preceding pages. These descriptions of Mr. Bourne were, at that time, thought by multitudes *incredible, and* probably, even by some abolitionists, who had never given much reflection to the subject. We are happy to furnish the reader with the following testimony of a Virginia slaveholder to the accuracy of Mr. Bourne's delineations. Especially as this slaveholder is a native of one of the counties (Culpepper) near to which the atrocities described by Mr. B. were committed:

Testimony of **Mr. William Hansborough**, of Culpepper, County, Virginia, the "owner" of sixty slaves, to Mr. Bourne's "Picture of Slavery" as a *true* delineation:

Lindley Coates, of Lancaster Co., Pa., a well known member of the Society of Friends, and a member of the late Pennsylvania Convention for revising the Constitution of the State, in a letter now before us, describing a recent interview between him and Mr. Hansborough, of several days continuance, says,—"I handed him Bourne's "Picture of Slavery" to read. *After reading it,* he said, that all of the sufferings of slaves therein related, were *true delineations, and that he had seen all those modes of torture himself."*

"John M'Cue of Augusta County, Virginia, a *Presbyterian preacher,* frequently on the Lord's day morning, tied up his slaves and whipped them; and left them bound, while he went to the meeting house and preached— and after his return home repeated his scourging. That fact, with others more heinous, was known to all persons in his congregation and around the vicinity; and so far from being censured for it, he and his brethren justified it as essential to preserve their 'domestic institutions.'

Mrs. Pence, of Rockingham County, Virginia, used to boast,—' I am the best hand to whip a *wench* in the whole county'. She used to pinion the girls to a post in the yard on the Lord's Day morning, scourge them, put on the 'negro *plaster'* of salt, pepper, and vinegar, leave them tied, and walk away to church as demure as a nun, and after service repeat her flaying, if she felt the whim. I once expostulated with her upon her cruelty. 'Mrs. Pence, how can you whip your girls so publicly and disturb your neighbors so on the Lord's Day morning.' Her answer was memorable. 'If I were to whip them on any other day 1 should lose a day's work; but by whipping them on Sunday, their backs get well enough by Monday morning.' That woman, if alive, is doubtless a member of the church now, as then.

Rev. Dr. Staughton, formerly of Philadelphia, often stated, that when he lived at Georgetown, S.C. he could tell the doings of one of the slaveholders of the Baptist church there by his prayers at the prayer meeting. 'If,' said he, 'that man was upon good terms with his slaves, his words were cold and heartless as frost; if he had been whipping a man, he would pray with life; but if he had left a woman whom he had been flogging, tied to a post in his cellar, with a determination to go back and torture her again; O! How he would pray!' The Rev. Cyrus P. Grosvenor of Massachusetts can confirm the above statement by Dr. Staughton.

"William Wilson, a Presbyterian preacher of Augusta County, Virginia, had a young colored girl who was constitutionally unhealthy. As no means to amend her were availing, he sold her to a member of his congregation, and in the usual style of human flesh dealers, warranted her 'sound,' &c. The fraud was instantly discovered; but he would not refund the amount. A suit was commenced, and was long continued, and finally the plaintiff recovered the money out of which he had been swindled by slave-trading with his own preacher, No Presbytery censured him, although Judge Brown, the chancellor, severely condemned the imposition.

"In the year 1811, Jehab Graham, a preacher, lived with Alexander Nelson a Presbyterian elder, near Stanton, Virginia, and he informed me that a man had appeared before Nelson, who was a magistrate, and swore falsely against his slave—that the elder ordered him thirty-nine lashes. All that wickedness was done as an excuse for his dissipated owner to obtain money. A negro trader had offered him a considerable sum for the 'boy' and under the pretence of saving him from the punishment of the law, he was trafficked away from his woman and children to another state. The magistrate was aware of the perjury, and the whole abomination, but all the truth uttered by every colored person in the southern states would not be of any avail against the notorious false swearing of the greatest white villain who ever cursed the world. 'How,' said Jehab Graham, 'can I preach to-morrow?' I replied, 'Very well; go and thunder the doctrine of retribution in their ears. Obadiah 15, till by the divine blessing you kill or cure them.' My friends, John M. Nelson of Hillsborough, Ohio, Samuel Linn, and Robert Herron, and others of the same vicinity, could 'make both the ears of everyone who heareth them tingle' with the accounts which they can give of slave-driving by professors of religion in the Shenandoah Valley, Virginia.

"In 1815, near Frederick, in Maryland, a most barbarous planter was killed in a fit of desperation, by four of his slaves *in self-defense.* It was declared by those slaves while in prison that, besides his atrocities among their female associates, he had deliberately butchered a number of his slaves. The four men were murdered by law, to appease the popular clamor. I saw them executed on the twenty-eighth day of Jan'y, 1816. The facts I received from the Rev. Patrick Davidson of Frederick, who constantly visited them during their imprisonment—and who became an abolitionist in consequence of the disclosures which he heard from those men in the jail. The name of the planter is not distinctly recollected, but it can be known by an inspection of the record of the trial in the clerk's office, Frederick.

"A minister of Virginia, still living, and whose name must not be mentioned for fear of Nero Preston and his confederate-hanging myrmidons, informed me of this fact in 1815, in his own house. "A member of my church", said he, "lately whipped a colored youth to death. What shall I do?" I answered, "I hope you do not mean to continue him in your church." That minister replied, "'How can we help it! We dare not call him to an account. We have no legal testimony." Their communion season was then approaching. I addressed his wife,—"Mrs. do you mean to sit at the Lord's table with that murderer?" "Not I," she answered, "I would as soon commune with the devil himself." The slave killer was equally unnoticed by the civil and ecclesiastical authority.

"John Baxter, a Presbyterian elder, the brother of that slaveholding doctor in divinity, George A. Baxter, held as a slave the wife of a Baptist colored preacher, familiarly called 'Uncle Jack.' In a late period of pregnancy he scourged her so that the lives of herself and her unborn child were considered in jeopardy. Uncle Jack was advised to obtain the liberation of his wife. Baxter finally agreed, I think, to sell the woman and her children, three of them, I believe for six hundred dollars and an additional hundred if the unborn child survived a certain period after its birth. Uncle Jack was to pay one hundred dollars per annum for his wife and children for seven years, and Baxter held a sort of mortgage upon them for the payment. Uncle Jack showed me his back in furrows like a ploughed field. His master used to whip up the flesh, then beat it downwards, and then apply the *'negro plaster'*, salt, pepper, mustard, and vinegar, until all Jack's back was almost as hard and un-impressible as the bones. There is slaveholding religion! A Presbyterian elder receiving from a Baptist preacher seven hundred dollars for his wife and children. James Kyle and Uncle Jack used to tell that story with great Christian sensibility; and Uncle Jack would weep tears of anguish over his wife's piteous tale, and tears of ecstasy at the same moment that he was free, and that soon, by the grace of God, his wife and children, as he said, 'would be all free together.'"

Rev. James Nourse, a Presbyterian clergyman of Mifflin Co. Penn., whose father is, we believe, a slaveholder in Washington City, says:

"The Rev. Mr. M____, now of the Huntingdon Presbytery, after an absence of many months, was about visiting his old friends on what is commonly called the 'Eastern Shore.' Late in the afternoon, on his journey, he called at the house of Rev. A. C. of P___ town, Md. With this brother he had been long acquainted. Just at that juncture Mr. C. was about proceeding to whip a colored female, who was his slave. She was firmly tied to a post in FRONT of his dwelling house. The arrival of a clerical visitor at such a time occasioned a temporary delay in the execution of Mr. C.'s purpose. But the delay was only temporary; for not even the presence of such a guest could destroy the bloody design. The guest interceded with all the mildness yet earnestness of a brother and new visitor. But all in vain, 'the woman had been SAUCY and must be punished.' The cowhide was accordingly produced, and the *Rev. Mr. C,* a large and very stout man, applied it' manfully 'on' woman's' bare and shrinking flesh.' I say *bare* because you know that the slave women generally have but three or four inches of the arm near the shoulder covered, and the neck is left entirely exposed. As the cowhide moved back and forward, striking right and left, on the head, neck and arms, at every few strokes the sympathizing guest would exclaim, 'O, brother C. desist.' But brother C. pursued his brutal work till, after inflicting about *sixty* lashes, the woman was found to be suffused with blood on the hinder part of her neck, and under her frock between the shoulders. Yet this Rev. gentleman is well esteemed in the church—was, three or four years since, moderator of the synod of Philadelphia, and yet walks abroad, feeling himself un-rebuked by law or gospel. Ah, sir, does not this narration give fearful force to the query—' *"What has the church to do with slavery?"* Comment on the facts is unnecessary, yet allow me to conclude by saying, that it is my opinion such occurrences *are not rare in the south.*   J. N."

Rev. Charles Stewart Renshaw, of Quincy, Illinois, in a recent letter, speaking of his residence, for a period, in Kentucky, says:

"In a conversation with Mr. Robert Willis, he told me that his negro girl had run away from him some time previous. He was convinced that she was lurking round, and he watched for her. He soon found the place of her concealment, drew her from it, got a rope, and tied her hands across each other, then threw the rope over a beam in the kitchen, and hoisted her up by the wrists; 'and,' said he, 'I whipped her there till I made the lint fly, I tell you.' I asked him the meaning of making 'the lint fly,' and he replied, *'till the blood flew.'* I spoke of the iniquity and cruelty of slavery, and of its immediate abandonment. He confessed it an evil, but said, 'I am a *colonizationist*—I believe in that scheme.' Mr. Willis is a teacher of sacred music, and a member of the Presbyterian Church in Lexington, Kentucky."

Mr. R. speaking of the Presbyterian minister and church where he resided, says:

"The minister and all the church members held slaves. Some were treated kindly, others harshly. *There was not a shade of difference* between their slaves and those of their *infidel* neighbors, either in their physical, intellectual, or moral state; in some cases they would *suffer* in the comparison.

"In the kitchen of the minister of the church, a slave man was living in open adultery with a slave woman, who was a member of the church, with an 'assured hope' of heaven—whilst the man's wife was on the minister's farm in Fayette County. The minister had to bring a cook down from his farm to the place in which he was preaching. The choice was between the wife of the man and this church member. He *left the wife,* and brought the church member to the adulterer's bed.

"A Methodist preacher last fall took a load of produce down the river. Amongst other *things* he took down five slaves. He sold them at New Orleans—he came up to Natchez—bought seven there—and took them down and sold them also. Last March he came up to preach the Gospel again. A number of persons on board the steamboat (the Tuscarora,) who had seen him in the slave-shambles in Natchez and New Orleans, and now, for the first time, found him to be a preacher, had much sport at the expense of 'the fine old preacher who dealt in slaves.'

"A non-professor of religion, in Campbell County, Ky. sold a female and two children to a Methodist professor, with the proviso that they should not leave that region of country. The slave-drivers came, and offered $50 more for the woman than he had given, and he sold her. She is now in the lower country, and *her orphan babes are in Kentucky.*

"I was much shocked once, to see a Presbyterian elder's wife call a little slave to her to kiss her feet. At first the boy hesitated—but the command being repeated in tones not to be misunderstood, he approached timidly, knelt, and kissed her foot.

Rev. W. T. Allan, of Chatham, Illinois, gives the following in a letter dated Feb. 4, 1839:

"Mr. Peter Vanarsdale, an elder of the Presbyterian Church in Carrollton, formerly from Kentucky, told me, the other day, that a Mrs. Burford, in the neighborhood of Harrodsburg, Kentucky, had *separated a woman and her children from* their husband and father, taking them into another state. Mrs. B. was a member of the *Presbyterian Church.* The bereaved husband and father was also a professor of religion.

"Mr. V. told me of a slave woman who had lost her son, separated from her by public sale. In the anguish of her soul, she gave vent to her indignation freely, and perhaps harshly. Sometime after, she wished to become a member of the church. Before they received her, she had to make humble confession for speaking as she had done. *Some of the elders that received her, and required the confession, were engaged in selling the son from his mother.*"

The following communication from the **Rev. William Bardwell,** of Sandwich, Massachusetts, has just been published in "Zion's Watchman", New York City:

"*Mr. Editor:*—The following fact was given me last evening, from the pen of a shipmaster, who has traded in several of the principal ports in the south. He is a man of unblemished character, a member of the M..E. Church in this place, and familiarly known in this town. The facts were communicated to me last fall in a letter to his wife, with a request that she would cause them to be published. I give them verbatim, as they were written from the letter by brother Perry's own hand while I was in his house.

"A Methodist preacher, Wm. Whitby by name, who married in Bucksville, S.C, and by marriage came into possession of some slaves, in July, 1838, was about moving to another station to preach, and wished, also, to move his family and slaves to Tennessee, much against the will of the slaves, one of which, to get clear from him, ran into the woods after swimming a brook. The parson took after him with his gun, which, however, got wet and missed fire, when he ran to a neighbor for another gun, with the intention, as he said, of killing him; he did not, however, catch or kill him; he chained another for fear of his running away also. The above particulars were related to me by William Whitby himself.

Thomas C. Perry,March 3, 1839."

"I find by examining the minutes of the S.C. Conference, that there is such a preacher in the Conference, and brother Perry further stated to me that he was well acquainted with him, and if this statement was published, and if it could be known where he was since the last Conference, he wished a paper to be sent him containing the whole affair. He also stated to me, verbally, that the young man he attempted to shoot was about nineteen years *of* age, and had been shut up in a corn-house, and in the attempt of Mr. Whitby to chain him, he broke down the door and made his escape as above mentioned, and that Mr. W. was under the necessity of hiring him out for one year, with the risk of his employer's getting him. Brother Perry conversed with one of the slaves, who was so old that he thought it not profitable to remove so far, and had been sold; *he* informed him of all the above circumstances, and said, with tears, that he thought he had been so faithful as to be entitled to liberty, but instead of making him free, he had sold him to another master, besides parting one husband and wife from those ties rendered a thousand times dearer by an infant child which was torn for ever from the husband.

William Bardwell, *Sandwich, Mass.,* March 4, 1839."

Mr. William Poe, till recently a slaveholder in Virginia, now an elder in the Presbyterian Church at Delhi, Ohio, gives the following testimony: "An elder in the Presbyterian Church in Lynchburg had a most faithful servant, whom he flogged severely and sent him to prison, and had him confined as a felon a number of days, for being *saucy.* Another elder of the same church, an auctioneer, habitually sold slaves at his stand—very frequently *parted families—would* often go into the country to sell slaves on execution and otherwise; when remonstrated with, he justified himself, saying, 'it was his business;' the church also justified him on the same ground.

"A Doctor Duval, of Lynchburg, Va. got offended with a very faithful, worthy servant, and immediately sold him to a negro trader, to be taken to New Orleans; Duval *still keeping the wife* of the man as his slave. This Duval was a *professor of religion."*

Mr. Samuel Hall, a teacher in Marietta College, Ohio, says, in a recent letter:

"A student in Marietta College, from Mississippi, a professor of religion, and in every way worthy of entire confidence, made to me the following statement. [If his name were published it would probably cost him his life.]

"When I was in the family of the Rev. James Martin, of Louisville, Winston County, Mississippi, in the spring of 1838, Mrs. Martin became offended at a female slave, because she did not move faster. She commanded her to do so; the girl quickened her pace; again she was ordered to move faster, or, Mrs. M. declared, she would break the broomstick over her head. Again the slave quickened her pace; but not coming up to the *maximum* desired by Mrs. M. the latter declared she would *see* whether she (the slave) could move or not; and, going into another apartment, she brought in a raw hide, awaiting the return of her husband for its application. In this instance I know not what was the final result, but I have heard the sound of the raw-hide in at least *two* other instances, applied by this same reverend gentleman to the back of his *female* servant."

Mr. Hall adds—"The name of my informant must be suppressed, as" he says, "there are those who would cut my throat in a moment, if the information I give were to be coupled with my name." Suffice it to say that he is a professor of religion, a native of Virginia, and a student of Marietta College, whose character will bear the strictest scrutiny. He says:

"In 1838 at Charlestown, Va. I conversed with several members of the church under the care of the Rev. Mr. Brown, of the same place. Taking occasion to speak of slavery, and of the sin of slaveholding, to one of them who was a lady, she replied, 'I am a slaveholder, and I *glory* in it.' I had a conversation, a few days after, with the pastor himself, concerning the state of religion in his church, and who were the most exemplary members in it The pastor mentioned several of those who were of that description; the *first* of whom, however, was the identical lady who *gloried* in being a slaveholder! That church numbers nearly two hundred members.

"Another lady, who was considered as devoted a Christian as any in the same church, but who was in poor health, was accustomed to flog some of her female domestics with a raw-hide till she was exhausted, and then go and lie down till her strength was recruited, rising again and resuming the flagellation. This she considered as not at all derogatory to her Christian character."

Mr. Joel S. Bingham, of Cornwall, Vermont, lately a student in Middlebury College, and a member of the Congregational Church, spent a few weeks in Kentucky in the summer of 1838. He relates the following occurrence which took place in the neighborhood where he resided, and was a matter of perfect notoriety in the vicinity:

"Rev. Mr. Lewis, a Baptist minister in the vicinity of Frankfort, Ky. had a slave that ran away, but was retaken and brought back to his master, who threatened him with punishment for making an attempt to escape. Though terrified the slave immediately attempted to run away again. Mr. L. commanded him to stop, but he did not obey. *Mr. L. then took a gun, loaded with, small shot and fired at the slave, who fell;* but was not killed, and afterward recovered. Mr. L. did not probably intend to kill the slave, as it was his legs which were aimed at and received the contents of the gun. The master asserted that he was driven to this necessity to maintain his authority. This took place about the first of July, 1838."

The following is given upon the authority of **Rev. Orange Scott**, of Lowell, Mass. for many years a presiding elder in the Methodist Episcopal Church:

"Rev. Joseph Hough, a Baptist minister, formerly of Springfield, Mass. now of Plainfield, N. H. while traveling in the south, a few years ago, put up one night with a Methodist family, and spent the Sabbath with them. While there, one of the female slaves did something which displeased her mistress. She took a chisel and mallet, and very deliberately cut off one of her toes!"

SLAVE BREEDING
An Index of 'Public Opinion'
AMONG THE 'HIGHEST CLASS OF SOCIETY'
In Virginia and other Northern Slave States

But we shall be told, that 'slave-breeders' are regarded with contempt, and the business of slave breeding is looked upon as despicable; and the hot disclaimer of Mr. Stevenson, our Minister Plenipotentiary at the Court of St. James, in reply to Mr. O'Connell, who had intimated that he might be a slave breeder,' will doubtless be quoted.*

* The following is Mr. Stevenson's disclaimer: it was published in the 'London Mail' Oct. 30, 1838:

To the Editor of the Evening Mail:

Sir—I did not see until my return from Scotland the note addressed by Mr. O'Connell, to the editor of the Chronicle, purporting to give an explanation of the correspondence which has passed between us, and which I deemed it proper to make public. I do not intend to be drawn into any discussion of the subject of domestic slavery as it exists in the United

States, nor to give any explanation of the motives or circumstances under which I have acted. Disposed to regard Mr. O'Connell as a man of honor, I was induced to take the course I did; whether justifiable or not, the world will now decide. The tone and report of his last note in which he disavows responsibility for anything he may say) precludes any further notice from me, than to say that the charge which he has thought proper again to repeat, of my being a breeder of slaves for sale and traffick, is wholly destitute of truth; and that I am warranted in believing it has been made by him without the slightest authority. Such, too, I venture to say, is the case IN RELATION TO HIS CHARGE OF SLAVE-BREEDING IN VIRGINIA.

I make this declaration, not because I admit Mr. O'Connell's right to call for it, but to prevent my silence from being misinterpreted.

A. Stevenson, 23 *Portland Place, Oct.* 29

In reply, we need not say what everybody knows, that if Mr. Stevenson is not a 'slave breeder,' he is a solitary exception among the large slaveholders of Virginia. What! Virginia slaveholders not 'slave-breeders?' the pretence is ridiculous and contemptible; it is meanness, hypocrisy, and falsehood, as is abundantly proved by the testimony which follows:

Mr. Gholson, of Virginia, in his speech in the Legislature of that state, Jan. 18, 1831, (see Richmond Whig,) says:

"It has always (perhaps erroneously) been considered by steady and old-fashioned people, that the owner of land had a reasonable right to its annual profits; the owner of orchards, to their annual fruits; the owner of *brood mares,* to their product; and the owner *of female slaves, to their increase.* We have not the fine-spun intelligence, nor legal acumen, to discover the technical distinctions drawn by gentlemen. The legal maxim of '*Partus sequitur ventrem*' is coeval with the existence of the rights of property itself, and is founded in wisdom and justice. It is on the justice and inviolability of this maxim that the master foregoes the service of the female slave; has her nursed and attended during the period of her gestation, and raises the helpless and infant offspring. The value of the property justifies the expense; and I do not hesitate to say, that in its *increase consists* much *of our wealth*"

Hon. Thomas Mann Randolph, of Virginia, formerly Governor of that state, in his speech before the legislature in 1832, while speaking of the number of slaves annually sold from Virginia to the more southern slave states, said:

"The exportation has *averaged* EIGHT THOUSAND FIVE HUNDRED for the last twenty years. Forty years ago, the whites exceeded the colored 25,000, the colored now exceed the whites 81,000; and these results too during an exportation of near 260,000 slaves since the year 1790, now

~ 448 ~

perhaps the fruitful progenitors of half a million in other states. It is a practice and an increasing practice, in parts of Virginia, to rear slaves for market. How can an honorable mind, a patriot and a lover of his country, bear to see this ancient dominion converted into one grand menagerie, where men are to be reared for market, like oxen for the shambles."

Professor Dew, now President of the University of William and Mary, Virginia, in his Review of the Debate in the Virginia Legislature, 1831.2, says, p 49:

"From all the information we can obtain, we have no hesitation in saying that upwards of six thousand [slaves] are yearly exported [from Virginia] to other states.' Again, p. 61: 'The 6000 slaves which Virginia annually sends off to the south, are a source of wealth to Virginia.'— Again, p. 120: 'A full equivalent being thus left in the place of the slave, this emigration becomes an advantage to the state, and does not check the black population as much as, at first view, we might imagine—because it furnishes every inducement to the master to attend to the negroes, to ENCOURAGE BREEDING and to cause the *greatest number possible to be raised &c.*"

"*Virginia is, in fact, a negro-raising state for other states.*"

Extract from the speech of Mr. Faulkner, in the Va. House of Delegates, 1832. [See Richmond Whig.]:

"But he [Mr. Gholson,] has labored to show that the Abolition of Slavery, were it practicable, would be *impolitic,* because as the drift of this portion of his argument runs your slaves constitute the entire wealth of the state, all the *productive capacity* Virginia possesses. And, sir, as things are, I *believe he is correct.* He says, and in this he is sustained by the gentleman from Halifax, Mr. Bruce, that the slaves constitute the entire available wealth at present, of Eastern Virginia. Is it true that for 200 years the only increase in the wealth and resources of Virginia, has been a remnant of the natural *increase* of this miserable race?—Can it be, that on this *increase,* she places her sole dependence? I had always understood that indolence and extravagance were the necessary concomitants of slavery; but, until I heard these declarations, I had not fully conceived the horrible extent of this evil. These gentlemen state the fact, which the history and *present aspect of the Commonwealth but too well sustain.* The gentlemen's facts and argument in support of his plea of impolicy, to me, seem rather unhappy. To me, such a state of things would itself be conclusive at least, that something, even as a measure of policy should be done. What, sir, have you lived for two 'hundred years, without personal effort or productive industry, in extravagance and indolence, sustained alone *by the return from sales of the increase of slaves,* and retaining merely such a number as your now impoverished lands can sustain, as stock, *depending, too, upon a most uncertain market?* When that market is closed, as in the nature of things it must be, what then will become of this gentleman's hundred millions worth of slaves, and the annual product?"

In the debates in the Virginia Convention, in 1829, **Judge Upsher** said: "The value of slaves as an article of property [and it is in that view only that they are legitimate subjects of taxation] depends *much on the state of the market abroad.* In this view, it is the value of land *abroad,* and not of land here, which furnishes the ratio. It is well known to us all, that nothing is more fluctuating than the value of slaves. A late law of Louisiana reduced their value 25 per cent, in two hours after its passage was known. IF IT SHOULD BE OUR LOT, AS I TRUST IT WILL BE, TO ACQUIRE THE COUNTRY OF TEXAS, THEIR PRICE WILL RISE AGAIN." p. 77.

Mr. Goode, of Virginia, in his speech before the Virginia Legislature, in Jan. 1832, [See Richmond Whig, of that date,] said:

"The superior usefulness of the slaves in the south will constitute an *effectual demand,* which will remove them from our limits. We shall send them from our state, because *it will be our interest to do so.* Our planters are already becoming farmers. Many, who grew tobacco as their only staple, have already introduced, and commingled the wheat crop. They are already semi-farmers; and in the natural course of events, they must become more and more so.—As the greater quantity of rich western lands are appropriated to the production of the staple of our planters, that staple will become less profitable.—We shall gradually divert our lands from its production, until we shall become actual farmers.—Then will the necessity for slave labor diminish; then will the effectual demand diminish, and then will the quantity of slaves diminish, until they shall be adapted to the effectual demand.

"But gentlemen are alarmed *lest the markets of other states be closed against the introduction of our slaves.* Sir, the demand for slave labor MUST INCREASE through the South and West. It has been heretofore limited by the want of capital; but when emigrants shall be relieved from their embarrassments, contracted by the purchase of their lands, the annual profits of their estates, will constitute an accumulating capital, which they will *seek to invest in labor*. That the demand for labor must increase in proportion to the increase of capital, is one of the demonstrations of political economists; and I confess, that for the removal of slavery from Virginia, I look to the efficacy of that principle; together with the circumstance that our southern brethren are constrained to continue planters, by their position, soil and climate."

The following is from Niles' Weekly Register, published at Baltimore, Md. vol. 35. p.4:

"*Dealing in slaves has become a large business;* establishments are made in several places in Maryland and Virginia, at which they are sold like cattle; these places of deposit are strongly built, and well supplied with thumb-screws and gags, and ornamented with cow-skins and other whips oftentimes bloody."

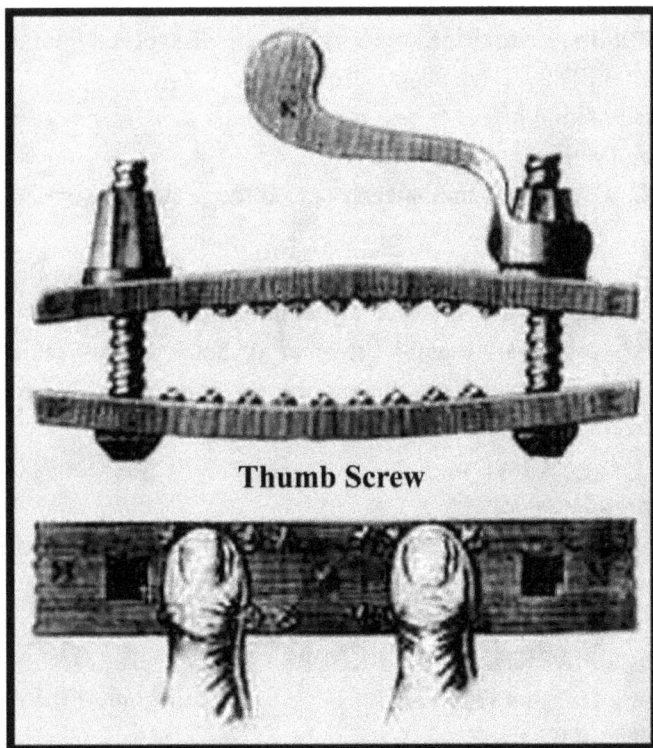

Thumb Screw

R. S. Finley, Esq. late General Agent of the American Colonization Society, at a meeting in New York, 27th Feb. 1833, said:

"In Virginia and other grain-growing slave states, the blacks do not support themselves, and the only profit their masters derive from them is, repulsive as the idea may justly seem, in breeding them, like other live stock for the more southern states."

Rev. Dr. Graham, of Fayetteville, N.C.at a Colonization Meeting, held in that place in the fall of 1837 said:

"He had resided for 15 years in one of the largest slaveholding counties in the state, had long and anxiously considered the subject, and still it was dark. There were nearly 7000 slaves offered in New Orleans market last winter. From Virginia alone 6000 were annually sent to the south; and from Virginia and N.C. there had gone, in the same direction, in the last twenty years, 300,000 slaves. While not 4000 had gone to Africa. What it portended, he could not predict, but he felt deeply, that *we must awake in these states and consider the subject.*"

Hon. Philip Doddridge, of Virginia, in his speech in the Virginia Convention, in 1829, [Debates p. 89.] said:

"The acquisition of Texas will greatly *enhance the value of the property in* question, [Virginia slaves.]"

Hon. C. F. Mercer, in a speech before the same Convention, in 1829, says:

"The tables of the natural growth of the slave population demonstrate, when compared with the increase of its numbers in the commonwealth for twenty years past, that an annual revenue of not less than a million and a half of dollars is derived from the exportation of a part of this population." (Debates, p. 199.)

Hon. Henry Clay, of Ky., in his speech before the Colonization Society, in 1829, says:

"It is believed that nowhere in the farming portion of the United States, would slave labor be generally employed, if the proprietor were not tempted TO RAISE SLAVES BY THE HIGH PRICE OF THE SOUTHERN MARKET WHICH KEEPS IT UP IN HIS OWN."

The New Orleans Courier, Feb. 15, 1839, speaking of the prohibition of the African slave trade, while the internal slave-trade is plied, says:

"The United States law may, and probably does, put millions *into the pockets of the people living between the Roanoke, and Mason and Dixon's line;* still we think it would require some casuistry to show that *the present slave-trade from that quarter* is a whit better than the one from Africa. One thing is certain—that its results are more menacing to the tranquility of the people in this quarter, as there can be no comparison between the ability and inclination to do mischief, possessed by the Virginia negro, and that of the rude and ignorant African."

That the New Orleans Editor does not exaggerate in saying that the internal slave-trade puts 'millions' into the pockets of the slaveholders in Maryland and Virginia, is very clear from the following statement, made by the editor of the Virginia Times, an influential political paper, published at Wheeling, Virginia. Of the exact date of the paper we are not quite certain, it was, however, sometime in 1836, probably near the middle of the year—the file will show. The editor says:

"We have heard intelligent men estimate the number of slaves exported from Virginia within the last twelve months, at 120,000—each slave averaging at least $600, making an aggregate at $72,000,000. Of the number of slaves exported, not more than *one-third* have been sold, (the others having been carried by their owners, who have removed,) *which would leave in the state the* SUM OF $24,000,000 ARISING FROM THE SALE OF SLAVES."

According to this estimate about FORTY THOUSAND SLAVES WERE SOLD OUT OF THE STATE OF VIRGINIA IN A SINGLE YEAR, and the 'slave-breeders' who sold them, put into their pockets Twenty-four MILLIONS OF DOLLARS, the price of the 'souls of men.'

The **New York Journal of Commerce** of Oct. 12, 1835, contained a letter from a Virginian, whom the editor calls 'a very good and sensible man,' asserting that Twenty Thousand Slaves had been driven to the south from Virginia *during that year,* nearly one-fourth of which was then remaining.

The **Maryville (Tenn.) Intelligencer,** sometime in the early part of 1836, (we have not the date,) says, in an article reviewing a communication of Rev. J. W. Douglass, of Fayetteville North Carolina: "Sixty thousand slaves passed through a little western town for the southern market, during the year 1835."

The **Natchez (Miss.) Courier,** says "that the states of Louisiana, Mississippi, Alabama, and Arkansas, imported TWO HUNDRED AND

FIFTY THOUSAND SLAVES from the more northern slave states in the year 1836."

The Baltimore American gives the following from a Mississippi paper, of 1837:

"The report made by the committee of the citizens of Mobile, appointed at their meeting held on the 1st instant, on the subject of the existing pecuniary pressure, states, among other things: that so large has been the return of slave labor, that purchases by Alabama of that species of property from other states since 1833, have amounted to about Ten Million Dollars Annually."

Further the *inhumanity* of a slaveholding 'public opinion' toward slaves, follows legitimately from the downright ruffianism of the slaveholding *spirit* in the 'highest class of society.' When roused, it tramples upon all the proprieties and courtesies, and even common decencies of life, and is held in check by none of those considerations of time, and place, and relations of station, character, law, and national honor, which are usually sufficient, even in the absence of conscientious principles, to restrain other men from outrages. Our National Legislature is a fit illustration of this. Slaveholders have converted the Congress of the United States into a very bear garden. Within the last three years some of the most prominent slaveholding members of the House, and among them the late speaker, have struck and kicked, and throttled, and seized each other by the hair and with their fists pummeled each other's faces, on the floor of Congress. We need not publish an account of what everybody knows, that during the session of the last Congress, Mr. Wise of Virginia and Mr. Bynum of North Carolina, after having called each other "liars, villains" and "damned rascals" sprung from their seats "both sufficiently armed for any desperate purpose," cursing each other as they rushed together, and would doubtless have butchered each other on the floor of Congress, if both had not been seized and held by their friends.

The **New York Gazette** relates the following which occurred at the close of the session of 1838:

"The House could not adjourn without another brutal and bloody row. It occurred on Sunday morning immediately at the moment of adjournment, between Messrs. Campbell and Maury, both of Tennessee. He took offense to some remarks made to him by his colleague, Mr. Campbell, and the fight followed."

The **Huntsville (Ala.) Democrat** of June 16, 1838, gives the particulars which follow:

"Mr. Maury is said to be badly hurt. He was near losing his life by being knocked through the window; but his adversary, it is said, saved him by clutching the hair of his head with his left hand, while he struck him with his right."

The same number of the **Huntsville Democrat** contains the particulars of a fist-fight on the floor of the House of Representatives, between Mr. Bell, the late Speaker, and his colleague Mr. Turney of Tennessee. The following is an extract:

"Mr. Turney concluded his remarks in reply to Mr. Bell, in the course of which he commented upon that gentleman's course at different periods of his political career with great severity.

"He did not think his colleague [Mr. Turney,] was actuated by private malice, but was the willing voluntary instrument of others, the fool of fools.

Mr. Turney. "It is false! It is false!"

Mr. Stanley called Mr. Turney to order.

At the same moment both gentlemen were perceived in personal conflict, and blows with the fist were aimed by each at the other. Several members interfered, and suppressed the personal violence; others called order, order, and some called for the interference of the Speaker.

The Speaker hastily took the chair, and insisted upon order; but both gentlemen continued struggling, and endeavoring, notwithstanding the constraint of their friends, to strike each other."

The correspondent of the New York Gazette gives the following, which took place about the time of the preceding affrays:

The House was much agitated last night, by the passage between Mr. Biddle, of Pittsburgh, and Mr. Downing, of Florida. Mr. D. exclaimed "do you impute falsehood to me!" at the same time catching up some missile and making a demonstration to advance upon Mr. Biddle. Mr. Biddle repeated his accusation, and meanwhile, Mr. Downing was arrested by many members."

"The last three fights all occurred, if we mistake not, in the short space of one month. The fisticuffs between Messrs. Bynum and Wise occurred at the previous session of Congress. At the same session Messrs. Peyton of Tenn. and Wise of Virginia, went armed with pistols and dirks to the meeting of a committee of Congress, and threatened to shoot a witness while giving his testimony. We begin with the first on the list. Who are Messrs. Wise and Bynum? Both slaveholders, Who are Messrs. Campbell and Maury? Both slaveholders. Who are Messrs. Bell and Turney? Both slaveholders. Who is Mr. Downing, who seized a weapon and rushed upon Mr. Biddle? A slaveholder. Who is Mr. Peyton who drew his pistol on a witness before a committee of Congress? A slaveholder of course. All these bullies were slaveholders, and they magnified their office, and slaveholding was justified of her children. We might fill a volume with similar chronicles of slaveholding brutality. But time would fail us. Suffice it to say, that since the organization of the government, a majority of the distinguished men in the slaveholding states have gloried in strutting over the stage in the character of murderers. Look at the men whom the people delight to honor. President Jackson, Senator Benton, the late Gen Coffee,—it is but a few years since these slaveholders shot at, and stabbed, and stamped upon each other in a tavern oil. General Jackson had previously killed Mr. Dickenson. Senator Clay of Kentucky has immortalized himself by shooting at a near relative Chief Justice Marshall, and being wounded by him; and not long after by shooting at John Randolph of Virginia. Governor McDuffie of South Carolina has signalized himself also, both by shooting and being shot,—so has Governor Poindexter, and Governor Rowan, and Judge McKinley of the U. S. Supreme Court, late senator in Congress from Alabama,—but we desist; a full catalogue would fill pages. We will only add, that a few months since, in the city of London, Governor Hamilton, of South Carolina, went armed with pistols, to the lodgings of Daniel O'Connell, 'to stop his wind' in the bullying slang of his own published boast. During the last session of Congress Messrs. Dromgoole and Wise* of Virginia, W. Cost Johnson and Jenifer of Maryland, Pickens and Campbell of South Carolina, and we know not how many more slaveholding members of Congress have been engaged, either as principals or seconds, in that species of murder dignified with the name of dueling. But enough; we are heart-sick. What meaneth all this? Are slaveholders worse than other men? No! But arbitrary power has wrought in them its mystery of iniquity, and poisoned their better nature with its infuriating sorcery.

*Mr. Wise said in one of his speeches during the last session of Congress, that he was obliged to go armed for the protection of his life in Washington. It could not have been for fear of Northern men.

Their savage ferocity toward each other when their passions are up is the natural result of their habit of daily plundering and oppressing the slave. **The North Carolina Standard** of August 30, 1837, contains the following illustration of this ferocity exhibited by two southern lawyers in settling the preliminaries of a duel.

"The following conditions were proposed by Alexander K. McClung, of Raymond, in the State of Mississippi, to H. C. Stewart, as the laws to govern a duel they were to fight near Vicksburg:

Article 1st. The parties shall meet opposite Vicksburg, in the State of Louisiana, on Thursday the 29th inst. precisely at 4 o'clock, P. M. Agreed to.

2d. The weapons to be used by each shall weigh one pound two and a half ounces, measuring sixteen inches and a half in length, including the handle, and one inch and three-eighths in breadth. Agreed to.

3d. Both knives shall be sharp on one edge, and on the back shall be sharp only one inch at the point. Agreed to.

4th. Each party shall stand at the distance of eight feet from the other, until the word is given. Agreed to.

5th. The second of each party shall throw up, with a silver dollar, on the ground, for the word, and two best out of three shall win the word. Agreed to.

6th. After the word is given, either party may take what advantage he can with his knife, but on throwing his knife at the other, shall be shot down by the second of his opponent. Agreed to.

7th. Each party shall be stripped entirely naked, except one pair of linen pantaloons; one pair of socks, and boots or pumps as the party please. Acceded to.

8th. The wrist of the left arm of each party shall he tied tight to his left thigh, and a strong cord shall be fastened around his left arm at the elbow, and then around his body. Rejected.

9th. After the word is given, each party shall be allowed to advance or recede as he pleases, over the space of twenty acres of ground, until death ensues to one of the parties. Agreed to—the parties to be placed in the centre of the space.

10th. The word shall be given by the winner of the same, in the following manner, viz: "Gentlemen are you ready? Each party shall then answer, "I am!" The second giving the word shall then distinctly command—*strike*. Agreed to.

If either party shall violate these rules, upon being notified by the second of either party, he may be liable to be shot down instantly. As established usage points out the duty of both parties, therefore notification is considered unnecessary."

The Favorite Amusements of slaveholders, like the gladiatorial shows of Rome and the Bull Fights of Spain, reveal a public feeling insensible to suffering, and a degree of brutality in the highest degree revolting to every truly noble mind. One of their most common amusements is cock fighting. Mains of cocks, with twenty, thirty, and fifty cocks on each side, are fought for hundreds of dollars aside. The fowls are armed with steel spurs or 'gafts,' about two inches long. These 'gafts' are fastened upon the legs by sawing off the *natural* 'spur,' leaving enough only of it to answer the purpose of a *stock* for the tube of the "gafts," which are so sharp that at a stroke the fowls thrust them through each other's necks and heads, and tear each other's bodies till one or both dies, then two others are brought forward for the amusement of the multitude assembled, and this barbarous pastime is often kept up for days in succession, hundreds and thousands gathering from a distance to witness it. The following advertisements from the Raleigh Register, June 18, 1838, edited by Messrs. Gales and Son, the father and brother of Mr. Gales, editor of the National Intelligencer, and late Mayor of Washington City, reveal the public sentiment of North Carolina:

"**CHATHAM AGAINST NASH,** or any other county in the State. I am authorized to take a bet of any amount that may be offered, to FIGHT A MAIN OF COCKS, at any place that may be agreed upon by the parties—to be fought the ensuing spring.

Gideon Alston, Chatham County, June 7, 1838."

Two weeks after, this challenge was answered as follows:

"TO MR. GIDEON ALSTON, of Chatham County, N.C.

"Sir: In looking over the North Carolina Standard of the 20th inst. I discover a challenge over your signature, headed 'Chatham against Nash,' in which you state that you are 'authorized to take a bet of any amount that may be offered, to fight a main of cocks, at any place that may be agreed upon by the parties, to be fought the ensuing spring,' which challenge I accept: and do propose to meet you at Rolesville, Wake County, N.C. on the last Wednesday May next, the parties to show thirty-one cocks each— fight four days, and be governed by the rules as laid down in Turner's Cock Laws—which, if you think proper to accede to, you will signify through this or any other medium you may select, and then I will name the sum for which we shall fight, as that privilege was surrendered by you in your challenge.

I am, sir, very respectfully, &c.

Nicholas W. Arrington, near Hilliardston, Nash Co. North Carolina. June 22nd, 1838."

The following advertisement in the **Richmond Whig,** of July 12, 1837, exhibits the public sentiment of Virginia:

MAIN OF COCKS.—A large 'MAIN OF COCKS,' 21 a side, for $25 'the fight,' and $500 'the odd,' will be fought between the County of Dinwiddie on one part, and the Counties of Hanover and Henrico on the other.

"The 'regular" fighting will be continued three *days,* and from the large number of "game'uns' on both sides and in the adjacent country, will be prolonged no doubt a *fourth.* To prevent confusion and promote 'sport,' the pit will be enclosed and furnished with *seats;* so that those having a curiosity to witness a species of diversion originating in a better day (for they had no rag money then,) can have *that* very *natural* feeling gratified.

"The Petersburg Constellation is requested to copy."

Horse-racing too, as everybody knows, is a favorite amusement of slaveholders. Every slave state has its race course, and in the older states almost every county has one on a small scale. There is hardly a day in the year, the weather permitting, in which crowds do not assemble in the south to witness this barbarous sport. Horrible cruelty is absolutely inseparable from it. Hardly a race occurs of any celebrity in which some one of the coursers are not lamed, 'broken down,' or in some way seriously injured, often for life, and not un-frequently they are killed by the rupture of some vital part in the struggle. When the heats are closely contested, the blood of the tortured animal drips from the lash and flies every leap from the stroke of the rowel. From the breaking of girths and other accidents, their riders (mostly slaves) are often thrown and maimed or killed. Yet these amusements are attended by thousands in every part of the slave states. The wealth and fashion, the gentlemen and *ladies* the 'highest circles' at the south, throng the race course.

That those who can fasten steel spurs upon the legs of dunghill fowls, and goad the poor birds to worry and tear each other to death—and those who can crowd by thousands to witness such barbarity—that those who can throng the race-course and with keen relish witness the hot pantings of the life-struggle, the lacerations and fitful spasms of the muscles, swelling through the crimsoned foam, as the tortured steeds rush in blood-welterings to the goal—that such should look upon the sufferings of their slaves with indifference is certainly small wonder.

Perhaps we shall be told that there are thronged race-courses at the North. True, there are a few, and they are thronged chiefly by *Southerners,* and 'Northern men with *Southern* principles,' and supported mainly by the patronage of slaveholders who summer at the North. Cock-fighting and horse-racing are "*Southern* institutions." The idleness, contempt of labor, dissipation, sensuality, brutality, cruelty, and meanness, engineered by the habit of making men and women work without pay, and flogging them if they demur at it, constitutes a congenial soil out of which cock-fighting and horse racing are the spontaneous growth.

Again,—the kind treatment of the slaves is often argued from the liberal education and enlarged views of slaveholders. The facts and reasoning of the preceding pages have shown, that 'liberal education,' despotic habits and ungoverned passions work together with slight friction. And every day's observation shows that the former is often a stimulant to the latter.

But the notion so common at the north that the majority of the slaveholders are persons of education is entirely erroneous. A *very few* slaveholders in each of the slave states have been men *of ripe* education, to whom our national literature is much indebted. A larger number may be called *well* educated—these reside mostly in the cities and large villages, but a majority of the slaveholders are ignorant men, thousands of them notoriously so, *mere boors* unable to write their names or to read the alphabet.

No one of the slave states has probably so much general education as Virginia. It is the oldest of them—has furnished one half of the presidents of the United States—has expended more upon her university than any state in the Union has done during the same time upon its colleges—sent to Europe nearly twenty years since for her most learned professors, and in fine, has far surpassed every other slave state in her efforts to disseminate education among her citizens, and yet, the Governor of Virginia in his message to the legislature (Jan. 7, 1839) says, that of four thousand six hundred and fourteen adult males in that state, who applied to the county clerks for marriage licenses in the year 1837, 'One Thousand and Forty-seven *were unable to write their names.'* The governor adds,' These statements, it will be remembered, are confined to one sex; the education of females, it is to be feared, is in a condition of *much greater neglect.'*

The **Editor of the Virginia Times**, published at Wheeling, in his paper of Jan. 23, 1839, says:

"We have every reason to suppose that one fourth of the people of the state cannot write their names, and they have not, of course, any other species of education."

Kentucky is the child of Virginia; her first settlers were some of the most distinguished citizens of the mother state; in the general diffusion of intelligence amongst her citizens Kentucky is probably in advance of all the slave states except Virginia and South Carolina; and yet Governor Clark, in his last message to the Kentucky Legislature, (Dec 5,1838) makes the following declaration:

"'From the computation of those most familiar with the subject, it appears that 'AT LEAST ONE THIRD OF THE ADULT POPULATION OF THE STATE ARE UNABLE TO WRITE THEIR NAMES.'

The following advertisement in the "Milledgeville (Geo.) Journal" Dec. 26, 1837, is another specimen from one of the 'old thirteen:'

"**Notice.**—I, Pleasant Webb, of the State of Georgia, Oglethorpe County, being an *illiterate man, and not able to write my own name,* and whereas it hath been represented to me that there is a certain promissory note or notes out against me that I know nothing of, and further that some man in this State holds a bill of sale for *a certain negro woman named Ailsey and her increase, a part of which is now in my possession,* which I also know nothing of. Now I do hereby certify and declare, that I have no knowledge whatsoever of any such papers existing in my name as above stated and I hereby require all or any person or persons whatsoever holding or pretending to hold any such papers, to produce them to me within thirty days from the date hereof, showing their authority for holding the same, or they will be considered fictitious and fraudulently obtained or raised, by some person or persons for base purposes after my death.

"Given under my hand this 2nd day of December, 1837.

His

" PLEASANT X WEBB.

Mark

THAT SLAVES MUST HABITUALLY SUFFER GREAT CRUELTIES FOLLOWS INEVITABLY FROM THE BRUTAL OUTRAGES WHICH THEIR MASTERS INFLICT ON EACH OTHER.

Slaveholders, exercising from childhood irresponsible power over human beings, and in the language of President Jefferson, "giving loose to the worst of passions" in the treatment of their slaves, become in a great measure unfitted for self control in their intercourse with each other. Tempers accustomed to riot with loose reins, spurn restraints, and passions inflamed by indulgence, take fire on the least friction. We repeat it, the state of society in the slave states, the duels, and daily deadly affrays of slaveholders with each other—the fact that the most deliberate and cold-blooded murders are committed at noon day, in the presence of thousands, and the perpetrators eulogized by the community as "honorable men," reveals such a prostration of law, as gives impunity to crime—a state of society, an omnipresent public sentiment reckless of human life, taking bloody vengeance on the spot for every imaginary affront, glorying in such assassinations as the only true honor and chivalry, successfully defying the civil arm, and laughing its impotency to scorn.

When such things are done in the green tree, what will be done in the dry? When slaveholders are in the habit of caning, stabbing, and shooting *each other* at every supposed insult, the unspeakable enormities perpetrated by such men, with such passions, upon their defenseless slaves, *must* be beyond computation. To furnish the reader with an illustration of slaveholding civilization and morality, as exhibited in the unbridled fury, rage, malignant hate, jealousy, diabolical revenge, and all those infernal passions that shoot up rank in the hot-bed of arbitrary power, we will insert here a mass of testimony, detailing a large number of affrays, lynchings, assassinations, &c., &c., which have taken place in various parts of the slave states within a brief period—and to leave no room for cavil on the subject, these extracts will be made exclusively from newspapers published in the slave states, and generally in the immediate vicinity of the tragedies described. They will not be made second hand from *northern* papers, but from the original *southern* papers, which now lie on our table.

Before proceeding to furnish details of certain classes of crimes in the slave states, we advertise the reader—1st. That we *shall not* include in the list those crimes which are ordinarily committed in the free, as well as in the slave states. 2d. We shall not include any of the crimes perpetrated by whites upon slaves and free colored persons, who constitute a majority of the population in Mississippi and Louisiana, a large majority,in South Carolina, and, on an average, two-fifths in the other slave states. 3d. Fist fights, canings, beatings, biting off noses and ears, gougings, knockings down, &c., unless they result in *death,* will not be included in the list, nor will *ordinary* murders, unless connected with circumstances that serve as a special index of public sentiment. 4th Neither will *ordinary, formal duels* be included, except in such cases as just specified. 5th. The only crimes which, as the general rule, will be specified, will be deadly affrays with bowie knives, dirks, pistols, rifles, guns, or other death weapons, and *lynchings.* 6th. The crimes enumerated will, for the most part, be only those perpetrated *openly,* without *attempt at concealment.* 7th. We shall not attempt to give *a full* list of the affrays, &c., that took place in the respective states during the period selected, as the only files' of southern papers to which we have access are very imperfect.

The reader will perceive, from these preliminaries, that only a *small* proportion of the crimes actually perpetrated in the respective slave states during the period selected, will be entered upon this list. He will also perceive, that the crimes which will be presented are of a class rarely perpetrated in the free states; and if perpetrated there at all, they are, with scarcely an exception, committed either by slaveholders, temporarily resident in them, or by persons whose passions have been inflamed by the poison of a southern contact—whose habits and characters have become perverted by living among slaveholders, and adopting the code of slaveholding morality.

We now proceed to the details, commencing with the new state of Arkansas.

ARKANSAS

At the last session of the legislature of that state, Col. John Wilson, President of the Bank at Little Rock, the capital of the state, was elected Speaker of the House of Representatives. He had been elected to that office for a number of years successively, and was one of the most influential citizens of the state. While presiding over the deliberations of the House, he took umbrage at words spoken in debate by Major Anthony, a conspicuous member, came down from the Speaker's chair, drew a large bowie knife from his bosom, and attacked Major A., who defended himself for some time, but was at last stabbed through the heart, and fell dead on the floor. Wilson deliberately wiped the blood from his knife, and returned to his seat. The following statement of the circumstances of the murder, and the trial of the murderer, is abridged from the account published in the Arkansas Gazette, a few months since—it is here taken from the **Knoxville (Tennessee) Register,** July 4, 1838:

"On the 14th of December last, Maj. Joseph J. Anthony, a member of the Legislature of Arkansas, was murdered, while performing his duty as a member of the House of Representatives, by John Wilson, Speaker of that House.

The facts were these: A bill came from the Senate, commonly called the *Wolf Bill.* Among the amendments proposed, was one by Maj. Anthony, that the signature of the President of the Real Estate Bank should be attached to the certificate of the wolf scalp. Col. Wilson, the Speaker, asked Maj. Anthony whether he intended the remark as personal. Maj. Anthony promptly said, *"No, I do not."* And at that instant of time, a message was delivered from the Senate, which suspended the proceedings of the House for a few minutes. Immediately after the messenger from the Senate had retired, Maj. Anthony rose from his seat, and said he wished to explain, that he did not intend to insult the Speaker or the House; when Wilson, interrupting, peremptorily ordered him to take his seat. Maj. Anthony said, as a member, he had *a* right to the floor, to explain himself. Wilson said, in an angry tone, 'Sit down, or you had better;' and thrust his hand into his bosom, and drew out a large bowie knife, 10 or 11 inches in length, and descended from the Speaker's chair to the floor, with the knife drawn in a menacing manner. Maj. Anthony, seeing the danger he was placed in, by Wilson's advance on him with a drawn knife, rose from his chair, set it out of his way, stepped back a pace or two, and drew his knife. Wilson caught up a chair, and struck Anthony with it. Anthony, recovering from the blow, caught the chair in his left hand, and a fight ensued over the chair. Wilson received two wounds, one on each arm, and Anthony lost his knife, either by throwing it at Wilson, or it escaped by accident. After Anthony had lost his knife, Wilson advanced on Anthony, who was then retreating, looking over his shoulder. Seeing Wilson pursuing him, he threw a chair. Wilson still pursued, and Anthony raised another chair as high as his breast, with a view, it is supposed, of keeping Wilson off. Wilson then caught hold of the chair with his left hand, raised it up, and with his right hand deliberately thrust the knife, up to the hilt, into Anthony's heart, and as deliberately drew it out, and wiping off the blood with his thumb and finger, retired near to the Speaker's chair.

"As the knife was withdrawn from Anthony's heart, he fell a lifeless corpse on the floor, without uttering a word, or scarcely making a struggle; so true did the knife, as deliberately directed, pierce his heart.

"Three days elapsed before the constituted authorities took any notice of this horrible deed; and not then, until a relation of the murdered Anthony had demanded a warrant for the apprehension of Wilson. Several days then elapsed before he was brought before an examining court. He then, in a carriage and four, came to the place appointed for his trial. Four or five days were employed in the examination of witnesses, and never was a clearer case of murder proved than on that occasion. Notwithstanding, the court (Justice Brown dissenting) admitted Wilson to bail, and positively refused that the prosecuting attorney for the state should introduce the law, to show that it was not a bailable case, or even to hear an argument from him.

"At the time appointed for the session of the Circuit Court, Wilson appeared agreeably to his recognizance. A motion was made by Wilson's counsel for *change of venue,* founded on the affidavits of Wilson, and two other men. The court thereupon removed the case to Saline County, and ordered the Sheriff to take Wilson into custody, and deliver him over to the Sheriff of Saline County.

"The Sheriff of Pulaski never confined Wilson one minute, but permitted him to go where he pleased, without a guard, or any restraint imposed on him whatever. On his way to Saline, he entertained him freely at his own house, and the next day delivered him over to the Sheriff of that county, who conducted the prisoner to the debtor's room in the jail and gave him the key so that he and everybody else had free egress and ingress at all times. Wilson invited everybody to call on him, as he wished to see his friends, and his room was crowded with visitors, who called to drink grog, and laugh and talk with him. But this theatre was not sufficiently large for his purpose. He afterwards visited the dram-shops, where he freely treated all that would partake with him, and went fishing and hunting with others at pleasure, and entirely without restraint. He also ate at the same table with the Judge, while on trial.

"When the court met at Saline, Wilson was put on his trial. Several days were occupied in examining the witnesses in the case. After the examination was closed, while Col. Taylor was engaged in a very able, lucid, and argumentative speech, on the part of the prosecution, some man collected a parcel of the rabble, and came within a few yards of the court-house door, and bawled in a loud voice, 'part them—part them!' Everybody supposed there was an affray, and ran to the doors and windows to see; behold, there was nothing more than the man, and the rabble he had collected around him, for the purpose of annoying Col. Taylor while speaking. A few minutes afterwards, this same person brought a horse near the court-house door, and commenced crying the horse, as though he was for sale, and continued for ten or fifteen minutes to ride before the court-house door, crying the horse, in a loud and boisterous tone of voice. The Judge sat as a silent listener to the indignity thus offered the court and counsel by this man, without interposing his authority.

"To show the depravity of the times, and the people, after the verdict had been delivered by the jury, and the court informed Wilson that he was discharged, there was a rush toward him; some seized him by the hand, some by the arm, and there was great and loud rejoicing and exultation, directly in the presence of the court; and Wilson told the Sheriff to take the jury to a grocery, that he might treat them, and invited everybody that chose to go. The house was soon filled to overflowing. The rejoicing was kept up till near supper time, but to cap the climax, soon after supper was over, a majority of the jury, together with many others, went to the rooms that had been occupied several days by the friend and relation of the murdered Anthony, and commenced a scene of the most ridiculous dancing, (as it is believed,) in triumph for Wilson, and as a triumph over the feelings of the relations of the departed Anthony. The scene did not close here. The party retired to a dram-shop, and continued their rejoicing until about half after 10 o'clock. They then collected a parcel of horns, trumpets, &c., and marched through the streets, blowing them, till near day, when one of the company rode his horse in the porch adjoining the room which was occupied by the relations of the deceased."

This case is given to the reader at length, in order fully to show, that in a community where the law sanctions the commission of every species of outrage upon one class of citizens, it fosters passions which will paralyze its power to protect the other classes. Look at the facts developed in this case, as exhibiting the state of society among slaveholders.

1st. That the members of the legislature are *in the habit* of wearing bowie knives. Wilson's knife was 10 or 11 inches long.*

* A correspondent of the "Frederick Herald," writing from Little Rock, says, "Anthony's knife was about *twenty-eight inches* in length. They *all* carry knives here, or pistols. There are several kinds of knives in use—a narrow blade, and about twelve inches long, is called an "Arkansas tooth-pick."

2d. The murderer, Wilson, was a man of wealth, president of the bank at the capital of the state, a high military officer, and had, for many years, been Speaker of the House of Representatives, as appears from a previous statement in the Arkansas Gazette.

3d. The murder was committed in open day, before all the members of the House, and many spectators, not one of whom seems to have made the least attempt to intercept Wilson, as he advanced upon Anthony with his knife drawn, but "made way for him," as is stated in another account.

4th. Though the murder was committed in the State-house, at the capital of the state, days passed before the civil authorities moved in the matter; and they did not finally do it, until the relations of the murdered man demanded a warrant for the apprehension of the murderer. Even then, several days elapsed before he was brought before an examining court. When his trial came on, he drove to it in state, drew up before the door with "his coach and four," alighted, and strided into court like a lord among his vassals; and there, though a clearer case of deliberate murder never reeked in the face of the sun, yet he was admitted to bail, the court absolutely refusing to hear an argument from the prosecuting attorney, showing that it was not a bailable case.

5th. The sheriff of Pulaski county, who had Wilson in custody, "never confined him a moment, but permitted him to go at large wholly unrestrained." When transferred to Saline co. for trial, the sheriff of that county gave Wilson the same liberty, and he spent his time in parties of pleasure, fishing, hunting, and at houses of entertainment.

6th. Finally, to demonstrate to the world, that justice among slaveholders is consistent with itself; that authorizing man-stealing and patronizing robbery, it will, of course, be the patron and associate of murder also; the judge who sat upon the case, and the murderer who was on trial for his life before him, were boon-companions together, eating and drinking at the same table throughout the trial. Then came the conclusion of the farce—the uproar round the court-house during the trial, drowning the voice of the prosecutor while pleading, without the least attempt by the court to put it down—then the charge of the judge to the jury, and their unanimous verdict of acquittal—then the rush from all quarters around the murderer with congratulations—the whole crowd in the court room shouting and cheering—then Wilson leading the way to a tavern, inviting the sheriff, and jury, and all present to "a treat"—then the bacchanalian revelry kept up all night, a majority of the jurors participating—the dancing, the triumphal procession through the streets with the blowing of horns and trumpets, and the prancing of horses through the porch of the house occupied by the relations of the murdered Anthony, adding insult and mockery to their agony.

A few months before this murder on the floor of the legislature, George Scott, Esq., formerly marshal of the state was shot in an affray at Van Buren, Crawford Co., Arkansas, by a man named Walker; and Robert Carothers, in an affray in St. Francis co., shot William Rachel, just as Rachel was shooting at Carothers' father. *(National Intelligencer. May* 8, 1837, *and Little Hock Gazette, August* 30,1837.)

While Wilson's trial was in progress, Mr. Gabriel Sibley was stabbed to the heart at a public dinner, in St. Francis Co., Arkansas, by James W. Grant. *(Arkansas Gazette, May* 30, 1838.)

Hardly a week before this, the following occurred:

"On the 16th ult., an encounter took place at Little Rock, Ark., between David F. Douglass, a young man of 18 or 19, and Dr. Wm. C. Howell. A shot was exchanged between them at the distance of 8 or 10 feet with double-barreled guns. The load of Douglass entered the left hip of Dr.

Howell, and a buckshot from the gun of the latter struck a negro girl, 13 or 14 years of age, just below the pit of the stomach. Douglass then fired a second time and hit Howell in the left groin, penetrating the abdomen and bladder, and causing his death in four hours. The negro girl, at the last dates, was not dead, but no hopes were entertained of her recovery. Douglass was committed to await his trial at the April term of the Circuit Court."—*Louisville Journal.*

"The Little Rock Gazette of Oct. 24, says, "We are again called upon to record the cold blooded murder of a valuable citizen. On the 10th instant, Col. John Lasater, of Franklin Co., was murdered by John W. Whitson, who deliberately shot him with a shot gun, loaded with a handful of rifle balls, six of which entered his body. He lived twelve hours after he was shot.

"Whitson is the son of William Whitson, who was unfortunately killed, about a year since, in a encounter with Col. Lasater, (who was fully exonerated from all blame by a jury,) and, in revenge of his father's death, committed this bloody deed."

These atrocities were all perpetrated within a few months of the time of the deliberate assassination, on the floor of the legislature by the speaker, already described, and are probably but a small portion of the outrages committed in that state during the same period. The state of Arkansas contains about forty-five thousand white inhabitants, which is, if we mistake not, the present population of Litchfield County, Connecticut. And we venture the assertion, that a public affray, with deadly weapons, has not taken place in that county for fifty years, if indeed ever since its settlement, a century and a half ago.

MISSOURI
Missouri became one of the United States in 1821. Its present white population is about two hundred and fifty thousand. The following are a few of the affrays that have occurred there during the years 1837 and '38:

The "Salt River Journal" March 8, 1838, has the following:
"Fatal Affray.—An affray took place during last week, in the town of New London, between Dr. Peake and Dr. Bosley, both of that village, growing out of some trivial matter at a card party. After some words, Bosley threw a glass at Peake, which was followed up by other acts of

violence, and in the quarrel Peake stabbed Bosley, several times with a dirk, in consequence of which, Bosley died the following morning. The court of inquiry considered Peake justifiable, and discharged him from arrest."

From the **"St. Louis Republican"** of September 29, 1837:

"We learn that a fight occurred at Bowling. Green, in this state, a few days since, between Dr. Michael Reynolds and Henry Lalor. Lalor procured a gun, and Mr. Dickerson wrested the gun from him; this produced a fight between Lalor and Dickerson, in which the former stabbed the latter in the abdomen. Mr. Dickerson died of the wound."

The following was in the same paper about a month previous, August 21, 1837:

"*A Horse Thief Shot.*—A thief was caught in the act of stealing a horse on Friday last, on the opposite side of the river, by a company of persons out sporting. Mr. Kremer, who was in the company, leveled his rifle and ordered him to stop; which he refused; he then fired and lodged the contents in the thief's body, of which he died soon afterwards. Mr. K. went before a magistrate, who after hearing the case, REFUSED TO HOLD HIM FOR FURTHER TRIAL!"

On the 5th of July, 1838, Alpha P. Buckley murdered William Yaochum in an affray in Jackson County, Missouri. (**Missouri Republican,** July 24, 1838.)

General Atkinson of the United States Army was waylaid on the 4th of September, 1838, by a number of persons, and attacked in his carriage near St. Louis, on the road to Jefferson Barracks, but escaped after shooting one of the assailants. **The New Orleans True American** of October 29, '38, speaking of this says: "It will be recollected that a few weeks ago, Judge Dougherty, one of the most respectable citizens of St. Louis, was murdered upon the same road."

The same paper contains the following letter from the murderer of Judge Dougherty.

"*Murder of Judge Dougherty.*—The St. Louis Republican received the following mysterious letter, unsealed, regarding this brutal murder:"— "Natchez, Miss., Sept. 24. "Messrs. Editors:—Revenge is sweet. On the night of the 11th, 12th, and 13th, I made preparations, and did, on the 14th July kill a rascal, and only regret that I have not the privilege of telling the circumstance. I have so placed it that I can never be identified; and further,

I have no compunctions of conscience for the death of Thomas M. Dougherty."

But instead of presenting individual affrays and single atrocities, however numerous, (and the Missouri papers abound with them,) in order to exhibit the true state of society there, we refer to the fact now universally notorious, that for months during the last fall and winter, some hundreds of inoffensive Mormons, occupying a considerable tract of land, and a flourishing village in the interior of the state, have suffered every species of inhuman outrage from the inhabitants of the surrounding counties—that for weeks together, mobs consisting of hundreds and thousands, kept them in a state of constant siege, laying waste their lands, destroying their cattle and provisions, tearing down their houses, ravishing the females, seizing and dragging off and killing the men. Not one of the thousands engaged in these horrible outrages and butcherings has, so far as we can learn, been indicted. The following extract of a letter from a military officer of one of the brigades ordered out by the Governor of Missouri, to terminate the matter, is taken from the North Alabamian of December 22, 1838:

Correspondence of the Nashville Whig.

THE MORMON WAR. Millersburg, Mo. November 8."

Dear Sir—A lawless mob had organized themselves for the express purpose of driving the Mormons from the country, or exterminating them, for no other reason, that I can perceive, than that these poor deluded creatures owned a large and fertile body of land in their neighborhood, and would not let them (the Mobocrats) have it for their own price. I have just returned from the seat of difficulty, and am perfectly conversant with all the facts in relation to it. The mob meeting with resistance altogether unanticipated, called loudly upon the kindred spirits of adjacent counties for help. The Mormons determined to die in defense of their rights, set about fortifying their town "Far West," with a resolution and energy that kept the mob (who all the time were extending their cries of help to all parts of Missouri) at bay. The Governor, from exaggerated accounts of the Mormon depredations, issued orders for the raising of several thousand mounted riflemen, of which this division raised five hundred, and the writer of this was *honored* with the appointment of_____to the Brigade.

"On the first day of this month, we marched for the "seat of war," but General Clark, Commander-in-chief, having reached Far West on the day previous with a large force, the difficulty was settled when we arrived, so we escaped the infamy and disgrace of a bloody victory. Before General Clark's arrival, the mob had increased to about four thousand, and determined to attack the town. The Mormons upon the approach of the mob, sent out *a* white flag, which being fired on by the mob, Jo Smith and Rigdon, and a *few* other Mormons of less influence, gave themselves up to the mob, with a view of so far appeasing their wrath as to save their women and children from violence. Vain hope! The prisoners being secured, the mob entered the town and perpetrated every conceivable act of brutality and outrage—forcing fifteen or twenty Mormon girls to yield to their brutal passions!!! Of these things I was assured by many persons while I was at Far West, in whose veracity I have the utmost confidence. I conversed with many of the prisoners, who numbered about eight hundred, among whom there were many young and interesting girls, and I assure you, a more distracted set of creatures I never saw. I assure you, my dear sir, it was peculiarly heart rending to see old gray headed fathers and mothers, young ladies and innocent babes, forced at this inclement season, with the thermometer at 8 degrees below zero, to abandon their warm houses, and many of them the luxuries and elegances of a high degree of civilization and intelligence, and take up their march for the uncultivated wilds of the Missouri frontier.

"The better informed here have but one opinion of the result of this Mormon persecution, and that is, it is a most fearful extension of "Judge Lynch's" jurisdiction."

The present white population of Missouri is but thirty thousand less than that of New Hampshire, and yet the insecurity of human life in the former state to that in the latter, is probably at least twenty to one.

ALABAMA

This state was admitted to the Union in 1819. Its present white population is not far from three hundred thousand. The security of human life in Alabama may be inferred from the facts and testimony which follow:

The Mobile Register of Nov. 15, 1837, contains the annual message of Mr. McVay, the acting Governor of the state, at the opening of the Legislature. The message has the following on the frequency of homicides:

"We hear of homicides in different parts of the state *continually,* and yet how few convictions for murder, and still fewer executions? How is this to be accounted for? In regard to 'assault and battery with intent to commit murder,' why is it that this offense continues so common—why do we hear of stabbings and shootings *almost daily* in some part or other of our state?"

The "Montgomery (Alabama) Advertiser" of April 22, 1837, has the following from the Mobile Register:

"Within a few days a man was shot in an affray in the upper part of the town, and has since died. The perpetrator of the violence is at large. We need hardly speak of another scene which occurred in Royal Street, when a fray occurred between two individuals, a third standing by with a cocked pistol to prevent interference. On Saturday night a still more exciting scene of outrage took place in the theatre.

"An altercation commenced at the porquett entrance between the check-taker and a young man, which ended in the first being desperately wounded by a stab with a knife. The other also drew a pistol. If some strange manifestations of public opinion, do not coerce a spirit of deference to law, and the abandonment of the habit of carrying secret arms, we shall deserve every reproach we may receive, and have our punishment in the unchecked growth of a spirit of lawlessness, reckless deeds, and exasperated feeling, which will destroy our social comfort at home, and respectability abroad."

From the **"Huntsville Democrat," of Nov. 7, 1837"** A trifling dispute arose between Silas Randal and Pharaoh Massingale, both of Marshall County. They exchanged but a few words, when the former drew a Bowie knife and stabbed the latter in the abdomen fronting the left hip to the depth of several inches; also inflicted several other dangerous wounds, of which Massengale died immediately.—Randal is yet at large, not having been apprehended."

From the **"Free Press"** of August 16, 1838."The streets of Gainesville, Alabama, have recently been the scene of a most tragic affair. Some five weeks since, at a meeting of the citizens, Col. Christopher Scott, a lawyer of good standing, and one of the most influential citizens of the place, made a violent attack on the Tombeckbee Rail Road Company. A Mr. Smith, agent for the T. R. R. Company, took Col. C's remarks as a personal insult, and demanded an explanation. A day or two after, as Mr. Smith was passing Colonel Scott's door, he was shot down by him, and after lingering a few hours expired.

"It appears also from an Alabama paper, that Col. Scott's brother, L. S. Scott Esq., and L. J. Smith Esq., were accomplices of the Colonel in the murder."

The following is from the **"Natchez Free Trader"** June 14, 1838.

"An affray, attended with fatal consequences, occurred in the town of Moulton, Alabama, on the 12th May. It appears that three young men from the country, of the name of J. Walton, Geo. Bowling, and Alexander Bowling, rode into Moulton on that day for the purpose of chastising the bar-keeper at McCord's tavern, whose name is Cowan, for an alleged insult offered by him to the father of young Walton. They made a furious attack on Cowan, and drove him into the bar room of the tavern. Sometime after, a second attack was made upon Cowan in the street by one of the Bowlings and Walton, when pistols were resorted to by both parties. Three rounds were fired, and the third shot, which was said to have been discharged by Walton, struck a young man by the name of Neil, who happened to be passing in the street at the time, and killed him instantly. The combatants were taken into custody, and after an examination before two magistrates, were bailed."

The following exploits of the "Alabama Volunteers," are recorded in the **Florida Herald,** Jan. 1, 1838.

"Save Us From Our Friends.—On Monday last, a large body of men, calling themselves Alabama Volunteers, arrived in the vicinity of this city. It is reported that their conduct during their march from Tallahassee to this city has been a series of excesses of every description. They have committed almost every crime except murder, and have even threatened life.

"Large numbers of them paraded our streets, grossly insulted our females, and were otherwise extremely riotous in their conduct. One of the squads, forty or fifty in number, on reaching the bridge, where there was a small guard of three or four men stationed, assaulted the guard, overturned the sentry-box into the river, and bodily seized two of the guards, and threw them into the river, where the water was deep, and they were forced to swim for their lives. At one of the men while in the water, they pointed a musket, threatening to kill him; and pelted with every missile which came to hand."

The following Alabama tragedy is published by the **"Columbia (S.C.) Telescope"** Sept. 16, 1837, from the Wetumpka Sentinel:

"Our highly respectable townsman, Mr. Hugh Ware, a merchant of Wetumpka, was standing in the door of his counting-room, between the hours of 8 and 9 o'clock at night, in company with a friend, when an assassin lurked within a few paces of his position, and discharged his musket, loaded with ten or fifteen buckshot. Mr. Ware instantly fell, and expired without a struggle or a groan. A coroner's inquest decided that the deceased came to his death by violence, and that Abner J. Cody, and his servant John, were the perpetrators. John frankly confessed, that his master, Cody, compelled him to assist, threatening his life if he dared to disobey; that he carried the musket to the place at which it was discharged; that his master then received it from him, rested it on the fence, fired and killed Mr. Ware."

From the **"Southern (Miss.) Mechanic"** April 17, 1838:

"**Horrid Butchery.**—A desperate fight occurred in Montgomery, Alabama, on the 28th ult. We learn from the Advocate of that city, that the persons engaged were Wm. S. Mooney and Kenyon Mooney, his son, Edward Bell, and Bushrod Bell, Jr. The first received a wound in the abdomen, made by that fatal instrument, the Bowie knife, which caused his death in about fifteen hours. The second was shot in the side, and would doubtless have been killed, had not the ball partly lost its force by first striking his arm. The third received a shot in the neck, and now lies without hope of recovery. The fourth escaped unhurt, and, we understand has fled. This is a brief statement of one of the bloodiest fights that we ever heard of."

From the **"Virginia Statesman"** May 6, 1837:

"Several affrays, wherein pistols, dirks and knives were used, lately occurred at Mobile. One took place on the 8th inst., at the theatre, in which a Mr. Bellum was so badly stabbed that his life is despaired of. On the Wednesday preceding, a man named Johnson shot another named Snow dead. No notice was taken of the affair."

From the **"Huntsville Advocate"** June 20, 1837:

Desperate Affray.—On Sunday the 11th inst., an affray of desperate and fatal character occurred near Chater's Landing, Marshall County,

Alabama. The dispute which led to it arose out of a contested right to *possession* of a piece of land. A Mr. Steele was the occupant, and Mr. James McFarlane and some others, claimants. Mr. F. and his friends went to Mr. Steele's house with a view to take possession, whether peaceably or by violence, we do not certainly know. As they entered the house a quarrel ensued between two of the opposite parties, and some blows perhaps followed; in a short time, several guns were discharged from the house at Mr. McFarlane and friends. Mr. M. was killed, a Mr. Freamster dangerously wounded, and it is thought will not recover; two others were also wounded, though not so as to endanger life. Mr. Steele's brother was wounded by the discharge of a pistol from one of Mr. M's. friends. We have heard some other particulars about the affray, but we abstain from giving them, as incidental versions are often erroneous, and as the whole matter will be submitted to legal investigation. Four of Steele's party, his brother, and three whose names are Lemen, Collins and Wilis, have been arrested, and are now confined in the jail in this place."

From the **"Norfolk Beacon"** July 14, 1838:

"A few days since at Claysville, Marshal Co., Alabama, Messrs. Nathaniel and Graves W. Steele, while riding in a carriage, were shot dead, and Alex. Steele and Wm. Collins, also in the carriage, were severely wounded, (the former supposed mortally,) by Messrs. Jesse Allen, Alexander and Arthur McFarlane, and Daniel Dickerson. The Steeles, it appears, last year killed James McFarlane and another person in a similar manner, which led to this dreadful retaliation."

From the **"Montgomery (Ala.) Advocate"**, Washington, Autauga Co., Dec. 28, 1838:

"Fatal Rencontre.—On Friday last, the 28th ult., a fatal rencontre took place in the town of Washington, Autauga County, between John Tittle and Thomas J. Tarleton, which resulted in the death of the former. After a patient investigation of the matter, Mr. Tarleton was released by the investigating tribunal, on the ground that the homicide was clearly justifiable."

The **"Columbus (Ga.) Sentinel"** July 6, 1837, quotes the following from the Mobile (Ala.) Examiner:

"A man by the name of Peter Church was killed on one of the wharves night before last. The person by whom it was done delivered himself to the proper authorities yesterday morning. The deceased and his destroyer were friends, and the act occurred in consequence of an immaterial quarrel."

The **"Milledgeville Federal Union"** of July 11, 1837 has the following:

"In Selma, Alabama, resided lately messrs. Philips and Dickerson, physicians. Mr. P. is brother to the wife of W. Bleevin Esq., a rich cotton planter in that neighborhood; the latter has a very lovely daughter, to whom Dr. D. paid his addresses. A short time since a gentleman from Mobile married her. Soon after this, a schoolmaster in Selma set a story afloat to the effect, that he had heard Dr. D. say things about the lady's conduct before marriage which ought not to be said about any lady. Dr. D. denied having said such things, and the other denied having spread the story; but neither denials sufficed to pacify the enraged parent. He met Dr. D. fired at him two pistols, and wounded him. Dr. D. was unarmed, and advanced to Mr. Bleevin, holding up his hands imploringly, when Mr. B. drew a Bowie knife, and stabbed him to the heart. The doctor dropped dead on the spot: and Mr. Bleevin has been held to bail."

The following is taken from the **"Alabama Intelligencer"** Sept. 17, 1838:

"On the 5th instant, a deadly rencounter took place in the streets of Russelville, (our county town,) between John A. Chambers, Esq., of the city of mobile, and Thomas L. Jones, of this county. In the rencounter, Jones was wounded by several balls which took effect in his chin, mouth, neck, arm, and shoulder, believed to be mortal; he did not fire his gun.

"Mr. Chambers forthwith surrendered himself to the Sheriff of the county, and was on the 6th, tried and fully acquitted, by a court of inquiry."

The **"Maysville (Ky.) Advocate"** of August 14, 1838, gives the following affray, which took place in Girard, Alabama, July 10th:

"Two brothers named Thomas and Hal Lucas, who had been much in the habit of quarrelling, came together under strong excitement, and Tom, as was his frequent custom, being about to flog Hal with a stick of some sort, the latter drew a pistol and shot the former, his own brother, through the heart, who almost instantly expired!"

The **"New Orleans Bee"** of Oct. 5, 1838, relates an affray in Mobile, Alabama, between Benjamin Alexander, an aged man of ninety, with Thomas Hamilton, his grandson, on the 24th of September, in which the former killed the latter with a dirk.

The **"Red River Whig"** of July 7, 1838, gives the particulars of a tragedy in Western Alabama, in which a planter near Lakeville, left home for some days, but suspecting his wife's fidelity, returned home late at night, and finding his suspicions verified, set fire to his house and waited with his rifle before the door, till his wife and her paramour attempted to rush out, when he shot them both dead.

From the **"Morgan (Ala.) Observer"** Dec. 1838:

"We are informed from private sources, that on last Saturday, a poor man who was moving westward with his wife and three little children, and driving a small drove of sheep, and perhaps a cow or two, which was driven by his family, on arriving in Florence, and while passing through, met with a citizen of that place, who rode into his flock and caused him some trouble to keep it together, when the mover informed the individual that he must not do so again or he would throw a rock at him, upon which some words ensued, and the individual again disturbed the flock, when the mover, as near as we can learn, threw at him upon this the troublesome man got off his horse, went into a grocery, got a gun, and came out and deliberately shot the poor stranger in the presence of his wife and little children. The wounded man then made an effort to get into some house, when his murderous assailant overtook and stabbed him to the heart with a Bowie *knife*. This revolting scene, we are informed, occurred in the presence of many citizens, who, report says, never even lifted their voices in defense of the murdered man."

A late number of the **"Flag of the Union"** published at Tuscaloosa, the seat of the government of Alabama, states that since the commencement of the late session of the legislature of that state, "no less than thirteen fights had been had within sight of the capitol."*Pistols and Bowie knives were used in every case.*

The present white population of Alabama is about the same with that of New Jersey, yet for the last twenty years there have not been so many public deadly affrays, and of such a horrible character, in New Jersey, as have taken place in Alabama within the last eight months.

MISSISSIPPI

Mississippi became one of the United States in 1817. Its present white population is about one hundred and sixty thousand.

The following extracts will serve to show that those who combine together to beat, rob, and manacle innocent men, women and children, will stick at nothing when their passions are up.

The following murderous affray at Canton, Mississippi, is from the **"Alabama Beacon"** Sept, 13, 1838:

"A terrible tragedy recently occurred at Canton, Miss., growing out of the late duel between Messrs. Dickins and Drane of that place. A Kentuckian happening to be in Canton, spoke of the duel, and charged Mr. Mitchell Calhoun, the second of Drane, with cowardice and unfairness. Mr. Calhoun called on the Kentuckian for an explanation, and the offensive charge was repeated. *A challenge and fight with Bowie knives, toe to toe,* were the consequences. Both parties were dreadfully and dangerously wounded, though neither was dead at the last advices. Mr. Calhoun is a brother to the Hon. John Calhoun, member of Congress."

Here follows the account of the duel referred to above, between Messrs. Dickins and Drane:

"Intelligence has been received in this town of a fatal duel that took place in Canton, Miss., on the 28th ultl., between Rufus K. Dickins, and a Mr. Westley Drane. They fought with double barreled guns, loaded with buckshot—both were mortally wounded."

The **"Louisville Journal"** publishes the following, Nov. 23:

"On the 7th instant, a fatal affray took place at Gallatin, Mississippi. The principal parties concerned were, Messrs. John W. Scott, James G. Scott, and Edmund B. Hatch. The latter was shot down and then stabbed twice through the body, by J. G. Scott."

The **"Alabama Beacon"** of Sept. 13, 1838, says: "An attempt was made in Vicksburg lately, by a gang of Lynchers, to inflict summary punishment on three men of the name of Fleckenstein. The assault was made upon the house, about 11 o'clock at night. Meeting with some resistance from the three Fleckensteins, a leader of the gang, by the name of Helt, discharged his pistol, and wounded one of the brothers severely in the neck and jaws. A volley of four or five shots was almost instantly returned, when Helt fell dead, a piece of the top of the skull being torn off, and almost the whole of his brains dashed out. His comrades seeing him fall, suddenly took to their heels. There were, it is supposed, some *ten or fifteen* concerned in the transaction."

The **"Manchester (Miss.) Gazette"** August 11, 1838, says:

"It appears that Mr. Asa Hazeltine, who kept a public or boarding house in Jackson, during the past winter, and Mr. Benjamin Tanner, came here about five or six weeks since, with the intention of opening a public house. Foiled in the design, in the settlement of their affairs some difficulty arose as to a question of veracity between the parties. Mr. Tanner deeply excited, procured a pistol and loaded it with the charge of death, sought and found the object of his hatred in the afternoon, in the yard of Messrs. Kezer & Maynard, and in the presence of several persons, after repeated and ineffectual attempts on the part of Capt. Jackson to baffle his fell spirit, shot the unfortunate victim, of which wound Mr. Hazeltine died in a short time.

O" "We understand that Mr. Hazeltine was a native of Boston."

The **"Columbia (S.C.) Telescope"** Sept. 16, 1837, gives the details below:

"By a letter from Mississippi, we have an account of a rencontre which took place in Rodney, on the 27th July, between Messrs. Thos. J. Johnston and G. H. Wilcox, both formerly of this city. In consequence of certain publications made by these gentlemen against each other, Johnston challenged Wilcox. The latter declining to accept the challenge, Johnston informed his friends at Rodney that he would be there at the term of the court then not distant, when he would make an attack upon him. He repaired thither on the 26th and on the next morning the following communication was read aloud in the presence of Wilcox and a large crowd:

"Rodney July 27, 1837.

"Mr. Johnston informs Mr. Wilcox, that at or about 1 o'clock of this day, he will be on the common, opposite the Presbyterian Church of this town, waiting and expecting Mr. Wilcox to meet him there.

"I pledge my honor that Mr. Johnston will not fire at Mr. Wilcox, until he arrives at a distance of one hundred yards from him, and I desire Mr. Wilcox or any of his friends, to see that distance accurately measured.

"Mr. Johnston will wait there thirty minutes. "J. M. DUFFIELD.

"Mr. Wilcox declined being a party to any such arrangement, and Mr. D. told him to be prepared for an attack. Accordingly, about an hour after this, Johnston proceeded towards Wilcox's office, armed with a double-barreled gun, (one of the barrels rifled,) and three pistols in his belt. He halted about fifty yards from W's door and leveled his gun. W. withdrew before Johnston could fire, and seized a musket, returned to the door and flashed. Johnston fired both barrels without effect. Wilcox then seized a double barrel gun, and Johnston a musket, and both again fired. Wilcox sent twenty-three buck shot over Johnston's head, one of them passing through his hat, and Wilcox was slightly wounded on both hands, his thigh and leg."

From the **"Alabama Beacon"** May 27, 1838:

"An affray of the most barbarous nature was expected to take place in Arkansas opposite Princeton, on Thursday last. The two original parties .have been endeavoring for several weeks, to settle their differences at Natchez. One of the individuals concerned stood pledged, our informant states, to fight three different antagonists in one day. The fights, we understand, were to be with pistols; but a variety of other weapons were taken along—among others, the deadly Bowie knife. These latter instruments, we are told, were whetted and dressed up at Grand Gulf, as the parties passed up, avowedly with the intention of being used in the field."

From the **"Southern (Miss) Argus"** Nov. 21, 1837:

"We learn that, at a wood yard above Natchez, on Sunday evening last, a difficulty arose between Captain Crosly, of the steamboat Galenian, and one of his deck passengers. Capt. C. drew a Bowie knife, and made a pass at the throat of the passenger, which failed to do any harm, and the captain then ordered him to leave his boat. The man went on board to get his baggage, and the captain immediately sought the cabin for a pistol. As the passenger was about leaving the boat, the captain presented a pistol to his breast, which snapped. Instantly the enraged and wronged individual seized Capt. Crosly by the throat, and brought him to the ground, when he drew a dirk and stabbed him eight or nine times in the breast, each blow driving the weapon into his body up to the hilt. The passenger was arrested, carried to Natchez, tried and acquitted."

The **"Planter's Intelligencer"** publishes the following from the Vicksburg Sentinel of June 19, 1838:

"About 1 o'clock, we observed two men ' pummeling" one another in the street, to the infinite amusement of a crowd. Presently a third hero made his appearance in the arena, with Bowie knife in hand, and he cried out, 'Let me come at him!' Upon hearing this threat, one of the pugilists ' took himself off,' our hero following at full speed. Finding his pursuit was vain, our hero returned, when an attack was commenced upon an. other individual. He was most cruelly beat, and cut through the skull with a knife; it is feared the wounds will prove mortal. The sufferer, we learn, is an inoffensive German."

From the **"Mississippian"** Nov. 9, 1838:

"On Tuesday evening last, 23d, an affray occurred at the town of Tallahassee, in this county, between Hugh Roark and Captain Flack, which resulted in the death of Roark. Roark went to bed, and Flack, who was in the bar-room below, observed to some persons there, that he believed they had set up Roark to whip him; Roark, upon hearing his name mentioned, got out of bed and came down stairs. Flack met and stabbed him in the lower part of his abdomen with a knife, letting out his bowels. Roark ran to the door, and received another stab in the back. He lived until Thursday night, when he expired in great agony. Flack was tried before a justice of the peace, and we understand was only held to bail to appear at court in the event Roark should die."

From the **"Grand Gulf Advertiser"** Nov. 7, 1838:

Attempt at Riot at Natchez.—The *Courier* says, that in consequence of the discharge of certain individuals who had been arraigned for the murder of a man named Medill, a mob of about 200 persons assembled on the night of the 1st instant, with the avowed purpose of *lynching* them. But fortunately, the objects of their vengeance had escaped from town. Foiled in their purpose, the rioters repaired to the shantee where the murder was committed, and precipitated it over the bluff. The military of the city were ordered out to keep order."

From the **"Natchez Free Trader:"**

"A violent attack was lately made on Captain Barrett, of the steamboat Southerner, by three persons from Wilkinson Co., Miss., whose names are Carey, and one of the name of J. S. Towles. The only reason for the outrage was, that Captain B. had the assurance to require of the gentlemen, who were quarreling on board his boat, to keep order for the peace and comfort of the other passengers. *Towles* drew a Bowie knife upon the

Captain, which the latter wrested from him. A pistol, drawn by one of the Careys was also taken, and the assailant was knocked overboard. Fortunately for him he was rescued from drowning. The brave band then landed. On her return up the river, the Southerner stopped at Fort Adams, and on her leaving that place, an armed party, among whom were the Careys and Towles, fired into the boat, but happily the shot missed a crowd of passengers on the hurricane deck."

From the **"Mississippian"** Dec. 18, 1838:

"Greer Spikes, a citizen of this county, was killed a few days ago, between this place and Raymond, by a man named Pegram. It seems that Pegram and Spikes had been carrying weapons for each other for some time past. Pegram had threatened to take Spikes' life on first sight, for the base treatment he had received at his hands.

"We have heard something of the particulars, but not enough to give them at this time. Pegram had not been seen since."

The **"Lynchburg Virginian"** July 23, 1838, says:

"A fatal affray occurred a *few* days ago in Clinton, Mississippi. The actors in it were a Mr. Parham, Mr. Shackleford, and a Mr. Henry. Shackleford was killed on the spot, and Henry was slightly wounded by a shot gun with which Parham was armed."

From the **" Columbus (Ga.) Sentinel"** Nov. 22, 1838.

"*Butchery.*—A Bowie knife slaughter took place a few days since in Honesville, Miss. A Mr. Hobbs was the victim; Strother the butcher."

The **"Vicksburg Sentinel"** Sept. 28, 1837, says: "It is only a few weeks since humanity was shocked by a most atrocious outrage, inflicted by the Lynchers, on the person of a Mr. Saunderson of Madison Co. in this state. They dragged this respectable planter from the bosom of his family, and mutilated him in the most brutal manner—maiming him most inhumanly, besides cutting off his nose and ears and scarifying his body to the very ribs! We believe the subject of this foul outrage still drags out a miserable existence—an object of horror and of pity. Last week a club of Lynchers, amounting to four or five individuals, as we have been credibly informed, broke into the house of Mr. Scott of Wilkinson Co., a respectable member of the bar, forced him out, and hung him dead on the next tree. We have heard of numerous minor outrages committed against the peace of society, and the welfare and happiness of the country; but we mention these as the most enormous that we have heard for some months.

"It now becomes our painful duty, to notice a most disgraceful outrage committed by the Lynchers of Vicksburg, on last Sunday. The victim was a Mr. Grace, formerly of the neighborhood of Warrenton, Va., but for two years a resident of this city. He was detected in giving free passes to slaves and brought to trial before Squire Maxcy. Unfortunately for the wretch, either through the want of law or evidence, he could not be punished and he was set at liberty by the magistrate. The city marshal seeing that a few in the crowd were disposed to lay violent hands on the prisoner in the event of his escaping punishment by law, resolved to accompany him to his house. The Lynch mob still followed, and the marshal finding the prisoner could only be protected by hurrying him to jail, endeavored to effect that object. The Lynchers, however, pursued the officer of the law, dragged him from his horse, bruised him, and conveyed the prisoner to the most convenient point of the city for carrying their blood-thirsty designs into execution. We blush while we record the atrocious deed; in this city, containing nearly 5,000 souls, in the broad light of day, this aged wretch was stripped and flogged, we believe within hearing of the lamentations and the shrieks of his afflicted wife and children."

In an affray at Montgomery, Mississippi, July 1, 1838, Mr. A. L. Herbert was killed by Dr. J. B. Harrington. See **Grand Gulf Advertiser, August 1, 1838.**

The **"Maryland Republican"** of January 30, 1838, has the following:

"A street rencounter lately took place in Jackson, Miss., between Mr. Robert McDonald and Mr. W. H. Lockhart, in which McDonald was shot with a pistol and immediately expired. Lockhart was committed to prison."

The **"Nashville Banner,"** June 22, 1838, has the following:

"On the 8th inst. Col. James M. Hulet was shot with a rifle without any apparent provocation in Gallatin, Miss., by one Richard M. Jones."

From the **"Huntsville Democrat"** Dec. 8, 1838:

"The Aberdeen (Miss.) Advocate, of Saturday last, states that on the morning of the day previous, (the 9th) a dispute arose between Mr. Robert Smith and Mr. Alexander Eanes, both of Aberdeen, which resulted in the death of Mr. Smith, who kept a boarding-house, and was an amiable man and a good citizen. In the course of the contradictory words of the disputants, the lie was given by Eanes, upon which Smith gathered up a piece of iron and threw it at Eanes, but which missed him and lodged in the walls of the house. At this, Eanes drew a large dirk knife, and stabbed

Smith in the abdomen, the knife penetrating the vitals, and thus causing immediate death. Smith breathed only a few seconds after the fatal thrust.

"Eanes immediately mounted his horse and rode off, but was pursued by Mr. Hanes, who arrested and took him back, when he was put under guard to await a trial before the proper authorities."

From the **"Vicksburg Register"** Nov. 17, 1838:

"On the 2d inst. an affray occurred between one Stephen Scarbrough and A. W. Higbee of Grand Gulf, in which Scarbrough was stabbed with a knife, which occasioned his death in a few hours. Higbee has been arrested and committed for trial."

From the "Huntsville (Ala.) Democrat" Nov. 10, 1838:

"Life in the Southwest.—A friend in Louisiana writes, under date of the 31st ult., that a fight took place a few days ago in Madison parish, 60 miles below Lake Providence, between a Mr. Nevils and a Mr. Harper, which terminated fatally. The police jury had ordered a road on the right bank of the Mississippi, and the neighboring planters were out with their forces to open it. For some offense, Nevils, the superintendent of the operations, flogged two of Harper's negroes. The next day the parties met on horseback, when Harper dismounted, and proceeded to cowskin Nevils for the chastisement inflicted on the negroes. Nevils immediately drew a pistol and shot his assailant dead on the spot. Both were gentlemen of the highest respectability.

"An affray also came off recently, as the same correspondent writes us, in Raymond, Hinds co., Miss., which for a serious one, was rather amusing. The sheriff had a process to serve on a man of the name of Bright, and, in consequence of some difficulty and intemperate language, thought proper to commence the service by the application of his cowskin to the defendant. Bright thereupon floored his adversary, and, wresting his cowhide from him, applied it to its owner to the extent of at least five hundred lashes, meanwhile threatening to shoot the first bystander who attempted to interfere. The sheriff was carried home in a state of insensibility, and his life has been despaired of. The mayor of the place, however, issued his warrant, and started three of the sheriff's deputies in pursuit of the delinquent, but the latter, after keeping them at bay till they found it impossible to arrest him, surrendered himself to the magistrate, by whom he was bound over to the next Circuit Court. From the mayor's office, his honor and the parties litigant proceeded to the tavern to take a drink by way of ending hostilities. But the civil functionary refused to sign articles of peace by touching glasses with Bright, whereupon the latter made a furious assault upon him, and then turned and flogged 'mine host' within an inch of his life because he interfered. Satisfied with his day's work, Bright retired. Can we show any such specimens of chivalry and refinement in Kentucky!"

From the **"Grand Gulf (Miss.) Advertiser"** June 27, 1837:

"Death By Violence.—The moral atmosphere in our state appears to be in a deleterious and sanguinary condition. *Almost every exchange paper which reaches us contains some inhuman and revolting case of murder or death by violence. Not less than fifteen deaths by violence have occurred, to our certain knowledge, within the past three months.* Such a state of things, in a country professing to be moral and Christian, is a disgrace to human nature, and is well calculated to induce those abroad unacquainted with our general habits and feelings, to regard the morals of our people in no very enviable light; and does more to injure and weaken our political institutions than years of pecuniary distress. The frequency of such events is a burning disgrace to the morality, civilization, and refinement of feeling to which we lay claim, and so often boast, in comparison with the older states. And unless we set about and put an immediate and effectual termination to such revolting scenes, we shall be compelled to part with what all genuine southerners have ever regarded as their richest inheritance, the proud appellation of the *'brace, high-minded and chivalrous sons of the south.'*

"This done, we should soon discover a change for the better—peace and good order would prevail, and the ends of justice be effectually and speedily attained, and then the people of this wealthy state would be in a condition to bid defiance to the disgraceful reproaches which are now daily heaped upon them by the religious and moral of other states."

"The present white population of Mississippi is but little more than half as great as that of Vermont, and yet more horrible crimes are perpetrated by them Every Month, than have ever been perpetrated in Vermont since it has been a state, now about half a century. Whoever doubts it, let him get data and make his estimate, and he will find that this is no random guess.

LOUISIANA

Louisiana became one of the United States in 1811. Its present white population is about one hundred and fifteen thousand.

The extracts which follow furnish another illustration of the horrors produced by passions blown up to fury in the furnace of arbitrary power. We have just been looking over a broken file of Louisiana papers, including the last six months of 1837, and the whole of 1838, and find ourselves obliged to abandon our design of publishing even an abstract of the scores and *hundreds* of affrays, murders, assassinations, duels, lynchings, assaults, &c. which took place in that state during that period. Those which have taken place in New Orleans alone, during the last eighteen months, would, in detail, fill a volume. Instead of inserting the details of the principal atrocities in Louisiana, as in the states already noticed, we will furnish the reader with the testimony of various editors of newspapers, and others, residents of the state, which will perhaps as truly set forth the actual state of society there, as could be done by a publication of the outrages themselves.

From the **"New Orleans Bee"** of May 23, 1838:

"Contempt of human life.—In view of the crimes which are *daily* committed, we are led to inquire whether it is owing to the inefficiency of our laws, or to the manner in which those laws are administered, that this *frightful deluge of human blood flows through our streets and our places of public resort.*

"Whither will such contempt for the life of man lead us? The unhealthiness of the climate mows down annually a part of our population; the murderous steel dispatches its proportion; and if crime increases as it has, the latter will soon become *the most powerful agent in destroying life.*

"We cannot but doubt the perfection of our criminal code, when we see that *almost every criminal eludes the law,* either by boldly avowing the crime, or by the tardiness with which legal prosecutions are carried on, or, lastly, by the convenient application of *bail* in criminal cases."

The **"New Orleans Picayune"** of July 30, 1837, says:

"It is with the most painful feelings that we *daily* hear of some *fatal* duel. Yesterday we were told of the unhappy end of one of our most influential and highly respectable merchants, who fell yesterday morning at sunrise in a duel. As usual, the circumstances which led to the meeting were trivial."

The New Orleans correspondent of the **New York Express,** in his letter dated New Orleans, July 30, 1837, says:

"Thirteen Duels have been fought in and near the city during the week; five *more were to take place this morning."*

The **"New Orleans Merchant"** of March 20, 1838, says:

"Murder has been rife within the two or three weeks last past; and what is worse, the authorities of those places where they occur are *perfectly regardless of the fact."*

The **"New Orleans Bee"** of September 8, 1838, says:

"Not two months since, the miserable Barba became a victim to one of the most cold-blooded schemes of assassination that ever disgraced a civilized community. Last Sunday evening an individual, Gonzales by name, was seen in perfect health, in conversation with his friends. On Monday morning his dead body was withdrawn from the Mississippi, near the ferry of the first municipality, in a state of terrible mutilation. To cap the climax of horror, on Friday morning, about half past six o'clock, the coroner was called to hold an inquest over the body of an individual, between Magazine and Tchoupitoulas Streets. The head was entirely severed from the body; the lower extremities had likewise suffered amputation; the right foot was completely dismembered from the leg, and the left knee nearly severed from the thigh. Several stabs, wounds and bruises, were discovered on various parts of the body, which of themselves were sufficient to produce death."

The **"Georgetown (South Carolina) Union"** of May 20, 1837, has the following extract from a New Orleans paper:

"A short time since, two men shot one another down in one of our bar rooms, one of whom died instantly. A day or two after, one or two infants were found murdered, there was every reason to believe, by their own mothers. Last week we had to chronicle a brutal and bloody murder, committed in the heart of our city: the very next day a murder-trial was commenced in our criminal court: the day ensuing this, we published the particulars of Hart's murder. The day after that, Tibbetts was hung for attempting to commit a murder; the next day again we had to publish a murder committed by two Spaniards at the Lake—this was on Friday last. On Sunday we published the account of another murder committed by the

Italian, Gregorio. On Monday, another murder was committed, and the murderer lodged in jail. On Tuesday morning another man was stabbed and robbed, and is not likely to recover, but the assassin escaped. The same day Reynolds, who killed Barre, shot himself in prison. On Wednesday, another person, Mr. Nicolet, blew out his brains. Yesterday, the unfortunate George Clement destroyed himself in his cell; and in addition to this dreadful catalogue we have to add that of the death of two brothers, who destroyed themselves through grief at the death of their mother; and truly may we say that 'we know not what tomorrow will bring forth.'

The **"Louisiana Advertiser"** as quoted by the Salt River (Mo.) Journal of May 25, 1837, says: Within the last ten or twelve days, three suicides, four murders, and two executions, have occurred in the city!"

The **"New Orleans Bee"** of October 25, 1837, says:

"We remark with regret the frightful list of homicides that are *daily* committed in New Orleans."

The **"Planter's Banner"** of September 30,1838, published at Franklin, Louisiana, after giving an account of an affray between a number of planters, in which three were killed and a fourth mortally wounded, says that "Davis (one of the murderers) was arrested by the by-standers, but a *justice of the peace* came up and told them, he did not think it right to keep a man 'tied in that manner,' and 'thought it best to turn him loose.' *It was accordingly so done.*"

This occurred in the parish of Harrisonburg. The Banner closes the account by saying:

"Our informant states that *five white men* and *one* negro have been murdered in the parish of Madison, during the months of July and August." This *justice of the peace,* who bade the bystanders unloose the murderer, mentioned above, has plenty of birds of his own feather among the law officers of Louisiana. Two of the leading officers in the New Orleans police took two witnesses, while undergoing legal examination at Lexington, near New Orleans, "carried them to a bye-place, and *lynched* them, during which inquisitorial operations, they divulged everything to the officers, Messrs. Foyle and Grossman." The preceding fact is published in the Maryland Republican of August 22, 1837.

Judge Lansuge of New Orleans, in his address at the opening of the criminal court, Nov. 4,1837, published in the "Bee" of Nov. 8, in remarking upon the prevalence of out-breaking crimes, says:"Is it possible in a civilized country such crying abuses are *constantly* encountered? How many individuals have given themselves up to such culpable habits! Yet we find magistrates and juries hesitating to expose crimes of the blackest dye to eternal contempt and infamy, to the vengeance of the law.

"As a Louisianian parent, *I reflect with terror* that our beloved children, reared to become one day honorable and useful citizens, may be the victims of these votaries of vice and licentiousness. Without some powerful and certain remedy, *our streets will become butcheries overflowing with the blood of our citizens.*"

The Editor of the "New Orleans Bee" in his paper of Oct. 21, 1837, has a long editorial article, in which he argues for the virtual legalizing of "Lynch Law", as follows:

"We think then that in the circumstances in which we are placed, the Legislature ought to sanction such measures as the situation of the country render necessary, by giving to justice *a convenient* latitude There are occasions when the delays inseparable from the administration of justice would be inimical to the public safety, and where the most fatal consequences would be the result.

"It appears to us, that there is an urgent necessity to provide against the inconveniences which result from popular judgment, and to check the disposition for the speedy execution of justice, resulting from the unconstitutional principle of a pretended Lynch law, by authorizing the parish court to take cognizance without delay, against every free man who shall be convicted of a crime, from the accusations arising from the mere provocations to the insurrection of the working classes.

"All judicial sentences ought to be based upon law, and the terrible privilege which the populace now have of punishing with death certain crimes, *ought to be consecrated by law,* powerful interests would not suffice in our view to excuse the interruption of social order, if the public safety was not with us the supreme law.

"This is the reason that whilst we deplore the imperious necessity which exists, we entreat the legislative power to give the sanction of principle to what already exists in fact."

The Editor of the "New Orleans Bee" in his paper, Oct. 25, 1837, says:

"We remark with regret the frightful list of homicides, whether justifiable or not, that are daily committed in New Orleans. It is not through any inherent vice of legal provision that such outrages are perpetrated with impunity: it is rather in the neglect of the *application of the law* which exists on this subject.

"We will confine our observation to the dangerous facilities afforded by this code for the escape of the homicide. We are well aware that the laws in question are intended for the distribution of equal justice, yet we have too often witnessed the acquittal of delinquents whom we can denominate by no other title than that of homicides, while the simple affirmation of others has been admitted (in default of testimony) who are themselves the authors of the deed, for which they stand in judgment. The *indiscriminate system of accepting bail* is a blot on our criminal legislation, and is one great reason why so many violators of the law avoid its penalties. To this doubtless must be ascribed the non-interference of the Attorney General. The law of *habeas corpus* being subjected to the interpretation of every magistrate, whether versed or not in criminal cases, a degree of arbitrary and incorrect explanation necessarily results. How frequently does it happen that the Mayor or Recorder decides upon the gravest case without putting himself to the smallest trouble to inform the Attorney General, who sometimes only hears of the affair when investigation is no longer possible, or when the criminal has wisely commuted his punishment into temporary or perpetual exile.

That morality suffers by such practices, is beyond a doubt; yet moderation and mercy are so beautiful in themselves, that we would scarcely protest against indulgence, were it not well known that the acceptance of bail is the safeguard of every delinquent who, through wealth or connections, possesses influence enough to obtain it. Here arbitrary construction glides amidst the confusion of testimony; there it presumes upon the want of evidence, and from one cause or another it is extremely rare, that a refusal to bail has delivered the accused into the hands of justice. In criminal cases, the Court and Jury are the proper tribunals to decide upon the reality of the crime, and the palliating circumstances; *yet it is not un-frequent* for the public voice to condemn as an odious assassin, the very individual who by the acquittal of the judge, walks at large and scoffs at justice.

"It is time to restrict within its proper limits this pretended right of personal protection; it is time to teach our population to abstain from mutual murder upon slight provocation. Duelling...Heaven knows, is dreadful enough, and quite a sufficient means of gratifying private aversion, and avenging insult. Frequent and serious brawls in our cafes, streets and houses, everywhere attest the insufficiency or misapplication of our legal code, or the want of energy in its organs. To say that unbounded license is the result of liberty is folly. Liberty is the consequence of well regulated laws—without these, Freedom can exist only in name, and the law which favors the escape of the opulent and aristocratic from the penalties of retribution, but consigns the poor and friendless to the chain-gang or the gallows, is in fact the very essence of slavery!!

The editor of the same paper says (Nov. 4, 1837.) "Perhaps by an equitable, but strict application of that law, (the law which forbids the wearing of deadly weapons concealed,) the effusion of human blood might be stopt *which now defiles our streets and our coffee-houses as if they were shambles!* Reckless disregard of the life of man is rapidly gaining ground among us, and the habit of seeing a man whom it is taken for granted was armed, murdered merely for a *gesture,* may influence the opinion of a jury composed of citizens, whom, LONG IMPUNITY TO HOMICIDES OF EVERY KIND has persuaded, that the right of self-defense extends even to the taking of life for *gestures,* more or less threatening. So many Daily instances of outbreaking passion which have thrown whole families into the deepest affliction, teach us a terrible lesson."

From the **"Columbus (Ga.) Sentinel"** July 6, 1837:

"Wholesale Murders.—No less than three murders were committed in New Orleans *on* Monday evening last. The first was that of a man in Poydras, near the corner of Tehapitoulas. The murdered individual had been suspected of a *liason* with another man's wife in the neighborhood, was caught in the act, followed to the above corner and shot.

"The second was that of a man in Perdido Street. Circumstances not known.

"The third was that of a watchman, on the corner of Custom House and Burgundy Street, who was found dead yesterday morning, shot through the heart. The deed was evidently committed on the opposite side from where he was found, as the unfortunate man was tracked by his blood across the street. In addition to being shot through the heart, two wounds in his breast, supposed to have been done with a Bowie knife, were discovered. No arrests have been made to our knowledge."

The editor of the "Charleston, (S.C.) Mercury" of April, 1837, makes the following remarks:

"The energy of a Tacon is much needed to vivify the police of New Orleans. In a single paper we find an account of the execution of one man for robbery and intent to kill, of the arrest of another for stabbing a man to death with a carving knife; and of a third found murdered on the Levee on the previous Sunday morning. In the last case, although the murderer was known, *no steps had been taken for his arrest;* and to crown the whole, it is actually stated in so many words, that the City guards are not permitted, according to their instructions, to patrol the Levee after night, for fear of attacks from persons employed in steamboats!"

The present white population of Louisiana is but little more than that of Rhode Island, yet more appalling crime is committed in Louisiana *every day, than* in Rhode Island during a year, notwithstanding the tone of public morals probably is lower in the latter than in any other New England state.

TENNESSEE

Tennessee became one of the United States in 1796. Its present white population is about seven hundred thousand.

The details which follow go to confirm the old truth that the exercise of arbitrary power tends to make men monsters.

The following, from the **"Memphis (Tennessee) Enquirer"** was published in the Virginia Advocate, Jan. 26, 1838:

"Below will be found a detailed account of one of the most unnatural and aggravated murders ever recorded. Col. Ward, the deceased, was a man of high standing in the state, and very much esteemed by his neighbors, and by all who knew him. The brothers concerned in this ' murder, most foul and unnatural,' were Lafayette, Chamberlayne, Caesar, and Achilles Jones, (the nephews of Col. Ward.)

"The four brothers, all armed, went to the residence of Mr. A. G. Ward, in Shelby co., on the evening of 22d instant. They were conducted into the room in which Col. Ward was sitting, together with some two or three ladies, his intended wife amongst the number. Upon their entering the room, Col. Ward rose, and extended his hand to Lafayette. He refused, saying he would shake hands with no such d——d rascal. The rest answered in the same tone. Col. Ward remarked that they were not in a proper place for a difficulty, if they sought one. Col. Ward went from the room to the passage, and was followed by the brothers. He said he was unarmed, but if they would lay down their arms, he could whip the whole of them; or if they would place him on an equal footing, he could whip the whole of them one by one. Caesar told Chamberlayne to give the Col. one of his pistols, which he did, and both went out into the yard, the other brothers following. While standing a few paces from each other, Lafayette came up, and remarked to the Col., 'If you spill my brother's blood, I will spill yours,' about which time Chamberlayne's pistol fired, and immediately Lafayette bursted a cap at him. The Colonel turned to Lafayette, and said, 'Lafayette, you intend to kill,' and discharged his pistol at him. The ball struck the pistol of Lafayette, and glanced into his arm. By this time Albert Ward, being close by, and hearing the fuss, came up to the assistance of the Colonel, when a scuffle amongst all hands ensued. The Colonel stumbled and fell down—he received several wounds from a large bowie knife; and, after being stabbed, Chamberlayne jumped upon him, and stamped him several times. After the scuffle, Caesar Jones was seen to put up a large bowie knife. Colonel Ward said he was a dead man. By the assistance of Albert Ward, he reached the house, distance about 15 or 20 yards, and in a few minutes expired. On examination by the Coroner, it appeared that he had received several wounds from pistols and knives. Albert Ward was also badly bruised, not dangerously."

The **"New Orleans Bee"** Sept. 22, 1838, published the following from the "Nashville (Tennessee) Whig:"

"The Nashville Whig, of the 11th ult., says: Pleasant Watson, of De Kalb County, and a Mr. Carmichael, of Alabama, were the principals in an affray at Livingston, Overton County, last week, which terminated in the death of the former. Watson made the assault with a dirk, and Carmichael defended himself with a pistol, shooting his antagonist through the body, a few inches below the heart. Watson was living at the last account. The dispute grew out of a horse race."

The New Orleans Courier, April 7, 1837, has the following extract from the **"McMinersville (Tennessee) Gazette:**

"On Saturday, the 8th instant, Colonel David L. Mitchell, the worthy sheriff of White County, was most barbarously murdered by a man named Joseph Little. Colonel Mitchell had a civil process against Little. He went to Little's house for the purpose of arresting him. He found Little armed with a rifle, pistols, &c. He commenced a conversation with Little upon the impropriety of his resisting, and stated his determination to take him, at the same time slowly advancing upon Little, who discharged his rifle at him without effect. Mitchell then attempted to jump in, to take hold of him, when Little struck him over the head with the barrel of his rifle, and literally mashed his skull to pieces; and, as he lay prostrate on the earth, Little deliberately pulled a large pistol from his belt, and placing the muzzle close to Mitchell's head, be shot the ball through it. Little has made his escape. *There were three men nearby when the murder was committed, who made no attempt to arrest the murderer."*

The following affray at Athens, Tennessee, is from the **Mississippian,** August 10, 1838.

"An unpleasant occurrence transpired at Athens on Monday. Captain James Byrnes was stabbed four times, twice in the arm, and twice in the side, by A. R. Livingston. The wounds are said to be very severe, and fears are entertained of their proving mortal. The affair underwent an examination before Sylvester Nichols, Esq., by whom Livingston was let to bail."

The **"West Tennessean"** Aug. 4, 1837, says— "A duel was fought at Calhoun, Tenn., between G. W. Carter and J. C. Sherley. They used yaugers at the distance of 20 yards. The former was slightly wounded, and the latter quite dangerously."

June 23d, 1838, Benjamin Shipley, of Hamilton Co., Tennessee, shot Archibald McCallie. *(Nashville Banner, July 16, 1838.)*

June 23d, 1838, Levi Stunston, of Weakly Co., Tennessee, killed William Price, of said county, in an affray. *(Nashville Banner, July 6, 1838.)*

October 8, 1838, in an affray at Wolf's Ferry, Tennessee, Martin Farley, Senior, was killed by John and Solomon Step. *(Georgia Telegraph, Nov. 6, 1838.)*

Feb. 14, 1838, John Manie was killed by William Doss at Decatur, Tennessee. *(Memphis Gazette, May 15, 1838.)*

"From the **Nashville Whig.**

"Fatal Affray in Columbia, Tenn.—A fatal street encounter occurred at that place, on the 3d inst., between Richard H. Hays, attorney at law, and Wm. Polk, brother to the Hon. Jas. K. Polk. The parties met, armed with pistols, and exchanged shots simultaneously. A buck-shot pierced the brain of Hays, and he died early the next morning. The quarrel grew out of a

sportive remark of Hays', at dinner, at the Columbia Inn, for which he offered an apology, not accepted, it seems, as Polk went to Hays' office, the same evening, and chastised him with a whip. This occurred on Friday, the fatal result took place on Monday."

In a fight near Memphis, Tennessee, May 15, 1837, Mr. Jackson, of that place, shot through the heart Mr. W. F. Gholson, son of the late Mr. Gholson, of Virginia. *(Raleigh Register, June 13, 1837.)*

The following horrible outrage, committed in West Tennessee, not far from Randolph, was published by the Georgetown (S.C.) Union, May 26, 1837, from the **Louisville Journal:**

"A feeble bodied man settled a few years ago on the Mississippi, a short distance below Randolph, on the Tennessee side. He succeeded in amassing property to the value of about $14,000, and, like most of the settlers, made a business of selling wood to the boats. This he sold at $2.50 a cord, while his neighbors asked $3.00. One of them came to remonstrate against his underselling, and had a fight with his brother-in-law Clark, in which he was beaten. He then went and obtained legal process against Clark, and returned with a deputy sheriff, attended by a posse of desperate villains. When they arrived at Clark's house, he was seated among his children—they put two or three balls through his body. Clark ran, was overtaken and knocked down; in the midst of his cries for mercy, one of the villains fired a pistol in his mouth, killing him instantly. They then required the settler to sell his property to them, and leave the country. He, fearing that they would otherwise take his life, sold them his valuable property for $300, and departed with his family. *The sheriff was one of the purchasers."*

The Baltimore American, Feb. 8, 1838, publishes the following from the **Nashville (Tennessee) Banner:**

"A most atrocious murder was committed a few days ago at Lagrange, in this state, on the body of Mr. John T. Foster, a respectable merchant of that town. The perpetrators of this bloody act are E. Moody, Thomas Moody, J. E. Douglass, W. R. Harris, and W. C. Harris. The circumstances attending this horrible affair are the following:—On the night previous to the murder, a gang of villains, under pretence of wishing to purchase goods, entered Mr. Foster's store, took him by force, and rode him through the streets *on a rail.* The next morning, Mr. F. met one of the party, and gave him a caning. For this *just* retaliation for the outrage which had been committed on his person, he was pursued by the persons above named, while taking a walk with a friend, and murdered in the open face of day."

The following presentment of a Tennessee Grand Jury sufficiently explains and comments on itself:

The Grand Jurors empanelled to inquire for the county of Shelby, would separate without having discharged their duties, if they were to omit to notice public evils which they have found their powers inadequate to put in train for punishment. The evils referred to exist more particularly in the town of Memphis.

The audacity and frequency with which outrages are committed, forbid us, in justice to our consciences, to omit to use the powers we possess, to bring them to the severe action of the law; and when we find our powers inadequate, to draw upon them public attention, and the rebuke of the good.

An infamous female publicly and grossly assaults a lady; therefore a public meeting is called, the mayor of the town is placed in the chair, resolutions are adopted, providing for the summary and lawless punishment of the wretched woman. In the progress of the affair, *hundreds of citizens* assemble at her house, and raze it to the ground. The unfortunate creature, together with two or three men of like character, are committed, in an open canoe or boat, without oar or paddle, to the middle of the Mississippi River.

Such is a concise outline of the leading incidents of a recent transaction in Memphis. It might be filled up by the detail of individual exploits, which would give vivacity to the description; but we forbear to mention them. We leave it to others to admire the manliness of the transaction, and the courage displayed by a mob of hundreds, in the various outrages upon the persons and property of three or four individuals who fell under its vengeance.

The present white population of Tennessee is about the same with that of Massachusetts, and yet more out-breaking crimes are committed in Tennessee in a *single month,* than in Massachusetts during a whole year; and this, too, notwithstanding the largest town in Tennessee has but six thousand inhabitants; whereas, in Massachusetts, besides one of eighty thousand, and two others of nearly twenty thousand each, there are at least a *dozen* larger than the chief town in Tennessee, which gives to the latter state an important advantage on the score of morality, the country being so much more favorable to it than large towns.

KENTUCKY

Kentucky has been one of the United States since 1792. Its present white population is but six hundred thousand.

The details which follow show still further that those who unite to plunder of their rights one class of human beings regard as *sacred* the rights of no class.

The following affair at Maysville, Kentucky, is extracted from the **Maryland Republican**, January 30, 1838:

"A fight came off at Maysville, Ky. on the 29th ultimo, in which a Mr. Coulster was stabbed in the side and is dead; a Mr. Gibson was well hacked with a knife; a Mr. Farris was dangerously wounded in the head, and another of the same name in the hip; a Mr. Shoemaker was severely beaten, and several others seriously hurt in various ways."

The following is extracted from the **N.C.Standard**:

"A most bloody and shocking transaction took place in the little town of Clinton, Hickman Co. Ken. The circumstances are briefly as follows:

A special canvass for a representative from the county of Hickman, had for some time been in progress. A gentleman by the name of Binford was a candidate. The State Senator from the district, Judge James, took some exceptions to the reputation of Binford, and intimated that if B. should be elected, he (James) would resign rather than serve with such a colleague. Hearing this, Binford went to the house of James to demand an explanation. Mrs. James remarked, in a jest as Binford thought, that if she was in the place of her husband she would resign her seat in the Senate, and not serve with such a character. B. told her that she was a woman, and could say what she pleased. She replied that she was not in earnest. James then looked B. in the face and said that, if his wife said so, it was the fact— he was an infamous scoundrel and d—d rascal.' He asked B. if he was armed, and on being answered in the affirmative, he stepped into an adjoining room to arm himself. He was prevented by the family from returning, and Binford walked out. J. then told him from his piazza, that he would meet him next day in Clinton.

True to their appointment, the enraged parties met on the streets the following day. James shot first, his ball passing through his antagonist's liver, whose pistol fired immediately afterwards, and missing J., the ball pierced the head of a stranger by the name of Collins, who instantly fell and expired. After being shot, Binford sprang upon J. with the fury of a wounded tiger, and would have taken his life but for a second shot received through the back from Bartin James, the brother of Thomas. Even after he received the last fatal wound he struggled with his antagonist until death relaxed his grasp, and he fell with the horrid exclamation, '*I am a dead man!.*"

"Judge James gave himself up to the authorities; and when the informant of the editor left Clinton, Binford, and the unfortunate stranger lay shrouded corpses together."

The "N.O. Bee" thus gives the conclusion of the matter:

"Judge James was tried and acquitted, the death of Binford being regarded as an act of justifiable homicide."

From the **"Flemingsburg Kentuckian"** June 23, '38.

Affray.—Thomas Binford, of Hickman County, Kentucky, recently attacked a Mr. Gardner of Dresden, with a drawn knife, and cut his face pretty badly. Gardner picked up a piece of iron and gave him a side-wipe above the ear that brought him to terms. The skull was fractured about two inches. Binford's brother was killed at Clinton, Kentucky, last fall by Judge James.

The **"Red River Whig"** of September 15,1838, says:—" A ruffian of the name of Charles Gibson, attempted to murder a girl named Mary Green, of Louisville, Ky. on the 23d ult. He cut her in six different places with a Bowie knife. His object, as stated in a subsequent investigation before the Police Court, was to cut her throat, which she prevented by throwing up her arms."

From the **"Louisville Advertiser"** Dec. 17th, 1838:—" A startling tragedy occurred in this city on Saturday evening last, in which A. H. Meeks was instantly killed, John Rothwell mortally wounded, William Holmes severely wounded, and Henry Oldham slightly, by the use of Bowie knives, by Judge E. C. Wilkinson, and his brother, B. R. Wilkinson, of Natchez, and J. Murdough, of Holly Springs, Mississippi. It seems that Judge Wilkinson had ordered a coat at the shop of Messrs. Varnum & Redding. The coat was made; the Judge, accompanied by his brother and

Mr. Murdough, went to the shop of Varnum & Redding, tried on the coat, and was irritated because, as he believed, it did not fit him. Mr. Redding undertook to convince him that he was in error, and ventured to assure the Judge that the coat was well made. The Judge instantly seized an iron poker, and commenced an attack on Redding. The blow with the poker was partially warded off— Redding grappled his assailant, when a companion of the Judge drew a Bowie knife, and, but for the interposition and interference of the unfortunate Meeks, a journeyman tailor, and a gentleman passing by at the moment, Redding might have been assassinated in his own shop. Shortly afterwards, Redding, Meeks, Rothwell, and Holmes went to the Gait House. They sent up stairs for Judge Wilkinson, and he came down into the bar room, when angry words were passed. The Judge went up stairs again, and in a short time returned with his companions, all armed with knives. Harsh language was again used. Meeks, felt called on to state what he had seen of the conflict, and did so, and Murdough gave him the d—d lie, for which Meeks struck him. On receiving the blow with the whip, Murdough instantly plunged his Bowie knife into the abdomen of Meeks, and killed him on the spot.

"At the same instant B. R. Wilkinson attempted to get at Redding, and Holmes and Rothwell interfered, or joined in the affray. Holmes was wounded, probably by B. R. Wilkinson; and the Judge, having left the room for an instant, returned, and finding Rothwell contending with his brother, or bending over him, he (the Judge) stabbed Rothwell in the back, and inflicted a mortal wound."

Judge Wilkinson, his brother, and J. Murdough, have been recently tried and acquitted.

From the **"New Orleans Bee"** Sept. 27, 1838:
"It appears from the statement of the Lexington Intelligencer, that there has been for some time past, an enmity between the drivers of the old and opposition lines of stages running from that city. On the evening of the 13th an encounter took place at the Circus between two of them, Powell and Cameron, and the latter was so much injured that his life was in imminent danger. About 12 o'clock the same night, several drivers of the old line rushed into Keizer's Hotel, where Powell and other drivers of the opposition-line boarded, and a general melee took place, in the course of which several pistols were discharged, the ball of one of them passing

through the head of Crabster, an old line driver, and killing him on the spot. Crabster, before he was shot, had discharged his own pistol which had burst into fragments. Two or three drivers of the opposition were wounded with buck shot, but not dangerously."

The "Mobile Advertiser" of September 15, 1838, copies the following from the **Louisville (Ky.) Journal**:

"A Mr. Campbell was killed in Henderson County on the 31st ult. by a Mr. Harrison. It appears, that there was an affray between the parties some months ago, and that Harrison subsequently left home and returned on the 31st in a trading boat. Campbell met him at the boat with a loaded rifle and declared his determination to kill him, at the same time asking him whether he had a rifle and expressing a desire to give him a fair chance. Harrison affected to laugh at the whole matter and invited Campbell into his boat to take a drink with him. Campbell accepted the invitation, but, while he was in the act of drinking, Harrison seized his rifle, fired it off, and laid Campbell dead by striking him with the barrel of it."

The "Missouri Republican" of July 29, 1837, published the details which follow from the **Louisville Journal**:

Mount Sterling, Ky. July 20, 1837.

"Gentlemen:—A most unfortunate and fatal occurrence transpired in our town last evening, about 6 o'clock. Some of the most prominent friends of Judge French had a meeting yesterday at Col. Young's, near this place and warm words ensued between Mr. Albert Thomas and Belvard Peters, Esq., and a few blows were exchanged, and several of the friends of each collected at the spot. Whilst the parties were thus engaged, Mr. Wm. White, who was a friend of Mr. Peters, struck Mr. Thomas, whereupon B. F. Thomas Esq. engaged in the combat on the side of his brother and Mr. W. Roberts on the part of Peters —Mr. G. W. Thomas taking part with his brothers. Albert Thomas had Peters down and was taken off by a gentleman present, and whilst held by that gentleman, he was struck by White; and B. F. Thomas having made some remark White struck him. B. F. Thomas returned the blow, and having a large knife, stabbed White, who nevertheless continued the contest, and, it is said, broke Thomas's arm with a rock of a chair. Thomas then inflicted some other stabs, of which White died in a few minutes. Roberts was knocked down twice by Albert Thomas, and, I believe, is much hurt. G. W. Thomas was somewhat hurt also. White and B. F. Thomas had always been on friendly terms. You are acquainted with the Messrs. Thomas. Mr. White was a much larger man than either of them, weighing nearly 200 pounds, and in the prime of life. As you may very naturally suppose, great excitement prevails here, and Mr. B. F. Thomas regrets the fatal catastrophe as much as anyone else, but believes from all the circumstances that he was justifiable in what he did, although he would be as far from doing such an act when cool and deliberate as any man whatever.

The "New Orleans Bulletin" of Aug. 24, 1838, extracts the following from the **Louisville Journal**:

"News has just reached us, that Thomas P. Moore, attacked the Senior Editor of this paper in the yard of the Harrodsburg Springs. Mr. Moore advanced upon Mr. Prentice with a drawn pistol and fired at him; Mr. Prentice then fired, neither shot taking effect. Mr. Prentice drew a second pistol, when Mr. Moore quailed and said he had no other arms; whereupon Mr. Prentice from superabundant magnanimity spared the miscreant's life."

From **"The Floridian"** of June 10, 1837:

MURDER. Mr. Gillespie, a respectable citizen aged 50, was murdered a few days since by a Mr. Arnett, near Mumfordsville, Ky., which latter shot his victim twice with a rifle.

The **"Augusta (Ga.) Sentinel"** May 11, 1838, has the following account of murders in Kentucky:

"At Mill's Point, Kentucky, Dr. Thomas Rivers was shot one day last week, from out of a window, by Lawyer Ferguson, both citizens of that place, and both parties are represented to have stood high in the estimation of the community in which they lived. The difficulty we understand to have grown out of a law suit at issue between them.

Just as our paper was going to press, we learn that the brother of Dr. Rivers, who had been sent for, had arrived, and immediately shot Lawyer Ferguson. He at first shot him with a shot gun, upon his retreat, which did not prove fatal; he then approached him immediately with a pistol, and killed him on the spot."

The Right **Rev. B. B. Smith**, Bishop of the Episcopal diocese of Kentucky, published about two years since an article in the Lexington (Ky.) Intelligencer, entitled "Thoughts on the frequency of homicides in the state of Kentucky." We conclude this head with a brief extract from the testimony of the Bishop, contained in that article:

"The writer has never conversed with a traveled and enlightened European or eastern man, who has not expressed the most undisguised horror at the frequency of homicide and murder within our bounds, and at the *ease with which the homicide escapes from* punishment.

"As to the frequency of these shocking occurrences, the writer has some opportunity of being correctly impressed, by means of a yearly tour through many counties of the State. He has also been particular in making inquiries of our most distinguished legal and political characters, and from some has derived conjectural estimates which were truly alarming. A few have been of the opinion, that on an average one murder a year may be charged to the account of every county in the state, making the frightful aggregate of 850 human lives sacrificed to revenge, or the victims of momentary passion, in the course of every ten years.

"Others have placed the estimate much lower, and have thought that thirty for the whole state, every year, would be found much nearer the truth. An attempt has been made lately to obtain data more satisfactory than conjecture, and circulars have been addressed to the clerks of most of the counties, in order to arrive at as correct an estimate as possible of the actual number of homicides during the three years last past. It will be seen, however, that statistics thus obtained, even from every county in the state, would necessarily be imperfect, inasmuch as the records of the courts *by no means show all the cases* which occur, some escaping without *any* of the forms of a legal examination, and there being *many affrays* which end only in wounds, or where the parties are separated.

"From these returns, it appears that in 27 counties there have been, within the last three years, of homicides of every grade, 35, but only 8 convictions in the same period, leaving 27 cases which have passed wholly unpunished. During the same period there have been from eighty-five counties, only eleven commitments to the state prison, nine for manslaughter, and two for shooting with intent to kill, *and not an instance of capital punishment in the person of any white offender.* Thus an approximation is made to a general average, which probably would not vary much from one in each county every three years, or about 280 in ten years.

"It is believed that such a register of crime amongst a people professing the protestant religion and speaking the English language is not to be found, with regard to any three-quarters of a million of people, since the downfall of the feudal system. Compared with the records of crime in Scotland, or the eastern states, the results are ABSOLUTELY SHOCKING! *It is believed there are more homicides, on an average of two years, in any of our more populous counties, than in the whole of several of our states, of equal or nearly equal white population with Kentucky.*

"The victims of these affrays are not always, by any means, the most worthless of our population.

"It too often happens that the enlightened citizen, the elevated lawyer, the affectionate husband, and precious father, are thus instantaneously taken from their useful stations on earth, and hurried, all unprepared, to their final account!

"The question is again asked, what could have brought about, and can perpetuate, this shocking state of things?"

As an illustration of the recklessness of life in Kentucky, and the terrible paralysis of public sentiment, the bishop states the following fact:

"A case of shocking homicide is remembered, where the guilty person was acquitted by a sort of acclamation, and the next day was seen in public, with two ladies hanging on his arm!"

Notwithstanding the frightful frequency of deadly affrays in Kentucky, as is certified by the above testimony of Bishop Smith, there are fewer, in proportion to the white population, than in any of the states which have passed under review, unless Tennessee may be an exception. The present white population of Kentucky is perhaps seventy thousand more than that of Maine, and yet more public fatal affrays have taken place in the former, within the last six months, than in the latter during its entire existence as a state.

The seven slave states which we have already passed under review are just one half of the slave states and territories, included in the American Union. Before proceeding to consider the condition of society in the other slave states, we pause a moment to review the ground already traversed. The present entire white population of the states already considered, is about two and a quarter million; just about equal to the present white population of the state of New York. If the amount of crime resulting in loss of life, which is perpetrated by the white population of those states upon the *whites alone,* be contrasted with the amount perpetrated in the state of New York, by *all* classes, upon *all,* we believe it will be found, that more of such crimes have been committed in these states within the last 18 months, than have occurred in the state of New York for half a century. But perhaps we shall be told that in these seven states, there are scores of cities and large towns, and that a majority of all these deadly affrays, &c., take place in *them;* to this we reply, that there are *three times as many* cities and large towns in the state of New York, as in all those states together, and that nearly all the capital crimes perpetrated in the state take place in these cities and large villages. In the state of New York, there are more than *half a million* persons who live in cities and villages of more than two thousand inhabitants, whereas in Kentucky, Tennessee, Alabama, Mississippi, Louisiana, Arkansas and Missouri, there are on the largest computation not more than *one hundred thousand* persons, residing in cities and villages of more than two thousand inhabitants, and the white population of these places (which alone is included in the estimate of crime, and that too *inflicted upon whites only,)* is probably not more than sixty-five *thousand.*

But it will doubtless be pleaded in mitigation, that the cities and large villages in those states are *new;* that they have not had sufficient time thoroughly to organize their police, so as to make it an effectual terror to evil doers; and further, that the rapid growth of those places has so overloaded the authorities with all sorts of responsibilities, that due attention to the preservation of the public peace has been nearly impossible; and besides, they have had no official experience to draw upon, as in the older cities, the offices being generally filled by young men, as a necessary consequence of the newness of the country, &c. To this we reply, that New Orleans is more than a century old, and for half that period has been the center of a great trade; that St. Louis, Natchez, Mobile, Nashville, Louisville and Lexington, are all half a century old, and each had arrived at years of discretion, while yet the sites of Buffalo, Rochester, Lockport, Canandaigua, Geneva, Auburn, Ithaca, Oswego, Syracuse, and other large towns in Western New-York, *were a wilderness.* Further, as *a number* of these places are larger than *either* of the former, their growth must have been more *rapid,* and, consequently, they must have encountered still greater obstacles in the organization of an efficient police than those south western cities, with this exception, they WERE NOT SETTLED BY SLAVEHOLDERS!"

The absurdity of assigning the *newness* of the country, the unrestrained habits of pioneer settlers, the recklessness of life engendered by wars with the Indians, &c., as reasons sufficient to account for the frightful amount of crime in the states under review, is manifest from the fact, that Vermont is of the same age with Kentucky; Ohio, ten years younger than Kentucky, and six years younger than Tennessee; Indiana, five years younger than Louisiana; Illinois, one year younger than Mississippi; Maine, of the same age with Missouri, and two years younger than Alabama; and Michigan of the same age with Arkansas. Now, let anyone contrast the state of society in Maine, Vermont, Ohio, Indiana, Illinois, and Michigan with that of Kentucky, Tennessee, Alabama, Missouri, Louisiana, Arkansas, and Mississippi, and candidly ponder the result. It is impossible satisfactorily to account for the immense disparity in crime, on any other supposition than that the latter states were settled and are inhabited almost exclusively by those who carried with them the violence, impatience of legal restraint, love of domination, fiery passions, idleness, and contempt of laborious industry, which are engendered by habits of despotic sway, acquired by residence in communities where such manners, habits and passions, mould society into their own image.*

* Bishop Smith of Kentucky, in his testimony respecting homicides, which is quoted on a preceding page, thus speaks of the influence of slave-holding, as an exciting cause.

"Are not some of the indirect influences of a system, the existence of which amongst us can never be sufficiently deplored, discoverable in these affrays? Are not our young men more heady, violent and imperious in consequence of their early habits of command? And are not our taverns and other public places of resort, much more crowded with an inflammable material, than if young men were brought up in the staid and frugal habits of those who are constrained to earn their bread by the sweat of their brow? Is not intemperance more social, more inflammatory, more pugnacious where a fancied superiority of gentlemanly character is felt, in consequence of exemption from severe manual labor? Is there ever stabbing where there is not idleness and strong drink?"

The Bishop also gives the following as another exciting cause; it is however only the product of the preceding:

"Has not a public sentiment which we hear characterized as singularly high minded and honorable, and sensitively alive to every affront, whether real or imaginary, but which strangers denominate rough and ferocious, much to do in provoking these assaults, and then in applauding instead of punishing the offender."

The Bishop says of the young men of Kentucky, that they "grow up proud, impetuous, and reckless of all responsibility;" and adds, that the practice of carrying deadly weapons is with them "Nearly Universal."

The practical workings of this cause are powerfully illustrated in those parts of the slave states where slaves abound, when contrasted with those where very few are held. Who does not know that there are fewer deadly affrays in proportion to the white population—that law has more sway and that human life is less insecure in East Tennessee, where there are very few slaves, than in West Tennessee, where there are large numbers. This is true also of northern and western Virginia, where few slaves are held, when contrasted with eastern Virginia, where they abound; the same remark applies to those parts of Kentucky and Missouri, where large numbers of slaves are held, when contrasted with others where there are comparatively few.

We see the same cause operating to a considerable extent in those parts of Ohio, Indiana and Illinois, settled mainly by slaveholders and others, who were natives of slave states, in contrast with other parts of these states settled almost exclusively by persons from free states; that affrays and breaches of the peace are far more frequent in the former than in the latter, is well known to all.

We now proceed to the remaining slave states. Those that have not yet been considered are Delaware, Maryland, Virginia, North and South Carolina, Georgia, and the territory of Florida. As Delaware has hardly two thousand five hundred slaves, arbitrary power over human beings is exercised by so few persons, that the turbulence infused thereby into the public mind is but an in considerable element, quite insufficient to inflame the passions, much less to cast the character of the mass of the people; consequently, the state of society there, and the general security of life is but little less than in New Jersey and Pennsylvania, upon which states it borders on the north and east. The same causes operate in a considerable measure, though to a much less extent, in Maryland and in Northern and Western Virginia. But in lower Virginia, North and South Carolina, Georgia and Florida, the general state of society as it respects the successful triumph of passion over law, and the consequent and universal insecurity of life is, in the main, very similar to that of the states already considered. In some portions of each of these states, human life has probably as little real protection as in Arkansas, Mississippi and Louisiana; but generally throughout the former states and sections, the laws are not so absolutely powerless as in the latter three. Deadly affrays, duels, murders, lynchings, &c., are, in proportion to the white population, as frequent and as rarely punished in lower Virginia as in Kentucky and Missouri; in North Carolina and South Carolina as in Tennessee; and in Georgia and Florida as in Alabama.

To insert the criminal statistics of the remaining slave states in detail, as those of the states already considered have been presented, would, we find, fill more space than can well be spared. Instead of this, we propose to exhibit the state of society in all the slaveholding region bordering on the Atlantic, by the testimony of the slaveholders themselves, corroborated by a few plain facts. Leaving out of view Florida, where law is the *most* powerless, and Maryland where probably it is the *least* so, we propose to select as a fair illustration of the actual state of society in the Atlantic slaveholding regions, North Carolina whose border is but 250 miles from the free states of Pennsylvania and New Jersey, and Georgia which constitutes its south western boundary.

We will begin with Georgia. This state was settled more than a century ago by a colony under General Oglethorpe. The colony was memorable for its high toned morality. One of its first regulations was an absolute prohibition of slavery in every form: but another generation arose, the prohibition was abolished, a multitude of slaves were imported, the exercise of unlimited power over them lashed up passion to the spurning of all control, and now the dreadful state of society that exists in Georgia, is revealed by the following testimony out of her own mouth.

The editor of the **Darien (Georgia) Telegraph,** in his paper of November 6, 1838, published the following:.

"Murderous Attack.—Between the hours of three and four o'clock, on Saturday last, the editor of this paper was attacked by FOURTEEN armed ruffians, and knocked down by repeated blows of bludgeons. All his assailants were armed with pistols, dirks, and large clubs. Many of them are known to us; but *there is neither law nor justice to be had in Darien! We are doomed to death* by the employers of the assassins who attacked us on Saturday, and no less than our blood will satisfy them. The cause alleged for this unmanly, base, cowardly outrage, is some expressions which occurred in an election squib, printed at this office, and extensively circulated through the county *before the election.* The names of those who surrounded us, when the attack was made, are, A. Lefils, Jr. (son to the representative), Madison Thomas, Francis Harrison, Thomas Hopkins, Alexander Blue, George Wing, James Eilands, W. I. Perkins, A. J. Raymur; the others we cannot at present recollect. The two first, Lefils and Thomas struck us at the same time. Pistols were leveled at us in all

directions. We can produce the most respectable testimony of the truth of this statement."

The same number of the "Darien Telegraph," from which the preceding is taken,-contains a correspondence between six individuals, settling the preliminaries of duels. The correspondence fills, with the exception of a dozen lines, *five columns* of the paper. The parties were Col. W. Whig Hazzard, commander of one of the Georgia regiments in the recent Seminole campaign, Dr. T. F. Hazzard, a physician of St. Simons, and Thomas Hazzard, Esq. a county magistrate, on the one side, and Messrs. J. A. Willey, H. W. Willey, and H. B. Gould, Esqs. of Darien, on the other. In their published correspondence the parties call each other "liar," "mean rascal," "puppy," "villain," &c.

The magistrate, Thomas Hazzard, who accepts the challenge of J. A. Willey, says, in one of his letters, "Being a magistrate, under a solemn oath to do all in my power to keep the peace," &c., and yet this personification of Georgia *justice* superscribes his letter as follows: "To the Liar, Puppy, Fool, and Poltroon, Mr. John A. Willey." The magistrate closes his letter thus:

"Here I am; call upon me for personal satisfaction (in *propria forma)*; and in the Farm Field, on St. Simon's Island, *(Deo juvante,)* I will give you a full front of my body, and do all in my power to satisfy your thirst for blood! And more, I will wager you $100, to be planked on the scratch! That J. A. Willey will neither kill or defeat T. F. Hazzard."

The following extract from the correspondence is a sufficient index of slaveholding civilization.

"ARTICLES OF BATTLE BETWEEN JOHN A. WILLEY AND W. WHIG HAZZARD:

Condition 1. The parties to fight on the same day and at the same place, (St. Simon's Beach, near the lighthouse,) where the meeting between T. F. Hazzard and J. A. Willey will take place.

Condition 2. The parties to fight with broadswords in the right hand, and a dirk in the left.

Condition 3. On the word "Charge," the parties to advance, and attack with the broad-sword, or close with the dirk.

Condition 4. The Head of the vanquished to BE CUT OFF BY THE VICTOR, AND STUCK UPON A POLE on the Farm Field Dam, the original cause of dispute.

Condition 5. Neither party to object to each other's weapons; and if a sword breaks, the contest to continue with the dirk."

This Col. W. Whig Hazzard is one of the most prominent citizens in the southern part of Georgia, and previously signalized himself, as we learn from one of the letters in the correspondence, by "three deliberate rounds in a duel."

The **Macon (Georgia) Telegraph** of October 9, 1838, contains the following notice of two affrays in that place, in each of which an individual was killed, one on Tuesday and the other on Saturday of the same week. In publishing the case, the Macon editor remarks:

"We are compelled to remark on the inefficiency of our laws in bringing to the bar of public justice, persons committing capital offenses. Under the present mode, a man has nothing more to do than to leave the state, or step over to Texas, or some other place not farther off, and he need entertain no fear of being apprehended. So long as such a state of things is permitted to exist, just so long will every man who has an enemy (and there are but few who have not) *be in constant danger of being shot down in the streets.*"

To these remarks of the Macon editor, who is in the centre of the state, near the capital, the editor of the Darien Telegraph, two hundred miles distant, responds as follows, in his paper of October 30. 1838:

"The remarks of our contemporary are not without cause. They apply, with peculiar force, to this community. *Murderers and rioters will never stand in need of a sanctuary as long as Darien is what it is.*"

It is a coincidence which carries a comment with it that in less than a week after this Darien editor made these remarks, he was attacked in the street by *"fourteen* gentlemen," armed with bludgeons, knives, dirks, pistols, &c., and would doubtless have been butchered on the spot if he had not been rescued.

We give the following statement at length as the chief perpetrator of the outrages, Col. W. N. Bishop, was at the time a high functionary of the State of Georgia, and, as we learn from the Macon Messenger, still holds two public offices in the State, one of them from the direct appointment of the governor.

From the **"Georgia Messenger"** of August 25, 1837:

"During the administration of Wilson Lumpkin, WILLIAM N. BISHOP received from his Excellency the appointment of Indian Agent, in the place of William Springer. During that year (1834,) the said governor gave the command of a company of men, 40 in number, to the said W. N. Bishop, to be selected by him, and armed with the muskets of the State. This band was organized for the special purpose of keeping the Cherokees in subjection, and although it is a notorious fact that the Cherokees in the neighborhood of Spring Place were peaceable and by no means refractory, the said band were kept there, and seldom made any excursion whatever out of the county of Murray. It is also *a notorious fact,* that the said band, from the day of their organization, never permitted a citizen of Murray County opposed to the dominant party of Georgia, to exercise the right of suffrage at any election whatever. From that period to the last of January election, the said band appeared at the polls with the arms of the State, rejecting every vote that "was not of the true stripe," as they called it. That they frequently seized and dragged to the polls honest citizens, and compelled them to vote contrary to their will.

"Such acts of arbitrary despotism were tolerated by the administration. Appeals from the citizens of Murray County brought them no relief—and incensed at such outrages, they determined on the first Monday in January last, to turn out and elect such Judges of the Inferior Court and county officers, as would be above the control of Bishop, that he might thereby be prevented from packing such a jury as he chose to try him for his brutal and unconstitutional outrages on their rights. Accordingly on Sunday evening previous to the election, about twenty citizens who lived a distance from the county site, came in unarmed and unprepared for battle, intending to remain in town, vote in the morning and return home. They were met by Bishop and his State band, and asked by the former 'whether they were for peace or war.' They unanimously responded "we are for peace." At that moment Bishop ordered a fire and instantly *every musket of his band was discharged on those citizens,* 5 of whom were wounded, and others escaped with bullet holes in their clothes. Not satisfied with the outrage, *they dragged an aged man from his wagon and beat him nearly to death.*

"In this way the voters were driven from Spring Place, and before day light the next morning, the polls were opened by order of Bishop, and soon after sun rise they were closed; Bishop having ascertained that the band and Schley men had all voted. A runner was then dispatched to Milledgeville, and received from Governor Schley commissions for those self-made officers of Bishop's, two of whom have since runaway, and the rest have been called on by the citizens of the county to resign, being each members of Bishop's band, and doubtless runaways from other States. "After these outrages, Bishop apprehending an appeal to the judiciary on the part of the injured citizens of Murray County, had a jury drawn to suit him and appointed one of his band Clerk of the Superior Court. For these acts, the Governor and officers of the Central Bank rewarded him with an office in the Bank of the State, since which his own jury found *eleven true bills* against him."

In the Milledgeville Federal Union of May 2, 1837, we find the following presentment of the Grand Jury of Union County, Georgia, which as it shows some relics of a moral sense, still lingering in the state we insert:

Presentment of the Grand Jury of Union Co., March term, 1837

"We would notice, as a subject of painful interest, the appointment of Wm. N. Bishop to the high and responsible office of Teller, of the Central Bank of the State of Georgia—an institution of such magnitude as to merit and demand the most un-slumbering vigilance of the freemen of this State; as a portion of whom, we feel bound to express our *indignant reprehension* of the promotion of such a character to one of its most responsible posts— and do exceedingly regret the blindness or *depravity* of those who can sanction such a measure.

"We request that our presentment be published in the "Miners' Recorder and Federal Union. John Martin, Foreman."

On motion of Henry L. Sims, Solicitor General, "Ordered by the court, that the presentments of the Grand Jury, be published according to their request." Thomas Henry, Clerk.

The same paper, four weeks after publishing the preceding facts, contained the following: we give it in detail as the wretch who enacted the tragedy was another public functionary of the state of Georgia and acting in an official capacity.

"**Murder.**—One of the most brutal and inhuman murders it has ever fallen to our lot to notice, was lately committed in Cherokee County, by Julius Bates, the son of the principal keeper of the Penitentiary, upon an Indian.

"The circumstances as detailed to us by the most respectable men of both parties, are these. At the last Superior Court of Cass County, the unfortunate Indian was sentenced to the Penitentiary. Bates, as *one of the*

Penitentiary guard, was sent with another to carry him and others, from other counties to Milledgeville. He started from Cassville with the Indian ironed and barefooted; and walked him within a quarter of a mile of Canton, the C. H. in Cherokee, a distance of twenty-eight to thirty miles, over a very rough road in little more than half the day. On arriving at a small creek near town, the Indian [who had walked until the *soles of his feet were off and those of his heel turned black,]* made signs to get water, Bates refused to let him, and ordered him to go on: the Indian stopped and finally set down, whereupon Bates dismounted and gathering a pine knot, commenced and continued beating him and jerking him by a chain around his neck, until the citizens of the village were drawn there by the severity of the blows. The unfortunate creature was taken up to town and died in a few hours.

"An inquest was held, and the jury found a verdict of murder by Bates. A warrant was issued, but Bates had departed that morning in charge of other prisoners taken from Canton, and the worthy officers of the county desisted from his pursuit, 'because they apprehended he had passed the limits of the county.' We understand that the warrant was immediately sent to the Governor to have him arrested. Will it be done? We shall see."

Having devoted so much space to a revelation of the state of society among the slaveholders of Georgia, we will tax the reader's patience with only a single illustration of the public sentiment —the degree of actual legal protection enjoyed in the state of North Carolina.

North Carolina was settled about two centuries ago; its present white population is about five hundred thousand.

Passing by the murders, affrays, &c. with which the North Carolina papers abound, we insert the following as an illustration of the public sentiment of North Carolina among 'gentlemen of property and standing.'

The '**North Carolina Literary and Commercial Journal,**' of January 20,1838, published at Elizabeth City, devotes a column and a half to a description of the lynching, tarring, feathering, ducking, riding on a rail, pumping, &c., of a Mr. Charles Fife, a merchant of that city, for the crime of 'trading with negroes.' The editor informs us that this exploit of vandalism was performed very deliberately, at mid-day, and *by a number of the citizens,* The Most Respectable in The City,' &c. We proceed to give the reader an abridgement of the editor's statement in his own words:

"Such being the case, a number of the citizens, The Most Respectable In This City, collected, about ten days since, and after putting the fellow on a rail, carried him through town with a duck and chicken tied to him. He was taken down to the water and his head tarred and feathered; and when they returned he was put under a pump, where for a few minutes he underwent a little cooling. He was then told that he must leave town by the next Saturday—if he did not he would be visited again, and treated more in accordance with the principles of the laws of "Judge Lynch".

"On Saturday last, he was again visited, and as Fife had several of his friends to assist him, some little scuffle ensued, when several were knocked down, but nothing serious occurred. Fife was again mounted on a rail and brought into town, but as he promised if they would not trouble him he would leave town in a few days, he was set at liberty. Several of our magistrates *took no notice of the affair,* and rather seemed to tacitly acquiesce in the proceedings. The whole subject every one supposed was ended, as Fife was to leave in a few days, when What Was Our Astonishment to hear that Mr. Charles R. Kinney had visited Fife, advised him not to leave, and actually took upon himself to examine witnesses, and came before the public as the defender of Fife. The consequence was that all the rioters were summoned by the Sheriff to appear in the Court House and give bail for their appearance at our next court. On Monday last the court opened at 12 o'clock, Judge Bailey presiding. Such an excitement we never witnessed before in our town. A great many witnesses were examined, which proved the character of Fife beyond a doubt. At one time rather serious consequences were apprehended—high words were spoken, and luckily a blow which was aimed at Mr. Kinney was parried off, and we are happy to say the court adjourned after ample securities being given. The next day Fife was taken to jail for trading with negroes, but has since been released on paying $100. The interference of Mr. Kinney was wholly unnecessary; it was an assumption on his part which properly belonged to our magistrates. Fife had agreed to go away, and the matter would have been amicably settled but for him. We have no unfriendly feelings towards Mr. Kinney: no personal animosities to gratify; we have always considered him as one of our best lawyers. But when he comes forth as the supporter of such a fellow as Fife, under the plea that the laws have been violated—when he arraigns the acts of thirty of the inhabitants of this place, it is high time for him to reflect seriously on the consequences. The Penitentiary system is the result of the refinement of the eighteenth century. As man advances in the sciences, in the arts, in the intercourse of social and civilized life, in the same proportion does crime and vice keep an equal pace, and always makes demands on the wisdom of legislators. Now, what is the "Lynch" law but the Penitentiary system carried out to its full extent, with a little more steam power? Or more properly, it is simply thus: *There are some scoundrels in society on whom the laws take no effect; the most expeditious and short way is to let a majority decide and give them* JUSTICE."

Let the reader notice,

1st, that this outrage was perpetrated with great deliberation, and after it was over, the victim was commanded to leave town by the next week: when that cooling interval had passed, the outrage was again deliberately repeated.

2d. It was perpetrated by "thirty persons,' "*the most respectable in the city.*"

3d. That at the second lynching of Fife, several of his neighbors who had gathered to defend him, (seeing that all the legal officers in the city had refused to do it, thus violating their oaths of office,) *were knocked down,* to which the editor adds, with the business air of a professional butcher, "nothing *serious* occurred!"

4th. That not a single magistrate in the city took the least notice either of the barbarities inflicted upon Fife, or of the assaults upon his friends, knocking them down, &c., but, as the editor informs us, all "seemed to acquiesce in the proceedings."

5th. That this conduct of the magistrates was well pleasing to the great mass of the citizens, is plain, from the remark of the editor that "every one supposed that the whole subject was ended," and from his wondering exclamation, "What Was Our Astonishment to hear that Mr. C. R. Kinney had actually took upon him to examine witnesses," &c., and also from the editor's declaration, " Such an excitement we never before witnessed m our town." Excitement at what? Not because the laws had been most impiously trampled down at noon-day by a conspiracy of thirty persons, "the most respectable in the city;" not because a citizen had been twice seized and publicly tortured for hours, without trial, and in utter defiance of all authority; nay, verily! This was all complacently acquiesced in; but because in this slaveholding Sodom there was found a solitary Lot who dared to uplift his voice for *law* and the *right of trial* by *jury;* this crime stirred up such an uproar in that city of "most respectable" lynchers as was *"never witnessed before"* and the noble lawyer who thus put everything at stake in invoking the majesty of law, would, it seems, have been knocked down, even in the presence of the Court, if the blow had not been "parried."

6th. Mark the murderous threat of the editor—"when he arraigns the *acts,"* (no matter how murderous)" of thirty citizens of this place, it is high time for him to reflect seriously *on the consequences."*

7th. The open advocacy of "Lynch law" by a set argument, boldly setting it above all codes, with which the editor closes his article, reveals a public sentiment in the community which shows, that in North Carolina, though society may still rally under the flag of civilization, and insist on wrapping itself in its folds, barbarism is none the less so in a stolen livery, and savages are savages still, though tricked out with the gauze and tinsel of the stars and stripes. It may be stated, in conclusion, that the North Carolina "Literary and Commercial Journal," from which the article is taken, is a large six columned paper, edited by F. S. Proctor, Esq., a graduate of a University, and of considerable literary note in the South.

Having drawn out this topic to so great a length, we waive all comments, and only say to the reader, in conclusion, *ponder these things,* and lay it to heart, that slaveholding "is justified *of her children."* Verily, they have their reward!" With what measure ye mete withal it shall be measured to you again." Those who combine to trample on others will trample on *each other.* The habit of trampling upon *one,* begets a state of mind that will trample upon *all.* Accustomed to wreak their vengeance on their slaves, indulgence of passion becomes with slaveholders a second law of nature, and, when excited even by their equals, their hot blood brooks neither restraint nor delay; *gratification* is the first thought—prudence generally comes too late, and the slaves see their masters fall a prey to each other, the victims of those very passions which have been engendered and infuriated by the practice of arbitrary rule over them. Surely it need not be added, that those who thus tread down their equals, must trample as in a wine-press their defenseless vassals. If, when in passion, they seize those who are *on their own level* and dash them under their feet, with what a crushing vengeance will they leap upon those who are *always* under their feet?

Index

A

A speculator with his drove of negroes, 248
Abbott, Jordan
  Slaveholder, 175
Abdie, P
  Slaveholder, 378, 379
Abraham / Slave, 214
Abraham Gray,
  Slaveholder, 199
Abram / Slave, 405, 414
Acclimation, 397
Adams
  Surname, 163
  Surname, 393
Adolphe / Slave, 216
Advertisements, 84, 332, 379
Alabama Volunteers, 474
Alexander
  Surname, 260
Alexander / Slave, 209
Alexander, Benjamin, 478
Alfred / Slave, 384
Alick / Slave, 209
Allan, James M., 97
Allan, Rev. W. T., 432, 443
Allan, Rev. William T., 95, 97
Allen / Slave, 194
Allen, Jesse, 476
Alston, J. A.
  Slaveholder, 206
Alvis, J.
  Slaveholder, 410
Amanda / Slave, 416
Ambrose / Slave, 174
American Anti-Slavery Society, iii, 1, 52, 230
Amos / Slave, 175
Anderson, Benjamin, 87
Anthony / Slave, 160, 161, 194, 467
Anthony Major, 464
Anthony, Julius C., 160

Anthony, Maj. Joseph J., 464
Antrim, Joshua
  Slaveholder, 199
Appleton, John James, 231
Armstrong, William, 388
Arthur / Slave, 190
Artop, James
  Slaveholder, 192
Ashford, J. J.
  Slaveholder, 376
  Slaveholder, 190
Ashford, J. P.
  Slaveholder, 190
Ashurst
  Surname, 234
Atkinson
  Surname, 470
Aunt Grace / Slave, 112
Aunt Grace's freedom given and taken away., 112
Avery, George A., 87, 89, 94, 318, 423, 427
Aylethorpe, Thomas
  Slaveholder, 212

B

Bahi, P.
  Slaveholder, 380, 413
Bailey
  Surname, 514
Bailey, E. D.
  Slaveholder, 407
Baker, William, 202
Baldwin, J. G., 150
Baldwin, Jonathan F., 183
Ballinger, A. S., 206
Barba
  surname, 488
Bardwell, Rev. William, 444
Barker, Jacob, 351, 354
Barnard, Alonzo, 151
Barnes, George W.

Slaveholder, 215
Barr
    Surname, 99
Barr, James
    Slaveholder, 204
Barr, Rev. H., 98, 101
Barr, Rev. Hugh, 100
Barr, William P., 100
Barre
    Surname, 489
Barrer, B. G.
    Slaveholder, 196
Barrett, Captain, 482
Barton, David W.
    Slaveholder, 342
Bateman, William
    Slaveholder, 192
Bates, Julius, 513
Baxter, John, 441
Bayhi, P., 178, 205
Beall, Samuel, 416
Beasley, John C.
    Slaveholder, 379
Beasley, Robert
    Slaveholder, 146, 196
Beazley, A. G. A.
    Slaveholder, 214
Beckman, Wm., 232
Beckwith, Elisha, 2
Beebe, Isaac, 1
Beebe, Lodowick, 1
Beene, Jesse
    Slaveholder, 147
Bell
    Surname, 455
Bell, Abraham, 151
Bell, Bushrod, 475
Bell, Edward, 475
Belt, Samuel, 416
Ben / Slave, 9, 191, 202, 208, 407
Ben Fox / Slave, 385
Bennett, D. S., 147
Besson, Jacob
    Slaveholder, 380

Betsey / Slave, 174, 178, 376
Betty / Slave, 375
Bezou
    Surname, 196
Bill / Slave, 146, 192, 199, 200
Billy / Slave, 147, 385
Binford
    Surname, 498
Binford, Thomas, 499
Bingham, Joel S., 446
Birdseye, Ezekiel, 229, 388, 435
Birney, James G., 74
Bishop, J.
    Slaveholder, 190
Bishop, William N., 511
Blackwell, Samuel, 78
Blake, Jim / Slave, 195
Bland, R. J., 145
Bleevin
    Surname, 477
Bliss, Philemon, 58, 70, 71, 74, 77, 83,
    91, 261, 343
Blocker
    Surname, 100
Blount
    Surname, 153
Blue, Alexander, 508
Bob / Slave, 197, 207
Bolles, William, 2
Bolton, W. J.
    Slaveholder, 176
Bosley, Dr., 469
Boudinot, Tobias, 50, 236
Bouldin, T. T.
    Slaveholder, 81
Bourne, Rev. George, 50, 113, 437
Bowen
    Surname, 385
Bowen, James
    Slaveholder, 342
Bowling, Alexander, 474
Bowling, Geo., 474
Boyd, Thomas, 404
Bradburn, George, 350

Bradley
Surname, 167
Bradley, Henry, 387
Bragg, Thomas
Slaveholder, 409
Branded by a hot iron, 29
Brasseale, W. H., 146
Breaking and tearing out teeth., 216
Brewster, Jarvis, 54
Bringing their infants into the field, 20
Britt, Benjamin W., 234
Brove, A.
Slaveholder, 203
Brown
Surname, 394
Brown, J. A., 189, 207
Brown, John
Slaveholder, 100
Brown, Rev. Abel Jr., 226
Brown, Thos.
Slaveholder, 201
Brown, William
Free/Kidnapped and sold into
bondage., 399
Slaveholder, 201
Brubecker
Surname, 226
Buchanan, Dr. George, 286, 298
Buchanan, George Dr., 81, 129
Buck / Slave, 204
Buckels, William D.
Slaveholder, 198
Buckley, Alpha P., 470
Burford
Surname, 443
Burk, Littleton L.
Slaveholder, 416
Burned face with a hot iron., 375
Burned to death., 384, 386
Burned with a smoothing iron., 161
Burvant
Surname, 425
Burvant, Madame
Slaveholder, 189

Bush, Moses E.
Slaveholder, 205
Buster
Surname, 167
Butt, Moses
Slaveholder, 415
Bynum
Surname, 454
Bynum, Jesse
Slaveholder, 408
Byrnes, Captain James, 495

C

Caesar / Slave, 198
Cain / Slave, 406
Caleb / Slave, 193
Calhoun, John C., 422
Calhoun, Mitchell, 479
Calvert
Surname, 171
Calvert, Robert
Slaveholder, 214
Cameron
Surname, 500
Campbell
Surname, 501
Carey
Surname, 482
Carmichael
Surname, 494
Carney, R. P.
Slaveholder, 188
Caroline / Slave, 380, 414, See
Carried his head home., 13
Carter, Elizabeth L.
Slaveholder, 198
Slaveholder, 425
Carter, G. W., 495
Cary / Slave, 208
Case of Crawford vs. Cherry, 368
Case of Gomez vs. Bonneval, 402
Case of the State vs. Cheetwood, 356
Case of the State vs. Mann, 368

Case of the State vs. Mann, 1829, 356
Casey
    Surname, 162
Cat-hauling, 438
Caulkins, Nehemiah, 1, 2, 18, 55, 58, 71
Celia / Slave, 144, 379
Chambers, John A., 477
Chambers, William
    Slaveholder, 416
Channing, Rev. Dr., 76, 318
Chapin, William A., 267
Chapman B. F., 414
Chapman, Gurdon, 217
Charles / Slave, 6, 97, 175, 414
Charlotte / Slave, 406
Chatham against Nash cock fight, 458
Cherry, John W.
    Slaveholder, 201
Child, David L., 231
Chilton, Joseph, 44
Choules, Rev. John O., 79
Church, Peter, 476
Clark
    Surname, 472, 496
Clark, W. G.
    Slaveholder, 409
Clarke, John, 222
Clay, Henry, 74, 428, 452
Clay, Thomas
    Slaveholder, 61
    Slaveholder, 50, 57
Clay, Thos.
    Slaveholder, 54
Cleft his skull with an axe., 100
Clement, George, 489
Clendenon, Benjamin, 424
Coates, Lindley, 236, 438
Cobb, O. B.
    Slaveholder, 398
Cobb, W. D..
    Slaveholder, 385
Cody, Abner J., 475
Coffee
    Surname, 456

Coffield, Josiah
    Slaveholder, 409
Colborn, J. L.
    Slaveholder, 216
Cole, Nathan, 137, 229
Coleman / Slave, 195
Coleman, Edmund / Slave, 178
Collins, Wm., 476
Comstock, Peter, 1
Constant
    Surname, 157
Cook, Giles,
    Slaveholder, 342
Cook, H. L.
    Slaveholder, 406
Cooner, L. E.
    Slaveholder, 148
Cooper, Charity
    Slaveholder, 426
Cooper, Dr. Thomas, 298
Cornelius, Rev. Elias, 396, 397
Corprew, G. W.
    Slaveholder, 405
Coulster
    Surname, 498
Couper, J. H., 66
Covered with scars and filled with
    worms., 233
Cowan
    Surname, 474
cow-hide, 11, 120
Cowles, Mary, 219, 220
Cowles, Rev. Sylvester, 436
Cox
    Surname, 346
Crabster
    Surname, 501
Craiqe, Charles
    Slaveholder, 380
Craze, William, 145
Crosly, Captain, 481
Crutchfield, Thomas
    Slaveholder, 206
Cuffee / Slave, 192

Cuffee/ Slave, 206
Cuggy, T.
    Slaveholder, 380
Curener, Charles
    Slaveholder, 177
Curtiss, Rev. John H., 149
Cut his back to mince-meat., 166
Cut to pieces from shoulder to hips., 153
Cutting up a slave with a broad axe., 237
Cuyler, J.
    Slaveholder, 414
Cy / Slave, 206

D

Daily ration, 61
Daniel / Slave, 175
Darrow, Francis, 2
Dave / Slave, 17, 414
David / Slave, 174, 320
Davidson, Rev. Patrick, 440
Davies, John, 69
Davis
    Surname, 489
Davis / Slave, 408
Davis, Benjamin
    Slaveholder, 412
Davis, Henry
    Slaveholder, 416
Davis, John, 335
Davis, Samuel, 230
Davis, T.
    Slaveholder, 410
Davis, Thomas
    Slaveholder, 425
De Jarnett, James J.
    Slaveholder, 144
De Jarnett, James T.
    Slaveholder, 379
De Wolf, James, 288
De Yampert, T. J.
    Slaveholder, 177
Dean, Jethro, 416
Deas, Colonel Henry, 430

Death by the six pound paddle., 169
Debruhl, Jesse, 212, 215
Demming, Dr., 78
Dennis / Slave, 189
Densler, T. S., 381
Derrah, James, 148
Description of a Slave Ship, 347
Dew, Philip A.
    Slaveholder, 214
Diana / Slave, 409
Dick / Slave, 145, 195, 203, 214, 405
Dickerson
    Surname, 477
Dickerson, Daniel, 476
Dickey, Rev. James H., 320
Dickey, Rev. William, 237
Dickins, Rufus K., 479
Dickinson
    Surname, 78
Dickinson, Francis
    Slaveholder, 407
Died of excessive whipping, 43
Dillahunty, John N.
    Slaveholder, 200
Doddridge, Philip, 452
Dogerty, Leaven, 352
Donnell, Rev. Mr.
    Slaveholder, 167
Doss, William, 495
Dougherty
    Surname, 470
Dougherty, Thomas M., 471
Douglass, J. E., 496
Douglass, Rev. J. W., 453
Downman, Lucy M.
    Slaveholder, 410
Dr. K.
    Slaveholder, 155
Drane, Mr. Westley, 479
Drier, David / Slave, 201
Dromgoole
    Surname, 456
Drown, William, 184
Dudley, Rev. John, 180

Dufflefield, J. M., 480
Duggan, John
  Slaveholder, 380
Dunham, Capt. Jacob, 436
Dunham, Jacob, 436
Dunn, John L.
  Slaveholder, 408
Durell, Daniel M., 327
Durett, Francis
  Slaveholder, 175, 178
Dustin, W., 155
Duval, Doctor, 445
Dyer, William, 174

E

E. W. Morris,, 208, 400
Eanes, Alexander, 484
Eastman, Rev. D. C., 52, 161
Eaton / Slave, 203
Eaton, General William, 319
Edmund / Slave, 201
Edmund, Martha, John and Louisa
  Free Family/ Kidnapped and
    imprisoned as slaves., 399
Edmunds, Nicholas
  Slaveholder, 189
Edward / Slave, 193
Edwards, F. L. C..
  Slaveholder, 194
Eells, Richard Dr., 85
Eels, Dr. Richard, 185
Eilands, James, 508
Elijah / Slave, 189
Eliza / Slave, 384
Ellic / Slave, 193
Ellis / Slave, 198
Ellis, Orren
  Slaveholder, 199
Ellison, Samuel, 87, 149
Ellsworth, Col. Elijah, 153
Emerson
  Surname, 227
Enggy, T.

  Slaveholder, 174
English, Walter R.
  Slaveholder, 198
Ephraim / Slave, 207
Esther / Slave, 380
Evans, R. A.
  Slaveholder, 147
Everett, Wm., 400
Ewall, Merry
  Free/Imprisoned as a slave to be
    sold., 402
Excellent Dogs!, 393

F

F. Wisner,, 213
Fanny / Slave, 84, 408
Farley, Martin, 495
Farr, James, 254
Farris
  Surname, 498
Ferguson
  Surname, 502
Fetter, 180
Fife, Charles, 514
Finley, Dr. James C., 136
Finley, R. S., 136, 452
Fisher
  Surname, 85
Fisher, E. H.
  Slaveholder, 340
Fisher, Rev. Ezra, 185
Fitzhugh, William H., 297
Five hundred blows were inflicted., 45
Five hundred lashes., 164
Flack, Captain, 482
Fleckenstein
  Surname, 479
Flim
  Surname, 271
Forced to eat tobacco worms., 226
Ford, John, 208
Foster, Francis
  Slaveholder, 381

Foster, John T., 496
Fountain / Slave, 146, 196
Four hundred lashes for crooked corn rows., 231
Fox, John B.
    Slaveholder, 207
Foy, Enoch
    Slaveholder, 385
Foyle
    Surname, 489
Fractured his skull., 169
Frank / Slave, 9, 405
Frazier / Slave, 194
Freamster
    Surname, 476
Frederick / Slave, 405
Frederick, John
    Slaveholder, 212, 214
Free colored men hung without trial., 389
French
    Surname, 501
Fuller, Isaac C., 235
Fullerton, G. S., 52, 163
Furman, R.
    Slaveholder, 195

G

Gabriel / Slave, 196
Gadsden, Thomas N., 407, 428, 429
Gaines, Rev. Ludwell G., 236
Gales
    Surname, 458
Galloway
    Cruel Overseer, 4
Gardner
    Surname, 499
Garland, Maurice H.
    Slaveholder, 341
Gates, Seth M., 322
Gayle, John
    Slaveholder, 424
Gearrall

Surname, 377
George / Slave, 148, 167, 176, 190
    Chopped up with broadaxe, 237
Gholson
    Surname, 448
Gholson, W. F., 496
Gibbs
    Surname, 166
Gibson
    Surname, 498
Gibson, Charles, 499
Giddings, Ohio Congressman, 186
Gilbert, M. E. W.
    Slaveholder, 215
Gildersleeve, W. C., 54, 71, 74, 84, 91, 109, 312
Givins, John
    Slaveholder, 408
Glasgow / Slave, 148
Glidden
    Surname, 163
Gonzales
    Surname, 488
Goode
    Surname, 450
Goodwin, James
    Slaveholder, 408
Gordon, Charles, 230
Gormley, William
    Slaveholder, 75
Gould, H. B., 509
Grace, Byrd M.
    Slaveholder, 215
Graham, Jehab, 439, 440
Graham, Rev. Dr., 452
Graham, Rev. John, 39
Green
    Surname, 388
Green, James R.
    Slaveholder, 174
Green, Mary, 499
Greene, R. A.
    Slaveholder, 197
Gregory, Ossian

Slaveholder, 340
Gridly, H., 176
Grimke, Sarah M., 33, 93, 115, 140, 212
Grimke, Thomas S., 33, 93, 113, 431
Grisee / Slave, 177
Grossman
    Surname, 489
Grosvenor, Rev. C. P., 226
Grosvenor, Rev. Cyrus P., 439
Grovenstine
    Surname, 405
Guex, D. F., 177
Gunn, Gabriel
    Slaveholder, 411
Gunnell, John J. H.
    Slaveholder, 342
Guthrie, A. A., 95
Guyler, J.
    Slaveholder, 188
Gwatney, Joseph, 254

H

Hall, Samuel, 163, 181, 185, 235, 445
Halley, Preston
    Slaveholder, 200
Hambleton / Slave, 191
Hamilton
    Surname, 456
Hamilton, Thomas, 478
Hammond
    Surname, 335
Hampton, General Wade, 52, 53, 433
Han, E.
    Slaveholder, 204
Hand half cooked in boiling water., 222
Hand, J. H., 177
Hand, John H., 148
Hannah / Slave, 396
Hansborough, William, 236, 438
Hanson, Peter
    Slaveholder, 199
Harding, Rev. N. H.
    Slaveholder, 138

Hardy / Slave, 202
Harman, Samuel
    Slaveholder, 216
Harper
    Surname, 485
Harper / Slave, 197
Harrington. Dr. J. B., 484
Harris, Benjamin James, 43
Harris, W. R., 496
Harrison
    Surname, 501
Harrison, Francis, 508
Harrison, General William H., 297
Harrison, Gov. William Henry, 131
Harry / Slave, 4
Harry, Elias
    Slaveholder, 418
Hart
    Surname, 222, 488
Hart, F. A., 234
Harvet, J., 404
Hatch, Edmund B., 479
Hawley, David, 149, 234
Hawley, Rev. Francis, 241, 433
Haws, C.
    Slaveholder, 408
Hayne, Gen. R. Y.
    Slaveholder, 409, 425
Hayne, General R. Y.
    Slaveholder, 425
Hays, Richard H., 495
Hazeltine, Asa, 480
Hazzard, Col. W. Whig, 509, 510
Hazzard, Dr. T. F., 509
Hazzard, Thomas, 509
He drew from beneath his cloak, the
    head of the slave., 396
He refused to be taken alive., 393
Head stuck on a high pole., 37
Heavy iron yoke on his neck., 102
Heddings
    Surname, 110
Helt
    Surname, 479

Helton, James, 98
Henderson, Chief Justice, 322
Henderson, John
    Slaveholder, 174, 376
Hendron, H.
    Slaveholder, 340
Henry
    Surname, 483
Henry / Slave, 202, 215
Henry, Thomas, 512
Herbert, A. L., 484
Hermon /Slave, 205
Herring, D., 204, 216
Herron, Robert, 440
Heyward, Nathaniel, 429, 430
Hickson, Timothy, 404
Higbee, A. W., 485
Hight, James
    Free / kidnapped & sold into
        bondage., 351
His back was one gore of blood, 34
Hitchcock, H.
    Slave holder/ Supreme Court Judge,
        428
    Slaveholder/ Supreme Court Judge,
        197
Hite, S. N.
    Slaveholder, 202
Hobbs
    Surname, 483
Hodges, B. W., 178
Hodges, Rev. Coleman S., 224
Holcombe, John P.
    Slaveholder, 208
Holmes William, 351, 499
Holmes, George, 391
Holmes, William
    Free / Kidnapped & sold into
        bondage., 351
Honerton, Philip, 194
Hopkins, Rev. Henry T., 226
Hopkins, Thomas, 508
Hough, Rev. Joseph, 447
House slaves suffer a great deal., 122

Houston, General Felix, 398
Houstoun, Edward
    Slaveholder, 407
Hover / Slave, 202
Hown / Slave, 177
Hudnall, Thomas
    Slaveholder, 191
Hughes, Benj.
    Slaveholder, 398
Hughes, Philip O., 255, See
Hulet, Col. James M., 484
Hung for stealing a piece of
    gingerbread., 230
Hunt, John
    Slaveholder, 212
Hunt, Rev. Thomas P., 16
Hussey, George P. C., 186
Hutchings, A. J.
    Slaveholder, 214

I

Ida / Slave, 407
Ide, Joseph, 257
Inadequate Clothing if any., 81
Inhuman treatment of the sick., 92
Insurrection, 18, 111, 234, 246, 389,
    430, 490
Irby
    Surname, 435
Iron band around his head., 181
Iron collar around her neck., 179
Isaac / Slave, 190, 407, 425
Isham / Slave, 205

J

Jack / Slave, 111, 204, 208, 214
Jackson
    Surname. See
Jackson / Slave, 214
Jackson, Stephen M.
    Slaveholder, 194
Jacob / Slave, 202, 208

James / Slave, 108, 177, 411
James, Joseph
    Slaveholder, 193
James, Judge, 498
Jane / Slave, 380
Janes, Mr. Dwight P., 2
Jarrett / Slave, 196
Jenkins, John
    Slaveholder, 198
Jenks, Samuel H., 351
Jerry / Slave, 105, 196, 206
Jesse / Slave, 406
Jett, Marshall
    Slaveholder, 207
Jim / Slave, 147, 173, 177, 197, 406, 407
Jim Dragon / Slave, 101
Joe / Slave, 147, 406
Joe Dennis / Slave, 203
John / Slave, 108, 148, 176, 177, 178,
    197, 201, 205, 208, 213, 409
John Hunt
    Slaveholder, 212, 407
John Tidd,
    Free / Kidnapped & sold into
        bondage., 351
Johnson / Slave, 146
Johnson, Bryant
    Slaveholder, 144, 195
    Slaveholder, 195
    Slaveholder, 385
Johnson, Cornelius, 70
Johnson, Isaac
    Slaveholder, 191
Johnson,Cornelius, 73, 90, 151
Johnston, Thos. J., 480
Jolliffe, John
    Slaveholder, 342
Jones, Achilles, 493
Jones, Alexander
    Slaveholder, 79
Jones, Anson, 260
Jones, Caesar, 493
Jones, Chamberlayne, 493
Jones, Dr. Anson, 433

Jones, Hardy
    Slaveholder, 407
Jones, Henry, 229
Jones, Hill, 408
Jones, James
    Free / Kidnapped and imprisoned as
        a slave., 394
Jones, Lafayette, 493
Jones, R. H., 414
Jones, Richard M., 484
Jones, Thomas L., 477
Jordan / Slave, 413
Joshua / Slave, 192, 197
Jourdan, Green B., 209
Jourdan, vs. Patton, 361
Judd, D., 144
Judd, Nancy, 226
Judy / Slave, 199
Jupiter / Slave, 146, 200, 415

K

Kate / Slave, 148
Kearney, Joe, 417
Keeton, G. W., 75, 398
Kennedy, John
    Slaveholder, 213
Kentucky Tom / Slave, 194
Kephart, Geo.
    Slaveholder, 416
Kernin, Charles
    Slaveholder, 178
Keyes, Willard, 167
Kezer
    Surname, 480
Kidnapping of Free negroes in the
    north., 349
Kimball, George, 423
Kimborough, James
    Slaveholder, 196
King
    Surname, 417
King, John H.
    Slaveholder, 207

King, Nehemiah
    Slaveholder, 408
Kinney, Charles R., 514
Knapp, Henry E., 72
Knapp, Isaac, 166
Knocking out the teeth and eyes., 210
Kremer
    Surname, 470
Kyle, James, 438, 441

L

Lacy, Theo. A.
    Slavleholder, 409
Ladd, William, 51, 54, 82, 89, 220, 343
Laid 60 strokes on his back., 167
Lains, O. W.
    Slaveholder, 189
Laman / Slave, 188
Lambeth, William L.
    Slaveholder, 177
Lambre
    Surname, 176
Lancette, R.
    Slaveholder, 203
Lansuge
    Surname, 489
Larkin, Ephraim
    Free / Kidnapped and sold into
        bondage., 352
Larrimer, Thomas, 52, 162
Lasater, Col. John, 469
Latimer, W. K.
    Slaveholder, 339
Law, Nathan
    Slaveholder, 409
LeCont
    Surname, 405
Ledwith, Thomas
    Slaveholder, 193
Lee, Charles S., 75
Lefils, A., 508
Leftwich, William, 51, 71, 84, 90
Legare, Hugh S., 422

Lemos, Ferdinand
    Slaveholder, 176
LeMoyne, Dr. F. Julius, 227
Leverich, J. H.
    Slaveholder, 380
Levi / Slave, 200
Lewis / Slave, 198
Lewis, Benjamin, 437
Lewis, Isham
    Brother of Lilburn Lewis, 240
Lewis, John / Slave, 408
Lewis, Kerkman
    Slaveholder, 405
Lewis, Letitia, 239
Lewis, Lilburn
    Murderer / Butcher, 237, 433
Liby / Slave, 377
Liley / Slave, 216
Linn, Samuel, 440
Little, Joseph, 494
Little, Sophia, 182
Livingston, A. R., 495
Lockhart, W. H., 484
Lock-jaw iron head frame, 184
Lockman, William
    Free / Kidnapped & imprisoned as a
        slave., 353
Lofiano, Hazlet
    Slaveowner, 174
Long, Lucy
    Slaveholder, 426
Long, Reuben, 108
Lonnon, Eral
    Free / Kidnapped & imprisoned as a
        slave., 352
Loomis, Henry H., 222
Loring, R.
    Slaveholder, 339
Lowry, Nancy, 108
Lucas
    Surname, 418
Lucas, Hal, 477
Lucas, Thomas, 477
Lucy / Slave, 256

Luke / Slave, 12
Luminais, A.
    Slaveholder, 191
Lumpkin, Wilson, 511
Lyman, Judge, 183
Lyman, Rev. H., 87, 152, 320
Lyman, Rev. Huntington, 435
Lynchers, 479, 483, 484

M

M'Coy
    Surname, 254
Mackey, John, 168
Macoin, J.
    Slaveholder, 176
Macoin, John, 84
Macy, F. C., 55
Macy, Reuben G., 51, 83, 250
Macy, Reuben L., 91
Macy, Richard, 55, 84, 250, 253
Macy, T.D.M. & F.C., 269
Madame La Laurie, 233
Magee, William, 413
Magee, Wm., 208, 399
Malcolm
    Surname, 320
Males, Henry, 168
Mallix
    Surname, 152
Maltby, Stephen E., 83, 89, 150
Manie, John, 495
Manning, P. J.
    Slaveholder, 177
Maria / Slave, 195, 379, 407, 408
Mark / Slave, 192
Marking slaves., 211, 212
Marks, James
    Slaveholder, 204
Marshall
    Surname, 456
Marshall, John T.
    Slaveholder, 409
Martha / Slave, 144, 199, 207

Martin, John, 512
Mary / Slave, 188, 190, 196, 198, 212,
    215, 319, 376, 380, 416
Mason, George
    Slaveholders, 426
Mason, Samuel
    Slaveholder, 193
Massingale, Pharaoh, 473
Matilda / Slave, 410, 414
Maxcy
    Surname, 484
May, Rev. Samuel J., 395
Maynard
    Surname, 480
Mazyck, Wm.
    Slaveholder, 418
McCallie, Archibald, 495
McCargo T.
    Slaveholder, 406
McClung, Alexander K., 457
McCue, Moses, 406
McDonald, Robert, 484
McDonnell, James
    Slaveholder, 201
McDowell, Robert
    Slaveholder, 179
McDuffie
    Surname, 456
McFarlane, Alexander, 476
McFarlane, Arthur, 476
McFarlane, James, 476
Mcgehee, Edmund James
    Slaveholder, 385
McGregor, Henry M.
    Slaveholder, 209
McIntosh / Slave, 386
McKinley
    Surname, 456
McKitchen
    Surname, 227
McMurrain, John
    Slaveholder, 191
    Slaveholder, 213
M'Cue, John, 438

Mead, Whitman, 133
Means
  Surname, 426
Medill
  Surname, 482
Meeks, A. H., 499
Menard
  Surname, 176
Menifee, R. H.
  Slaveholder, 414
Menzies, Judge
  Slaveholder, 225
Mercer, C. F., 452
Metcalf, A. J.
  Slaveholder, 376
Metcalf, Asa B.
  Slaveholder, 188
Mike / Slave, 200
Miles, Lemuel
  Slaveholder, 195
Miller
  Surname, 159
Miller, C.
  Slaveholder, 407
Miller, William
  Slaveholder, 408
Minard, Pierre, 131
Mince / Slave, 105
Minor, Slave, 416
Mitchell
  Surname, 227
Mitchell, Colonel David L., 494
Mitchell, Isaac
  Slaveholder, 204
M'Neil
  Surname, 161
M'Neilly
  Surname, 383
Mongin, R. P. T.
  Slaveholder, 406
Montesquieu, 299
Montgomery, W. H.
  Slaveholder, 414
Moody, E., 496

Moody, Thomas, 496
Mooney, Wm. S., 475
Moor
  Surname, 409
Moore, Thomas P., 502
Moorehead, John H., 154
Morgan, John, 152
Morgan, Philip, 1
Morgan, William / Slave, 289
Morton, Thomas C., 432
Mose / Slave, 192
Mosely, William, 100
Moses
  Surname, 377
Moses / Slave, 198, 213, 409, 424, 425
Moulton, Horace, 19
Moulton, Rev. Horace, 50, 54, 57, 95,
  226, 278, 286, 339, 346
Mrs. Maxwell
  Slaveholder, 157
Muggridge, Matthew
  Slaveholder, 407
Muir, J. G.
  Slaveholder, 380
Murat, A.
  Slaveholder, 175
Murdough, J., 499, 500
Murphy, S. B., 148, 191
Murray, John
  Free / Kidnapped and imprisoned as
    a slave., 394
Mushat, Rev. John, 435
Myal / Slave, 213
Myra / Slave, 178

N

Nailed the negro's ear to a tree., 155
Nancy / Slave, 414, 418
Napier
  Surname, 414
Nat / Slave, 210, 410
Ned / Slave, 108, 112, 191, 212, 215,
  312

Neely
  Surname, 103
Neglect of the aged, 95
Negro plaster, 439, 441
Neil
  Surname, 474
Nelly / Slave, 414
Nelson / Slave, 209, 408
Nelson, Dr. David, 221, 319
Nelson, John M., 111, 179, 312, 440
Nesbitt, Wilson
  Slaveholder, 340
Nevils
  Surname, 485
Newman, B.
  Slaveholder, 425
Neyle, S.
  Slaveholder, 190
  Slaveholder, 213
Nicholas, Samuel S., 297
Nichols, A. B., 44
Nicoll, Robert
  Slaveholder, 144, 377
Nightingale, P. M., 66
Noe, James
  Slaveholder, 145
Nourse, Rev. James, 441
Nye, Major Horace, 150, 154, 179

O

O'Rorke, John, 407
O'Byrne, D.
  Slaveholder, 409
O'Connell
  Surname, 456
Ocra / Slave, 269

I

'Oh Missee, don't kill me!", 109

O

Old at middle age, 76
Oldham, Henry, 499
Oliver, Colonel, 417
Oliver, Thomas W.
  Slaveholder, 406
One hundred lashes were laid on his bare
  body., 109
Oneill, Peter
  Slavaeholder, 407
Orme, Moses
  Slaveholder, 192
Osnaburgh cloth, 82
Otis, D. G., 1
Overseer gave him four hundred lashes.,
  231
Overstreet, Richard
  Slaveholder, 195
Overworked., 74
Owen Cooke,
  Slaveholder, 174
Owen, Captain W. F. / Royal Navy, 310
Owen, John W.
  Slaveholder, 342
Owens
  Surname, 162
Owens, J. G.
  Slaveholder, 406
Oxford, James
  Free / Kidnapped & sold into
    bondage., 351

P

Paclin, John, 404
Painter
  Surname, 152
pancake sticks, 115
Parham
  Surname, 483
Parker, Job
  Slaveholder, 409
Parker, Rev. Joel, 435

Parrish, John, 55, 82, 382
Parrott
    Surname, 260
Paterson, Willie
    Slaveholder, 205
Patience / Slave, 380
Patrick / Slave, 175, 203
Patsey / Slave, 381, 407
Patterson, Willis
    Slaveholder, 208
Pauladore / Slave, 409
Paulding, James K., 186, 227
Paulladore / Slave, 425
Payne, Wm.
    Slaveholder, 377
Peacock, Jesse, 416
Peake, Dr., 469
Peggy / Slave, 408, 414
Pegram
    Surname, 483
Penny / Slave, 425
Perkins, A. P. Dr., 1
Perkins, W. I., 509
Perry / Slave, 212
Perry, Thomas C., 444
Peter / Slave, 176, 206, 213, 408, 409
Peters, Belvard, 501
Phil / Slave, 209
Philip / Slave, 409
Philips
    Surname, 477
Phillips
    Surname, 166, 230
Pickard, Y. S., 414
Pierce, Cyrus, 269
Pilot, Frank
    Free / Kidnapped and held in
        bondage., 400
Pinckney, H. L.
    Slaveholder, 409, 425
Pinckney, William, 128
Piney / Slave, 108
Pinkney, Col. Thomas
    Slaveholder, 418

Poe, William, 43, 445
Poindexter
    Surname, 456
Polk, Jas. K., 495
Polk, Wm., 495
Poor shelter from the elements, 89
Porter
    Surname, 154, 158
Powel, Eleazar, 71
Powell
    Surname, 500
Powell, Eleazar, 51, 58, 253
Prentice
    Surname, 502
President Edwards the younger, 298
President Edwards, the younger, 50
Price, William, 495
Prince / Slave, 215
Pringle, Thomas, 310
Priscilla / Slave, 210
Prisley, Thomas
    Slaveholder, 377
Pritchard, William H., 394
Professor Dew, 449
Purdon, James
    Slaveholder, 214
Purnell, Capril
    Free / Imprisoned as a slave to be
        sold., 402
Pursued by the dogs, 31
Putrid flesh of their lacerated backs., 116

R

R. W. Barber,, 401
Rachel / Slave, 189, 269, 416, 425
Ragland, Samuel
    Slaveholder, 205
Ralston, Samuel
    Slaveholder, 400
Randal / Slave, 194
Randal, Silas, 473
Randall, J. B., 200, 415
Randolph, John, 88, 291, 426, 456

Slaveholder, 129
Randolph, Thomas Mann, 448
Rankin, Rev. John, 49, 81, 91, 133, 158, 236, 237
Ransom / Slave, 384
Rascoe, Wm. D.
Slaveholder, 409
Ratcliffe, William K., 200
Ratliff
Surname, 406
Rawlins, Samuel
Slaveholder, 209
Raworth, Egbert A
Slaveholder, 213
Reading, Joseph, 404
Redden, J. V.
Slaveholder, 341
Redding
Surname, 499
Redmond
Surname, 410
Reed, Rev. Doctor, 79
Reed, William H., 182
Rees, Thomas, 404
Reese, Enoch, 405
Reeves, W. P., 175
Remley
Surname, 164
Renshaw, Rev. C. S., 56, 59, 85, 225, 410
Renshaw, Rev. Charles Stewart, 415, 442
Reynolds
Surname, 489
Reynolds, Dr. Michael, 470
Rhett, Robert Barnwell, 422, 429, 431
Rhodes, Durant H.
Slaveholder, 384
Rice, H. W., 175
Richard / Slave, 384
Richards, James R.
Slaveholder, 342
Richards, Stephen M.
Slaveholder, 203

Richardson, G. C.
Slaveholder, 203
Ricks, Micajah
Slaveholder, 375
Slaveholder, 188
Rigdon
Surname, 472
Rigdon / Slave, 385
Riley, W.
Slaveholder, 193
Ripley, George B., 217
Ritter, Thomas, 273
Rivers, Dr. Thomas, 502
Roach, Philip
Slaveholder, 340
Roark, Hugh, 482
Robarts, Wm.
Slaveholder, 405
Robbins, Asher, 182
Robbins, Welcome H.
Slaveholder, 200
Roberts, J. K., 145
Roberts, W., 501
Robertson, Daniel S.
Slaveholder, 416
Robin, C. C., 131
Robin, Monsieur C. C., 80, 298
Robinson, John J.
Free / Kidnapped and imprisoned as a slave., 400
Robinson, N. M. C., 206
Robinson, William
Slaveholder, 379
Roebuck, George, 161
Rogers, Col. Thomas, 170
Rogers, James Dr., 1
Rogers, N. P., 327, 423
Ross, Abner
Slaveholder, 377
Rothwell, John, 499
Rowan
Surname, 456
Rowland, John A., 145
Royston, Grandison D., 398

Ruff, John
  Slaveholder, 406
Ruffin, Judge
  Supreme Court of N.C., 135
Ruffner, John
  Slaveholder, 108
Russel, Benjamin, 197, 213
Russell, W., 395
Rynes, Littlejohn
  Slaveholder, 206

S

Sadd, Rev. Joseph M., 89, 139, 151, 322, 327
Sally / Slave, 202, 213, 426
Sally/ Slave, 409
Salvo, Conrad
  slaveholder, 202
Sam / Slave, 189
Saman / Slave, 414
Sampson / Slave, 385
Sappington, Lemuel, 83, 106
Sarah / Slave, 414
Saunders, James
  Slaveholder, 198
Saunders, Seller / Slave, 215
Saunderson
  Surname, 483
Savage, Rev. Thomas, 184, 223
Savery, William, 55, 81, 152
Sawyer, Zadock
  Slaveholder, 199
Say
  Surname, 158
Scales, Rev. William, 160, 267
Scales, William, 256
Scarbrough, Stephen, 485
Schmidt, Louis
  Slaveholder, 202
Scott
  Surname, 483
Scott, Col. Christopher, 473
Scott, James G., 479

Scott, John W., 479
Scott, Rev. Orange, 447
Scrivener, J.
  Slaveholder, 189
Seabrook, Whitmarsh B., 430
Separated from his wife, 35
Set his blood hounds upon them., 275
Sevier, Senator Ambrose H.
  Slaveholder, 197
Sewall, Stephen, 218, 286
Shackleford, Henry, 483
Shafter, M. M., 234
Sheith, Col. M. J.
  Slaveholder, 203
Shepherd
  Surname / Slaveowner, 52
Sherley, J. C., 495
Sherrod, Col. Ben
  Slaveholder, 101
Shields, Polly C.
  Slalveholder, 409
Shipley, Benjamin, 495
Shoemaker
  Surname, 498
Shoolbred
  Surname, 418
Shoulders to his heels there was not a spot un-ridged!, 264
Shropshire, David, 408
Siby / Slave, 144
Siglar, Michael, 152
Simmons, B. G.
  Slaveholder, 192
Simon / Slave, 190
Simpson, Jno.
  Slaveholder, 401
Sims, Henry L., 512
Sizer, R. W.
  Slaveholder, 189
Skinner, W.
  Slaveholder, 382
Skinner, Wm., 404
Slaughter
  Surname, 153

Slaves are severely driven., 67
Smith, A. G. Professor, 57
Smith, Gerrit, 157, 221, 396
Smith, James
  Free / Kidnapped & sold into
    bondage., 351
Smith, Mary
  Free / Kidnapped & sold into
    bondage., 351
Smith, Rev. B. B., 502
Smith, Rev. Phineas, 58, 82, 95, 139,
  259, 278, 286, 343
Smith, Robert, 484
Smith, Sen.William, 432
Smith, William
  Free / Kidnapped & imprisoned as a
    slave., 352
Smyth, Alexander
  Slaveholder, 68
  Slaveholder, 48
Snow
  Surname, 475
Snow, Henry H., 167
Snowden, J., 414
Snowden, Rev. Samuel, 351
Southmayd, Rev. Daniel S., 434
Sparks, William, 232
Speece, Rev. Dr., 113
Spikes, Greer, 483
Squire /Slave, 174
Stallard, David, 228
Stanley
  Surname, 455
Stansell, William
  Slaveholder, 197
Starky
  Surname, 162
Starved a female slave to death., 36
Staughton, Rev. Dr., 439
Steele
  Surname, 476
Steele, Alex., 476
Steele, Graves W., 476
Steele, Nathaniel, 476

Step, John, 495
Step, Solomon, 495
Stevenson
  Surname, 447
Steward, Elizabeth / Slave, 216
Stewart
  Surname, 405
Stewart, H. C., 457
Stewart, Samuel
  Slaveholder, 147
Stoddard, Major, 87
Stone, Asa A., 49, 69, 139
Stone, Silas, 412
Strickland, William, 192
Stroud, George M., 349
Stuart, Charles, 311
Stuart, Hinds, 256
Stunston, Levi, 495
Suffering from Hunger., 47
Summers, Lewis, 296
Surgette, James
  Slaveholder, 194
Swain, B., 135
Swain, Moses, 49, 134
Swain, William, 49, 134
Swan, John, 3
Sweeny
  Surname, 261

T

Tanner, Benjamin, 480
Tappan, Arthur, 101, 137, 229, 273, 363
Tappan, Lewis, 211
Tarleton, Thomas J., 476
Tart, John
  Slaveholder, 195
Tate, Calvin H., 225
Taylor
  Surname, 406
Taylor, James H.
  Slaveholder, 205
Taylor, John Sen., 66, 342
Thatcher

Surname, 423
The case of the State vs. M'Gee, 383
The Mormon War, 471
The torture of his fetter was severe., 181
Their flesh is mangled to the very bones, 133
They have no stoves or chimneys, 23
Thomas, Albert, 501
Thomas, J. B., 131
Thomas, Madison, 508
Thome, Arthur, 390
Thome, Rev. James A., 137, 390
Thompson
    Surname, 100
    Surname, 327
Thompson, Henry P., 224
Thomson
    Surname, 403
Thomson, Sanford
    Slaveholder, 408
Three hundred and five blows with the paddle., 263
Thrust her hand into the fire., 220
Thumb screw., 139
Tibbetts
    Surname, 488
Tier, Henry
    Free / Kidnapped & imprisoned as a slave., 353
Tittle, John, 476
Todd, R. S., 341
Toler, William, 173
Tolin, Cornelius J.
    Slaveholder, 146
Tom / Slave, 145, 191, 194, 199, 207, 213, 389
Toothache, 9
Top / Slave, 204
Towles, J. S., 482
Townsend, Ely
    Slaveholder, 190
Townsend, Samuel
    Slaveholder, 214
Toy / Slave, 148

Truly, James, 256
Tucker, Judge
    Slaveholder, 311
Turnbull, R. J.
    Slaveholder, 70
    Slaveholder, 59
    Slaveholder, 92
Turnbull, Robert
    Slaveholder, 51
Turner, Fielding S., 222, 433
Turner, Isaac
    Free / Kidnapped & imprisoned as a slave., 394
Turner, John
    Slaveholder, 147
Turner, John D.
    Slaveholder, 196
Turner, L., 99
Turner, Nat, 246
Turton, S. B., 207, 208
Tuston, S. B., 199
Twenty-seven whipped at one time, 42
Two million seven hundred thousand slaves., v

U

Uncle Jack, 441
Upsher
    Surname, 450
Ustick, G. S., 52, 163

V

Vanarsdale, Peter, 443
Vance, John, 152
Varillat, J.
    Slaveholder, 146
Varnum
    Surname, 499
Victorine / Slave, 380

W

W. C. Harris,, 496
Wadmalaw / Slave, 407
Walker
    Surname, 101
Walker, John
    Slaveholder, 147
Wall
    Surname, 232
Walsh, Sarah
    Slaveholder, 190
    Slaveholder, 425
Walton
    Surname, 474
Walton, George, 413
Walton, J., 474
Walton, John W.
    Slaveholder, 194
Walton, Thomas
    Kidnapper of the free., 399
Walton, Thomas J.
    Slaveholder, 406
Ward
    Surname, 493
Ware, Hugh, 475
Warren / Slave, 215
Washington / Slave, 201, 214
Waters
    Surname, 388
Watkins, Col. Robert J.
    Slaveholder, 101
Watkins, Robert H. Col,, 95, 432
Watson, Pleasant, 494
Waugh, Dr. Jeremiah S., 435
Webb, Carroll, 268
Webb, Pleasant, 461
Weld, Angelina Grimke, 113
Wells, Thomas J.
    Slaveholder, 408
West, Eli, 162
Westgate, George W., 56, 72, 73, 86, 90,
    171, 172
Weston
    Surname, 409
Whipped and burned a young girl to
    death., 43
Whipped and burned to death., 43
Whipped to death, 129, 150, 153, 154,
    162, 172, 223, 231, 232, 427
Whipped with a holed paddle, 97
Whipping pregnant women., 28
Whitbread
    Surname, 299
Whitby, William, 444
White, Hiram, 110
White, Peter, 232
White, Wm., 501
Whitefield, Needham
    Slaveholder, 203
Whitefield, Rev. George, 49, 127, 286
Whitehead
    Surname, 147
Whitehead, W. M. .
    Slaveholder, 202
Whitfield, Elizabeth
    Slaveholder, 407
Whitson, John W., 469
Whitson, William, 469
Wightman, Rev. William M., 430
Wilberforce
    Surname, 299
Wilcox, G. H., 480
Wilkins, C. W., 205
Wilkinson, Alfred, 156, 181
Wilkinson, B. R., 499, 500
Wilkinson, E. C., 499
Willey, H. W., 509
Willey, J. A., 509
William / Slave, 192
William Adams,
    Free / Kidnapped & sold into
        bondage., 351
Williams
    Surname, 44
Williams, George W.
    Slaveholder, 341
Williams, Samuel, 220

Willis
  Surname, 415
Willis, Robert, 442
Willis, William, 232
Wilson
  Surname, 100
Wilson / Slave, 406, 416
Wilson, Col. John, 464
Wilson, John, 464
Wilson, Rev. Joseph G., 232
Wilson, William, 439
Winfield, Robert
  Free / Kidnapped and imprisoned as
    a slave., 401
Wing, George, 508
Winston, George / Slave, 214
Winter / Slave, 204
Wirt, Attorney Gen. of the U.S., 277
Wise
  Surname, 454

Woodward, Jeremiah
  Slaveholder, 209
Woolman, John, 127, 288
Work from daylight till dark, 7
Wotton, John
  Slaveholder, 146
Wounded by a wild hog., 41
Wright, Isaac
  Free / Kidnapped and sold into
    slavery. Escaped, 402
Wright, Professor E., 273
Wright, Spencer P.
  Slaveholder, 418

Y

Yaochum, William, 470
Young
  Surname, 501

For more great stories from our past, please visit the Historical Collection at our website.

www.BadgleyPublishingCompany.com

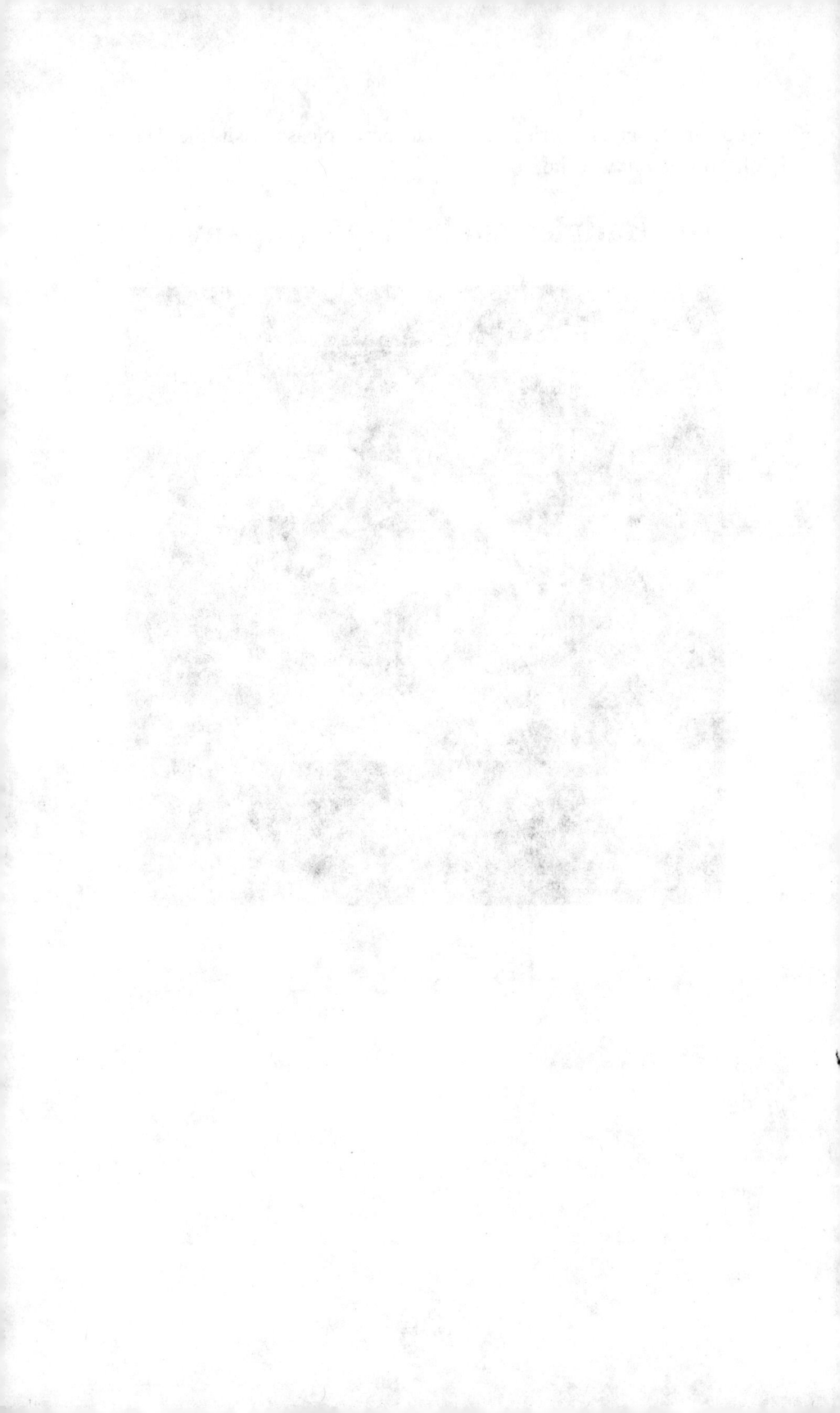